ICCA
CONGRESS SERIES NO. 15

INTERNATIONAL ARBITRATION CONFERENCE
RIO DE JANEIRO, 23 - 26 MAY 2010

INTERNATIONAL COUNCIL FOR COMMERCIAL ARBITRATION

ARBITRATION ADVOCACY IN CHANGING TIMES

GENERAL EDITOR:
ALBERT JAN VAN DEN BERG

with the assistance of the
Permanent Court of Arbitration
Peace Palace, The Hague

ISBN 978-90-411-3366-3

Published by:
Kluwer Law International
PO Box 316
2400 AH Alphen aan den Rijn
The Netherlands
Website: www.kluwerlaw.com

Sold and distributed in North, Central and South America by:
Aspen Publishers, Inc.
7201 McKinney Circle
Frederick, MD 21704
United States of America
Email: customer.service@aspenpublishers.com

Sold and distributed in all other countries by:
Turpin Distribution Services Ltd.
Stratton Business Park
Pegasus Drive, Biggleswade
Bedfordshire SG18 8TQ
United Kingdom
Email: kluwerlaw@turpin-distribution.com

Printed on acid-free paper.

© 2011 Kluwer Law International BV, The Netherlands

All Rights Reserved. No part of this publication may be reproduced, stored in a retrieval system, or transmitted in any form or by any means, mechanical, photocopying, recording or otherwise, without prior written permission of the publishers.

Permissions to use this content must be obtained from the copyright owner. Please apply to: Permissions Department, Wolters Kluwer Legal, 76 Ninth Avenue, Seventh Floor, New York, NY 10011, United States of America. E-mail: permissions@kluwerlaw.com.

Printed and bound by CPI Group (UK) Ltd, Croydon, CR0 4YY, United Kingdom.

Preface

This fifteenth volume in the ICCA Congress Series contains the proceedings of the XX International Arbitration Congress organized in Rio de Janeiro, 23-26 May 2010. It was the first ICCA Congress to be held in South America, and we are grateful to the Host Organization, the Comité Brasileiro de Arbitragem, for their warm hospitality and efficiency, which made this Congress such a success.

The Congress Sessions explored the landscape of arbitration advocacy in changing times from practical, theoretical and ethical perspectives. The closing Keynote Address proposed a uniform code of ethics for lawyers practicing before international arbitral tribunals.

I would like to extend my thanks to the Panel chairs, who are as follows:

— Effective Advocacy in Arbitration: Arthur Mariott, QC, chair
— Strategic Management in Commencing an Arbitration: Yves Derains, chair
— Effective Advocacy in the Written and Procedural Phases of Arbitration: Carlos NehringNetto, chair
— Experts: Neutrals or Advocates? Bernard Hanotiau, chair
— The Hearing: Emmanuel Gaillard, chair
— Advocacy After the Issue of the Arbitral Award: Michael Pryles, chair
— Arbitration Advocacy and Constitutional Law: Francisco Orrego Vicuña, chair.

I also wish to thank the Congress Programme Committe: Bernardo Cremades, chair; Arthur Marriott, QC; Carlos Nehring Netto; Donald Donovan; Guillermo Aguilar Álvarez; Emmanuel Gaillard; Francisco Orrego Vicuña; Guido Tawil; Fathi Kemicha; William K. Slate II; and William W. Park.

This volume would not be complete without a word of thanks to the Secretary General of the Permanent Court of Arbitration, Mr. Christiaan Kröner, for hosting the staff of ICCA Publications at its headquarters in the Peace Palace as well as to the staff of the PCA for their administrative and technical support. My final word of thanks to the staff of ICCA Publications, in particular Ms. Alice Siegel and Ms. Helen Pin, for their invaluable assistance in compiling and editing this volume.

The next ICCA Congress will be held in Singapore on 10-13 June 2012. Information on the Congress is posted on the ICCA website <www.arbitration-icca.org> and the Singapore 2012 Organizing Committee website <www.iccasingapore2012.org>.

Albert Jan van den Berg
August 2011

TABLE OF CONTENTS

PREFACE
    Albert Jan van den Berg, General Editor   v

TABLE OF CONTENTS   vii

Effective Advocacy in Arbitration

Donald Francis Donovan
    The Transnational Advocate   3

Antonio Crivellaro
    Advocacy in International Arbitration: An Art, a Science or a Technique?   9

Strategic Management in Commencing Arbitration

V.V. Veeder
    Strategic Management in Commencing an Arbitration   27

John M. Townsend
    Promoting Peace Before Conflict: Integrating Alternative Methods of Dispute Resolution into the Arbitration Process   35

Meg Kinnear and Aïssatou Diop
    Use of the Media by Counsel in Investor-State Arbitration   40

Effective Advocacy in the Written and Procedural Phases of Arbitration

Guillermo Aguilar Alvarez
    Written Advocacy   55

Jalal El Ahdab and Amal Bouchenaki
    Discovery in International Arbitration: A Foreign Creature for Civil Lawyers?   65
    Annex I: Timing and Other Issues of Time Management   114

Nigel Blackaby
    Witness Preparation – A Key to Effective Advocacy in International Arbitration   118

Experts: Neutrals or Advocates?

Dr. Klaus Sachs with the assistance of Dr. Nils Schmidt-Ahrendts
    Protocol on Expert Teaming: A New Approach to Expert Evidence   135

Dushyant Dave
    Should Experts Be Neutrals or Advocates?   149

Paul Friedland and Kate Brown de Vejar
    Discoverability of Communications Between Counsel and Party-Appointed Experts in International Arbitration   160

The Hearing

David J.A. Cairns
    Oral Advocacy and Time Control in International Arbitration   181
    Annex I: The Economics of Oral Advocacy and Time Control   199

Marinn Carlson
    The Examination and Cross-Examination of Witnesses   202

Dr. Claus von Wobeser
    The Effective Use of Legal Sources: How Much Is Too Much and What Is the Role for *Iura Novit Curia*?   207

Alejandro A. Escobar
    The Relative Merits of Oral Argument and Post-Hearing Briefs   221

Advocacy After the Issue of the Arbitral Award

Eduardo Zuleta
    Post-Award Advocacy: The Relationship Between Interim and Final Awards – Res Judicata Concerns   231

Luiz Olavo Baptista
    Correction and Clarification of Arbitral Awards   275

Gabriela Alvarez Avila
    ICSID Annulment Procedure: A Balancing Exercise Between Correctness and Finality   289

TABLE OF CONTENTS

Arbitration Advocacy and Constitutional Law

Laurence Boisson de Chazournes
   Fundamental Rights and International Arbitration: Arbitral Awards and
   Constitutional Law   309

Guido Santiago Tawil
   On the Internationalization of Administrative Contracts, Arbitration and
   the Calvo Doctrine   325

Josefa Sicard-Mirabal
   Mandatory Rules: What's a Lawyer to Do?   348

Teresa Cheng, SC
   State Immunity, Public Policy and International Commercial Arbitration   362

Keynote Address: Advocacy and Ethics in International Arbitration

Doak Bishop
   Ethics in International Arbitration   383

Doak Bishop and Margrete Stevens
   The Compelling Need for a Code of Ethics in International Arbitration:
   Transparency, Integrity and Legitimacy   391

   International Code of Ethics for Lawyers Practicing Before International
   Arbitral Tribunals   408

LIST OF SESSION REPORTERS   421

LIST OF PARTICIPANTS   423

LIST OF ICCA OFFICERS AND MEMBERS   463

Effective Advocacy in Arbitration

The Transnational Advocate

Donald Francis Donovan[*]

TABLE OF CONTENTS	Page
I. Introduction	3
II. International Arbitration as a Transnational Justice System	3
III. Expectations of Transnational Advocates	5

I. INTRODUCTION

It's great to be here in Rio for the ICCA 2010 Congress. It is clear already that Carlos Nehring Netto, Adriana Braghetta, Eduardo Damião Gonçalves and the rest of the Organizing Committee have done a spectacular job, and it is wonderful to be here with so many friends from Brazil and elsewhere.

We here in this opening panel have been asked to address the topic of effective advocacy in international arbitration, and we immediately face the obstacle that all the speakers here will face: it's a bit difficult to *talk* about effective advocacy. The best way to consider effective advocacy, whether oral or written, is to demonstrate it, or witness it. Still, there is much to be said, and I look to make my contribution in two steps.

First, given that we are leading off, I'd like to consider the international arbitration system in which the advocacy that we are examining happens. I want to identify the features of that system that make it a transnational system of justice.

Second, I'd like to consider the international arbitration advocate as one of the critical actors in that system. In other words, I want to draw out the implications of this transnational system of justice for our expectations of the advocate.

II. INTERNATIONAL ARBITRATION AS A TRANSNATIONAL JUSTICE SYSTEM

So let me take in turn each component of the term transnational system of justice.

First, it's a system. I do not need to rehearse for this audience the systemic attributes of international arbitration – those attributes that make it an interconnected legal system rather than a disjointed series of legal phenomena. National jurisdictions throughout the world have enacted modern arbitration laws, including various versions of the UNCITRAL Model Law on International Commercial Arbitration, whose purpose is to promote a transjurisdictional process. Adherence to the 1958 New York Convention is nearly universal, and the ICSID and other conventions have wide adherence as well. States have increasingly recognized the arbitrability of public law claims previously reserved to their national courts, and, by more than 2,000 bilateral and multilateral

---

[*] Partner, Debevoise & Plimpton LLP; Honorary Vice President of ICCA.

investment treaties, states have subjected their treatment of foreign investors to independent review by international arbitration tribunals.

Second, this is a dispute resolution system – a system intended to deliver *justice*. I will come back to this point and so won't linger on it here. We all understand that the enterprise in which we're engaged is an attempt to provide a fair and efficient means of resolving commercial, public law and investment disputes between parties from different countries, from different economic systems, and from different legal cultures, while applying a wide range of norms drawn from national law, international law, industry custom and transnational sources. And we engage in that enterprise with the conviction that putting in place a just and reliable system of dispute resolution will contribute to the economic and social development of the affected states and communities.

Finally, and this is a point on which I *do* want to linger for a moment, the system is *transnational*. The starting point for the international arbitration system is, of course, party consent. In the face of this consent, the state takes a fundamentally different role in the resolution of the dispute. The international arbitration tribunal's authority is ultimately grounded in national and international law, but the tribunal, and the process it supervises, actually forms part of a well-defined transnational legal order that operates outside the structure of any state or body of states.

I should emphasize that I use the term "transnational legal order" to refer to the structural features of the system, not to any body of substantive law. I am not talking about any form of lex mercatoria, or harmonization of national laws of contract, or competition, or other subject matter. Instead, I speak about the legal architecture that gives shape to the contemporary system of international arbitration.

I want to identify four features of this transnational justice system that have implications for the role of the advocate.

The *first*, and most fundamental, is the delegation of dispute resolution authority, by states and by the parties in dispute, to decision-makers the state does not directly appoint (except when acting in the capacity of a party) or regulate. One of the core functions of the modern state is to fairly and impartially resolve disputes, and then to bring its coercive authority to bear in order to give effect to that resolution. International arbitration involves the delegation of that authority to individuals with whom the state does not have a direct relationship. The national and international law of international arbitration provides the structure within which the process operates, but no state actually runs the system.

The result is that national courts routinely enforce decisions in civil matters from juridical bodies that have operated not only outside their own jurisdiction, but outside the jurisdiction of any state. So the recognition and enforcement of an arbitral award has a fundamentally different basis than the recognition and enforcement of a foreign judgment, which is grounded in interstate comity and interstate relations.

The system is also structurally different than the institutions of international adjudication. An international court is established on the direct authority, not of a single state, but of a body of states defined by treaty. The authority exercised by that court thereby derives directly from those states, and while the court maintains at all times its adjudicatory independence, it is subject otherwise to the control of that body of states. The source of the court's authority is therefore different than that of the transnational tribunals we consider here.

The *second* feature of the transnational legal order I want to highlight is the constitution of not simply international, but *transnational*, arbitration tribunals. Any one international tribunal will frequently include members who come from several different jurisdictions and perhaps legal cultures. So will the advocates before them. But it goes further than that.

Arbitration panels are transnational in the sense that their members are not directly subject to national legal orders and are not dependent for their appointment upon their own governments or any group of governments. Hence, they are divorced from the traditional conception of "inter-*national* relations" as government-to-government interactions between states.

The *third* feature of this transnational legal order we should consider here is that arbitral tribunals routinely deal with cases requiring the application of various national laws and international law as well. Yet, as I am not the first to say, in an international arbitration all of these laws are the law of the forum; in international arbitration, there is no such thing as foreign law.

Fourth, and finally, is the use and development of transnational procedure. The civil procedure used in national courts is inapplicable to international arbitration, and the provisions of both national law and institutional and ad hoc rules that frequently govern the conduct of arbitral proceedings leave a wide degree of discretion for procedural autonomy.

III. EXPECTATIONS OF TRANSNATIONAL ADVOCATES

If we have now placed the international arbitration advocate in a transnational system of justice, we're in a position to consider what we should expect from the advocate as a critical actor in that system. My proposition is that the character of international arbitration as a transnational justice system allows us – indeed *requires* us – to develop standards and expectations of advocates within that system. Those standards and expectations must be designed to promote the effectiveness of the system. They must draw their content from, but not be bound by, the rich mixture of legal traditions that contribute to international arbitration. And they must be capable of direct application by the relevant authorities within that system – that is, arbitration tribunals.

Let me pause to draw a distinction here.

One way to think about our expectations of an advocate involved in international arbitration is in terms of the ethical regulations or constraints that govern the advocate's conduct. By this I mean the ethical rules whose violation would subject a lawyer to discipline by his or her licensing or regulatory authority. While we regularly talk about the ethical norms governing arbitrators, we have paid little attention to the norms that govern arbitration practitioners, perhaps because we have usually assumed that those norms would be supplied by either or both of the lawyer's licensing jurisdiction or the place of arbitration. Some initial work has been done in this area, and the 20th Annual Workshop of the Institute for Transnational Arbitration, held in Dallas in June 2009, illustrated the kinds of issues of which we all need to be aware.[1] I think it's still fair to say, as Jan Paulsson observed at the start of his 1992 article, that at this point the subject of the ethical constraints attaching to the international arbitration practitioner is underexamined,[2] but perhaps it will be less so after we hear what Doak Bishop has to say on the subject in his keynote address on Wednesday.[3]

Given the topic of this panel, though, I have a different goal here. Considering again three key features of the transnational justice system I have described — *first*, that it is consent-based; *second*, that it is transnational and hence not directly supervised by state authorities; and *third*, that it administers justice — I want to propose that we have as our goal the development, within this transnational justice system, of a community of transnational advocates, with a set of standards and expectations that are regulated within the system itself.

To start, we should consider what it means for the advocate that the arbitration is consent-based. It means that the advocate is appearing as an agent of a party that *has agreed to the procedure*, and, I submit, it imposes an obligation on the advocate to carry through on that agreement in good faith.

Concretely what does that mean? In a word, *collaboration*: good faith and constructive conduct in pursuing the parties' commitment to resolving the dispute in arbitration. The arbitrators are not a national court or other national authority — the parties are there because they have granted the arbitrators the authority to act as adjudicators. Others have made the basic point in various ways, but it remains fundamental.

Both as agents of the parties and in their own right, counsel have just as important a role as the arbitrators in collaborative arbitration. And that role is principled — and hence, I'd like to suggest, effective — advocacy.

The effective advocate adheres to three principles — candor, cooperation, and professionalism.

First, candor. On procedural matters no less than the merits, the principled and hence effective advocate owes it to the tribunal to lay out the represented party's position fully and forcefully, but candidly. It simply wastes time when counsel tries to hide the ball, or lays out a misleadingly incomplete picture of the situation he or she is addressing.

The principle of candor goes beyond the ethical obligation not to sponsor perjury or misstate facts. And it does not preclude forceful and zealous advocacy. It just means engaging the tribunal and the adversary as a trustworthy advocate ready to deal with the real issues.

And that leads to the *second* principle — cooperation. The principled and hence effective advocate is prepared fully to communicate on procedure and to make a diligent effort to work issues out. She's fully sensitive to the balance between fairness and efficiency that must be struck on all procedural issues, and she is prepared to play hardball when hardball is necessary to protect those values as they affect her client. But

---

1. The proceedings of the 20th Annual ITA Workshop are published in 3 World Arbitration and Mediation Review (2009, no. 3).
2. Jan PAULSSON, "Standards of Conduct in International Arbitration, 3 Am. Review Int'l Arb. (1992) pp. 214-222.
3. See this volume, pp. 383-390.

she has the judgment to distinguish between important points and trivia, and the smarts to propose solutions that anticipate, as good advocates almost always can, the tribunal's disposition.

And *finally*, the principled and hence effective advocate is *professional* in dealing with the adversary and tribunal. By professionalism I mean the fundamental reliability and competence that we appreciate from our colleagues in virtually all endeavors. You deal with people straightforwardly, you do what you say you are going to do, and you get it done when you say are going to get it done.

Surely we can give greater content to these three principles, and I would humbly suggest that the Debevoise Protocol my colleagues and I recently proposed would be a good place to start.[4] But start we surely should, by recognizing this advocacy community as a group of practitioners committed to principled advocacy.

So let me now try to take account of the transnational character of the system – that is, its character as a system not directly regulated or supervised by states. Given that character, how do we foster principled advocacy and enforce ethical norms?

I don't propose here to assess the wisdom or prudence of proposals to develop detailed codes of ethics, including proposals to back those codes with the prospect of sanctions that invoke the authority of national governments or local licensing authorities. For my purposes it's enough to observe that no such scheme is imminent. I'd instead like to focus on how we might use the tools *already* at our disposal to foster principled and hence effective advocacy.

As a matter of substance, arbitrators have great capacity to make sure that they have been provided what they need, on the law and the facts, to decide the dispute on a fully informed basis. And in making this point, I don't mean to refer only to the unusual case in which a tribunal will draw adverse inferences from a failure to produce available evidence. On a much broader scale, arbitral tribunals can make clear far before the award their expectations of the assistance they need from the advocates in order to properly decide the dispute.

As a matter of procedure, the tools are there as well. Arbitrators can craft their procedural rulings in a manner that will provide the right incentives and disincentives, and they can use cost awards to make sure that the responsible party bears the cost of unreasonable advocacy or conduct.

Finally, we should make sure that we are fully employing the best policing mechanism of all – the imperative to be effective. On that score, we should strive mightily to make virtue its own reward. Advocacy is all about credibility, and these principles – candor, responsibility, and professionalism – all result in credibility. I have not tried to discuss the role of the arbitrator in the model of the collaborative arbitration, but the reciprocal part that arbitrators need to play should largely be clear. Arbitrators can *demand* principled advocacy by making that advocacy most effective – by penalizing procedural gamesmanship, by pressing advocates hard when they present unsupported arguments,

---

4. Available at <http://www.debevoise.com/files/News/2cd13af2-2530-40de-808a-a903f5813bad/Presentation/NewsAttachment/79302949-69b6-49eb-9a75-a9ebf1675572/DebevoiseProtocolToPromoteEfficiencyinInternationalArbitration.pdf>.

and by pushing parties to present the most useful evidence and expertise and to do so in the manner in which it can be most effectively tested.

And that leads to my final point about the role of the advocate in the transnational justice system of international arbitration. We cannot remind ourselves frequently enough that we are all, in the end, participants in a *justice* system, though a largely autonomous one. To borrow Pierre Lalive's taxonomy in the realm of public policy, I'd like to suggest that this is an area in which we should develop transnational, or truly international, standards of advocacy.[5] Oscar Schachter spoke some time ago of the invisible college of international lawyers.[6] We should be thinking in terms of a very visible college of transnational advocates.

Just as advocates who regularly appear before national courts must understand their ethical obligations and the advocacy tools and expectations that will make them most effective, we, too, as actors in this transnational justice system, must develop a similar set of standards and expectations. Whether we are acting as advocates or arbitrators, we should have always as our objective that point at which principled advocacy, on the one hand, and high-quality, client-serving, supremely effective advocacy, on the other, perfectly converge.

Many thanks.

---

5. "Transnational (or Truly International) Public Policy and International Arbitration" in *Comparative Arbitration Practice and Public Policy in Arbitration*, ICCA Congress Series no. 3 (Kluwer 1987) p. 257.
6. "The Invisible College of International Lawyers", 72 Nw. U. L. Rev. (1977-1978) p. 217.

Advocacy in International Arbitration: An Art, a Science or a Technique?

Antonio Crivellaro[*]

TABLE OF CONTENTS	Page
I. From Ancient to Modern Times	9
II. The Great Traditions on Presentation of Evidence: Anglo-American Versus Continental European Legal Systems	11
III. What Tradition Has Mostly Influenced International Arbitration?	13
IV. International Arbitration Versus Standing Courts: From Strict to Flexible Procedures	14
V. Arbitral Advocacy as an "Art of Writing"	16
VI. Techniques for Oral Advocacy: The Hearing	18
VII. Does a Cultural "Conflict" Still Exist in International Arbitration?	21
VIII. Conclusions	23

I. FROM ANCIENT TO MODERN TIMES

How best to put advocacy into effect is not such a modern topic, as we commonly tend to consider it.

Two thousand four hundred years ago Aristotle deeply reflected on an equivalent notion: of course, he did not have in mind the "advocate" in its contemporary meaning. Rather, he philosophized about the "art of rhetoric", writing admirable pages on how "rhetoricians" should practice it.[1]

In his view, rhetoric is the typical "art of persuasion", or the "ability of observing in any given case the available means of persuasion". As an art implemented "by spoken word", it is exclusively reserved to "speakers", who have three "modes of persuasion" available.

The first mode is *ethos*, that is, the speaker's "power of evincing a personal character which will make his speech credible". Aristotle thought that, quite understandably, the predominant appeal to the audience is given by the personality of the speaker.

The second is *pathos*, that is, the speaker's "power of stirring the emotions of the hearers", or the emotional attractiveness insinuated in the message; said otherwise, the ability of putting the audience into a certain frame of mind.

---

[*] Of Counsel and former Head of the Arbitration Practice, Bonelli Erede Pappalardo Studio Legale. Former Professor of International Trade Law, Padua University. Member, ICC Institute of International Business Law. Counsel and arbitrator in many ad hoc (UNCITRAL or FED) and institutional arbitrations, including International Chamber of Commerce (ICC), International Centre for Settlement of Investment Disputes (ICSID), LCIA (London Court of International Arbitration), Stockholm Chamber, Cairo Centre, Bangkok Centre, Milan Chamber.

1. ARISTOTLE, *Rhetoric*, Book I, Chapter 2.

The third mode is *logos*, the speaker's "power of proving the truth, or an apparent truth, by means of persuasive arguments": this is attracting the listener by the use of logical reasoning.

He went on to specify that the persuasive arguments are: (a) the examples, corresponding to inductions in dialectic; (b) the enthymeme, corresponding to the syllogism; (c) the apparent enthymeme, corresponding to the apparent syllogism. The enthymeme is a rhetorical syllogism, and the example a rhetorical induction. In the end, argumentative persuasion is a "sort of demonstration" which "stands for proof".

Those who are in command of this art must "be able, reason logically, understand human character and goodness in their various forms and understand the emotions", which implies "to name them, to know their causes and the way in which they are excited".

Reading this language, one should not infer that the kind of speaker depicted by Aristotle is comparable to a sort of shaman or magician. Aristotle constantly insisted on the result that the speaker eventually has to achieve, which is "persuading through logic". The "understanding and excitation of emotions" is just a means to obtain the result: "[e]veryone who effects persuasion through proof does in fact use either enthymemes or examples; there is no other way". [2]

In Cicero's time, approximately three centuries after Aristotle, rhetorical and philosophical works were still confused. Cicero wrote *De Oratore* in 55 B.C. and *Orator* in 46 B.C. (and died in 43 B.C.). The work in which he better defined the art of *eloquentia* in terms that to some extent apply to the present topic was *De Oratore – Liber III*. Reading this book, one gathers that also in Cicero's view advocacy was typically an "oral" exercise. However, Cicero describes the *orator* more as what in modern language we would call an "intellectual" rather than an "artist" in Aristotle's meaning. The *orator* persuades the audience by his *elocutio* or *loquendi elegantia*, which however is not self-sufficient and must be supported by a consistent and publicly renowned *actio*: that is, his visible conduct and the *doctrinae possessio* typically belonging to *homine erudito*. In Cicero's

---

2. The following passage – self-explanatory and still valid today – is worth quoting:

> "And since every one who proves anything at all is bound to use either syllogisms or inductions (and this is clear to us from the Analytics), it must follow that enthymemes are syllogisms and examples are inductions. The difference between example and enthymeme is made plain by the passages in the Topics where induction and syllogism have already been discussed. When we base the proof of a proposition on a number of similar cases, this is induction in dialectic, example in rhetoric; when it is shown that, certain propositions being true, a further and quite distinct proposition must also be true in consequence, whether invariably or usually, this is called syllogism in dialectic, enthymeme in rhetoric. It is plain also that each of these types of oratory has its advantages. Types of oratory, I say: for what has been said in the Methodics applies equally well here; in some oratorical styles examples prevail, in others enthymemes; and in like manner, some orators are better at the former and some at the latter. Speeches that rely on examples are as persuasive as the other kind, but those which rely on enthymemes excite the louder applause."

Quoted from the translation made by Professor W. Rhys Roberts.

view, the best advocacy coincides with the best speeches (*sermones*) and the best example is given by Demosthenes' *orationes*.[3]

Therefore, also according to Cicero the art of advocacy is exclusively aimed at "persuading other human minds" and its highest expression is given by a "persuasive speech".

At the time of Aristotle and Cicero, the subjective emotions of the listener were more decisive than the objective credibility of the speaker, or even more decisive than the evidence in the speaker's hands: the victory of the advocate mainly depended on his ability to mentally captivate the adhesion of the listener.

After more than two thousand years, the end purpose of advocacy remains the same – persuading the listener – but the techniques have progressed – or perhaps regressed. It is quite hard to assert that advocacy has maintained the fascinating components of the "artistic" or "rhetorical" mission described by Aristotle and Cicero. One should modestly recognize that it is now a profession much closer to craft than to art. To win the case, the modern advocate must count more on a huge amount of disciplined training on how to build up the case defences, and much less on his instinctive inspiration or artistic inclination.

Advocacy has become a "learned" profession: the ancient tools of persuasion have been replaced by techniques which are meant to identify the most apt "process" assisting a panel in finding the truth in a given case. This requires fewer spectacular speeches and more humble preparatory work at the counsel desk.

An advocate now recognizes that the process of persuasion involves concrete means of communication, requiring long and burdensome preparation, such as written submissions, witness statements, documentary evidence, direct and cross-examinations, demonstrative electronic devices, oral arguments: in brief very pedestrian tools.

I would therefore be tempted to summarize these introductory notes by offering the following realistic proposition: initiated as an "art", century by century advocacy has become a "technique". This does not downgrade our profession, in that a "science" element is still inevitably involved. However, science is here represented by the underlying legal know-how which, however, cannot itself alone amount to advocacy. An additional technique is needed to make legal know-how a tool for persuasion. The scientific or cultural support strengthening the advocate's argument will thus give to it a "logic" which is not purely "rhetorical", but objective.

II. THE GREAT TRADITIONS ON PRESENTATION OF EVIDENCE: ANGLO-AMERICAN VERSUS CONTINENTAL EUROPEAN LEGAL SYSTEMS

As is well known, the common law tradition is typically featured through a mix of oral advocacy and adversarial process. This is why one party has an almost unlimited right to obtain documents from the other; why documents assume full evidential weight when exhibited and discussed via a witness at the hearing; particularly, why antagonistic cross-examinations of witnesses are admitted and normally practiced; and why the principal

---

3. *De Oratore,* Book III, Sects. VII to XI and Sects. XXXI to XXXV.

(final) hearing constitutes the most crucial and decisive phase of the entire proceedings, capable of determining its outcome.

Differently from the rigorous civil law tradition, there is no restriction on the admissibility of a witness who is an employee of the party. Moreover, experts are normally appointed by the parties and their reports become part of the appointing party's evidence.

Hearings are not numerous, but quite extensive and mainly devoted to the understanding of the factual evidence through witness examination. The examination of witnesses is conducted by the parties rather than the judge (or arbitrator), through adversarial and somehow aggressive confrontation. In cross-examination, a party has virtually no restriction on the liberty to raise questions to the adverse witness, especially when a party needs to discredit the witness. Briefly, the principal hearing coincides with the "court trial" in domestic litigations. Finally, the last word is not the strict prerogative of the respondent only.

The procedural scenario is quite different in civil law tradition, where mostly written advocacy and an inquisitorial process are employed. Accordingly, the admitted documents are those produced and commented by counsel in his written submissions. A party may have access to the documents of the other party only in exceptional circumstances and generally must rely on its own documents.

In rigorous terms, witnesses are *third* persons, who have personal independent knowledge of the relevant facts. Experts are appointed by the court (or tribunal) and their reports are an auxiliary aid which is meant to assist the court (or tribunal) in understanding technical issues involved in the evidence already received from the parties. Experts do not substitute for the parties' evidence, which must be provided by the parties autonomously, not through the experts. This rule is applied to the extent that if a party has failed to discharge properly its burden of proof, it has no right to obtain from the judge the appointment of an expert: absent the party's proof, the expert has nothing to evaluate or check.

Hearings are numerous, short and may be devoted to either specific procedural or merit issues, or both.

Witnesses appear in the proceedings only to the extent they are summoned or admitted by the judge, and are exclusively examined by the judge himself, the party having a limited power to request the judge to put a given question to the witness. Cross-examinations of adverse witnesses are rarely admitted and still conducted by the judge himself, on petition by the party concerned. Submissions of advance written statements are normally prohibited: they are viewed as an inadmissible opportunity for unethical parties and counsel to exert influence upon the witness during his pre-hearing preparation.

Generally, the last word solely belongs to respondent.

In one respect, both traditions almost coincide. This concerns the burden of proof, in that each party shall have the burden of proving the facts relied on to support its claim or defence. The similarity does not impede some slight differences: the civil law system gives, indeed, a more rigorous application to this rule than the common law system, which tolerates some degree of departure from the general maxim (see infra).

III. WHAT TRADITION HAS MOSTLY INFLUENCED INTERNATIONAL ARBITRATION?

International arbitration has borrowed its own procedural rules from both traditions, although it has, of course, created its own autonomous system in addition to the rules inherited from common or civil law.

The civil law system has undoubtedly influenced the presently prevailing international arbitration practice whereby greater reliance is put on written rather than oral procedure. Documents and written pleadings are thus submitted by the parties in view of preparing the future oral hearing and the hearing is focused on debating the most intricate and relevant aspects and clarifying factual divergences which remain unresolved after the closing of the written exchanges.

By contrast, the common law tradition exerted its cultural influence in transposing into international arbitration the practice of pre-hearing witness statements; the modalities for examination and, particularly, cross-examination of witnesses and experts; and the disclosure of documents on one party's application.[4]

Seen from a civil lawyer's perspective, common law has also transplanted into the international arbitration arena its peculiar sensitivity to the primary importance of facts upon law, and the decisive relevance of the way factual evidence is presented. Continental lawyers are inclined to prematurely rush towards the elaboration of legal theories and conclusions, whereas their Anglo-American colleagues are – if I may say so – less anxious to immediately find the proper legal solution. They give priority to an exhaustive fact-finding permitting full and precise acquaintance with the facts; law is presented after completion of this due diligence. The need to conclude in law is common to both cultures, but in one case it risks being unsupported on or contradicted by the facts; in the other the possible disadvantage is given by the longer and harder preparatory work (according to some colleagues this is, inter alia, why Anglo-American counsel are the most costly).

The above Anglo-American approach has become the state of the profession in the presentation of evidence in international arbitration. In my view, considering the obvious relevance of the factual determination (not only in arbitration, but in any type of judicial proceedings), the transposition of this method from common law enriches and improves international arbitration advocacy.

That the burden of proving a claim or a defence belongs to the claimant or respondent respectively, is an obvious proposition also in international arbitration, which however has progressively derived from common law certain flexible variants of the above classic maxim. I refer, for instance, to the practice of postponing the exhaustion of the burden of proof to the end of the proceedings. This would depart from a mandatory civil law tradition that requires the discharge of this burden either immediately or never again.

In arbitration, the pre-hearing written pleadings fundamentally have the purpose of providing the arbitrators with a broad spectrum of facts and arguments. The arbitrators remain, at least temporarily, relatively indifferent as to which party first supplies the relevant proof in the course of the proceedings. Some facts are often undisputed and no

---

4. See the comments by Karl-Heinz BÖCKSTIEGEL, "Presenting Evidence in International Arbitration", 16 ICSID Review–Foreign Investment Law Journal (Spring 2001, no. 1) p. 2.

evidence will be needed in their respect; for the rest, any evidentiary lacuna is progressively cured by either the claimant or the respondent before or, at the latest, in the hearing. Where a lacuna remains unfilled, the arbitrators will make the appropriate procedural directions. What counts at the end is that the evidence is produced, no matter by whom.

In abstract terms, this system departs from the formalistic application of the time-bar rules on the submission of evidence, but it is normally tolerated. From a fair-justice perspective, what is more important: making available to the arbitrators an exhaustive file before the deliberation stage no matter who was the first to produce evidence, or applying the strict rule which rewards the party who first takes action and sanctions a belated submission discarding some pieces of evidence? It seems clear that the first approach is preferable. Sometimes it is also the inescapable solution in consideration of the different cultural origins and traditions of the players (lawyers and arbitrators).

IV.   INTERNATIONAL ARBITRATION VERSUS STANDING COURTS: FROM STRICT TO FLEXIBLE PROCEDURES

Advocacy is exercised before standing domestic courts pursuant to a body of pre-existing rules, established in procedural codes or regulations. The court "imposes" its own rules and little room is left to the advocate's freedom to frame or propose procedural rules different from those which are known from the outset.

In similar proceedings, advocacy is substantially confined to arguing on the merits. It is within this precise ambit, not in matter of procedure, that the advocate has ample freedom to present the case and advocacy may display its almost unlimited facets.[5]

The same procedural regime applies before international standing courts (the Permanent Court of Arbitration; the International Court of Justice) or ad hoc tribunals in State-to-State disputes, where the procedural rules are pre-established. In general, the scheme is repetitive: first, one or two substantial rounds of written pleadings with documentary appendices, followed by oral development of the arguments of the parties. No new evidence is admitted after the close of written pleadings. Therefore, oral development means "recapitulation" or "interchange of argument", depending, inter alia, on how interactive the court or tribunal is; but it cannot include integration of evidence through new proofs.[6]

In international arbitration, what prevails – on the contrary – is the rule that favours *procedural flexibility*. No fixed rules exist and, whenever possible, a mixed system is derived from common or civil law traditions, thus achieving a variable degree of

---

5. For a comparative analysis of the regional systems, see the contributions by Peter LEAVER and Henri Forbes SMITH (The British Perspective), Teresa GIOVANNINI (The Continental European Perspective), R. Doak BISHOP and James H. CARTER (The US Perspective), Christopher LAU (The Asian Perspective) in R. Doak BISHOP and Edward G. KEHOE, eds., *The Art of Advocacy in International Arbitration*, 2nd edn. (JurisNet LLC May 2010).
6. See James CRAWFORD, "Advocacy Before International Tribunals in State-to-State Cases" in *The Art of Advocacy in International Arbitration*, fn. 5 above, p. 303 et seq.

harmonization of the two judicial cultures. Decisive influence is frequently exercised by the personal inclination and legal education of arbitrators and counsel.

Domestic laws on arbitration and institutional regulations provide for the parties' and arbitrators' right to agree or fix the applicable procedural rules. This liberty gives the parties (and counsel) a wide range of options, so that procedural rules are normally "tailored" to fit the specific needs of the individual case.

"Procedural liberty" is now common to arbitration conducted in all European countries and applies to method and timing for: (I) submission of written briefs; (ii) acquiring evidence through documents; (iii) acquiring evidence through witnesses; (iv) acquiring "auxiliary" evidence through experts.

Parties may agree on conducting lengthy witness hearings (pursuant to the Anglo-American style), if they so wish, or no witness hearing at all, if it is commonly accepted that the documentary evidence presented in the written exchanges is sufficient. They may proceed through extensive discovery, or no discovery at all. They may exchange written pleadings only, or – in the alternative – limit the proceedings to oral arguments. Finally, they may opt for mixing written and oral procedures, which is the most frequent practice.

The key issue is that the parties must agree on the procedural rules. Failing their agreement, the arbitral tribunal has the authority to conduct the proceedings as it considers fit, provided that (I) *due process* and (ii) *equality* of the parties are preserved.

The parties' autonomy includes their right to opt for either the procedural rules of a given arbitral institution, or for those of a given national law, or even for a-national rules of procedure (for instance the UNCITRAL Arbitration Rules or, in matter of evidence, the International Bar Association Rules on the Taking of Evidence (the IBA Rules).

A good example – which combines the parties' autonomy with the tribunal's supervision of the compliance with due process and equality – is given by Art. 15 of the International Chamber of Commerce Arbitration Rules (ICC Rules), which reads as follows:

> "15.1. The proceedings before the Arbitral Tribunal shall be governed by these Rules and, where these Rules are silent, by any rules which the parties or, failing them, the Arbitral Tribunal may settle on, whether or not reference is thereby made to the rules of procedure of a national law to be applied to the arbitration. 15.2. In all cases, the Arbitral Tribunal shall act fairly and impartially and ensure that each party has a reasonable opportunity to present its case."

A prudent tribunal will give reasons for its final choice. In particular, it will be careful to assure that the adopted procedural rules confer on the parties the same – and ample – opportunity to present their case, without discrimination or unreasonable restrictions.

Most of the generally applied arbitration rules contain provisions on the taking of evidence, which are commonly framed by primarily referring to the parties' autonomy and, subsidiarily conferring discretion to the arbitrators. Similar provisions may be found in Arts. 20 and 21 of the ICC Rules, Arts. 33 to 37 of the ICSID Rules, Arts. 19 to 22 of the LCIA Arbitration Rules and Arts. 24 and 25 of the UNCITRAL Rules.

V. ARBITRAL ADVOCACY AS AN "ART OF WRITING"

The trend of the last decades shows that in international arbitration advocacy is mostly carried out by written pleadings during the (long) first phase. Oral pleadings (including Anglo-American–style cross-examinations) are reserved to the (shorter) closing phase, but are not per se indispensable.

Thus, written advocacy is inevitable, whereas oral advocacy is an (important) "additive". In other words, in international arbitration the art of advocacy is the art of drafting written submissions. The advocate must persuade the members of the tribunal at a distance by means of written arguments and evidence. He should not wait until the hearing to persuade them by oral eloquence: unfortunately for him, this could be too late.

The advocate must consider that diligent arbitrators (we have to assume that all arbitrators are by definition diligent) come to the hearings after careful analysis of the briefs and documents. Prior to the hearing, they have inevitably made up their minds on the case and reached a feeling about its probable outcome. Certainly they will approach the hearing with an open mind, ready to receive further clarifications which could dispel the original "sentiment" on the chances of one or the other party. However, a diligent advocate will avoid submitting confusing, deficient or misguiding written arguments which create in the reader the conviction that the case is unsupported or otherwise wrong. And he will not forget that persuading in writing is not confined to the briefs as such: he has many other opportunities to send written messages to the tribunal through the regular correspondence exchanged between the parties and the tribunal outside the scheduled briefs.

Moreover, the advocate has the burden of persuading all or at least the majority of the tribunal's members and must consider that, when reading his written submissions, they are not sitting together: one could be sitting in New York, one in Zurich, one in Singapore. The arbitrators will normally start exchanging views on the case on the eve of or during the hearing. Efficient advocacy therefore requires the best efforts at this stage to convince the arbitrators one by one, when they are still working in isolation from co-panellists, as if each would be the one who decides the case alone.

By the "art of writing", I do not mean the art exhibited by novelists or journalists. I more humbly refer to the professional techniques and expertise needed to file an exhaustive and convincing written defence.

The present audience does not need an academic lecture, nor do I have the ambition to impose on it an exhaustive lesson, but I wish to recommend a number of rules which, in my view, make the "art of writing" more effective.

(i) One should avoid inundating or submerging the arbitrator's office with an excessive production of written materials, something that is sometimes called the "Anglo-Saxonization" of the arbitration proceedings. When extensive documentation of thousands of pages and a large number of witnesses and experts are objectively needed, the logistics in the presentation become essential to avoid that the arbitrators lose track of the facts and evidence. Arbitrators must be helped: it is surprising to see how many colleagues fail to realize the importance of the most obvious logistic methods, such as separate tables of contents, chronological lists, pagination, numbering of the exhibits, proper separators between different tabs and the like.

(ii) Do not "unload" into the hands of the arbitrators a massive and disordered collection of documents, not accompanied by specific references and guidance. Facts must be narrated and proved orderly and clearly one by one: avoid generic references such as "see exhibits R-74 to R-83" and insert in your submission consistent references to each document together with clear explanation of its content, the fact or facts that the document is meant to prove and its evidentiary weight. In brief, give support to each fact by referral to the corresponding document.

(iii) An international litigator should be aware that the merits of most of the disputes referred to an arbitral tribunal will be disposed of more on facts than on law. Law is what it is, and it is frequently clear in itself. In any case, law is easier to explain than an intricate factual background, especially when the dispute arises from long-term contracts and a long history of past events. Therefore, deploy your "art of writing" to provide the arbitrators with a precise factual understanding. In order to establish the facts, chronological summaries are extremely useful and continuous linkages between the pleading as such and the attached supporting documents are strongly recommended.

(iv) Concerning presentation of law, every legal ground and relief sought should be addressed specifically one by one. Even more important, quote the relevant law or contract provisions entirely in your written submissions and link your defences to the quoted text, as commented or underlined. Do not overvalue the extent of the legal culture of the arbitrators: while in domestic litigation the mere reference to the number of a given article (of a law, or of a contract) may suffice under the principle *iura novit curia*, in international arbitration full quotation and interpretation of the governing law is a burden for the counsel. Arbitrators cannot be familiar with every type of applicable law.

(v) Exhaustive guidance by counsel in matters of law will, inter alia, help arbitrators in avoiding *extra petita*. It is common knowledge that imprudent arbitrators sometimes also refer to legal authorities or precedents on which none of the parties had relied or pleaded. This risk is removed if, through an exhaustive discussion of the law and presentation of legal authorities, you assist the arbitrators to remain within the boundaries of what is relied on and pleaded by the parties during the proceedings.

(vi) The *onus probandi* also applies to *legal* arguments, at least whenever the proceedings are governed by a law requiring that the law applicable to the merits must be proven by the parties and cannot be determined by the tribunal itself. The maxim *iura novit curia* is indeed of a limited and uncertain application in international arbitration.

(vii) In all cases, keep in mind that arbitrators have the tendency to expect to be persuaded by the party's own efforts; they expect to be "guided" in the understanding of facts and law and, rightly, presume that counsel knows the file best. If the counsel omits an argument or a reference, do not take for granted that the arbitrator will fill your gap on his own. Arbitration is a "party-driven" process and the arbitrator is not supposed to be more active or pro-active than the parties' counsel, who are responsible for the mastery of the case.

(viii) Do not forget that the burden of proof applies to *all* factual assertions: no such assertion may stand by itself without reference to the supporting documentary evidence. If it does, the arbitrator cannot give it any probative relevance.

(ix) Is there any standard style to be recommended for a written brief? Should it be argumentative or succinct? I would say exhaustive, but ordered. Order makes lengthy presentations intelligible and prevails over quantity. Frequent use of headings and sub-headings may be helpful. Moreover, specific complex topics might be conveniently addressed in separate attachments and briefly referred to in the general submission.

(x) Argue by reference to case law, whenever this is available. International arbitrators are in continuous search for precedents; satisfy their appetite in order to strength your case. Whenever you quote a previous judgment or award, describe also the underlying facts, so as to establish the pertinence and relevance of the quotation.

(xi) Be specific and clear in requesting the relief sought: this is also part of the party's burden.

(xii) When drafting the closing or post-hearing submissions, try to use them for "framing the award" that you claim or expect from the tribunal. If you are the probable winner, the arbitrators will be tempted to make an award symmetrical to your frame.

VI. TECHNIQUES FOR ORAL ADVOCACY: THE HEARING

At the hearing, oral advocacy is exercised for the opening statements, the examination of witnesses and experts and the closing pleadings (oral argument).

I find it extremely important for a tribunal to organize a "pre-hearing conference" (or meeting) where parties' counsel and arbitrators discuss and tend to agree on the format of the scheduled hearing – i.e., timing, sequence, duration, admissibility of electronic devices, admissibility or inadmissibility of witnesses and experts in the hearing room, etc. – and achieve an understanding on procedural solutions which is then incorporated in a procedural order issued by the chairman of the tribunal. The conference is conducted under the guidance of the chairman, a circumstance which permits the achievement of a result that will objectively benefit the efficiency of the hearing.

It is in this conference that a number of matters are definitely clarified: whether there will or will not be opening statements; how many witnesses and experts need to be heard and in what order; whether there will or will not be a direct examination before a cross-examination; whether cross-examination will be followed by re-direct examination; how long each such step will presumably last; how long each counsel estimates its oral argument will last so as to apportion equally the available time for the closing statements; whether or not there will be post-hearing briefs, this being also a question the solution of which the counsel should know in advance in order to frame his final oral defences accordingly.

Holding such a pre-hearing conference has become common practice, unless it is replaced by correspondence between tribunal and parties with the purpose of defining the same preparatory issues and thus avoiding deadlocks or surprises at the hearing.

Looking at the practice, the oral openings (or opening statements) are frequently waived by agreement between parties and tribunal. However, this optional phase has in my view an undeniable importance, being a remarkable opportunity for briefing the tribunal in succinct terms on what the hearing is intended to establish. It should be exploited as a message on how the case should be disposed of by the tribunal, and why. As it is the first oral "approach" between counsel and tribunal, advocates should keep in mind the common saying whereby "there is only one chance to make a good first impression".

Of course, the openings must not be used for anticipating the presentation of the merits as such. This must be reserved for the last oral argument, in order to avoid repetition and, more importantly, not prematurely disclose to the opposite party the core of the advocate's strategy.

When, however, the openings cannot but merely anticipate part of the final argument and the hearing time-frame is limited, this first presentation may be renounced with no irreparable harm to the proceedings.[7]

Much more important is the examination of witnesses. It usually starts by the "direct" examination or "examination-in-chief", whereby a party questions its own witness. It is frequently excluded, first to save time and second because the parties prefer to question their own witness in the "re-direct" examination. This occurs when direct examination has a purely formalistic or ritualistic purpose, such as having the witness introduce himself and confirm that the witness statement in front of all persons in the room is indeed his own statement, the signature appended to it on a certain date is his own signature and the statement stands as presented.

However, in other cases direct examination may become more substantial. It is advisable to use it, for instance, to give the witness an opportunity to correct some errors in his written statement, if he so wishes, or to respond to new matters raised in the other party's last written pleadings or witness statements, which were unknown to the witness when he delivered his own statement, or to update his testimony to any new fact that has subsequently occurred. In the case of complex depositions from experts, arbitrators tend to use this phase to allow the expert to make a brief introductory presentation of the crucial issues involved in the expertise and the method followed in the preparation of the expert report.

It is my understanding that a limited direct examination is beneficial to the process: the tribunal can obtain an initial impression of the witness when he is still relaxed, prior to obliging him to assume a defensive posture as soon as cross-examination begins.

Once direct examination is over, the floor is given to the opposite party, which will cross-examine the same witness. Much has been written on what counsel should not do when cross-examining an adverse witness.[8] Surely, any questions on contract interpretation or on damage evaluation, or other "forensic" questions, are not only inadmissible but patently pointless and not helpful to the questioning party's case. They waste time unnecessarily and, especially, risk annoying the tribunal. What the advocate should ask an adverse witness is to explain certain assertions in his witness statement or in a document made by him included in the file, with the intent of establishing a

---

7. Toby LANDAU and R. Doak BISHOP, "Opening Statements" in *The Art of Advocacy in International Arbitration*, fn. 5 above, p. 359 et seq., who conclude admitting that: "If there is one point above all others that should be born in mind with respect to opening statements, it is that there exists no single, correct form for such a presentation. Procedural flexibility remains at the heart of international arbitration...", p. 385.
8. Michael HWANG, "Ten Questions Not to Ask in Cross-examination in International Arbitration", in *The Art of Advocacy in International Arbitration*, fn. 5 above, p. 431 et seq.

contradiction, or an incorrect or insincere assertion, or wavering behaviour, in brief with the intent to discredit his reliability.[9] There are questions that must be absolutely avoided because of the high probability of provoking a response that is harmful to the party asking the question. What tribunals like are specific and non-leading questions that go directly to the point in dispute, be it technical, factual or behavioural.

In general, the advocate should use witness examination as a means to go through the documents, and thus help the arbitrators grasp the relevance of the principal documents which are decisive for disposing of the matter.[10] In addition, the advocate should keep in mind that the target is not the adverse witness himself and that insisting on humiliating him is pointless. The advocate must conduct the dialogue between himself and the witness remembering that the real and more important "dialogue" is between himself and the arbitrators. Examination must be seen as an opportunity for sending messages to the arbitrators in order either to reinforce their apparent understanding of the matter, or correct an apparent misunderstanding.

Re-direct examination is the last chance for the advocate to redress poor testimony by a witness, although the only questions admissible in re-direct are those which fall within the ambit of the cross-examination. As a general tendency, I would recommend reserving re-direct examination only for cases of emergency or real necessity. Do not abuse it for a purely ceremonial need. Arbitrators have the tendency to see it, especially when it is unduly protracted, as a sign of weakness. It should be exploited only when you need to minimize the risk of a misunderstanding concerning certain documentary evidence on which your witness was obscure or failed to give the most convincing explanation, whilst you have good reasons to assume that he knows the precise answer: give him the opportunity to rectify.

Of course, the same techniques are advisable for the direct, cross- and re-direct examination of experts.

Common law lawyers are certainly better equipped for the above exercise, whereas civil law lawyers should improve their training and skills in direct, cross- and re-direct examination and oral advocacy in general. This is not a question of legal culture as such, in my experience, but rather a question of specific education and training. It is rare for continental European or Latin American law firms to make the necessary investment to train their young associates in examination techniques. The legal culture in itself does not play a fundamental role, because the above techniques are capable of working efficiently when the advocate is in full command of them, regardless of his legal background.

A few suggestions will be sufficient for closings: make them succinct and schematic and make use of skeleton and PowerPoint or similar presentations. Do not be repetitive and do not abuse your time: save time for the arbitrators' questioning.[11]

---

9. Guido Santiago TAWIL, "Attacking the Credibility of Witnesses and Experts" in *The Art of Advocacy in International Arbitration*, fn. 5 above, p. 451 et seq.
10. Stephen JAGUSCH, "Organization and Presentation of Documents to the Tribunal" in *The Art of Advocacy in International Arbitration*, fn. 5 above, p. 281 et seq.
11. Richard C. WAITES and James E. LAWRENCE, "Psychological Dynamics in International Arbitration Advocacy" and Audley SHEPPARD, "Closing Arguments" in *The Art of Advocacy in International Arbitration*, fn. 5 above, p. 69 et seq. and p. 465 et seq., respectively.

VII. DOES A CULTURAL "CONFLICT" STILL EXIST IN INTERNATIONAL ARBITRATION?

It is not infrequent to read comments according to which the encounter between different legal cultures in international arbitration "raises suspicion on both sides" or causes "mutual incomprehension, confusion and cultural confrontation" to the extent of giving rise to "a melting pot of cultures ... similar to a courtship between two legal systems that seek a marriage of convenience".[12]

The cultural differences that affect international arbitration are emphasized as follows:

> "In its fullest sense, culture provides us with a sense of security about who we are, where we belong, how we should act and what we should do. When we are confronted by someone who does not share or understand these 'assurances', that is to say, someone who does not respond to the same cultural signals and codes of conduct, a sense of exile and insecurity is created."[13]

and:

> "International commercial arbitration gives rise to procedural asperities, which, even though on the surface they appear to be technical disputes, at bottom represent cultural values in conflict."[14]

I find these expressions exaggerated and unjustified. As a civil lawyer, I never felt "a sense of exile" when pleading in London or Bangkok against American colleagues, nor did I ever see them as "insecure" because – for instance – the governing law was the law of a continental European country or the majority of the tribunal were non-American arbitrators. I have no recollection, after so many years in the profession, of any mutual "courtship" in the search for a "marriage of convenience" or other similarly sad relationships.

There are obvious over-statements in the above caricatures. Some of the depicted difficulties were partly in existence until approximately twenty years ago. Subsequently, practice has been allowed to produce solutions gradually and, at present, the solutions that have been found in the concrete life of international arbitration prove to be amply suitable.

The above-quoted opinions are principally based on the alleged insuperable obstacles that would exist in reconciling an arbitration procedure partly conducted under the civil

---

12. Ignacio GÓMEZ-PALACIO, "International Commercial Arbitration: Two Cultures in a State of Courtship and Potential Marriage of Convenience", 20 The American Review of International Arbitration, (2009, no. 2) pp. 235 to 239. According to the author, "In the air is a sense that 'I want to get you know' along with doubt, pride, alternating cloudy and blue skies, attraction and reluctance. The sweethearts, already mature, at once desire and distrust the marriage that both know to be inevitable," *ibid.* p. 239.
13. *Ibid.*, p. 248.
14. *Ibid.*, p. 249.

law tradition with two Anglo-American predominant procedural features, namely pre-trial discovery and the cross-examination.[15]

Undoubtedly, if pre-trial discovery means obtaining verbal information (depositions) and written information (document production, interrogatories and deposition on written questions) with the purpose of preparing an arbitration hearing, this is something that is seldom seen in international arbitration, if ever. This is rather the common practice in Anglo-American courts, where the object of pre-trial discovery is to obtain information to be used at the trial against the opposite party before the court. It is often used for discovering weaknesses in the testimony of the opponent's witnesses or experts.

This is certainly in contrast with the civil law tradition, where the proof is offered at the time of the demand or legal submission, and a party is not permitted to wait until the hearing to exhibit his proofs.

However, none of these two procedures apply in modern international arbitration, which has found its own way to resolve the issue in question. This consists in allowing one party to request the other to produce additional documents or disclose unknown documents, the existence of which may be reasonably assumed. This practice has become very common.

The typical procedure is framed as follows. *First*, the parties are required to exhibit all documents and witness statements at the same time they file a brief referring to facts that should be proved by means of those documents or testimonies. *Second*, the tribunal has the permanent power to order the parties to produce documents within a given deadline. *Third*, a party has the right to request the other party to produce certain other documents or, failing spontaneous disclosure, to request the tribunal to order their production, being however obliged to describe and identify the document or the narrow and specific category of documents requested, to give the reason why the documents are relevant to the case and to specify that the documents in question are not in its possession. *Fourth*, the party to whom the request is addressed may either spontaneously comply or object to the disclosure of some or all of the documents requested, specifying the relevant reasons. *Fifth*, the arbitral tribunal determines whether the requested evidence is admissible in terms of relevance, materiality and weight of evidence. *Sixth*, the party so directed complies with the tribunal's order, frequently using what is known as the "Redfern Schedule".[16]

This is a procedure which is unreservedly accepted by counsel and arbitrators from all regions of the world, irrespective of their native legal background. The "melting pot of cultures" has caused no mutual "suspicion", "incomprehension" or "confrontation". Quite the contrary, all legal cultures participating in the arbitration arena have contributed to create a level playing field where the best has been picked up from each contributor.

Certainly this obstacle has been successfully overcome and, by the way, the arbitration hearing is far from resembling an Anglo-American "court trial".

---

15. *Ibid.*, p. 251 et seq.
16. The above-described procedure substantially corresponds to what is provided, inter alia, in Arts. 3 and 9 of the IBA Rules on the Taking of Evidence.

The same is true for cross-examination, which has become a commonly adopted method for acquiring oral evidence in international arbitration. I see no abuse in it, nor cultural obstacles which would impede its acceptance by non-Anglo-American counsel or arbitrators. As a player coming from a civil law country, I have no difficulty in recognizing that this system fits well with the purpose of obtaining, at the end, the truth – or at least the most likely or plausible truth – from oral testimony. All that I regret, as I said before, is that civil lawyers are less trained in making proper use of it.

Cross-examination is generally criticized because it is too aggressive and hostile. In my view, first, this is not necessarily true in all cases because it depends on the character of the players, not on the objective needs of the process; second, cross examination is conducted under the supervision of the tribunal, which tends to intervene whenever impermissible excesses must be either prevented or discontinued.

Although cross-examination as such is not unknown in the civil law countries, including the many jurisdictions inspired by it (see the Spanish "*contra-interrogación oral*", or the Italian "*controinterrogatorio*", or the French "*contre-interrogatoire*"), one must recognize that it is unable to convey to the tribunal the same precise appraisal of the facts. The civil law cross-examination is made by the judge himself and little or no room is given to the party-to-witness confrontation.

One must recognize that it is the "adversarial" confrontation allowed under the common law system that helps the tribunal in better distinguishing sincere and correct from false or incorrect testimonies.

To close on this point, international arbitration does not deserve the above-mentioned criticism.

VIII. CONCLUSIONS

Advocacy in international arbitration has reached a level playing field and has found its own fundamental common features. This was made possible by the players' openness to accepting variations and adaptations of their own national traditions and by their readiness to enter into new worlds and new cultures.

The players have accepted to cross the borders, to be taken away from their native environment and play the game in another field.

The journey is not bad at all. You might frequently discover that the "other" field is sometimes more advantageous, for it drives your case to a more favourable conclusion or gives you more freedom to select the most suitable technique. Sometimes you might discover that both fields, the old and the new, are equally efficient or generous in terms of procedural flexibility and that, in the end, all systems tend to be guided by nothing other than "common sense".

The position of advocates practicing in both fields is comparable to that of travellers having acquired two nationalities and two passports. In my experience, I have only received benefits: I now feel a bit civil law lawyer, a bit common law lawyer and I play in a cultural world where a sense of being on familiar ground is permanently preserved, irrespective of where I am actually playing. I tried to learn from both traditions and this has certainly enriched my professional life.

In conclusion, what is true for all litigation is also true for international arbitration: "advocate" is the person who pleads, intercedes or speaks for another person or for a certain cause. "Advocacy" is still the "art of persuasion" on behalf of a person or cause in Aristotle's terms, but it has developed its own techniques.[17]

The only distinctive feature is that the tools that are at present available derive from distinct historical and cultural traditions, but this is what makes international arbitration attractive for those who practice advocacy.

---

17. David J.A. CAIRNS, "Advocacy and the Functions of Lawyers in International Arbitration" in M.A. FERNANDEZ-BALLESTEROS, D. ARIAS, eds., *Liber Amicorum Bernardo Cremades* (La Ley, Madrid 2010) p. 291 et seq.

Strategic Management

in Commencing Arbitration

Strategic Management in Commencing an Arbitration

V.V. Veeder[*]

TABLE OF CONTENTS	Page
I. Introduction	27
II. International Commercial Arbitration	28
III. Investor-State Arbitration	29
IV. Arbitrator Nomination	30
V. Jurisdiction	31
VI. Language	32
VII. Pleading Objections	32
VIII. Strategic Use of National Courts	33
IX. Conclusion	34

I. INTRODUCTION

"Advocacy" in transnational arbitration is now largely written advocacy, beginning with the claimant's written request for arbitration initiating the arbitration proceedings.[1] It extends through the arbitration's written phase with the parties' respective memorials; and after the oral phase it usually resumes with the parties' written post-hearing submissions. Oral advocacy remains important and occasionally decisive, but for all that a party's counsel ever says orally to a tribunal, it could not be said without the writing; and of all the writing, the most significant is often the request for arbitration. That request reflects the most important "strategic" decisions influencing the course of the arbitration proceedings, including its chances of eventual success or failure, both for claimant and, paradoxically, the respondent also.

This is true for most forms of international commercial arbitration, especially arbitration under institutional rules intended for commercial parties. It is even more true for investor-State arbitration, especially arbitration under bilateral investment treaties (BITs).

The form and content of transnational arbitration is thus largely driven initially by the claimant and not the respondent. And unlike the respondent's initial answer, the claimant usually has months, if not years, to plan and prepare its request for arbitration. A well-advised claimant and its counsel will prepare the request with painstaking care; but, ironically, if that job is well done, after the arbitration's initial phase, little or no

---

[*] Essex Court Chambers, London; Visiting Professor on Investment Arbitration, King's College, London University; Member of ICCA.

[1] This change extends even to litigation in certain common law countries: see A. SCALIA and B.A. GARNER, *Making Your Case: The Art of Persuading Judges* (West Publishing 2008). In the United States, that art lies in the *written* case.

reference may be made to the request for arbitration. If the claimant's counsel have done their job properly, the request is the proverbial dog that does not bark.

This paper looks first, separately, at international commercial arbitration and investor-State arbitration. They are similar in most parts but significantly different in others. It then looks at several common features to the early stages of transnational arbitration, each requiring "strategic management" by counsel (using the phrase designated for this collection of papers).

II.   INTERNATIONAL COMMERCIAL ARBITRATION

Historically, it used to be so easy, cheap and quick. One ship broker would walk across the floor of the Baltic Exchange in the City of London, with a short telex in his hand (still warm), touch a colleague on his shoulder, and say "we've got a dispute, the owner wants to send his claim to arbitration, so bring your charterer's file and meet you in the pub after work tonight". That was how, traditionally many maritime and commodity arbitrations were commenced in England between arbitrator-advocates, until we invented arbitral institutions, three-arbitrator tribunals and slow-track arbitration.

Why is it now so formalistic, so labour intensive, so expensive and so necessary to engage specialist arbitration counsel, to start an international arbitration? Why is there, at that early stage, such need for any "advocacy", still less such a high degree of "strategic management"? With recent technical advances, why is the modern equivalent of the Baltic Exchange not the simple "bumping" of two iPhones?

If we look at the institutional rules setting out the requirements for a claimant's request for arbitration, the first part of the answer is obvious. These arbitration rules generally impose a heavy task, increasingly front-loaded with significant legal costs, effort and time by counsel; and the heaviest are imposed by the older European institutions. For example, the Arbitration Rules of the International Chamber of Commerce (ICC) list six separate topics under Art. 4(3) for an ICC Request for Arbitration; the LCIA Rules list seven separate matters under Art. 1; the Stockholm Chamber of Commerce (SCC) Rules list six separate matters under Art. 2; the Rules of the Netherlands Arbitration Institution (NAI) list eleven matters under Art. 6(3); and, perhaps worst of all, the new UNCITRAL Arbitration Rules (2010), influenced by the older European States and the United States, list ten items under Art. 3.

There is another burdensome requirement, namely, the need for the formal service of the claimant's notice on the intended respondent, often in multiple original versions. Art. 2 of the New UNCITRAL Rules 2010 provides for service in no less than 244 separate words, thereby creating several complicated technical procedures for what should be and what once was a short and simple exercise for most cases – a colleague's tap on the shoulder. It is noteworthy that Professor Sanders, in his magisterial historical work on "Arbitration" for the *International Encyclopaedia of Comparative Law*, did not even think it necessary to address the commencement of an arbitration, still less the problems of service of the notice or request for arbitration.[2]

These modern arbitration rules impose an onerous task on claimants wishing to start an arbitration, because, over the years, the rules were modified to cater for the worst of cases, always the outliers not representative of the more traditional arbitrations. Accordingly, that task must now be discharged with the help of specialist arbitration practitioners for *all* cases. But does it need to be so in the future? We live in the age of computers, the internet, email, iPhones and apps; and there must surely be a better way to start a traditional arbitration than with a laborious and expensive drafting exercise requiring ever-more specialist counsel. Could it not be done by electronic means, with a claimant filling out a standard form template on the website of an arbitration institution: succinct, multilingual, simple, paperless and green; that form being electronically transmitted by the institution to all parties and arbitrators; and with the claimant also paying its institutional starting-fee on line? Certain new arbitral bodies have started to do this; others are considering similar procedures; but given that several barely caught up with the twentieth century before its expiry, patience may be required for users of transnational arbitration.

However, all this external rule-based activity is only the tip of the modern arbitral iceberg. Underneath, still more internal activity is required of a claimant before it can safely start an arbitration; i.e. more "strategic management".

III.   INVESTOR-STATE ARBITRATION

Under most investor-State arbitrations under BITs, the claimant investor has a choice of one of several forms of arbitration, whether non-institutional such as UNCITRAL arbitration or institutional such as ICSID, ICC or SCC. The choice will be made by the investor according to its particular claim and its own needs, whether geographic, cultural or juridical.

For example, an investor with a claim dependent on an investment qualifying under the BIT's broad definition of "investment", but not manifestly meeting the narrower definition of Art. 25 of the ICSID Convention, will now generally avoid ICSID arbitration in favour of another form of arbitration. Conversely, an investor with limited financial resources, wishing to avoid the intervention of State courts, will generally prefer the protection of the ICSID Convention, particularly its effect on the award's finality and enforcement more easily ensured under the ICSID Convention than the 1958 New York Convention. The initial choice is important. It is a choice exercisable only once.

---

2. P. SANDERS, "Arbitration" in *International Encyclopedia of Comparative Law*, Vol. VI, Civil Procedure (1996).

IV. ARBITRATOR NOMINATION

Having settled upon the form of arbitration and the applicable rules of arbitration, the claimant's next task is directed at the composition of the arbitration tribunal. Much has been written elsewhere about this increasingly difficult, time-consuming and important task for counsel advising a client. That task now resembles an elaborate chess-game, particularly with the new problems of disclosure by and independence of arbitrators revealed (or compounded) by the IBA Guidelines on Conflict of Interest (2004) and the more recent ICC standard form (2009).

The claimant will want to nominate or appoint a safe candidate free of the risk of challenge from the respondent which could delay the arbitration proceedings significantly. For that reason, the "orange" matters in the IBA's Guidelines operate, in practice, as "red" matters, precluding a claimant from considering many arbitral candidates as arbitrators. This cautious approach is understandable on the part of claimants; it is mirrored in other areas of public life where, for example, a nation's president dare not appoint an "orange" candidate to the nation's supreme court with any previous judicial experience, out of a rational fear that a candidate's public court judgments could only provide fodder for his political opponents – whereas a person who has kept his (or her) judicial views hidden can much more easily survive legislative scrutiny. In arbitration, the new safety-factor creates an unfortunate imbalance of arms between claimant and respondent, the latter with much less to fear from delay can select both "green" and "orange" arbitrators, with the claimant limited to "green" candidates.

As regards disclosure by both a claimant and its appointed arbitrator, an emerging problem arises from the practice of arbitral "beauty-parades". It is now a fact of arbitral life that many parties undertake the beauty-parading of potential arbitrators before selecting their most favoured candidate. At worst, this exercise resembles the excesses of jury-selection in US courts; but at best, in a simple form with appropriate safeguards, it can be a necessary tool in levelling the playing field for arbitration users and counsel. The family of specialist arbitrators is relatively small and well-known to specialist practitioners (from conferences and kindred professional links); but an outside practitioner may want to know an arbitrator more than by name; or a specialist practitioner may likewise want to know a new or younger arbitrator. A short meeting, not raising any likely issue in the arbitration, under the famous guidelines long established by Mr. Aksen ("the Aksen Rules") or more recently (but controversially) by the Chartered Institute of Arbitrators, can build confidence both in the specific arbitration and the arbitral process generally.

There remains, however, the awkward question as to whether and, if so, how much of this beauty-parading should be transparent and disclosed to the other party, other members of the tribunal and the arbitral institution. Under current standards of disclosure, it should be disclosed – but does this in fact happen? It seems that disclosure of beauty-parades is inhibited because, given that such disclosure remains haphazard amongst different arbitrators, arbitral institutions and national cultures, any disclosure could immediately attract an arbitral challenge by the other party. To many, this may not now seem a good enough reason for non-disclosure; but it is significant that the ICC Court, having drafted its new form, has apparently decided that an ICC arbitrator should disclose a beauty-parade before appointment (as was confirmed by the President of the

ICC Court during the ICCA Rio Conference). If so, will the ICC Court now uphold an arbitral challenge under the ICC Rules if an arbitrator has failed to disclose a beauty-parade?

V. JURISDICTION

Under most arbitration rules, the request for arbitration determines not only the tribunal's jurisdiction but also the scope of the issues requiring determination in that particular arbitration. Under a BIT with an investor-State provision for arbitration, it will be the claimant's request which usually invokes and completes the bilateral arbitration agreement founding the tribunal's jurisdiction. Whether the resulting arbitration agreement between the claimant investor and the respondent State is governed by international law, national law or none, a wrong choice of arbitration provision by the claimant at the outset of the proceedings can prove fatal to its claim as a matter of jurisdiction. So too a misstated description of the dispute, issues or claimed relief in the request for arbitration.

These hazards are aggravated if the claimant's request is subject to institutional registration or like procedure as a pre-qualifying condition for submission to the tribunal (such as ICSID); or where the parties' dispute is only referable to arbitration if previously subjected to a pre-arbitration procedure between the parties, such as a standstill agreement or compulsory conciliation.

It seems that where a claimant selects one of several available forms of arbitration under a BIT, that choice is final. For example, having chosen ICSID arbitration offered under the BIT, the claimant cannot later transform these ICSID proceedings by exercising a different choice in favour of other forms of arbitration offered by the same BIT. A tribunal appointed under the ICSID Convention therefore cannot, upon the unilateral act of the claimant, be converted into a tribunal appointed under the UNCITRAL or ICC or SCC Rules. There can be no switching of arbitral horses in mid-stream.

This analysis (if correct) can give rise to logical difficulties when a claimant invokes a most-favoured-nation (MFN) provision in the BIT made between its home State and the respondent host State in order to invoke a different provision for investor-State arbitration in a second BIT made by the respondent State with a third State. If, as many surmise, an arbitration provision in any BIT is a conditional offer or option granted by the State and exercisable by the claimant-investor, would it follow logically that the claimant must exercise that grant at the latest by its request for arbitration?

The first difficulty is whether the request for arbitration (invoking an MFN clause) can simultaneously invoke two different forms of arbitration: could an ICSID arbitration simultaneously be an SCC or ICC arbitration, or even a non-institutional arbitration under the UNCITRAL rules? If not, an investment arbitration remains a one-horse race.

The second difficulty is timing. After the request for arbitration invoking the arbitration grant in the first BIT (still more after any requisite institutional registration), would it then be too late to invoke the MFN clause and seek to trigger the arbitration provision in the second BIT? That attempt could produce, at best, a new arbitration agreement with different legal effects. For example, could an investor initiating arbitration proceedings under the ICSID Convention and meeting an insuperable jurisdictional obstacle for want of an "investment" narrowly defined under Art. 25, later, midway through those ICSID proceedings, invoke an MFN clause to re-constitute the arbitration proceedings as an ICC, SCC or UNCITRAL arbitration?

If the claimant cannot invoke two or more arbitration provisions in the same BIT in its initial request, it would not seem logically possible for the claimant to switch horses using an MFN clause triggering a different form of arbitration in another BIT. Even if the MFN clause produced a second ICSID arbitration, could it really be the same ICSID arbitration as the first ICSID arbitration? Would it require re-registration and the appointment of a fresh tribunal? These are technical problems extending into substance and not mere form.

VI. LANGUAGE

The request for arbitration will seek to establish the basic elements of the arbitration, such as seat, applicable law and language. For international commercial arbitrations, the universal language of arbitration is now English which has, regrettably, displaced French. This latter change is not mitigated by Francophone arbitration specialists speaking French but using English words. Whereas the French language was generally comprehensible to the world, English is generally not. As Sir Winston Churchill said long ago, it was only the English language which divided England and the United States; and the divisions between (for example) English-English, Scottish-English, Indian-English and Australasian-English have become even more accentuated. It is now necessary in literary and political circles to distinguish between starkly different uses of native English, from "Estuarine" to "Strine".

In transnational arbitration, however, non-native English speakers have taken over the English language. It is perhaps no accident that both the ICSID Convention and the New York Convention were drafted in Dutch-English and that the chairmen of UNCITRAL's Working Group on Arbitration (revising the UNCITRAL Model Law and Arbitration Rules) have not been native English speakers. English works for transnational arbitration, with the most pedantic grammarians now coming from non-native English speakers. It is not a little humiliating for a native English-speaking arbitrator to have his award's English grammar corrected by a polyglot secretary at ICSID or the SCC.

VII. PLEADING OBJECTIONS

The request for arbitration must survive what is now the almost inevitable response from the respondent in transnational arbitration, particularly investment arbitration: a challenge to the tribunal's jurisdiction. It may serve no purpose in setting out too fully in the request a party's detailed case on jurisdiction, still less on the merits. Here saying more early is saying less later, because it may facilitate the respondent's jurisdictional challenge to the request for arbitration.

On the other hand, a succinct recitation of the factual basis for the claimant's claim may be necessary to meet a jurisdictional and like challenge. Under the doctrine derived from Judge Higgins' judgment in the *Oil Platforms Case*, such facts pleaded in good faith will usually be determined by the tribunal in the claimant's favour at the jurisdictional stage.[3] There may be an exception if such facts relate only to jurisdiction: it would make no sense a tribunal assuming provisionally disputed facts alleged by the claimant in finding jurisdiction if the tribunal never again addresses those jurisdictional facts with evidence.

The request for arbitration may next meet an admissibility objection, based on a procedure analogous to the US court procedure for summary judgment or the English court procedure for striking out a claim. It is questionable whether Anglo-Saxon court procedures should play any part in transnational arbitration, still less investment arbitration, as opposed to the well-known procedures for an award on assumed facts or a partial award on a preliminary issue. The US influence, however, remains strong, even as regards arbitral terminology in English.[4]

For ICSID arbitration, the position has been formally resolved in favour of an express admissibility objection based on the Rule 41(6) of the new ICSID Arbitration Rules: "If the Tribunal decides ... that all claims are manifestly without legal merit, it shall render an award to that effect." An ICSID tribunal can thus make an "award" dismissing the claimant's claim at an early stage of the proceedings, at the first session or promptly thereafter, if it finds that the claim is manifestly without legal merit. It is perhaps only the word "manifestly" which has protected ICSID proceedings from this procedure's abuse to date.[5] Yet, as Professor Schreuer and his distinguished co-authors warn: "In many cases it [the new rule] is likely to lead to an additional procedural layer, thereby delaying proceedings and increasing costs."[6]

VIII. STRATEGIC USE OF NATIONAL COURTS

Under the ICSID Convention, there is very limited opportunity for parties to resort to national courts, given the terms of Art. 26 of the ICSID Convention. This is not so in

---

3. The *Oil Platforms case (Iran v. US)*, 1996 I.C.J. 803, 856, applied by ICSID tribunals in materials the Decision on Jurisdiction of 29 January 2004 in *SGS v. Philippines* (ICSID Case No. ARB/02/06 (para. 26)); the Decision on Jurisdiction of 8 February 2005 in *Plama v. Bulgaria* (ICSID Case No. ARB/03/24 (para. 118)); the Decision on Jurisdiction of 22 April 2005 in *Impregilo v. Pakistan* (ICSID Case No. ARB/03/03 (para. 254)), the Decision on Jurisdiction of 22 February 2006 in *Continental Casualty v. Argentina* (ICSID Case No. ARB/03/9 (para. 63)); and the Decision on Jurisdiction etc of 21March 2007 in *Saipem v. Bangladesh* (ICSID Case No. ARB/05/07 (para. 85)), as well as by several non-ICSID tribunals.
4. J. PAULSSON, "Jurisdiction and Admissibility" in *Global Reflections on International Law, Commerce and Dispute Resolution: Liber Amicorum in Honour of Robert Briner* (ICC 2005).
5. See "Suggested Changes to the ICSID Rules and Regulations", Working Paper of the ICSID Secretariat of 12 May 2005; A. PARRA, "The Development of the Regulations and Rules of the International Centre for Settlement of Investment Disputes", 41 Int. Law. (2007) p. 47; Aurélia ANTONIETTI, "The 2006 Amendments to the ICSID Rules and Regulations and the Additional Facility Rules", 21 ICSID Review-Foreign Inv. L.J. (2006) p. 427 at p. 439; and Ch. SCHREUER et al., *The ICSID Convention: A Commentary*, 2nd edn. (Cambridge University Press 2009) p. 544.
6. Ch. SCHREUER et al., *The ICSID Convention: A Commentary*, op. cit., fn. 5, p. 544.

regard to arbitrations under the rules of UNCITRAL and other forms of arbitration. These differences can be illustrated by the difficulties now existing within the European Union under the Brussels Regulation I regarding the New York Convention, enacted in all EU Member States but, in several States, notoriously more honoured in the breach in the form of the "Italian torpedo" negating Art. II of the New York Convention.

The uneven decisions of the European Court of Justice in *West Tankers*, *van Uden* and *Marc Rich* and of the French Courts in *Putrabali, Fincantieri* and *SNF v. Sytec* have created procedural risks for transnational arbitration, not limited to the outset of an arbitration. These risks are widely regarded as unsatisfactory to users of arbitration within the European Union. To some, however, any reform entrusted to the European Commission can only promise worse for transnational arbitration; and to others, any reform has to be an improvement if based upon the European Commission's Consultative Report and Green Paper (2009), following the earlier "Heidelberg Report" by Professors Peter Schlosser, Burkhard Hess and Thomas Pfeiffer (2008).

The position in England is now probably the most unsatisfactory of all in the European Union, given the structure of the Arbitration Act 1996 codifying the English common law rules relating to the jurisdiction of the English Court over arbitrations taking place in England. However, after *West Tankers,* the English Court cannot impede, directly or indirectly, court proceedings in EU Member States brought and maintained in deliberate violation of an arbitration agreement – not even by declaration where London is the expressly chosen arbitral seat or lex loci arbitri. Yet the English Courts can still issue anti-suit injunctions impeding anti-arbitration litigation outside the European Union, in support of transnational arbitration. To many, this split jurisdiction seems odd and illogical.

What is needed is better respect, in good faith, by all EU courts for Art. II of the New York Convention (to which all EU States are parties) with an effective power to compel arbitration in accordance with the parties' arbitration agreement. *"Pacta sunt servanda"* should not be a controversial principle, together with the negative effect of *Kompetenz-Kompetenz*. But how to achieve this in the European Union may still take years, given the strength of political feeling this topic engenders and the role exercised by the European Commission. No solution is offered here, save to predict, regrettably, still more malign interference in the conduct of transnational arbitration by the State courts of certain EU Member States.

IX. CONCLUSION

There can be, of course, no general conclusion on this broad topic save to look back with a heavy heart to a foreign country far away where it all seemed to be so much easier, without any elaborate "advocacy" or "strategic management" in starting an arbitration. In moving from the recent past, progress in arbitration should be, perhaps, more simple.

Promoting Peace Before Conflict: Integrating Alternative Methods of Dispute Resolution into the Arbitration Process

John M. Townsend[*]

TABLE OF CONTENTS	Page
I. Introduction	35
II. Multi-tier Clauses	35
III. Roles of the Arbitral Tribunal	37

I. INTRODUCTION

Other papers have covered the subjects of how to prepare for and manage conflict in arbitration. It falls to this one to discuss how to prepare for and manage attempts to avoid conflict and achieve peace.

The topics addressed in this paper – the uses of multi-tier dispute resolution clauses; and how and when an arbitral tribunal may promote settlement discussions – approach this task from two different perspectives: first, from the perspective of the drafter of the dispute resolution clause before any dispute has emerged, and second, from the perspective of the arbitrators after the dispute has commenced. This paper will address those perspectives separately.

II. MULTI-TIER CLAUSES

A multi-tiered dispute resolution clause is one that requires certain steps to be taken – usually negotiation or mediation or one and then the other – before an arbitration or litigation may be commenced. From the perspective of the drafter of a dispute resolution clause, the principal purpose of designing a multi-tiered clause is to avoid the need ever to go to court or to appoint arbitrators, and thus to prevent the second issue (what the arbitrators should do) from arising. Before the drafter even starts drafting, however, he or she must confront a series of decisions about how to structure the dispute that he or she hopes to avoid.

These decisions are normally approached from the back end: Should a dispute ultimately, if all else fails, be referred to litigation or to arbitration – or even to a combination of the two? That is a choice that involves many factors, none of which this paper will address. Rather, this discussion will start at the point at which the decision between litigation and arbitration as the ultimate means of dispute resolution is made,

---

[*] Partner in the Washington, DC office and Chair, Arbitration and ADR Group, Hughes Hubbard & Reed LLP; Chairman of the Board of Directors, American Arbitration Association (2007-2010); Chairman, Mediation Committee of the International Bar Association (2005-2006).

when the drafter should back up to address whether the process for ultimate decision should be preceded by any non-binding procedure.

Before specifying whether one of the possible non-binding processes should precede the binding process, the drafter should first consider whether the clause should require some form of last-ditch, high level negotiation before either process may commence. This may be a question better answered by reference to human nature than to legal analysis.

By the time a dispute between two commercial entities is ready to refer to arbitration or litigation, the positions of the managers (business and legal) responsible in each organization for dealing with the other are likely to have hardened. Positions will have been taken, both with the other side, and perhaps more important, internally. Words will have been exchanged in anger. Egos will be on the line. In such a situation, there can be advantages to a contractual requirement to refer the dispute to a higher level within each corporation. In the most important disputes, the highest level will probably already be fully informed and may possibly be involved, so this approach may well have less value. But most disputes are managed on a day-to-day basis at a mid-management level.

There can be real advantages to requiring top management to step in before battle is joined. It requires the middle managers to make an effort to avoid bothering the boss, and this alone can sometimes lead to resolution of the dispute. If the boss has to become involved, the result will often be a fresh look from a corporate executive with less ego invested in the outcome than the manager dealing with the dispute may have. And top management is sometimes more sensitive to the importance of managing long-term relationships than their subordinates.

Requiring top management of each company to meet also has the often bracing effect of exposing each company to an unfiltered look at the other company's position. The other company's case often looks more compelling if not pre-packaged by subordinate managers invested in the outcome. Such exposure can be dangerous if one's own case is not properly prepared, but a top executive also has to trust his or her subordinates to brief him or her on the strengths, and weaknesses, of the company's case. And there is not much downside. At a minimum, one always learns something from listening to the other side.

Once a decision has been made about whether to require high level negotiation, the drafter of a dispute resolution clause has to confront whether to provide for a non-binding process, either in addition to or instead of negotiation, before the dispute can be sent to litigation or arbitration. Many of the same considerations apply: A fresh look often brings a fresh perspective, and one always learns something from the effort.

In addition, however, such non-binding processes are often remarkably effective. At the American Arbitration Association, which keeps statistics, more than 80 percent of mediations voluntarily commenced result in settlements. That figure results in some measure from self-selection. But even mediation resulting from contractual requirements has a high success rate, somewhere between voluntary mediation and court-ordered mediation (which has the lowest success rate).

The non-binding processes each have special characteristics. Mediation, for example, works best with a skilled mediator who has some hook to work with, such as a continuing relationship between the parties. I have never heard two people define the difference between mediation and conciliation the same way, so I do not propose to try.

Early neutral evaluation, however, is different from both mediation and conciliation and can often be remarkably useful. It involves simply presenting each side's position to an agreed neutral, and then listening to what the neutral's reaction is. That often provides enough of a dose of cold water to both sides to persuade each to moderate its position. This process works particularly well if the evaluator has some expertise in the subject matter. And the evaluation, if properly set up, will remain confidential, so that it cannot be used in the binding proceeding if no settlement can be achieved.

Non-binding arbitration sounds at first like a waste of time. But if it is used, not as a dress rehearsal, but as a preview, it can be very effective. It works best under very tight time limits. Each side gets an unvarnished look at the other side's case. And each side also gets a neutral "arbitrator's" reaction to both cases. Like early neutral evaluation, non-binding arbitration can often bring the parties to a more realistic assessment of their respective positions, and thus closer to settlement.

A mini-trial can be a more complex process, but is best thought of as a non-binding proceeding focused on opening presentations by each side under tight time limits, with the CEOs of each party required to be present and to listen to the other side and then to talk to each other. It is not often used, because CEOs don't like to be on the front lines, but it can also be very effective at dislodging parties from entrenched positions and making them more receptive to some form of settlement.

For all these reasons, the drafter of an arbitration clause should give serious thought to including in the clause the requirement for some non-binding step prior to commencing arbitration (or litigation). It may well provide the last opportunity for a peaceful resolution of the dispute before the bullets begin to fly. That can save a lot of time. And money.

III.   ROLES OF THE ARBITRAL TRIBUNAL

Once the bullets have been fired, and the arbitrators are in place, the dynamic is very different.

It sometimes happens, after hearing initial presentations in a case, or following an application for interim relief, or even during the hearings on the merits, that the arbitrators say to themselves or to each other that this case really should be settled. An arbitration may, for example, involve disputes about how an ongoing relationship is to be managed. The parties will clearly be more qualified to design a solution for such a dispute than arbitrators would be. Or the dispute may present technical issues that should be addressed by experts. Or the arbitrators may conclude that they have identified a path to a reasonable solution, but not one that they can impose in an award. Or occasionally, issues of trust or feelings are involved that might be solvable by an agreement, but that cannot really be resolved by an award.

In such situations, the arbitrators are presented with the question of whether they can say or do anything to encourage the parties to talk to each other. Doing so involves some risk. The arbitrators will not wish to cast doubt on any award they may ultimately arrive at by seeming to have made a decision too early or on incomplete information. Nor will they want to expose themselves to a charge of bias. But often they will feel that they owe it to the parties to say something.

Approaches to this dilemma differ widely among legal systems, cultures, and individual arbitrators, and there is no universal answer to how to approach it. In some legal systems – in Germany, for example – judges in the state courts are expected to make efforts to mediate disputes before them. Arbitrators in those systems are expected to make similar efforts. Parties to disputes in those systems are used to this participation, and seem to welcome it.

In others, however, both judges and arbitrators are expected to confine themselves to deciding the dispute, and are not expected to suggest consensual solutions. In still others – in the American system, for example – judges may attempt to promote a mediated solution, but such an effort by an arbitrator is viewed with deep suspicion. One explanation for this difference is that factual issues are often decided by juries in America, so that judges may feel relatively unconcerned about voicing informal views on factual issues. Some American judges will attempt to mediate cases in which the factual issues would go to a jury if the mediation were unsuccessful, but would never make a similar attempt in a case in which the facts would be tried to the court without a jury.

Where the legal system and the parties expect the judge or the arbitrator to intervene, there is relatively little difficulty for the arbitrator. The arbitrator must be careful in how he or she suggests mediation or settlement, in case the dispute ultimately has to be decided, but need not hesitate to suggest either. The question ultimately becomes one of the arbitrator's own temperament, and how far he or she feels comfortable in mediating between the parties or encouraging them to negotiate.

Where the arbitrator is not expected to engage in mediation, however, the challenge is more difficult. Under American federal law, for example, an arbitration award may be set aside for "evident partiality" on the part of the arbitrator, or for "any other misbehavior [on the part of the arbitrator] by which the rights of any party may have been prejudiced". For an arbitrator to act as a mediator, and especially for an arbitrator to engage in the type of discussions with one party at a time, out of the hearing of the other, in which a mediator typically engages, simply invites a challenge to the eventual award if the case cannot be settled as a result of those efforts.

How far can the arbitrator go? Most arbitrators would feel comfortable telling the parties, or their counsel, in the presence of each other, that the case, or some aspect of it, seems to the arbitrators to be one that the parties should talk to each other about trying to resolve between them. Such a message may be easiest to deliver where part of the dispute turns on a technical issue affecting future conduct – such as how to use a piece of machinery under a license agreement – that the parties are obviously better equipped to solve than the arbitrators.

Most arbitrators would also feel comfortable suggesting that the parties take the dispute, or a discrete portion of it, to mediation. The arbitrators could offer to adjust the arbitration schedule to accommodate an effort to mediate. They could also offer to help the parties to find an appropriate mediator. Most American arbitrators, at least, would stop there. The parties may take the hint, or they may not. But straying farther than these steps from the role of deciding fairly the issue presented for arbitration is generally considered to present too great a risk. It may cause the parties to lose confidence in the neutrality of the arbitrators. And it can put the enforceability of the ultimate award at risk.

An additional complication is sometimes introduced by a request from one of the parties that the arbitrator help to find an acceptable solution. That may be something the arbitrator may be prepared to do if both parties join in the request. But it would be highly risky if the other party resists, or even fails to consent. And the arbitrator who accepts such a mandate should probably be prepared to resign as arbitrator if the effort is unsuccessful.

These are not lines that can be drawn for all purposes for all arbitrators. As noted already, there are legal systems in which arbitrators are expected to go farther, and in which they may be derelict in their duties if they do not. But if the proceeding is in any way connected with any American jurisdiction, or if the award would need to be enforced in the United States, it would be prudent for the arbitrator to stop with suggesting settlement discussions or mediation, and not to engage in either. Compared to the expense of completing, or, especially, of repeating an arbitration, the incremental cost of retaining a mediator who is not also the arbitrator will be relatively trivial.

Use of the Media by Counsel in Investor-State Arbitration

Meg Kinnear[*] *and Aïssatou Diop*[**]

TABLE OF CONTENTS	Page
I. Introduction	40
II. The Broader Context	41
III. The Nature of Media Coverage in Investment Arbitration	42
IV. Implications for Counsel and Clients	45
V. Conclusion	51

I. INTRODUCTION

Many observers would suggest that the single most significant development in international investment arbitration is the increasing transparency of the process. Traditionally it was assumed that international investment arbitration, like commercial arbitration, was private. Bilateral investment treaties (BITs) rarely addressed the nature of arbitration other than to make it available in principle, to designate broadly applicable procedural rules, and to assign arbitrators wide discretion where there was a lacuna in those rules.[1] In turn, the applicable rules usually assumed closed proceedings and arbitral practice followed suit. Hearings were attended only by the parties, their counsel, witnesses, arbitrators and necessary service providers. Pleadings were inaccessible to non-participants and tribunal awards were rarely available in the public domain. Requests to participate by *amici* were unheard of.

The traditional assumption that investor-State arbitration would be conducted in private seems to have been just that: an assumption, taken for granted by all involved in the process. In recent years the appropriateness of closed proceedings in investor-State arbitration has been debated, and in many instances, reversed by practice, treaty

---

[*] Secretary-General, International Centre for Settlement of Investment Disputes (ICSID); former General Counsel, Trade Law Bureau for Canada.
[**] Attorney, ICSID; former Associate, Sidley Austin, LLP.
  The views expressed in this paper are personal views of the authors and are not offered as official views of ICSID.
1. See, e.g., Art. 10 of the Belgium-Luxembourg/Malaysia BIT; Art. 8 of the UK/Senegal BIT; Art. 10 of the Singapore/Sri Lanka BIT; Art. 10 of the Hungary/Switzerland BIT; Art. IX of the Italy/Philippines BIT; Art. 9 of the Hungary/Finland BIT. See also, Art. 44 of the Convention on the Settlement of Disputes between States and National of Other States (the ICSID Convention) which gives tribunals the power to decide questions of procedure that are not covered by the Arbitration Rules or otherwise agreed on between the parties. Similarly, tribunals have the power to conduct arbitrations in such manner as they consider appropriate under Art. 15 of the UNCITRAL Arbitration Rules.

interpretation or formal rule amendment.[2] The media has played a key role in this debate by challenging the assumptions supporting closed arbitral proceedings and by advocating for full transparency. In turn, increased transparency in the system has complemented and encouraged continued media coverage of this field.

II. THE BROADER CONTEXT

A number of shifts in the global environment set the stage for the increased role of the media in investment arbitration. However, two phenomena deserve special mention.

First, the cultural phenomenon of the information age has altered virtually every aspect of communication, including communication about investment arbitration. The development of the internet, followed by the advent of the World Wide Web, has enabled unprecedented access to information and its transfer on a global scale. We live in a time when there are vast sources of information (some reliable and some not), information is usually available for free or at low cost, it is distributed with lightening speed and is received by virtual and actual audiences around the world.

Second, there has been a proliferation in the number of concluded BITs. The United Nations Conference on Trade and Development (UNCTAD) reports that the number of BITs rose to 2,676 by the end of 2008,[3] from 1,857 in 1999,[4] and that "[t]he most dramatic increase took place during the 1990s, when their number quintupled".[5] Investor-State arbitration clauses have become standard in most BITs, including Model BITs.[6] Many new BITs expressly address transparency in the arbitral process, and allow

---

2. See, for example, NAFTA Free Trade Commission, *Notes of Interpretation of Certain Chapter 11 Provisions*, 21 July 2001, available at <www.international.gc.ca/trade-agreements-accords-commerciaux/disp-diff/nafta-interpr.aspx?lang=en>; ICSID Secretariat, "Possible Improvements of the Framework for ICSID Arbitration", Discussion Paper, 22 October 2004. See also, *Amco Asia Corporation and others v. Republic of Indonesia* (ICSID Case No. ARB/81/1), Decision on Request for Provisional Measures of 9 December 1983, 1 ICSID Rep. (1993) 410, 412; *Metalclad Corporation v. United Mexican States* (ICSID Case No. ARB(AF)/97/1), Award, para. 13. Amokura KAWHARU, "Public Participation and Transparency in International Investment Arbitration: *Suez v. Argentina*", 4 N.Z. Y.B. Int'l L. (2007) p. 159; Christina KNAHR, "The Role of Non-state Actors in International Investment Arbitration", 32 S. Afr. Y.B. Int'l L. (2007) p. 455.
3. See UNCTAD, "Recent Developments in International Investment Agreements (2008-June 2009)", IIA Monitor No. 3 (2009) International Investment Agreements, UNCTAD/WEB/DIAE/IA/2009/8, p. 2, available at <www.unctad.org/en/docs/webdiaeia 20098_en.pdf>.
4. UNCTAD, "Bilateral Investment Treaties 1959-1999", UNCTAD/ITE/IIA/2 (2000) p. 1, available at <www.unctad.org/en/docs/poiteiiad2.en.pdf>.
5. *Ibid.* See also, UNCTAD, "Recent Development in International Investment Agreements (2008-June 2009)", IIA Monitor No. 3 (2009), UNCTAD/WEB/DIAE/IA/2009/8, available at <www.unctad.org/en/docs/webdiaeia20098_en.pdf>.
6. See Arts. 22 (Claim by an Investor of a Party on Its Own Behalf) and 23 (Claim by an Investor of a Party on Behalf of an Enterprise) of the Canada 2004 Model BIT; Art. 7 (Settlement of disputes between an investor and a Contracting Party) of the France 2006 Model BIT; Art. 10 (Settlement of disputes between a Contracting State and an investor of the other Contracting State) of the Germany 2008 Model BIT; Art. 9 (Settlement of Disputes Between an Investor and a Contracting

open hearings, public access to case documents, and non-disputing participation. More BITs, combined with increased international investment flows, have led to an increase in the number of investor-State disputes.[7] For instance, the caseload of the International Centre for Settlement of Investment Disputes (ICSID) rose to 280 cases by the end of 2008, more than four times what it was in 1999 (69 cases).[8] By May 2010, ICSID had registered its 315th case.[9]

The combination of the information age and the increase in BITs and BIT litigation has engaged media interest in this field and resulted in significant media coverage of investment arbitration. This coverage has come from a variety of sources and expressed a number of perspectives.

III. THE NATURE OF MEDIA COVERAGE IN INVESTMENT ARBITRATION

Broadly speaking, one can isolate three types of media that are active in investor-State arbitration: mass media, advocacy media and specialized media.[10] Mass media relays news regarding any subject matter to the general public. The most familiar means of mass media communication are electronic (television, radio and internet) and print (newspapers, journals, and magazines) media. The topics addressed by mass media are usually of interest to the public at large or at least to a significant portion of their audience. The treatment of a topic in mass media tends to be on a more general or descriptive, rather than technical or detailed, level.

Mass media coverage of investment arbitration was stimulated by the initial NAFTA Chapter Eleven cases, filed in the mid and late 1990s.[11] These cases claimed large amounts of damages from the respondent States, and many challenged high-profile government measures, such as the cross-border transport and disposal of PCBs (*Myers v. Canada*),[12] construction and operation of a hazardous waste landfill in rural Mexico (*Metalclad Corp. v. Mexico*),[13] or a ban on the gasoline additive, MTBE (*Methanex Corp. v.*

Party) of the India 2003 Model BIT; Art. 24 (Submission of a Claim to Arbitration) of the 2004 US Model BIT, all available at <http://ita.law.uvic.ca/investmenttreaties.htm>.

7. See Barton LEGUM, "Trends and Challenges in Investor-State Arbitration", 19 Arbitration International (2003, no. 2) p. 143.
8. See The ICSID Caseload – Statistics available at <http://icsid.worldbank.org/ICSID/FrontServlet?requestType=ICSIDDocRH&actionVal=CaseLoadStatistics>.
9. See <http://icsid.worldbank.org/ICSID/FrontServlet>.
10. The authors acknowledge that these categories are generalizations, but offer them as a helpful shorthand to describe the different media in this area and as a way to think about the topic.
11. These cases are *Ethyl Corp. v. Canada* (1997), *Pope & Talbot v. Canada* (1998), *S.D. Myers v. Canada* (1998), *Metalclad Corp. v. Mexico* (1996), *Azinian v. Mexico* (1997), *Feldman v. Mexico* (1998), *Waste Management v. Mexico* (1998), *Loewen v. United States* (1998), *Methanex v. United States* (1999) and *Mondev v. United States* (1999).
12. See *S.D. Myers, Inc. v. Canada*, Partial Award of 13 November 2000, paras. 88-128.
13. *Metalclad Corporation v. Mexico* (ICSID Case No. ARB(AF)/97/1), Award of 30 August 2000, paras. 28-69.

United States).[14] Media coverage of these cases was not restricted to the facts and legal issues in each case; it also focused on perceived deficiencies in the process of investor-State arbitration, and the extent to which information about a case was unavailable in the public domain. It critiqued what was characterized as a closed adjudication system allowing unknown and non-appointed judges to make decisions potentially affecting people to whom the process gave no input or appeal. At a minimum, the media saw this as an anomaly when contrasted with the presumption of open courts in most democratic States.[15]

For example, The New York Times published several articles reporting on *Metalclad Corp. v. United Mexican States*,[16] criticizing the secrecy of its proceedings. One article reported:

> "…[a] three-person panel, composed of arbitrators picked by the opposing sides, operates with broad latitude and almost complete institutional secrecy. Its sessions are private, its actions cannot be appealed except in limited circumstances, and its decisions may not be publicized unless the principals involved choose to make them known."[17]

Another article, under the headline "Nafta's Powerful Little Secret", began as follows:

> "… [t]heir meetings are secret. Their members are generally unknown. The decisions they reach need not be fully disclosed. Yet the way a small group of international tribunals handles disputes between investors and foreign governments has led to national laws being revoked, justice systems questioned and environmental regulations challenged. And it is all in the name of protecting the rights of foreign investors under the North American Free Trade Agreement."[18]

A documentary on PBS entitled "Trading Democracy" took the same perspective. The narrator introduced the story by explaining that,

---

14. *Methanex Corporation v. United State*, Final Award of the Tribunal on Jurisdiction and Merits, 3 August 2005, Part II, Chapter D, paras. 1-25.
15. See, Andrea J. MENAKER, "Piercing the Veil of Confidentiality: The Recent Trend Towards Greater Public Participation and Transparency in Investor-State Arbitration" in Katia YANNACA-SMALL, ed., *Arbitration Under International Investment Agreements: A Guide to the Key Issues* (2010) p. 131; See also, Meg KINNEAR, "Transparency and Third Party Participation in Investor-State Dispute Settlement", presentation to Symposium Co-organized by ICSID, OECD and UNCTAD (12 December 2005, Paris) p. 2.
16. *Metalclad Corporation v. Mexico* (ICSID Case No. ARB(AF)/97/1).
17. Anthony DEPALMA, "International Business; Mexico Is Ordered To Pay a U.S. Company $16.7 Million", The New York Times (31 August 2000). See also, Evelyn IRITANI, "Canadians Sue Over NAFTA Bias Clause; Trade Activists, Labor Leaders Claim Pact's Chapter 11 Favors Private Firms at the Expense of Citizens", Los Angeles Times (29 March 2001).
18. Anthony DEPALMA, "Nafta's Powerful Little Secret; Obscure Tribunals Settle Disputes, but Go Too Far, Critics Say", The New York Times (11 March 2001).

"... almost no one heard about one obscure section of NAFTA – Chapter 11 – except for multinational corporations who are using it to challenge democracy.... Today, foreign companies are exploiting Chapter 11 to attack public laws that protect our health – and our environment – even to attack the American judicial system.... Secret NAFTA Tribunals can force taxpayers to pay billions of dollars in lawsuits filed by corporations against the United States.... NAFTA's Chapter 11 threatens radical changes in public policy. But it's all happening out of sight. Citizens have no seat at the table."[19]

Similar observations have been made by the mass media in relation to non-NAFTA cases. These reiterate concerns about the secrecy of the process, unknown qualifications of arbitrators, large awards of damages and the potential to protect foreign investment at the expense of domestic policy prerogatives.[20]

The early emphasis by mass media on critiques of the investor-State process at large has been supplemented by coverage of individual investment arbitrations in the mass media. This type of coverage focuses on the facts of a particular case, specific holdings by a tribunal, or reports on a series of cases against a single State, rather than on the general discipline of investor-State arbitration. For example, the series of cases against Argentina arising out of its fiscal crisis in the late 1990s was carefully and frequently reported on in the Argentine press.

A second category of media coverage of investment arbitration can be termed advocacy media. Advocacy media not only describes the phenomenon of investor-State arbitration or a particular case, but also aims to persuade the reader to see the topic in a certain way or to draw conclusions urged by the author. Advocacy media coverage often extends its commentary to alleged linkages of investment arbitration with other areas of public policy such as health, the environment, public safety or public services. Some advocacy reporting takes the view that BITs and investor-State arbitration interfere with State sovereignty, fail to account for legitimate policy goals, benefit the (foreign) few over the (domestic) many and adversely affect the public good. A substantial portion of advocacy media critiques the closed nature of investor-State procedure, similar to critiques in the mass media.[21]

A third type of media coverage has grown up around arbitration generally, and often focuses on investment arbitration. This specialized media is subject-matter specific and usually reports on technical legal issues such as procedural mechanisms, the latest case holdings or the views of counsel and arbitrators involved in leading cases. It is usually

---

19. *"Bill Moyers reports: Trading Democracy"*, <www.pbs.org/now/printable/transcript_tdfull_print.html>.
20. Michael PEEL and Jane CROFT, "Arbitration: case closed", Financial Times (15 April 2010).
21. See, for example, the June 2008 press release by the Center for International Environmental Law and the International Institute for Sustainable Development calling for the revision of the UNCITRAL commercial arbitration rules to support transparency requirements for investment arbitration: "CIEL and IISD call for an end to an era of secrecy in investor-State arbitration: UN body must support transparency in new arbitration rules". CIEL web at <www.ciel.org/Tae/Investor_ Secrecy_27Jun08.html>.

directed to an audience with some interest in, and knowledge of, the topic and its coverage is often more in-depth than that of mass or advocacy media.

The traditional expression of the specialized media is through academic legal texts and periodicals. There has been a vast increase in publication of specialized investment texts in the last twenty years, including publication of awards, surveys of investment law and procedure, annotations of relevant treaties and rules, and edited compilations of articles on investment arbitration. Much of this publication is found exclusively on internet sites such as <http://naftalaw.org> or <http://ita.law.uvic.ca>.

A more recent variation of specialized media in international investment arbitration has been the development of publications that look not just at the law, but also at the influences on the law and those who are professionally involved in arbitral practice. A good example of this type of publication is Global Arbitration Review (GAR). GAR relays investment (and other) arbitration news, and tracks developments in the legal and arbitral profession such as appointments to tribunals or career movements of professionals in law firms. Some media outlets, such as the Oil, Gas, Energy, Mining, Infrastructure and Investment Disputes forum (OGEMID) or the Kluwer investment blog, go even further to serve as an almost "real-time" forum for the exchange of information and ideas. The Transnational Dispute Management (TDM) site states its mandate "[t]o provide intelligence on [investment arbitration] developments.... [It] is ... a combination of newsletter, review-journal, internet service and primary materials database...."[22] Likewise, Investment Treaty Arbitration (ITA) "serves as a resource for lawyers, academics, government officials, researchers and members of the public who are interested in international investment law".[23] The Investment Arbitration Reporter (IAReporter) describes itself as a "news and analysis service focusing on cross-border lawsuits between foreign investors and their host governments. [It] specializes in tracking and chronicling so-called investor-state arbitrations, [which, although] confidential in nature ... may have major financial, legal and policy impacts."[24]

Specialized media have become an indispensable source of investment arbitration information and jurisprudence. The variety of these outlets, the quantity of information they offer and the speed with which they disseminate information make them important resources, while their informal character makes them user-friendly.

IV.   IMPLICATIONS FOR COUNSEL AND CLIENTS

Media interest in investment arbitration presents both a challenge and an opportunity for counsel and their clients. While media coverage can complement a party's overall litigation approach, counsel should have a clear idea of the extent to which it is proper for them, or their clients, to comment publicly on a case.

From a legal perspective, the constraints on communication with the media are potentially found in a few sources. One might first check in the relevant treaty or

---

22. <http://transnational-dispute-management.com/about/welcome.html>.
23. <http://ita.law.uvic.ca/about.htm>.
24. <www.iareporter.com/categories/about-us>.

contract, although these documents are unlikely to address such issues. Another potential source is the applicable arbitration rules, although again, these are unlikely to address the question directly. For example, the ICSID Arbitration Rules have few provisions governing confidentiality of proceedings, and the ones that exist primarily bind the tribunal or the ICSID Secretariat, and not the parties to the arbitration.[25] A more likely source of guidance is in the procedural rules adopted for the particular case, usually by the first procedural order.

Perhaps the most important constraint is the one developed by jurisprudence: A long line of investment awards clearly states that there is no presumption of confidentiality in investment arbitration. However, this case law also holds that counsel and their clients must ensure that their communications concerning the case do not jeopardize the procedural integrity of the arbitration and do not aggravate the dispute between the parties. In *Amco v. Indonesia*, the respondent blamed the claimants for the publication of a newspaper article which the respondent contended was prejudicial to Indonesia, and requested provisional measures, inter alia, on confidentiality. The respondent wrote, "Claimants' actions are incompatible with the spirit of confidentiality which imbues these international arbitral proceedings."[26] The tribunal replied, finding that "as to the 'spirit of confidentiality' of the arbitral procedure, it is right to say that the Convention and the Rules do not prevent the parties from revealing their case."[27] The absence of a presumption of confidentiality was reiterated in *Metalclad v. United Mexican States*, in which Mexico filed a Request for a Confidentiality Order. In rejecting Mexico's request, the tribunal found,

> "…[t]here remains nonetheless a question as to whether there exists any general principle of confidentiality that would operate to prohibit public discussion of the arbitration proceedings by either party. Neither the NAFTA nor the ICSID (Additional Facility) Rules contain any express restriction on the freedom of the parties in this respect. Though it is frequently said that one of the reasons for recourse to arbitration is to avoid publicity, unless the agreement between the parties incorporates such a limitation, each of them is still free to speak publicly of the arbitration."[28]

---

25. ICSID Arbitration Rule 6 requires tribunal members to undertake to keep information coming to their attention in the course of their tribunal participation confidential; ICSID Arbitration Rule 15 prescribes that tribunal deliberations "shall take place in private and remain secret". ICSID Arbitration Rule 32(2) gives tribunals authority to open hearings to non-parties. Art. 48(5) of the ICSID Convention states that "[t]he Centre shall not publish the award without the consent of the parties". ICSID Administrative and Financial Regulation 22(2) contains complementary language permitting the Secretary-General to publish awards with the consent of both parties.
26. *Amco Asia Corporation and others v. Republic of Indonesia* (ICSID Case No. ARB/81/1), Decision on Request for Provisional Measures of 9 December 1983, 1 ICSID Rep. 410 (1993).
27. *Ibid*.
28. *Metalclad Corporation v. Mexico* (ICSID Case No. ARB(AF)/97/1), Award, para. 13; see also, *World Duty Free Company Limited v. Republic of Kenya* (ICSID Case No. ARB/00/7); *Loewen v. United States*, Decision on Hearing of Respondent's Objection to Competence and Jurisdiction, para. 26; *Marvin Roy Feldman Karpa v. Mexico* (ICSID Case No. ARB(AF)/99/1), Procedural Order No. 5

The tribunal in *Loewen v. United States* went even further, expressly recognizing the inherent value of making information about arbitrations public. As the *Loewen* tribunal noted, failure to make such information public would "preclude the Government (or the other party) from discussing the case in public, thereby depriving the public of knowledge and information concerning government and public affairs".[29] Today, tribunals almost unanimously acknowledge that there is no general duty of confidentiality or privacy in investment arbitration, other than that imposed expressly by the relevant treaty, procedural rules or by procedural agreement of the parties, and that there is value in giving the public access to relevant information.[30] That said, tribunals usually pair this acknowledgment with an admonition to the parties that public disclosure, including interaction with the media, should not jeopardize the orderly unfolding of the individual case. As explained by the *Metalclad* tribunal,

> "...it would be of advantage to the orderly unfolding of the arbitral process and conducive to the maintenance of working relations between the Parties if during the proceeding they were both to limit public discussion of the case to a minimum, subject only to any externally imposed obligation of disclosure by which either of them may be legally bound".[31]

From a practical perspective, the counsel team in an investment arbitration should address whether communication with the media concerning its case is either inevitable or would be beneficial. If so, it should develop a media strategy at an early stage. A first consideration will be to ensure that the procedural rules governing the arbitration allow sufficient openness to implement the media strategy. This should be reflected in the first procedural order. For example, counsel should consider which categories of documents will be public. From a media perspective, it is easier to answer media questions and to

---

concerning questions raised in connection with Procedural Order No. 4, 6 December 2000, paras. 9-11; *S. D. Myers Inc. v. Government of Canada*, Procedural Order No. 16 of 13 May 2000, paras. 2-18.

29. *The Loewen Group, Inc. and Raymond L. Loewen v. United States* (ICSID Case No. ARB/(AF)/98/3), Decision on Hearing of Respondent's Objection to Competence and Jurisdiction of 5 January 2001, para. 26.
30. See, for example, *Giovanna Beccara et al v. Argentine Republic* (ICSID Case No. ARB/07/5), Procedural Order No. 3 of 27 January 2010, paras. 67-73. In 2001, the North American Free Trade Commission issued a Note of Interpretation of certain provisions of Chapter 11 of the NAFTA, confirming that "nothing in the NAFTA imposes a general duty of confidentiality on the parties": NAFTA Free Trade Commission, *Notes of Interpretation of Certain Chapter 11 Provisions*, 21 July 2001, available at <www.international.gc.ca/trade-agreements-accords-commerciaux/disp-diff/nafta-interpr.aspx?lang=en>.
31. *Metalclad Corporation v. Mexico* (ICSID Case No. ARB/(AF)/97/1), Decision on a Request by the Respondent for an Order Prohibiting the Claimant from Revealing Information Regarding ICSID Case ARB/(AF)/97/1, 27 October 1997, para. 10; See also, *Giovanna Beccara et al v. Argentine Republic* (ICSID Case No. ARB/07/5), Procedural Order No. 3 of 27 January 2010, paras. 70, 85; *Biwater Gauff v. Tanzania* (ICSID Case No. ARB/05/22), Procedural Order No. 3 of 29 September 2006, paras. 147, 163; *Loewen v. United States*, Decision on Hearing of Respondent's Objection to Competence and Jurisdiction, para. 26.

ensure accurate reporting if pleadings and other documents relevant to the arbitration are in the public domain. The first procedural order should also address the extent to which awards and procedural orders can be made public. That order should also consider the extent to which hearings will be open to the public. An open hearing makes it easier for media to attend and report on a case and can reduce the burden on counsel to brief the media.

The media strategy should address a number of pragmatic considerations. For example, who will be designated as the media spokesperson? While counsel might wish to play this role, they are often too busy during the hearing to do so effectively. As a result, consideration should be given to having a designated media spokesperson, ideally one with media training and experience.

If a media spokesperson is designated, it is vital for that individual to understand the facts of the arbitration and the procedure sufficiently. The media spokesperson should be involved with counsel in designing the overall media strategy and key messages on behalf of the client. The spokesperson must also be kept current throughout the case so that he or she can ensure the media strategy evolves with case developments. It is often helpful for counsel and the media spokesperson to think through likely questions and how they should be answered. All representatives of the client should know who the designated spokesperson is and should refer media inquiries to that person. It is important for all clients to understand the importance of speaking with a single voice. It is equally important for clients to understand that media coverage that aggravates the dispute is also likely to aggravate the tribunal!

Another consideration is whether to compile a physical, or "take away", package for the media. This practice is increasingly seen in high profile cases, often by *amici*, but also by parties to the dispute. The advantage of a media package is that it makes key information available in an accessible format. It allows a party to ensure that the information shared is properly in the public domain, is factual and supports the overall media strategy adopted by that party. For example, in *Piero Foresti v. South Africa,* the non-disputing parties published various documents relating to the case, including the *amici* petition for participation to the tribunal, the tribunal's letter to the petitioners, and a press release stating, "[t]he group's aim is to assist the tribunal in resolving the dispute fairly while at the same time avoiding any conclusion that would create conflict between South Africa's legal obligations arising from bilateral investment treaties and its human rights obligations...".[32] In the same vein, one might consider whether a press briefing is appropriate to convey background information and the basic messages of the client. While such briefings are unusual, they are seen increasingly in high profile investment arbitration. For example, in the *Chevron* arbitration, environmental law organizations such as the Center for International Environmental Law (CIEL) held a public briefing, co-sponsored by Oxfam America, to explain the legal issues in the dispute.[33] In the same case, a group of Ecuadorian plaintiffs had a press spokesperson and press release that set

---

32. "South African and International Human Rights Groups Granted Permission to Intervene in Foreign Mining Companies' Complaint Against South African Government", available at <www.ciel.org/Publications/SouthAfrica_Media_19Oct09.pdf>.
33. <www.ciel.org/Hre/Ecuador_Chevron_17Nov09.html>.

out the case against Chevron's claim.[34] Press reports also quoted the views of Chevron's media relations advisor stating its position that private claimants had no legal grounds to claim for damages in Ecuadorian domestic proceedings. The General Counsel of Chevron was quoted in a company press release stating that "Because Ecuador's judicial system is incapable of functioning independently of political influence, Chevron has no choice but to seek relief under the treaty between the United States and Ecuador."[35]

If there is communication with the media concerning an arbitration, counsel must continuously assess whether this interaction with the media would aggravate the dispute or affect its procedural integrity. This is a highly fact-specific assessment. However, most tribunals urge counsel to err on the side of caution when making this assessment. For example, in the *Metalclad* example quoted above, after the claimant held a conference call discussing the case and the potential for settlement, the tribunal suggested that the parties limit public discussion to a minimum, subject only to legally binding external obligations of disclosure.

Procedural Order No. 3 in the *Biwater v. Tanzania* case provides useful guidance in drawing the line between legitimate and inappropriate use of the media in investment arbitration. That arbitration concerned the cancellation of a contract for water in Dar Es Salaam, Tanzania. It garnered significant media and public attention, and ultimately both disputing parties complained to the tribunal that the opposing party had launched media campaigns which both aggravated the dispute and undermined its procedural integrity. The claimant requested a provisional measure on confidentiality, asking that the parties discuss all publication on a case-by-case basis, and that they refrain from publishing pleadings, documents and correspondence in respect of the arbitration except by mutual agreement. In support of this request the claimant alleged that counsel for the respondent had given misleading statements to The Guardian newspaper, had unilaterally published tribunal minutes without authorization, had facilitated numerous commentaries in investment treaty newsletters and that this publicity had led to a public e-mail campaign urging the Chair of the claimant company to discontinue the proceedings.

The procedural order in *Biwater* began by recognizing the need to balance transparency of proceedings with procedural integrity of the arbitration. It noted that there is no general duty of confidentiality in ICSID arbitration absent an agreement between the parties on the issue, but noted equally that no provision imposed a general rule of transparency or non-confidentiality. The tribunal continued to hold that actual harm need not be established to justify a provisional order regulating public sharing of information in arbitration and that some form of control is warranted where a sufficient risk of harm or prejudice exists. In the result, the tribunal opted for narrowly delimited restrictions: it allowed the parties to publish their own documents and tribunal decisions so long as these did not contain information likely to exacerbate the dispute. At the same time, it refused to allow publication of minutes, of documents produced by the opposing

---

34. "Guy Walks Into A Court-house. Sky Does Not Fall", Luke Eric Petersen, Kluwer Arbitration Blog (28March 2010).
35. Fernando CABRERA DIAZ, "Ecuadorians Battle Chevron in U.S. Court Over BIT Arbitration in Long-Running Environmental Damage Dispute", Investment Treaty News (March 2010) pp. 3-4.

party or of correspondence between the parties. It also permitted general discussion about the case in public so long as such discussion was not used to antagonize the parties, exacerbate their differences, unduly pressure either party or render resolution of the dispute more difficult.[36]

Another factor relevant to assessing whether media contact aggravates the dispute is the stage of the case: by definition, it is impossible to affect the procedural integrity of a case after the arbitration is concluded, and so extra caution is required while the matter is on-going. The first procedural order in *Beccara v. Argentina* specifically made the point that where disclosure occurs while proceedings are ongoing, considerations such as the orderly unfolding of the arbitration, respect for the parties' equality of rights and avoiding exacerbation of the dispute carry more weight and therefore require more caution than once the procedure has been completed and an award has been rendered.[37]

A final question concerns the remedy for communication with the media that goes beyond the proper limits and aggravates the dispute or adversely affects its procedural integrity. Of course, investment tribunals do not have contempt powers or other powers typically available to a domestic judge to ensure respect for the adjudicative process. Nonetheless, while a case is pending, a tribunal maintains some procedural tools to discipline unauthorized or inappropriate disclosure of information. The main remedy is an order for provisional or interim measures under the applicable procedure rules,[38] or a similar order made pursuant to the inherent power of the tribunal to regulate its proceedings. Ultimately, a tribunal might award costs against a party whose conduct with respect to media communications and confidentiality orders is inappropriate. In one case, *Pope & Talbot v. Canada*, a NAFTA tribunal awarded costs against claimants where claimants' counsel provided the media with a document that had been sent in error by an administrative officer of the respondent and where this error should have been obvious to counsel. In that case, the tribunal ordered the claimant to pay $10,000 forthwith and expressed its wish that claimants' counsel voluntarily pay this sum personally.[39] Arguably, a tribunal might draw adverse inferences against the disclosing party based on the disclosures made, although this would require a very particular set of circumstances to fall within the correct ambit of the doctrine of adverse inferences.

While tribunals have several tools to enforce confidentiality orders and to police contact with the media that jeopardizes the proper functioning of the tribunal during the hearing of a matter, it becomes more difficult to control such behaviour after a case has concluded.[40] Some parties have obtained confidentiality undertakings that are expressed

---

36. *Biwater Gauff v. Tanzania* (ICSID Case No. ARB/05/22), Procedural Order No. 3 of 29 September 2006.
37. *Giovanna Beccara v. The Argentine Republic* (ICSID Case No. ARB/07/5), Procedural Order No. 3 (Confidentiality Order) of 27 January 2010, para. 81.
38. ICSID Convention Art. 47 and ICSID Arbitration Rule 39 address provisional measures in ICSID Convention proceedings.
39. *Pope & Talbot, Inc. v. Canada* (UNCITRAL), Decision of Tribunal, 27 September 2000.
40. See *Giovanna Beccara et al. v. The Argentine Republic* (ICSID Case No. ARB/07/5), Procedural Order No. 3 of 27 January 2010, para. 120 where the tribunal imposed specific confidentiality requirements and noted, without deciding, that

to survive the conclusion of the arbitration, but it is difficult to understand how these could be enforced in a cost-effective way.

V.   CONCLUSION

At the end of the day, the professionalism and restraint of counsel will be vital to crafting a tailored and respectful media strategy in an investment arbitration. While communication with the media can be effective and appropriate, a media strategy must give priority to the orderly and fair unfolding of the arbitral proceedings.

"[T]he question will arise whether the tribunal has the power and authority to decide, either on its own initiative or upon request of a Party, on the continuation of some or all of these restrictions beyond the conclusion of the present proceedings. This question will be dealt with when concluding the present proceedings."

Effective Advocacy in the Written and Procedural Phases of Arbitration

Written Advocacy

Guillermo Aguilar Alvarez[*]

TABLE OF CONTENTS	Page
I. Introduction	55
II. Preparation	56
III. Drafting	62

> "*I keep six honest serving men. (They taught me all I know); Their names are What and Why and When and How and Where and Who.*"
>
> Rudyard Kipling

I. INTRODUCTION

There is only one opportunity to make a first impression. For advocates, this opportunity comes in the form of a written submission. While naturally there is a chance to address the court orally, it comes much later, and by that time the parties' written submissions will have already set the stage of the dispute. The court's approach to the hearing and to adjudication will be influenced by preliminary views formed in reviewing the memorials of the parties, the documentary and testimonial evidence, and the legal authorities tendered in support for their respective positions. Whether in the context of domestic litigation or international arbitration, the orientation, strength and permanence of these views will be determined by the focus, clarity and effectiveness of the advocate's written argument.

Persuasion in the context of international arbitration presents additional challenges.[1] Arbitrators and counsel from different nationalities, cultural backgrounds and legal instruction converge in a single proceeding. A diversity of languages is frequently involved. Competing normative frameworks may govern the merits of the dispute and the conduct of the proceedings. It is not uncommon in international arbitration for

---

[*] Past General Counsel, International Court of Arbitration of the International Chamber of Commerce; Principal Legal Counsel for the Government of Mexico for the Negotiation and Implementation of NAFTA; Visiting Scholar, Yale Law School; Partner, King & Spalding; Vice President of ICCA.

[1] "Many of today's largest and most important legal disputes have changed almost unrecognizably from traditional court litigation: they are resolved by private arbitral tribunals, apparently apply multiple legal systems to achieve their final award and, at times, involve a stunning number of languages and cultures." (F.G. SOURGENS, "Comparative Law as Rhetoric: An Analysis of the Use of Comparative Law in International Arbitration", 8 Pepperdine Dispute Resolution Law Journal (2007)).

counsel to face the challenge of arguing at venues, in languages and under legal norms that are not familiar to all of the arbitrators. Finally, upon completion of the arbitral proceedings, an international legal regime looms over the recognition and enforcement of the award.

This paper briefly explores how advocates meet the challenge of written persuasion in international arbitration. Part II addresses the preparatory stages of a written submission. Part III discusses the drafting process.

II. PREPARATION

There is a perception that British and American influence has been the engine of an arbitration proceeding that places great emphasis on oral advocacy. This perception overstates reality because it underestimates the importance of the written record.[2] International arbitration comprises several stages of written submissions. Typically the sequence goes something like this: claimant will file statement of claim, respondent submits its statement of defense, claimant presents a reply and respondent concludes with a rejoinder. In addition, the parties may request the right to file simultaneous or successive post-hearing briefs. Having said this, factors that might affect the number and cadence of written submissions include the participation of a State or a State enterprise, the type and complexity of the case, the nature of jurisdictional objections, applications for interim measures of protection or bifurcation of the proceedings,[3] and the existence of counterclaims or cross-claims.

In any event, long before counsel address the tribunal orally at the hearing, written submissions provide an opportunity to present, improve and rebut factual and legal arguments. Fact and expert witnesses are also generally required to file written testimony that will replace their direct examination at the hearing. Finally, arbitrators have little tolerance for surprise documents or testimony at the hearing – all documentary and testimonial evidence that a party intends to rely on must at the latest be filed with the last pre-hearing written memorial,[4] and a rule requiring the parties to exchange demonstrative exhibits before the hearing may also be enforced. As a result, "... arbitral counsel will have little chance to dazzle [the] audience at the merits hearing ... Perry Mason-styled advocacy simply fails to convince in international arbitration due

---

2. Art. 31 of the International Centre for Settlement of Investment Disputes (ICSID) Rules of Procedure for Arbitration Proceedings provide for two rounds of written submissions. The UNCITRAL Arbitration Rules (Art. 22), the American Arbitration Association International Arbitration Rules (Art. 17(1)) and the LCIA Arbitration Rules (Art. 15) provide for one round, although it is possible for the arbitrators to determine if the parties shall file a second round of memorials (see G.S. TAWIL, "Advocacy in International Commercial Arbitration: Argentina" in R. Doak BISHOP, ed., *The Art of Advocacy in International Arbitration*, (Juris, Huntington (2004) p. 385). The International Chamber of Commerce (ICC) Rules of Arbitration provide for a Request for Arbitration and an Answer (Arts. 4 and 5) but then grant the arbitrators discretion to determine the procedural timetable in consultation with the parties (Art. 18(4)).
3. For instance jurisdiction and the merits, or liability and quantum.
4. Exceptions may be made for justifiable cause, with the leave of the tribunal.

to a process strongly favoring balanced written advocacy."[5] While the oral hearing is designed for the parties to test the accuracy and strength of each other's evidence and arguments, the risk of exposure of inconsistencies and weaknesses can largely be avoided by careful preparation and drafting of the written submissions.

Paradoxically, the bulk of time required to prepare a written submission is not spent writing. Rather, an advocate must set aside a considerable amount of time to investigate the facts of the case, research the relevant legal principles, and find a place to stand – a place where the facts and the law converge to maximize the likelihood of success.

1. The Facts

Good advocates know their case cold. But, perhaps more importantly, successful advocates know the other party's case better. Getting to this point requires mastering the underlying contract and its genesis, and working with the client in the meticulous investigation of the facts.

In commercial arbitration counsel's starting point is usually the disputed contract. The relevant agreement or agreements and their negotiating history will be carefully reviewed to provide an initial understanding of the parties' bargain and to put preliminary questions to the client as to the ensuing dispute. Comprehension of the deal will facilitate identification of the relevant facts and development of a strategy – facts fall into place more naturally and persuasively when they tell the story of the parties' shared expectations at the time of contracting.[6]

Moreover, the approach towards contract interpretation ordinarily applied in international commercial arbitration often focuses on the intentions of the parties, since the transactions with which it is concerned are between individuals and commercial entities from different linguistic and cultural systems, between whom the possibilities of lack of congruence in the use of terms is comparatively high. Even between

---

5. F.G. SOURGENS, *op. cit.*, fn. 1, p. 5.
6. In investment arbitration under bilateral investment treaties, the investor and the host State do not typically "contract" with each other – the treaty is entered into by the host State and the State of the investor, and the investigation tends to focus not on "shared" expectations but rather on the expectations of the investor at the time of making the investment (See, *Plama Consortium Limited v. Bulgaria* (ICSID Case No. ARB/03/24), Award of 27 August 2008; *Tecnicas Medioambientales Tecmed v. Mexico* (ICSID Case No. ARB(AF)/00/2), Award of 29 May 2003; *Enron Corp. v. Argentina* (ICSID Case No. ARB/01/03), Award of 22 May 2007; *LG&E Energy Corp., LG&E Capital Corp., LG&E International, Inv. v. Argentine Republic* (ICSID Case No. ARB/02/1), Award of 3 October 2006; *CMS Gas Transmission Company v. Argentine Republic* (ICSID Case No. ARB/01/8), Award of 12 May 2005; *Occidental Exploration and Production Company (OEPC) v. Ecuador* (UNCITRAL case UN3467), Award of 1 July 2004); *Rumeli Telekom A.S. v. Kazakhstan* (ICSID Case No. ARB/05/16), Award of 29 July 2008; *Biwater Gauff Ltd. v. Tanzania* (ICSID Case No. ARB/05/22), Award of 24 July 2008; *PSEG Global Inc. v. Turkey* (ICSID Case No. ARB/02/5), Award of 19 January 2007); *Saluka Investments BV v. Czech Republic*, UNCITRAL, Award of 17 March 2006; *MTD v. Chile* (ICSID Case No. ARB/01/7), Award of 25 May 2004).

sophisticated parties served by competent counsel it would not be at all surprising that key terms might be misunderstood, or have different acceptances on each side.[7]

For many reasons, it is key to develop a good working relationship with the client's general counsel. Close cooperation is key to a common understanding of the estimated duration, cost and possible outcome of the arbitration. Additionally, the general counsel will gauge adaptation of the advocate's strategy to the client's goals and, where appropriate, seek business guidance from senior management. The client's legal department also provides an organized central point of access to the relevant cast of characters and to documentary evidence.[8] The general counsel will identify the location of documents, employees who may have left the company, employees or documents not under the control of the client or individuals who may be cooperative or harmful. In sum, the client's legal officer is the advocate's point of entry to witnesses and documents, the necessary inputs of the factual investigation.

Counsel will gather available documents in the client's possession from the designated locations. Counsel will also interview personnel with first-hand knowledge of the underlying project and the dispute. These interviews will yield not only a better understanding of events, they also lead to the location of additional relevant documents, to the identification of possible fact witnesses and to early determination as to the need for expert evidence.

Counsel will organize the facts, frequently in the form of a timeline supported by documents and notes from interviews. Analysis of the facts and supporting evidence in chronological order provides insight into motivations and permits spotting of evidentiary gaps. This is typically the first of many readings, one that will provide the big picture. Subsequent visits to the counsel's record will be more focused, and they will produce a preliminary sense of strengths and weaknesses. This preliminary assessment may subsequently vary, as the gaps in available evidence are filled.

2. The Law

It is beyond the scope of this paper to explore the much debated issue of the proper substantive or procedural rules in international arbitration. Nonetheless, a brief assessment of the normative framework in international arbitration is a useful reminder of the diversity in which the international arbitration bar operates.

---

7. Under some legal systems the court may review the negotiating history to determine which party is responsible for inserting the disputed contractual provision. Under the *contra proferentem* rule of interpretation, an ambiguous term will then be construed against the interests of the party that imposed its inclusion in the contract. This rule applies only where the ambiguous clause was included at the unilateral insistence of one party. However, even counsel who has determined that it is in the client's best interest to argue strict application of the contract should review the negotiating history and be mindful of a possible *contra proferentem* defense.
8. Some multinational companies keep project-specific databases with remote access capabilities, or that are easily transferable. This considerably facilitates the investigation of the facts, and it saves time and money in the preparation of electronic files for the tribunal.

National laws,[9] international conventions,[10] authoritative international instruments[11] and commentators[12] recognize the right of the parties to designate the substantive rules that will govern in case of dispute. In fact, parties make that choice in an overwhelming majority of cases. According to International Chamber of Commerce (ICC) statistical information for 2008, the parties selected the proper law in 86.8 percent of the relevant contracts. In 84 percent of cases, the choice was a national law.[13] However, parties also specified international rules in 3 percent of their contracts: e.g., the UN Convention on Contracts for the International Sale of Goods, the UNIDROIT Principles of International Commercial Contracts, the Law of the Organization for the Harmonization of Business Law in Africa, EC law, international law or universally recognized principles of law. Consider, however, the geographic origin of the parties (120 countries), the arbitrators (74 countries) and the arbitral venues (93 cities in 50 countries),[14] and realize how rare it is to find a case in which counsel on both sides and the three arbitrators are all trained in the law selected by the parties, or in the law of the place of arbitration. By design, advocates in international arbitration face the challenge of persuasion using tools that are frequently foreign to them, and to a majority of the arbitrators.

Advocates are drawn to legal principles quite early, as they gather the facts. However, this process is quite dynamic. Legal research intensifies and expands as relevant facts are organized and analyzed, and as the opposite side presents rebuttal factual and legal arguments. While the starting point is typically the contract, if a clear solution does not readily emerge from the ordinary meaning of the agreement, apposite rules will be researched in the applicable statutes, in the decisions of the courts, in the works of legal scholars, or in other relevant sources mandated by the stipulated arbitration rules. For instance, Art. 17(2) of the ICC Rules of Arbitration directs the arbitrators to "… take account of the provisions of the contract and the relevant trade usages". Interestingly, while Art. 17(1) of the ICC Rules is a testament to the importance of the parties' choice of law, Art. 17(2) provides arbitrators with some common ground: the contract and

---

9. Argentina (Art. 14 of the Civil Code); Austria (see W. MELIS, "National Report Austria" in P. SANDERS and A.J. VAN DEN BERG, eds., ICCA *International Handbook on Commercial Arbitration* (Kluwer, The Hague) (hereinafter *Handbook*), vol. I; Denmark (Sect. 12 of the Arbitration Act of 1972); England (see V.V. VEEDER, "National Report England", *Handbook*, vol. II); Finland (Art. 31(2) of the Arbitration Act of 1992); France (Art. 1496 of the New Code of Civil Procedure); Mexico (Art. 1445 of the Code of Commerce); Netherlands (Art. 1054 of the Code of Civil Procedure) and Switzerland (Art. 187 of the Swiss Private International Law Act).
10. Art. VII of the 1961 Geneva Convention and Art. 42 of the 1965 Washington Convention (ICSID).
11. Art. 28(1) of the UNCITRAL Model Law.
12. See, for instance, H. BATTIFOL, "*L'affirmation de la loi d'autonomie dans la jurisprudence francaise*", *Festschrift für Hans Lewald* (Basel 1953); B. GOLDMAN, "*La volonte des parties et le role de l'arbitre dans l'arbitrage international*", Revue de l'arbitrage (1981) p. 469; T. IONASCO and I. NESTOR, "The Limits of Party Autonomy – I" in C.M. SCHMITTHOFF, ed., *The Sources of the Law of International Trade* (Stevens & Sons, London 1964); F.E. KLEIN, "*Autonomie de la Volonte et arbitrage*", Revue Critique de Droit International Privé (1958) p. 255; H.E. YNTEMA, "Autonomy in Choice of Law", 1 American Journal of Comparative Law (1952, no. 4) p. 341.
13. 20 ICC International Court of Arbitration Bulletin, "Statistical Report" (2009, no. 1) p. 12.
14. All for 2008 *(ibid.*, pp. 6, 10 and 11).

relevant trade usages. Journals and commentators report on arbitral awards where, the choice of the parties notwithstanding, arbitrators applied other rules on grounds that the law selected by the parties was insufficient to solve the dispute. There has been controversy over the appropriateness of this *démarche*.[15] This paper does not dwell on this debate. Rather, it highlights the importance of matching the selection of an arbitrator to the nucleus of the advocate's legal arguments. If counsel's legal case hinges on the interpretation of a contractual provision, the nationality of the arbitrator is not a compelling factor that restricts the advocate's choice. Conversely, if the matter turns on the interpretation and application of domestic law, counsel may be well advised to consider an arbitrator who is familiar with that law.

Finally, advocates must decide how best to convey the law to the tribunal. In general, counsel deal with the applicable law as a matter of evidence. Written expert witness statements are submitted and the legal experts are cross-examined at the hearing, such that the members of the tribunal that are not conversant with the applicable law may contrast this evidence with the views of their colleague arbitrator who is trained in the relevant law. Alternatively, other tribunals may take a more direct approach and require counsel to present the law directly, without the support of legal experts. Either way, counsel not trained in the proper law of the contract will be assisted by local counsel.

3. *Cracking the Code*

The advocate's central contribution lies in finding the place where the facts and the law intersect to yield the outcome sought by the client in the arbitration. Law and facts are critical inputs, but they are not the only source for the theory of the case. It is equally important that the advocate understand the client's business, and that the theory of the case leads to an award that achieves the desired business objectives. For instance, law and fact may support a finding of termination of contract. However, if the client's business objective is to preserve the contract as a means to gain leverage, counsel must find a different place to stand.

---

15. In *SPP v. Arab Republic of Egypt* (ICSID Case No. ARB/84/3), Award of 20 May 1992, the arbitrators resolved the question of calculation of interest by reference to international law, on grounds that the law selected by the parties (Egyptian law) was silent on this point. See also ICC Award No. 7792 (1995 Journal de Droit International 993), where the arbitrators circumnavigate the contractual choice of Argentinean law to interpret a provision of the contract in the light of Texas precedents. For a critical view, see M. MUSTILL, "The New *Lex Mercatoria*: The First Twenty Five Years" in *Liber Amicorum for Lord Wilberforce* (Oxford/Clarendon Press 1987) p. 104 ("[t]he arbitrator is mandated to decide the dispute in accordance with the contract; and the contract includes an agreement to abide by the denominated law. An arbitrator who decides according to some other law, whether anational or otherwise, presumes to rewrite the bargain. He has no right to do this. However good his motives, he does a disservice to the parties and to the institution of international arbitration.") For a different view, see E. GAILLARD, "Thirty Years of *Lex Mercatoria*: Towards the Selective Application of Transnational Rules, 10 ICSID Review – Foreign Investment Law Journal (1995, no. 2) pp. 208-231.

Like judges, arbitrators are also sensible to the equities of the case. A good advocate will develop a case plan that seeks to compel victory not just as a matter of law, but also as a matter of fairness. Bishop writes:

> "Inherent in the facts are the 'equities' of the case – the human sense of 'fairness' or 'unfairness' arising from the acts of the parties in their dealings, the 'wrongs' that were committed by one party against another, and the injury that was suffered by one party as a result. These are the engines that drive the case. The saying goes that the law follows the equities. This means that the law may often be molded or interpreted to do justice as the equities dictate. The advocate should focus on the equities to persuade the arbitrators."[16]

Naturally, the theory visualized by the advocate may falter with the development of the facts or the law as the case progresses. A skilled advocate will recognize this and will make adjustments to strategic decisions by asking new questions and developing new areas of investigation.[17] It is also inevitable that one of the two parties to the arbitration will have the stronger connection between facts, law and equities. If so, the case plan should also be viewed as a useful tool in the management and adjustment of client expectations. For instance, an advocate with a losing hand on liability may still have a winning hand on quantum. Greed often turns the moral compass of the arbitrators against the party with the stronger case on liability.

As a final point, the case plan is also a valuable scheduling and strategic tool. It will provide the advocate and the client with a road map setting out:

— staffing details;
— dates for completion of a first draft of the written submission;
— dates for the client to provide comments on the first draft;
— an indication of areas for fact or expert testimony, and a calendar for witness and expert witness interviews;
— dates for completion of written witness and expert witness statements;
— an inventory of available and required documentary evidence, productions lists and privilege logs;
— target dates for a possible mock arbitration to simulate the hearing and the outcome of the arbitration;[18] and
— a more accurate cost estimate to completion of the arbitration.

---

16. R.D. BISHOP, "Toward a Harmonized Approach to Advocacy in International Arbitration" in *The Art of Advocacy in International Arbitration*, *op. cit.*, fn. 2, p. 454.
17. *Ibid.*, p. 464.
18. See *ibid.*, p. 467 ("... parties have conducted mock arbitrations in some major international arbitrations in recent years in order to refine both the issues to be argued and the presentation of the case. These parties have selected mock arbitrators, subject to strict obligations of confidentiality, whose backgrounds are similar to the real arbitrators in the case. For example, a party will select mock arbitrators of the same nationality as each real arbitrator and from the same profession – professor, barrister, practicing international lawyer, etc.").

III. DRAFTING

The theory of the case developed by the advocate must be effectively communicated to the arbitrators if it is going to translate into a favorable decision. A strident prose, hyperbole, poor organization, and bad translation may all be fatal to even the most brilliant theory. On the other hand, an effective written submission may greatly enhance the persuasiveness of an otherwise weaker case.

First, advocates must be mindful of their audience. Their dispute will be adjudicated by arbitrators, not judges or a jury. This carries immediate style implications. While an aggressive style of advocacy may be the norm in domestic litigation, it does not go over well in international arbitration. In fact, clients who expect hostile advocacy must be educated on the advantages of courteous restraint in international adjudication:

> "Within the United States, many ... clients have come to expect a rather aggressive style of advocacy. This is what they are accustomed to. This is what they've come to expect. And there are times they don't feel they're being well served unless they see you taking that sort of aggressive stance. And yet, within the context of an international arbitration under other choices of law and in other fora, it may be the worst possible thing you can do."[19]

Second, it is very helpful to sketch out the legal and factual theory of the case in the form of an outline that brings out the themes developed by the advocate, and leads the arbitrators through the issues of fact and law to the desired outcome. Use of full sentences to identify the headings and sub-headings in the outline will later assist counsel in the drafting process, and the arbitrators in navigating the memorial.[20] Arbitrators also appreciate an accurate table of contents, and a table of authorities that separately identifies domestic court decisions, arbitral awards, statutes, international legal materials (e.g., international treaties or the resolutions of international organizations) and scholarly writing. Arbitral tribunals frequently also require that exhibits be bound separately and numbered sequentially throughout the proceedings, and that they be preceded by an index that identifies each document, its exhibit number and the volume where it is located. While this requirement may sound trivial, it is key to all future reference to the record, and to the drafting of the award by the arbitrators.

Third, style is, well, a question of style. Personal habits or preferences will yield different approaches and there is nothing wrong with this. However, personal styles should not interfere with the persuasive quality of a written submission. Here are some

---

19. Opinion expressed by Bill Cason in the context of the King & Spalding-Sponsored Roundtable, "Complex Issues in International Arbitration: Inside and Outside Counsel Debate Best Practices for Resolving Important Transnational Disputes" held on 4 November 2002. At the time, Bill Cason was listed as Vice-President and Assistant General Counsel of Oceana International Ltd.
20. "Without subheadings, the reader would face a vexatious reading experience." (S.A. VAUGHAN, "Persuasion Is An Art ... But It Is Also An Invaluable Tool In Advocacy", 61 Baylor Law Review p. 635). See also A. SCALIA and B. GARNER, *Making Your Case: The Art of Persuading Judges* (Thomson/West 2008) p. 59 ("The primary purpose of written submissions in legal proceedings is to assist the court in the adjudication of a dispute.").

recommendations on effective written briefing by Justice Scalia of the US Supreme Court and Bryan Garner:

(a) master language;[21]
(b) be clear;[22]
(c) be brief;[23]
(d) make it interesting;[24]
(e) don't misstate the facts;[25]
(f) don't misstate the law;[26]
(g) don't stray from your legal argument;[27]
(h) keep it simple;[28]
(I) use examples;[29] and
(j) revise, revise, revise.[30]

---

21. A. SCALIA and B. GARNER, *op. cit.*, fn. 20, p. 61 ("Lawyers possess only one tool to convey their thoughts: language. They must acquire and hone the finest, most effective version of that tool available. They must love words and use them exactly.").
22. *Ibid.*, p. 107 ("In brief-writing, one feature of a good style trumps all others. Literary elegance, erudition, sophistication or expression – these and all other qualities must be sacrificed if they detract from clarity.").
23. *Ibid.*, p. 98 ("Judges often associate the brevity of the brief with the quality of the lawyer. Many judges ... say that good lawyers often come in far below the page limits – and that bad lawyers almost never do.").
24. *Ibid.*, p. 112 ("Three simple ways to add interest to your writing are to enliven your word choices, to mix up your sentence structure, and to vary your sentence lengths. With words, ask yourself whether there is a more colorful way to put it. With sentences, guard against falling into a monotonous subject-verb-object rut – especially when it's the same subject sentence after sentence. And remember that an occasional arrestingly short sentence can deliver real punch.").
25. *Ibid.*, p. 93 ("Omitting a fact crucial to your case is a critical mistake. An even worse one is misstating a fact. Nothing is easier for the other side to point out, and nothing can so significantly damage your credibility.") and p. 95 ("A fair statement of the facts includes relevant facts that are adverse to your case. They will come out anyway, and if you omit them you simply give opposing counsel an opportunity to show the court that you're untrustworthy.").
26. *Ibid.*, p. 123. ("The impression you want to make on the court – that you're knowledgeable and even expert – will be compromised by any misdescription that opposing counsel brings to the court's attention. If a case is only close but not completely on point, say so. Then explain why the difference is insubstantial and should not affect the outcome.").
27. *Ibid.*, p. 98 "... keep your eye on the ball. Write down at the outset, and keep before you throughout your drafting of the Argument, the syllogism that wins your case. Each aspect of the argument must be consistent with this and should be no more sweeping than necessary to support it. Nothing should be irrelevant to it.").
28. *Ibid.*, p. 113 ("Banish jargon, hackneyed expressions, and needless Latin.").
29. *Ibid.*, p. 111 ("Legal briefs are necessarily filled with abstract concepts that are difficult to explain. Nothing clarifies their meaning as well as examples.") In international arbitration, recourse to comparative law may also be a valuable device to explain the contours of legal concepts that may be foreign to one or more of the arbitrators (for use of comparative law as an instrument of persuasion see F.G. SOURGENS, *op. cit.*, fn. 1).
30. A. SCALIA and B. GARNER, *op. cit.*, fn. 20, pp. 80-81.

Keeping to these simple guidelines will produce a written submission more likely to assist the arbitrators in the efficient adjudication of the dispute, and it will also strengthen the credibility of counsel.

Discovery in International Arbitration: A Foreign Creature for Civil Lawyers?

Jalal El Ahdab and Amal Bouchenaki***

TABLE OF CONTENTS	Page
I. Introduction	65
II. Discovery and Documentary Evidence in Common Law and Civil Law Systems: Some Shared Foundations With Significant Practical Differences	71
III. The Taking of Evidence in International Arbitration: a Marriage of Convenience	89
IV. Conclusion	112
Annex I: Timing and Other Issues of Time Management	114

"Say not, 'I have found the truth,' but rather, 'I have found a truth.'"

Khalil Gibran[1]

I. INTRODUCTION

1. Irresistible Influence of American Legal Culture?

The influence of American culture, values or power is the subject of continuing discussion, lament, and/or fascination. As the weight of United States economic interests grew in the nineteenth and twentieth centuries, so did the bearing of the procedural expectations of US entities and counsel engaged in international disputes outside the United States. It is widely accepted that international commercial arbitration is the preferred mode of resolution of international business disputes. Businesses, it is said, would rather litigate in their home courts. But with international conflict comes the need for neutrality. And with business disputes comes the need for greater flexibility and, often, greater confidentiality. Arbitration, a contract-based dispute resolution mechanism, is viewed to fulfill, more or less satisfactorily, these objectives. Arbitration is the creature of the parties' intent. As such, it is assumed to respond to parties' expectations of what the arbitral process should be.

---

* Of Counsel, Orrick, Paris; admitted to practice in France and Lebanon.
** Of Counsel, Gibson Dunn, New York; admitted to practice in France and California.
  The authors are grateful for the assistance provided by Orrick associates James Claxton, Yann Schneller, and Michelle Sequeira, and by Thiara Moraes, attorney in Paris.
1. *The Prophet* (Self Knowledge).

Expectations of users, arbitrators and counsel regarding the international arbitral process differ depending on their legal systems of origin.[2] Setting up a system of international adjudication that would conciliate diverse legal traditions has been the preoccupation of international jurists for many decades. Today, some practitioners and scholars view international arbitration as a "system" that has achieved a certain level of transnationality, bridging the divide between legal traditions:[3] a forum for international merchants. Many, however, disagree with the view that the practice of international arbitration has somehow evolved into an autonomous adjudicatory mechanism, unmoored from one single system of law. Yet, "arbitration fascinates", wrote Professor Oppetit, precisely because of the "impression it gives to escape from the grasp of organized societies, because of the ambiguity, source of liberty, resulting from its loose geographical roots…".[4]

---

2. P. MAYER, *"Le pouvoir des arbitres de régler la procédure une analyse comparative des systèmes de civil law et de common law"*, Rev. arb. (1995) p. 163 at p. 170. Pierre Mayer, refers to a "psychological phenomenon", which consists of the arbitrator's conviction that "the sole 'right' manner to conduct the proceeding is the one complying with the fundamental principles, or even merely the rooted customs, that govern arbitration in his country". Then at p. 181: the "legal culture", as opposed to procedural rules per se, "is extraterritorial" as "it haunts the arbitrator's brain and travels with him". See also: I. FADLALLAH, "Arbitration Facing Conflicts of Culture", 25 Arb. Int'l (2009, issue 3) p. 303, sp. at p. 311 et seq.
3. F. TERRÉ, ed., *"L'américanisation du droit"*, 45 Arch. de phil. du droit, (LGDJ 2001); "ALI/UNIDROIT Principles and Rules of Transnational Civil Procedure: Proposed Final Draft (9 March 2004)", Philadelphia: American Law Institute, 2004/Rome: UNIDROIT, 2004; about which: Ph. FOUCHARD's criticisms in *"Discours de clôture du colloque"*, Vers un procès universel? Les règles transnationales de procédure civile de l'Amercian Law Institute (ed. Panthéon-Assas, LGDJ 2001, no. 201) p. 153; C. KESSEDJIAN, *"La modélisation procédurale"* in E. LOQUIN and C. KESSEDJIAN, eds., La mondialisation du droit (Litec, 2000) p. 238; see also M. CAPPELLETTI, ed., International Encyclopedia of Comparative Law, Vol. 16: Civil Procedure (J.C.B. Mohr, Tubingen 1973); F. CARPI and M. A. LUPOI, eds., Scritti sul diritto processuale civile transnazionale e comparator (Giappichelli 2001); M.-L. NIBOYET, *"La globalisation du procès civil international dans l'espace judiciaire européen et mondial"*, JDI (2006) p. 937.
4. B. OPPETIT, Théorie de l'arbitrage, (PUF 1998) p. 9.

As illustrated by the vast number of articles on the topic,[5] the taking of evidence in

---

5. *L'administration de la preuve, Journées d'études de Londres*, 15 Feb. 1974: Rev. arb. (1974) p. 117 et seq.; C. DIERYCK, *"Procédure et moyens de preuve dans l'arbitrage commercial international"*, Rev. arb. (1988) p. 267-282; Cl. REYMOND, "Civil Law and Common Law Procedures: Which is the More Inquisitorial? A Civil Lawyer's Response", 5 Arb. Int'l (1989, no. 4) pp. 357-368; A.L. MARRIOTT, "Evidence in International Arbitration", 5 Arb. Int'l, (1989, no. 3) pp. 280-290; M. DE BOISSÉSON, *Le droit français de l'arbitrage interne et international*, 2nd edn. (GLN July 1990) no. 745 et seq.; W. MELIS, "Presentation of Documentary Evidence and Witnesses" in *Preventing Delay and Disruption of Arbitration, and Effective Proceedings in Construction Cases*, ICCA Congress series no. 5 (Kluwer 1991) pp. 511-515; L.W. NEWMAN and R. CASTILLA, "Production of Evidencethrough U.S. Courts for Use in International Arbitration", 9 J. Int'l Arb. (1992, no. 2), pp. 61-70; H. SMIT, "Roles of the Arbitral Tribunal in Civil Law and Common Law Systems with Respect to Presentation of Evidence" in *Planning Efficient Arbitration Proceedings and the Law Applicable in International Arbitration,* ICCA Congress series no. 7 (Wolters Kluwer 1996) p. 161 (hereinafter *ICCA Congress Series no. 7*); Andrew ROGERS, "Improving Procedures for Discovery and Documentary Evidence" in *ICCA Congress Series no. 7*, p. 131; J. PAULSSON, "Overview of Methods of Presenting Evidence in Different Legal Systems" in *ICCA Congress Series no. 7*, p. 112; M. PATOCCHI and I. MEAKIN, "Procedure and the Taking of Evidence in International Commercial Arbitration – The Interaction of Civil and Common Law Procedures", IBLJ (1996) p. 884; P. FRIEDLAND, "Combining Civil Law and Common Law Elements in the Presentation of Evidence in International Commercial Arbitration", 12-9 Mealey's Intl. Arb. Rep. 13 (1997); G.C. HAZARD, Jr., "Discovery and the Role of the Judge in Civil Law Jurisdictions", 73 Notre Dame L. Rev. (1997-1998) p. 1017; E. GAILLARD and J. SAVAGE, eds., *Fouchard Gaillard Goldman on International Commercial Arbitration* (Kluwer Law International 1999) paras. 1251 and 1261 et seq.; S.A. SALEH, "Reflections on Admissibility of Evidence: Interrelation Between Domestic Law and International Arbitration", 15 Arb. Int'l (1999, no. 2) pp. 141-160; D.B. KING and L. BOSMAN, *"Repenser la Problématique de la Discovery dans l'Arbitrage International au-delà du clivage entre common law et droit romain"*, 12 ICC Bull. (2001, no. 1) p. 21; T.H. WEBSTER, "Obtaining Documents from Adverse Parties in International Arbitration", 17 Arb. Int'l (2001, no. 1); W.L. CRAIG, W.W. PARK and J. PAULSSON, *International Chamber of Commerce Arbitration*, 3rd edn. (2001) paras. 23-01 et seq.; A. BAUM, "Reconciling Anglo-Saxon and Civil Law Procedure: The Path to a Procedural Lex Arbitrationis" in R. BRINER, L.Y. FORTIER, K.-P. BERGER and J. BREDOW, eds., *Recht der Internationalen Wirtschaft und Streiterledigung im 21. Jahrhundert: Liber Amicorum Karl-Heinz Böckstiegel* (Carl Heymanns Verlag 2001); J.H. RUBINSTEIN and Britton B. GUERRINA, "The Attorney-Client Privilege and International Arbitration", 18 J. Int'l Arb. (2001, no. 6) pp. 587-602; S.H. ELSING and J.M. TOWNSEND, "Bridging the Common Law-Civil Law Divide in Arbitration", 18 Arb. Int'l (2002, no. 1) p. 59; H. RAESCHKE-KESSLER, "The Production of Documents in International Arbitration – A Commentary on Article 3 of the New IBA Rules of Evidence", 18 Arb. Int'l (2002, no. 4) p. 411; S. ELSING, *Internationale Schiedsgerichte als Mittler zwischen prozessualen Rechtskulturen*, BB 2002, IDR-Beilage, p. 19 et seq. (at pp. 21-22); V. TRIEBEL and J. ZONS, *Discovery of Documents in internationalen Schiedsverfahren*, BB (2002) IDR-Beilage, p. 26; M. WIRTH, *"Ihr Zeuge, Herr Rechtsanwalt"*, SchiedsVZ (2003) p. 9 et seq. (at pp. 11 to 13); K. SACHS, "Use of Documents and Document Discovery: 'Fishing Expeditions' Versus Transparency and Burden of Proof", 5 SchiedsVZ (2003) pp. 193-198; G.M. VON MEHREN and Cl.T. SALOMON, "Submitting Evidence in an International Arbitration: The Common Lawyer's Guide", 20 J. Int'l Arb. (2003, no. 3) pp. 285-294; G. KAUFMANN-KOHLER, "Globalization of Arbitral Procedure", 36 Vand. J. Transnat'l L. (2003) p. 1313; J.D.M. LEW, L.A. MISTELIS and S.M. KRÖLL, *Comparative International Commercial Arbitration* (2003) p. 553; Y. DERAINS, *"La pratique de l'administration de la preuve dans l'arbitrage commercial international"*, Rev. arb. (2004) p. 780; G. KAUFMANN-KOHLER and Ph. BÄRTSCH, "Discovery in

international arbitration is an important piece of the debate on "transnationality" of the arbitral process. Users are sometimes frustrated with how evidence tends to be administered in a number of international arbitral proceedings. At the ICCA 50th Anniversary Conference,[6] a panel of "clients" identified the evidentiary phase of the arbitral process as one of the principal defects and main source of added costs and delays in international arbitration.

Lawyers from both the Romano-Germanic and common law traditions readily attribute the perceived ineffectiveness of the evidentiary process in arbitration to the spread of discovery "*à l'américaine*". Could lack of familiarity with common law-inspired procedures be the reason for US-style discovery taking the blame? While lack of familiarity can be an explanation for the Romano-Germanic lawyers'[7] discontent, surely

---

International Arbitration: How Much Is Too Much?", SchiedsVZ (2004, no. 1) pp. 13-21; B. HANOTIAU, "Civil Law and Common Law Procedural Traditions in International Arbitration: Who Has Crossed the Bridge?" in *Arbitral Procedure at the Dawn of the New Millenium*, Coll. CEPANI (Bruylant 2005) p. 83; Y. DERAINS and E.A. SCHWARTZ, *A Guide to the ICC Rules of Arbitration*, 2nd edn. (Kluwer Law International 2005) p. 270 et seq.; *Document Production in International Arbitration*", ICC Bull., 2006 Special Supplement (hereinafter ICC Bull. Sp. Suppl. 2006); R. PIETROWSKI, "Evidence in International Arbitration", 22 Arb. Int'l (2006, no. 3) pp. 373-410; U.M. LAEUCHLI, "Civil and Common Law: Contrast and Synthesis in International Arbitration", 62 Disp. Resol. J. (2007) pp. 81-82; J.-F. POUDRET and S. BESSON, *Comparative Law of International Arbitration*, 2nd edn. (Sweet & Maxwell 2007) at paras. 649 et seq.; C. BROWN, *A Common Law of International Adjudication* (Oxford University Press 2007) p. 83 et seq.; A. DE LOTBINIÈRE MCDOUGALL and N. BOUCHARDIE, "How International Arbitral Tribunals Establish the Facts of a Case Through Documentary Evidence", IBLJ (2008, no. 4) p. 509; T. GIOVANNINI and A. MOURRE, eds., *Written Evidence and Discovery in International Arbitration, New Issues and Tendencies*", Dossiers ICC Institute of World Business Law (ICC Publication no. 698, 2009); F.T. SCHWARZ, Ch. W. KONRAD, *The Vienna Rules, A Commentary on International Arbitration in Austria* (Kluwer Law International 2009) no. 20-224 et seq.; G.B. BORN, *International Commercial Arbitration* (Kluwer Law International 2009) p. 1876 et seq.; A. Redfern and M. Hunter with N. BLACKABY, C. PARTASIDES, *Redfern and Hunter on International Arbitration*, 5th edn. (2009) at para. 6.82 et seq.; M. MÜLLER-CHEN, "The Use of Evidence Obtained in US-American Discovery in International Civil Procedure Law and Arbitration in Switzerland", 27 ASA Bull. (2009, no. 2) at p. 196; *L'administration de la preuve en matière d'arbitrage – De bewijsregeling in arbitrage*, Coll. CEPANI, 12 November 2009 (Bruylant 2009); Pedro J. MARTINEZ-FRAGA, *The American Influence on International Commercial Arbitration: Doctrinal Developments and Discovery Method* (Cambridge 2009) pp. 51 and 62; J. H. CARTER and J. FELLAS, *International Commercial Arbitration in New York* (Oxford 2010) p. 280 et seq.; K.-H. BÖCKSTIEGEL, K.-P. BERGER, J. BREDOW, eds., *The Taking of Evidence in International Commercial Arbitration*, German Institution of Arbitration (DIS) Series, Vol. 26 (Carl Heymanns Verlag 2010).

6. "Clients Lament Delays and Discovery, ICCA Hears", GAR 24 May 2011. See also J.-Cl. NAJAR, "Inside Out: A User's Perspective on Challenges in International Arbitration", 25 Arb. Int'l (2009, no. 4) p. 515, sp. at pp. 516 and 518; see also: E. TUCHMANN, General Counsel of the AAA, quoted in B. BAR, "Some Attorneys Questioning Advantages of Arbitration", New York Law Journal, 18 May 2007; see also the article by Esso UK's General Counsel: A. CLARKE, "*Arbitrage international: sujets de préoccupation actuels des enterprises*", 20 ICC Bull. (2009, no. 2) p. 47, sp. at 52.
7. To speak of a Romano-Germanic or common law category of lawyers is a generalization. These categories include multiple jurisdictions. With respect to the civil law jurisdictions, the authors primarily considered the French legal system, while providing a less comprehensive overview of

that cannot form the basis for the criticisms of many US- or UK-trained international arbitration practitioners and users against a perceived inflation in the scope of disclosure in international arbitration. In fact, arbitration has traditionally been seen in the United States as a mechanism that permits parties to escape the burden of court discovery.[8] Couldn't it be said, then, that pragmatism and strategy[9] rather than legal tradition are what determine whether one will favor or stand against restraint in requesting and producing evidence?

2. Impact of Counsel's and Users' Legal Background

> "Sanity literally depends on the connection between the individual and the local reality that each has constructed in the context of a particular culture. This ... explains the emotion with which people embrace or reject (as the case may be) a Disney-fied or Sony-fied world. Our procedural systems are hardly immune from this dialogue...."[10]

"US-style discovery" and "fishing expeditions" are accusations often thrown at US-trained arbitration counsel who commit the heresy of requesting excessively broad categories of documents, or worse, of seeking to obtain depositions and interrogatories in the context of international arbitral proceedings. While, at least with regards to documentary evidence, lawyers from civil law jurisdictions resort to requests for categories of documents or information, one has to wonder how much of the evidentiary process in international arbitration is inspired by US/common law evidentiary rules, and how "foreign" that evidentiary process is to civil lawyers? More importantly, how should the response to these questions impact a party's strategic and procedural choices? The purpose of this paper is to explore the state of mind, reasoning and predispositions of civil law arbitrators, counsel or parties in the context of the evidentiary process in international arbitration.[11] To do that, we found it pertinent to first clarify the contours

---

other Romano-Germanic traditions in Brazil, Egypt or Germany.

8. Many US parties continue to resort to (domestic) arbitration and other ADR methods, precisely to avoid the costs and delays associated with state-court discovery; see: "Cost of Discovery a Driving Force in Settling Cases, Study Shows", The National Law Journal, 10 September 2008; see also *Commercial Solvents Corp. v. Louisiana Liquid Fertilizer Co.*, 20 F.R.D. 359 (S.D.N.Y. 1957) where the court considered pre-trial discovery superfluous and utterly incompatible with arbitration, refusing to compel the taking of depositions of party employees pursuant the Federal Rules of Civil Procedure.
9. H. GRIGERA NAÓN, "Document Production in International Commercial Arbitration: A Latin American Perspective" in ICC Bull. Sp. Suppl. 2006, *op. cit.*, fn. 5, p. 19: rather than a vacuum, it is "strategic preferences leading [Latin American] practitioners to import local procedural techniques into international arbitration" that "transform the arbitral process into a hybrid...".
10. O.G. CHASE, "Some Observations on the Cultural Dimension in Civil Procedure Reform", 45 Am. J. Comp. L. (1997) p. 862.
11. See, e.g., A. REDFERN and M. HUNTER, with N. BLACKABY and C. PARTASIDES, *The Law and Practice of International Commercial Arbitration*, 4th edn. (Sweet & Maxwell 2004) at para. 6-74:

    "in part, it is a matter of cultural differences. A US businessman will know that in the event of

of the "Anglo-American" judicial evidentiary process that is said to have invaded arbitral procedure, and, the roots of the predispositions of lawyers with a civil law procedural background in civil law judicial proceedings.[12]

3. *Caveat: An Imperfect Divide*

To clarify, reference to lawyers with a "civil law or common law background" encompasses diverse legal traditions within each system. Civil law traditions are often categorized as "Romano-Germanic",[13] and generally based on the primacy of a written *civil code,* such as the *Code Napoleon* of 1804 or the German 1896 *Bürgerliches Gesetzbuch* (BGB), rather than on court precedents. Civil code systems have been adopted in most European countries (save England), in Latin America (save for Guyana), but also in a majority of African and Arab countries (save for Jordan and, to some extent, the Gulf countries). A rough and unofficial estimate would place at least two thirds of the countries on the planet in the civil code family.[14]

Additionally, any attempt to draw an accurate dividing line between the civil law and common law traditions, especially in the context of international arbitration, is doomed to be approximate. One has to accept the "fallacy of the Great Divide".[15] It has been rightly pointed out that "civil law procedure [was] not monolithic"[16] and that "there were as many systems of civil procedure as there are countries in continental Europe"[17] and, one might add, as there are countries in Latin America, the Middle East and Africa. Is a lawyer qualified in Quebec, Canada, or Louisiana, which have codes, a "civil lawyer"? "Belonging to the same legal family does not create an identity among the different

---

litigation, all his internal correspondence, memoranda, computer disks and emails may have to be disclosed to an opposing party. As a result, he will either be careful about what he writes down (or creates in electronic form); or involve his lawyers in the 'paper trail' in the hope of invoking privilege; or accept possible disclosure of damaging documents as a fact of life. A French businessman, by contrast, will be appalled if he finds that the internal documentation he handed to his own lawyers for their information is being passed on by them to the opposing party's lawyers."

12. French law and procedure will constitute the principal basis for the analysis of the predispositions of lawyers from a civil law tradition. However, reference will be made to other civil law jurisdictions in Europe, the Middle East and South America.
13. For a subtle approach on the frontiers and content of this legal family; see R. DAVID and C. JAUFFRET-SPINOSI, *Les grands systèmes de droit contemporain*, Précis Dalloz, 8th edn., (2002, no. 17); see also: R. DAVID, "*L'arbitrage dans le commerce international*", Economica (1982, no. 115).
14. Ottowa University's JuriGlobe world map on World Legal Systems at <www.juriglobe.ca/eng/rep-geo/cartes/monde.php> (last accessed 22 April 2011). See also <http://foreignlawguide.com> (last accessed 22 April 2011) and <www.commonlii.org> (last accessed 22 April 2011). This rough estimation attempts to take into account the fact that there exists a third category (where customary law and *Shari'a* prevail) and that the legal system of some countries can sometimes be hybrid.
15. J. PAULSSON, *op. cit.*, fn. 5, at p. 112.
16. H. SMIT, *op. cit.*, fn. 5, p. 160.
17. Cl. REYMOND, *op. cit.*, fn. 5, p. 357.

national traditions, sometimes characterized by significant divergences, especially as far as the taking of evidence is concerned."[18]

4.   Structure

However, despite the imperfections and approximations inherent to the analysis of the civil law/common law divide, this paper identifies core similarities and differences between evidentiary principles common to the civil law legal tradition, focusing mainly on France, and the common law legal tradition, looking mainly at the United Kingdom and the United States (II). The paper then examines the attempt of arbitration practitioners to reconcile common law and civil law principles of and approaches to evidence (III). The conclusion (IV) will open up on Annex I (pp. 114-117) that will include a few suggestions on how to best approach the concerns and challenges posed by the new era of documents and devices: electronic discovery.

II.   DISCOVERY AND DOCUMENTARY EVIDENCE IN COMMON LAW AND CIVIL LAW SYSTEMS: SOME SHARED FOUNDATIONS WITH SIGNIFICANT PRACTICAL DIFFERENCES

Discovery is a mechanism specific to modern civil procedure in the United States.[19] It is rooted in the English common law, where trials used to have a key role in a civil suit. Trial continues to hold a predominant role in the US system, allowing discovery to occupy a paramount place in the evidentiary phase of a civil or commercial action and even beyond (*1*). The historical sources of English and US discovery explains why discovery never spread to civil law systems, with France as an example. Not that mechanisms to obtain evidence from another party do not exist in France, but court practices differ so significantly (*2*). This difference in degree between evidentiary systems can be perceived as one of nature but should not: there are routes allowing the two systems to reconcile, behind the so-called Great Divide(*3*).

1.   Discovery and Document Production in American and English Civil Procedure

a.   Origins, rationale and present perception

i.   Jury as finder of the facts
"US-style discovery, like any procedural device, reflects the unique features of the legal system in which it was developed."[20] Discovery used in the United States has its roots in equity, which can be traced back to England. The particularity of US discovery and of

---

18. Y. DERAINS, *op. cit.*, fn. 5, p. 780 at p. 784.
19. G. FISHER, "Preface", *Fisher's Evidence*, 2nd edn. (Foundation Press 2008) p. 1: "[U.S.] Evidence law is about the limits we place on the information juries hear."
20. L.F. REED and G. HANCOCK, "US-Style Discovery: Good or Evil?" in T. GIOVANNINI and A. MOURRE, *Written Evidence and Discovery in International Arbitration*, *op. cit.*, fn. 5, p. 349 at pp. 339, 341.

common law procedural rules rests on the existence of jury trial, the right to a jury being today, at least in the United States, a fundamental political right with constitutional weight.[21]

The difference in approaching the taking and collection of evidence between the civil law and common law traditions is generally attributed to the role of juries in early English civil procedure, continued and developed in US civil procedure. "Common law has developed elaborated rules of evidence," which "principal task is to keep from the juries evidence it is judged they, composed as they are of lay persons, are unable to evaluate properly."[22] The jurors were the adjudicators of the facts, but had no legal background. They were therefore assumed to be unable to see through the trickeries and pleadings of the lawyers appearing before them. As a result, an initial phase, preliminary to the trial, was dedicated to collecting the evidence – documentary and oral – that would be admissible for presentation to the jury, and on the basis of which the parties would prove the truth of their allegations. The role of the judge, in that process, was intended to be limited to choosing the version of the truth that was supported by the most credible evidence. This pre-trial phase was also intended to enable the judge and the parties to narrow down the scope of the dispute so that only truly disputed facts would be debated at trial.

While the historical root of the mechanism, the jury trial, was abandoned a long time ago in England, discovery remained available until 1999. The 1999 Woolf Reform of English Civil Procedure Rules (Rule 31), which sought to narrow the scope and the nature of discovery in the United Kingdom, now only refers to "disclosure" and "inspection of documents". The English lawmaker's "overriding objective" was for courts to deal with every case "justly". The scope of the taking of evidence now depends on the "track" to which a dispute is assigned, and this track, in turn, depends on the amount at

---

21. The Seventh Amendment to the United States Constitution codifies the right to a jury trial in certain civil trials.
22. H. SMIT, *op. cit.*, fn. 5, at p. 163. However, see Joseph W. GLANNON, *Civil Procedure,* 5th edn. (Aspen Publishers 2006) p. 361:

"The big news in civil procedure over the last century has been the demise of pleading and the rise of discovery. In the early common law, pleading played a central role in defining the issues and the factual contentions of the parties. Plaintiffs learned as much as they could about their cases before commencing suit, and then pleaded their cases based on their best guess as to what they would be able to prove. Once the pleadings were closed, the shape of the case was settled; it only remained to be seen whether the parties could prove what they had alleged.... Modern civil practices turns this approach on its head. Under our current notice pleading rules, the complaint and the answer provide a tentative view of the parties' positions, based on preliminary research and investigation. Once issue is joined [sic], full development of the parties' positions evolves through the process of discovery, the court-mandated production of information from other parties and non-party witnesses. As discovery puts flesh on the bare-bones cases presented in the pleadings, the parties may usually amend those pleadings to conform to their evolving understanding of the dispute."

This does not expressly implicate the jury-based system but makes note of the general historical shift in Western discovery practices.

stake and/or the difficulty of the case.[23] The 1999 English Rules have also introduced conditions of reasonableness and proportionality in the search to be undertaken by the disclosing party.[24] However, the taking of evidence in the United Kingdom continues to be viewed as a rather heavy process that does not make an overall contribution to ranking the UK judiciary amongst the cheapest systems in the world.[25]

ii.   Overview of US discovery practices

In the United States, the adoption of the Federal Rules of Civil Procedure (FRCP) in 1938 created one codified system for processing discovery in both cases decided in equity and law. The FRCP provided tools to aid discovery including interrogatories,[26] depositions,[27] requests for admission and written discovery.[28] Thus discovery in the United States extends far beyond documentary materials. Interrogatories, depositions, and oral examination and cross-examination are central to the unearthing of the truth before judges and juries in the United States. In the authors' experience, while requests for the production of documents have spread to arbitration, the use of depositions and interrogatories is often resisted by international arbitration practitioners, regardless of their legal background. Of note, the practice of depositions and interrogatories is virtually absent from civil law litigation.

Another point of difference with civil law jurisdictions stems from the fact that discovery rules, designed to facilitate the gathering and exchange of information, may lead a party to provide information that will not be used as proof in support of a claim. In fact, documents really relevant to the issues in dispute will often be buried in massive volumes of production that will not be used for the adjudication of the case. In common law jurisdictions, the inquiry is not "What evidence is required to reach a justifiable decision?", as a civil law judge may put it, but rather "What evidence should be heard to understand the *whole* case?"[29] When codified into the FRCP, the US rules of evidence were intended to ensure proceedings would be more accusatorial and emphasize the role

---

23. A. REDFERN and M. HUNTER, *Redfern and Hunter on International Arbitration*, 3rd edn. (Sweet & Maxwell) p. 316.
24. That is, the burden represented by the volume of documents to be searched and disclosed must not outweigh the evidentiary value of these documents.
25. See indirectly V.V. VEEDER, "Document Production in England: Legislative Developments and Current Arbitral Practice" in ICC Bull. Sp. Suppl. 2006, *op. cit.*, fn. 5, at p. 57. See also Sir H. LADDIE, "A Legal System We Can't Afford", The Times, 22 May 2007, in which the former Justice Laddie explains that litigation – he mainly discusses IP– in England costs between three and ten times more than similar cases in Germany and the Netherlands and writes: "Any civil lawyer will identify why our proceedings cost so much; lengthy cross-examination and oral argument and, above all else, disclosure of documents." See also the costs incurred in *BskyB v. Electronic Data*, reported to exceed £ 70 million (as of 9 June 2010, for 110 court days, 70 witnesses and over 500,000 documents involved, "Litigation Costs Come Under Scrutiny with Launch of New E-Disclosure Regime", 1 Oct. 2010 <www.thelawyer.com>.
26. FRCP Rule 33.
27. FRCP Rules 30 and 31.
28. FRCP Rule 36.
29. G.C. HAZARD, Jr., *op. cit.*, fn. 5, at p. 1022.

of parties in litigation, to the detriment of the judge. The judge was perceived to enjoy too much power in the conduct of the proceedings. The Rules specifically contemplate discovery managed by the parties. As summarized by Professor Raeschke-Kessler,[30] discovery's rationale is

> "that all cards must be put on the table at the very beginning of court proceedings and none may be withheld. Each party is to supply the other parties with all documentary or other information (on paper or nowadays electronically stored) that may be relevant to the outcome of a case, even if the information may have or even evidently does have a negative effect on the position of the requested party. The 'may' indicated that documents which are only potentially relevant are also included in the discovery process."

Indeed, under the FRCP, any party may seek specific documents or categories of documents from other parties to the litigation or from third parties.[31] For the purposes of the Rules, "document" includes nearly every type of written, digitized or recorded information. The threshold for relevance is low, despite recent attempts at stricter relevancy criteria.[32] Parties may seek discovery of "any matter, not privileged, that is relevant to the claim or defense of any party".[33] The aim is to help the truth emerge and thus facilitate the decision-making by the jury, through a very broad exchange of information and materials. "The discovery rules in particular were intended to promote the search for truth that is the heart of our judicial system. However, the success with which the rules are applied toward the search for truth greatly depends on the professionalism and integrity of the attorneys involved."[34] What appears almost inconceivable for civil lawyers is that under US law "the professional standards and ethical obligations of lawyers are redirected by requiring attorneys to come forward with information even when it may be damaging to their client"[35] and "parties who withhold information on privilege grounds must provide an explanation of the basis for their claim".[36]

The far-reaching scope of parties' discovery rights under US law is perfectly exemplified by the liberal approach taken by the Supreme Court[37] when it comes to

---

30. H. RAESCHKE-KESSLER, *op. cit.*, fn. 5, p. 45.
31. FRCP Rules 34(c) and 45.
32. Indeed, as recalled below, Rule 26(b)(1) was changed in 2000 precisely in an attempt to limit the scope of discovery, which in the previous drafting included any element "relevant to the subject matter involved in the pending action"; whereas Rule 26(b)(1) now requires that the request pertains to a "matter, not privileged, that is relevant to the claim or defense of a party".
33. FRCP Rule 26(b)(1).
34. Judge Peter FAYE in *Malautea v. Suzuki Motor Co.*, 987 F.2d 1536 (11th Cir. 1993) at p. 1546, quoted in L.F. REED and G. HANCOCK, *op. cit.*, fn. 20, at p. 341.
35. S.B. BURBANK and L.J. SILBERMAN, "Civil Procedure Reform in Comparative Context: The United States of America", 45 Am. J. Comp. L. (1997) p. 682; see also: Brazil, "Ethical Perspectives on Discovery Reform," 3 Rev. Litig. (1982-1983) p. 51.
36. Under FRCP Rule 26(b)(5).
37. *Intel Corp. v. Advanced Micro Devices, Inc.*, 542 US 241 (2004).

determining the scope of Art. 28 USC 1782: as commonly known, even by many non-US lawyers, this provision offers foreign or international tribunals and parties access to discovery and allows a US court to order (third) persons or entities in its jurisdiction to produce documents[38] (or testify), which can in turn serve as evidence within that foreign proceeding. That led some Federal lower courts[39] to apply that provision to arbitral tribunals, whether or not "situated" in the United States, and could thus theoretically allow parties to an arbitration with no connection whatsoever to the United States, for instance located in France or Switzerland,[40] to rely on a US judge to obtain discovery in the course of the arbitral proceeding.

The differences between the US and other civil law-based legal systems, appear from the very beginning of litigious proceedings. Unlike the requirement, in most civil law jurisdictions, for the claimant to produce the documents on which it relies when the notice of a case is first filed, the FRCP only requires a "short and plain statement of claim".[41] While certain mandatory disclosures must be made before substantive pleadings are filed under the FRCP,[42] at the outset, the parties are left to sort out the strengths and weaknesses of their respective positions through pre-trial discovery. Because of the division of a civil suit into these two distinct phases (discovery/disclosure on the one hand, and trial on the other), American and British counsel for a claimant will typically initiate their lawsuit without presenting the evidence that supports their case.

That is not to say that the principle of *actori incumbi probatio* – which is a cornerstone of the theory of evidence in civil law jurisdictions – is not recognized in common law countries. It has been argued that the fact that common law systems impose no requirement for claimants to submit evidence at the same time as they file a claim was irrelevant to the issue of who bears the burden of proof.[43] Rather than burden of proof, discovery, and the amount of evidence introduced in support of an initial statement of claim, addresses the question of how a party claiming a right may have access to those factual elements that can support her claim. It is then another question, this time directly relevant to burden of proof, to determine which information, data or documents obtained in discovery will be put in evidence. That determination, however, only takes place after discovery is complete. Accordingly, because of the requirement, under US discovery rules, that all information even remotely relevant to a case be produced, issues

---

38. Even if, some courts have ruled, located outside the US: see, e.g.: *In re Gemeinshcaftpraxis*, 2006 US Dist. Lexis 94161, 2006 WL 3844464 at 85 (S.D.N.Y. 2006).
39. *In re Roz Trading Ltd.*, 469 F.Supp.2d 1221, 1223 (ND Ga. 2006); *In re Hallmark Capital Corp.*, 534 F.Supp.2d 951 (D. Minn., 2007); *In re Oxus Gold plc*, MISC 06-82-GEB, 2007 WL 1037387 (D.N.J., 2007); *In re Babcock Borsig AG*, 583 F.Supp.2d 233 (D. Mass. 2008).
40. See M. Müller-Chen, "The Use of Evidence Obtained in US-American Discovery in International Civil Procedure Law and Arbitration in Switzerland", 27 ASA Bull. (June 2009, no. 2) p. 196, at p. 205 et seq.
41. FRCP Rule 8(a).
42. FRCP Rule 26(a)(1).
43. Y. DERAINS, "Towards Greater Efficiency in Document Production Before Arbitral Tribunals – A Continental Viewpoint" in ICC Bull. Sp. Suppl. Supplement 2006, *op. cit.*, fn. 5, at p. 83, no. 11.

of burden of proof and shifting of the burden of proof are much less litigated in the United States than they are in France.

iii.   Importance of admissibility thresholds to counterbalance the burden resulting from discovery

A corollary to the extensive reach of the right to obtain discovery is an elaborate system of exclusionary rules and objections to discovery. Privilege rules, for example, are more intricate and provide tools to limit the breadth of discovery. By the same token, other strict exclusionary and technical rules (best evidence and parole evidence rules, hearsay, leading questions, work-product) fulfill the same function.

b.   *More evil than good?*

i.   Assessment

The result of this often heavy process of discovery is that most cases either settle during the discovery phase or are brought to resolution through a successful motion for summary judgment – a tool by which a party can terminate proceedings on a showing that the evidence reveals no disputed material issues of fact.[44] These results have led commentators to observe that discovery has the effect of encouraging settlement and discouraging frivolous claims. Empirical data also suggest that the attacks against discovery may be overstated.[45] Abuse of the discovery process may, for example, give rise to severe penalties. If a request does not have a factual or legal basis, courts may award costs to the party forced to respond.[46] Non-compliance with requests, misleading disclosure or incomplete disclosure may result in sanctions, the severity of which will depend on the seriousness of the misconduct.[47] Sanctions include an award of costs and attorneys' fees, the loss of the right of the culpable party to make certain claims in the litigation, default judgment or contempt of court. However, circumstances in which attorneys are sanctioned for abuse of process due to discovery requests remain rare.[48] Additionally, a request giving rise to a large volume of production, cannot alone serve as the basis for a finding of abuse of process.

The volumes involved make the evidentiary phase a significant source of costs and delays in the resolution of disputes before US courts. With the emergence of electronically stored evidence, an entire industry of vendors and attorneys developed for the sole field of discovery. Zealous counsel logically seek to utilize discovery rules to the limits of what is available to them under the law, often adding to the massive volume of production. In high-stake cases, discovery will be a strategic tool for each side. As a result of the volumes involved, the costs of discovery can pressure a party into settling a case when it would not have otherwise been in its interest to do so. On the cost of discovery, the US Supreme Court recently commented: "Litigation, though necessary

---

44. FRCP Rule 56.
45. L.F. REED and G. HANCOCK, *op. cit.*, fn. 20, sp. at pp. 342, 345 and 346.
46. FRCP Rule 26(g).
47. FRCP Rule 37(b)-(d).
48. See, e.g., *Wine Mkts. Int'l v. Bass*, 977 F.Supp. 601, 605 (E.D.N.Y. 1997).

to ensure that officials comply with the law, exacts heavy costs in terms of efficiency and expenditure of valuable time and resources that otherwise would be directed to the proper execution of the work of the government."[49]

While US litigators are not oblivious to the weight that discovery places on the overall efficiency of US litigation, discovery stems from principles and procedural guarantees that few are willing to relinquish. "The rest of the world needs to understand why the American observer is perplexed at the willingness in other countries to countenance what seems to us a remarkable indifference to getting out the truth in civil litigation."[50] To many US-trained lawyers, the narrowly construed rights to obtain evidence in civil law jurisdictions are detrimental to ferreting out the truth of a case. The approach to discovery before US courts has influenced the position of US-trained arbitration practitioners with respect to the taking of evidence in international arbitration.

2. *Documentary Evidence Under (French) Rules of Civil Procedure*

Is that to say that bringing the truth of a matter to light is not central to how civil law jurisdictions have shaped their procedure? "One feature common to Civil Law systems of procedure that distinguish them from the Common Law tradition: we never had a *jury* in civil matters.... The result of this situation is that in Civil Law countries, it was never found necessary to elaborate refined rules aimed at providing exclusively the best possible evidence in order not to mislead the jury; neither had we the necessity of a basically oral hearing. By contrast with jurors from ancient times, judges are expected to be able to read documents, pleadings, statutes and law reports."[51] "[T]here is no such thing in our civil procedures as a trial Common Law Style."[52]

a. *No proof equals no right and the predominance of written evidence*

i. *Idem est non esse aut non probari*

To the outside observer, proof under French law and most Continental legal systems, does not appear to bear the same weight and importance as in common law jurisdictions. For example, evidence is not taught as a stand-alone subject in French law schools, and rules governing evidence are spread over different codes and areas of the law.[53] Yet, these observations should not be seen as an indication that the French and other civil law systems would somehow consider evidence as a minor area of the law.[54] Already under

---

49. *Ashcroft v. Iqbal*, 556 U.S. 129 S.Ct. 1937 (2009) at p. 18.
50. R.L. MARCUS, "Retooling American Discovery for the 21st Century: Towards a New World Order?" in M. TARUFFO, ed., *Abuse of Procedural Rights: Comparative Standards of Procedural Fairness* (Kluwer Law International, Nov. 1999) pp. 281-329, sp. at p. 286.
51. Cl. REYMOND, *op. cit.*, fn. 5, at p. 358.
52. *Ibid.*
53. No autonomous developments on the rules of evidence are recognized by the French *Code civil*. Rules of evidence are provided in Arts. 1315 to 1369 on the section relating to *obligations* (contracts and torts) whereas they have a broader material scope.
54. P. THÉRY, "*Les finalités du droit de la preuve en droit privé*", Revue Droits (1996) p. 41 et seq.

the Roman rule, it was affirmed that the existence of a right was conditioned by the ability of a party to prove it.[55]

As in many other civil law systems, Art. 1315(1) of the French Civil Code recognizes several types of admissible evidence: documentary evidence (*"preuve littérale"*), which can be on paper or in electronic format),[56] witness evidence, presumptions, admissions of parties and declarations under oath. Two main principles direct the theory of evidence in civil law systems: the principle of legality of evidence, pursuant to which it is the legislator that establishes a hierarchy among the various types of evidence; and the principle of free evidence, under which the judge will have a wide discretion to choose, among the facts that the parties are free to submit in evidence, those that will help him reach a determination of the case. While for criminal, administrative and commercial matters, French law leans increasingly towards a more flexible system of free evidence, in tort and contractual matters, contemporaneous written evidence – whether paper or electronic – carries a higher probative value than oral witness testimony.[57] It follows that hearings play a much more limited role in civil law procedures, which are mainly conducted through exchanges of written submissions and attached written documentary evidence. As a result, French lawyers, when bringing an action, tend to submit an initial statement of claim that attaches the main exhibits and pieces of evidence on which the claimant intends to rely. This aspect of the civil law process has influenced arbitral proceedings,[58] where documents are the prevailing proof.[59]

ii. The burden of proof in civil law jurisdictions: a constantly shifting rule

A foundational purpose of rules of evidence in civil law jurisdictions is to determine which party will eventually bear the burden of proving an allegation. In turn, the burden of proof will condition the judge's power to draw negative inferences from a party's failure to substantiate a claim. Under French law, if the proof of a fact or right is not established, the claim of the party that bears the burden of proof will fail and the

---

55. *Idem est non esse aut non probari*.
56. See Art. 1316 of the French Civil Code: "literal evidence, or documentary evidence, is constituted of a set of letters, characters, figures or any other signs or symbols with an intelligible meaning, whatever is the support and the modalities of transmission".
57. The idea being that the system does not trust the parties with some interest in the dispute to tell the entire truth in a neutral manner. Hence the French *Cour de cassation* adage against self-serving evidence: *"nul ne peut se constituer de preuve à soi-même"* (no one can be a witness of her own case). See e.g. Civ. 1, 2 April 1996: Bull. Civ. I, no. 170; see also in German civil litigation (bearing in mind that these rules do not apply in arbitration), where parties may only testify at trial in very narrow situations (Sects. 445-447 ZPO) and where a party (e.g., company representative or executive) is not considered to be a "witness". See: J. H. LANGBEIN, "The German Advantage in Civil Procedure", 52 U. CHI. L. Rev., p. 823 at p. 834; S. TIMMERBEIL, "The Role of Expert Witnesses in German and U.S. Civil Litigation", 9 Annual Survey of International & Comparative Law (2003, issue 1) Art. 8, p. 163 at p. 178.
58. J.-F. POUDRET and S. BESSON, *op. cit.*, fn. 5, at para. 649, p. 554.
59. See, however, A.-V. SCHLAEPFER, Ph. BÄRTSCH, "A Few Reflections on the Assessment of Evidence by International Arbitrators", IBLJ (2010, no. 3) p. 211 at p. 216.

opposite party's claim will succeed. A party bears the burden of proving that what appears to exist is not what really exists.

Under French general theory of law, social cohesion presumes that a claimant should establish the reason or reasons for its claim.[60] Thus, Art. 1315(1) of the French *Code civil* provides that a party claiming the performance of an obligation must prove it.[61] This is a mere application of the Roman law *adage: actori incombit probatio*. As a result of this principle, a claimant in Germany, France, Egypt or Argentina will be required to substantiate an initial submission with key documents. Art. 56 of the French Code of Civil Procedure requires the claimant's submission to include a description of the legal arguments *and* factual allegations made (Art. 56(1)(2)). Art. 56 also refers to the evidence underlying the claim (Art. 56(2)).[62] Similar provisions can be found in Art. 333 of the Argentine *Código de Procesal Civil*, or Art. 65 of the Egyptian Code of Civil and Commercial Procedure, as well as in the Lebanese Rules on Civil Procedure.[63] This is the case in most civil law systems in Europe,[64] the Middle East and North Africa,[65] and Latin America.[66]

But the burden of proof often shifts. For example, Art. 1315(2)[67] of the French *Code civil* states that the party claiming to be released from its obligation shall prove the payment or the fact that extinguished such obligation. This burden-shifting mechanism derives naturally from a claimant's general duty to substantiate her claim. The shifting ends when one of the parties can no longer satisfy her duty to prove the relevant elements of her claim. A claim that cannot be supported by adequate proof will generally be dismissed. Accordingly, the practice went from determining the bearer of the burden of proof, to determining the bearer of the risk of proof: a party unable to lift the doubts attached to her allegations will lose. The principle of *actori incombit probatio* thus weighs on *both* parties, not simply the claimant.

The common law and civil law systems share the principle that only a claim supported by evidence can succeed, and that, generally speaking, the party making a claim bears the burden of proving it. The main difference between the law of evidence in the civil law and common law systems rather lies in the amount of evidence *not in her possession* that a party can obtain in order to prove her claim. A party's ability to request documents and information not in her possession somewhat softens the rule of *actori incombit probatio*. Here, it is admitted that, to a certain extent, a party has a right to investigate outside of

---

60. F. TERRÉ, *Introduction générale au droit*, 6th edn., Précis Dalloz 2003, no. 474, p. 466.
61. Art. 1315(1): "a person who claims the performance of an obligation must prove it" (translation provided by Légifrance).
62. French CPC, Art. 56(1)(2) and (2).
63. Arts. 389, 443(4), 445, 655.
64. F.T. SCHWARZ, Ch.W. KONRAD, *op. cit.*, fn. 5, at p. 503, paras. 20-230 and 20-231.
65. See, e.g., in the UAE: Arts. 42-47 of the Emirati CCP.
66. E.g., Art. 335 of the Argentinean National Code of Civil and Commercial Procedure and Arts. 323 and 324 of the Mexican Federal Code of Civil Procedure, quoted by H. GRIGERA NAÓN, *op. cit.*, fn. 9, p. 16.
67. Art. 1315(2): "reciprocally, a person who claims to be released must substantiate the payment or the fact which has produced the extinguishment of his obligation" (translation provided by Légifrance).

what is in its custody in order to establish the truth of its case. The question then is the extent to which that right is allowed to be exercised in civil law jurisdictions.

b.   *Obtaining evidence not in the requesting party's possession or control*

i.   A theoretical "right to obtain evidence" not in a party's possession

A mechanism to investigate and seek production of documents necessary to the *manifestation of the truth*[68] exists in most civil law systems of procedure. In fact the Justinian Code had already provided for the principle of *actio ad exhibendum*.[69] French courts, for instance, applied this principle as early as 1879[70] and it was codified in the Code of Civil Procedure.[71] As a result, French commentators have even spoken of a "right to evidence", a right to obtain evidence not within one's possession. From such right stems the ability for a party to ask for production of documents from another party, or from a third party, a mechanism referred to as *"production forcée"* (compulsory production).[72]

This right to evidence seems to have gone even further in Germany.[73] Germany recently (2002 and 2006) modified its Civil Procedure Code *(Zivilprozessordnung* – ZPO), in particular Sect. 142 (and to some extent Sect. 421 et seq.) of the German ZPO, to allow for court-ordered production of documents and other data in the possession of a party, where the documents or data are referred to by either party in oral or written submissions.[74] The right to obtain evidence not in one's possession can also be

---

68. The expression flows, as mentioned below, from Art. 10 of the French Civil Code which provides that: *"chacun est tenu d'apporter son concours à la justice en vue de la manifestation de la vérité"* ("everyone must cooperate with the judiciary with the aim of making the truth emerge"); a similar article exists in other civil law countries (see, e.g., in Brazil: Art. 339 CPC; and in Portugal: Art. 519(1) CPC).
69. Brahic LAMBREY, *Production forcée des pièces*, Rép. Pr. Civ. (Dalloz April 2007) para. 3.
70. The French previous *Chambre des Requêtes* then stated that: "for the sake of the truth manifestation, courts may ... order production of some documents which have been neither notified nor used" (Cass. Req., 17 June 1879, Patureau-Mirand, DP 1880. 1. 427, S. 1881. 1. 116., in Brahic LAMBREY, *op. cit.*, fn. 69, para. 4).
71. Arts. 11, 40 and 42 of decree no. 71-740 of 9 September 1971, amended by decree no. 72-788 of 28 August 1972 and Arts. 73-77 of decree no. 72-684 of 20 July 1972; see notably Art. 11(2) CPC: "In case a party holds a piece of evidence, a judge may, further to the other requesting party, enjoin its production, under penalty if necessary."; and Art. 142 CPC, which governs the form of document-production requests.
72. G. GOUBEAUX, *"Le droit à la preuve"* in C. PERELEMAN, P. FORIERS, *La preuve en droit* (Bruylant 1981) p. 277 et seq.; J.-A. JOLOWICZ, *La production forcée des pièces dans le procès civil* (Mél. Perrot, Dalloz 1995) p. 167.
73. F.T. SCHWARZ, Ch.W. KONRAD, *op. cit.*, fn. 5, at p. 502.
74. Dr. Christof SIERFATH, *Document Production: New Developments in German Litigation and International Arbitration* (Kyoto University 30 September 2008).

encountered in almost all countries in Continental Europe,[75] Latin America[76] and in the Arab world.[77] Similar rules apply to court-ordered production of documents in the possession of a third party to the dispute.[78]

Generally, when an order for production is directed at a third party, the third party can oppose production[79] on grounds of "legitimate impediment" (*"empêchement légitime"*). Parties themselves, on the other hand, can make no such objection to a production order pursuant to the French Code of Civil Procedure.[80] Even the defense of "privilege against self-incrimination", available under European law[81] and paradoxically rooted in common law,[82] would not protect a party against an order to produce issued by a French judge. Privilege against self-incrimination is considered to be a weak objection to production,[83] not absolute,[84] and meant to only apply to criminal or anti-trust investigations. It is generally considered that, in French litigation, the protection afforded by these objections is not available to a party because, in practice, a French judge would not issue a broad order for production. To be granted, a request for documents or data must meet strict standards of specificity and relevance.[85]

---

75. See for example in *Italy*: Art. 210 (and Art. 421) of the Italian CPC; in *Portugal*: Art. 528 et seq. of the Portuguese CPC; in *Switzerland*: Art. 186 of the Swiss Federal CPC; in *Belgium*: Art. 877 of the Belgian Judiciary Code; in *Luxembourg*: Art. 279 et seq. of the Luxembourg NCPC.
76. See *Brazil*: Art. 130 of the Brazilian CPC and Arts. 355 and following CPC.
77. See in *Egypt*: Art. 20 et seq. (pertaining to document production) of the Law of Evidence no. 25 of 1968; in *Lebanon*: Art. 203 et seq. of the Lebanese "Code" of Civil Procedure; in the *UAE*: Art. 18 et seq. of Federal Law no. 10, 1992, on the Law of Proof in Civil and Commercial Transactions.
78. Art. 142 of the French CPC provides that production of evidentiary materials held by the parties is governed by Arts. 138-139, applicable to the production of documents in the possession of third parties.
79. Art. 11(2) French CPC: The judge "may, following either party's request, request or order, under the same penalty if necessary, the production of any document held by a third party, unless there exists a legitimate impediment" (see also Art. 141 French CPC).
80. Production of documents by parties is governed by Art. 142 which refers to Arts. 138 and 139 none of which allows a party to object to the tribunal's order to produce. Moreover, French case law, appears to be clear on the fact that the defendant may never object on the grounds of a *"legitimate impediment"* (see: S. GUINCHARD and F. FERRAND, *Procédure civile – Droit interne et droit communautaire*, Dalloz, 28th edn. (2006, no. 1171) p. 915.
81. See European Court of Human Rights (ECHR), 25 Feb. 1993, *Funke c/ France* A 256-A.
82. M. REDMAYNE, "Rethinking the Privilege Against Self-Incrimination", 27 Oxford Journal of Legal Studies (2007, no. 2) pp. 209-232.
83. See D. ROETS, *Le droit de ne pas contribuer à sa propre incrimination dans la jurisprudence de la Cour Européenne des droits de l'homme, Actualité Juridique Pénal* (2008) p. 119, who explains that, even in criminal proceedings, this right is often limited by the fact that the prevailing evidence in this field continues to be the confession.
84. See the recent ECHR cases of 11 July 2006, *Jalloh v. Germany*, 54810/00, and of 29 June 2007, *O'Halloran & Francis v. United Kingdom*, 15809/02 & 25624/02, which restricted this privilege rather severely.
85. See how the French *Cour de cassation* construes the scope of Art. 145 CCP (according to which any interested party may require, on the basis of a justified ground, the court's assistance to preserve before the beginning of a trial any piece of evidence which may impact the litigation's outcome)

Failure to disclose or late disclosure of a document can lead the judge to exclude it from the case file[86] (see, for example, a document produced three days before the hearing).[87] Similarly, a judgment cannot be rendered on the basis of evidentiary materials that have not been disclosed.[88] A court is thus obligated to rule on the basis of evidentiary material properly submitted before it. If the court has not been made aware of the failure by one of the parties to disclose a document and has rendered a decision regardless of such undisclosed evidentiary material, the decision can be set aside.[89] At first glance, the standards we describe here are not unlike UK disclosure or US discovery.

ii.   Rarely used in practice

Evidentiary practice, however, differs significantly between civil law and common law jurisdictions. In practice, the *scope* of document requests allowed in most civil law jurisdictions limits significantly the extent to which documents may be obtained from the other side or a third party in a civil trial. The *Tribunal de Grande Instance* (first instance civil court) of Marseilles[90] thus denied a request for documents, holding that allowing a broad document request would mean "imposing on one of the parties to produce all documents including official and internal documents or correspondence, without knowing which specific documents are concerned and whether such documents can be tied to a piece of evidence relevant to the issues in dispute". The court added that were it to order the document request on such broad terms, it would be acting in "an inquisitorial manner against a party in order to lead that party to uncover unidentified or unidentifiable documents merely to allow for a piece of evidence that the requesting party is not certain to find. This would constitute a serious infringement to individual freedom to which every party is entitled." This holding of a French court in 1954 is illustrative of the approach concerning document production in civil law jurisdictions to this date.

Still today, a request to order production of a document will be granted by a state court under strict conditions of relevancy and narrowness.[91] A French judge, for

---

by requiring any documentary search that could be granted to be circumscribed to the limits prescribed by the judge in her order: Com., 8 Dec. 2009, case no. 08-21253.
86. Art. 135 French CPC: "[t]he judge may exclude from the debate those documents which have not been served in due time".
87. Soc. 29 nov. 2006, Bull. civ. V, no. 364.
88. See Art. 16(2) French CPC: "[i]n his decision, the judge may take into consideration grounds, explanations and documents relied upon or produced by the parties only if the parties had an opportunity to discuss them in an adversarial manner" (translation provided by Légifrance). French case law has constantly ruled in such way since Civ. 3e, 16 March 1976, Bull. Civ. III, no. 120.
89. Civ. 3e, 16 March 1976, Bull. Civ. III, no. 120.
90. TGI Marseille, 20 February 1954, Gaz. Pal. 1974. 2. 544.
91. James Beardsley observed in this respect that: "the unwillingness of the judge to compel the parties to produce evidence under their control is an attitude that has not much changed even under the impact of a New Code of Civil Procedure which, on its face, gives the judge broad powers to require the production of evidence". James BEARDSELY, "Proof of Fact in French Civil Procedure", 34 Am. J. Comp. L. p. 459.

instance, will enjoin production only if the requesting party has no other way of proving its claim. Thus an order for document production simply to address a party's inability to meet its burden of proof is not an option in a civil law trial.[92] On the other hand, if the existence of the element of proof requested is certain or very likely,[93] or if the evidence is sufficiently identified in the request[94] and, if the judge is satisfied that such evidence would be likely to help the determination of the case,[95] then a civil law judge would be in a position to grant a request for documents.

The same apparent dichotomy exists between practice and legal provisions with respect to the judicial taking of evidence in other civil law countries. For example, although Argentinean civil procedure provides for a mechanism of document request,

> "the wording of these provisions would seem to suggest that from the beginning of the proceedings the parties have broad discovery obligations matching those under the US discovery system. In practice, however, although the parties have a general duty to contribute to establishing the true facts and circumstances of the case, it is widely recognized that such duty does not extend to the spontaneous production of documents contrary to the interest of the party in whose possession they lie."[96]

Indeed, courts in many Continental European countries, such as Italy[97] and Portugal,[98] and in other civil law countries, such as Brazil[99] or Egypt,[100] tend to construe their

---

92. Art. 146(2) French CPC; see also, TGI Marseille, 20 February 1954, Gaz. Pal. 1974. 2. 544, and CA Aix-en-Provence, ord., 21 Nov. 1995
93. Civ. 2e, 17 Nov. 1993, Bull. Civ. II, no. 330.
94. Com., 12 March 1979 et Civ. 2e, 15 March 1979.
95. Art. 144 French CPC.
96. H. GRIGERA NAÓN, *op. cit.*, fn. 9, p. 18.
97. Cass. civile, 5.8.2002, no. 11709 (the requesting party must prove the existence of the document); Cass. civile, 8.9.2003, no. 13072 (documents must be indispensable to the requesting party); Cass. civile, 20 October 2010, no. 22196 (the judge enjoys a discretionary power to grant the request or not); Cass. 10.12.2003, no. 18833 (there is no compulsory penalty attached to such orders); see also: F. CORSINI, "*Le proposte di 'privatizzazione' dell'attivita istruttoria alla luce delle recenti vincedi della 'discovery' anglosassionne*", Riv. trim. proc. civ. 2002, 04, 1273.
98. Or when they are granted, no or very limited adverse consequences follow from non-compliance with such requests or orders: Acórdão do Supremo Tribunal de Justiça, 17-04-2008 (at <www.dgsi.pt>; Processo 08S149); Acórdão do Supremo Tribunal Português, 01-03-2007 (at <www.dgsi.pt>; Processo 06S3210); Acórdão do Tribunal da Relação de Lisboa, 05-06-2008 (at <www.dgsi.pt>; Processo 3861/2008-6); Acórdão do Tribunal da Relação de Lisboa, 17-03-2004 (at <www.dgsi.pt>; Processo 10400/2003-4); Acórdão do Tribunal da Relação do Porto, 12-12-2000 (at <www.dgsi.pt>; Processo 0020607).
99. See "The request for exhibition of document shall strictly provide the maximum specification of the document, as well as the purpose of this evidence," TRF-5 [regional federal court of appeals], AG no. 9005013940, Relator Francisco Falcão, 06.25.1990.
100. Ruling of 5 March 1979, Recourse no. 24, judicial year 44; Ruling of 21 November 1989, Recourse no. 2117, judicial year 52; Ruling of 29 April 1981, Recourse no. 417, judicial year 48.

evidentiary laws rather restrictively, and impose requirements (specificity, materiality, proof of existence, absence of burden for the producing party) so strictly that document-production requests are rarely granted. Commenting on Egypt, Professor El-Kosheiri and Mohamed Saleh Abdel Wahab noted that "pre-trial discovery is foreign to civil law and Arab legal systems. Courts usually rely on documents and other forms of evidence submitted by the parties on their own initiative, and have long been loath to order a party or a third party to submit documents that might not be in their interest."[101]

iii.   A limited evolution of the judge's role in the French evidentiary process

In France, the respective roles of the parties and the judge within a typical civil trial have evolved in France. With the adoption of the (*Nouveau*) *Code de procédure civile*, French judges have become more active in managing the evidentiary process. While the parties continue to define the limits of their claims, judges are to ensure the proper conduct of the proceedings and *may* order any measure of inquiry that might be relevant for the outcome of the case. As a result, all parties to the proceedings must, under the judge's supervision, search for the elements of proof that are relevant to the case, and assist the judiciary in their task.[102] This evolution has been viewed as a move of the French civil trial towards a more inquisitorial system.[103] The role of the judge after the reform materialized in the mechanism of "*production forcée*", or forced production.

In practice however, the role of the French judge in the taking of evidence remains limited. The judge has not gone beyond his supervisory role and is far from enjoying the inquisitorial powers common lawyers tend to attribute to judges in civil law jurisdictions. In a French civil trial, the classical principles described above continue to apply: if evidence could not be obtained despite the other party's collaboration as well as the judge's initiatives, the claimant's claim is likely to be dismissed and the opponent's claim will succeed. The judge will do little to order production. French judges continue to view themselves "as a neutral umpire who must not intervene in the unfolding of the dispute that the parties bring before [them]",[104] considering "any action on [their] part [as] likely to disturb the balance between the parties".[105] In this respect, while it provides for

---

101. A.S. EL-KOSHERI and M. S. ABDEL WAHAB, "Trends in Document Production in Egypt and the Arab World" in ICC Bull. Sp. Suppl. 2006, *op. cit.*, fn. 5, at Sect. II, p. 10.
102. Art. 10(1) of the French Civil Code.
103. F. TERRÉ, *op. cit.*, fn. 60, no. 482, p. 471.
104. J. BEARDSLEY, *op. cit.*, fn. 91, p. 462. See also S. GUINCHARD and F. FERRAND, *op. cit.*, fn. 80, p. 576, who explain the tendency, in the French tradition, to insist on the fact that the parties draw the frame of the suit, in which the judge is a mere referee, neutral and passive, unable to call a witness unrelated to one of the parties or to request the production of a document concealed by them.
105. James BEARDSLEY, *op. cit.*, fn. 91, p. 462, also citing BARTIN (12 AUBRY AND RAU, *Cours de Droit Civil Pratique Français* at p. 74 (5th edn., Bartin 1922)) at p. 461, explaining that the judge:

"... 'is to decide the claims that the parties submit to him, and, consequently, to decide these claims as they are submitted to him. It is not his task to seek out himself the facts, documents or

no right to or duty of discovery,[106] "in some of its aspects, civil fact-finding comes closer to the Anglo-American style, in which the court supervises rather than participates in proof-taking activity".[107]

c. *Evidence in the quest for truth*

i. Evidence, truth and competing considerations

The adjudicatory process in civil law jurisdictions is generally viewed as a mechanism intended to bring truth to light, albeit a relative truth.[108] Evidence and, more particularly, means to deter allegations of falsehoods, are therefore central to the process.[109] It is inaccurate to oppose a supposed focus of the criminal trial on truth[110] to the civil trial where the judge would "merely" settle a dispute opposing two private interests,[111] with little regard for the pursuit of truth. Rather, it is commonly accepted among civil law scholars[112] that all trials, whether criminal, commercial, civil or administrative, must shed light on the truth of the facts and the reality of each party's rights. This is viewed, in civil law jurisdictions as the way to place the judge in the best position to properly apply the rule of law. The pursuit of truth is embodied in the French *Code civil*.[113] Yet, the civil law systems have not determined that to effectively establish truth, a party needed or was entitled to a broad right to seek evidence and information not already in her possession.

Competing considerations are taken into account. Thus, in addition to truth, other policy objectives apply, for example: social peace (which a lawsuit can be viewed to

---

> [other written] evidence which may support or weaken these claims. Any initiative on his part in this respect violates the fundamental rule that no fact may be invoked against a party except insofar as it has been submitted to him in advance and he has had the opportunity to challenge it....'"

106. Cl. REYMOND, *op. cit.*, fn. 5, at p. 359. Claude Reymond further comments that discovery is viewed by civil lawyers as an invasion of privacy by the courts that is only acceptable in criminal cases, where the public interest is at stake.
107. M. DAMAŠKA, "The Uncertain Fate of Evidentiary Transplants: Anglo-American and Continental Experiments", 45 Am. J. Comp. L. (1997) p. 839 at p. 843.
108. J. L. BAUDOUIN, "*La vérité dans le droits des personnes: aspects nouveaux, rapport général*" in *Travaux de l'association Henri Capitant* (1989) p. 21 et seq.; G. CORNU, "*La vérité et le droit*" in *L'art du droit en quête de la sagesse* (1998) p. 211 et seq.; see also: R. TRITTMANN, "Basics and Differences of the Continental and Common Law System and State Court Proceedings" in K.-H. BÖCKSTIEGEL, K.-P. BERGER, J. BREDOW, eds., *The Taking of Evidence in International Commercial Arbitration*, op. cit., fn. 5, Sect. III, p. 20.
109. P. GODÉ, "*Le mensonge dans le procès civil (impressions d'audience)*" in *Mélanges Weil* (1983) p. 259 et seq.
110. Evidentiary devices in French criminal law are sometimes likened to certain common law evidentiary mechanisms.
111. F. TERRÉ, *op. cit.*, fn. 60, p. 448.
112. Ch.-F. PONSARD, "*Vérité et justice (la vérité et le procès), rapport français*" in *La vérité et le droit*, *Trav. H. Capitant, Journées canadiennes*, Vol. XXXVIII, (1987) p. 673 et seq.
113. Art. 10(1): "everyone must cooperate with the judiciary so that truth may emerge".

disturb), legal security (e.g., against the abuse or excess of judicial process), reliability (the certainty of a written proof over the fallibility of oral testimony) and equity (the need for proportionality between the evidentiary means to be deployed and the end pursued). These competing considerations explain why contemporary written evidence has generally prevailed as the most secure and reliable basis in the overall French hierarchy of proof.[114]

The perception in civil law jurisdictions is that these competing concerns have little value in the United States, where, it is thought, pursuit of truth leaves little room for other policy considerations,[115] such as the legality and proportionality of the evidentiary methods used in light of the fundamental right for privacy,[116] loyalty,[117] protection of personal data[118] or even attorney-client confidentiality rules.[119] A "Blocking Statute", first enacted in France in 1968, then confirmed in 1980,[120] and still in force today, is a telling

---

114. F. TERRÉ, *op. cit.*, fn. 60, no. 452, pp. 448-449.
115. See Lord DENNING:

> "The reason for compelling discovery of documents in this way lies in the public interest of discovering the truth so that justice may be done between the parties. That public interest is to be put into the scales against the public interest in preserving privacy and protecting confidential information. The balance comes down in the ordinary way in favour of the public interest of discovering the truth, i.e. in making full disclosure."

quoted in M. DE BOISSÉSON, *op. cit.*, fn. 5, no. 747.
116. See ECHR, *L.L. v. France*, 10 October 2006, no. 7508/02; *N.N. & T.A. v. Belgium*, 13 May 2008, no. 65097/01.
117. See Paris (1ère Ch. accus.), 26 April 1990, JCP 1991 II 21704 note PANNIER: "General principles of the law prohibit the search for the truth by any means and preclude a judge from admitting some evidence that could have been obtained by fraud"; see also the recent and key decision by the higher chamber of the French *Cour de cassation*: Ass. Plén., 7 Jan. 2011, no. 09-14.316 09-14.667; Ph. DELEBECQUE, J.-D. BRETZNER, Th. VASSEUR, *Droit de la preuve* (Dalloz 2009) p. 2714 et seq.; M.-E. BOURSIER, *"Le principe de loyauté en droit processuel"*, vol. 23 (Dalloz NBT 2003) at p. 316 et seq.
118. CNIL Deliberation no. 2009-474 of 23 July 2009 containing recommendations with respect to personal data transfer in the frame of US judicial proceedings called "Discovery": JORF no. 0190 of 19 August 2009, which, further to Law no. 78-17of 6 January 1978 related to IT, files and liberties, modified by Law no. 2004-801 of 6 August 2004 regarding the protection of individuals against personal data treatment, poses some conditions of legitimacy and proportionality of personal data requests made in the framework of US discovery and entitles the CNIL (the French supervising public authority that plays the role of guardian of the liberties in this field) to reject massive requests.
119. As opposed to many jurisdictions, especially in the United States, where a waiver is more liberally admitted, an attorney may never relinquish the privilege attached to his correspondence and communication, such that if he discloses confidential information, even with his client's permission, he is subject to criminal liability; see Cass. Crim., 27 October 2004, Bull. crim. (2004, no. 259) p. 969.
120. Law no. 68-678 of 26 July 1968, which was first aimed at protecting French maritime companies from foreign overreaching laws (notably US antitrust laws) by giving the former (or any individual or company) a legal ground to refuse to communicate documents or information pertaining to maritime transport, was extended by Law no. 80-538 of 16 July 1980 to encompass

illustration of the distrust by lawyers from civil law countries regarding the weight given to these competing policy considerations in the United States. The French Blocking Statute thus aims at protecting parties based in France against abuse that could result from injunctions issued by US courts.[121] The statute applies to injunctions rendered outside the scope of "rogatory commissions" contemplated by the 1970 Hague Convention on the Taking of Evidence Abroad in Civil or Commercial Matters.[122] The criminal division of the French *Cour de cassation* went so far as to fine, on criminal grounds, a lawyer for having sought information pursuant to a US discovery injunction and related rogatory commissions, while not strictly complying with the exact mechanisms contemplated by the Hague Convention on the Taking of Evidence.[123]

Pursuit of truth, both in France and in the United States needs, however, to be put in perspective. A recent study on the concept of evidence in France concludes that evidentiary rules do not aim, primarily, at finding truth.[124] Rather, behind that objective is the judiciary's concern to show the legitimacy of its decisions. Legitimacy is a concern that is also present in international arbitration, which makes this analysis pertinent to understanding the evolution of the evidentiary process before international arbitral tribunals.

ii. Evidence, a tool in the hands of the parties

Also, despite the "principle of legality of the evidence", pursuant to which the legislator determines what weight to attribute to various elements of proof, French law admits that the parties may contract out of these rules.[125]

---

the communication of "documents or information of economic, commercial, industrial, financial or technical nature" to foreign public authorities, if this communication "is susceptible to harm France's sovereignty, security, essential economic interests or to public policy" (Art. 1). And Art. 1*bis* even "prevents any person from requesting, seeking or communicating, in writing, orally or by any other form" such documents or information which pertain to the taking of evidence for foreign judicial or administrative proceedings".

121. See the preparatory Report by the French Legislative Commission: the law's main goal is to protect French companies from potential overreaching effects by US laws in so far as "these requests for information are expensive for [French] companies" and "the communication of the requested documents is ... *dangerous*" (Rapport AN, no. 1814, session 1978/1980, p. 12).

122. The Hague Convention on the Taking of Evidence Abroad in Civil or Commercial Matters dated 18 March 1970, for which France, like many other States (including the United Kingdom) has made a reservation by excluding US "pre-trial discovery" from the scope of judicial cooperation.

123. Crim., 12 December 2007, *Armeniadès*: JCP E 2008.1206, n. M. DANIS; Rev. crit. DIP (3) (July-Sept. 2008) 626, n. D. CHILSTEIN.

124. X. LAGARDE, *Réflexion critique sur le droit de la preuve* (LGDJ 1994) preface by J. GHESTIN, p. 10 et seq.; see also by X. LAGARDE: *Finalités et principes du droit de la preuve. Ce qui change*, La semaine juridique, gen. ed. (27 April 2005), no. 17 doctrine I, 133, p. 771-777.

125. Save for some fundamental public policy considerations, such as the necessity to debate any evidence through the *principe du contradictoire*. See M. MEKKI and C. GRIMALDI, *Réflexions sur le risque de la preuve en droit des contrats (1ère partie)*, Revue des Contrats (July 2008) p. 681; "*La gestion contractuelle du risque de la preuve (2nde partie)*, Revue des Contrats (April 2009) p. 453.

Parties can agree on different rules to govern admissibility or burden of proof.[126] Indeed, in a civil law trial, evidence remains a means for the parties to ensure the efficiency of the rights they assert.[127] The French judge, on the other hand, remains a neutral observer[128] and takes no action in the establishment of the underlying facts. Only the parties, most of the time by their own means, can put forward the evidence supporting their claims.

3. *Behind the Clichés, A Realistic View of the Divide*

> "It has been demonstrated, amongst others, by Professor Goldman, that whatever the legal background of the arbitrators, they will generally tend to adopt a similar approach concerning the burden of proof: they adopt from the civil law system and the common law system those types of evidentiary methods which will give them the possibility to come closer to the truth of the case and confirm or invalidate the various possible solutions which they have extracted from their reading of the parties' briefs and documents."[129]

An exploration of the theories that underlie the rules of evidence in common law and civil law jurisdictions offers a realistic grasp of the roots of the evidentiary practice in international arbitration. This review of the civil law and common law theories of evidence hence shows that:

– The pursuit of truth is a policy objective in both common law and civil law jurisdictions. The differences observed in the rules that govern fact-finding stem from the weight that each system gives to other competing considerations and policies.
– These differences are rooted in the history of each family of legal systems. "[F]or cultural, historic and constitutional reasons, there is a deeply-seated resistance in many [Civil Law] jurisdictions to requiring a party to legal proceedings to assist the other side in gathering information that might be used against the producing party in court."[130] Accordingly, while both the common law and civil law systems allow for document requests, such requests are the subject of strict, narrowly construed requirements of relevancy, materiality and likelihood that the party asked to produce has the evidence in its possession and control. The duty for a claimant to bear the burden of proof and the

---

126. See M. MEKKI and C. GRIMALDI, "*Réflexions sur le risque de la preuve en droit des contrats (1ère partie), op. cit.*, fn. 125, p. 681; *La gestion contractuelle du risque de la preuve (2nde partie), op. cit.*, fn. 121, p. 453.
127. F. TERRÉ, *op. cit.*, fn. 60, no. 454, p. 450.
128. AUBRY amd RAU (BARTIN, ed.), *Cours de droit civil*, 5th ed. Vol. XII (1922) Sect. 749, p. 73.
129. See, e.g., B. HANOTIAU, "The Standards and Burden of Proof in International Arbitration", 10 Arb. Int'l. (1994, no. 3) pp. 317-364 at p. 348: "… They are not much interested in the rules relating to the burden of proof, except in the situation where they reach the conclusion that in the particular case, the party who had the burden of proof has not satisfied it and therefore that his contentions or claims should be set aside."
130. Report by the ICC Task Force on the Production of Electronic Documents in International Arbitration, Finally Adopted in March 2011, Sect. 1.4.

so-called right against self-incrimination[131] do not defeat this right to obtain disclosure of narrowly and specifically described information or documents.

– "Judges' powers [in common law jurisdictions] are not of lesser importance, but are differently oriented."[132] Similarly, in practice, the inquisitorial role of civil law judges is fairly limited. Judges in civil law jurisdictions tend to act as neutral observers and assessors of the facts presented to them.

– Oral testimony plays a more important role in common law jurisdictions. But it is not absent from civil law procedures. Arguably, both systems are suspicious of the credibility of non-contemporaneous evidence created by a party. But each system addresses its suspicions in its own way. Common law systems tackle this credibility issue through cross-examination, while civil law systems address it by affording less probative value to non-written, non-contemporaneous evidence.

– Documentary evidence, on the other hand, has significant probative value in both common law and civil law jurisdictions.

> "True, the procedural conceptions adopted on each shore of the Atlantic are not identical for they have roots in cultures that do not share the same history, as they evolve in an institutional, and even constitutional, environment where the respective roles of private interests and public interest, of the individuals and the State, of the civil society and the administration are assigned differently. Yet, these differences do not preclude neither resemblances nor connections."[133]

Looking behind or beyond the clichés of the "Big Divide" allows a realistic assessment of the predispositions and level of comfort of arbitrators, counsel and parties from civil law jurisdictions vis-à-vis the evidentiary process in international arbitration.

III. THE TAKING OF EVIDENCE IN INTERNATIONAL ARBITRATION: A MARRIAGE OF CONVENIENCE

As rightly summarized by a renowned Swiss arbitrator, in international arbitration, "*nobody feels really at home*".[134] One could add: while everyone should feel at home, no one actually is. This is so because today's international arbitration has traced a route where both cultures have been combined and in which, rather than divorcing, practitioners from both legal systems have agreed to compromise[135] by reaching a

---

131. See *contra*: B.M. CREMADES, "Managing Discovery in International Arbitration", 57 Disp. Resol. J. (Nov. 2002-Jan. 2003, no. 4) p. 2.
132. Y. DERAINS, "*La pratique de l'administration de la preuve dans l'arbitrage commercial international*", *op. cit.*, fn. 5, p. 786, para. 12.
133. L. CADIET, "*Quelles preuves? Discovery, témoins, experts, rôle respectif des parties et du juge*" in "*Vers un procès universel?*" *op. cit.*, fn. 3, p. 117.
134. *Ibid.*
135. See the Commentary on the Revised Text of the 2010 IBA Rules on the Taking of Evidence, by the 1999 IBA Working Party and 2010 IBA Rules of Evidence Review Subcommittee, which uses this term repeatedly (at pp. 8 and 9), but also, that of "*balance*" (*ibid.*) and "*consensus*"(at p. 7).

reasonable balance, a sort of cherry-pick of procedural rules from here and there. A photograph of this *mariage de raison* will be displayed (*1*). But as for almost all marriages, life is not a bed of roses and difficulties continue to arise in this field, for civil lawyers as well as for common lawyers: these differences will be exposed here (*2*). The biggest challenge that faces written evidence for practitioners, whatever their legal background, is the rise of electronic documents: practical advice, also addressed to civil lawyers, will also be suggested to help better cope with what is sometimes seen as a "documentary deluge" (*3*).

1. *"Mariage de Raison" Between Common Law and Civil Law Practices*

Like most arbitration agreements, national laws and institutional rules are silent on the particular issue of the parties' rights and duties to produce documents to the adversary, as well as on the arbitrator's powers to rule over and sanction them. The initiative of finding a compromise eventually came from a rather neutral organization and not from an arbitration center: the Rules of the International Bar Association on the Taking of Evidence in International Arbitration (the IBA Rules), which are said to constitute a fair balance between various legal traditions and thus to incorporate the civil law approach to documentary evidence. These rules will be explained (*a*), so that the common principles that seem to have been agreed upon by international practitioners on that matter can be understood and presented (*b*).

a.   *What do the rules say?*

i.   A deafening silence

First, if one puts aside the fundamental source that should be governing that issue – the arbitration agreement – which almost never encompasses any stipulation on document production, and if we turn to national arbitration laws, very few will contemplate expressly, and even less specifically, a party's faculty to request an arbitral tribunal to order document production from the other party.[136] Most national laws, whether or not inspired by the UNCITRAL Model Law,[137] are silent on this matter, probably because this is a typical procedural issue the details of which a lawmaker will not get into, leaving

---

Maybe rather than a "happy merger", the analogy with a *"mariage de raison"* seems to better fit the reality; some other authors have used the more neutral and clinical words of *"synthesis"* or *"syncretism"*: see Y. DERAINS, *"La pratique de l'administration de la preuve dans l'arbitrage commercial international"*, op. cit., fn. 5, no. 17.

136. See, e.g., Sect. 34(2)(d) of the English Arbitration Act 1996 or, in the United States, Sect. 7 U.S. Federal Arbitration Act and Sect. 7 of the Uniform Arbitration Act; see also Art. 1467(3) (formerly Art. 1460 of the French CPC): "If a party holds a piece of evidence, the arbitral tribunal may enjoin her to produce it according to such manner it deems appropriate and if need be under the threat of a civil fine."

137. Which, unsurprisingly, is rather vague on that issue, as Art. 19(2) provides "… the arbitral tribunal may, subject to the provisions of this Law, conduct the arbitration in such manner as it considers appropriate. The power conferred upon the arbitral tribunal includes the power to determine the admissibility, relevance, materiality and weight of any evidence."

it to the parties' will, including arbitration rules the parties would have agreed upon. It is also quite symptomatic to note that very few arbitral institutional rules take a clear position, if any, as to (i) the parties' duties and rights to disclose/obtain documents as per the opponent's request and (ii) scope in relation to the tribunal's power to enjoin such document production. When they do, the rules of arbitral institutions bear on disclosure with varying degrees of specificity. Most will merely recognize, absent any agreement between the parties, the authority – and discretion – of arbitral tribunals to conduct proceedings as they see fit –[138] from which tribunals will easily assume their jurisdictional power and authority to order document production – and may even go a bit further on this particular issue, but with no detail at all as to the document-production process.[139] For example, the Rules of the London Court of International Arbitration (LCIA Arbitration Rules), contain express language about the power of tribunals to seek disclosure. As an initial matter, they empower tribunals: "to order any party to make any property, site or thing under its control and relating to the subject matter of the arbitration available for inspection by the Arbitral Tribunal, any other party, its expert or any expert to the Arbitral Tribunal".[140] The Rules go on to endow tribunals with the power: "to order any party to produce to the Arbitral Tribunal, and to the other parties, for inspection, and to supply copies of, any documents or classes of documents in their possession, custody or power which the Arbitral Tribunal determines to be relevant".[141] Although the Rules expressly contemplate written disclosure, they do not provide a specific procedural mechanism whereby parties may seek and obtain disclosure. Most institutional rules grant similar authority to tribunals but in terms that are far less express. The rules of the Vienna International Arbitral Centre (Vienna Rules) provide an example.[142] They begin by recognizing the broad power of tribunals to manage arbitral proceedings: in the context of the Vienna Rules and the agreements between the parties, the sole arbitrator (arbitral tribunal) may conduct the arbitration proceedings at his (its) absolute discretion.[143] The Rules go on to state: "If the sole arbitrator (arbitral tribunal) considers it necessary, he (it) may on his (its) own initiative collect evidence, and in particular may question parties or witnesses, may request the

---

138. See Art. 15(2) of the ICC Rules, Art. 14(2) of the LCIA Rules, Art. 17(1) of the UNCITRAL Rules; see also, on a legislative level, Art. 1464(1) (former Art. 1460(1)) and Art. 1509(2) (former Art. 1494(2)) of the French CPC; Art. 182 (2) of the Swiss LPIL; Sect. 1047 of the German ZPO; Sect. 587(1) of the Austrian ZPO; Art. 1693 of the Belgian Judicial Code; Sect. 34(1) of the English Arbitration Act; (and for a quasi-legislative example: Art. 19(2) of the UNCITRAL Model Law).
139. Among the rules that explicitly provide the arbitral tribunal's power to order document production are: Art. 24(3) of the UNCITRAL Rules, Art. 20(5) of the ICC Rules (see infra, Sect. III.1.a.ii), Art. 34(2) of the ICSID Rules; Art. 27(1) of the DIS Rules; see also Art. 37 of the Japan Commercial Arbitration Association Commercial Arbitration Rules
140. Art. 22(1)(d).
141. Art. 22(1)(e).
142. Termed the "Rules of Arbitration and Conciliation of the International Arbitral Centre of the Austrian Federal Economic Chamber in Vienna."
143. Art. 20(1).

parties to submit documents and visual evidence and may call in experts."[144] Like the LCIA Arbitration Rules, the Vienna Rules do not provide an express procedure whereby parties may seek disclosure.

ii. ICC and ICDR

Strangely, the 1998 version of the Rules of Arbitration of the International Court of Arbitration of the International Chamber of Commerce, although amongst the most used, are even less explicit. Art. 20(1) states: "The Arbitral Tribunal shall proceed within as short a time as possible to establish the facts of the case by all appropriate means," while Art. 20 (5) provides that at "any time during the proceedings, the Arbitral Tribunal may summon any party to provide additional evidence." Documentary evidence is not expressly mentioned. Despite the lack of specificity, however, some believe it is beyond doubt that the rule extends to written disclosure.[145] Moreover, the ICC addressed written disclosure directly in a report issued in August 2007.[146] Although non-binding, the report suggests approaches and encourages parties and tribunals to "think of [the 2007 ICC Report] as a basis from which to develop the procedures to be used". The ICC Rules encourage using the so-called "Redfern Schedule" – a four-column chart identifying the documents requested, the justification for the requests, objections raised against such requests and the tribunal's decision –[147] as well as the guidelines for document production established in the IBA Rules. However, they also suggest a variety of ways in which the scope and burden of production can be reduced. Some of these include limiting the number of document requests,[148] establishing reasonable time limits for production, avoiding unnecessary duplication of production with filings, minimizing the creation of hard copies of documents and minimizing the need for certified translations.[149] With the same aim of avoiding broad, burdensome or excessive document-production requests, the recent Report by the Task Force of the ICC Commission on Arbitration on the Production of Electronic Documents in International Arbitration, also referring to the IBA Rules as well as to the 2007 ICC Report, has rightly recalled some basic principles aimed at excluding any type of "fishing

---

144. Art. 20(5).
145. See, e.g., G.B. BORN, *op. cit.*, fn. 5, pp. 1885 and 1889.
146. International Chamber of Commerce, Publication no. 843, "Techniques for Controlling Time and Costs in Arbitration" (2007), available at <www.iccwbo.org/uploadedFiles/TimeCost_E.pdf> (last accessed 15 February 2010).
147. About which, see: *Redfern and Hunter on International Arbitration*, 5th edn., *op. cit.*, fn. 5, para. 6-114.
148. It is noteworthy to mention that para. 53 poses the principle that "The parties will normally each produce the documents upon which they intend to rely. Each party should consider avoiding requests for production of documents from another party unless such production is relevant and material to the outcome of the case. When the parties have agreed upon non-controversial facts, no documentary evidence should be needed to prove those facts."
149. *Ibid.*, at paras. 55-60.

expeditions"[150] and "broad, US-style discovery"[151] and containing the scope of production, when and if at all necessary or desirable.[152]

A more dramatic effort to use guidelines to introduce specific written disclosure provisions into institutional rules was undertaken by the American Arbitration Association's International Centre for Dispute Resolution (ICDR).[153] The ICDR Rules themselves do not take up either written disclosure or even related powers of tribunals.[154] In 2008, the ICDR issued guidelines which address written disclosure (ICDR Guidelines).[155] Unlike the ICC 2007 Report, the ICDR Guidelines are binding on all cases administered by the ICDR commenced after 31 May 2008. The ICDR Guidelines mirror the IBA Rules in many respects. The operative language states that tribunals may:

> "upon application, require one party to make available to another party, documents in the party's possession, not otherwise available to the party seeking the documents, that are reasonably believed to exist and to be relevant and material to the outcome of the case. Requests for documents shall contain a description of specific documents or classes of documents, along with an explanation of their relevance and materiality to the outcome of the case."[156]

The ICDR Guidelines contain express limitations on production requests and go further than any other institutional rules considered in setting forth a procedure for compelling document production.

iii.   Finally, the IBA Rules. From 1983 ...

Given the usual silence of the three major sources of rules likely to govern such issues – the arbitration agreement, rules issued by centers and referred to by parties and national laws applicable in the seat's jurisdiction – alternative sources emerged from practice to supplement this vacuum. In that respect, the International Bar Association, originally created in 1947 in New York by lawyers to promote an exchange of information between legal associations worldwide, played a key role in supplying arbitration users a "soft-law" in that field, which started as guidelines and have today become almost binding rules,[157] given their widespread authority.[158] As early as 1983,

---

150. See Sect. 5(6)(a).
151. See Sect. 5(6)(d).
152. See, e.g., the Introduction at Sect. 1(5), as well as Sects. 5(6), 5(7), 5(8), 5(9) and 5(10).
153. See Art. 19(3) of the AAA Rules which provides that the "tribunal may, if it deems it necessary at any stage of the proceedings: (a) call upon the party to produce documents...".
154. The rules have historically been read to imply the right to written disclosure.
155. International Centre for Dispute Resolution, ICDR Guidelines for Arbitrators Concerning Exchanges of Information (2008) available at <www.adr.org/si.asp?id=5288> (last accessed 15 February 2010).
156. *Ibid.*, at Art. 3.
157. Even if not incorporated into the parties' arbitration agreement, which happens very rarely.
158. See for instance: Robert KARRAR-LEWSLEY, "Developments in Arbitration – The Revised IBA Rules of Evidence, Law Update (February 2011, issue 237), according to whom those rules would be "widely used in arbitrations in the Middle East".

the IBA issued rules governing discovery and the presentation of evidence in international arbitration.[159] Seeking to strike a balance between the common and civil law traditions, the rules provided an elective procedural framework for interested parties. The rules were changed and reissued as the "Rules on the Taking of Evidence in International Commercial Arbitration" (IBA Rules) in 1999.

The 1999 IBA Rules address mandatory and elective document production. In the first instance, they placed an affirmative obligation on parties to produce all documents on which they rely to support their claims.[160] This provision was likely to be familiar to practitioners from a civil law background. In the second instance, however, they created a mechanism whereby a party could obtain relevant documents not in its possession. This was more unsettling to civil lawyers. Procedurally, a party seeking disclosure could identify documents sought from its adversary to the tribunal.[161] The opposing party is then given some time to produce the documents.[162] If it resists disclosure, it could then lodge objections with the tribunal,[163] and the tribunal is to decide whether production should be ordered.[164]

It is now firmly admitted that elective disclosure under these IBA Rules did and does not amount to "American-style" discovery. The party seeking documents, or a narrow category of documents, must demonstrate that they are "relevant and material" to the outcome of the case.[165] The party must also explain why the documents sought are believed to be in the "possession, custody or control" of its adversary.[166] Aside from these express limitations, there are practical hurdles. Although the rules authorize tribunals to take steps to compel document production by a non-party, with limited exceptions, tribunals are not authorized by national laws to use the apparatus of the state to compel production.[167] It has been observed that document production under the IBA Rules is narrower than discovery under the FRCP in the United States, similar in scope to disclosure in the United Kingdom and broader than disclosure in most civil law systems. Whether or not this is accurate, the rules continue to gain traction as a common point of reference in international commercial arbitration. Therefore, even if parties do not

---

159. Supplementary Rules Governing the Presentation and Reception of Evidence in International Commercial Arbitration, ICCA *Yearbook Commercial Arbitration* X (1985) p. 145.
160. Art. 3(1).
161. Art. 3(2).
162. Art. 3(4).
163. Art. 3(5).
164. Art. 3(6).
165. Art. 3(3)(b). Relevance, of course, need only be shown to be likely since actual relevance can only be ascertained after the document has been produced. See, e.g., V. HAMILTON, "Document Production in ICC Arbitration", ICC Bull. Sp. Suppl. 2006, *op. cit.*, fn. 5.
166. At least one commentator emphasizes the tendency of courts in common law jurisdictions to interpret "control" liberally. See G.B. BORN, "Disclosure and Discovery in International Arbitration – B. Discovery and Disclosure Powers of International Arbitral Tribunals" in *International Commercial Arbitration*, *op. cit.*, fn. 5, pp. 878, 1898 citing G.B. BORN and P. RUTLEDGE, *International Civil Litigation in United States Courts* (4th edn. 2007) pp. 929-932; P. MATTHEWS and H. MALEK, *Disclosure* (Sweet & Maxwell 2008) paras. 5.39-5.42.
167. Art. 3(8).

agree to their express application, their presence may be felt, and civil lawyers must anticipate their influence.[168]

iv. ... Up to the 2010 IBA Rules on Evidence

As many practitioners felt the need to further "improve"[169] the 1999 Rules, a new version[170] thereof was adopted by the IBA Council on 29 May 2010 and is worth mentioning here since it has not only taken into account a new generation of (electronic) evidence, but has also consolidated the balance referred to above and has probably even gone slightly beyond. First, the 2010 Rules[171] have introduced, in the Preamble under (3), a new standard of "good faith" by which parties must abide and they should now be entitled to know the evidence on which the other parties rely, not only in advance of any evidentiary hearing but also before "determination on the merit". This new drafting seems to clearly strengthen the parties' duties to disclose the documents that have a bearing on their case, whether on their own initiative or at the request of the other party or parties. On the other hand, the drafter of the 2010 Rules clearly intended to address and contain the risk that the document-production process drifts in an uncontrollable manner. Hence, the arbitral tribunal's new obligation to "consult the parties and invite them to consult each other with a view to agreeing on an efficient, economical and fair process for the taking of evidence" (Art. 2(1)), as well as the indication that it may consult them "at the earliest appropriate time in the proceedings regarding the scope, timing and manner of the taking of evidence", which includes, by way of example, "the requirements and procedure applicable to the production of Documents". In short, seeking efficiency and avoiding excessive burdens, and even more "fishing expeditions", through the process of document production are practical considerations the drafters of the 2010 Rules had clearly in mind.[172] Beyond their content, what is also interesting

---

168. See, e.g., Jan PAULSSON, "Cross-Enrichment of Public and Private Law Dispute Resolution Mechanisms in the International Arena", 9 J. Int'l Arb. (1992, no. 1) p. 59 at p. 63 and V.V. VEEDER, op. cit., fn. 25.
169. V.V. VEEDER, "Are the IBA Rules Perfectible?" in T. GIOVANNINI and A. MOURRE, Written Evidence and Discovery in International Arbitration, op. cit., fn. 5, at p. 321; see also R. KREINDLER, "Possible Future Revisions to the IBA Rules on the Taking of Evidence in International Commercial Arbitration" in K.-H. BÖCKSTIEGEL, K.-P. BERGER, J. BREDOW, eds., The Taking of Evidence in International Commercial Arbitration, op. cit., fn. 5, at p. 85.
170. Now called the "Rules on the Taking of Evidence in International Arbitration" (to include investment arbitrations in the scope of disputes likely to refer to these rules) and which shall apply to all contracts concluded on or after 29 May 2010.
171. For a presentation, see R. KREINDLER, "The IBA Rules on the Taking of Evidence in International Arbitration, Presentation of the 2010 Revised Text", lecture presented at the Swedish Arbitration Association, Stockholm, 27 January 2011. See also: Judith GILL, Guido S. TAWIL and R. KREINDLER, "The 2010 Revisions to the IBA Rules on the Taking of Evidence in International Arbitration", 1 PJIA (2011) p.23.
172. See, e.g., the very first lines of the second paragraph of the Foreword to the 2010 version by Guido TAWIL and Judith GILL which not only point to considerations of efficiency and economy, but have also now added a fairness criterion; similarly for Art. 1 of the Preamble of the Rules as well as (ii) of the Preamble of the Commentary: "it is important for parties and arbitral tribunals to find methods to resolve their disputes in the most effective and least costly manner";

about the 2010 Rules is that they aim to be more accessible – that is, they are available in multiple languages,[173] which was barely the case with the previous versions. To that extent, it is likely that these translations will help many civil lawyers, unfamiliar with the very principle of document production, to make themselves more familiar with this device. By the same token, in relation to the admission and assessment of evidence, it seems important to note that the new IBA Rules now expressly allow the tribunal, when assessing if a document should or should not be produced with regard notably to privilege, "to take into account the need to maintain fairness and equality as between the Parties, particularly if they are subject to different legal or ethical rules" (Art. 9(3)(e)). This renewed[174] reference to fairness and equality appears to be another clear indication that the IBA drafters confirmed their intention to enable the tribunal to rightly cope with legal, ethical and, ultimately, cultural differences.[175] As already mentioned, the 2010 version has also incorporated some further guidance directed to the arbitrator(s) on how to address the question of production of electronic documents.

Eventually, apart from this preliminary, early and efficiency-oriented consultation with the tribunal as to the framework and details of the document-production process, the following five fundamental rules currently govern documentary evidence under the latest IBA Rules:

(i) the "principle" continues to be – or so it seems – the parties' obligation to produce any document on which they rely (Art. 3(1));
(ii) document-production requests by the opponent are permissible (Art. 3(2));
(iii) these "Requests to Produce" are, however, subject to strict conditions, which are: specificity and narrowness,[176] the fact the documents requested have to reasonably be believed to exist (Art. 3(3)(a)(ii)), must be relevant to the case and material to its outcome (Art. 3(3)(b), Art. 3(7), Art. 3(9), Art. 3(11) and Art. 9(2)(a)), not in the possession, custody or control of the requesting party[177] but in that of the producing

---

Art. 3(3)(a)(ii) which imposes some restrictions to the party requesting electronic documents and introduces an "efficient and economic" standard; see also the new Art. 3(3)(c)(i) which requires from the requesting party, inter alia, "a statement of the reasons why it would be unreasonably burdensome for the [latter] to produce such Documents"; Art. 3(12)(b) which requires, for electronic document production, a "form most convenient or economical to" the producing party; Art. 9(2)(g) which introduces (compared with its previous version) some new considerations of "procedural economy".

173. Versions in other languages than English and already posted (as of April 2011) include Chinese, French, German, Greek, Italian, Japanese, Korean, Spanish and Turkish; and yet to come are Arabic, Portuguese and Russian.
174. See that reference already made in former Art. 9(2)(g), which has been slightly amended by the 2010 version (see fn. 172).
175. See the end of the second paragraph of Guido S. TAWIL's and Judith GILL's Foreword to the 2010 version of the Rules, which paraphrases David W. RIVKIN's formula in his Foreword to the 1999 version: "The IBA Rules of Evidence reflect procedures in use in many different legal systems, and they may be particularly useful when the parties come from different legal cultures."
176. The documents must be sufficiently identified (Art. 3(3)(a)(i)) and the Request to Produce must pertain to a "narrow and specific" category of documents.
177. Or be too burdensome for the requesting party to produce them.

party (Art. 3(3)(c)(i) and (ii)) and at last, to a lesser extent, that they not be unreasonably burdensome for the producing party to produce them (Ar. 9(2)(c));
(iv) conversely and equally admitted[178] are the objections to such document-production requests, made on specific grounds, such as privilege or confidentiality;
(v) failure to produce a requested document, with no valid justification, *may* entail possible adverse inference,[179] as well as financial sanctions,[180] on the part of the tribunal.

v. Beyond the Rules?
If the IBA Rules have undeniably filled a gap in this field in that it framed a process that was too often left blank, they must serve as a reference, and not exclusively, to appreciate whether common principles governing documentary evidence exist in international arbitration. As rightly pointed out by some practitioners,[181] even if the IBA Rules offer a degree of certainty and efficiency by posing a detailed framework that would otherwise require long discussions between the tribunal and the parties, "there may be benefit to a party to arbitration in not adopting the IBA Rules, and instead seeking to retain a greater degree of procedural flexibility throughout the proceedings. Alternatively, there may be benefit to a party to arbitration in requesting that the tribunal adopt a purely civil, or common, law approach to the procedure." Thus, the question becomes the following: Beyond the IBA rules, is it possible to identify a consensus or some fundamental commonly accepted principles in the area of documentary evidence? If the answer is somehow positive, it should also be much nuanced.

b. *Some agreed principles: from an ambitious merger to a few smallest common denominators*

i. A difference of degree, not of nature
Admittedly, it is impossible to say today which of the civil law or the common law traditions prevails, at least insofar as issues of documentary evidence in international arbitration are concerned. Some may say, of course, that the very fact that document-production requests are available to parties suffices to say that common law has marked the arbitral process with an indelible fingerprint and in an overwhelming way. We have seen that this is clearly an overstatement as civil law procedure knows such a device very well. Others will also counter-argue that this mechanism, as it exists in international arbitration, has little, if anything, to do with the actual US-style "discovery" device, such that it is simply impossible to accept there has been some "evidentiary transplant"– to borrow an expression from a US expert[182] – from common law into the principles governing this area. Hence, the focus should not be on what is sometimes, wrongly in our view, presented as a difference in nature between the two systems, as both seem to

---

178. Art. 3(5) to (8), Art. 9(2)(b) and (e) and (3).
179. Art. 9(5) and (6).
180. Art. 9(7).
181. See Herbert Smith's Japan dispute avoidance newsletter "International Arbitration: Documentary Evidence and the Revised IBA Rules" (Sept. 2010, issue no. 97).
182. M. DAMAŠKA, *op. cit.*, fn. 107, at p. 843.

accept the idea that a party may request from the other party, documents that the former wants to rely upon but does not have in his or her possession (and, to some extent, obtain an order from the tribunal enjoining that party to produce these documents). Rather, the fundamental difference remains one of scope and degree. And it is true that, once the principle is deemed to have been commonly accepted, the scale of the document production permitted by a tribunal continues and will continue to be hard fought by the parties and to generate some uncertainty.

ii.   Four points of agreement

It is therefore possible to synthesize the following principles as they appear to emerge from the international practice of international arbitration, whether they directly flow from the IBA Rules, which are themselves an attempt to encapsulate that common practice, or whether they flow from beyond this soft law. Those principles must be seen as the smallest common denominators on which each system has agreed to compromise, rather than as obvious, natural or universally admitted principles.

– First, there should be no room for US-style discovery in international arbitration,[183] or, by the same token, for what is called today "fishing expeditions",[184] namely overwhelmingly broad document productions, that are also systematic and repetitive, unreasonably expensive, very remote to the issue at stake and aimed solely, at best, at making up for the requesting party's own failure to provide the documents he or she is supposed to rely upon for his or her claim and, at worst, at putting some undue burden and pressure on the producing party.

– Second, even if the starting point or rule of any international arbitration remains the claimant's duty to produce from the outset the documents he or she intends to rely upon to ground his or her claim, the very admission of document-production requests makes it difficult to treat this fact-finding device as a mere exception to the broader rule imposing the burden of proof mainly on the claimant's shoulders. This firm (automatic?) admission[185] of this device is confirmed by the producing party's obligation to comply

---

183. See the Commentary on the revised text of the 2010 IBA Rules on the Taking of Evidence in International Arbitration, at p. 8, which provides: "Article 3.3 is designed to prevent a broad 'fishing expedition'."
184. See W.L. CRAIG, W.W. PARK, J. PAULSSON, *op. cit.*, fn. 5, Sect. 26.01.
185. It is rather symptomatic to note that very few sources dare admit explicitly that this device is now firmly rooted and no longer some exception to a broader restrictive rule: many, like the drafters of the IBA Rules (1999 and 2010) will say that, while US-style discovery is "inappropriate", there is a "general consensus, even among practitioners from civil law countries, that *some level* of document production is *appropriate*" (see Commentary on the revised text of the 2010 IBA Rules at p. 7 (emphasis added)); of course the "appropriateness" means not only that the use of the device is admitted, but also that it may be desirable or encouraged; see also the Report by the ICC Task Force on Production of Electronic Documents, *op. cit.*, fn. 130, which states that "there is no *automatic* right" to obtain documentary evidence from the other party in international arbitration (at Sects. 1.5 and 5.6(b) (emphasis added)), which also implies that, if there is no automaticity, there still remains a *right* in that respect; see also A. REDFERN, M. HUNTER with N. BLACKABY and C. PARTASIDES, *Law and Practice of International Commercial Arbitration*, 4th edn., *op. cit.*, fn. 11, at para. 6-71, who state that there "is no practice of *automatic* discovery in

with the requests (or the corresponding order issue by the tribunal),[186] but also by the fact that objections to such requests – the first of which being privilege – are also admitted and even regulated with a great level of detail. This is all the more true in that it seems that the ability for a party to request from his or her opponent certain documents in its possession – along with its corollary, the ability to revert to the tribunal to order such document production should the producing party refuse to provide the requested documents – is being progressively treated as a "right" and more specifically as one of procedural or fundamental nature and pertaining to due process, which arbitral tribunals, by principle and in practice, are increasingly reluctant to overlook and thus to refuse to grant.

– Third, if document-production requests are allowed in international arbitration, they impose a set of very demanding conditions (as discussed below)[187] on the requesting party. But above these technical requirements, there are other unique policy considerations that will counterbalance the depth and scope of such requests: proportionality and efficiency, on one side – that is, the insurance to weigh the alleged importance of the documents requested with the cost that their being retrieved and produced will entail for the producing party – and, on the other side, fairness and equality: that is, the concern that such requests will not make up an undue burden for the producing party and will not put him or her in an unbalanced situation compared with the other party that might be more acquainted with this device.

– Fourth, it is a consensus that ... there is precisely no (possible?) consensus of principle over the standard scale, scope and depth of a document-production process in international arbitration since, despite all the efforts – including those of the IBA drafters – undertaken to better frame this device, improve its efficiency, limit its burden and excesses and make it more predictable, the fundamental power to regulate it continues – and will continue – to lie with the arbitrators' discretionary and broader power[188] to manage the proceedings.[189] On these procedural issues, it seems generally accepted, although sometimes contested, that the tribunal has the last say, for better or worse. Thus, as already mentioned, what a party may expect from this device, how it will be

---

international arbitration" (but, then, made it clearer in the subsequent edition that "the process known as 'discovery' has no place in international arbitration" (at para. 6.107, fn. 65 of the 5th edn.); see also B. HANOTIAU, "Document Production in International Arbitration: A Tentative Definition of 'Best Practices'", in ICC Bull. Sp. Suppl. 2006, *op. cit.*, fn. 5, at p. 114, which states that, beyond the different legal cultures, "it is generally agreed that document production *has a place* in international arbitration" (emphasis added).

186. See, e.g., the compelling language of Art. 3(4) of the 2010 IBA Rules: "Within the time ordered by the Arbitral Tribunal, the Party to whom the Request to Produce is addressed *shall* produce to the other Parties and, if the Arbitral Tribunal so orders, to it, all the Documents requested in its possession, custody or control as to which it makes no objection." (emphasis added).
187. Specificity, narrowness, relevance, materiality, absence of undue burden for the producing party, proof of their existence and of their being under the control of the other party (see supra, Sect. III.*1*.*a*.iv.
188. See G. KAUFMANN-KOHLER and Ph. BÄRTSCH, "Discovery in International Arbitration: How Much Is Too Much?", *op. cit.*, fn. 5, at p. 17.
189. Absent the parties' agreement.

treated – contained or broadened – by an arbitral tribunal, will vary from one arbitration to another and will greatly depend, not that much on whether the parties and/or the tribunal opted to follow the IBA Rules, but rather on the parties', counsels' and, at the end of the day, the arbitrators' legal background and on whether they are familiar with (and favorable to) this device or, to the contrary, are prejudiced against it.

iii.   True love or love by default?

If these principles seem to reflect a reasonable compromise, which is the *mariage de raison* referred to above, this does not mean, however, that it led to a "happy marriage",[190] where "life is a long quiet river". On the contrary, there continue to be major issues, both in the actual practice of the document-production process and in terms of legal remedies, which clearly pollute its efficiency as well as the way this mechanism is perceived by users and counsel all over the globe, especially when they come from civil law countries.

2.   *Some Pitfalls That Continue to Make the Document-Production Process Relatively Uncertain.*

Two types of difficulties must be mentioned here. First, those encountered in practice, the importance of which, although of a technical nature and despite the welcomed emergence of best practices in this field,[191] should not be underestimated, especially for counsel who come from a legal background that did not accustom them to the technicalities of this device (*a*). Equally important, some serious legal issues continue to surround this process, especially when it comes to identifying the proper remedy notably to the situation where a party does not comply with an order enjoining it to produce certain documents (*b*).

a.   *Practical issues still encountered in document production*

i.   Overwhelming

Take two basic elements already covered: one, the fact that the divergence between practitioners is not about admitting document production but rather about its scope and, two, that scope is eventually determined by the tribunal with a great amount of discretion. This can lead to situations where, in fact, and despite the limits and restrictions discussed below, the document production allowed by a tribunal is not significantly different than a discovery ordered by a US court,[192] both in terms of volume and costs. Hence the very acceptance of this device within international arbitration could be seen as opening a Pandora's box, in theory, and sometimes in practice. Whatever the prima facie position vis-à-vis document production (favorable or against), the past ten

---

190. In reference to the article by G. KAUFMANN-KOHLER and Ph. BÄRTSCH, "Discovery in International Arbitration: How Much Is Too Much?", *op. cit.*, fn. 5, p. 21, who use the term "happy merger".
191. See B. HANOTIAU, *op. cit.*, fn. 185, p. 113.
192. See for a similar idea: J.-F. POUDRET and S. BESSON, *op. cit.*, fn. 5, para. 653, p. 555-556.

years have indeed seen a commonly shared and growing concern that this device could be, and sometimes actually was, mutating into a "monster"[193] or a "tsunami",[194] given the enormous number of documents resulting from that process, which not only are burdensome for the producing party to store, retrieve, review, classify and provide, but also for the other party to digest and treat efficiently within the limited amount of time that has been assigned by the procedural calendar set up by the tribunal. Some will explain it by the influence of common lawyers who are more concerned about having a comprehensive grasp of the facts and whose document-production requests will be far-reaching.[195] It might be the case that US lawyers are better trained to cope with such large amounts of documentary evidence, but this advantage does not go very far, and, in fact, this tendency to "over-produce" is also the natural result of the actual functioning of all of our modern societies, regardless of their legal features, where quantity often prevails over quality and in which technology, copying and storage are more and more systematically used.[196] In addition, this uncontrollable drift does not flow merely from the parties' and its counsels' variable appetite for documentary evidence: it can also be imputable to the arbitrators' practice and their unwillingness to refuse document-production requests, even when excessively broad or burdensome, out of fear of violating the parties' due process rights.[197] Whatever the causes of this pitfall, it does address a serious challenge to the fate of international arbitration, beyond differences in legal backgrounds: not only to the overall efficiency of this device (is the potential benefit of finding all relevant documents adverse to the interests of the producing party worth its actual cost?),[198] but more fundamentally with regard to the risks related to the way the arbitrators will render their decision, faced with an ocean of documents (it is not uncommon in arbitrations where significant amounts are at stake to see several million involved). Can three individuals (sometimes even one) constituting a tribunal – however competent or accustomed to this mechanism they are and whatever their due compensation – truly cope with that ocean without bearing the risk of overlooking some of its waves?[199] Beyond cost considerations, and despite (or with the help of) further

---

193. See S.P. FINIZIO, "Discovery in International Arbitration: Frankenstein's Monster in the Digital Age" in K.-H. BÖCKSTIEGEL, K.-P. BERGER, J. BREDOW, eds., *The Taking of Evidence in International Commercial Arbitration*, op. cit., fn. 5, p. 57.
194. M.E. SCHNEIDER, "The Paper Tsunami in International Arbitration – Problems, Risks for the Arbitrators' Decision Making and Possible Solutions" in T. GIOVANNINI and A. MOURRE, eds., *Written Evidence and Discovery in International Arbitration*, op. cit., fn. 5, p. 365; see also: B. HANOTIAU, "Massive Production of Documents and Demonstrative Exhibits" in *ibid.*, p. 357.
195. Y. DERAINS, op. cit., fn. 43, at p. 83.
196. See infra Sect. III.3.a, re the specific question of production of electronic documents.
197. R. ZIADÉ and Ch.-H. de TAFFIN, Commentary on Paris Court of Appeal's decision of 26 Nov. 2009, 2 International Journal of Arab Arbitration (2010, no. 3) pp. 138-158.
198. The cost alone of retrieving, following a tribunal's order, the requested documents, without even knowing whether they, or even some of them, will be relevant to the dispute, can in certain instances, reach over US$ 1 million.
199. See M.E. SCHNEIDER, op. cit., fn. 194, p. 367.

guidelines in this direction,[200] this will probably be the most serious challenge document production will have to face in the future. It must be admitted that no efficient remedy has emerged today to respond to this frightening drift.

ii. Timing and other issues of case-management

Although it is undeniable that a great number of arbitrations take place in a manner where parties are capable of agreeing over how to efficiently manage the document-production process,[201] points of divergence are also quite frequent and they can occur about little details, which tribunals are often obliged to get into to allow the process to move forward. For instance, a more specific issue of case management has recently arisen about the exact timing of that production phase within the arbitral process and only a few authors have raised the issue and proposed some guidance – [202] mainly advising to date the document-production process after the first exchange of submissions. Yet, again, these case-management issues fall within the discretionary power of the tribunal, and in case of disagreement, this "best practice" might not be applied, for example for reasons of bifurcation. It can indeed happen that because a jurisdictional challenge was raised by a party and the tribunal has decided to settle that issue first, the tribunal decides that document-production requests will be allowed right after the claimant has filed its first submission. In that case, such requests will come mainly, if not exclusively, from the respondent who may tailor its requests (to obtain documents supporting the absence of jurisdiction) according to the claimant's submission, while the claimant, not having seen any pleadings from the respondent as the requesting party, will not be able to raise the proper objections against its requests. While this situation may be understandable from a practical standpoint, it can also raise serious issues of equality between the parties. Conversely, it may happen that a non-signatory to an arbitration agreement is brought by a claimant as a party to an arbitration: if the tribunal decides to join the merits to the jurisdictional issues, the non-signatory defendant might be caught up in an arbitration in which the claimant will file very burdensome document-production requests against it at a very early stage of the proceedings, whereas the tribunal might eventually find it does not have jurisdiction against that non-signatory respondent. Again, because of these unpredictable timing issues, the dramatic and additional costs incurred, actually unjustly, by such a party –[203] not to mention the possible disclosure of some confidential documents due to a claim that will turn out to be ill-grounded – may seriously undermine the fairness of this process.

---

200. It is doubtful that cost-shifting (i.e., shifting the cost of the document production from the responding party to the requesting party), as practiced notably in the US judiciary, can address this issue.
201. See G.B. BORN, *op. cit*, fn. 5, p. 1893; see also S.P. FINIZIO, *op. cit.*, fn. 193, p. 68, who suggests that the US practice, where parties are invited to confer on this process, be taken as a source of inspiration.
202. See G. KAUFMANN-KOHLER and Ph. BÄRTSCH, *op. cit.*, fn. 5, p. 20; B. HANOTIAU, *op. cit.*, fn. 185, p. 115, para. 10; S.P. FINIZIO, *op. cit.*, fn. 193.
203. True, that may be reimbursed if the respondent ultimately prevails in its jurisdictional challenge, but only much later and with the risk it may not recover this cost at all because of enforcement issues.

If it is undeniable that the Redfern Schedule, already mentioned above,[204] became a standard and very practical support to help parties and tribunals make the document-production process as efficient as possible, the frame and content of this device continue to be, in some instances at least, eagerly fought, often because of seemingly incidental issues that turn out to be of critical importance for parties from different legal backgrounds. Many examples can be provided here: besides the four "core" columns, how many more can be admitted, for instance to allow the requesting party to make objections to the producing party's objections? By the same token, who must have the last word in this document? If a timetable was set up in detail for each party to fill up its column, may the requesting party modify its columns in light of the other party's objection when they eventually submit the common Redfern Schedule? How can parties avoid filing this joint submission with the tribunal in an indigestible fashion (too many columns, too many pages)? Can explanatory memoranda accompany this Schedule precisely to make it more readable[205] and, if so, how and when should this side document be filed? Many other issues, which could sound like mere technical and practical ones to be merely regulated by the parties or the tribunal's procedural authority to manage the proceedings, can also raise, inadvertently, serious issues of due process, such as the language in which the documents requested or produced should be filed – in their original version (if this involves hundreds of thousands of documents) that the requesting party may not be capable of understanding, or in translated version, with the costs this may entail. Other tools, more or less related to the Redfern Schedule, such as the Master Referee[206] or the privilege log, originally aimed at facilitating the document-production process, are also not used without hurdles. They both concern another practical, though important, aspect: privilege.

iii. Managing privilege

It is only recently that authors have started examining this issue, often presented as a practical one, left, like many other "technical" ones, to the tribunal's discretion to manage the proceedings, but which is gaining importance as practitioners are becoming increasingly aware of its critical role in the proper conduct and outcome of the arbitration.[207] There too, behind what is often described technically as "evidentiary

---

204. See supra, Sect. III.1.a.ii.
205. This has increasingly become the case.
206. Recognized by the new Art. 3(7) of the 2010 IBA Rules.
207. H. ALVAREZ, "Evidentiary Principles in International Arbitration" in *International Arbitration 2006: Back to Basics?* ICCA Congress Series no. 13 (Kluwer 2007) p. 663 (hereinafter *ICCA Congress Series no. 13*); see also F. VON SCHLABRENDORFF and A. SHEPPARD, "Conflict of Legal Privileges in International Arbitration: An Attempt to Find a Holistic Solution" in G. AKSEN, et al., *Global Reflections on International Law, Commerce and Dispute Resolution: Liber Amicorum in Honour of Robert Briner* (ICC 2005) p. 743; K.-P. BERGER, "Evidentiary Privileges", in *Best Practices in International Arbitration*, ASA Special Series no. 26 (2006), p. 19; Pierre HEITZMANN, "Confidentiality and Privileges in Cross-Border Legal Practice: The Need for a Global Standard?", 26 ASA Bulletin (2008, no. 2) p. 213; Amy F. COHEN, "Options for Approaching Evidentiary Privilege in International Arbitration" in T. GIOVANNINI and A. MOURRE, eds., *Written Evidence and Discovery in International Arbitration, op. cit.*, fn. 5, p. 423 at

privilege" (as it primarily aims at excluding otherwise relevant evidence), actually lies great difficulty, mainly due to the fundamental differences between various legal systems, not only as to the terminology, but also in terms of the meaning, value, scope and depth of this category. If it is admitted today that this field of law continues to be a "grey area in international commercial arbitration",[208] it is probably because of this culture clash, which raises challenges in terms of fairness and equality. For instance, even if one were to put aside the question of the lack of international procedural rules or standards[209] to identify the applicable law to govern that question,[210] there is even no agreement today as to whether it must be deemed as an issue of substance or of procedure. As two authors have observed, in civil law countries such as France, legal privilege "is considered a matter of professional ethics rather that a rule of disclosure and evidence",[211] while privilege under US law is a pure evidentiary issue, making the client the ultimate beneficiary of any right to claim privilege which he can also waive. Put differently, while the US privilege seems *in rem*, i.e., attached to a document in particular, in France it is *ad personam*, i.e., intertwined with the person of the counsel. This is also why civil lawyers are subject to stricter rules, such as in France where an attorney may not waive his professional secrecy, even with his client's permission, and where even fee issues or accessory documents are covered by privilege. This also explains why devices, such as the privilege log (or the appointment of an independent referee) aimed at facilitating the process of identifying the documents withheld on the basis of a privilege, can pose a problem. For the log, not only does it require the actual disclosure of features of documents that should be confidential per se but it also runs the risk of involuntary disclosure of a document that would be otherwise withheld as privileged. But counsel on the other side of the Atlantic are also better protected from

---

pp. 437-440; Matthieu DE BOISSÉSON, "Evidentiary Privileges in International Arbitration" in *ICCA Congress Series no. 13*, p. 712; Javier H. RUBINSTEIN and Britton B. GUERRINA, "The Attorney-Client Privilege and International Arbitration", *op. cit.*, fn. 5, p. 587 at p. 599.

208. J. LEW, "Document Disclosure, Evidentiary Value of Documents and Burden of Evidence" in T. GIOVANNINI and A. MOURRE, eds., *Written Evidence and Discovery in International Arbitration, op. cit.*, fn. 5, p. 11 at p. 18.

209. See AAA – ICDR Arbitration Rules (Amended and effective as at 1 June 2009), Art. 20(6): "The tribunal shall determine the admissibility, relevance, materiality and weight of the evidence offered by any party. The tribunal shall take into account applicable principles of legal privilege, such as those involving the confidentiality of communications between a lawyer and client." See also, ICC Rules, Art. 20(7): "The Arbitral Tribunal may take measures for protecting trade secrets and confidential information."

210. The standards generally considered by arbitral tribunals to determine the rules applicable to legal privilege objections include: (i) the law of the domicile of the party claiming privilege, (ii) the law of the place where a document was sent; (iii) the law of the professional domicile of the lawyer or the applicable rules of professional ethics; (iv) the law of the place where a document is located.

211. V. CAMERER, Ch. G. HIOUREAS, "*Glamis Gold, Ltd. v. United States:* A Case Study on Disclosure Procedures in International Arbitration", 2 World Arbitration and Mediation Review (2008, no. 3) p. 33.

another angle: while the Court of Justice of the European Union has, once again,[212] stated that in-house counsel could not invoke any privilege, US lawyers employed in US corporations do benefit from privilege as much as outside attorneys. In order to find the right balance among these different, sometimes conflicting rules, more and more tribunals are guided by principles of equality and fairness, which often dictate the opting for a "most favorable privilege" approach.[213] The 2010 IBA Rules (Art. 9(3)(c) and (e)) also invite arbitrators to follow that direction.

b. *Legal remedies including in case of a failure to produce documents in international arbitration*

i. A right per se?

If indeed document production is deemed to be admitted both legally (as nothing in the law would actually prevent it) and in practice (whether from institutional rules or on the basis of the IBA rules), a first fundamental question must then be addressed, which is whether some *effective* entitlement by a party to request from his opponent that the latter produce documents in his possession exists and, above all, whether this right can be sanctioned by tribunals *and* courts? We have seen that this "right" is implicitly admitted in practice,[214] although rarely explicitly recognized.[215] Yet, the question posed here is not theoretical, but much more practical, as there cannot be any right without an efficient sanction attached thereto. The first available sanction, in the realm of international arbitration, is the tribunal's faculty to draw adverse inferences, which is broadly accepted.[216] Published awards[217] show that tribunals do use this faculty, although not that frequently. Indeed, even if it is said that the threat of adverse inferences encourages fairness and efficiency and may help to encourage parties to produce all of the documents a tribunal has judged necessary to decide a case – and eventually should result in awards that are more likely to be enforced –[218] it is also acknowledged that adverse inference

---

212. Court of Justice of the European Union, 14 Sept. 2010, *Akzo Nobel Chemicals et Akcros Chemicals v. Commission*, aff. C-550/07 P.
213. Matthieu DE BOISSÉSON, *op. cit.*, fn. 207, p. 713, stating that the "most favorable privilege" approach: "allows any party to an international arbitration to claim the same privilege that are available to any other party". See also, Henri ALVAREZ, *op. cit.*, fn. 207, p. 686.
214. See Art. 3(4) of the 2010 IBA Rules which explicitly compels the receiving party, subject to certain conditions, to produce the requested documents.
215. See infra, Sect. III.*1.b*.ii, fn. 230 about the uncomfortable language surrounding this admission.
216. Although most institutional rules do not contain provisions on adverse inferences, they are expressly contemplated in the IBA Rules, and some national arbitration laws even contemplate this rationale, such as, for example, the English Arbitration Act (Sect. 41(7)(b), Chapter 23) which expressly provides that they may be drawn if a party fails to comply with an order.
217. See, e.g., the straightforward language used in an ICC award (no. 8694), quoted by Y. DERAINS, *op. cit.*, fn. 5, p. 792 (fn. 21) and published in JDI (1997) p. 1056, obs. Y DERAINS.
218. J.K. SHARPE, "Drawing Adverse Inferences from the Non-production of Evidence", 22 Arb. Int'l, (2006, no. 4) p. 549 at p. 550; see also Ch. N. BROWER, "Evidence Before International Tribunals: The Need for Some Standard Rules", 28 The International Lawyer (1994, no. 1) p. 47 at p. 57.

presents inherent limits, especially as it recalls the tribunal's lack of *imperium* and ability to force parties to produce documents. For example, an experienced arbitrator has written that adverse inferences may not be the "fearsome weapon some lawyers would seem to imagine, given the fact that most arbitrators would be disturbed at the thought of deeming the burden of proof discharged by *inference*."[219] It is indeed commonly observed that adverse inferences, as indirect proof, will not change outcome of case[220] and do not actually shift the burden of proof,[221] not to mention the fact this mechanism is subordinated to a set of very strict criteria[222] and constitutes only a faculty for the tribunal[223] which will also use this tool only if it is satisfied that due-process requirements have been met.[224]

ii. The court sanction

The other question that then comes to mind is whether the so-called right for document production can go beyond these adverse inferences and be more effectively sanctioned by courts. Of course, the requesting party may go to state courts, as many arbitration laws (from common and civil law countries) permit,[225] to seek assistance in compelling the reluctant party, or even a non-party,[226] to produce the requested documents, although this may require that an enjoining order from the tribunal had already been granted.[227] But what if a party refuses to comply with a request to produce certain

---

219. J. PAULSSON, *op. cit.*, fn. 5, p. 550.
220. See, e.g., V. VAN HOUTTE, "Adverse Inferences in International Arbitration" in T. GIOVANNINI and A. MOURRE, eds., *Written Evidence and Discovery in International Arbitration*, *op. cit.*, fn. 5, p. 206.
221. See, e.g., J.K. SHARPE, *op. cit.*, fn. 218, pp. 552-553.
222. As systematized by an author (see J.K. SHARPE, *ibid.*): awards tend to show that tribunals are most likely to draw inferences where (1) the document in question is material and relevant, (2) the parties were warned that non-production could lead to adverse inferences, (3) the party from which the document is sought was responsible for non-production, and (4) the document was expressly sought by the tribunal.
223. Art. 9(5) and (6) of the 2010 IBA Rules.
224. See, e.g., V. VAN HOUTTE, *op. cit.*, fn. 220, p. 208.
225. See in the US the rather far-reaching and famous Art. 28 USC 1782, already mentioned previously (see supra Sect. II.12.a.ii); see also Art. 184 of the Swiss International Private Law Federal Act; Sect. 1036 of the German ZPO; Sect. 602 of the Austrian ZPO.
226. Even French law has become almost as liberal in that area as other common law countries, with broad geographical scope (such as Art. 28 USC 1782): the new Art. 1469 of the French CPC (applicable to both domestic and international arbitration), allows a party, with the tribunal's invitation and through a court order, to compel a third party to produce some relevant documents; see in contrast Sect. 44(2) of the English Arbitration Act (about which see *AssiminaMaritime v. Pakistan Shipping* [2004] EWHC 3005 (Commercial Court)).
227. See in the United Kingdom, the court's previous power to order "disclosure" under Sect. 12(6)(b) of the 1950 Arbitration Act was revoked in 1990 and, under Sects. 34 and 35 of the 1996 Act, especially Sect. 34(2)(d), the 1996 Arbitration Act makes disclosure by the parties a matter for the Arbitral Tribunal. (*BNP Paribas v. Deloitte & Touche LLP* [2003] EWHC 2874 (Comm)), which does not prevent a court from enforcing a peremptory disclosure order by the tribunal (under Sect. 42); see also in the United States: *In Re Technostroyexport*, 853 F.Supp. 695 (S.D.N.Y. 1994).

documents in its possession and the tribunal declines to grant a corresponding order enjoining the receiving party to comply with the request from the requesting party: What would then be the legal remedy available at law? More radically than resorting to state courts in the course of the proceedings, it has been argued[228] that the final award that would result from these proceedings could be challenged (or refused enforcement) on various related grounds: failure to comply with the procedure agreed by the parties[229] or violation of the right to be heard. If the first cause of action seems weaker than the second, even a challenge based on such a due process violation has proved very difficult before state courts, mainly because, as previously seen, this issue is encompassed in the broad and discretionary powers of the tribunal to manage the proceedings in general and the taking of evidence in particular.[230] Even in the case where document production has proved to be deficient, the party claiming that it has been harmed by that deficiency, will have to meet, even on the basis of an alleged fraud,[231] a very high standard of proof to successfully challenge the resulting award.[232] Conversely, what if a party felt "obliged" to go through a process of document production, with which it (or its counsel) is unfamiliar or which it did not anticipate or contemplate (for instance due to their legal background), and which the tribunal would have imposed? Could it argue that it rendered the proceedings fundamentally unbalanced, which resulted in the violation of its right to a fair and equal treatment?[233] Some authors considered that this argument would hardly be sustainable. Beyond certain valid reasons put forward, this alleged

---

228. G. KAUFMANN-KOHLER and Ph. BÄRTSCH, *op. cit.*, fn. 5, p. 17.
229. For issues of enforcement, see Art. V(*d*) of the New York Convention; one could also think of grounds related to an award rendered *infra petita* (Art. V(*c*) of the New York Convention) or, to a lesser extent, in violation of procedural public policy.
230. See in France, the consistent case law in that respect: Paris Court of Appeal, 21 Jan. 1997, *White Knight*, 3 Rev. arb. (1997) pp. 429, with obs. by Y. DERAINS; Paris Court of Appeal, 9 Sept. 1997, *M. Heilmann*, Rev. arb. (1998, issue 4) p. 712, with obs. by Y. DERAINS; Paris Court of Appeal, 19 Jan. 1999, *CIC International Ltd.*, Rev. arb. (1999 issue 3, p. 601) with obs. by Ch. JARROSSON; Paris Court of Appeal, 22 Jan. 2004, *Nafimco*, Cahiers de l'Arbitrage (2004, no. 1/2) *Gaz. Pal.* 21-22 (May 2004) p. 22; Paris Court of Appeal, 15 June 2006, Rev. arb. (2006, issue 4) p. 1002, with obs. by J.-Y. GARAUD and C.-H. de TAFFIN; Paris Court of Appeal, 26 Nov. 2008, *Sarah*, 25 Mealey's International Arbitration Report, (March 2010, no. 3) with a case note by J. KIRBY and D. BENSAUDE at p. 8; Paris Court of Appeal, 26 Nov. 2009, International Journal of Arab Arbitration (2010, no. 3) p.131; International Journal of Arab Arbitration (2010, no. 4) with a case note by R. ZIADÉ and Ch.-H. DE TAFFIN, pp. 138-158.
231. See the major precedent in France: Civ. 1ère, 25 May 1992, *Fougerolle*, Rev. arb. (1993, no. 1) p. 91, with an article by M. DE BOISSÉSON, p. 3; confirmed by subsequent cases, such as: Civ. 1ère, 9 March 2011, *CAT v. GTT*, case no. 10-18.763; see also in the United Kingdom: *Elektrim S.A. v. Vivendi Universal S.A.* [2007] EWHC 11 (Comm.), Rev. 1 [2007] APP.L.R. 01/19, judgment rendered by Justice Aikens on 19 January 2007.
232. For a successful, though rare, challenge, see Paris Court of Appeal, 1 July 1999, *Brasoil*, 14 Mealey's IAR, (1999, no. 8) XXIVa ICCA *Yearbook Commercial Arbitration*, pp. 296-302, Rev. arb. (1999, issue 4) p. 834, with a case note by Ch. Jarrosson.
233. See F. SCHÄFFLER, *Zulässigkeit und Zweckmässigkeit der Anwendung angloamerikanischer Beweismethoden in deutschen und internationalen Schiedsverfahren*, (Sellier European Law Publisher, Munich 2003) at p. 96, quoted by F. T. SCHWARZ and Ch. W. KONRAD, *op. cit.*, fn. 5, para. 20-247, fn. 499.

inequality should also be nuanced by the fact that document production does not necessarily create an unfair disadvantage vis-à-vis the party unacquainted with that device. Indeed, parties from common law jurisdictions are likely to be retaining common law counsel and, US parties, US counsel, who happen to be – contrary to civil law attorneys – legally, ethically and specifically obligated to comply with orders to produce according to a much higher standard.[234] Because a US attorney is under an affirmative duty to disclose, in some cases he may be left with no choice but to withdraw representation[235] and may even be liable should a client conduct an inadequate search for documents ordered to be produced. In one notable case, a district court in California sanctioned attorneys on such grounds.[236] There are no such equivalent duties in civil law countries, which, in turn, may constitute a procedural advantage and is thus likely to neutralize the counter-argument.[237] Yet, that does not mean that tribunals, beyond legal and cultural differences, are not wary of the principle of equality in this stage of the proceedings.[238]

---

234. This obligation comes from both state laws and professional standards promulgated by the American Bar Association (ABA), which is a voluntary association of law students and lawyers comprised of over 400,000 members and is influential in drafting and maintaining rules governing ethical standards for lawyers. Rule 3(4) of the ABA Model Rules of Professional Conduct specifically prohibits attorneys from obstructing access to evidence and from helping a client to obstruct access to evidence. California, the outlier, has an autonomous code of professional responsibility which similarly prohibits suppression of evidence sought by a court (see California Rules of Professional Conduct, Rule 5-220).
235. ABA Model Rules of Professional Conduct, Rule 1.16(a); California Rules of Professional Conduct, Rule 3-700.
236. *Qualcomm Inc. v. Broadcom Corp.*, 2008 U.S. Dist. LEXIS 911 (S.D. Cal. 7 Jan. 2008):

    "[T]hese attorneys did not conduct a reasonable inquiry into the adequacy of [Defendant's] document search and production and, accordingly, they are responsible, along with [Defendant], for the monumental discovery violation *(Id.* at pp. 56-57).... Attorneys' ethical obligations do not permit them to participate in an inadequate document search and then provide misleading and incomplete information to their opponents and false arguments to the court *(Id.* at fn. 10, p. 49)."

237. One may want to remember, though, that French lawyers were for some time placed at a significant disadvantage vis-à-vis non-French lawyers, especially in arbitrations having their seat in Paris, because before a resolution was recently passed by the Paris Bar (*Résolution du Conseil de l'Ordre des avocats*, dated 26 Feb. 2008, published in Bulletin du Barreau de Paris, 4 March 2008, no. 9), they were prevented from preparing a witness.
238. See *Libananco Holding Co. Ltd. v. Republic of Turkey* (ICSID Case no. ARB/06/8), Decision on Preliminary Issues of 23 June 2008.

3. *Electronically Stored Evidence: A Practical Application of the Evidentiary Compromise Among International Arbitration Practitioners*

a. *The emergence of new regulations and practices*

The taking of electronically stored evidence is the most recent challenge facing the arbitral process.[239] Because of the volume of information that can be stored electronically, an expansive interpretation of the scope of the information to be produced can significantly impact the time and cost dimensions of a proceeding. When parties are faced with the risk of excessive burden and cost of production, principles of proportionality, privilege, relevance and materiality or good faith must be fiercely litigated. In that context, both the parties and the tribunals need a predictable and precise frame of references and standards.

The 2010 IBA Rules suggest early agreement between the parties and the tribunal as to the conduct of the proceedings. And it is recommended that in the event of a disagreement, the parties apply promptly to obtain an order from the Tribunal.[240] But in the event of a disagreement, on what standards should a party rely to argue that a request for backed-up data lacks proportionality? In what format and pursuant to which guidelines should parties address the unavoidable risk of inadvertent production of privileged or confidential documents? Pursuant to which practice should claw-back agreements be drafted in the context of international arbitral proceedings between parties from civil law and common law countries? Should metadata fall within the scope of an order to produce? What format should be followed to create an "arbitration hold"? Is an arbitration hold even desirable in the context of international arbitration?

A French party is likely to find production of metadata to be overly intrusive and unacceptable. How should arbitral tribunals and counsel address the vastly divergent information retention policies in various regions of the world? What to do about personal emails? The 1995 EU Data Protection Directive protects personal data, broadly defined, to include any information relating to an identifiable individual.[241] For example, in Austria, as a general rule, all e-mails addressed to an employee's personal e-mail account will be considered to be private even if the company policy prohibits the use of

---

239. As a telling example, see Report by the ICC Task Force on the Production of Electronic Documents in International Arbitration, Finally Adopted in March 2011, *op. cit.*, fn. 130.
240. Carole MALINVAUD, "Will Electronic Evidence and E-Discovery Change the Face of Arbitration" in T. GIOVANNINI and A. MOURRE, eds., *Written Evidence and Discovery in International Arbitration, op. cit.*, fn. 5, p. 373. See also: Nicolas FLETCHER, "The Use of Technology in the Production of Documents", in ICC Bull. Sp. Suppl. 2006, *op. cit.*, fn. 5, at p. 101; Richard D. HILL, "The New Reality of Electronic Document Production in International Arbitration: A Catalyst for Convergence?" 25 Arb. Int'l. (2009, no. 1) p. 87; Aren GOLDSMITH, "Requests for the Production of Electronic Documents in International Arbitration: Some Threshold Issues", IBLJ, (2010, no.3) p. 313; C. Mark BAKER, "The Role of the Institution in Taming Electronic Disclosure", 24 News and Notes from the ITA (Winter/Spring 2010) pp. 1 and 6.
241. Directive 95/46/EC of the European Parliament and of the Council on the Protection of Individuals with Regard to the Processing of Personal Data and on the Free Movement of Such Data.

e-mail for private messages. A violation of privacy can result in sanctions ranging from damages to imprisonment. Likewise, in France, privacy is a fundamental legal right.[242] Under the French Data Protection Law, an argument can successfully be made that an electronic document is the personal property of the person towards whom the information request is targeted. Violation of such right of privacy is punishable under both civil and criminal law. The United States, on the other hand, has no comprehensive data-protection legislation, relying instead on a sectorial approach, mixing legislation, regulation and self-regulation.

In addition to the standards that should apply to the production of electronically stored information, the divergent practices in collection and identification of responsive documents continues to be a source of delay and, at times, inequality between parties. Practitioners before US courts for example, have developed a thorough and systematic approach to gathering the information in their clients' custody. But while counsel from all legal backgrounds who are routinely engaged in international arbitral proceedings have developed systematic ways of managing the evidentiary process, there continues to be a lack of homogeneity in the scope of collection and identification of responsive evidence in the international arbitral process. Thus when US trained counsel will include, as custodians of the information requested, all people who might have created, received or shared relevant electronic information, i.e., assistants and support personnel, counsel from a civil law jurisdiction might limit the search to the mailbox and the documents created and received by the executive who is the target of the search. Further, counsel from a civil law jurisdiction might feel compelled not to produce responsive but adverse documents, while US-qualified counsel will have the ethical obligation to produce such documents. Unquestionably, it is crucial to ascertain the standards and scope of the search at preliminary procedural conferences and in the tribunal's production order.

But are these preliminary hearings and conferences sufficient to address the deeper issue of predictability of the evidentiary practice in international arbitration? To cater to the need for flexibility, the IBA Rules set out general guidelines rather than specific rules. Practitioners in need of specific standards to address the specific questions mentioned above, will therefore have to draw parallels with court decisions that have already provided answers to those questions. There is a difference between emulating an approach in its entirety and merely drawing lessons from the experience of the US courts.[243]

For example, the US courts have directly addressed questions of document retention in recent decisions targeting electronically stored information. The act of specially preserving documents when a party reasonably anticipates litigation is frequently

---

242. French CCP, Art. 11.
243. See, for a brief discussion of possible inspiration from US-developed standards regarding electronically stored evidence, Amal BOUCHENAKI and Dylan MEFFORD, "The IBA Rules Lay the Grounds for Solutions to Address Electronic Document Production Disputes", 13 International Arbitration Law Review (2010, issue 5) pp. 180-185.

referred to as creation of a "litigation hold".[244] The creation of an "arbitration hold" would fall perfectly within the IBA's suggestion that the parties agree early on in the procedure as to how it should be conducted. Likewise, US courts have developed an approach to privilege-related disputes that can be of use to parties and tribunals in international arbitration. There are several examples of arbitral tribunals looking to US-court evidentiary decisions on privilege. For example, the *Glamis Gold* tribunal referred to the five factors set out in *Koch Materials Co. v. Shore Slurry Seal, Inc.*, 208 F.R.D. 109, 118 (D.N.J. 2002) to determine whether an inadvertent production of privileged documents should amount to waiver.[245] The tribunal stated that it "finds these five factors to reflect considerations generally applicable to the analysis of waiver of privilege on the grounds of partial disclosure". The tribunal in another NAFTA case, *Vito G. Gallo v. Government of Canada*, used a similar case-by-case approach, but came to a different result.[246] In *V.G. Gallo*, the tribunal began by stating that "according to Canadian law (which is taken into consideration to the extent that it conforms to international practice) and also international law on the subject, where information covered by solicitor-client privilege is disclosed inadvertently, as a general rule there is no waiver of privilege". After finding that the documents at issue would normally be covered by the solicitor-client privilege, the tribunal then went on to take "other considerations" into account: "The Tribunal is influenced by the way in which the erroneous production of the unredacted Cabinet documents has unfolded in the instant case."[247] Interestingly, the tribunal in *V.G. Gallo* considered that given the cross-border nature of the dispute, it would look not just to Canadian legal authorities, but also "to those of other common law jurisdictions such as Australia, England, and the United States".

b.   A pragmatic compromise in international arbitration
The efforts and guidelines mentioned above aim at improving the cost-effectiveness of an evidentiary process that is, at times, crippled by the inflation of information exchange.[248] One has to accept that, but for a lax interpretation of the right of a party to obtain evidence not in its possession, the volumes of information involved would be reduced significantly. That is not to say, however, that the increase in the volume of documents requested is due to the US- or UK-trained practitioners' attempt to impose their home procedural devices. As mentioned in the Introduction, strategy and pragmatism, rather than legal tradition, are the driving factors of the scope of production requested and ordered.

---

244. "'The obligation to preserve evidence arises when the party has notice that the evidence is relevant to litigation or when a party should have known that the evidence may be relevant to future litigation.'" *Zubulake v. UBS Warburg*, 220 F.R.D. 212, 216 (S.D.N.Y. 2003) (quoting *Fujitsu Ltd. v. Fed. Express Corp.*, 247 F.3d 423, 436 (2d Cir. 2001)).
245. *Glamis Gold, Ltd. v. United States*, at para. 51.
246. *Vito G. Gallo and Government of Canada* ("*V.G. Gallo*"), 21 Dec. 2009, Procedural Order No. 4, at para. 27.
247. *Ibid.*, at para. 39.
248. The authors suggest some time- and cost-management considerations in Annex I to this article (see this volume, pp. 114-117).

If we are to take the IBA Rules as a reliable marker of current evidentiary practices in international arbitration, one has to recognize that in many respects, the IBA Rules reflect practices that are more developed in common law jurisdictions. The mere admission in the IBA Rules of a right to request from another party or a third party information in categories, and its corollary, the right to lodge objections against such requests, reflects a practice that is entrenched in common law jurisdictions. Likewise, the practice of cross-examining witnesses, also available under the IBA Rules, and also extensively practiced in today's international arbitral proceedings, is virtually absent from civil law evidentiary practice. The expansion of electronically stored information is likely to increase the influence of common law and US-inspired procedures. Allowing a relatively wide category of electronically stored information to be produced leads to challenges and questions that are inherent to the larger volume of information stored electronically. The challenges and questions have only been addressed in the Unites States and, to a lesser extent, in other common law jurisdictions.

Accordingly, while there is no "evidentiary transplant",[249] the fact that practitioners from civil law jurisdictions do not have in their systems of origin references and standards that regulate questions of evidence as they arise in international arbitration, warrants a de facto influence of US/common law evidentiary practices. It also follows that, on a number of issues, such as electronically stored information, if arbitrators or counsel are to look at judicial standards of evidentiary determinations, decisions of civil law courts will be of little help. They will therefore turn to US- or UK-court-developed standards. While a large number of lawyers practicing international arbitration today are trained in multiple legal systems, more likely than not, counsel's and arbitrators' approach to procedure and to evidence, will be influenced by the legal system in which they were originally trained.[250] That is not to say that practitioners with common law backgrounds will feel at home in international arbitral procedures. Principles of good faith, assessments of narrowness, relevance and materiality, are concepts that are more familiar to lawyers from the civil law traditions. "Nobody feels really at home,"[251] it has been observed.

IV. CONCLUSION

To conclude, the influence of common law evidentiary practices in international arbitration is undeniable. But does this influence, along with a less predictable procedural framework, make international arbitration a less effective or more challenging dispute resolution mechanism? In reality, the weight of disclosure devices in arbitration should

---

249. M. DAMAŠKA, *op. cit.*, fn. 107, at p. 843.
250. P. MAYER, *op. cit.*, fn. 2, at p. 170.; see also: I. FADLALLAH, *op. cit.*, fn. 2, p. 303, esp. at p. 311 et seq.
251. Cl. REYMOND, *op. cit.*, fn. 5, p. 366.

be neither underestimated nor given too much importance.[252] As our overview of the principles that underlie fact-finding in common law and civil law jurisdictions demonstrates, truth and justice have many ways to emerge; they are not constrained in one "right manner to conduct proceedings".[253] Compliance with and mastery of complex evidentiary rules or hierarchies in the weight of evidence do not replace effective advocacy. "Proof is the core of evidentiary proceedings in all legal fora, but a formal set of evidentiary rules does not tell anyone how to decipher the documentary evidence or how to make a sound assessment of the truthfulness of a witness's testimony ... proof and the pursuit of truth are cross-cultural goals ... [and] powerful legal arguments are not culturally bounded."[254]

---

252. A renowned UK Justice mentioned, for instance, at a conference in Houston in May 2010 that he had rarely experienced, both as a judge and an arbitrator, an arbitration where the document production process had changed the entire face of the dispute.
253. P. MAYER, *op. cit.*, fn. 2, p. 163 at p. 170.
254. L. SHORE, "Arbitration, Rhetoric, Proof" in A. ROVINE, ed., *Contemporary Issues in International Arbitration and Mediation: The Fordham Papers* (Martinus Nijhoff 2009) pp. 293-304.

Annex I: Timing and Other Issues of Time Management

Gathering the answers to the four questions - Who, What, When, and Where – will enable parties to successfully negotiate the hurdles of electronic discovery.

I. WHAT?

The types of electronic documents created can vary greatly. Data gathered might include word processing, spreadsheets, email, web applications, images (e.g., scanned photographs), video images, stored voice data and many other forms of electronic communication.[255] Your client may have various departments within the organization which each use different software, i.e., the finance department might rely primarily on Microsoft Excel to create spreadsheets, whereas the members of the executive board might use Microsoft Word or Powerpoint more frequently to create letters and presentations. Metadata[256] provides interesting concerns as it is normally hidden from the electronic document/information but rather provides a "behind the scenes" view of the relevant document. However, as it provides a digital record, metadata shares the same characteristics as any other electronic data: it can be searched for, and it is vulnerable to change and duplication.

As a practical consideration, it is important to acknowledge that in international arbitration, where parties may be from different cultures, metadata may be considered as 'background' information revealing private information about the parties. As discussed below, parties from civil law countries such as France would view this as intrusive and unacceptable. Furthermore, a party requesting metadata should be required to demonstrate that the relevance and materiality of the requested metadata outweighs the cost and burden of producing the same.[257]

II. WHO?

When you have received the document request for your client, there are three initial questions to ask: 1. Who are the document custodians? 2. Who are the holders of electronic evidence relevant to the requests? And, 3. Who would be the authority to ask how and where the electronic documents are located? Answering these questions will help create an overall electronic disclosure strategy. It will help to identify the key

---

255. Cher Seat DEVEY, "Electronic Discovery/Disclosure: From Litigation to International Commercial Arbitration", 74 Arbitration (2008) pp. 369-384.
256. Record data pertaining to how electronic data is manipulated including by whom and when such manipulation took place.
257. David J. HOWELL, "Introduction. Electronic Disclosure in International Arbitration: A Changing Paradigm" in T. GIOVANNINI and A. MOURRE, eds., *Written Evidence and Discovery in International Arbitration, op. cit.*, fn. 5. A terabyte is 1,000 gigabyte; a petabyte is 1000 terabytes.

people involved in the dispute and also help to identify the custodians of relevant documents. This stage involves open communication with the client to help identify all of the people who may have created, received or shared relevant electronic information. For example, beyond identifying key players, would review of support staff be considered critical, i.e., secretaries and assistants? It is quite possible such persons might have created relevant electronic documents on behalf of a key player. Similarly, an IT department will have more than one person managing corporate data (or databases) and so establishing the custodian of such data will be required. To address this question and to obtain the most accurate information, this stage usually involves discussions with the client, the client's information technology department and the lawyers. This is crucial as it creates an overall organizational structure to make the gathering of information efficient and accurate.

III. WHERE?

This practical question requires thinking about where the electronic information resides. It is not uncommon for parties to request documents located in different countries on different servers. Along this line additional questions can arise, such as where the backup data is stored? On what networks would the information be stored? This question would be particularly important for an international client with many offices. Where are the e-mails stored? Is information stored on the local disk of a key person's computer?

In a modern business, electronic information may be found on a mainframe, servers, networked workstations, desktops and laptops, home computers, removable media (such as CDs, DVDs and USB drives) and handheld devices (such as PDAs, mobile phones, iPods and so on). As well as the types of places to search, issues can arise over duplication of information. This usually arises when e-mails can be sent to multiple recipients, replied to, forwarded, received on multiple devices and so on.

It is imperative to begin thinking about this question as soon as it seems likely that arbitration is imminent as document preservation obligations can arise. Furthermore, addressing such issues early can save considerable time and expense during the arbitration process which could bring resolution of the dispute much faster. Once information is determined on location of electronic information, further information is needed to search for the data. Employing keywords to search the identified servers is critical at this stage. A common approach would be to decide on keywords between the parties and such words might include party names, company names and the location of the dispute for example.

IV. WHEN?

Two "when" questions must be addressed: 1. When does the duty to preserve electronic data attach? And, 2. when was the responsive data created? In relation to question one, to avoid allegations of spoliation of evidence, you must take precautions as soon as arbitration is pending or imminent. With regard to question two, it is important to bear in mind that responsive electronic documents may have been created many years before a dispute becomes pending. The author notes a recent case where documents had to be reviewed over a ten-year span for potential responsive materials. It involved the review of upwards of 750,000 documents, and the man-hours of an extensive team made up of partners, many associates and legal assistants. The entire process involved a time span of many months. Even though the initial documents were filtered with a general keyword search and then narrowed down with a more tailored keyword search, this still left thousands of documents to be individually reviewed by the team to determine responsive, irrelevant, and privileged documents.

V.   MISCELLANEOUS

A small sampling of miscellaneous issues which can arise are addressed here to bear in mind when undertaking the electronic disclosure process:

1.   Inadvertent Disclosure of Privileged Documents

The ease and low cost of creation and storage of electronic information can lead to massively large volumes of electronic data. Just one gigabyte of files in Microsoft Word format is equivalent to approximately 50,000 pages of text. Large businesses frequently deal in terabytes, or even petabytes of electronic data. As a consequence of the potentially voluminous amount of electronic disclosure to be reviewed, the possibility of inadvertently disclosing confidential information can arise. When such a situation arises, an arbitral tribunal must decide whether to allow an opposing party to rely on any such document. As reflected by the IBA Rules, the considerations for making this decision are similar to those applied in the context of privilege which arise in court systems. A tribunal will consider the context of how the inadvertent disclosure was made (e.g., as a result of searching a voluminous batch of information that made failsafe checking impossible) when it is conducting its balancing exercise. Where appropriate, parties should consider the inclusion of a claw-back agreement and also consider obtaining an order from the tribunal relieving them of the obligation to conduct a pre-production review of all electronic documents for privilege, and specifically ordering that the attorney-client and work-product privileges are not waived by the production of documents.

2.   Personal E-mails

Even though many companies enact policies which forbid the transmission of personal emails, it is still quite common for employees to send and receive such e-mail. How this issue is tackled in an electronic disclosure exercise can vary by law system and country. In Europe, the 1995 EU Data Protection Directive protects personal data, broadly defined to include any information relating to an identifiable individual.[258] For example, in Austria, as a general rule all e-mails addressed to a personal e-mail account of an employee will be considered to be private even if the company policy prohibits the use of e-mail for private messages. Violation of privacy is sanctioned by civil law (damages) and criminal law (imprisonment). In French law, privacy is a fundamental legal right.[259] Under the French Data Protection law, an argument can successfully be made that an electronic document is incontestably the personal property of the key player and such a document is disclosed, such a violation of privacy could be punishable under civil and criminal law. Ascertaining the precise nature of the protection covering particular data can be troublesome, as it can be difficult to decide which jurisdiction a particular document is under for data protection purposes. This becomes particularly relevant, as the level of protection granted inside and outside the European Union can be very different. This is exacerbated by the fact that the United States has no comprehensive data-protection legislation, relying instead on a sectoral approach, mixing legislation, regulation and self-regulation. The combination of jurisdictions can result in a mixed bag of views of parties with regard to what is potentially disclosable.

3. *Computer Upgrades*

If it is determined that relevant information might be stored on the local disk drive of a key player's computer and the dispute requires document-searching over a time span of many years, it is common to raise a challenge that the computer would have been upgraded and such information lost. However, this argument might be weakened, especially in the case of large corporations, as it is common for IT departments to transfer locally saved data to a new computer when such upgrade takes place.

4. *Broad Keyword Search Terms*

The agreed upon keywords for the search of documents might include words which would result in the procurement of thousands of irrelevant documents. For example, if a keyword necessarily includes a company which has an acronym that can double as a generally used word and such acronym must also be searched (e.g., the company can be abbreviated to "AT"), such a search would yield many false positives as plugging in the word "AT" would result in many irrelevant words. To overcome this, the use of Boolean terms and symbols could be employed to decrease the likelihood of false positives. Currently, there are a wide range of sophisticated products and search engines to assist with electronic disclosure, making the ability to tailor searches for specific requests more accessible and user-friendly.

---

258. Directive 95/46/EC of the European Parliament and of the Council on the Protection of Individuals with Regard to the Processing of Personal Data and on the Free Movement of Such Data.
259. French CPC, Art. 11.

Witness Preparation – A Key to Effective Advocacy in International Arbitration

Nigel Blackaby[*]

TABLE OF CONTENTS	Page
I. Introduction	118
II. Purpose of Witness Preparation	119
III. Preparation of Witness Statements	120
IV. Preparation for Oral Testimony	123
V. Conclusion	132

I. INTRODUCTION

It is no secret that lawyers like to be in control. Written submissions can be researched, reviewed and perfected. Oral submission is a little more risky: who knows what questions the tribunal may ask? However, a good lawyer will rehearse, analyse all permutations of the issues and have the answers ready. There is, however, a time when the lawyer loses this control, when an untrained third party takes centre stage. And it is a moment that most lawyers view with fear, trepidation and a degree of excitement. This is the moment when live factual and expert witnesses take the stand without a script, to be thrown to the mercy of the other party's counsel's cross-examination and the piercing questions of the arbitral tribunal. For the lawyer presenting the witness, watching cross-examination is like watching a close family member perform acrobatics with no safety net save the very limited insurance policy provided by re-examination (otherwise known as re-direct). A case can be won or lost on responses. So should the lawyer just stand back and assume destiny will play its role or can something be done to limit the risks?

Witness testimony provides the factual foundation of a case. If the witness fails to provide clear and credible evidence, the case that is built upon their testimony may crumble. For this reason, it is crucial that the witness be prepared to provide testimony before the tribunal. This is not a process whereby the witness is told the answers. Rather, it is a process which ensures that the witness has had the opportunity to refresh recollections of relevant events that may have taken place a long time ago, reviewed contemporaneous documents authored or copied to them, and prepared for what is likely to happen in the examination process.

It is well established that witnesses may be interviewed and prepared prior to giving testimony, be it written or oral, in an international arbitration. This is expressly set out in certain arbitration rules, including, the International Bar Association (IBA) Rules on

---

[*] Partner and head of the US international arbitration practice, Freshfields Bruckhaus Deringer LLP, based in Washington DC.
   The author wishes to thank Caroline Richard, an associate of his firm, for assistance in the preparation of this paper.

the Taking of Evidence in International Commercial Arbitration and the LCIA Arbitration Rules:

> *Art. 4(3) IBA Rules*:
> "It shall not be improper for a Party, its officers, employees, legal advisors or other representatives to interview its witnesses or potential witnesses."
>
> *Art. 20(6) LCIA Rules*:
> "Subject to the mandatory provisions of any applicable law, it shall not be improper for any party or its legal representatives to interview any witness or potential witness for the purpose of presenting his testimony in written form or producing him as an oral witness."

Witness preparation is key to successful advocacy and the efficient conduct of arbitral proceedings. Without it, putting a credible and persuasive case before the arbitral tribunal may prove difficult or impossible.

But what is the purpose of witness preparation, and what methods for preparing a witness are considered appropriate? The answers to these questions are not provided in any arbitration rules or guidelines, and may differ depending on counsel's legal culture and ethical duties; although these differences are sometimes exaggerated. Ultimately, this much is clear: witness preparation does not involve putting words in the witness's mouth, but rather enabling the witness effectively to assist the tribunal by fully and accurately describing the facts that are relevant to the issues in dispute.

Witness preparation begins with the selection of witnesses and the preparation of their statements. It also involves preparing them for the crucible of cross-examination, as well as for direct and re-direct examination. Before examining effective strategies to prepare witnesses for each of these stages of the proceedings, we first turn to the purpose of witness preparation which underpins and justifies these strategies.

II.   PURPOSE OF WITNESS PREPARATION

The purpose of witness preparation, like all advocacy, is to assist and ultimately persuade the tribunal by enabling the witness to proffer relevant and credible testimony.

Let us take an example. Ms. Jones, a witness in an arbitration arising out of a contractual dispute has been asked to testify on events that took place several years ago, namely the negotiation of the commercial terms of a contract. As the dispute has been ongoing for several months, with one round of pleadings already exchanged by the parties, the parties have delved down into the details of the contract negotiations, and the terms of reference require the tribunal to decide fine issues of fact. Ms. Jones, however, has only recently become aware of the dispute, and has been asked to provide a statement and testify at the upcoming hearing. Ms. Jones is not a lawyer. She has never been involved in arbitration or court proceedings before, let alone testified. As someone who has never liked public speaking, she is apprehensive at the idea of being examined before the tribunal.

Without adequate preparation, Ms. Jones may be unable fully to assist the tribunal. When asked to prepare a witness statement describing the negotiation of the contract, if unaided by counsel, she may focus on the issues that were contentious at the time, not those that are relevant to the dispute now. Indeed, she may not understand the finer issues in dispute. When questioned on the stand, without any prior preparation, she may not be readily in a position to testify about the factual issues in dispute because she will not have turned her mind to them or reviewed the relevant documents. Whilst she could refresh her memory by going through the various stages of the negotiation of the contract and the relevant documents on the stand, her testimony would likely take a day or two to complete. However, the timetable for the arbitration hearing may only provide for only ten minutes of direct, and ninety minutes of cross-examination. Moreover, without adequate preparation, Ms. Jones may be too nervous to fully and accurately answer difficult cross-examination questions that have caught her off guard. After reading her statement and hearing two hours of testimony, the tribunal may not have been enlightened on the issues in dispute and may well regard her testimony as irrelevant.

Counsel for the party presenting Ms. Jones as a witness could have avoided this outcome by helping Ms. Jones to prepare to testify.

This preparation should be aimed at ensuring that the witness can confidently and truthfully describe the facts that she has witnessed to the tribunal. The goal, therefore, is to give the witness the support she needs to tell her story.

This is a fine balancing act. On the one hand, witness preparation that seeks to put words in the witness's mouth or that turns the witness into an advocate for the party will harm that witness's credibility. The witness must tell the story based on their own experience and in their own words. A witness who gives an answer that sounds rehearsed, that repeats the words used by counsel (or the "party line"), or that seeks to draw legal conclusions will not persuade the tribunal and will open them up to attack from the other side. On the other hand, an underprepared witness who does not understand the arbitration process or which issues are in dispute may not be able to focus on or to recall the relevant issues or may be too intimidated or caught by surprise to provide a full answer to difficult questions.

The preparation described below seeks to achieve a balance between these two extremes.

III. PREPARATION OF WITNESS STATEMENTS

1. Choosing a Witness

As a first step early in the case, one or several witnesses will need to be chosen. This is arguably one of the most critical strategic decisions in an arbitration. A good witness is one who has direct knowledge of facts and information relevant to the issues in the case.

a. The minimum number of witnesses necessary to prove the case

A good first rule in choosing a witness is to select the minimum number of witnesses necessary to effectively prove the case I need to prove subject to III.*1* above. The relevant facts to a case may span several years from the initial negotiation of a contract or a decision to invest up to the date of an alleged breach or (in investment cases) the adverse government action. There should be a live witness available to testify for all relevant periods. If there has been one general manager throughout the relevant period then you may get away with a single factual witness. However, it is advisable to have at least two witnesses as a safety net just in case one freezes on the day! But subject to the minimum of two, do not think that there is safety in numbers. The greater the number of factual witnesses, the greater the risk of contradiction and the less time for preparation. If I see that the other party has advanced three witnesses to cover the same meeting, I rub my hands for there will surely be a contradiction I can exploit on cross-examination.

b. *Choose a witness for their direct and detailed knowledge of facts, not their seniority*

Choosing a witness for their seniority rather than for their first hand knowledge is a mistake made all too often. Some believe that parading the Chief Executive of the parent company will impress the tribunal and show the importance given to the matter by the party. However, senior executives are unlikely to have been close to the details and may only have received their information second-hand. They are also less likely to spend the time necessary refamiliarizing themselves with the key documents and facts which may leave them as easy prey to effective cross-examiners. Senior executives are more used to respect and deference than to being questioned in a hostile manner, which may lead to a certain arrogance or resentment which is easily read by a tribunal. I recall a senior investment banker presented by the opposite party informing the tribunal at the beginning of his examination that he only had an hour and that he would only answer questions on a limited list of topics. This was not well received.

In general terms middle managers who were directly involved on a day-to-day basis with the contract or the investment tend to make far better witnesses. They have a better and deeper knowledge of most of the facts, they are usually prepared to invest more time in preparation and tend to be less arrogant. The honest, hard-working, loyal middle manager is a good first port of call when identifying witnesses and the Chief Executive of the parent corporation is usually best left out of the picture unless there is a very specific reason to include them.

c. *Party representatives and employees may give evidence*

It is important to clarify that, unlike in certain domestic court systems, any person may present evidence as a witness in an international arbitration, including a party or a party's employees or other representatives.[1] The relationship between the party and the witness should therefore not influence the decision to designate a person with directly relevant knowledge as a witness. In real life, given the absence of coercive powers of the arbitral tribunal to command the attendance of third parties, most witnesses are employees or former employees of the disputing parties.

---

1. International Bar Association (IBA) Rules on the Taking of Evidence, Art. 4(2) provides that: "Any person may present evidence as a witness, including a Party or a Party's officer, employee or other representative."

2. Preparing the Written Witness Statement

Once the relevant witnesses are identified, their statements must be prepared.

In arbitration proceedings, the written statement will typically stand as the witness's direct testimony (sometimes known as evidence-in-chief),[2] which may be challenged or tested through cross-examination at a hearing.[3] As such, it must tell the witness's story, and describe the relevant facts and events within that witness's knowledge.

It is accepted that counsel in international arbitrations may assist with the preparation of the witness's statement.[4] This ensures that the statement will be focused on the issues in dispute and describe all the pertinent facts supported by the relevant contemporaneous documents. It is usually helpful candidly to state the counsel's role in the preparation of the statement in the statement itself (e.g., "counsel have assisted me in the drafting of this statement"). This transparent approach will assist in defusing any cheap questions on cross-examination.

The drafting exercise can only begin following extensive interviews of the witness and the review of all evidence and contemporaneous documents. Undertaking this exercise early on in the case – even if the submission of witness statements is only to occur at a later stage of the proceedings – is strongly advised. Witness testimony is, together with documentary evidence, the foundation of a case. Building a case that later turns out not to be fully supported will cause it to founder. Involving witnesses in case preparation is therefore good practice: it is crucial for the preparation of case theory and is key to effective advocacy.

In drafting or assisting with the drafting of the witness's statement, counsel should ensure that it is focused on the key issues in dispute, and that it tells a story and describes facts and events within the witness's direct knowledge. This story should be told in a logical (and usually chronological) manner, using the witness's own words.

Witness statements that reproduce passages from the party's pleadings are unpersuasive. Similarly, a statement that attempts to turn a witness into an advocate for one of the parties will only cause problems on cross-examination. This is especially important when preparing rebuttal statements where it is easy to drift into advocacy. The witness should respond to factual assertions made by the other party or its witnesses, without drawing conclusions (which should be in the party's pleadings).

Witnesses are presented to describe the facts that are within their own knowledge. To the extent that the statement describes facts or events that are not within the witness's direct knowledge, the witness should say so and explain how they came to know this information. But this should be the exception. By and large, the statement should describe events of which the witness had direct knowledge, and refer to contemporaneous documents which the witness authored or reviewed at the relevant

---

2. See Gary B. BORN, *International Commercial Arbitration* (Kluwer 2009) at 1828.
3. IBA Rules on the Taking of Evidence, Arts. 4(7) and 8(2).
4. See Georg VON SEGESSER, "Witness Preparation in International Commercial Arbitration", 20 ASA Bulletin (2002, no. 2) p. 222 at p. 223 noting that "it would not make much sense to provide for the submission of witness statements if the parties and/or their legal representatives are not allowed to contact witnesses in order to discuss the preparation of such statements".

time. If the witness is being stretched to cover facts not known personally, it exposes them in cross examination. It would be far better to identify another witness who has personal experience of those facts.

Ideally, the statement should be drafted in the language in which the witness will testify, usually the witness's native tongue or a language in which the witness is comfortable enough to be cross-examined. This ensures that the witness will be able to accurately check the full content of their statements and credibly tell their story using their own words. A witness will always be more comfortable and confident, and therefore more credible, testifying in a language they master. If a witness signs a statement in English and then demands to be cross-examined in another language, there is an easy first cross-examination question as to whether they understood what they signed.

Whether a statement is primarily drafted by counsel, or drafted by the witness with the assistance of counsel, before signing it, the witness must confirm that every sentence of the statement is true and must understand that by signing the statement, they are committing to be cross-examined on its contents. It is wise to explain the process of cross-examination to the witness prior to the signature of the statement as this can have a sobering influence on the quality of the witness's recollection and the depth of their review.

IV. PREPARATION FOR ORAL TESTIMONY

1. The Ethical Debate

The preparation of witnesses prior to their oral testimony before a tribunal has been a source of controversy, owing to differences in legal cultures and ethical rules in various jurisdictions. Whilst contact with witnesses prior to hearings is frowned upon, or even prohibited, in court proceedings in certain jurisdictions, particularly in civil law countries,[5] lawyers in other jurisdictions not only are not subject to such limitations,[6] but would be professionally negligent if they did not undertake comprehensive witness preparation before putting the witness on the stand.[7]

---

5. See, e.g., Art. 11 of the *Us et Coutumes* of the Geneva Bar Association. Similar rules also apply in Germany (see Brian COOPER, "Ethics for Party Representatives in International Commercial Arbitration: Developing a Standard for Witness Preparation", 22 Georgetown Journal of Legal Ethics (2009) p. 779 at p. 785) and, as established by case law, to members of the Paris Bar (see Jan PAULSSON, "Standards of Conduct for Counsel in International Arbitration", 3 American Review of International Arbitration (1992) p. 214 at p. 216). Cf. Art. 1, section 8 of the Rules on the Exercise of the Legal Profession and for the Supervision of the Duties of Attorneys of the Austrian Bar.
6. See, e.g., Rule 4.03 of the Rules of Professional Conduct of the Law Society of Upper Canada.
7. See John M. TOWNSEND, "Clash and Convergence on Ethical Issues in International Arbitration", 36 University of Miami Inter-American Law Review (2004) p. 1 ("To a common lawyer, or at least an American lawyer, it would border on malpractice to allow a witness to testify without having been prepared by a lawyer"); Brian COOPER, *op. cit.*, fn. 5, p. 779 at p. 785; and Detlev F.

That said, these cultural differences may be exaggerated since even civil lawyers will coordinate closely with their clients and their employees to prepare their written submissions to the courts, which will serve as the basis for these employees and officers to prepare for their appearance in court as witnesses. As one commentator points out:

> "[I]n civil law jurisdictions, the same process often occurs in a slightly different sequence. Legal representatives invariably prepare all written submissions in close consultation with those employees of their client who were involved in the dispute before any such submissions are filed with the court. When these employees are subsequently called to testify as witnesses, they very often will prepare by re-reading these written submissions and then will confirm and repeat the facts as set out in the written submissions before the court. Consequently, at the end of the day, there is not, in practice, a great deal of difference between the civil law and common law approaches to contact with witnesses, at least insofar as a party's employees are concerned."[8]

Moreover, the rules applicable in court proceedings are typically relaxed when it comes to international arbitration[9] and a general practice of conducting witness preparation has emerged.[10] Indeed, this is required by the very structure of the

---

VAGTS, "Professional Responsibility in Transborder Practice: Conflict and Resolution", 13 Georgetown Journal of Legal Ethics (2000) p. 677 at p. 690. See also D.C. Bar Opinion 79 (1979) reproduced in G. BORN, *op. cit.*, fn. 2, at 2308-2309 ("The mere fact of a lawyer's having prepared the witness for the presentation of testimony is simply irrelevant: indeed, a lawyer who did not prepare his or her witness for testimony, having had an opportunity to do so, would not be doing his or her professional job properly").

8. Georg VON SEGESSER, *op. cit.*, fn. 4, p. 222 at pp. 223-224.
9. See Georg VON SEGESSER, *ibid.*, p. 228. See also Jan PAULSSON, *op. cit.*, fn. 5, p. 214 at p. 219 noting that "it is salutary for national legal systems to adapt their restrictions on professional conduct to international usages; usages widely accepted in international practice should not be sanctioned in the context of international arbitration because they are inconsistent with national norms". However, there are no ethical rules or guidelines regarding party representatives' conduct in international arbitration, See Brian COOPER, *op. cit.*, fn. 5, p. 779 at p. 781 (noting that whilst international bodies have created rules governing the conduct of arbitrators, no equivalent rules or guidelines have been adopted with respect to the conduct of counsel). This may change now that the International Bar Association formed a "Task Force on Attorney Ethics in Arbitration" whose role is "to survey and report on worldwide ethical practices and principles with respect to attorneys who handle international arbitration matters". See <www.ibanet.orgiLPD/Dispute Resolution SectionJArbitration/Subcommittees.aspx> (last visited 20 April 2010).
10. See *Redfern and Hunter on International Commercial Arbitration*, 5th edn. (OUP 2009) at para. 6.140; E. GAILLARD and John SAVAGE, eds., *Fouchard Gaillard Goldman on International Commercial Arbitration* (Kluwer 1999) at para. 1285; Gary B. BORN, *op. cit.*, fn. 2, at 2308-2311; Brian COOPER, *op. cit.*, fn. 5, p. 779; Georg VON SEGESSER, *op. cit.*, fn. 4, p. 222; David P. RONEY, "Effective Witness Preparation for International Commercial Arbitration: A Practical Guide for Counsel", 20 Journal of International Arbitration (2003, no. 3) p. 429 at p. 430; Christian OETIKER, "Witnesses Before the International Arbitral Tribunal", 25 ASA Bulletin (2007, no. 2) p. 253 at pp. 262-263; Baiju S. VASANI, "So You're Going to Be a Witness in an International Arbitration? Twenty Golden Rules to Help You to Get Through It", 4 TDM (June

arbitration process which involves hearings that are typically significantly shorter than in court proceedings[11] (with cases with hundreds of millions of dollars at stake frequently heard by arbitrators within a one-week period, rather than a period of several months before a judge and/or jury), and a procedure which relies on written statements (rather than oral evidence) as the witness's evidence in chief. These features of the arbitral process – which lead to its efficiency and attractiveness to commercial parties – make it necessary for counsel to assist witnesses to focus their testimony on the issues in dispute.

Nevertheless, methods for preparing witnesses differ across jurisdictions, influenced in part by their legal traditions. Whilst lawyers in England may naturally tend to opt for "witness familiarization", involving an explanation of the examination process, a description of the room and the actors involved and a series of generic tips for testifying (such as speak up, sit straight, understand the question or ask for it to be repeated),[12] lawyers in other jurisdictions such as the United States will go a step further, undertaking "witness training" involving aggressive mock cross-examinations.[13]

There is nothing sinister in such training. On the contrary, it equips the witness with the knowledge and experience needed to be able to assist the tribunal by providing relevant and accurate evidence as part of an efficient process. Moreover, there are inbuilt safeguards which incentivize lawyers not to cross the line between witness training and witness tampering, namely, ethical and penal rules,[14] and the significant risk that the

---

2007, no. 3); Jane JENKINS and Simon STEBBINGS, *International Construction Arbitration Law* (Kluwer 2006) at p. 265; and John P. MADDEN, "How to Present Witness Evidence in an Arbitration – American Style", ASA Bull (1993) p. 438.

11. See Georg VON SEGESSER, *op. cit.*, fn. 4, p. 222 at p. 225, who points out that "In state court proceedings where the parties are precluded from contacting witnesses, a great deal of time is often wasted in hearing witness testimony which is either irrelevant or only marginally relevant to the substance of the dispute. In international arbitration, the use of witness statements, and the associated preparation of witnesses, enable both the parties and the arbitral tribunal to identify and concentrate on the critical issues in dispute. This usually results in much more efficient hearings."

12. See the Code of Conduct of the Bar of England and Wales, Rule 705: "A barrister must not ... rehearse, practise or coach a witness in relation to his evidence ... " and "The Preparation of Witness Statements", Guidance for Members of the Bar, para. 9(v):

"Rule 705 of the Code of Conduct provides that a barrister must not rehearse, practice or coach a witness in relation to his evidence. This does not prevent Counsel giving general advice to a witness about giving evidence e.g. speak up, speak slowly, answer the question, keep answers as short as possible, ask if a question is not understood, say if you cannot remember and do not guess or speculate. Nor is there any objection to testing a witness's recollection robustly to ascertain the quality of his evidence or to discussing the issues that may arise in cross-examination. By contrast, mock cross-examinations or rehearsals of particular lines of questioning that counsel proposes to follow are not permitted.... "

13. See, e.g., David P. RONEY, *op. cit.*, fn. 10, p. 429.
14. Indeed, this is one reason why it is preferable for witness preparation to be undertaken by lawyers subject to ethical rules of conduct, see David P. RONEY, *ibid.*, at p. 430. Examples of ethical and penal rules include Rule 705 of the Code of Conduct of the Bar of England and Wales, Disciplinary Rule 7-109 of the New York Lawyer's Code of Professional Responsibility, and Rule 17 of the Queensland Law Society's Legal Professional (Solicitors) Rules 2007.

other party or tribunal will uncover any untruth, affecting not only the credibility of the witness but of that party's case as a whole. Lawyers trained in common law tradition strongly believe that cross-examination is the most powerful tool for uncovering the truth. A skillful cross-examiner will uncover and highlight any untruths; and experienced arbitrators will detect and discount coached responses.[15]

To the extent that the parties to an arbitration may have different expectations as to the acceptable limits to witness preparation, the arbitral tribunal has a role to play to elucidate these expectations at an early stage and ensure transparency and equal treatment of the parties.[16] This can be done by setting out acceptable practices in the first procedural order. This ensures a level playing field.

2. *The Three Stages of Preparation for Oral Testimony*

There are three stages to effective witness preparation.[17] These involve familiarizing the witness with the issues in dispute and the relevant documents, familiarizing the witness with the examination process and, finally, subjecting the witness to mock examinations.

a.   Step one: Familiarization with the issues in dispute and relevant documents
Much of the first stage of witness preparation will have been undertaken when assisting the witness with the preparation of their witness statement. Nevertheless, the exercise should be repeated ahead of the hearing to refresh the witness's memory (as several months may have passed since the witness submitted their statement) as well as update it in light of new factual developments or new allegations or arguments raised by the opposing party.

This first preparation phase mainly consists of a self-study exercise to be undertaken by the witness alone. The witness should read and re-read their statement, familiarize themselves with the documents and exhibits that are relevant to their testimony, and acquaint themselves with the issues in dispute. To assist the witness in doing this, counsel should prepare a bundle of documents for the witness which should include their statement, excerpts of the statements of the other party's witnesses that are relevant to the subject matter of the witness's testimony, as well as the relevant documents and exhibits. The relevant documents and exhibits should include all documents on the record authored by the witness or on which the witness was copied. The witness should be instructed to review these documents carefully.

---

15. See David P. RONEY, *op. cit.*, fn. 10, p. 429 at p. 430, who cautions that "counsel must not propose, either directly or indirectly, that a witness should tell a specific 'story'. This is not only unethical, it is also invariably counterproductive. A witness who is coached to recount a specific story will not be credible and, in all likelihood, this story will not hold up under questioning from opposing counsel or the arbitral tribunal."
16. The tribunal should encourage the parties to reach agreement on such procedural issues. See Georg VON SEGESSER, *op. cit.*, fn. 4, p. 222 at p. 223.
17. Different authors describe different numbers and categories of stages for the witness preparation process, see, e.g., David P. RONEY, *op. cit.*, fn. 10, p. 429 at p. 430 (setting out the "Six Steps to Successful Witness Preparation"), however, these are broadly equivalent.

b. *Step two: Familiarization with the process*

The aim of this second phase is to familiarize the witness with what can be an unknown and intimidating process – and one that will be unlike any preconceived notions stemming from television or the movies – and to give common-sense guidelines for testifying before an arbitral tribunal.

The witness should be guided as to what will happen when they take the stand. The sequence of events (namely the affirmation of truth, confirmation of the authenticity of the statements, the direct examination, followed by cross-examination by the other side and potentially a short re-direct examination), and the roles of each person in attendance should be fully explained. The witness should also be guided as to what the "stand" (normally, a chair at a table, facing the tribunal) and surroundings will look like, and who the interlocutors will be. To help the witness visualize the hearing environment, it may be helpful to provide a diagram of the hearing room as well as the biographies (ideally with pictures) of the arbitrators and opposing counsel. If there is to be simultaneous or sequential interpretation, this process should also be explained to the witness (including the need to allow time for interpretations to be complete before continuing with an answer).

More importantly, the fundamental objective of the examination process should be explained to the witness. The aim is to defend the truth of the contents of the witness's testimony (written and oral) and to show that the witness is credible and trustworthy. Throughout the examination process, no one in the room matters more than the members of the tribunal. For this reason, even though questions are asked by counsel, the witness should be told to maintain eye contact with the tribunal, to the extent possible, when answering questions. The witness should keep in mind that the tribunal controls the examination process and may intervene at any time to ask questions of the witness.

On the flip side, the witness should try to forget that the party that has called them to testify and its counsel are in the room. There is an unhealthy tendency for witnesses called by a party to look at the party's counsel after responding to a question. A witness who looks to a party or counsel when answering difficult questions will appear as though they are seeking assistance or approval, and will not seem credible.

With this in mind, the witness should be given basic common-sense guidelines on testifying and answering cross-examination questions. These can be boiled down to the following ten tips:[18]

(i) Tell the truth

To be credible and trustworthy, the witness must, obviously, always tell the truth. This is of paramount importance.

If during the course of the examination, the witness realizes that one of the answers is incorrect or incomplete, they should correct or add to the previous answer, even if the topics have moved on. Similarly, if the witness feels that they have not clearly expressed

---

18. For other lists of guidelines, see David P. RONEY, *op. cit.*, fn. 10, p. 429 at p. 434; and Baiju S. VASANI, *op. cit.*, fn. 10.

themselves, and examining counsel seizes upon the answer, the witness should feel free to clarify what they intended to say or rephrase the answer.

Moreover, the witness should not try to memorize answers to possible questions in advance as the answer will appear rehearsed and therefore suspect.

(ii)   Understand the question

Before answering a question, the witness must ensure that they fully understand the question that has been put. There is a risk that the witness will feel under pressure to advance the process and will be embarrassed to request a repetition of the question. However, a witness should never guess what the question means or where the question is leading to. If the question is unclear, the witness should explain that they do not understand and ask for the question to be repeated or rephrased. Sometimes the confusion can result from an unclear translation, in which case, the witness should feel free to ask the interpreter to clarify. Other times, a question can be difficult to answer because it has several parts or sub-questions, or it includes a statement within a question. Witnesses should be instructed not to attempt to answer multiple questions, but rather to ask examining counsel to break the multiple question down so it may be answered one stage at a time. The witness should also be wary of statements embedded into a question, and address (rather than ignore) any statement with which they disagree.

(iii)   Take time when answering

The witness should not allow themselves to be hurried by examining counsel. If the witness needs time to think before answering a question, they should do so; a thoughtful pause after a question is perfectly proper. However, the pause should be to reflect on the answer as a question of fact and not for the witness to seek to understand the objective of the question. I recall one witness called by opposing counsel who took a full minute before answering any question. Such a delay would not be necessary simply to recollect a fact and affected that witness's credibility.

It is particularly important for a witness to take time when asked questions about a document. The witness should feel free to take the necessary time to read the document or relevant portions before answering, particularly if it is a document they have never seen before. Cross examination thrives on small passages of documents taken out of context.

(iv)   Answer the question succinctly

The witness should answer questions asked by the cross-examiner succinctly, then stop. The witness should only answer the question asked, not the question the witness thinks the questioner should have asked or what the witness thinks the next question will be. The witness should not go beyond the scope of the question which has been asked or feel the need to fill in silences. If examining counsel requires further information, he or she will ask for it.

Once the question has been answered succinctly, the witness should resist the temptation to elaborate too much on their answer. The witness should answer the question clearly and then provide any relevant context as briefly as possible. If examining counsel does not give the witness the opportunity to provide context, the witness should request the right to finish (counsel presenting the witness may also intervene if this occurs).

(v)   Do not pretend to know the answer
Whilst a witness may want to be helpful or appear to be knowledgeable, they should resist the temptation to answer a question if they are unsure of the answer. The witness cannot be expected to know the answer to every question. If they do not know the answer or do not remember, or if the subject matter of the question falls outside the witness's direct knowledge or area of responsibility, they should say so. They should not guess at the answer to be helpful, as the answer may be wrong which could damage their credibility. For the same reason, the witness should refuse to be drawn to comment or speculate on matters they do not know (e.g., other people's intentions, understandings, motives or state of mind). If the witness is asked to speculate, they should make it clear that that is what they are doing.

(vi)   Stay calm and courteous at all times
The witness should strive to remain calm, polite, serious and courteous at all times during the examination. Even if the cross-examiner is hostile, or the questions become pointed or difficult, the witness should avoid becoming aggressive or flustered. Hostility or aggression on the part of the opposing lawyer will reflect poorly on him or her, not on the witness.

(vii)   Speak slowly and clearly
The hearing will be transcribed by a court reporter and may be translated by an interpreter. The arbitrators may be elderly. It is therefore important that the witness speak clearly and slowly so that the transcript writers and translators have the time to do their jobs accurately. It is easy to forget that a movement of the head cannot be recorded on the transcript, or heard by the translator. The witness should therefore say "yes" or "no" clearly. Similarly, the witness should speak in clear terms and avoid jargon and technical terms where possible.

(viii)   Avoid absolutes
The witness should avoid words like "never" and "always", as examining counsel will no doubt have the one exception at their fingertips.

(ix)   Be helpful
A witness that is evasive or deliberately difficult will not appear credible in the eyes of the tribunal. The witness should not feel that it is their duty not to agree with the cross-examiner or avoid concessions. Cross-examination is not about scoring points against the cross-examiner. Answering questions directly is the best policy. Avoiding conceding an obvious point only damages credibility. That said, actions and decisions should be explained in light of the situation prevailing at the time and the information available.

(x) Be yourself

Lastly, it is important that witnesses be themselves and let their personality come through. A witness who tries to take on a persona in cross-examination will seem phony and untrustworthy.

By the end of this second phase of preparation, the witness should have a good understanding of the mechanics and purpose of the examination process and understand the basic guidelines for providing testimony.

c. *Step three: Conducting mock examinations*

Whilst describing the examination process along the lines above is helpful, ultimately, there is no substitute to putting a witness through a mock examination.[19] It is one thing to be given a description of a pool of water, but quite another to find oneself immersed in it and needing to swim. Nothing other than first-hand experience can truly prepare an individual for the rather unnatural experience of cross-examination involving one-sided skillful and sometimes aggressive questioning by an opposing party before a panel of arbitrators tasked with judging one's credibility. With a little experience, anyone can learn to get comfortable with the process and to confidently and truthfully answer difficult questions. This is the ultimate goal of this third stage of witness preparation.[20]

Mock examinations should be conducted in the weeks or days prior to the hearing, and only after the first two preparatory stages have been completed. The witness should experience a mock direct as well as cross-examination, ideally in an environment that resembles the hearing room (i.e., in a conference room set up similarly to the hearing room). The idea is to give the witness an experience that is close to the "real thing".

i. Mock direct examination

Because a witness's written statement normally stands as evidence-in-chief, direct examination in international arbitration is often limited to a ritualistic request by the party presenting their evidence to confirm that the statements are indeed the witness's statements and that it is their signature that is appended to them, and to confirm whether the witness wishes to change or add anything to that statement?[21] Whilst there is usually no need (and no procedural opportunity) for extensive "storytelling" direct examination as might be found in court, limiting the direct examination to the extent described above entails foregoing an opportunity to let the witness acclimatize to their surroundings and

---

19. See David P. RONEY, *op. cit.*, fn. 10, p. 429 at p. 434 ("The best possible preparation for the rigours of cross-examination is to subject the witness to several rounds of aggressive mock cross-examination").
20. It also levels the playing field between opposing counsel who will have spent hours (perhaps days) preparing for cross-examination (and often years honing cross-examination skills) and the witness who is expected to spontaneously answer these skillful questions on the spot.
21. See, e.g., Art. 8(3) of the IBA Rules on the Taking of Evidence in International Commercial Arbitration which provides: "Any witness providing testimony shall first affirm, in a manner determined appropriate by the arbitral tribunal, that he or she is telling the truth. If the witness has submitted a Witness Statement or an Expert Report, the witness shall confirm it…."

to let the tribunal form its first impression of the witness's character and demeanor before they are put in a defensive posture.

In preparing the direct examination, counsel should discuss with the witness the likely scope of the questions to be asked on direct. These should include questions aimed at reminding the tribunal who the witness is, highlighting positive aspects of their background and their relevance to the dispute. Not only are such questions helpful to refresh the tribunal's memory and to establish the relevance and credibility of the witness, but they also tend to help the witness relax and get comfortable answering questions. Other potential areas for questioning that should be discussed with the witness beforehand include:

(1) whether there are any new facts that have arisen since the date of the witness's statement that the witness should address during the direct examination;
(2) whether there are any new matters arising from the opposing party's last written pleadings that the witness should be given an opportunity to respond to in direct examination;
(3) whether there are any corrections or weaknesses in the statement (for instance, in light of rebuttal testimony from the opposing party's witnesses) that should be addressed preemptively on direct examination so as to lessen the impact of cross-examination.

Once the scope of the questions has been discussed, it may be helpful to do a mock direct examination with the witness, complete with the affirmation of truth and the formulaic procedural questions aimed at having them confirm their statement, in order to familiarize them with the process. However, the witness should not be over-prepared for direct examination. Answers that sound memorized or rehearsed will lose credibility.

ii.   Mock cross-examination

Mock cross-examinations should cover a broad range of areas on which the witness may be questioned by the opposing party, and should be focused on the issues in dispute. The exercise achieves several objectives. First, it provides an opportunity for the witness to put the tips learned during the witness familiarization process into practice. (Experienced counsel can attest that after painstakingly reviewing a list of tips for testifying, the witness will invariably proceed to forget each and every one of them.) Given the opportunity, witnesses can learn to put these tips into practice, giving them a heightened sense of confidence and control over the cross-examination process. Second, it significantly reduces the element of surprise. A good mock cross-examination will, if nothing else, cause the witness to be aware of and begin reflecting on difficult questions. A witness presented with these questions for the first time at the hearing can be thrown off guard or intimidated, and consequently inhibited from providing a full response.[22] Worse, effective advocacy by opposing counsel could cause the witness to become

---

22. See Brian COOPER, *op. cit.*, fn. 5, p. 779 at pp. 786-787 ("While ethical concerns prohibit lawyers and witnesses from collaborating over 'concocted' testimony, such concerns should not allow otherwise meritorious cases to be damaged by 'surprise' evidence to which a prepared witness might have readied a succinct and truthful explanation").

confused and to provide an inaccurate response, or an incomplete response that neglects to put facts into context. Putting the witness through a mock cross-examination should reduce the risk that, as a result of surprise or confusion, the witness is made to agree to a conclusion put to them by the cross-examiner, only to realize later (when it is too late) that the answer was wrong or incomplete. Whilst re-direct examination can be used to salvage such situations, it is far better from an advocacy perspective that the witness avoid these situations altogether by being alert to the issues and to the ruses of the cross-examiner. This should permit counsel for the party presenting the witness to minimize (or forgo) objections during cross-examination as well as questions in re-direct – both of which are optimal from an advocacy perspective.

Following the completion of this third stage of preparation, the witness will be less likely to be intimidated, frustrated or caught by surprise during cross-examination and they can therefore better tell their story and put answers to difficult questions in context. In sum, they will come across as a more credible witness.

V.   CONCLUSION

Witness preparation is key to persuading the tribunal through effective advocacy. Ultimately, good witness preparation ensures that the witness tells their story accurately, relevantly and truthfully, both in writing and orally, in a way that can withstand the crucible of cross-examination.

Experts:

Neutrals or Advocates?

Protocol on Expert Teaming: A New Approach to Expert Evidence

Dr. Klaus Sachs with the assistance of Dr. Nils Schmidt-Ahrendts***

TABLE OF CONTENTS	Page
I. Introduction	135
II. Regulations	136
III. Advantages and Disadvantages	139
IV. "New Techniques" for Party-Appointed Experts	141
V. Expert Teaming	144
VI. Conclusions	147

I. INTRODUCTION

The subject our panel has been asked to address centres on the independence and impartiality of experts. The way the subject is formulated – "Experts: Neutrals or Advocates" suggests that we are talking exclusively about party-appointed experts. It would be odd to ask this question if we were talking about tribunal-appointed experts; they are rarely perceived as being advocates. The situation is different when it comes to party-appointed experts where one increasingly often hears complaints that their evidence is of little value because it advocates too much in the interest of the party presenting it. The result is that tribunals then find themselves faced with deciding between the opinions of opposing experts who have arrived at diametrically opposite and hardly reconcilable conclusions: no damages vs. US$ 100 million damages; insurmountable regulatory hurdles to proceed with a project vs. no impediments whatsoever; state-of-the-art construction of a product vs. serious engineering mistakes.

That is a rather unsatisfactory situation for a tribunal, in particular in complex cases where the stakes are often high and much depends on technical, regulatory or financial issues. After all, is it not the role of experts, be they tribunal- or party-appointed, to assist, educate and advise the tribunal, in a fair and impartial manner, in specific fields in which the arbitrators do not themselves have the relevant expertise?[1]

Hence, a preliminary question to our topic is whether it has become a given in international arbitration practice that expert evidence should be provided only by party-appointed experts? Or, is there still a case to be made for using a tribunal-appointed expert?

---

* Partner CMS Hasche Sigle, Munich, Germany; head of the Practice Group Arbitration.
** Associate, CMS Hasche Sigle, Munich, Germany; member of the Practice Group Arbitration.
1. Martin HUNTER, "Techniques for Eliciting Expert Testimony: Expert Conferencing and New Methods" in *International Arbitration 2006: Back to Basics?*, ICCA Congress Series no. 13 (2006) p. 820 et seq.

In analyzing this question, we will start by looking into the regulatory framework, i.e., first, the various arbitration laws, from both common law and civil law countries and, second, the rules of the leading institutions and those reflecting best practices, such as the IBA Rules:[2] Do they provide further guidance as to the circumstances under which the one or the other method is more suitable?

In a second step, we will briefly point out the main advantages and disadvantages of both types of expert testimony.

In a third step, we will briefly address some of the techniques which have been introduced in international arbitration proceedings to cope with the disadvantages commonly connected with party-appointed experts, such as "pre-hearing meetings", "witness conferencing" and "codes of conduct". We submit that these remedies can indeed be helpful but that they are not always sufficient to do away with the disadvantages of using party-appointed experts.

For all these reasons, in a final step, we will describe an alternative approach to expert evidence which may be referred to as "expert teaming" and to present an outline for a protocol setting forth such approach. Instead of remedying potential disadvantages connected with the use of party-appointed experts, the concept of "expert teaming" rather seeks to address the concerns commonly expressed with regard to tribunal-appointed experts.

II. REGULATIONS

1. *National Laws*

It is true that arbitration practice still reflects a certain divide between the common law and the civil law approach to expert evidence. It is a common law tradition for parties to present "their" expert witness, a tradition built on the notion of a fully adversarial system. Civil lawyers, by contrast, have historically been more sceptical about the benefits and costs of party-appointed expert witnesses. This is a result of the civil law tradition of attributing only limited evidentiary value to expert opinions put forward by the parties. Thus, civil law arbitrators still tend to favour the appointment of experts who follow the tribunal's and not the parties' instructions. However, there is a clear trend in international arbitration to rely primarily on the testimony of party-appointed experts, with tribunal-appointed experts being used only in exceptional circumstances.

Interestingly, national arbitration laws do not exactly mirror this divide in the approach to expert evidence. Most national arbitration laws, from both common law and civil law countries, if at all, primarily deal with tribunal-appointed experts, and only secondarily with party-appointed experts. This is certainly due to the fact that until the 1990s tribunal-appointed experts were more commonly used in arbitration than today.

Thus, the 1985 UNCITRAL Model Law on International Commercial Arbitration (the Model Law) – the mother of most modern arbitration laws – deals in Art. 26 only with experts appointed by the tribunal. Party-appointed experts are only mentioned in the

---

2. The IBA Rules on the Taking of Evidence in International Commercial Arbitration (the IBA Rules).

context of the parties' right to put questions to the tribunal-appointed expert at the hearing. However, there is no doubt that evidence by means of party-appointed experts is admissible under the Model Law. This principle follows from the parties' general right to submit evidence pursuant to Sect. 23(1) of the Model Law. It includes the right to present expert evidence from their own party-appointed experts.

Similarly, the English Arbitration Act 1996 mainly deals with tribunal-appointed experts although it is unusual for a tribunal in England to appoint its own experts. Interestingly, Sect. 37 of the English Arbitration Act mentions not only experts in the usual sense but also legal advisors and so-called assessors, the role of whom is to assist the tribunal on technical matters. The Swedish Arbitration Act, in turn, simply states that the parties shall supply the evidence; however, the arbitrators may appoint experts, unless both parties are opposed thereto. See Sect. 25 of the Swedish Arbitration Act. By contrast, none of the French, the Swiss or the US arbitration laws contain specific provisions for expert evidence. Nevertheless, also in these countries, the admissibility of both types of expert evidence is beyond doubt.[3]

Interestingly, some of the laws enacted more recently in UNCITRAL Model Law countries, such as Austria and Spain, now expressly address the parties' right to appoint their own experts. Thus, the Austrian Code of Civil Procedure (*Zivilprozessordnung* – ZPO) provides in Sect. 601(2) that "in the hearing, the parties shall have the opportunity ... to present their own expert witnesses in order to testify on the points at issue"; and states in Sect. 601(4) that "unless otherwise agreed by the parties, each party has the right to produce reports from his own expert". It is noteworthy that the Austrian legislator specifically included these additions to the text of the Model Law in recognition that the use of party-appointed experts is increasingly common in international arbitration, even though it does not follow the tradition in civil law systems.[4]

To summarize: It can safely be said that national arbitration laws permit both types of expert evidence without giving a clear preference. It is further commonly accepted that the decision whether or not the tribunal should appoint its own expert is left to the tribunal's discretion. However, national arbitration laws offer no guidance as to how to exercise such discretion.

2. *Institutional Rules*

Most institutional rules are not much more specific than the national arbitration laws when dealing with expert evidence. This is true, for example, for Art. 27 of the UNCITRAL Arbitration Rules 1976 which corresponds more or less to Art. 26 of the Model Law and thus primarily deals with tribunal-appointed experts. A similar provision

---

3. For Switzerland, Pierre A. KARRER and Peter A. STRAUB, "I. Switzerland" in Frank-Bernd WEIGAND, ed., *Practitioner's Handbook on International Arbitration* (C.H. Beck/DJØF 2002) (hereinafter *Practitioner's Handbook*) p. 1047 et seq. at p. 1064; for the United States, Thomas E. CARBONNEAU, "J. United States" in *Practitioner's Handbook*, p. 1087 et seq. at p. 1064; and for France, Emmanuel GAILLARD and Jenny EDELSTEIN, "C. France" in *Practitioner's Handbook*, p. 643 et seq. at p. 664 (referring to Art. 10 French Code of Civil Procedure).
4. Franz T. SCHWARZ and Christian W. KONRAD, *The Vienna Rules, A Commentary on International Arbitration in Austria* (Wolters Kluwer 2009) p. 532 (margin note 21-015).

appears in Art. 21 of the Arbitration Rules of the LCIA (London Court of International Arbitration).

The Arbitration Rules of the International Chamber of Commerce (ICC) provide for the two mechanisms in a distinct manner, though in very broad terms, with Art. 20(3) dealing with party-appointed experts and Art. 20(4) dealing with tribunal-appointed experts. It is not expected that the current revision of the ICC Rules will become more specific in this respect, except possibly for providing certain case management techniques. Although Art. 20(4) might arguably be said to give the tribunal the right to appoint an expert even if none of the parties desire it, Derains and Schwarz[5] in their commentary are of the view that there is no way in which the tribunal can, as a practical matter, impose an expert on the parties against their wishes as the expert has to be paid by the parties.

3. *The IBA Rules*

The 1999 version of the IBA Rules provides more detailed procedures both for party-appointed and tribunal-appointed experts.

Art. 5 of the IBA Rules specifically confirms the well-established principle that a party may rely on a party-appointed expert as a means of evidence. It further sets forth in detail the required content of an expert report; the general obligation of an expert to give his testimony at an evidentiary hearing; the consequences of a failure to appear; and the possibility for a tribunal to order the party-appointed experts, if they have submitted reports on related issues, to meet and confer with each other in order to reach agreement on issues upon which they had disagreed in their reports.

Art. 6 of the IBA Rules confirms that the tribunal has the right to appoint its own "independent" expert but requires it to consult with the parties before selecting its expert and in establishing the expert's terms of reference. The parties, in turn, are required to raise any objections to the independence of the tribunal-appointed expert within the time limit set by the tribunal. Art. 6 further provides that the tribunal-appointed expert is entitled to request any relevant and material information directly from the parties and requires him to report in writing to the tribunal and to describe in his report the method, evidence and information used in arriving at his conclusions. Art. 6 makes clear that the tribunal-appointed expert may be questioned at the hearing by any party-appointed expert on issues raised in his report.

As one can see, the IBA Rules set forth rather comprehensive and well-balanced rules for each of the two procedures, however, without giving any preference. Both procedures are dealt with on an equal footing, which should not come as a surprise since the IBA Rules have an overall tendency to find compromise solutions between civil law and common law practices.

---

5. Yves DERAINS and Eric A. SCHWARTZ, *A Guide to the ICC Rules of Arbitration*, 2nd edn. (Kluwer Law International 2005) p. 276.

III. ADVANTAGES AND DISADVANTAGES

The question therefore remains as to how arbitrators should exercise their discretion to appoint their own expert. To answer this question, we shall analyze the most common concerns expressed with regard to each type of expert testimony.

1. Party-Appointed Experts

The most common concern expressed with regard to party-appointed experts is that their expertise is often tainted by a lack of impartiality. Party-appointed experts are accused of acting like "hired guns" or of producing evidence "bought by the party presenting it".[6] Their statements often resemble arguments made by the party that appointed them. In particular, party-financed reports on issues of quantum tend to come to extreme conclusions.[7]

A second concern is that the reports submitted by these experts suffer from a lack of clarity. They tend to be too long and too complex.[8] In addition, since the experts preparing the reports have been instructed by the party and not by the tribunal, the reports tend to have a different focus than the tribunal has.[9]

A third concern is the lack of coordination among the party-appointed experts. In particular, if the reports are submitted simultaneously, they do not correspond to each other. They are often based on different facts, different scientific approaches and different assumptions, and they address different issues. In other words: it is often difficult, if not impossible, for the tribunal to bridge the gap between the reports without the help of yet another expert. As a consequence, actual or potential points of agreement remain unclear.

A fourth concern is that the traditional method of examining party-appointed experts by direct and cross-examination often proves to be inefficient. At the same time, experts guided by counsel may develop points which are not decisive for the tribunal's decision.

2. Tribunal-Appointed Experts

In light of these criticisms, the obvious response appears to be that tribunals should instead seek to appoint their own "independent" experts. However, such approach also suffers from a number of disadvantages and gives cause for substantial concern.

---

6. See Bob DAVIS and Damian WILKINSON, "High Noon for Hired Guns – the Duties and Standard of Expert Witnesses", at <www.armstrongdavis.co.uk/downloads/ADA_high_noon_for_hired_guns.pdf> (last accessed 10 June 2010); see also Doug JONES, "Party Appointed Expert Witnesses in International Arbitration: A Protocol at Last", 24 Arbitration International (2008, no. 1) p. 137 et seq. at p. 138.
7. Rolf TRITTMAN and Boris KASOLOWSKY, "Taking Evidence in Arbitration Proceedings between Common Law and Civil", 31 UNSW Law Journal (2008) p. 330 et seq. at p. 338.
8. D. JONES, "Party Appointed Expert Witnesses in International Arbitration: A Protocol at Last", *op. cit.*, fn. 6, p. 138.
9. Wolfgang PETER, "Witness 'Conferencing'", 18 Arbitration International (2002, no. 1), p. 47 et seq. at p. 49.

The main concern, at least from a common law perspective, is that the parties distrust the tribunal-appointed experts because they feel that they are unable to control the manner in which what may be the most critical element in their case will be presented.[10] This concern is understandable but does not speak against tribunal-appointed experts per se if one accepts that their focus should be to advise the tribunal.

A second and closely related concern is that tribunal-appointed experts render a report despite a potential lack of factual information. Undisputedly, the flow of factual information between the party and the corresponding party-appointed expert is usually much smoother than between a party and the tribunal-appointed expert, who, at least in case of non-compliance, has to obtain the assistance of an intermediary, i.e., the arbitral tribunal.

A third concern is that the reports prepared by tribunal-appointed experts are as likely to suffer from a lack of clarity as those prepared by party-appointed experts. At times it appears that when talking about the same set of facts, lawyers and experts use different languages.

Another concern of the parties is that their dispute is in effect decided by the experts instead of the tribunal. It has been said that: "When appointing an independent expert, an arbitral tribunal seeks to obtain technical information that might guide it in the search for truth."[11] Yet, in practice, one can observe that the experts' tasks may go well beyond this. In some cases, tribunals have assigned experts the task of "establishing the facts of the case by identifying the evidence provided and assessing its probative value". In other cases, experts have been asked to express their "opinion on a claim" without identifying any specific aspects to be addressed.[12]

This last concern is a more serious one: Although a tribunal-appointed expert has to be competent and neutral and is subject to the same standards of impartiality and independence as the members of the tribunal, he is not the person chosen by the parties to resolve their dispute. Any suggestion that the expert should be called in and included in the tribunal's deliberations and the preparation of the final award[13] is therefore highly problematic and is likely to raise further suspicion as to tribunal-appointed experts in general.

The ability to select the person who will resolve the dispute is one of the major reasons why parties choose to submit their disputes to arbitration.[14] Therefore, it is expected that special efforts will be made by the tribunal to resolve the dispute itself.

---

10. M. HUNTER, Techniques for Eliciting Expert Testimony: Expert Conferencing and New Methods", *op. cit.*, fn. 1.
11. Michael SCHNEIDER, "Technical Experts in International Arbitration", ASA Bulletin (1993) p. 446 et seq. at p. 449.
12. The corresponding examples from cases are reprinted as abstracts and cited in M. SCHNEIDER, Techniques for Eliciting Expert Testimony: Expert Conferencing and New Methods", *op. cit.*, fn. 11, p. 450.
13. Karl SPÜHLER and Myriam A. GEHRI, "*Die Zulassung von Experten zur Urteilsberatung: Neue Wege für Schiedsverfahren?*", ASA Bulletin (2003) p. 16 et seq. at p. 24.
14. Nigel BLACKABY, Constantine PARTASIDES, Alan REDFERN and Martin HUNTER, *Redfern and Hunter on International Arbitration*, 5th edn. (Oxford University Press 2009) p. 246 referring to such option as one of the "unique distinguishing factors of arbitration".

Thus, while the perception that a dispute is – in fact – decided by someone else may raise substantial concerns in state court proceedings, it is unacceptable in arbitration, or to quote the Latin phrase: *delegatus non potest delegare*.

IV. "NEW TECHNIQUES" FOR PARTY-APPOINTED EXPERTS

Although national laws, institutional rules and other sets of rules, such as the IBA Rules, do not favour one type of expert testimony over the other, there is no doubt that, as of today, the standard approach in international arbitration proceedings is to rely primarily on the testimony of party-appointed experts, with tribunal-appointed experts being used in exceptional circumstances.[15]

With the aim of responding to the criticisms and complaints related to the use of party-appointed experts, certain techniques have been proposed and introduced in international arbitration proceedings which seek to address some of the concerns and perceived disadvantages of relying exclusively on party-appointed experts. Two techniques should be mentioned in particular: "pre-hearing meetings" and "expert witness conferencing" or "hot-tubbing"; further, "specific codes of conduct"[16] for party-appointed experts have been initiated.

It is interesting to note that similar techniques, for similar reasons, have been introduced in English and Australian state court proceedings: In England, the techniques were introduced as a consequence of the so-called "Lord Woolf reforms".[17] In Australia, such techniques were introduced by reforms adopted by the Federal Court of Australia and the State Supreme Courts.[18]

Since these techniques have been carefully and comprehensively explained in scholarly contributions by esteemed colleagues,[19] this paper shall be limited to a brief summary of the content and put an emphasis on the evaluation of the techniques.

1. *"Pre-hearing Meetings"*

The instrument of pre-hearing meetings is expressly foreseen by Art. 5(3) of the IBA Rules which reads as follows:

---

15. See R. TRITTMAN and B. KASOLOWSKY, "Taking Evidence in Arbitration Proceedings between Common Law and Civil", *op. cit.*, fn. 7, p. 338.
16. The terms attributed to such techniques vary and shall not be regarded as fixed terms.
17. Right Hon. Lord WOOLF MR, "Access to Justice: Final Report to the Lord Chancellor on the Civil Justice System in England and Wales" (Stationery Office Books 1996). See, for example, Rule 35.12 Civil Procedure Rules.
18. The Guidelines for Expert Witnesses in Proceedings in the Federal Court of Australia were produced in 1998 and last amended in June 2008.
19. See W. PETER, "Witness 'Conferencing'", *op. cit.*, fn. 9, p. 49. See also R. TRITTMAN and B. KASOLOWSKY, "Taking Evidence in Arbitration Proceedings between Common Law and Civil", *op. cit.*, fn. 7, p. 330.

"The Arbitral Tribunal in its discretion may order that any Party-Appointed Experts who have submitted Expert Reports on the same or related issues meet and confer on such issues. At such meeting, the Party-Appointed Experts shall attempt to reach agreement on those issues as to which they had differences of opinion in their Expert Reports, and they shall record in writing any such issues on which they reach agreement."

It lies in the discretion of the tribunal and the parties to amend and/or further specify such provision.

A much more detailed description of how "pre-hearing meetings" shall be conducted is contained in Art. 6 of the Protocol for the Use of Party-Appointed Expert Witnesses in International Arbitration which was issued by the Chartered Institute of Arbitrators in September 2007 (CIArb Expert Protocol).[20] The foreword to the protocol provides that the protocol has "been aligned with" and "expands upon" the IBA Rules.

For example, different from the IBA Rules, the protocol requires the experts to meet before they prepare their first report, to agree on issues, analysis and methods and also to record the issues on which they disagree and indicate the reasons of their disagreement.[21]

2. *"Witness Conferencing"*

A second instrument, which ideally builds upon the results of "pre-hearing meetings", has been introduced under the label "witness conferencing". As already indicated by the term "witness conferencing", the technique is not limited to expert witnesses but also extends to fact witnesses. According to the definition given by my colleague Wolfgang Peter, it consists of *"the simultaneous joint hearing of all fact witnesses, expert witnesses, and other experts involved in the arbitration"*.[22]

It is for that reason that the instrument is not foreseen by Art. 5 of the IBA Rules, which deals with party-appointed experts, but rather by Art. 8(2) of the IBA Rules, which provides rules for the evidentiary hearing and thus applies to all types of witnesses. In its relevant part, the provision reads:

"The Arbitral Tribunal, upon request of a Party or on its own motion, may vary this order of proceeding, including the arrangement of testimony by particular issues or in such a manner that witnesses presented by different Parties be questioned at the same time and in confrontation with each other."

---

20. For a detailed analysis of the protocol and its background, see D. JONES, "Party Appointed Expert Witnesses in International Arbitration: A Protocol at Last", *op. cit.*, fn. 6, p. 137 et seq.
21. See Art. 6 of the Protocol for the Use of Party-Appointed Expert Witnesses in International Arbitration at <www.ciarb.org/information-and-resources/The%20use%20of%20party-appointed%20experts.pdf> (last accessed 10 June 2010).
22. See W. PETER, "Witness 'Conferencing'", *op. cit.*, fn. 9, p. 47 et seq.

However, there is agreement that witness conferencing is particularly useful for examining party-appointed expert witnesses.[23]

In sum, this approach may elicit much clearer evidence than having a single expert more or less lecture the tribunal. Being placed next to their peers may well compel experts to present their opinions more independently and objectively.[24] The approach has also been successfully introduced in the national court systems in England and Australia where it has colloquially become known as "*hot tubbing*".

3.   *"Code of Conduct"*

National laws and institutional sets of rules are silent as to the duties and obligations of party-appointed experts. Although the IBA Rules, in Art. 5, provide for some obligations closely related to the expert's duties in preparing the report, they do not contain any provisions dealing with the general duties and obligations of party-appointed experts.

In response to the criticism that party-appointed experts have the tendency to view themselves as assistants to the party appointing (and paying) them, rather than as assistants to the tribunal in determining the objective facts, the Australian and English[25] legislators decided to introduce certain rules of conduct applicable to party-appointed experts in state court proceedings. The above-mentioned CIArb Expert Protocol has expanded on this idea. In Art. 4, it sets forth specific rules of conduct which, among others, provide that:

> "An expert's opinion shall be impartial, objective, unbiased and uninfluenced […]. An expert's duty […] is to assist the Arbitral Tribunal to decide the issues in respect of which expert evidence is adduced."

4.   *Preliminary Assessment*

There can be no doubt that the above-mentioned instruments are quite beneficial to the process of taking evidence by means of party-appointed experts. Since it is standard practice in international arbitration proceedings for the parties to appoint experts, there is also no doubt that these instruments have already had and promise to continue having a significant and very positive impact on the way international arbitration proceedings are conducted.

In particular, "pre-hearing meetings" and "witness conferencing" with the opposing experts are useful in order to

---

23. *Ibid.*, p. 49; see also R. TRITTMAN and B. KASOLOWSKY, "Taking Evidence in Arbitration Proceedings between Common Law and Civil", *op. cit.*, fn. 7, p. 339.
24. Robert MACPHERSON, Richard SMITH and Roy MITCHELL, "Innovations in Arbitration: Improving the Presentation of Evidence in Construction Arbitration", Dispute Resolution Journal (2003) p. 1 et seq. at p. 3.
25. The Civil Justice Council drafted a Protocol for the Instruction of Experts to give Evidence in Civil Claims which applies since 5 September 2005 and replaces the Code of Guidance on Expert Evidence.

(i) clarify technical and factual issues,
(ii) outline areas of agreement and disagreement,
(iii) focus on relevant points,
(iv) narrow down the differences between expert reports,
(v) encourage scientific debate and, as a consequence,
(vi) render the taking of expert evidence more time- and cost-efficient.

Further, the introduction of specific codes of conduct for party-appointed experts, such as the one proposed by the CIArb Expert Protocol, should have a positive impact on the impartiality of the experts and thus on the objectivity and quality of their work.[26]

Nevertheless, from my own practice as an arbitrator, and from the discussions I have had with many of my colleagues, I have to acknowledge that in some cases, these methods are not always sufficient to ensure an efficient (measured in terms of time and costs) and successful (measured in terms of clarity, quality and objectivity of the expert's finding before the tribunal) process of taking expert evidence.

As long as an expert is appointed and paid by a particular party, there will always be an incentive for him to sympathize with that party's position. There will often be a reluctance to cooperate with the expert appointed by the opposing party. And counsel will always try to control the evidence submitted by their expert and to prevent him from making statements which might turn out to be unfavourable to the client.

Metaphorically speaking: "pre-hearing meetings" and "witness conferencing" might downsize the ring in which the experts confront each other, coached by the counsel who appointed them, and thus make it less burdensome for the arbitrators as referees to oversee the fight and to detect fouls and lack of sportsmanship. However, they will not stop them from fighting altogether.

V. EXPERT TEAMING

We have seen that the standard approach in international arbitration proceedings is the use of party-appointed experts. By contrast, tribunal-appointed experts are being used only in exceptional circumstances due to the strong remaining scepticism of many of my colleagues, in particular those with a common law background, as to the benefits compared to the disadvantages of this form of expert evidence.

At least from my knowledge and review, few efforts have been made in practice or literature to address and remove the concerns expressed in relation to tribunal-appointed experts.

Therefore, the final part of the paper is dedicated to the description of an instrument which seeks to respond to the concerns expressed in relation to tribunal-appointed experts. In fact, the instrument provides for an effort to combine the advantages of party-appointed and tribunal-appointed experts. As far as my review has shown, this

---

26. For the advantages and benefits of such techniques, see also W. PETER, "Witness 'Conferencing'", *op. cit.*, fn. 9, p. 49, and D. JONES, "Party Appointed Expert Witnesses in International Arbitration: A Protocol at Last", *op. cit.*, fn. 6, p. 143.

instrument has not been described in greater detail in the literature and, for the purpose of this paper, shall be referred to as "expert teaming".

1. Characteristics

In the following, we will briefly describe the characteristics and general functioning of the instrument:

Instead of relying exclusively on party-appointed experts or appointing its own expert of choice, the tribunal could consult with the parties at an early stage in the proceedings and invite them to each provide the tribunal and the opposing party with a short list of candidates who they consider could serve as an expert to give evidence on the issues at stake. The tribunal should then invite the parties to briefly comment on the experts proposed by the other party, in particular as to whether there are any conflicts of interest. Then the tribunal chooses two experts, one from each list, and appoints these experts jointly as an "expert team". Following such appointment, the tribunal will meet with the expert team and the parties in order to establish a protocol on the expert team's mission.

Based on the terms of the protocol, the expert team prepares a preliminary joint report which is circulated to the tribunal and the parties. The parties and the tribunal are given the opportunity to comment on this preliminary report. The experts then review these comments and take them into consideration in preparing their final joint report which will be submitted to the parties and the tribunal.

Finally, upon request by one of the parties or the tribunal, the members of the expert team shall be present at the evidentiary hearing and they may be questioned by the tribunal, the parties or any party-appointed expert on issues raised in the experts' report.

2. The Outline of a Protocol

As regards the duties and obligations of the expert team, it is advisable that the protocol provides, inter alia, that

(i) both experts retained must be impartial and independent;
(ii) the task of the expert team is to assist the tribunal in deciding the issues in respect of which expert evidence is adduced;
(iii) the expert team shall only address issues identified in the terms of reference;
(iv) the expert team is expected to submit a joint report providing only the joint and mutual findings;
(v) each member of the expert team shall refrain from communicating separately with the parties, the tribunal or any third party;
(vi) the expert team shall prepare its report "from scratch" and shall rely only on its own expertise;
(vii) the expert team shall seek any input and assistance required from the parties;
(viii) in the preparation of the report, the expert team shall carefully examine all briefs and documents submitted by the parties and shall address the parties' views and concerns; and

(ix) the expert team shall be prepared to testify during an oral hearing and to respond to questions asked by the tribunal and the parties, their counsel and consultants.

Areas of disagreement on which the experts cannot reach a joint conclusion should be identified and, if necessary, the parties will be permitted to comment or submit additional (expert) evidence on these.

3.   Advantages

My experience has shown that the appointment of a team of experts selected equally from proposals made by both sides is likely to remove most of the concerns commonly connected with tribunal-appointed experts.

   a.   *Advantages compared to a single tribunal-appointed expert*
First, it removes the concern that the tribunal will select an expert of its own choice although the parties, due to their better knowledge of the factual and technical details of the case, would be in a much better position to make such choice.

   Second, it removes the concern that the tribunal will select a person whose personal skills and business-related expertise could not be carefully examined and tested by the parties prior to the appointment.

   Third, it removes the concern that the report will be prepared by a single individual who is not under the supervision of anyone possessing sufficient knowledge and technical expertise to challenge the technical findings and to correct potential errors by the expert. By appointing an expert team, the tribunal introduces a system of checks and balances.

   Fourth, as regards the concern that, in the case of tribunal-appointed experts, the dispute will be decided by the experts rather than by the tribunal, I submit that this is more an issue of properly drafting the experts' terms of reference. It is the task of the tribunal and the parties alike to ensure that the expert team is provided with a clear mandate which precisely defines the issues which the expert team shall determine and those which are left to the tribunal to decide.

   b.   *Advantages compared to party-appointed experts*
The principal advantage compared to party-appointed experts lies in the general status of the experts. Although the experts have been proposed by the parties, they are appointed by the tribunal and, thus, under the applicable laws and regulations, qualify as tribunal-appointed. Consequently, they are subject to special duties of independence and impartiality.[27] Probably, even more important, the experts themselves regard themselves as facilitators to the tribunal and not as assistants to the party appointing them. In addition, the experts are not paid by the party who proposed the expert. Instead, the fees of each expert are shared by the parties and are subject to the final determination of costs by the tribunal in its final award.

---

27. For example, according to Sect. 1049(3) German Code of Civil Procedure and Art. 27(5) Swiss Rules, tribunal-appointed experts are subject to the same rules regarding independence and impartiality as the members of the tribunal.

A second advantage is that when making proposals for their member of the expert team, the parties will be guided by different thoughts and concerns than when selecting their own experts. The parties themselves will ensure that the proposed expert's competence, independence and impartiality are beyond doubt since otherwise this person will have little chance of being selected by the tribunal.

Third, the fact that both the parties *and* the tribunal meet with and instruct the experts also addresses the concern that reports from party-appointed experts always run the risk of missing the points which the parties and the tribunal regard as relevant and material for the outcome of the case. In other words, this method appears much more likely to be successful as regards effectiveness, time and ultimately costs. Of course, this method also eliminates the risk of multiple expert reports which come to completely contradictory results or, worse, are not even responsive to each other.

Finally, for the avoidance of doubt, it should be reiterated that the parties, of course, remain free to comment on the expert team's report in writing and to question the experts during an oral hearing. In this regard, the parties naturally also remain entitled to seek the assistance of one or several experts of their choice, a so-called "expert consultant".[28] The consultant shall be entitled to assist the parties in the same manner as they are assisted by their counsel in legal matters. Such consultant shall be entitled to be present at oral hearings and to question the expert team. He may also argue before the tribunal, but since the consultant does not testify, his submissions may only qualify as arguments, not as evidence.

It is true that the appointment of additional experts by the parties would also lead to additional costs. Yet, since the focus of those experts' task would be more precise and the scope of their work more limited, it is submitted that the overall costs for experts will still be significantly less compared to the costs if both parties had solely retained party-appointed experts.

VI. CONCLUSIONS

It is a fact that experts are essential and indispensable for the process of dispute resolution in complex international proceedings. Thus, determining the most efficient and successful forms and methods for the taking of evidence by expert witness testimony is essential for the process.

National laws on arbitration and national and international institutional rules provide for the possibility of taking evidence either by party-appointed or by tribunal-appointed experts, yet offer very little guidance as to the details of such procedures. The IBA Rules contain more sophisticated provisions relating to both forms of expert testimony but, like the laws and institutional rules, they do not address which form should be applied under which circumstances.

---

28. For a distinction between the different types of experts in international arbitration proceedings and their respective functions and duties, see "Issues for Experts Acting under the ICC Rules for Expertise or the ICC Rules of Arbitration", 20 ICC Bulletin (2009, no. 1) p. 23 et seq.

The taking of evidence by means of party-appointed experts does raise substantial concerns and has often led to frustration among arbitrators and counsel alike. Nevertheless, it has become standard practice in international proceedings to rely mainly on party-appointed experts. In recent years, substantial efforts have been made to address the concerns resulting from this technique and to minimize potential disadvantages. In particular, procedures such as "pre-hearing meetings" and "witness conferencing" have proven quite successful. The CIArb Expert Protocol issued by the Chartered Institute of Arbitrators probably reflects most closely today's standards of best practice for party-appointed experts in international arbitration.

Much fewer efforts have been made to remedy the potential disadvantages of tribunal-appointed experts and to address the respective concerns, in particular those of practitioners and parties with a common law background. The concept of "expert teaming" seeks to combine the advantages of party-appointed and tribunal-appointed experts and thus may serve as an alternative approach to assist the tribunal, in an impartial and objective manner, to decide the issues in respect of which expert evidence is adduced.

Should Experts Be Neutrals or Advocates?

*Dushyant Dave**

TABLE OF CONTENTS	Page
I. Introduction	149
II. Expert Witness Must Be Led and Shown as Neutral in Examination-in-Chief	152
III. Expert Witness Attacked as Advocate in Cross-examination	155
IV. What Then Is the Solution?	157
V. Conclusions	158

I. INTRODUCTION

In *R. v. Abbey*, Dickson J. emphasized the need for experts in trials in following words:

> "Witnesses testify as to facts. The judge or jury draws inferences from facts. With respect to matters calling for special knowledge, an expert in the field may draw inferences and state his opinion. An expert's function is precisely this: to provide the judge and jury with the ready-made inference which the judge and jury, due to the technical nature of the facts, are unable to formulate. An expert's opinion is admissible to furnish the court with scientific information, which is likely to be outside the experience and knowledge of a judge or jury."

Redfern and Hunter on International Arbitration", fifth edition, has emphasized the need for expert evidence pithily:[1]

> "The third method of presenting evidence to an arbitral tribunal is by the use of expert witnesses. Some issues of fact can only be determined by the arbitral tribunal becoming involved in the evaluation of elements that are essentially matters of opinion. Thus, in a construction dispute, the contemporary documents, comprising correspondence, progress reports and other memoranda, and the evidence of witnesses who were present on the site may enable the arbitral tribunal to determine what actually happened. There may then be a further question to be determined; namely whether or not what actually happened was the result of, for example, a design error or defective construction practices. The determination of such an issue can only be made by the arbitral tribunal with the assistance of experts, unless it possesses the relevant expertise itself. Equally, in shipping arbitrations, the performance of a vessel or its equipment may need to

---

* Senior Advocate, Supreme Court of India; Board Member, American Arbitration Association; former member, LCIA Court; former Vice Chair, IBA Arbitration Committee; Member of ICCA.
1. Nigel BLACKABY, Constantine PARTASIDES, Alan REDFERN and Martin HUNTER, *Redfern and Hunter on International Arbitration*, 5th edn. (Oxford University Press) p. 406.

be evaluated by experts, so that the arbitral tribunal may make the relevant findings of fact."

Experts can help the arbitral tribunal to understand technical matters, can clarify technical issues and facts, can summarize extensive technical evidence so as to put it in a simplified form and can even obtain evidence. In international arbitration experts play a significant role and have been characterized to be "the most frequent evidence".

Experts can be presented through "expert evidence" by the parties or can be appointed by the arbitral tribunals as such. Either way experts have a significant role in international commercial arbitration and will continue to do so, if not dominate, in future. The fact remains that international commercial disputes are getting more and more complex, be they technological-, financial-, accounting- or construction-related. Added to these are the financial stakes involved. Disputes involving large public projects may also affect lives of millions and involving environmental and human rights issues. Arbitral tribunals will have to lean more and more on experts in times to come.

But as was said in 1873:

> "Undoubtedly there is a natural bias to do something serviceable for those who employ you and adequately remunerate you. It is very natural, and it is so effectual that we constantly see persons, instead of considering themselves witnesses, rather consider themselves as the paid agents of the person who employs them."[2]

And repeated in 1994 by Macdonald J.:

> "If the person rendering the evidence assumes the role of advocate, he or she can no longer be viewed as an expert in the legally correct sense; instead, he or she must be viewed as advocating the case of a party with the attendant diminishment in the credibility of the report. Expert opinions guide the court but they do not determine the matters which are to be determined by the court."[3]

In *Government v. The Century Spinning and Manufacturing Co., Ltd.*, AIR 1942 Bombay 105, it was observed by John Beaumont, Kt., CJ, and Sen, J.:

> "The evidence of expert witnesses is generally of assistance to the court, but it has also its limitations. I think it is well known that in all these cases of valuation too much is often claimed and too little is offered as between the opposing parties. As the Privy Council pointed out in the same case which I have referred to before. 'Every expert witnesses has his own set of conjectures of more or less weight according to his experienced and personal sagacity with the result that the enquiry abounds with uncertainty and give[s] more than ordinary room for guess work.' Further, the expert witness sometimes begins with a predetermined conclusion.

---

2. *Lord Arbinger v. Ashton*, (1873) 17 LR Eq 358 at 374.
3. *Perricone v. Baldassarra*, [1994] O.J. No. 2199.

It is to my mind reversing the ordinary logical process of reasoning to let the conclusion justify the premises rather than let the premises justify the conclusion."

Experts have earned the infamous title of being 'Advocates'. One of the best summations of the Duties and Responsibilities of expert witnesses is to be found in the words of Justice Cresswell in the "*Ikarian Reefer*" case as follows:[4]

> "1. Expert evidence presented to the Court should be, and should be seen to be, the independent product of the expert uninfluenced as to form or content by the exigencies of litigation (*Whitehouse v. Jordan*, [1981] 1 W.L.R. 246 at p. 256, per Lord Wilberforce).
> 2. An expert witness should provide independent assistance to the Court by way of objective unbiased opinion in relation to matters within his expertise (see *Polivitte Ltd. v. Commercial Union Assurance Co. Plc.*, [1987] 1 Lloyd's Rep. 379 at p. 386 per Mr. Justice Garland and Re J, [1990] F.C.R. 193, per Mr. Justice Cazalet). An expert witness in the High Court should never assume the role of an advocate.
> 3. An expert witness should state the facts or assumptions upon which his opinion is based. He should not omit to consider material facts which could detract from his concluded opinion (Re J sup.).
> 4. An expert witness should make it clear when a particular question or issue falls outside his expertise.
> 5. If an expert's opinion is not properly researched because he considers that insufficient data is available, then this must be state[d] with an indication that the opinion is no more than a provisional one (Re J sup.). In cases where an expert witness who has prepared a report could not assert that the report contained the truth, the whole truth and nothing but the truth without some qualification, that qualification should be stated in the report (*Derby & Co. Ltd. and Others v. Weldon and Others*, The Times, November 9, 1990 per Lord Justice Staughton).
> 6. If, after exchange of reports, an expert witness changes his view on a material matter having read the other side's expert report or for any other reason, such change of view should be communicated (through legal representatives) to the other side without delay and when appropriate to the Court.
> 7. Where expert evidence refers to photographs, plans, calculations, analysis, measurements, survey reports or other similar documents, these must be provided to the opposite party at the same time as the exchange of reports (see 15.5 of the Guide to Commercial Court Practice)."

This must apply with equal force to arbitration.

Even in the face of well-defined rules of international institutions as well as the IBA Rules on the Taking of Evidence in International Arbitration, the experts, as noted in the leading textbooks and the personal experience of most practitioners, are more advocates and less neutrals. A respected arbitral tribunal comprised of Böckstiegel, Noori and

---

4. *National Justice Compania S.A. v. Prudential Assurance Co. Ltd.*, [1993] 2 Lloyds Rep. 68.

Holtzmann in *Rockwell*[5] critically examined the evidence of an expert before it and observed:

> "The Ministry has requested that an expert be appointed to evaluate Rockwell's alleged performance under the Contracts, in particular to assess the scope of the work done and whether it conforms with the contractual requirements. In the Tribunal's view, the question whether to appoint an expert need only be reached in a case where the party requesting the appointment has sufficiently substantiated its claims or defense. It is not the task of an expert appointed by the Tribunal to argue a party's case."

Undoubtedly the role of an expert is twofold: first, to advance the case of the party calling him, so far as it can properly be advanced on the basis of information available to the expert in the professional exercise of his skill and experience; and, second, to assist the court or the tribunal, which does not possess the relevant skill and experience, in determining where the truth lies. How best to balance these two is a challenge faced by every arbitrator and every practitioner. But can these two at all be balanced? And if yes, then how to go about doing the same is the subject of today's discussion.

Experts must be led and shown as neutrals in examination in chief but should be exposed as advocates in cross-examination.

II. EXPERT WITNESS MUST BE LED AND SHOWN AS NEUTRAL IN EXAMINATION-IN-CHIEF

More often than not parties lead expert evidence through affidavits. Tribunals mostly encourage this manner of submission of evidence by parties. It is quite common to find that such evidence is either prepared by or under direct supervision of parties' lawyers. It therefore loses its purpose, significance and most of all credibility. It is not uncommon to find expert witnesses signing their statement that has been prepared by lawyers on dotted lines as evidenced by the following story:

> "In a domestic arbitration involving substantial disputes of financial implication between the Acquirer of Government shares in Fertilizer Company through disinvestment process and Government of India, expert evidence was led on behalf of Government of India in the form of an affidavit evidence of a Chartered Accountant. His cross examination revealed how mechanically he had given the evidence.
>
> Q21. Do you recall when you were first approached by Ms. X?
> A.   For this matter one Mr. Y, first approached me and then Ms. X had a discussion with me when she handed over these papers to me. That was in Nov. 2006.
> Q22. From your memory do you remember that name of the Notary before whom you affirmed the affidavit?

---

5. *Rockwell International Systems Inc. v. Iran,* 23, Iran-US CTR (1989), 150.

A. I don't remember.
Q23. Where was the affidavit affirmed?
A. That was in Noida."

The affidavit was actually affirmed in New Delhi, thus disclosing how casually the affidavit-in-chief was prepared by lawyers and signed by the expert who did not even remember where he had affirmed the affidavit.

Justice Laddie in *Cala Homes (South) Ltd. v. Alfred McAlpine Homes East Ltd.*[6] exposed the pitfalls of this approach when he said:

> "The whole basis of Mr. Goodall's approach to the drafting of an expert's report is wrong. The function of a court of law is to discover the truth relating to the issues before it.... That some witnesses of fact, driven by a desire to achieve a particular outcome to the litigation, feel it necessary to sacrifice the truth in pursuit of victory is a fact of life.
>
> The court tries to discover it when it happens. But in case of an expert witness the court is likely to lower its guard. Of course the court will be aware that a party is likely to choose its expert someone whose view is most sympathetic to its position. Subject to that caveat, the court is likely to assume that the expert witness is more interested in being honest and right that in ensuring that one side or another wins.
>
> An expert should not consider that it is his job to stand shoulder-to-shoulder through thick and thin with the side which is paying his bill. 'Pragmatic flexibility' as used by Mr. Goodall is a euphemism for 'misleading selectivity'. According to this approach the flexibility will give place to something closer to the true and balanced view of the expert only when he is being cross-examined and is faced with the possibility of being 'found out'.
>
> The reality, of course, will be somewhat different. An expert who has committed himself in writing to a report which is selectively misleading may feel obliged to stick to the views he expressed there when he is being cross-examined. Most witnesses would not be prepared to admit he was approaching the drafting of his report as a partisan hired gun. The result is that expert's report and then his oral evidence will be contaminated by this attempted sleight of mind. This deprives the evidence much of its value. I would like to think that in most cases cross-examination exposes the bias. Where there is no cross-examination, the court is clearly at much risk of being misled.
>
> In view of the above, it is relevant to remind those concerned with the preparation of expert's report of some of what Cresswell J. said in The '*Ikarian Reefer*'....
>
> In the light of the matters set out above, during the preparation of this judgment I re-read Mr. Goodall's report on the understanding that it was drafted as a partisan act with the objective of selling the defendant's case to the court and ignoring virtually everything which could harm that objective. I did not find it of significant assistance in deciding the issues."

---

6. (1996) C.I.L.L. 1083.

The simple solution therefore lies in leading the expert evidence as examination-in-chief before the tribunal rather than through affidavit evidence. Even though the party, its lawyers and the expert may have discussed the disputes as well as their viewpoints in relation thereto, the evidence led orally will look natural, convincing and inspiring in confidence. The tribunal will have the advantage of observing the demeanor of the witness. This offers a real opportunity to the lawyers for the parties leading evidence to demonstrate skills in advocacy in eliciting from the expert, first and foremost, the facts upon which his opinion is to be based and then leading to the opinion itself. It is a poor advocacy to leave the other side to elicit facts through cross-examination which may change the very basis of the opinion.

First and foremost, lawyers advising parties in an arbitration requiring expert evidence must be sure that such evidence, if honestly tendered, will support the case of the party they represent. It would be suicidal to tender an expert witness knowing full well that such a witness is being asked to depose contrary to honest and objective opinion that he or she may harbor. In such a situation it is better to leave out the expert witness and allow the other party or perhaps the tribunal to bring in the expert and then hope to shake him or her through cross- examination. But once the decision is taken to lead expert evidence the lawyer must first help the party in identifying the right witness and then acquaint him with full facts and evidence on record to the extent it is relevant to enable him to form solid, inspiring and objective opinion. He should be briefed but not tutored. It is my experience, that in-depth discussion by lawyers fully acquainted with facts and issues in presence of parties and even technical personnel goes a long way in apprising the expert fully while eliciting from him his views at the pre-evidence stage. Failure to do so will result in what happened in the award of *Arbitral Chamber for Fresh Fruits and Early Products* in a dispute between a French seller and a Dutch buyer:[7] The dispute was that the potatoes sold by French seller were for industrial use which fact was not disclosed to the expert who deposed that the goods were unfit to be packed in bags and for immediate consumption therefore forcing the Tribunal to reject his opinion straight away.

Once that is done the next task is how best to introduce the expert witness to the tribunal. He must be put to ease throughout examination. He must therefore be taken extensively through the journey as to his qualification, experience and credentials. Thereafter he should be slowly walked through facts and lastly left to form and express his opinion as an expert in his own words for the tribunal to hear for itself. The questioning-in-chief must be simple and uncomplicated. Technical issues admixtured with facts and legal technicalities once discerned from the larger controversy must be separated from "technical facts in issue" so as to allow the expert to address the latter.

Such an expert witness or his examination-in-chief will usually stand the scrutiny of cross-examination. It is also many a times necessary to ask the expert witness, in chief, inconvenient questions and elicit simple and convincing answers rather than leave them in cross where the chances are that the witness might falter.

---

7. *Arbitral Chamber for Fresh Fruits and Early Products (EEC)*, ICCA *Yearbook Commercial Arbitration* VIII (1983) p. 118.

III. EXPERT WITNESS ATTACKED AS ADVOCATE IN CROSS-EXAMINATION

Cross-examination by each party, whether or not it succeeds, contributes substantially to a proper decision. The value of destroying an opponent's evidence is immense, but cross-examination may sometimes even enhance the credibility of the evidence in the eyes of the tribunal. It is strategically wiser to refrain from cross-examination than to do it badly. Lawyers must therefore weigh the pros and cons of cross-examination of the expert witness and once the decision is taken to cross-examine, lawyers must be sure on what particular aspects in examination-in-chief questions must be directed to.

Is it possible to shake the very credibility of the expert's qualifications, experience and credentials? If yes, it must be done in a subtle and respectful manner. Is it possible to shake the witness on relevant facts? If yes, then the witness should be put short, quick and numerous questions allowing him to either fain ignorance on vital facts and/or contradict himself. But it must always be remembered that this journey must be as short as necessary and no further.

Once done on facts the witnesses must be confronted on his opinion. The best way to proceed is to allow him to admit that more than one opinion or interpretation is possible on the same set of facts or even on different facts. It is ill-advised to attack the expert through direct question on opinion which he is positively likely to reaffirm. Remember that before going to any form of destructive cross-examination, it would be better for the defendant's advocates to conduct cross-examination constructively by emphasizing favorable facts which could assist his case. At this stage the expert is cooperative and will be willing to speak freely, being unguarded.

In one international commercial arbitration while cross-examining an expert witness of the other party in respect of a contract which mandated a performance test upon commissioning of a large industrial plant, I confronted the expert with the following questions and his answers supported what was the case of the party I represented, namely, the performance test was not done because it involved costs:

> "Q. Would you say that various projects and plants with which you were associated based on CFB Technology between 1981 to 1999 were successfully commissioned?
> A. At the end, all the plans were commissioned successfully. But initially few started problems which had to be solved. The plants in two places have still not been commissioned.
> Q. In cases where plants were commissioned, were performance tests also conducted?
> A. Not in all the cases. Whether a performance/acceptance tests is conducted is the decision of the operator/utility. Since the performance/acceptance test is relatively expensive, sometimes the performance/acceptance test is avoided. In most of the cases, however, a performance/acceptance test has been conducted.
> Q. Is it correct that before giving your opinion in respect of the present disputed boilers, you did not visit the site and inspect the boilers at any stage?
> A. It is correct that I have not visited the site. In the case of the present dispute, which is mainly concerned with the design and operation of the boilers, the documents provided were detailed enough to make an evaluation."

Earlier the same witness contradicted his own evidence to the point of losing credibility, as follows:

> "Q. Could you turn to paragraph 3.2.d of your affidavit. Read the last two lines at the end of the page 'relating to ... fuel'. Would it not have been appropriate for any manufacturer/supplier to simply request new fuel for conducting a performance test if the fuel being used was not appropriate?
> A   The fuel for the performance test has been clearly specified in the contract, that is lignite. (Question repeated). Yes. For the performance test, the manufacturer would have demanded the correct fuel.
> Q.   Are you aware on the basis of the review of the documents that as late as April and May of 2000, company A and company B had jointly agreed that performance test will be conducted in respect of the three boilers first on coal and then on lignite?
> A.   No. Performance test with coal makes no sense. Because most of the guarantee values are not applicable for coal."

In the same arbitration another expert witness during my cross-examination undermined his own independence and objectivity, as follows:

> "Q. Before preparing this report along with Mr. X, did you not feel it appropriate to visit the boiler site in question?
> A.   The company A which had entrusted us with this task had not asked us to visit the site.
> Q.   Have you been associated in the past with Group A in any capacity?
> A.   No. This is my first job with Group A. Mr. X had worked with Group A earlier.
> Q.   In the team of yourself and Mr. X, was Mr. X a senior person in terms of qualification, experience etc.?
> A.   I know Mr. X from college days. We had studied together. We had started working independently in 1994, each one of us for himself. We have done many jobs together.
> Q.   Did Mr. X contact you for this job also?
> A.   Yes. It was his idea to include me."

In yet another international commercial arbitration my cross-examination revealed how poorly the expert was supplied and acquainted with relevant documents and had instead based his opinion on documents selectively supplied by the claimant.

> "Q. Would you kindly turn to paragraph 8 of your affidavit. Would it be correct therefore to assume that you did not seek any other document other than what Claimant had provided you, Sir?
> A.   I was provided with all documentation that the claimant had, which obviously included exchanges of correspondence from the respondent and the Claimant.

Q. No, Sir, my question is different. Did you seek any document other than what Claimant had provided you?
A. Sorry, I apologize. Obviously, during the course of my enquiry, I examined further supporting information in relation to manuals and other information that has been referred to in the statement of claimant's witness No. 1, because there was further information that was provided that I think wasn't in the original claim submission.
Q. No, other than claimant's witness No. 1's satisfaction or claimants satisfaction, my question, Sir, to you is did you seek any other document or other information to satisfy your own self other than what was provided?
A. The answer to that, I think is no."

Cross-examination, if conducted skillfully, can expose experts projecting themselves to be neutrals as advocates. The judicial criticisms emanating from courts and tribunals for over a hundred years are well founded.

IV. WHAT THEN IS THE SOLUTION?

One of the methods suggested and now successfully implemented is to have joint meetings between experts of both parties allowing them to agree on as many issues of dispute as possible, narrowing down the points in controversy. This method also has its advantage because most important facts on which respective opinions are based will also stand agreed upon if not admitted. The cross-examination then stands limited as to the points of difference and thus reduces time and costs. This method also allows the arbitral tribunals to have better and clearer understanding as to points in controversy and particularly as to technical aspects.

But perhaps an even stronger approach may be appointment of experts by arbitral tribunals. This method is now agreed upon in most international instruments like the UNCITRAL Model Law and is also provided in many domestic laws (for example, the English Arbitration Act 1996) and even the rules of arbitral institutions like the Arbitration Rules of the LCIA (London Court of International Arbitration), the Rules of the International Chamber of Commerce, American Arbitration Association, Singapore International Arbitration Centre and the Hong Kong International Arbitration Centre Administered Arbitration Rules. The Chartered Institute of Arbitrators has in fact framed exhaustive rules in this regard which throw substantial light on the manner and method of this technique. International Bar Association's Rules on the Taking of Evidence in International Arbitration also deal with this aspect quite clearly.

So strong is the acceptability of this approach that the US Court of Appeal, 11th Circuit, in its 1998 decision *Industrial Risk Insurers v. MAN Gutehoffnungshütte GmbH*[8] even upheld an award based on evidence of an expert who was initially retained by the appellant party, then dropped but was called by the Arbitral Panel to testify "sua sponte". The court rejected the argument of "side-switching" and even held that the same did not

---

8. 141 F.3d 1434 (11th Cir.1998).

violate any of the provisions of the 1958 New York Convention to enforce such an award.

True, this method is attacked on the ground that it may amount to delegation of decision-making powers by arbitrators to a third party. There is a fine line between blindly depending and receiving evidence from an expert. The established authority suggests:

(a) The arbitrators are bound to act judicially and cannot delegate the ultimate award to an expert.
(b) The arbitrators are free to accept the advice obtained from the expert and the weight to be given to that advice.
(c) In case of a conflict amongst experts, the arbitrators must make a factual finding as to which evidence they prefer.
(d) Any advice given by an expert must be disclosed to the parties and they must be offered reasonable opportunity to contest it and if necessary lead their own expert evidence.
(e) Arbitrators can seek expert advice on the form but not the content of the award.

V. CONCLUSIONS

To conclude experts – neutrals or advocates – have a firm place in international commercial arbitration in the modern world. Whether they remain neutrals or advocates depends on the parties and the lawyers representing them. Experts' usefulness to tribunals being immense, tribunals will increasingly exercise their powers to appoint their own experts.

But then there can always be a situation like the one in the following story of John Hutton Balfour-Browne, King's Counsel,

> "I remember in the inquiry into the Regent's Canal Railway Bill I was 'put up' to be impertinent by Mr. James Staats Forbes, who had a 'spice of the devil' in him. Sir Fredrick Bramwell ('Hogshed' Bramwell) was the witness and, as I have said before, he was a most admirable witness. But although he was excellent as a witness he had done very little as a constructive engineer. Afterwards, no doubt, he and his partner, Mr. Harris, were engineers for some important Power Bills, and for one sewage scheme, at least; but Bramwell's real forte was evidence. He was very often an Umpire in arbitrations, especially in arbitrations under Section 43 of the Tramways Act. Upon the occasion in question Mr. Forbes suggested that I should ask him what works he had designed or constructed, and being young I acted upon his somewhat cruel suggestion.
>
> 'We all know', I said, 'your eminence as a witness, but would you tell me what you have done as an engineer? What works have you designed or constructed?'
> 'Not very much,' he answered.
> 'Can I help you? You designed a floating dock for Bermuda, did you not?'
> He assented with a 'Yes' which sounded like a grunt.
> 'And it would not float?'

Again he grunted.
'And you also designed, if I am not mistaken, the Caterham Lunatic Asylum?'
But, as I say, it was Mr. Forbes' doing."[9]

---

9. Michael GILBERT, ed., *The Oxford Book of Legal Anecdotes* (Oxford University Press 1989).

Discoverability of Communications Between Counsel and Party-Appointed Experts in International Arbitration

Paul Friedland* and Kate Brown de Vejar**

TABLE OF CONTENTS	Page
I. Introduction	160
II. The Prevailing Practice in International Arbitration	161
III. Comment on the Rationale for Discoverability of Counsel-Expert Communications in International Arbitration	170
IV. Conclusion	177

I. INTRODUCTION

It is common for parties in international arbitration to engage and present experts to testify on technical matters, industry custom and legal issues.[1] It is also common and generally accepted that a party's counsel will work closely with a party-appointed expert, discussing substantive points of an expert's opinion, and providing comments on drafts of an expert's report, at least as to format, language and style.[2]

---

* Partner, White & Case LLP (New York). The authors thank Damien Nyer (Associate, White & Case LLP, New York) for his invaluable assistance.

** Counsel, Curtis, Mallet-Prevost, Colt & Mosle, S.C. (Mexico City). (Associate in the White & Case LLP International Arbitration Group (New York), 2005-2009).

1. This practice is a departure from the usual civil law approach where courts appoint their own experts to provide objective, technical guidance. Giorgio BERNINI, "The Civil Law Approach to Discovery: A Comparative Overview of the Taking of Evidence in the Anglo-American and Continental Arbitration Systems" in Lawrence W. NEWMAN and Richard D. HILL, eds., *The Leading Arbitrators' Guide to International Arbitration* (2008) p. 265 at p. 286 fn. 42. In France, for example, the judge typically appoints an *expert judiciaire*. See French Code of Civil Procedure, Arts. 232-248, 264-272. See also Brazilian Code of Civil Procedure, Arts. 420-439.

2. Rachel KENT, "Expert Witnesses in Arbitration and Litigation Proceedings", 4 Transnat'l Dispute Mgmt. (2007, no. 3) at p. 4, available at <www.transnational-dispute-management.com/>. See also Christopher NEWMARK, "Expert Evidence" in Lawrence W. NEWMAN and Grant HANESSIAN, eds., *International Arbitration Checklists* (2004) p. 107 at pp. 119-120 ("However, it is inevitable in complex cases that there will be discussion between experts and lawyers as to the form and content of an expert's report and it is entirely appropriate for lawyers and their clients to suggest changes, additions and rephrasing of a draft report, *provided* that the expert only adopts those proposals with which he agrees and provided that the final report remains one which expresses his own opinion." (Emphasis in original.)); George RUTTINGER and Joe MEADOWS, "Using Experts in Arbitration", 62 Disp. Resol. J. (2007) p. 46 at p. 49 ("If necessary, counsel should participate in drafting expert reports to make them persuasive and less subject to attack on cross-examination."); Dana H. FREYER, "Assessing Expert Evidence" in L.W. NEWMAN and R.D. HILL, eds., *The Leading Arbitrators' Guide to International Arbitration*, op. cit., fn. 1, p. 429 at

Cautious counsel in international arbitration wonder whether their written communications with an expert, including drafts and markups of the expert's report, may be subject to production to the other side and to the arbitrators. To answer this question, we reviewed the disclosure practice in numerous unreported cases and we submitted questions to a broad range of international arbitration practitioners and arbitrators from varying legal backgrounds and regions.[3] We also reviewed written authority on the issue. In this article, we seek to distill these sources into a summary of the prevailing practice and to offer guidance to practitioners. We also examine the trend that has led some common law jurisdictions to permit more extensive discovery of counsel-expert communications in the context of domestic litigation, and consider whether such an approach is desirable in international arbitration. We conclude that it is not.

II. THE PREVAILING PRACTICE IN INTERNATIONAL ARBITRATION

1. The Presumption of Non-Discoverability of Counsel-Expert Communications

Formal international guidelines on the discoverability of counsel-expert communications are rare.[4] National rules applicable to national court proceedings, where they exist,[5] vary

---

p. 431 ("expert testimony and reports may be the result of extensive collaboration").

3. In addition to surveying the collective experience of the White & Case International Arbitration Group, the authors contacted eighteen of the most prominent international arbitrators with extensive experience of international cases (both commercial and investment): eight in Continental Europe, two in Canada, four in the United States, two in the United Kingdom, one in Latin America and one in Asia.

4. The issue is not dealt with in any of the rules of major arbitral institutions. For instance, Art. 20 of the Rules of Arbitration of the International Chamber of Commerce (the ICC) refers only to the tribunal's authority to "establish the facts of the case by all appropriate means", and to "summon any party to provide additional evidence"; Art. 22(1)(e) of the Rules of the LCIA (London Court of International Arbitration) merely authorizes the arbitral tribunal to "order any party to produce to the Arbitral Tribunal, and to the other Parties for inspection ... any documents or classes of documents ... which the Arbitral Tribunal determines to be relevant"; Art. 19 of the International Arbitration Rules of the American Arbitration Association (the AAA) empowers the arbitral tribunal to "order parties to produce other documents, exhibits or other evidence it deems necessary or appropriate". Neither the 1999 Rules on the Taking of Evidence in International Commercial Arbitration of the International Bar Association (IBA) nor the UNCITRAL Notes on Organizing Arbitral Proceedings provide guidance on the subject. Only the Chartered Institute of Arbitrators has addressed the issue, with the 2007 publication of its Protocol for the Use of Party-Appointed Expert Witnesses in International Arbitration (the CIArb Protocol). For a commentary on the CIArb Protocol, see generally Doug JONES, "Party Appointed Expert Witness in International Arbitration: A Protocol at Last", 24 Arb. Int'l (2008, no. 1) p. 137 at pp. 152-153. We examine the approach adopted in the CIArb Protocol below, II.*2.b.*

5. In civil law countries, experts are ordinarily appointed by the court and pre-trial document disclosure is minimal or non-existent. See G. BERNINI, "The Civil Law Approach to Discovery: A Comparative Overview of the Taking of Evidence in the Anglo-American and Continental Arbitration Systems", *op. cit.*, fn. 1, pp. 273-274 and p. 286 fn. 42.

161

widely and are, in any case, inapposite to international arbitration.[6] Our experience and our survey nonetheless show shared expectations about the discoverability of counsel-expert communications in international arbitration. An overall presumption of non-discoverability, with certain common exceptions, can be discerned.[7] Production of documents reflecting such communications is rarely sought – almost all of the arbitrators questioned on the subject replied that they had *never* faced the question – and the overwhelming view among experienced international arbitrators is that, in the ordinary situation, production would not be warranted.[8] This view is shared by both civil law and common law arbitrators and, among the latter group, even by arbitrators from jurisdictions where mandatory production of counsel-expert communications is the rule in domestic litigation.[9]

Commentators support the view that, regardless of the rules applicable to domestic litigation, the practice in international arbitration is not to require disclosure of counsel-

---

6. The separateness of international arbitration from the evidentiary/procedural regime governing national court litigation is reflected in the laws of major arbitral jurisdictions. In the United States, it is well established that arbitrators are not constrained by formal rules of procedure or evidence. See, e.g., *Bernhardt v. Polygraphic Co. of America, Inc.*, 350 U.S. 198, 203 n. 4 (1956) (where the Supreme Court noted that "[a]rbitrators are not bound by the rules of evidence"). In England, the Arbitration Act 1996 confers a wide discretion on the arbitral tribunal to decide issues of procedure and evidence. Sect. 34 thus provides that "[i]t shall be for the tribunal to decide all procedural and evidential matters, subject to the right of the parties to agree any matter" and defines "procedural and evidential matters" as including "whether to apply strict rules of evidence (or any other rules)...". In Hong Kong, a tribunal may not order disclosure of documents privileged under Hong Kong law. Hong Kong Arbitration Ordinance, Chapter 341, Sect. 2GB(8). See also Art. 19(2) of the UNCITRAL Model Law, which provides in relevant part that "the arbitral tribunal may, subject to the provisions of this Law, conduct the arbitration in such manner as it considers appropriate. The power conferred upon the arbitral tribunal includes the power to determine the admissibility, relevance, materiality and weight of any evidence". Although issues of evidentiary privilege may, at their limit, touch on public policy concerns, questions as to which documents are subject to mandatory production and which are privileged have generally (and properly) been considered to fall within the arbitrators' overall procedural discretion. See Henri ALVAREZ, "Evidentiary Privileges in International Arbitration" in *International Arbitration 2006: Back to Basics?*, ICCA Congress Series no. 13 (hereinafter *ICCA Congress Series no. 13*) (2007) p. 662 at pp. 674-675 (noting the "increasing recognition that rules of privilege are more than merely procedural in nature and, in fact, are substantive rules which reflect public policy".). See generally infra, fn. 14.
7. As Craig, Park and Paulsson explain, a result of the often cosmopolitan makeup of international arbitral tribunals is that "procedural questions arising in the arbitration are resolved pragmatically rather than dogmatically". Hence, "[t]he prevailing rule is that of professional common sense, and good sense in this context tends to reflect an amalgam of three jurists' legal culture". W. Laurence CRAIG, William W. PARK and Jan PAULSSON, *International Chamber of Commerce Arbitration*, Sect. 23.04 (2000).
8. Of the eighteen international arbitrators – all with extensive experience – polled by the authors, only one expressed a willingness, "in the right circumstances", to order disclosure of drafts and counsel-expert communications. (Confidential communication on file with the authors.)
9. None of the four very experienced US-based international arbitrators polled by the authors considered that disclosure of counsel-expert communications was appropriate in the general case, and this even though such disclosure is available in domestic litigation in the United States. See below Sect. III.*1.a*.

expert communications.[10] Christopher Newmark explains: "In most international arbitration scenarios, communications between the party and the expert will be treated as privileged, and disclosure of those communications (including any draft expert reports) will not be required."[11]

On this basis, Dana Freyer advises that "[b]ecause communications between a party and its expert remain undisclosed, expert testimony and reports may be the result of extensive collaboration".[12]

The Chartered Institute of Arbitrators' 2007 Protocol for the Use of Party-Appointed Expert Witnesses in International Arbitration (the CIArb Protocol) offers additional support for this view. By providing for a limited waiver of privilege in respect of "instructions to, and any terms of appointment of, an expert" (a topic explored further below), Art. 5 of the CIArb Protocol presumes that counsel-expert communications as a general matter are privileged and therefore not subject to production. The CIArb Protocol also confirms the consensus that drafts and other expert work product are not discoverable. Art. 5(2) reads: "Drafts, working papers or any other documentation created by an expert for the purpose of providing expert evidence in the Arbitration shall be privileged from production and shall not be discloseable in the Arbitration."

It is doubtful that the apparent consensus about the non-discoverability of counsel-expert communications in international arbitration reflects a shared understanding among arbitration practitioners of the rules governing evidentiary privileges.[13] Given the diversity of rules (if any) governing document production, privilege and waiver of such privilege across different jurisdictions, a consensus about privilege cannot be identified[14]

---

10. R. KENT, "Expert Witnesses in Arbitration and Litigation Proceedings", *op. cit.*, fn. 2, at p. 2 ("By contrast, in international arbitration proceedings, expert witnesses are subject to far less discovery, and will rarely, if ever, be asked about their conversations with counsel."); G. RUTTINGER and J. MEADOWS, "Using Experts in Arbitration", *op. cit.*, fn. 2, p. 49 ("Since counsel's thoughts, impressions, and work product can be exchanged with experts without having to be produced to the adversary, counsel should take an active role when it comes to drafting expert reports and preparing experts for depositions or the actual hearing."); Javier H. RUBINSTEIN, "International Commercial Arbitration: Reflections at the Crossroads of the Common Law and Civil Law Traditions", 5 Chi. J. Int'l L. (2004) p. 303 at p. 307 ("The obvious concern arises, however, as to whether such communications between counsel and witness would be subject to disclosure.... [I]it is doubtful that many arbitral tribunals would be willing to permit such questioning [about counsel-witness communications].").
11. C. NEWMARK, "Expert Evidence", *op. cit.*, fn. 2, at p. 117.
12. D.H. FREYER, "Assessing Expert Evidence", *op. cit.*, fn. 2, p. 431. With respect to counsel-witness communications more generally, see J.H. RUBINSTEIN, "International Commercial Arbitration: Reflections at the Crossroads of the Common Law and Civil Law Traditions", *op. cit.*, fn. 10, p. 307.
13. Cf. C. NEWMARK, "Expert Evidence", *op. cit.*, fn. 2, p. 117 ("In most international arbitration scenarios, communications between the party and the expert will be treated as privileged....").
14. See generally H.C. ALVAREZ, "Evidentiary Privileges in International Arbitration", *op. cit.*, fn. 6; J.H. RUBINSTEIN, "International Commercial Arbitration: Reflections at the Crossroads of the Common Law and Civil Law Traditions", *op. cit.*, fn. 10, p. 306 ("There are no established rules to govern the nature or scope of the attorney-client privilege in international arbitration."); *Ibid.* at 307 ("There is thus a great deal of uncertainty over what sorts of communications between an attorney and a client are immune from discovery in international arbitrations – uncertainty

and a consensus therefore cannot be the explanation. Rather, the consensus is better understood as reflecting the broad view that, as a general matter, the production of counsel-expert communications and drafts is not ordered because these documents are not considered sufficiently relevant – let alone material – to the outcome of the case.[15] This view of what matters in a case must explain why arbitrators from legal cultures with widely diverging approaches to evidentiary privileges are in agreement about the non-discoverability of counsel-expert communications in the ordinary course.[16]

While counsel-expert communications may be relevant to a case to the extent that they assist in evaluating the credibility and independence of an expert, it would be highly unusual for an arbitral tribunal to grant production of communications between counsel and expert on the mere chance that some such communications might shed light upon the expert's independence. Rather, a production request of this nature would and should demonstrate that a certain communication exists and that there is a particular reason to conclude that it would be relevant and material to the arbitrators' determination of the case. This brings us to the following topic: the exceptions to the general prohibition against disclosure of counsel-expert communications.

2. *The Potential Exceptions*

Three potential exceptions to the non-discoverability of counsel-expert communications can be discerned. The first potential exception relates to materials relied upon, referenced by or reviewed by an expert; the second to communications between counsel and expert regarding the scope of an expert's engagement; and the third to cases of abuse.

a. Counsel-expert communications relied upon, referenced by or reviewed by an expert

There are three categories of documents which can be said to be used by an expert: documents *relied upon* by an expert in forming his or her opinions; documents *referenced* by an expert in his or her report; and documents *reviewed* by an expert, although not

---

further compounded by the absence of any established choice-of-law rules to determine which law will govern the existence and scope of the privilege, and the extent to which the privilege can be waived."); C. NEWMARK, "Expert Evidence", *op. cit.*, fn. 2, at p. 112 ("In England for example, the Civil Procedure Rules contain extensive provisions governing the circumstances in which expert evidence will be allowed.... This entire framework is missing from the world of international arbitration.").

15. This is the standard required for an order for production of documents under the IBA Rules on the Taking of Evidence in International Commercial Arbitration 1999, Art. 3(3)(b). See also Bernard HANOTIAU, "Document Production in International Arbitration: A Tentative Definition of 'Best Practices'" in *Document Production in International Arbitration*, ICC International Court of Arbitration Bulletin Special Supplement (2006) p. 113 at p. 116 ("Relevance and materiality are two related criteria which the arbitral tribunal will use when deciding whether or not to grant a document production request.").

16. To cite but one example among many, a prominent Swiss arbitrator has explained that, in the one case where he faced the issue, the request for production of counsel-expert communications was rejected, irrespective of any privilege, because the requesting party could not establish the relevance of the communications. (Confidential communication on file with the authors.)

necessarily relied upon or referenced. The first two categories (which in practice overlap to a significant extent) are considered together below. The third category – documents *reviewed* by an expert – is, plainly, the broadest of the three. We conclude that the first two categories are subject to production, and that documents in the third category usually are not.

i. Documents relied upon or referenced by an expert

A competent expert will usually attach as exhibits to the report all documents relied upon in forming his or her opinions. This practice is based on the principle of equality of arms, which requires that the opposing party be given an opportunity to review the same documents as the other party's expert. It is also necessary to permit an arbitral tribunal to evaluate properly the opinions and credibility of an expert.

The survey of practitioners and arbitrators shows a broad consensus among arbitration practitioners that counsel-expert communications, which would ordinarily benefit from a presumption against disclosure, become subject to production once relied upon by an expert, and in particular when referenced by an expert in his or her report.[17]

The authors' recent experience is consistent with this consensus. In a New York-based International Chamber of Commerce (ICC) arbitration in 2008, a party sought production of drafts of an expert report which had been shown to a second expert engaged by the same party. The document was inadvertently included in a list of documents attached to the second expert's report. The arbitral tribunal, comprised of three US-trained attorneys, ordered production of the drafts, with no discussion of what law governed the question of privilege and whether the draft was ever in fact privileged.

In a 2009 ICC arbitration in Stockholm, a party had produced an expert report that referenced certain preliminary opinion reports which the expert had prepared during the parties' negotiations, before the filing of the request for arbitration. When the opposing party requested production of these preliminary reports, the party proffering the expert report argued that these documents were privileged because they were mere drafts of the expert's final opinion, and because they were created in contemplation of litigation. The tribunal, composed of civil law lawyers, ordered production of the preliminary reports. The tribunal buttressed its decision by noting that the party resisting production had indicated a willingness to produce the document before the initiation of the arbitration.

These two examples demonstrate a clear principle: documents included in the list of materials relied upon by an expert are discoverable. This exception to the principle of non-discoverability of counsel-expert communications also has its basis in the relevance-and-materiality test for production of documents. That is, documents that would ordinarily not be relevant and material to the outcome of the case become so when an expert references them as bases for the opinions in his or her report.

In the first of the two cases described, the absence of any discussion as to whether the draft reports in question were subject to any attorney work-product privilege indicates that, in the view of the tribunal, applicable privileges (if any) were waived or overridden by the expert's reference to the document. Similarly, in the second example, the tribunal

---

17. None of the eighteen arbitrators surveyed questioned the applicability of this exception.

appears to have been of the view that the claimed litigation privilege attaching to the expert's preliminary reports was waived or overridden by the fact that the expert had referenced those documents in the final report. This suggests that the obligation to produce documents referenced by an expert would apply equally to documents prepared by counsel in contemplation of litigation and potentially covered by the attorney work-product doctrine. On this basis, if counsel provides an expert with notes of an interview with a key witness and these constitute part of the referenced factual underpinning for that expert's report, there is little doubt that the notes would be considered relevant and that that expert's reliance on them would suffice to waive any work-product protection, thus justifying disclosure.

A further question is whether the obligation to produce documents relied upon or referenced by an expert applies when such documents contain or reveal client confidences. Such documents might potentially be protected from disclosure by some form of attorney-client privilege or *secret professionnel*, a protection that is often regarded as more fundamental than that offered by the work-product doctrine,[18] and which can usually be waived only by the client. We see no blanket solution to this question; resolution of such a document production request would depend upon the circumstances. A tribunal faced with this issue would first need to understand properly the nature of the client information which would be revealed by production of the document (an in camera review of the document may assist). A tribunal may also need to consider the public policy implications of its ruling, and any applicable provisions of mandatory law. Given the strong consensus that documents relied upon or referenced by an expert should be produced, there is a reasonable prospect that an international arbitral tribunal would order production of such documents irrespective of any applicable attorney-client privilege or *secret professionnel* obligation.[19]

ii.   Documents reviewed by an expert

We now consider whether production can be expected not only of documents *relied upon* or *referenced* by an expert but also, more broadly, of all documents *reviewed* by an expert. The argument in favor of requiring production of this broader category of documents – including, potentially, counsel-expert communications – is that limiting disclosure to documents *relied upon* or *referenced* by an expert accords the expert too much discretion.

---

18. See, e.g., *Blank v. Canada (Minister of Justice)*, 2006 SCC 39, paras. 24-28. See also *Three Rivers District Council v. Governor and Co. of the Bank of England*, [2004] U.K.H.L. 48 (H.L.), para. 34.
19. The Hong Kong Court of First Instance explained the rationale for finding that reliance on a document by an expert waives privilege in that document:

   "Any material identified by the expert as having been considered by him in the formulation of his opinion must also be disclosed by him. It cannot be protected by a claim of legal professional privilege since the vehicle in which such an opinion has been expressed, has itself ceased to have that protection. It would of course constitute a nonsense if, a party seeking to adduce an expert's opinion, were to argue along the lines 'you have to admit and evaluate that opinion without being entitled to see all the material on which it is based'."

   Chan Mun Kui v. Lau Yuk Lai (1999) HCPI 301/98, para. 8.

An unscrupulous expert could always decide that he or she did not *rely* upon documents which, although relevant, upon review did not support his or her opinion.[20] At least one commentator argues that disclosure of all document reviewed by an expert is desirable in order to permit an arbitral tribunal to evaluate properly that expert's report.[21]

Experience shows that arbitral tribunals are reluctant, and rightly so, to order production of documents merely *reviewed* by an expert. For example, in a 2008 ICC arbitration in New York, the chairman, a US-trained lawyer, refused to grant a party's request for all documents *reviewed* by the other party's expert, even though such an order would have been consistent with the Federal Rules of Civil Procedure applicable to domestic US litigation.[22] Rather, the chairman ordered production only of those documents that the expert had *relied upon*. Such an approach is justified for two reasons. First, the concern that an expert may deliberately conceal damaging documents can be addressed by cross-examination: what materials an expert reviewed (or failed to review), or listed in the report (or failed to list in the report), often constitutes the first line of questioning at a hearing. An expert who pretends not to have reviewed documents *potentially* damaging to his party does so at peril to his or her credibility, and to the party's case as a whole. Second, if a party is able to show that certain documents were reviewed by an expert, but not referenced, and that such documents are relevant and material to the outcome of the case (i.e., that they go to the issues on which the expert was asked to opine), that party may be able to obtain production of such documents by requesting them *specifically*. A blanket request for all documents *reviewed* by, or *provided* to, an expert is overbroad and unlikely to be granted by an arbitral tribunal.

b.   *Counsel-expert communications regarding the scope of an expert's engagement*

A second potential exception to the presumption of non-discoverability of counsel-expert communications comprises those communications which have as their subject the scope of an expert's engagement, including directives received from counsel.

Expert reports can be difficult to understand, weigh and compare in the absence of information as to the scope of each expert's engagement, including the issues that an expert was asked to consider (or not).[23] There is an expectation that expert reports in

---

20. As explained below, for this reason, in the United States the Federal Rules of Civil Procedure require disclosure of "the data or other information *considered* by the witness in forming" his or her opinions. (Emphasis added.) See Sect. III.*1.a*.
21. John TACKABERRY, "Practical Considerations for Conducting the Hearing" in Rufus VON RHOADES, Daniel M. KOLKEY and Richard CHERNICK, eds., *Practitioner's Handbook on International Arbitration and Mediation* (2007) p. 155 at p. 182 ("An international panel, in all likelihood, would be unwilling to regard as privileged any of the documents reviewed by the expert (even though some might characterise those as communications between lawyer and witness) since the panel may not be able to evaluate the meaning of, and the weight to be given to the report, without sight of what the expert has relied upon.").
22. Fed.R.Civ.P. 26(a)(2).
23. For the same reasons, the Woolf Report in England ("Access to Justice: Final Report by the Right Honourable the Lord Woolf" (London: H.M. Stationery Office, 1996) available at <www.dca.gov.uk/civil/final/index.htm>) recommended that expert reports be required to include a statement of material "instructions" received from counsel and that such instructions be

international arbitration will include a statement summarizing the issues on which that expert was asked to opine and other material directives received from counsel. Expert reports may also include a statement of the financial terms of that expert's engagement (though this is not a common practice). There is broad agreement that a party should voluntarily disclose to the other party, and to the arbitral tribunal, the substance of the instructions provided to an expert.

The expectation that experts will voluntarily disclose the nature of their instructions does not answer the question whether information pertaining to an expert's instructions, beyond that voluntarily disclosed in that expert's report, can be obtained. The choices are, either, by cross-examination of the expert, or by an order for the production of the underlying document containing an expert's instructions. Requests to produce documents regarding the scope of an expert's engagement are rare in international arbitration, and, when faced with such a request, arbitrators are reluctant to order production.

John Tackaberry has written that "[i]ncreasingly, panels will expect to see the instructions that were given to the expert that led to the report…".[24] However, our experience does not support this expectation, and several of the arbitrators surveyed for the purpose of this article expressed hesitation at the idea that production of documents might be ordered on the topic of instructions, while emphasizing that cross-examination about the scope of an expert's engagement was allowed as a matter of course.

In a recent ICC case, a party submitted an expert report that did not specify the instructions that that expert had received from counsel. The other side requested production of the documents that reflected the terms and scope of the expert's engagement. The arbitral tribunal, composed of civil law arbitrators, refused to order production of the documents setting out such instructions.[25]

In summary, while cross-examination on the issue of an expert's instructions is always permissible, production of the documents containing an expert's instructions is *not* ordinarily an exception to the presumption of non-discoverability of counsel-expert communications.

The CIArb Protocol lends support to this view. Its Art. 4 recommends that an expert's report should include "a statement setting out all instructions the expert has received from the appointing Party and the basis of remuneration of the expert", which recommendation the authors understand contemplates a description by an expert in his or her report of the directives received from counsel. Art. 5(1) of the CIArb Protocol further provides:

> "1. All instructions to, and any terms of appointment of, an expert shall not be privileged against disclosure in the arbitration, but the Arbitral Tribunal shall not, in relation to the instructions or terms of appointment:

---

discoverable. *Ibid.*, Chapter 13, para. 32.
24. J. TACKABERRY, "Practical Considerations for Conducting the Hearing", *op. cit.*, fn. 21, p. 182.
25. As of the date of this writing, no hearing had been held in that case, and it cannot be known whether the tribunal will allow questioning.

(a) order disclosure of the instructions or appointment or any document relating thereto; or

(b) permit any questioning of the expert about such instructions or appointment unless it is satisfied that there is good cause."

Despite the emphasis in Art. 4 on the importance of voluntary disclosure of instructions, Art. 5(1)(b) of the CIArb Protocol precludes questioning of an expert regarding his or her instructions unless the tribunal is satisfied that there is good cause. In this respect, the CIArb Protocol is more restrictive than the prevailing practice in international arbitration.

While Arts. 4 and 5 of the CIArb Protocol can be read to take a pro-disclosure stance with respect to an expert's instructions, the emphasis is on the importance of *voluntary* disclosure in an expert's report. Art. 5 of the CIArb Protocol says that an arbitral tribunal is not to order production of the underlying documents containing the instructions to an expert absent "good cause". Although "good cause" is not defined in the Protocol, this concept was likely imported from the Civil Procedure Rules in England.[26] If English practice is a guide, "good cause" would include the situation where there are reasonable grounds to find that an expert's statement of his instructions is "inaccurate or incomplete".[27]

A word of caution is needed regarding this brief discussion of the purpose and scope of Arts. 4 and 5 of the CIArb Protocol. We have assumed that the term "instructions" refers to that particular set of counsel-expert communications which set out the scope of an expert's engagement, and any other directives received from counsel. However, English courts, interpreting the English Civil Procedure Rules from which Art. 5 of the CIArb Protocol was derived, have construed the term "instructions" widely to include all "the information being supplied by the claimant and all the material which a solicitor places in front of the expert in order to gain advice".[28] As such, under English law, the

---

26. Peter J. REES, "From Hired Gun to Lone Ranger – The Evolving Role of the Party-Appointed Expert Witness" (2008) at p. 13, available at <www.transnational-dispute-management.com/> ("In England, under the [Civil Procedure Rules] the instructions to experts are discloseable, but draft reports are considered not to be and that compromise is what the Protocol has largely incorporated in Article 5.").

27. The English Civil Procedure Rules specify that an expert must give a statement of all material instructions received from counsel, that such instructions are not privileged and that questioning or document disclosure in respect of such instructions may be ordered if the court is "satisfied that there are reasonable grounds to consider the statement of instructions given under paragraph (3) to be inaccurate or incomplete." Civil Procedure Rules 35.10(4).

28. Under English law, the only real guidance on this issue is that the term "instructions" has been construed widely to include all "the information being supplied by the claimant and all the material which a solicitor places in front of the expert in order to gain advice". *Lucas v. Barking, Havering and Redbridge Hospitals NHS Trust* [2003] 4 All ER 72 (CA), [2003] EWCA Civ. 1102, at paras. 30-31. Therefore, potentially, an English court satisfied that there is good cause, may order wide discovery of counsel-expert communications.

line between counsel-expert communications and "instructions" may be very faint.[29] Importing an expansive understanding of "instructions" into Art. 5 of the CIArb Protocol could result in requests for disclosure of the whole range of counsel-expert communications, which would run against the basic expectations of arbitration practitioners outlined above.

c. *Abuse*

A third potential exception to the presumption of non-discoverability of counsel-expert communications arises in circumstances of abuse by counsel (and by the expert insofar as he or she allows such conduct). Although it is accepted practice that counsel may assist an expert in writing his or her report, overly intrusive style is frowned upon, and counsel who exert excessive influence over the content of an expert report do so at the risk of their expert's, and their own, credibility. As a noted arbitrator commented in response to a question posed for the purposes of this article, "lawyerly ghostwriting" tends to annoy tribunals and may attract pointed questions by arbitrators about the precise circumstances of the genesis of an expert's report. The practice, though, is to deal with this abuse through questioning rather than through document production. While the concern that gives rise to questioning about abuse would logically lead to document production orders, that has not been the practice to date. The absence of known instances of document production orders arising from overly intrusive counsel is not, though, an argument that such orders would or should not be granted where warranted.

III. COMMENT ON THE RATIONALE FOR DISCOVERABILITY OF COUNSEL-EXPERT COMMUNICATIONS IN INTERNATIONAL ARBITRATION

In recent years, there has been growing concern in common law countries where party-appointed experts are used in domestic litigation that such experts tend to overlook their duty of independence to the court[30] and instead act as "hired guns" advocating for the

---

29. Despite this, even interpreting the term "instructions" in Art. 5 of the CIArb Protocol in light of English case law on the English Civil Procedure Rules, in the opinion of the authors the distinction between "instructions" (which are not privileged but which enjoy a strong presumption against disclosure absent "good cause") and other counsel-expert communications (which are subject to a privilege which may be waived) may not be material as a practical matter. Circumstances amounting to "good cause" may also constitute waiver of privilege. Indeed, the very same English case which proposed a wide interpretation of the term "instructions" in the Civil Procedure Rules also clarified that the presumption against disclosure of "instructions" absent good cause was "designed primarily to give protection to a party who would otherwise have waived privilege by being compelled to set out matters in an expert's report". *Lucas*, para. 31.
30. As a general matter, common law countries recognize that a party-appointed expert owes a duty to the court or tribunal to give an objective opinion, independent of any influence by the party which appointed him or her. In 1981, Lord Wilberforce stated that expert evidence presented in court should be, and be seen to be, "the independent product of the expert, uninfluenced as to form or content by the exigencies of litigation". *Whitehouse v. Jordan*, [1981] 1 WLR 246, 256-257. Similarly, in the much-cited 1993 English case, *National Justice Compania Naviera S.A. v. Prudential*

party that retained them with little or no objectivity.[31] This concern has led several common law jurisdictions to allow broader discovery of counsel-expert communications in an effort to promote greater independence and objectivity on the part of experts and to limit lawyer influence over the content of expert testimony.

As in common law jurisdictions, in international arbitration the role of party-appointed experts is to provide objective testimony aimed at assisting the arbitral tribunal,[32] and the problem of "hired guns" has led to calls for increased disclosure of counsel-expert communications.[33] Doug Jones explains:

> "It is likely that a court or arbitral tribunal would benefit from greater transparency as to how experts came to develop their opinion. This would enable the court or arbitral tribunal to make a fully informed determination and to better

---

Assurance Co. Tld. (The Ikarian Reefer), [1993] 2 Lloyd's Rep. 68, the English Commercial Court, Queen's Bench Division, developed this statement into a set of seven principles which have come to be regarded as a classic statement of good practice for experts. Of particular import in the context of this article is the second principle: "2. An expert witness should provide independent assistance to the Court by way of objective unbiased opinion relating to matters within his expertise. An expert witness in the High Court should never assume the role of an advocate." *Ibid.*, p. 81.

31. See *Lord Abinger v. Ashton*, [1873] 17 L.R. Eq. 358, 373-374 ("[I]n matters of opinion, I very much distrust expert evidence ... Expert evidence of this kind is evidence of persons who sometimes live by their business, but in all cases are remunerated for their evidence.... [I]t is natural that his mind ... should be biassed in favour of the person employing him, and accordingly we do find such bias."); *Cala Homes (South) Ltd. v. Alfred McAlpine Homes East Ltd.*, [1995] F.S.R. 818, 843-844 ("The whole basis of Mr. Goodall's approach to the drafting of an expert's report is wrong. The function of a court of law is to discover the truth relating to the issues before it.... That some witnesses of fact, driven by a desire to achieve a particular outcome to the litigation, feel it necessary to sacrifice truth in pursuit of victory is a fact of life.... An expert should not consider that it is his job to stand shoulder to shoulder through thick and thin with the side which is paying his bill."); *Great Eastern Hotel Co. Ltd. v. John Laing Constr. Ltd.*, [2005] EWHC 181 (TCC), para. 111 ("I reject the expert evidence of Mr. Celetka as to the performance of Laing as contract manager.... He has demonstrated himself to be lacking in thoroughness in his research and unreliable by reason of his uncritical acceptance of the favourable accounts put forward by Laing.").

32. See Art. 4 of the CIArb Protocol, which provides that "[a]n expert's opinion shall be impartial, objective, unbiased and uninfluenced by the pressures of the dispute resolution process or by any Party" and that "[a]n expert's duty, in giving evidence in the Arbitration, is to assist the Arbitral Tribunal to decide the issues in respect of which expert evidence is adduced". *See also* Kap-You (Kevin) KIM and John BANG, "Commentary on Using Legal Experts in International Arbitration", *ICCA Congress Series no. 13* (2006) p. 779 at p. 781.

33. Kevin T. JACOBS and Matthew G. PAULSON, "The Convergence of Renewed Nationalization, Rising Commodities, and 'Americanization'" in *International Arbitration and the Need for More Rigorous Legal and Procedural Defenses*, 43 Tex. Int'l. L.J. (2008) p. 359 at p. 399 ("additional mandatory disclosures would promote greater neutrality, transparency, and objectivity as well as allow the parties and arbitrators to better prepare for the experts' meetings and cross-examinations. These additional mandatory disclosures, which would be established early in the arbitration process, should include: the expert's entire file including draft reports, correspondence, data, documents, and notes used in the evaluation of the issues within his or her expertise....").

weigh the evidence of opposing experts. Moreover, ensuring that all communications between him or herself and the party by whom he or she is appointed are made available may be a good way to remind the expert that their overriding duty is to the court or tribunal and not to that party."[34]

Some US practitioners likewise argue in favor of *full* discoverability of counsel-expert communications in international arbitration in order to promote greater "*neutrality, transparency and objectivity*" in the use of party-appointed experts.[35]

In the remainder of this article, we survey the evidence of a trend towards greater discoverability of counsel-expert communications in domestic litigation. We then explain why the use of discovery as a means to promote greater independence and objectivity on the part of party-appointed experts should be resisted in international arbitration.

1. *The Use of Discovery to Promote Experts' Independence and Objectivity in Domestic Litigation*

a. United States

The trend towards greater discoverability of counsel-expert communications in litigation has been most evident in the United States. The Federal Rules of Civil Procedure[36] were amended in 1993 to broaden the disclosure obligations of party-appointed testifying experts.[37] Testifying experts must now disclose "the data or other information *considered* by the witness in forming" their opinions.[38] A narrower formulation requiring disclosure of those materials "relied upon" by the expert was rejected due to concern that experts might deliberately conceal relevant but adverse information by determining that they had not relied upon it.[39] The duty to disclose under the US Federal Rules of Civil Procedure extends to anything a testifying expert "generates, reviews, reflects upon, reads, and/or uses in connection with the formulation of his opinions, even if such information is ultimately rejected"[40] and includes counsel-expert communications and draft expert

---

34. D. JONES, "Party Appointed Expert Witness in International Arbitration: A Protocol at Last", *op. cit.*, fn. 4, pp. 152-153.
35. See supra fn. 33.
36. Each state also has its own particular rules regarding the discovery obligations of expert witnesses in state court litigation. However, a survey of the laws across the United States is beyond the scope of this article.
37. The extensive disclosure requirements apply only to testifying experts, not to mere consultants. Adam BAIN, "Working with Expert Witnesses in the Age of Electronic Discovery", 56 The United States Attorneys' Bulletin (2008) p. 35 at p. 40, available at <www.justice.gov/usao/eousa/foia_reading_room/usab5603.pdf>.
38. Fed.R.Civ.P. 26(a)(2) (emphasis added).
39. Gregory P. JOSEPH, "Emerging Expert Issues Under the 1993 Disclosure Amendments to the Federal Rules of Civil Procedure", 164 F.R.D. 97 (1996) pp. 103-104.
40. *Synthes Spine Co., L.P. v. Walden*, 232 F.R.D. 460, 463 (E.D. Pa. 2005). See also *Schwab v. Phillip Morris USA, Inc.*, No. 04-CV-1945 (JBW), 2006 WL 721368, at *2 (E.D.N.Y. 20 Mar. 2006); *Karn v. Ingersoll-Rand Co.*, 168 F.R.D. 633, 635 (N.D. Ind. 1996).

reports.[41] A testifying expert's duty to disclose any materials "considered" overrides the attorney work-product doctrine and other forms of privilege.[42] Litigation counsel in the United States can and do seek discovery of documents showing interactions between opposing counsel and their experts, including any exchanges of drafts. Counsel scrutinize changes in successive iterations of a testifying expert's report and cross-examine experts in connection with such changes in order to draw out any evidence of bias or undue attorney influence.[43]

The practical consequence of this broad discovery mandate is not that US litigation counsel distance themselves from the expert-report drafting process. Rather, attorneys litigating in the United States know that all materials considered by an expert, including communications with counsel, are discoverable,[44] and take steps to avoid generating discoverable communications.

b.   Other common law jurisdictions

The trend toward greater discoverability of counsel-expert communications is also perceptible in Australia, where measures to address the issue of partisan experts, including additional disclosure requirements, were adopted in the late 1990s.[45] The

---

41. See, e.g., *Bro-Tech Corp. v. Thermax, Inc.*, No. 05-2330, 2008 WL 356928, at *1-2 (E.D. Pa. 7 Feb. 2008); *Varga v. Stanwood-Camano Sch. Dist.*, No. C-06-0178P, 2007 WL 1847201, at *1 (W.D. Wash. 26 Jun. 2007); *Univ. of Pittsburgh v. Townsend*, No. 3:04-cv-291, 2007 WL 1002317, at *2-5 (E.D. Tenn. 30 Mar. 2007).
42. *Reg'l Airport Auth. of Louisville v. LFG, LLC*, 460 F.3d 697, 714, 717 (6th Cir. 2006) (reviewing a compilation of cases and finding that the general work-product doctrine in Federal Civil Procedure Rule 26(b)(3) must yield to the more specific expert disclosure requirement in Rule 26(a)(2)). *See also Karn v. Ingersoll-Rand Co.*, 168 F.R.D. 633, 635-641 (N.D. Ind. 1996) (finding that Rule 26(a)(2) creates a "bright-line" requirement of disclosure); *TV-3, Inc. v. Royal Ins. Co. of Am.*, 194 F.R.D. 585, 588 (S.D. Miss. 2000) (requiring full disclosure of information that an expert considered is necessary for effective cross-examination of experts, which is sufficient reason to override the attorney work-produce doctrine). Adam Bain notes that this interpretation is supported by the Advisory Committee's note to the 1993 amendment, which states that "litigants should no longer be able to argue that materials furnished to their experts to be used in forming their opinions – whether or not ultimately relied upon by the expert – are privileged or otherwise protected from disclosure when such persons are testifying or being deposed." A. BAIN, "Working with Expert Witnesses in the Age of Electronic Discovery", *op. cit.*, fn. 37, p. 36,. See also "Notes of Advisory Committee on 1993 Amendments to Rules" (1993), available at <www.law.cornell.edu/rules/frcp/ACRule26.htm>.
43. *Ibid.*, pp. 36 and 41.
44. *Ibid.*, at p. 38.
45. A catalyst for the reforms was the publication of an empirical study carried out by the Australian Institute of Judicial Administration which showed that one of the major concerns among the Australian judiciary was a perception of bias on the part of expert witnesses. See Ian FRECKELTON, Prasuna REDDY and Hugh SELBY, *Australian Judicial Perspectives on Expert Evidence: An Empirical Study* (1999). With respect to disclosure requirements, *Australian Federal Court Practice Note CM 7, Expert Witnesses in Proceedings in the Federal Court of Australia* (2009), available at <www.fedcourt.gov.au/how/practice_notes_cm7.html>, now requires at para. 2.7 that "[t]here should be included in or attached to the report: (i) a statement of the questions or issues that the expert was asked to address; (ii) the factual premises upon which the report

trend went the furthest in the State of Queensland. While counsels' instructions to an expert remain privileged,[46] the Queensland Uniform Civil Procedure Rules (the UCPR) provide that "[a] document consisting of a statement or report of an expert is not privileged from disclosure".[47] The UCPR then define a "report" widely to mean "a document giving an expert's opinion on an issue arising in the proceeding".[48] This broad definition has been interpreted to include written reports of an expert who is not called as a witness[49] as well as drafts, working papers, source materials and documents collated and copied by an expert in order to prepare a report.[50]

As Doug Jones points out, "[the Queensland approach] has potentially significant implications for the parties to a proceeding, as draft reports may contain differing opinions to those finally developed by the expert".[51] The discoverability of an expert's working papers means that an expert may be confronted on cross-examination with his or her own early notes and questioned as to how and why his or her early positions changed.

Similarly, in Canada some discovery of counsel-expert communications is allowed in certain common law provinces. The trend started in the late 1980s when British Columbia allowed full disclosure of an expert's "file" in an effort to promote experts' independence and impartiality. Ontario has now followed suit.[52]

---

proceeds; and (iii) the documents and other materials that the expert has been instructed to consider".

46. *Greenhill Nominees Pty. Ltd. v. Aircraft Technicians of Australia Pty Ltd.*, [2001] QSC 7, para. 20 ("instructions given by lawyers to an expert for the purpose of preparing an expert report were protected by legal professional privilege. The position has not been changed by the Uniform Civil Procedure Rules," citing *Interchase Corp. Ltd. (in liq) v. Grosvenor Hill (Queensland) Pty. Ltd. (No. 1)*, [1999] 1QdR 141, 156.).
47. Uniform Civil Procedure Rules (Queensland), Rule 212(2).
48. *Ibid.*, Rule 425.
49. Andrew KITCHIN, "The Expert Evidence Rules Under the UCPR – A General Outline, and Some Comments on the Practical Application of Parts of the Expert Evidence Rules", paper delivered on 23 November 2005 at the request of Australian Insurance Law Association, para. 9, available at <www.aila.com.au/speakersPapers/downloads/05-10-31_Andrew_Kitchin.pdf>.
50. See *Mitchell Contractors Pty. Ltd. v. Townsville-Thuringowa Water Supply Joint Bd.*, [2004] QSC 329; *Interchase Corp. Ltd. (in liq) v. Grosvenor Hill (Queensland) Pty. Ltd.*, [1999] 1QdR 141, 150. However, *oral* opinions or reports are not covered by the UCPR disclosure requirements. A. KITCHIN, "The Expert Evidence Rules Under the UCPR – A General Outline, and Some Comments on the Practical Application of Parts of the Expert Evidence Rules", *op. cit.*, fn. 49, para. 9(c) ("The consultation draft for the UCPR included a sub-rule that in effect provided that if a party obtained oral advice from an expert about the proposed contents of a report/draft report or a finding or conclusion of the expert, then the party must record the advice in writing and disclose it – that sub rule never found its way into the UCPR as we know them.").
51. Doug JONES, "Use of Experts in Arbitration; Independent Experts – The Common Law Approach", 2 Transnat'l Dispute Mgmt. (2005, no. 5) at p. 12, available at <www.transnational-dispute-management.com/>.
52. See Basile CHIASSON, "Litigation Privilege and Disclosure of Expert's File", 56 U.N.B.L.J. (2007) p. 208 at pp. 242-249.

2. *The Case Against Using Discovery to Promote Experts' Independence and Objectivity in International Arbitration*

The authors are unaware of any international arbitration proceedings where disclosure of counsel-expert communications was ordered. Several of the practitioners surveyed commented that a move towards wide disclosure of counsel-expert communications would be an undesirable "Americanization" of international arbitration procedure. In the opinion of the authors, there are at least five reasons why the trend towards greater discoverability of counsel-expert communications should be resisted in international arbitration.

First, in contrast to US domestic litigation, where experts often find themselves in front of juries, international arbitrators are sophisticated fact-finders, adept at discerning the truth. As Johnny Veeder remarked with respect to witness statements:

> 'It is perhaps surprising that many sophisticated practitioners have not yet understood that their massive efforts at reshaping the testimony of their client's factual witnesses is not only ineffective but often counter-productive. Most arbitrators have been or remain practitioners, and they can usually detect the 'wood-shedding' of a witness."[53]

Therefore, increased disclosure of counsel-expert communications is ordinarily unnecessary. Arbitral tribunals are usually well capable of determining when an expert has failed to examine an issue with an objective eye.

Second, anyone who has read an unedited expert report understands that counsel often play an important role in shaping the scope, form and internal consistency of an expert's report. An expert's trade is rarely drafting, and counsel may and should ensure that the report is clear, focused and free of unnecessary repetition and irrelevant material. Unrestrained communications between counsel and experts are also necessary to enable counsel and expert to explore theories of the case and to avoid factual misconceptions. The threat of disclosure of counsel-expert communications is likely to hamper counsel's efforts to strategize, theorize and fully develop the client's case. Were counsel-expert communications subject to production, an expert's ability to get to the bottom of the issues in the case, and to test various theories in conjunction with counsel, would be constrained to the detriment of both the client and the tribunal's fact-finding mission.[54]

Third, document production tends to increase the cost of a case. While document production requests could, in theory, be tailored to seek production of only a few specified documents, this has not been the result in practice. By opening up counsel-

---

53. V.V. VEEDER Q.C., "The 2001 Goff Lecture: The Lawyer's Duty to Arbitrate in Good Faith", 18 Arb. Int'l (2002) p. 431 at p. 445.
54. Diane SUMOSKY, "ABA Recommends Exempting Draft Expert Reports and Certain Attorney-Expert Communications from Discovery", 3 Expert Alert, Section of Litigation, American Bar Association (2007) p. 1 at pp. 4-5.

expert communications to document production requests, document production overall would increase in cost.

Fourth, as the US experience reveals, increased discoverability of counsel-expert communications rarely makes counsel-expert communications more transparent or experts more neutral. Instead, such discovery tends to result only in additional costs and inefficiencies. Faced with the threat of discovery of their communications with their experts, US litigation counsel have been forced to become shrewder, and have become accustomed to minimizing any interaction with testifying experts that might create a paper trail. US litigation counsel and testifying experts rarely exchange edited drafts,[55] and confine their discussions regarding possible edits to in-person meetings or marathon conference calls. Counsel also seek to evade the temporal reach of a production order by discussing an expert's theories and opinions well in advance of the drafting of any report and sometimes even before an expert is retained.[56] Because the strict disclosure requirements under the US Federal Rules of Civil Procedure apply only to testifying experts, parties with sufficient resources also frequently retain a second expert, who acts as a consultant with whom counsel can freely communicate.[57] This use of "shadow experts" is also widespread in other jurisdictions that allow broad discovery of counsel-expert communications.[58] Finally, counsel in the United States often agree with opposing counsel that draft expert reports and counsel-expert communications are protected from discovery,[59] thereby evading the effect of the broad discovery rules.

Fifth, if the objective is absolute expert impartiality, *party*-appointed experts are, by definition, problematic. There are many areas of technical and legal expertise where divergent opinions can validly be held.[60] It is natural for a party to appoint an expert whose opinions fit the party's theory of the case. In this context, the subtle benefit of enhanced independence that may be occasioned by the discoverability of counsel-expert communications is outweighed by the cost and harm to the process that arises when counsel-expert communications are constrained by fear of discovery.

The rules allowing extended disclosure of counsel-expert communications are now being rolled back in some jurisdictions because of the difficulties and costs discussed above. In the United States, the American Bar Association (the ABA) has recommended that the US Federal Rules of Civil Procedure be amended "to protect from discovery

---

55. R. KENT, "Expert Witnesses in Arbitration and Litigation Proceedings", *op. cit.*, fn. 2, at p. 4.
56. A. BAIN, "Working with Expert Witnesses in the Age of Electronic Discovery", *op. cit.*, fn. 37, p. 42.
57. R. KENT, "Expert Witnesses in Arbitration and Litigation Proceedings", *op. cit.*, fn. 2, at p. 2.
58. BC Justice Review Task Force, *Effective and Affordable Civil Justice* (2006) p. 33, available at <www.bcjusticereview.org/working_groups/civil_justice/cjrwg_report_11_06.pdf>.
59. A. BAIN, "Working with Expert Witnesses in the Age of Electronic Discovery", *op. cit.*, fn. 37, p. 43.
60. Elizabeth BIRCH, "The Widening Role of Experts in the Changing Fields of Arbitration and ADR", 2 Transnat'l Dispute Mgmt. (2005, no. 1) at p. 2, available at <www.transnational-dispute-management.com/> ("In the context of experts, I believe that it is often forgotten that there is seldom one truth and this applies not only in factual situations, but in relation to expert evidence as well. Equally eminent experts from the same field may hold different opinions, each validly held.").

draft expert reports and communications between an attorney and a testifying expert relating to an expert's report." The amendment is currently being considered by the US Supreme Court.[61] The ABA also recommended that, pending such amendment, counsel enter voluntary stipulations protecting from discovery draft reports and counsel-expert communications.[62] Similarly, in the Canadian province of British Columbia, a judicial reform task force has recommend narrowing the rules regarding discovery of counsel-expert communications because of the widespread use of "shadow experts" (i.e., consultants with whom counsel can freely discuss the case) alongside testifying experts, and the costs associated with such practice.[63] In England, although Lord Woolf, commissioned to draft a report on Access to Justice in the 1990s, initially recommended that all counsel-expert communications be discoverable to "prevent the suppression of relevant opinions or factual material which did not support the case put forward by the party instructing the expert", Lord Woolf's final report ultimately rejected wide-ranging disclosure of counsel-expert communications on the basis of similar concerns.[64]

IV. CONCLUSION

Counsel in international arbitration can feel free to communicate with their party's experts unconstrained by fear that, in the ordinary circumstance, their communications

---

61. The amendment would take effect as of 1 December 2010, unless the US Congress acts to prevent its implementation. EDITOR, "Proposed Amendment to Fed. R. Civ. P. 26 Would Change Expert Witness Disclosure And Discovery Requirements", Federal Evidence Review, 30 Oct. 2009, available at <http://federalevidence.com/print/554>.
62. ABA, "Resolution 120A, Discoverability of Expert Reports", Adopted by the House of Delegates 7-8 August 2006, available at <www.abanet.org/litigation/standards/docs/120a_policy.pdf>.
63. The BC Justice Review Task Force thus explained:

    "Parties need access to the facts upon which the expert's opinion is based, but we believe that the benefits to be gained from full disclosure of an expert's file are outweighed by the cost of the resulting incentive to hire a second consulting expert. We therefore recommend that experts whose reports are served must disclose only the facts, including test results, upon which the expert has relied in forming his or her opinion."

    BC Justice Review Task Force, "Effective and Affordable Civil Justice" (2006) p. 33, available at <www.bcjusticereview.org/working_groups/civil_justice/cjrwg_report_11_06.pdf>. The New Rules of the Supreme Court of British Columbia will take effect on 1 July 2010.
64. "Access to Justice: Final Report by the Right Honourable the Lord Woolf", *op. cit.*, fn. 23, Chapter 13, para. 31 ("The point has been made that experts must be free to submit drafts to clients and their legal advisers, so that factual misconceptions can be corrected. A further objection is that a great deal of time could be wasted if all these documents were disclosable, because the opposing party would have to comb through the various versions of a report to identify any changes, the reasons for which would not always be clear in any event. Another possibility is that lawyers and experts might begin to subvert the system by avoiding written communication in favour of off the record conversations."). See also "Access to Justice: Interim Report by the Right Honourable the Lord Woolf" (London: H.M. Stationery Office, 1995) available at <www.dca.gov.uk/civil/interim/woolf.htm>.

will be subject to production to the other side and to the arbitrators. There are exceptions to this rule, for documents referenced or relied upon by an expert, and (potentially) for documents pertaining to the scope of an expert's engagement. International arbitrators also retain discretion to require production if there is an adequate basis to find that the counsel-expert relationship has been abused and that a production order is needed. Experienced international arbitrators and practitioners remain, however, broadly opposed to the production of counsel-expert communications.

Opposition to production of counsel-expert communications is justified by the importance of unconstrained collaboration between counsel and experts, as such collaboration affects both the quality of the representation provided to the client and the quality and accessibility of the expert evidence submitted to the arbitral tribunal. Counsel activism in the expert report drafting process does not mean that the work product generated by a collaborative effort belongs to the counsel rather than to the expert, or that the expert will inevitably become an advocate for the party. An arbitral tribunal will quickly lose patience with expert evidence that is so tainted. Rather, counsel's assistance is often needed to edit and reformulate an expert draft in order to make the report of use to the arbitral tribunal. The suggestion that increased discoverability of counsel-expert communications promotes expert independence and neutrality is belied by the experience of those national jurisdictions which, having implemented broader expert disclosure requirements, are now rolling back those rules because of the associated costs and inefficiency.

Were counsel-expert communications subject to broad production in international arbitration, the consequences would be less-refined expert evidence and increased cost and inefficiency, but not enhanced independence or neutrality on the part of experts.

The Hearing

Oral Advocacy and Time Control in International Arbitration

David J.A. Cairns[*]

TABLE OF CONTENTS	Page
I. Introduction	181
II. The Limits of Time Control I: Advocacy Skills and Procedural Efficiency	183
III. The Limits of Time Control II: Due Process	187
IV. The Limits of Time Control III: Party Agreement	191
V. The Limits of Time Control IV: Summary of the Current Position	192
VI. Nine Guidelines for Effective Time Control of Arbitral Advocacy	193
VII. Conclusions	197
Annex I: The Economics of Oral Advocacy and Time Control	199

I. INTRODUCTION

Time control is a contemporary imperative of the international arbitration community. Effective time management is essential for the containment of costs and the minimization of the period between the request for arbitration and the award. The duration and costs of arbitration are in turn critical to maintaining the confidence of the commercial users of arbitration, as well as to attracting new users, and therefore to the competitive success of arbitration in the commercial dispute resolution market. The time and cost management imperatives coexist in a dynamic tension with the complexity of modern commercial and investment disputes and the legal sophistication required for their resolution. The challenge is to reduce time and costs and at the same time to maintain high standards in factual and legal decision making, due process and award enforceability.

All phases of the arbitral process have been scrutinized from a time and cost perspective. The hearing is no exception, and has not emerged favourably when examined from this perspective. The judgment of the ICC Commission on Arbitration in its *Techniques for Controlling Time and Costs in Arbitration* is representative:[1]

> "Hearings are expensive and time-consuming. If the length and number of hearings requiring the physical attendance of the arbitral tribunal and the parties are minimized, this will significantly reduce the time and cost of the proceedings."

---

[*] Partner, B. Cremades y Asociados, Madrid; LLB (Hons), LLM (Toronto), PhD (Cambridge); FCIArb; Solicitor; Abogado; Adjunct Professor, University Carlos III of Madrid.
    The author would like to thank Sonsoles Huerta de Soto, an Associate with B. Cremades y Asociados, for her research and assistance in the preparation of this article, particularly in respect of the economic analysis of oral advocacy and time control.
[1] Report from the ICC Commission on Arbitration, *Techniques for Controlling Time and Costs in Arbitration* (ICC Publication N° 843, 2007) para. 72 (available at: <www.iccwbo.org/uploadedFiles/TimeCost_E.pdf>).

The oral hearing, and particularly the lengthy oral hearing, is a characteristic of common law procedure. However, the flexibility of arbitral procedure together with the impulse towards harmonization of different legal traditions in international arbitration has substantially reduced the length of arbitral hearings in comparison with similar disputes in domestic courts in common law jurisdictions. Two common features of international arbitration procedure have already successfully reduced the length of hearings: firstly, the preference of written over oral presentations where this is possible, including the preference for the written statements of witnesses, written legal submissions, and post-hearing briefs over their oral equivalents at a hearing; secondly, the displacement of potential functions of an oral hearing to other parts of the arbitral process. The common requirement in international arbitration that documentary exhibits, witness statements and expert reports are attached to the pleadings at an early stage of the arbitration exemplifies this technique.

A particular feature of international arbitration that strongly favours written communication is the involvement of multiple languages. Simultaneous translation at an arbitration hearing is not only time-consuming and an added expense, but also has a detrimental effect on the rhythm and effectiveness of communications at a hearing. If a witness does not speak the arbitral language then it makes sense to use a written statement in the witnesses' native language with a translation, and to limit the laborious process of the oral questioning by means of the translation of questions and answers. Similarly, written expression provides greater security of precision and mutual understanding than oral exchanges involving either non-native speakers or the explanation of legal doctrine and jurisprudence in a foreign language.

The justification of time control over oral advocacy is therefore to save time and costs, or in other words, procedural efficiency. This has been successfully pursued by maximizing the use of written communications including, where necessary, re-ordering arbitral procedure to enable the presentation of evidence and submissions in writing instead of orally. The result is that written advocacy today is far more significant than oral advocacy in international arbitration.[2]

The ultimate form of time control of oral advocacy is to eliminate the oral hearing entirely, and so save all the costs and delays associated with a hearing. An arbitration can and sometimes is completed without an oral hearing, but this is not the normal practice in cases of any substance. The reason for the resilience of the oral hearing is that there are limitations on the time controls that can be placed on oral advocacy. This paper considers three limitations on time control of oral advocacy. Firstly, oral advocacy offers some advantages not capable of substitution by a written procedure; in other words, in some circumstances oral advocacy is an efficient procedural choice. Secondly, mandatory rules may in some circumstances require a minimum level of oral advocacy. Thirdly, party agreement may place limits on the time controls on oral advocacy.

The next three sections of this paper consider these limitations on time control and evaluate the advantages of oral advocacy. Taking into account these advantages and limitations, the paper then addresses proactive time management for the effective control of oral advocacy in international arbitration. The objectives are to identify how the

---

2. See review of *The Art of Advocacy in International Arbitration,* edited by R. Doak Bishop, 54 International and Comparative Law Quarterly (July 2005; David J.A. CAIRNS) pp. 801-803.

duration of an arbitral hearing should be determined, in terms both of process and decision, and the most effective methods of time distribution and control in international arbitration.

II. THE LIMITS OF TIME CONTROL I: ADVOCACY SKILLS AND PROCEDURAL EFFICIENCY

The essence of advocacy is the persuasive communication of a party's case to the arbitral tribunal.[3] The skills of the modern advocate in international arbitration are six-fold: expertise in law; powers of logical reasoning; mastery of questioning and answering techniques; skills of expression; understanding the ethics of advocacy and tactical dexterity.[4] These skills apply to written or oral advocacy, with one exception. The questioning and answering techniques are a specifically oral skill. They are the skills applied by the advocate in questioning witnesses on the one hand, and in dialogue with the arbitral tribunal, on the other.

When we look at the modern arbitral hearing it is this specifically oral skill of the advocate that has best survived the pressures to minimize the length of the hearing. Many years ago Sir Michael Kerr noted that the primary function of the arbitral hearing had become the cross-examination of witnesses by reason of the pressures in international arbitration to reduce the length of hearings as much as possible:[5]

> "It is a cliché that the objective of the users of arbitration is to achieve speedy finality with fairness and economy of costs. But, like all clichés, it is true. The essence of the emerging common procedural pattern in international arbitration is designed to achieve these objectives by a system of checks and balances in the form of mainly written proceedings which concentrate on the important issues ... and curtail oral hearings as much as possible.... Pleadings should be replaced by full written submissions covering both fact and law, with each side referring to, and exhibiting, all documents relied upon.... All witness statements should be supplied in writing and refer to and exhibit any documents relied upon.... Finally, since the arbitrators are likely to be busy professional people and often from different countries, the oral hearings will usually be remarkably short by English standards. Their main purpose is to hear the cross-examination of the witnesses, bracketed by short opening and closing remarks from both sides, which are then often supplemented by written post-hearing submissions."

---

3. See David J.A. CAIRNS, "Advocacy and the Functions of Lawyers in International Arbitration" in M.A. FERNÁNDEZ-BALLESTEROS and D. ARIAS, *Liber Amicorum Bernardo M. Cremades* (La Ley 2010) pp. 291-307, where four distinct functions of the lawyer in international arbitration are distinguished and defined, namely: strategy, case investigation, advocacy and management. Advocacy includes all communication, whether written or oral, with or for the benefit of the arbitral tribunal. This is the only legal function properly described as advocacy.
4. David J.A. CAIRNS "Advocacy and the Functions of Lawyers in International Arbitration", *op. cit.* fn. 3, where the content of these six skills is described in detail.
5. Sir Michael KERR, "Concord and Conflict in International Arbitration", 13 Arbitration International (Kluwer Law International 1997, no. 2) pp. 121-144 at pp. 125-126.

In certain circumstances oral advocacy may simply be "the quickest way to get things done"; in other words, the most efficient procedural option. The clearest example of an efficiency advantage of oral advocacy is in the questioning of witnesses where doubts and conflicts in the documentary record and the written testimony can be tested and clarified by counsel and the arbitral tribunal.

From an efficiency perspective, the key questions are to identify the determinants of efficient oral advocacy and to identify the optimum amount of time necessary to realize efficiency advantages. As to the first question, oral advocacy is likely to be more efficient where there are high benefits from contemporaneous preparation of participants, and poor substitutability of oral advocacy by written procedure.

1.   Contemporaneous Preparation

An arbitral hearing brings all the participants together. It forces the parties and their legal advisers to justify the claims and defences of the arbitrations not only before the arbitral tribunal but before each other. Parties, witnesses, experts, counsel and arbitrators must all prepare for the hearing, and the hearing is the only time in the arbitral process where all the participants are fully focussed on the case *at the same time.* An imminent hearing concentrates minds wonderfully and this contemporaneous focus is a powerful force. At this time parties may suddenly settle matters that previously proved intractable, and counsel dispense with witnesses and lines of argumentation that were previously deemed indispensable. Arbitrators must be fully familiar with all aspects of the case and identify the key questions around which their award will turn. The arbitral tribunal can harness the force of this preparation and concentration to review efficiently contested points and so shorten the overall procedure. Experts can be brought together to identify points of agreement and sharpen the focus on the real points of difference. Contemporaneous preparation can clarify the parties' positions and reduce the issues in dispute, which in turn can reduce time and costs, and improve quality at the time of drafting the award.

From the perspective of the arbitral tribunal, therefore, it is important to ensure, where possible, that counsel, the parties and their witnesses are well prepared for the hearing. Possible means at the tribunal's disposal are addressed later in this paper.[6]

2.   Written Substitutability

Oral advocacy is advantageous where it has no realistic written substitute or the written substitute is clumsy by comparison. The clearest example of this type of advantage is the oral questioning of witnesses, where witnesses are required to answer questions regarding possible inconsistencies or omissions in their written testimony, or to address facts raised by the documentary record or other witness statements (cross-examination). Witnesses could conceivably be required to answer questions of counsel in writing, but

---

6. A more difficult problem for the tribunal than lack of preparation is where counsel simply lack the necessary expertise. Advocates who are poorly prepared or trained provide little benefit to a tribunal and may raise additional costs in terms of confusion, irrelevancy, repetition and party dissatisfaction. The optimum length of hearing where the level of advocacy is low is therefore likely to be shorter than where the advocacy is professional. Put another way, poor advocacy quickly makes an oral hearing a waste of time (see Annex I: Example 2, pp. 200-201).

such a procedure would be slow, subject to undue party influence, and pose problems for the type of follow-up clarification questions that are a normal part of an oral exchange. The conferencing of experts and the questioning of counsel by the tribunal[7] are other occasions where oral procedure enjoys a comparative advantage.

In contrast, there is simply little benefit from taking the evidence of witnesses entirely orally (direct examination) where so much time can be saved by the simple expedient of a written witness statement,[8] or from a lengthy review by counsel of the documentary evidence where all evidence has already been introduced and fully explained in writing. Where there has been, as is normal in international arbitration, two exchanges of full argumentation, with documentary evidence, expert reports and witness statements attached, then the optimum length of hearing will be much shorter than under a traditional common law procedure. The extent of the written development of the arbitration is therefore a major factor in defining the functions of the arbitral hearing.

3. *Cost/Benefit Analysis of Oral Advocacy*

Once the activities to be dealt with by oral advocacy have been identified, the second and more difficult question is the optimum time to allow for these activities. This requires a cost/benefit analysis of the oral advocacy, as limited to the specific forensic functions already identified by the tribunal.

The returns of oral advocacy are the clarification and testing of evidence, and particularly the evidence of witnesses and experts; the elimination or resolution of uncertain or contested issues of fact or law; identifying the subject matter of further evidence or post-hearing briefs; finalizing the parties' position in preparation for the award; meeting the requirements of mandatory law or due process (discussed below); a better informed arbitral tribunal;[9] as well as less tangible or more subjective benefits such as satisfying the expectations of the parties. In short, a better quality and therefore more just decision-making process. However, it is important to note that oral advocacy suffers from diminishing returns over time. An advocate allowed fifteen minutes for argument will only address the most fundamental issues; an advocate allowed an entire day will address many peripheral questions. The same principle applies in cross-examination. The corollary of the diminishing returns of oral advocacy is that the

---

7. The questioning of counsel by the tribunal can be done in written form, but is probably more efficiently performed at an oral hearing. In this manner the tribunal can identify points of doubt and concern, and counsel can address them in each other's presence. The opposing counsel can respond immediately. Provided counsel are well prepared, the result is a form of Socratic dialogue. In this way, the tribunal can make rapid progress in its preparation to write the award, and counsel can identify the issues to address in their post-hearing briefs. Nevertheless, there is a cultural component to these exchanges, with some arbitrators and counsel more prepared to engage in these dialogues than others.
8. Notwithstanding this advantage some limited direct examination may be justified where the credibility of the witness is in issue, or to supplement the written statement to address new issues.
9. Cf. *International Arbitration 2006: Back to Basics?*, ICCA Congress Series no. 13 (Kluwer Law International 2007) at pp. 829-846 where distinguished arbitrators confirm the value of oral argument to arbitral decision-making.

imposition of the discipline of time control over counsel forces counsel to prioritize and allocate time to their arguments and their questioning of witnesses.

The costs of oral advocacy include firstly and most directly the monetary costs of physically bringing so many people together (airfares, accommodation and related disbursements) and hiring all the facilities for the hearing. Secondly, there are the substantial monetary costs of the preparation of all the participants for the hearing. These costs may be excessive where the case is not "ripe" for the hearing (in terms of the maximization of the written advocacy) or where the issues have not been sufficiently defined in advance. Thirdly, there are costs arising from the time needed to organize and conduct the oral hearing and consequent delay in delivering the award.

Fourthly, oral advocacy not only generates diminishing returns over time, but also additional indirect costs of forensic excesses such as repetition, confusion, pedantry, speculative questioning and the dissipation of energy in irrelevant or peripheral issues. Repetition is a particular danger of oral advocacy in international arbitration, where so much evidence and argument has already been submitted in written form. The costs of these excesses might go beyond the hearing to post-hearing demands to reply or to submit new evidence, loss of focus in post-hearing briefs, delays in completing the award as the tribunal untangles the confusion, and even possible grounds for annulment or refusal to enforce the award.

The efficient duration of the hearing is the period of time in which the benefits of oral advocacy are maximized.[10] This point of the maximization of the benefits of oral advocacy is achieved when the marginal costs of oral advocacy equal the marginal returns. After this point, any additional unit of time of hearing will increase the total cost of the hearing more (in terms of the direct costs of facilities, attendance and preparation, additional costs of forensic excess, and delay in rendering an award) than its total returns (in terms of clarification of factual and legal issues, due process, user satisfaction with arbitration, etc.) therefore decreasing the total benefits of the advocacy. Any termination of the hearing prior to this point would be premature because the marginal returns of further advocacy would exceed the marginal costs, and therefore further hearing time would increase the benefits of the oral advocacy. In every arbitral hearing there is therefore an optimum level of oral advocacy in terms of time.[11]

In practical terms of course the difficulty is in making comparative measurements of the costs and returns of oral advocacy, and to determine the marginal costs and rates of return so as to limit the oral advocacy to the optimum time. In practice, this judgment is made intuitively and not mathematically, but it is exactly what an arbitrator means when he or she tells counsel "I think I have heard enough."

It is hoped that this analysis of forensic efficiency will serve as a correction to any suggestion that arbitrators should always seek to shorten an arbitral hearing as far as possible in order to save time and minimize costs. If this implication is drawn from the

---

10. "Benefits" is used to refer to the difference between the total returns and total costs of oral advocacy.
11. The discipline of law-and-economics addresses the efficiency of legal rules. Annex I to this paper expresses the optimum level of advocacy graphically, and develops two simple examples to demonstrate the different optimum hearing durations depending on the degree of development of the written procedure (Example 1, p. 200) of the quality of the oral advocacy (Example 2, p. 201).

current focus on saving time and costs then there is a danger of false economy. *An efficient hearing requires an effort to identify the optimum length rather than the minimum practical hearing.*[12]

4. Conclusions: Procedural Efficiency

There are certain aspects of arbitral procedure that are most efficiently dealt with orally, and the arbitral tribunal should identify these features and reserve them for oral advocacy. These features are distinguished by an absence of good substitutes in written procedure and the need for contemporaneous preparation, and include questioning of witnesses by opposing counsel and the tribunal, questioning and confrontation of experts, and tribunal/counsel dialogue. The optimum amount of time required for these forms of oral advocacy requires an informed but ultimately intuitive cost/benefit calculation by the arbitral tribunal.

III. THE LIMITS OF TIME CONTROL II: DUE PROCESS

Mandatory procedural rules can be derived from the applicable law at the seat and the place of enforcement, as well as from the principles of international public policy. Fundamental rules of procedure are normally reinforced by institutional rules. These sources point to certain internationally recognized principles of due process, and raise the question as to their possible influence over time controls on oral advocacy. Any possible breach of the principles of due process in an effort to reduce the length of a hearing is likely to jeopardize the enforceability of the award under the 1958 New York Convention,[13] and to provide grounds for annulment at the seat.[14]

From an international perspective, due process consists of three distinct guarantees: the right to be heard (or the principle of contradiction), the right to equality and the right to an independent and impartial tribunal.[15] The formulation preferred in international arbitration for the right to be heard is 'the right of each party to a

---

12. The opposite error to seeking to minimize hearing time and costs, is to set the hearing length so as to maximize the total returns of oral advocacy, notwithstanding the marginal costs are exceeding marginal returns. Where marginal costs exceed marginal returns then the total returns may go on increasing but the actual benefit of oral advocacy (that is, total returns less total costs) is decreasing.
13. Convention on the Recognition and Enforcement of Foreign Arbitral Awards (1958 New York Convention) Art. V(1)(b) and V(2)(b) (due process) and V(1)(d) (arbitral procedure in accordance with the agreement of the parties).
14. For example, UNCITRAL Model Law on International Commercial Arbitration, Art. 34(2)(a)(ii) and (iv), and 34(2)(b)(ii).
15. Art. 10 of the Universal Declaration of Human Rights ("Everyone is entitled in full equality to a fair and public hearing by an independent and impartial tribunal, in the determination of his rights and obligations...."); Art. 6(1) European Convention for the Protection of Human Rights and Fundamental Freedoms. It is assumed that any decision relating to time control is reached by an independent and impartial tribunal so that this aspect of due process will not be further considered.

reasonable opportunity to present its case'.[16] The essence of the right to be heard is the right to know the allegations and proof of the other party and to have a real opportunity to respond to them within the legal (or arbitral) process.[17] These three guarantees are confirmed in domestic arbitration legislation and institutional rules, with minor variations (such as the substitution of "fairness" for "equality").[18]

Equality requires that the parties enjoy substantially equal or equivalent opportunities in the arbitration to state their positions. There must be a just balance between the parties so that each has a reasonable opportunity of presenting its case in circumstances that do not place it at a clear disadvantage in relation to the other party.[19] The principle

16. See Art. 18 of the UNCITRAL Model Law on International Commercial Arbitration and Art. 15 of the UNCITRAL Arbitration Rules ("a full opportunity of presenting his case"); Sect. 33(1) of the English Arbitration Act 1996 and Art. 14(1) of the LCIA Arbitration Rules ("a reasonable opportunity of putting its case and dealing with that of its opponent"); Art. 15(2) of the ICC Rules of Arbitration ("a reasonable opportunity to present its case"). The name of "the right to be heard" suggests oral communication and therefore the right to a hearing and the same implication exists in the Latin expression *audi alteram partem*, commonly used by English lawyers. This semantic endorsement of orality is an anachronism, and it is clear today that the right to be heard does not necessarily require an oral hearing.
17. Cf. *Kanda v. Government of Federation of Malaya* [1962] AC 322 (Privy Council) "... If the right to be heard is to be a real right which is worth anything, it must carry with it a right in the accused man to know the case which is made against him. He must know what evidence has been given and what statements have been made affecting him: and then he must be given a fair opportunity to correct or contradict them.", per Lord Denning (at 337); Emmanuel GAILLARD and John SAVAGE, eds., *Fouchard Gaillard Goldman On International Commercial Arbitration* (Kluwer Law International, The Hague 1999) paras. 1638-1644 (hereinafter *Fouchard Gaillard Goldman*).
18. E.g., Art. 18(1) of the UNCITRAL Model Law on International Commercial Arbitration; ("the parties shall be treated with equality and each party shall be given a full opportunity of presenting his case"); Art. 15(1) of the UNCITRAL Arbitration Rules (requirements of equality and that "at any stage of the proceedings each party is given a full opportunity of presenting his case"); Art. 15(2) of the ICC Rules ("In all cases, the Arbitral Tribunal shall act fairly and impartially and ensure that each party has a reasonable opportunity to present its case"); Sect. 33(i) of the English Arbitration Act 1996 and Art. 14(1) of the LCIA Arbitration Rules (fairness, impartiality and that each party has "a reasonable opportunity of putting its case and dealing with that of its opponent"); Art. 16(i) of the ICDR International Arbitration Rules (equality and that each party has "the right to be heard" and "a fair opportunity to present its case").
19. The European Court of Human Rights has considered "equality of arms" in the context of the right to a fair hearing pursuant to Art. 6(1) of the European Convention for the Protection of Human Rights and Fundamental Freedoms; e.g., in *Dombo Beheer B.V. v. The Netherlands*, 27 October 1993, the Court stated that

"as regards litigation involving opposing private interests, 'equality of arms' implies that each party must be afforded a reasonable opportunity to present his case – including his evidence – under conditions that do not place him at a substantial disadvantage vis-à-vis his opponent".

In *Yvon v France* (Judgment, 24 April 2003) the Court stated that

"this principle [of equality of arms] is one element of the broader concept of fair trial, within the meaning of Article 6 §1 of the Convention. It requires 'a fair balance between the parties': each party must be given a reasonable opportunity to present his case under conditions that do not place him at a substantial disadvantage vis-à-vis his opponent (see, among other authorities, the

of equality is therefore intimately related to the right to be heard, as neither party ought to be at a clear disadvantage in the exercise of its right to present its case.[20] The parties are not identical, nor are their circumstances; and so the right to equality requires substantially equal opportunities, rather than a formal or mechanistic equality in all procedural matters. It might be infringed, for example, when a party is not permitted to call its only witness on the existence of an oral contract when a witness has testified for the other party on this issue, but not where one of its two witnesses is not heard under the same conditions as the witness for the other party,[21] or when one party is permitted to file an extensive memorial with additional exhibits but the other party is not permitted to reply.[22]

There is no doubt that the principles of equality and the right to be heard might be satisfied in a written procedure without any oral hearing. Modern international arbitral procedure provides for the full written exchange of allegations and proof, so that the substantive content of the right to be heard might be satisfied before the hearing is reached, particularly where there was little or no factual dispute between the witnesses presented by the parties. Indeed, the very fact that an oral hearing can be waived by the parties suggests an oral hearing is not a fundamental right but merely an optional element inside a larger process. If the right to be heard does not necessarily require an oral hearing, it follows that nor is any particular element of an oral hearing *ipso facto* indispensable to the right to be heard. Accordingly, the right to be heard does not necessarily mean that a party has the right to present all the evidence or argument it wishes to present at a hearing, or to demand direct examination of its own witnesses or cross-examination of opposing witnesses at the hearing.[23] The rights to be heard and to

---

following judgments: *Ankerl v. Switzerland*, 23 October 1996, Reports of Judgments and Decisions 1996-V, pp. 1567-68, para. 38; *Nideröst-Huber v. Switzerland*, 18 February 1997, Reports 1997-I, pp. 107-08, para. 23; and *Kress v. France* [GC], no. 39594/98, para. 72, ECHR 2001-VI)."

20. "Indeed, in the practice of international tribunals, the issue of equality has mainly arisen as a question concerning the right to present one's case, most particularly in connection with orders and other decisions on written submissions" D. CARON, L. CAPLAN and M. PELLONPÄÄ, *The UNCITRAL Arbitration Rules: A Commentary* (OUP, 2006) p. 29 (footnote omitted).

21. Compare *Ankerl v. Switzerland* (ECHR, 23 October 1996), and *Dombo Beheer B.V. v. The Netherlands* (ECHR 27 October 1993).

22. D. CARON, L. CAPLAN and M. PELLONPÄÄ *The UNCITRAL Arbitration Rules: A Commentary*, *op. cit.*, fn. 20, p. 28.

23. Audiencia Provincial de Madrid, Sección 10ª, Decision of 6 July 2002, rec. 316/2001:

"... *[el derecho a utilizar los medios de prueba pertinentes para la defensa] no comprende un hipotético derecho a llevar a cabo una actividad probatoria ilimitada en virtud de la cual las partes estén facultadas para exigir cualesquiera pruebas que tengan a bien proponer, sino que atribuye sólo el derecho a la recepción y práctica de las que sean 'necesarias para acreditar los hechos que sirven de base a sus pretensiones'...*"

["... the right to adduce evidence relevant to the case does not include a hypothetical right to undertake unlimited probative activity in virtue of which the parties are empowered to demand whatever evidence they wish to propose, rather it includes only the right to the presentation and practice of that evidence necessary to demonstrate that facts that form the basis of its claims..."];

British Insurance Co. of Cayman v. Water Street Insurance Co. Ltd., 93 F.Supp.2d 506, United States

a fair hearing do not consecrate a right of reply and the last word to be party with the burden of proof, even in common law jurisdictions where this is the normal practice.[24]

Due process objections have been raised in international arbitration in the context of the refusal of an arbitral tribunal to extend a deadline to submit evidence or submissions.

> "The arbitral tribunal will only be obliged to accept the belated submission of documents or evidence where the party submitting them has a valid excuse for its delay. In the absence of a legitimate reason, the tribunal can take a firm position and simply reject the memorials or evidence submitted late.... The requirements of due process are in fact satisfied if the initial deadline was sufficient to enable the party in question to present its arguments and evidence."[25]

The same principle would apply in an oral hearing: where a tribunal has set a sufficient period of time for a party to, for example, question witnesses, the tribunal is not obliged to give extra time where counsel for that party has failed to comply with the prescribed time limit. Further, where the questioning or submissions of counsel are in the tribunal's opinion, irrelevant, repetitive or abusive the tribunal can interrupt and stop counsel, and direct counsel to continue in another manner or move to a relevant topic.[26]

District Court, Southern District of New York, 28 April 2000; *Griffin Industries, Inc. and Ocean Logistics Corporation v. Petrojam, Ltd*, 58 F.Supp.2d. 212, United States District Court, Southern District of New York, 21 July 1999; *InterCarbon Bermuda, Ltd., v. Caltex Trading and Transport Corporation*, 146 F.R.D. 64, United States District Court, Southern District of New York, 12 Jan. 1993.

24. *Margulead Ltd. v Exide Technologies* [2005] 1 Lloyds Rep 324; [2004] EWHC 1019 (Comm); [2004] 2 All ER (Comm) 727 (Court of Appeal); Nigel BLACKABY, Constantine PARTASIDES, Alan REDFERN and Martin HUNTER, *Redfern and Hunter on International Arbitration*, 5th edn. (OUP 2009) para. 6.231.
25. *Fouchard Gaillard Goldman*, op. cit., fn. 17, para. 1270.
26. See Art. 8(1) of the IBA Rules on the Taking of Evidence in International Commercial Arbitration; Reza MOHTASHAMI, "The Requirements of Equal Treatment with Respect to the Conduct of Hearings and Hearing Preparation in International Arbitration", 3 Dispute Resolution International (2009) pp.124-133 at pp. 129-130; A. DE LA OLIVA SANTOS; I. DÍEZ-PICAZO JIMÉNEZ; J. VEGAS TORRES, *Derecho Procesal Civil*, 3rd edn. (Editorial universitaria Ramón Areces) p. 327

("... *que la admisión de la prueba no puede ser desacertada e injusta, porque.... en materia de prueba 'lo que abunda no daña' [es errónea].... La verdad es ... que la admisión de una prueba que sea inútil o impertinente sí puede dañar, porque no siempre se refiere a la cantidad de pruebas sino que cabe que ataña a la calidad de las mismas; en especial las pruebas impertinentes – no así las simplemente inútiles – pueden introducir en el proceso hechos irrelevantes, que confunden y complican muy perjudicialmente el desarrollo del proceso y la emisión de la correspondiente sentencia*")

["...that the admission of evidence cannot be incorrect and unfair because in the matter of evidence 'that which abounds does not damage' is erroneous ... the truth is that the admission of evidence that serves no purpose or is irrelevant can damage, because [admission] does not always refer to the *quantity* of the evidence but it is proper that it concerns its *quality*; particularly *irrelevant* evidence – not the evidence that simply serves no purpose – can introduce into the process irrelevant facts that confuse and complicate very prejudicially the development of the case and the issue of the decision."].

The standard practice in both institutional rules and domestic legislation is that unless the parties have agreed that no hearings shall be held, then the arbitral tribunal must hold a hearing if requested by either party.[27] Certain rules confer a right of the parties to question tribunal-appointed experts at a hearing.[28] Institutional rules do not normally impose any further mandatory requirements for the conduct of hearings that may limit the tribunal's discretion in matters of time control and efficiency. In contrast, the right of the parties to question fact witnesses, including to cross-examine a witness on the contents of a written declaration submitted by the other party, is normally subject to the overriding discretion of the arbitral tribunal.[29]

IV. THE LIMITS OF TIME CONTROL III: PARTY AGREEMENT

Party autonomy is the foundation of international arbitration, and the arbitral tribunal may find itself limited in its powers of control over oral advocacy at the hearing by the parties' agreement.

Parties sometimes reach a detailed agreement on the conduct of the arbitral hearing, including the provision for direct oral testimony of witnesses, and generous time for cross-examination, opening and closing statements and legal submissions. This is particularly likely to occur where both parties are represented by lawyers from common law jurisdictions who agree on an extended oral hearing on the common law model.

The arbitral tribunal will offer its comments on the nature and length of a hearing procedure agreed by the parties. Where the tribunal considers the level of oral advocacy agreed by the parties is excessive, then it has the duty to exercise its authority and powers of persuasion. The result is likely to be some accommodation so as to reach a mutually acceptable procedure.[30]

---

27. Art. 24(1) UNCITRAL Model Law on International Commercial Arbitration; Art. 15(2) of the UNCITRAL Arbitration Rules Art. 20(6) ICC Rules of Arbitration; Art. 19(1) LCIA Arbitration Rules.
28. E.g., Art. 27(4) of the UNCITRAL Arbitration Rules ("At the request of either party the expert, after delivery of the report, may be heard at a hearing where the parties shall have the opportunity to be present and to interrogate the expert. At this hearing either party may present expert witnesses in order to testify on the points at issue..."); Art. 21(2) of the LCIA Arbitration Rules; Art. 32(2) of the Spanish Arbitration Act 2003.
29. E.g., Art. 20(4) LCIA Arbitration Rules.
30. On the interaction of tribunal discretion and party agreement in fixing the procedure for the arbitration, see Yves FORTIER, "The Minimum Requirements of Due Process in Taking Measures Against Dilatory Tactics: Arbitral Discretion in International Commercial Arbitration – A Few Plain Rules and A Few Strong Instincts" in *Improving the Efficiency of Arbitration Agreements and Awards: 40 Years of the Application of the New York Convention*, ICCA Congress Series no. 9 (Kluwer, The Hague 1999) pp. 396-409 at p. 402 ("In practice, arbitrators faced with a procedural issue in respect of which the parties have not specifically agreed do not simply note the lack of such agreement and then pronounce their decision 'from on high'. The experienced – and I dare say, effective-arbitrator will consult with the parties and counsel, and solicit their views and suggestions, going so far as to encourage settlement between them, prior to rendering a decision. Conversely, when faced with party consensus regarding a particular procedural matter, such an arbitrator might still choose to engage in discussion with all concerned.").

There are dangers from a time and cost perspective in the parties (or in practice their counsel) deciding by agreement on the parameters for oral advocacy at the hearing. Counsel are likely to over-estimate the time required for oral advocacy. There are many possible reasons for this: a misplaced zeal to maximize the opportunities of communication with the tribunal, inexperience or a desire to create and exploit tactical advantages through oral advocacy.[31] Counsel like the luxury of time. From an efficiency perspective the oral phase of the procedure should be compatible with the written phase, and the tribunal should not allow counsel to impose a more elaborate hearing procedure than is necessary. If the written phase has been modelled on the standard of international arbitral procedure and then the hearing is conducted on a common law model, there will be wasted duplication as the advantages of the written substitution inherent in the international arbitral procedure are lost. If the parties wish to have a hearing on the common law model then it is more efficient to decide at the outset of the arbitration to follow common law pleading practice without extensive written argumentation.[32]

V. THE LIMITS OF TIME CONTROL IV: SUMMARY OF THE CURRENT POSITION

There is a hierarchical relationship between the principles of due process, party agreement and arbitral efficiency. The arbitration must always be conducted in accordance with the principles of due process, which take priority over the agreement of the parties and procedural efficiency. Further, provided the requirements of due process are met then the parties can agree to an inefficient procedure for the hearing of their dispute.

The practice of international arbitration today is to give the parties reasonable and equal opportunities to present their cases in writing before an oral hearing is reached. A full and fair written process preceding the hearing will reduce the mandatory requirements of due process relating to the content or time allowed for the advocacy of counsel at the hearing. The parties may agree and insist on an extended oral procedure, but in practice the arbitral tribunal has the decisive voice in setting the content and time limits for oral advocacy at the hearing. The decisive role of the arbitral tribunal imposes the responsibility on the arbitral tribunal to set the procedure to ensure that advocacy at

---

31. David W. RIVKIN, "21st Century Arbitration Worthy of Its Name" in *Law of International Business and Dispute Settlement in the 21st Century*, Liber Amicorum Karl-Heinz Böckstiegel (Carl Heymanns Verlag KG, Köln 2001) pp. 661-669, at p. 662 ("Counsel representing parties, and the parties themselves, frequently wish to present to the arbitrators everything they know about the case or feel the need to rebut all the arguments made by the other side, for fear that anything left unsaid could hurt them. In addition, they frequently have less experience with international arbitration than the arbitrators, so they seek to rely upon the procedures to which they are accustomed in their own domestic litigation. Arbitrators have the power and the authority to set the rules by which the arbitration will be conducted, and they have the ability to persuade the parties of the advantages of those procedures").
32. See Annex I, Example 1, p. 200. The written substitution in international arbitral procedure means the returns from oral advocacy are likely to be lower and decline more quickly than under the conventional common law model. If notwithstanding the extensive written procedure the length of hearing is set on the common law model, then the result is much more time than is necessary for efficient advocacy.

the hearing is conducted efficiently and an optimum duration is established for the hearing. The optimization of hearing time requires proactive arbitration management from the tribunal.

VI.   NINE GUIDELINES FOR EFFECTIVE TIME CONTROL OF ARBITRAL ADVOCACY

What does the responsibility to optimize hearing time by proactive arbitration management require in practice? What are the best means to achieve optimal time distribution and control at the arbitral hearing?

The above analysis suggests the following nine guidelines for an arbitral tribunal seeking to optimize the use of time at the oral hearing:

1. Identify the oral advocacy minimum required by applicable mandatory rules: Mandatory rules, in the form of due process, applicable procedural law and institutional rules, may require the tribunal to hold a hearing where requested by one party, but normally impose few prescriptive requirements on the nature of oral advocacy at the hearing. Nevertheless, the tribunal obviously should always be aware of the minimum requirements of the hearing imposed by mandatory rules.

2. Take full advantage of the potential of written advocacy: The presentation of evidence, expertise and arguments in writing reduces the functions of the oral hearing, with substantial savings in time and costs. The most effective technique for time control of oral advocacy is to take maximum advantage of the potential of written advocacy.

3. Consult with counsel: The tribunal must consult with counsel regarding the conduct for the hearing. The starting point for the consultation should be the tribunal's own preliminary assessment of the appropriate procedure and time frames for the hearing. Counsel should be asked to respond to specific proposals, as well as provide their own proposals, within a set time frame.

4. Assess the costs and returns of oral advocacy to determine the objectives and time required for the hearing: After consulting with the Parties, the tribunal is in a position to identify the objectives of the hearing. The arbitral tribunal can classify these objectives by function (for example, questioning of witnesses, conferencing experts, short opening statements, etc) or by questions or issue, or both (for example, "at the hearing the parties will be able to question witnesses, with questioning confined to the issues of XYZ etc").[33] Where

---

33. Cf. Sir Michael KERR, "Concord and Conflict in International Arbitration", *op. cit.*, fn. 5, pp. 121-144 at p. 125 ("Oral cross-examination of witnesses should be permitted upon request, but only under the control of the tribunal. This may involve advance notice of the issues on which it is desired to cross-examine each witness, whereupon the tribunal may impose limits on the number of witnesses, on the issues which it considers to be relevant, and on the time available for cross-examination."); Art. 19(3) of the LCIA Rules specifically provide for the tribunal to provide a list of questions for the hearing ("The Arbitral Tribunal may in advance of any hearing submit to the parties a list of questions which it wishes them to answer with special attention").

appropriate, the tribunal may consider the possibility of summary adjudication.[34] The selection of the objectives of the oral hearing will require an intuitive assessment of the likely returns of oral advocacy, and the time necessary to achieve these returns.

The arbitral tribunal must then address the costs of these hearing objectives, including how much preparation will be required and how effective counsel are likely to be in their advocacy; and whether there are any more efficient alternative means to achieve the same objectives. *The proper enquiry, as explained above, is the optimum length of the hearing and not the minimum length.*

5. *Issue a procedural order defining the objectives and the available time for advocacy at the hearing*: The conduct of the hearing should be addressed in a procedural order issued prior to the hearing. It is usual at this stage to confirm that written statements from witnesses shall serve as direct evidence, and to require the parties to identify the witnesses proposed by the opposing party that will be required for cross-examination. This common practice eliminates oral examination-in-chief and the attendance of unnecessary witnesses at the hearing, saving time as a result. The tribunal might also propose or advise the parties that witness or expert conferencing will be used at the hearing.[35]

The procedural order sometimes also identifies the other forms of advocacy that will take place at the hearing and the time permitted for them ("Each party may make an opening statement, not exceeding 30 minutes in length").

The procedural order may also identify the questions or issues to be dealt with by witnesses or counsel, either in a prescriptive form (that is, the tribunal simply orders that cross-examination, questioning or oral submissions will be limited to defined issues) or a merely advisory manner.

The proper preparation of counsel, experts and witnesses for the hearing, and the efficient use by counsel of time, are imperative if the full benefits of an oral hearing are to be achieved. The procedural order should ensure that all participants are fully informed well in advance of the hearing of the matters to be addressed at the hearing and the time controls that will be respected. The procedural order should establish the tribunal's expectations regarding the use of time, including the expectation that counsel and the parties will co-operate and share the responsibility for ensuring that advocacy does not waste time at the hearing.

Participant preparation is fundamental to effective time control at the hearing, and the procedural order is the tribunal's best opportunity to influence preparation and set the expectations for the oral advocacy of counsel.

6. *Fix a time allocation for the advocacy of each party*: A now common technique to encourage efficient advocacy is the fixed time allocation for each party (the "chess clock"

---

34. DAVID W. RIVKIN, "21st Century Arbitration Worthy of its Name", *op. cit.* fn. 31, pp. 661-669, at pp. 663-664.
35. Some commentators suggest that witness conferencing clarifies issues quicker than conventional party questioning and therefore saves time at the hearing; see, for example, Bernard HANOTIAU, "The Conduct of the Hearings" in Lawrence W. NEWMAN, Richard D. HILL, eds., *The Leading Arbitrators' Guide to International Arbitration* (Juris Publishing 2004) pp. 369-389 at p. 387.

technique). Each party is allocated a fixed period of time for cross-examination, submissions and other forms of advocacy that will take place at the hearing. Counsel for each party then have the discretion to distribute this time according to their own forensic priorities at the hearing.

This method of time control of advocacy offers numerous advantages. It guarantees the completion of the hearing within a specific period of time. It forces counsel in advance at the hearing to consider how long each forensic intervention is likely to take, and to eliminate any unnecessary advocacy from his or her plans in advance, and not to waste any time during the hearing. It is a salutary discipline for counsel to have an eye on the clock at all times.[36] It has proved successful in practice and has attracted praise from senior lawyers.[37]

This method invariably begins from a premise of equal time to both parties. This might not always be appropriate; for example where there is a significant imbalance between the number of witness statements and expert reports prepared by each side, and therefore the time required for witness questioning. However, it must never be forgotten that the essence of this method is time allocation and not equality. Equality of time is simply the convenient starting point; the fact that one party might have more to do in the set time simply increases the necessity to allocate that time well. Conversely, the tribunal may grant one party additional time during the hearing if it wishes to hear more from that party's counsel. Equality must not be a distraction in a hair-splitting search for "fairness", as when parties try to elevate differences in time allocation into a matter of due process.[38] The fairness of this method of time control lies in its efficiency and in the fact that counsel are given prior notice of their time allocation and can adjust their cases accordingly.

A fixed time allocation is a salutary discipline for the oral advocacy of counsel. Its potential should not be overlooked or underestimated by an arbitral tribunal.

---

36. Cf. UNCITRAL Notes on Organizing Arbitral Proceedings para. 79 ("Such planning of time [by limiting the aggregate amount of time of each party], provided it is realistic, fair and subject to judiciously firm control by the arbitral tribunal, will make it easier for the parties to plan the presentation of the various items of evidence and arguments, reduce the likelihood of running out of time towards the end of the hearings and avoid that one party would unfairly use up a disproportionate amount of time.").

37. For example, see John FELLAS, "A Fair and Efficient International Arbitration Process", Dispute Resolution Journal (2004) pp. 74-83 at p. 82 ("I have always appreciated the discipline of this process of presenting my case within time constraints ... placing time limits on presentations is an effective method of getting the parties and their counsel to agree to use their time efficiently."); DAVID W. RIVKIN, "21st Century Arbitration Worthy of Its Name" *op. cit.* fn. 31, pp. 661-669, at p. 668 ("Within the hearing itself ... I have used time limits on several cases, and it has been enormously useful.... Having a strict time limit forces parties to concentrate on which evidence is necessary from which witness, and it avoids unnecessary and repetitive testimony. In none of the cases in which I have used a time clock have I found that important evidence was not presented.").

38. See *Fouchard Gaillard Goldman*, *op. cit.*, fn. 17, para. 1299 ("The principle of equal treatment of the parties requires that both must have the opportunity to present their case orally, but not, as some parties claim, that they should have exactly the same amount of time to do so.").

7. Consider other possible incentives for preparation and effective advocacy: Another method to encourage efficient advocacy is by advising the parties and counsel prior to the hearing that the tribunal will take the advocacy of the parties into account in its allocation of costs. The ICC Commission on Arbitration in its *Techniques for Controlling Time and Costs in International Arbitration*[39] notes that the *"allocation of costs can provide a useful tool to encourage efficient behaviour and discourage unreasonable behaviour"* and lists "excessive legal argument", "excessive cross-examination" and "dilatory tactics" amongst the examples of unreasonable behaviour. The 2010 revision of the *IBA Rules on the Taking of Evidence in International Commercial Arbitration* (Art. 9(7)) suggests that the tribunal take into account in the allocation of costs any lack of good faith of a party in respect of the taking of evidence.

Given the subjectivity of many of the decisions an advocate must make, it would probably require an egregious case to justify a finding that advocacy has been unreasonable, excessive or lacking in good faith. However, the warning by a tribunal that it may take into account the efficient use of time at the hearing in its assessment of costs will encourage counsel to focus on the effective use of time.

8. Curtail time-wasting advocacy: It is a counsel of perfection in advocacy to demand that counsel speak only when necessary, and say only what is required. Nevertheless, there are some readily identifiable vices of oral advocacy in international arbitration that could be eliminated relatively easily.

The common law tradition that the development of the case, including the selection, order and mode of the presentation of evidence and argument, is the responsibility of counsel and the judge should allow counsel to get on with it is an anachronism in this age of active case management by judges, or strict time limits for argument.[40] It is not a breach of due process or other mandatory rules in international arbitration that counsel are not permitted to present their client's case in their own manner at the hearing. The power of the tribunal to intervene to curtail a line of questioning, direct evidence or argument to particular issues, or simply to prevent counsel wasting time is clear from institutional rules and other instruments in international arbitration.[41]

Some specific types of advocacy that the tribunal might curtail is advocacy that addresses evidence and argument already sufficiently addressed in writing, as well as

---

39. Report from the ICC Commission on Arbitration *Techniques for Controlling Time and Costs in Arbitration*, op. cit. fn. 1, para. 85.
40. DAVID W. RIVKIN, "21st Century Arbitration Worthy of Its Name", *op. cit.* fn. 31, pp. 661-669, at p. 664 ("The time and expense involved in international arbitration now requires arbitrators and parties to give up the former belief that in an arbitration parties should be able to present all of the evidence they wish to present. Such an attitude leads to a greater burden and unnecessary costs for all the parties.").
41. See, for example, Art. 16(3) of the ICDR International Arbitration Rules (effective 1 June 2009) ("The tribunal may in its discretion direct the order of proof ... exclude cumulative or irrelevant testimony or other evidence and direct the parties to focus their presentations on issues the decision of which could dispose of all or part of the case."); Art. 8(2) of the IBA Rules on the Taking of Evidence in International Commercial Arbitration.

duplicative advocacy generally,[42] irrelevant questioning and argumentation, unnecessary aggression, cross-examination directed towards the credibility of witnesses,[43] and practices derived from inapplicable domestic rules of evidence. This last category includes certain objections to the form of the questioning of witnesses, formalities such as identifying and summarizing the contents of documents through witnesses, presenting evidence or argument only "for the (written) record", and the reading of extracts from authorities. These practices suggest either that counsel is unaccustomed to international arbitration, or lacks confidence in the diligence of the arbitrator in preparing for the hearing and drafting the award. Advocacy should respond exclusively to the demands of international arbitration, and not to the customs of counsel's domestic jurisdiction.

9. *Lead by example*: The full preparation of the arbitrators for the hearing means counsel do not need to spend valuable time in the explanation of facts, arguments and evidence already presented in writing. A tribunal that knows the issues that are important to its decision, and questions witnesses and counsel in a penetrating manner can narrow the matters in dispute, as well as transmit a sense of urgency and confidence to counsel that has the effect of improving the efficiency of the oral advocacy.

VII. CONCLUSIONS

The primary function of the oral advocacy in international arbitration today is to complete the process of the taking of evidence through the questioning of witnesses and experts. The oral hearing serves other purposes including meeting any requirements of mandatory law or due process, satisfying the agreement or expectations of the parties, and identifying the subject matter of further evidence or post-hearing briefs. The oral hearing also brings all the participants together and so offers benefits of contemporaneous preparation and personal interaction, including dialogue between counsel and the tribunal and a better informed tribunal.

An oral hearing has substantial costs, which have attracted considerable attention in recent years. However, the interests of international arbitration are best served by a focus on an efficient hearing rather than time or cost minimization. An efficient hearing requires the tribunal to consider and attempt to roughly quantify the costs and returns

---

42. Cf. Report from the ICC Commission on Arbitration *Techniques for Controlling Time and Costs in Arbitration*, op. cit., fn. 1, para. 79: ("Consideration should be given to whether it is necessary to repeat pre-hearing written submissions in opening oral statements. This is sometimes done because of concern that the arbitral tribunal will not have read or digested the written submissions. If the arbitral tribunal has been provided with the documents it needs to read in advance of the hearing and has prepared properly, this will not be necessary.").
43. The testing of credibility – a major function of cross-examination in common law jurisdictions – is problematic in international arbitration, complicated by differences in language, culture and the applicable rules of evidence in questioning. On unnecessary aggression and cross-examination as to credibility in international commercial arbitration see Bernardo M. CREMADES and David J.A. CAIRNS "Cross-Examination and International Arbitration" in Kaj HOBÉR, Annette MAGNUSSON and Marie ÖHRSTRÖM, eds., *Between East and West: Essays in Honour of Ulf Franke* (Juris Publishing 2010) and the references cited therein.

of the hearing over time. An efficient hearing requires an effort to identify the optimum length rather than the minimum practical hearing.

The arbitral tribunal has a responsibility to optimize hearing time, and the optimization of hearing time requires proactive time management. Proactive management requires time control to be addressed through a structured process that fixes expectations, defines objectives, allocates time and provides incentives to the disciplined preparation of counsel for the hearing.

ANNEX I

The Economics of Oral Advocacy and Time Control

The following analysis illustrates the explanation in the text of the optimum hearing length for oral advocacy in more explicitly economic terms, using graphical representations of marginal costs and revenue. This analysis therefore assumes that not only the costs but the returns of advocacy can be quantified in monetary terms.

For the purposes of analysis a constant relationship between time and hearing cost is assumed. In other words, each additional hour or day of hearing time has the same cost. This means the marginal cost is constant and hence graphically appears as a horizontal line.

As a starting point, let us also assume the returns of advocacy decline at a constant rate for each additional hour of advocacy: i.e, that the marginal returns decrease at a constant rate.

Graphically these assumptions would give the following result:

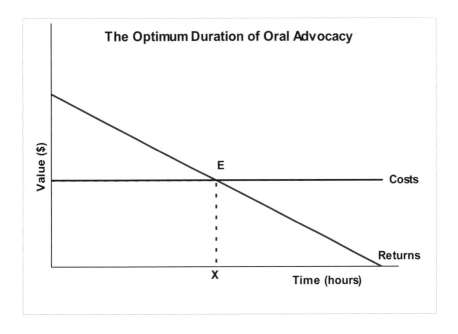

Point E represents the efficient or optimum level of oral advocacy. An efficient hearing will last for X hours, because it is at this point where the marginal cost is equal to the marginal returns and hence where the benefits of the hearing are maximized. Until point E is reached, each additional unit of time increases the total returns more than it increases the total costs; i.e, each additional unit of time keeps increasing the benefits or efficiency of orality. But from point E onwards each additional unit of time will increase the total costs more than it does the total returns and hence the benefits or efficiency of orality will start decreasing. We still obtain benefits, in other words, the returns of orality are still higher than its costs, but the benefits we obtain are diminishing with each additional unit of time. There is an overall loss of efficiency when we try to maximize the returns without taking into account the costs.

While it may be possible to accurately plot the marginal cost of advocacy curve in a particular arbitration, the position and slope of the returns curve presents insurmountable problems in practice. However, by concentrating on the possible effects of individual variables on the returns curve, the economics of advocacy can still provide certain insights. For example:

Example 1: The Effects of the Substitution of Written for Oral Proceedings.

The existence of a well-developed written phase, as in international arbitration, prior to the beginning of the oral hearing is likely to mean that the marginal returns of advocacy begin at a lower level and decline more quickly than at an oral hearing based on conventional common law procedure:

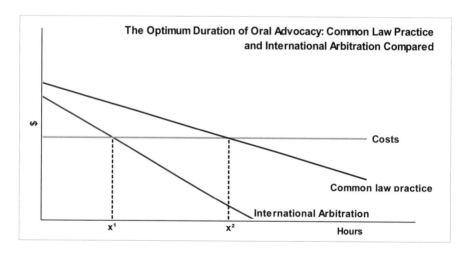

The result is that the optimum level of advocacy will require less time (graphically, the difference in hours between X^1 and X^2) with a well-developed written phase as the prior substitution of an extended written procedure lowers the returns of oral advocacy.

Example 2: The Quality of Advocacy

Another variable that affects the optimum length of hearing is the quality of advocacy (which is a function of the training, experience and preparation of the advocate). Highly professional advocacy is likely to initially produce a high marginal return, and may give high marginal returns for some time, but a point will be reached where the advocate has covered the most important issues, and further advocacy will mean rapidly diminishing marginal returns. Poor advocacy, in contrast, will have a low initial level of marginal return, but marginal returns will decline more gradually as the poor or ill-prepared advocate slowly makes the necessary arguments. Diagrammatically this appears as follows:

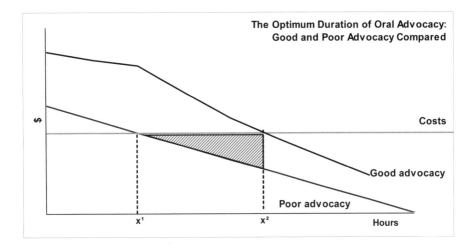

The conclusion, not surprisingly, is that good advocacy justifies a longer hearing than poor advocacy.

If the poor or ill-prepared advocate is allowed as much time as the good advocate then the shaded area represents the loss of benefits or wasted efficiency because of the inefficient allocation of time to the level of the forensic skill or preparation of counsel.

The Examination and Cross-Examination of Witnesses

Marinn Carlson[*]

TABLE OF CONTENTS	Page
I. Learning by Doing	202
II. Putting a Human Face on the Story	203
III. In Defense of Direct Examination	204
IV. Techniques for Effective Witness Examination	204

I. LEARNING BY DOING

I have been asked to speak about a topic – the examination of witnesses at a hearing – that is a bit difficult with this audience. Some of you have been examining witnesses, and watching their examinations, for decades. For others, this is relatively unfamiliar territory.

I also find it difficult because of the nature of the subject – witness examination is truly something that can only really be learned in part by seeing it done right, and most of all, it can only be learned by actually doing it. Someone like me talking about the examination of witnesses is a bit like someone talking about how one goes about riding a bicycle. No amount of theory in a conference room can even begin to substitute for actually getting on the bike. Frankly, a discussion about the theory really isn't much help at all when you are trying to balance, and get your feet on the pedals, and move forward, without falling off. If it has been a long time since you learned that skill, try to remember what it felt like to wobble down the sidewalk for the first time – as you were careening toward the bushes or the parked car, would it have helped you that before you got on the bicycle, someone said to you "push the pedals evenly in sequence"? Well, that's a lot like me sitting here saying things like "no leading questions in direct examination"....

That is why I would like to offer yet another plug for the program that Ank Santens mentioned yesterday morning – the Foundation for International Arbitration Advocacy's (FIAA) three-day, learning-by-doing workshops on examining fact witnesses and expert witnesses. In the interest of full disclosure, I am part of the faculty as well. In a salute to the rising importance of Brazil, and Latin America more generally, in international arbitration – as indicated by the location of this very conference – the program in São Paolo in October or November 2010 is our first outside of Europe. The program is not three days of lectures, it is three days of practicing examination skills, including with a full mock hearing. It is as close to real life as we can get it – because in real life, as we know, although we use this curious terminology of the "practice" of law, most clients do not wish to be the ones you "practice" upon, or that you try these techniques on for the first time.

---

[*] Partner, Sidley Austin LLP.

Having said all that, I have been asked to speak about the examination of witnesses, and so I shall dutifully try to do as I am told. As a threshold matter, I hope you'll allow me the luxury of setting aside the question of whether there should be examination of witnesses by the parties' counsel at all. The point has been made in a number of presentations already that that is not a given – that it is not a familiar thing, particularly for those in the civil law traditions, to have adversarial questioning of witnesses by the lawyers rather than the judge. (Well, perhaps it's familiar from the movies, or episodes of *Law & Order* on TV, but as you know by now, nothing is like the movies. The witness *never* breaks down crying on the stand and admits liability for breach of contract, or gives in and yells "you can't handle the truth!" like Jack Nicholson in the movie *A Few Good Men*. And in fact, if the witness starts crying, this august, well-mannered community of international arbitrators will probably hold it against you for being too much like an American litigator – I don't recommend it.)

II. PUTTING A HUMAN FACE ON THE STORY

But whether the examination of witnesses is familiar or not, the reality is that it is a known and, by this point, common phenomenon in international arbitration. I don't necessarily say that is a good thing or a bad thing – heaven only knows, American-style litigation is just as scary to me as to you (there's a reason why I do international arbitration!). But it is the done thing, and so it is an important part of effective advocacy to take advantage of the opportunity – and it *is* an opportunity – to use this means of presenting the case.

So assuming we are in a hearing where there will be examination of witnesses, why is so much attention paid to this aspect of the hearing? I would suggest that it is because the testimony of witnesses is the one thing that happens in the hearing that simply cannot be done on paper. As advocates, we can be very eloquent in oral argument, in our opening statements and our closing statements. But we could, if we had to, also put those same eloquent words in writing.

What we cannot do in writing is let the arbitrators assess the credibility and demeanor of witnesses. We can help the witnesses present their testimony in their written statements – we can put the facts on paper. But we cannot put the witness's candor on paper. And for your opponent's witnesses, we cannot test their candor on paper. I am very much a believer in the advice we received yesterday, that your written submissions are your first chance to make a first impression, and that both your submission and your witness's statements must tell a clear, straightforward story. But the witness's testimony is the opportunity to put a human face on that story. And it is the opportunity, in cross-examination, to probe the strengths and weaknesses of that story. If we did not examine the witness, we would have only words on paper, and untested words at that. If you come from a tradition that is not comfortable with party employees as witnesses, for example, imagine how you would feel if such testimony were only offered in writing, without a chance to put that witness under the spotlight of in-person testimony. I think we can agree that, as a matter of human nature, it can be a lot harder to stand by the accuracy or truth of a statement in person than it is to read and sign a piece of paper.

III. IN DEFENSE OF DIRECT EXAMINATION

So let us turn to the examination itself. First, let me say a word or two in defense of direct examination, which is much maligned – unfairly, in my view. Now, we all understand that the point of written witness statements is to substitute for a direct examination, to save time at the hearing since we don't have a jury that needs to be told the story from the beginning at the hearing itself. The arbitrators have read the pleadings, and they have read the witness statements, so before the hearing they already know how each side's story goes. So on this theory, we shouldn't need any direct examination, and after confirming the witness's name, we should just jump immediately into cross-examination as if the witness had just finished delivering orally the direct testimony in his witness statement. This sounds efficient, and we all want arbitration to be an efficient process. But in my view, as the advocate for the party putting that witness forward, there is something to be said for a little direct examination too. Not to repeat the entirety of the witness statement, but to hit the highlights, and perhaps to respond to allegations or developments that have arisen since the witness signed her statement. Why? Why resist the push – a push which, I must say, often comes from the arbitrators? Because as the advocate, I would like the tribunal to get to see my witness, and to get a sense of her or his candor and forthrightness – to get a measure of this person. And I want the tribunal to begin to develop that impression *before* the witness comes under hostile fire. That is, before he or she is on the defensive, and under stress.

IV. TECHNIQUES FOR EFFECTIVE WITNESS EXAMINATION

Now what does that mean for the techniques of direct examination? Well, the first and most important rule – which applies equally to direct and cross examination – is: keep the questions short, and simple. You the lawyer are not testifying. You are not the star of the show. (Again, remember, this is not the movies – here, the witness plays the starring role.) Your eloquence does not matter, and if you are too eloquent, the witness will lose track of what you are asking. The last thing you want is for your *own* witness to ask "what was the question?".

But the second rule of direct examination is "no leading questions" – no questions that suggest the answer in the question itself.

Now, as an aside, I have to be careful if I start talking about rules: this often comes up in the FIAA seminars, when we stop someone to point out that they have asked a leading question on direct examination, or that they have asked an open question on cross-examination – they get frustrated about these "rules" and what common law system invented them, and why do they have to follow them? The answer is of course you do not have to follow them – this is one of the best things about arbitration instead of litigation, that the actual mandatory rules are very few and far between, and the common techniques of witness examination are not those kinds of rules at all. But there are reasons behind them.

The reason behind "no leading questions on direct examination" is that your questions are there to launch the witness – *your* witness – to tell her own story. Your question opens the door for the witness, and maybe offers a gentle nudge as to which direction the witness should go, but then it is the witness who tells the tale. We heard very good advice yesterday from Nigel Blackaby[1] and John Gardiner that a witness who is coached, who sounds like she is reciting a rehearsed speech, or who just echoes the lawyer, is not persuasive. If that is what your witness does, then yes, you might as well have skipped direct examination and just relied on the written statement – in fact you may be worse off for having done a direct examination.

So this is why no leading questions on direct examination – because a leading question on direct examination just has the witness agreeing with what the lawyer said, rather than testifying for him- or herself. For example: "Mr. Jones, when you received the shipment on May 12 did you examine it and discover some defects in the equipment?" "Yes I did." "Were those defects serious and disruptive to your production schedule?" "Why yes they were." – Compare that to "Mr Jones, what happened when the shipment arrived?".

Now, let's consider cross-examination. There, the situation is reversed. Your job is to probe the weaknesses of Mr. Jones' testimony. On Sunday evening, in his opening remarks for the conference, Jan Paulsson characterized advocacy as the "art of persuasion" – and importantly he added, the art of possibly changing minds. If, as Guillermo Aguilar Alvarez said, the first impression is made in the written submission,[2] and if, as Professor Crivellaro said, the arbitrators likely come to the hearing with preliminary views about the case already developed,[3] then indeed, cross-examination may be your last opportunity to change their minds if they are leaning toward the other side. As Professor Crivellaro rightly said, cross-examination is not about humiliating the witness or badgering him or her. I promise you, there is very little to be gained from that. Cross-examination is about sending a message to the tribunal about the weaknesses of that witness's testimony. Not necessarily because the witness is lying or stretching the truth – often the message is about what the witness has not said, or how the witness's testimony might be incompatible with the party's legal theory.

Now, when it comes to technique, there is a tension in this idea of sending a message in cross-examination. You want it to be clear to the tribunal what you are asking about – so again, simple, short questions, and maybe some headings too ("Mr. Jones, I'd now like to ask you a few questions about the shipment that you received"). You also want it to be reasonably clear to the tribunal *why* you are asking what you are asking. But if it is clear to the tribunal where you are going and why, it may well be clear to the witness as well. And to be sure, the other side's witness is not there to help you. If Mr. Jones knows that you hope to show that he did not timely report any defect in the product, he is not about to help you by saying so. Again, there need not be any suggestion that Mr. Jones would lie to avoid saying that, but he is not going to offer it to you just because you ask him politely.

This is how we come to what I think of as a third basic rule: "no open questions on cross-examination". An open question is one that allows the witness to elaborate, to

---

1. See N. BLACKABY, "Witness Preparation – A Key to Effective Advocacy in International Arbitration", this volume, pp. 118-132.
2. See G. AGUILAR ALVAREZ, "Written Advocacy", this volume, pp. 55-64.
3. See A. CRIVELLARO, "Advocacy in International Arbitration: An Art, a Science or a Technique?", this volume pp. 9-16.

explain, to expound on a subject. The most obvious example is "why" or "why not"? "Mr. Jones, if the shipment was defective as you now say, why didn't you immediately report it to the seller?" Mr. Jones is now about to launch on a five minute long self-defense – this is not what you were looking for.

Instead, you ask closed questions – questions that admit of only a limited range of answers. "Mr. Jones, after you discovered the alleged defect on 12 May, you did not call the seller, did you?" Factually, his only answer is "no". "You did not write a letter or send an e-mail to the seller about this defect in the month of May, did you?" Again, "no". "In fact, the first time you mentioned this defect in writing was in your letter of 20 August, wasn't it?" And "yes".

To be sure, Mr. Jones will by this point interject some explanations and justifications, and you, appropriate to the decorum of international arbitration, will politely let him finish – but you have sent your message to the tribunal, and you have, to some degree, controlled the hostile witness by forcing him first to admit to the facts *before* he gets to offer his excuses. This is the theory of "closed questions" for cross-examination.

This is not the time or the place to get too far into the techniques of witness examination, or to talk about the differences between examining fact witnesses and expert witnesses, or to tell war stories about the famous pitfalls of "one question too many".

I hope here to have highlighted that there are some common techniques for effective witness examination, that there is some reasoning behind those techniques, and that the techniques are part of a useful and I submit necessary skill set for modern international arbitration practitioners. With them, you can do your best to persuade, and, if necessary for your side, to change some minds. And you can do so not through the medium of your own words or arguments, but through the medium of the witnesses – the most unpredictable, but sometimes the most powerful (because they connect to the arbitrators on a human level) pieces of evidence available to you.

The Effective Use of Legal Sources: How Much Is Too Much and What Is the Role for *Iura Novit Curia*?

Dr. Claus von Wobeser[*]

TABLE OF CONTENTS	Page
I. Preliminary Comments	207
II. Role of Arbitrators When Applying the Law	208
III. To What Extent Should Arbitrators Establish the Content of the Chosen Law?	212
IV. Practical Solution in International Arbitration in Establishing the Content of the Chosen Law	217
V. The Advocate's Perspective	219

I. PRELIMINARY COMMENTS

This paper considers the best practices for both counsel and arbitrators for the questioning of witnesses and the use of legal sources, when applying the substantive law governing the dispute submitted to arbitration, especially during the arbitration hearing. The subject of this paper has further been narrowed to focus on the role of *iura novit curia*.

The status of the law governing the merits of the dispute must be addressed with reference to international arbitration rules and practice. Reference to rules or principles applicable in national courts should be avoided, as these are very different from those applicable to international arbitration.

The same applies with the Latin aphorism *iura novit curia*, which literally means "the judge knows the law" and refers to a principle of procedural law, according to which the parties do not have to prove the content of the law before national courts.

There are different approaches taken by national courts when applying foreign law. Some jurisdictions, such as the Swiss, German or Mexican, consider foreign law as law and apply the principle. According to this approach, national courts have the obligation to know the law and apply it to the facts, even if it is foreign.

Some jurisdictions regard foreign law as a fact which must be proven. English and French law (unlike many civil law jurisdictions) adopt this view. In this approach,

---

[*] Managing Partner, Von Wobeser & Sierra, S.C., Mexico City; Bachelor of Law, Escuela Libre de Derecho, Mexico City; Doctorate of Law, Universidad de Droit, d'Economie et de Sciences Sociales de Paris; Vice Chairman, ICC Court of Arbitration; President of the Arbitration Commission, ICC Mexico; Member LCIA, Latin American Council; Member Board of Directors American Arbitration Association.

The author wishes to acknowledge Montserrat Manzano for her assistance in preparing this contribution.

national courts are not expected to research foreign law ex officio, and will apply foreign law only if proven as a fact, dismissing the application of the *iura novit curia* principle.

It has been said that reference to the rules applicable to national courts and their experience in applying foreign law is of limited use when applied to international arbitration. As there is no lex fori in international arbitration, the very concept of foreign law is misplaced.[1] Therefore, the conclusion that the principle of *iura novit curia* is not applicable to arbitral tribunals has been the view of most legal scholars.

According to our colleague Yves Derains "*L'adage Jura novit curia n'a pas sa place en matière d'arbitrage.*" [The *iura novit curia* adage has no place in arbitration.][2]

Gabrielle Kaufmann-Kohler also agrees that "a hard and fast *iura novit curia* rule would be inappropriate in international arbitration" and that a "pure 'law is fact' approach would not be appropriate either".[3]

Also, Julian Lew considers that "The situation in international arbitration is different. There are 'no forum' procedural requirements to follow. Rather, the composition of the Tribunal and the attitude of the arbitrators, often influenced by their own legal background, is a crucial factor. Equally there is no 'foreign law'."[4]

According to Fouchard, Gaillard and Goldman an "arbitral tribunal has no forum".[5]

Therefore, when it comes to international arbitration, the starting premise should necessarily be that an arbitrator must apply the law chosen by the parties and should not avoid this obligation with an argument that the law is foreign.

In order to determine the status of the substantive law in international arbitration and the role of arbitrators and counsel during the oral phase of the arbitration, however, it is essential to address the following questions: What is the role of arbitrators when applying the law? To what extent should arbitrators establish the law? How should arbitrators establish the content of the chosen law? What is the role of advocacy in this matter?

II. ROLE OF ARBITRATORS WHEN APPLYING THE LAW

1. Law as Fact Approach

Let us go back to Gabrielle Kaufmann-Kohler's Canadian co-arbitrator who "suggested dismissing a claim because – he said – 'they have not proven the law'".[6] There are

---

1. Gabrielle KAUFMANN-KOHLER, "The Governing Law: Fact or Law? – A Transnational Rule on establishing its contents" in M. Wirth, ed., *Best Practices in International Arbitration*, ASA Special Series, No. 26 (July 2006) p. 80.
2. Yves DERAINS, "Observations – *Cour d'appel de Paris* (1re Ch. C) 13 novembre 1997 – *Lemeur v. SARL Les Cités invisibles*", 1998 Revue de l'Arbitrage (Kluwer Law International, no. 4) pp. 709-711 at p. 711.
3. *Op. cit.*, fn. 1, p. 84.
4. J.D. LEW, L. MISTELIS, S. KRÖLL, *Comparative International Commercial Arbitration*, (Kluwer Law International 2003) pp. 442-443.
5. FOUCHARD, GAILLARD, GOLDMAN, *On International Commercial Arbitration*, (Kluwer Law International 1999) p. 692.
6. *Op. cit.*, fn. 1, p. 79.

arbitration practitioners who are of the view that foreign law should be proven as a fact, and that the burden of proof is on the parties to ascertain the contents of the law.

Some authors, like Fouchard, Gaillard and Goldman, support this position and have stated that: "… The idea that foreign laws should be treated as issues of fact is well established in both common law and civil law systems and should apply in international arbitral practice."[7]

This approach may not be applied rigidly to arbitration. It seems that even the English are moving away from a strict view of foreign law as a fact. This is reflected in the text of the 1996 English Arbitration Act, Sect. 34(1)(g), which indicates that the procedural powers of an arbitral tribunal include: "whether and to what extent the tribunal should itself take the initiative in ascertaining the facts and the law".[8]

In this regard, common law jurisdictions also recognize the flexibility and powers of an arbitral tribunal to ascertain the law and recognize that the law proven by the parties should not necessarily be the limit for the arbitrator's powers to decide on the legal solution.

2. *Balanced Approach*

According to Gabrielle Kaufmann-Kohler's proposition any appropriate transnational solution must be found between the two extremes, for instance along the following lines:

> "The parties shall establish the contents of the law applicable to the merits. *The arbitral tribunal shall have the power, but not the obligation*, to conduct its own research to establish such contents. If it makes use of such power, the tribunal shall give the parties an opportunity to comment on the result of the tribunal's research.
>
> If the contents of the applicable law are not established with respect to a specific issue, the Arbitral Tribunal *is empowered* to apply to such issue any rule of law which it deems appropriate."[9] (Emphasis added.)

According to this proposition, we may extract the following concepts:

(a) Foreign law is treated as law.
(b) The parties agree to establish the contents of the law applicable to the merits.
(c) When the parties have established the contents of the law, the arbitral tribunal shall have the power, but not the obligation, to conduct its own research to establish such contents.
(d) If the arbitral tribunal makes use of the power to establish such contents, it must give the parties an opportunity to comment on the results.

---

7. *Op. cit.*, fn. 5, p. 692.
8. English Arbitration Act, 1996 at <http://www.opsi.gov.uk/acts/acts1996/ukpga_19960023_en_1#aofs> (last accessed 1 June 2010).
9. *Op. cit.*, fn. 1, p. 84.

(e) If the contents of the applicable law are not established by the parties on a specific issue, the arbitral tribunal is empowered (but not obliged) to apply any rule it deems appropriate.

We have two comments on this proposition.

The first comment is that this proposition assumes that the parties have agreed to establish the contents of the law. However, in my experience this does not happen in practice, where normally there is no agreement on this issue during the procedural hearing. According to international arbitration rules, parties are not obligated to establish the contents of the law, just their statement of the facts, points at issue and remedy sought.

For example, according to the UNCITRAL Arbitration Rules (1976), Art. 18(2), there is no obligation to state the law, as may be read from the following text:

> "The statement of claim shall include the following particulars:
> (a) The names and addresses of the parties;
> (b) A statement of the facts supporting the claim;
> (c) The points at issue;
> (d) The relief or remedy sought."[10]

According to this rule, claimants should only state the facts supporting their claim and the relief or remedy sought and the respondent a defense thereof. However, there is no obligation to include reference to the substantive law or establish its content.

The second comment is that this proposition acknowledges that the arbitral tribunal is empowered to establish the contents of the law; however it imposes no obligation to do so. Should this "may" be a "must"? Are arbitrators obliged to make their own inquiries to establish such contents when there is no input from the parties?

The debate of whether this is an obligation or not has been highlighted in the *Brazilian Federal Loans* case:

> "'... although the Court does not consider itself bound to know the local law of the states appearing before it, at the same time it does not consider such law simply a question of fact to be proved by evidence produced by the parties. *This is important for it leaves the Court free,* **perhaps even obligated**, *to resolve through its own researches any uncertainty concerning such a law,* **if the parties fail to produce adequate proof**.*"*[11] (Emphasis added.)

This discussion leads us to the following analysis.

---

10. United Nations Commission on International Trade Law, Arbitration Rules, General Assembly Resolution 31/98, at <http://www.uncitral.org/uncitral/en/uncitral_texts/arbitration/1976 Arbitration_rules.html> (last accessed 1 June 2010) p. 13.
11. *Brazilian Federal Loans* case, as quoted in Gabrielle KAUFMANN-KOHLER, "The Arbitrator and the Law: Does He/She Know It? Apply It? How? And a Few More Questions", 21 Arbitration International, (Kluwer Law International 2005, no. 4) pp. 631-638 at p. 636.

3. Arbitrators' Mandate Approach

In my opinion the role of arbitrators when applying the law should be viewed in light of their mandate towards the parties. According to their mandate arbitrators are expected to resolve a dispute applying the law chosen by the parties.

The mandate of arbitrators to "apply the law" has been stated in the arbitration rules of mainly every arbitration institution, e.g.:

ICC Rules Art. 17: "The parties shall be free to agree upon the *rules of law to be applied* by the Arbitral Tribunal to the merits of the dispute…";[12]
LCIA Rules Art. 22(3): "The Arbitral Tribunal *shall decide* the parties' dispute *in accordance with the law(s) or rules of law chosen by the parties* as applicable to the merits of their dispute…";[13]
UNCITRAL Rules Art. 28: "(1) The arbitral tribunal *shall decide* the dispute in accordance with such *rules of law as are chosen by the parties* as applicable to the substance of the dispute…."[14] (Emphasis added.)

In the application of the law, there are different expectations as to whether arbitrators should know the law or whether it has to be proven, depending on the legal tradition of counsel and parties to the dispute. According to Julian Lew, the best solution would be to make the most out of each system, along the following lines:

> "The parties make full legal argument in writing and orally, about the applicable rules. They may support this with legal materials and independent expert reports. The tribunal may request further specific details about the applicable law. *It will, however, decide itself what the specific applicable rules are rather than rely on any expert.* This approach leaves considerable discretion to the tribunal and is increasingly the norm in international arbitration…. This approach reflects a neutral and international expectation that *the applicable law or rules must be ascertained and applied.* It recognizes that in international arbitration there is no domestic forum or foreign law. There is only the applicable law for the particular case."[15] (Emphasis added.)

My view is in line with this position, according to which the tribunal itself will decide the specific applicable rules, rather than rely solely on experts or be bound by the parties' submissions. It also, reflects the mandate that the applicable law or rules must be ascertained and applied. The bottom line is that parties have the expectation that the applicable law or rules must be ascertained and applied and that the arbitrators should

---

12. Rules of Arbitration, International Chamber of Commerce, in force as of 1 January 1998, at: <http://www.iccwbo.org/uploadedFiles/Court/Arbitration/other/rules_arb_english.pdf> (last accessed 1 June 2010) p. 11.
13. Arbitration Rules, London Court of International Arbitration, effective 1 January 1998, at: <http://www.lcia-arbitration.com> (last accessed 1 June 2010).
14. *Op. cit.*, fn. 10, p. 18.
15. *Op. cit.*, fn. 4, pp. 443-444.

know the law (or avail of enough information to know it) in order to be able to fulfill their mandate.

In sum, arbitrators "must" establish the contents of the law. If the parties fail to do so, the arbitral tribunal is not only "empowered" by the arbitral rules to establish such contents but must do so, in order to fulfill its mandate.

Therefore, arbitrators are obligated to address all claims brought forward by the parties, and provide a solution, applying the substantive law chosen by the parties (even when the content of the law has not been brought forward by them).

III. TO WHAT EXTENT SHOULD ARBITRATORS ESTABLISH THE CONTENT OF THE CHOSEN LAW?

Arbitrators in applying the substantive law chosen by the parties are faced with limits. Fouchard, Gaillard and Goldman have delineated them as follows:

> "For the arbitrators, the only limits, other than those resulting from the intentions of the parties, derive from the requirements of international procedural public policy. These include, in particular, equality between the parties and compliance with the requirements of due process, a breach of which would allow the award to be set aside."[16]

It seems that these limits lie in that: (1) arbitrators must not exceed their mandate and (2) arbitrators must conduct the arbitration in such a way that it leads to a valid award.

1. Compliance with Arbitrators' Mandate

When arbitrators rule *infra petita* or *ultra petita*, they will have exceeded their mandate and their award risks being set aside or refused enforcement. This will be the case where arbitrators exceed their powers under the applicable rules or law.[17]

It is relevant to distinguish at the outset that arbitrators may not base their decisions on arguments which were not put forward by the parties. However, the limit lies in that arbitrators may not award the parties more than they sought in their claims. For example, arbitrators may not award damages or interest absent a claim in such regard by the parties. In an arbitration in which I was arbitrator, the parties did not invoke the payment of interest. The arbitral tribunal did not apply the law, as the interest payment was not invoked by the parties and doing the contrary would have been *ultra petita*. This may also be the case where an arbitral tribunal awards consequential damages (where a contract excludes their application).[18]

On the other hand, when parties have not invoked a specific rule of law, but have asked for the remedy (e.g., interest payment), the arbitrator in order to resolve the claim is allowed to determine the content of the applicable legal provision, and this will

---

16. *Op. cit.*, fn. 5, p. 689.
17. See further: *op. cit.*, fn. 4, p. 280.
18. See further: *op. cit.*, fn. 4, p. 714.

not be *ultra petita*. It is not indispensable (although obviously it is convenient) for the parties to refer to the specific legal provision.

The limit regarding due process lies in the expectations of the parties as to the application of the law. In this regard, Gabrielle Kaufmann-Kohler has considered that: "Except for limits arising out of a possible agreement of the parties and the requirement that the arbitral tribunal must consult with the parties on the application of an unexpected legal rule, there appear to be no limits."[19]

According to this approach, arbitrators must allow the parties to comment on the application of any unexpected legal rule, in order to ensure due process and give the parties the opportunity to present their case in order to comply with the principle of adversarial proceedings.[20] Therefore, even if the parties did not invoke the law, the tribunal must, in order not to rule *ultra petita*, give the parties the opportunity to express their opinions on the rules of law which are to be applied when they are unexpected.

In the words of Laurent Levy:

> "In principle, there is no violation either of due process as the parties should know that the judges and the arbitrators, know the law and will apply it.... However, in extreme circumstances, due process, namely the right to put one's case in an adversarial proceeding, will bar the arbitrators from basing their award on a principle, a doctrine, a statute, a precedent etc., which the parties did not mention and of which they had no possibility to perceive the relevance and materiality.... The [Swiss Federal Tribunal] has always insisted that the arbitrators should not 'surprise' the parties, namely that the arbitrators should not find legal arguments that the parties could never have expected in view of their submissions and the briefing of the case."[21]

From the previous quotation we may conclude the following: (i) arbitrators may apply the governing law (beyond the submissions presented by the parties) and this will not be considered *ultra petita*; and (ii) the limit regarding compliance with due process lies in that parties must be afforded the opportunity to comment on the content of the law if the award will be based on legal material which the parties did not mention and did not perceive as relevant.

However, what is "unexpected" or "perceived as relevant" in a given case may not be clear. In a case related to these expectations, the Swiss Federal Supreme Court, on 9 June 2009, upheld an award stating that: "... the Hungarian company, represented by experienced business lawyers should have anticipated the application of contractual terms addressing the termination of the construction contract".[22]

---

19. *Op. cit.*, fn. 1, p. 83.
20. See further discussion on the principle of adversarial proceedings: *op. cit.*, fn. 2, p. 711.
21. Laurent LEVY, "Jura Novit Curia? The Arbitrator's Discretion in the Application of the Governing Law" at: <http://kluwerarbitrationblog.com/blog/2009/03/20/jura-novit-curia-the-arbitrator's-discretion-in-the-application-of-the-governing-law/> (last accessed 1 June 2010).
22. George VON SEGESSER, "Iura novit curia – the right to be heard (decision of the Swiss Federal Supreme Court as of 9 June 2009- 4a_108/2009)", at:<http://kluwerarbitrationblog.com/blog/2009/08/27/iura-novit-curia-the-right-to-be-heard-decision-of-the-swiss-federal-supreme-court-as-of-9-june-2009-4a_1082009/> (last accessed 1 June 2010).

In this matter Fouchard, Gaillard and Goldman give a practical solution. According to this view, as a general rule the arbitrators must afford the parties the opportunity to discuss a rule of law to be applied. The exception would be that: "the rule relied on by the arbitrators is so general in nature that it must have been implicitly included in the pleadings that the arbitrators can dispense with the need to call for a specific discussion on that point. This will be the case, for example, of the principle of good faith in the performance of contracts...."[23]

In order to further analyze the extent to which the arbitrator may ascertain the content of the law and identify legal issues the parties have not raised, the following cases serve as useful illustrations. In a case between the companies Comesa Gmbh and Polar Electro Europe BV[24] regarding a distribution agreement with a clause indicating that in the event of termination, the distributor was not entitled to compensation, the arbitral tribunal held that if the provision was not adjusted, the contract clause whereby the distributor gave up any rights to compensation would lead to an unreasonable result due to changed circumstances. The tribunal found legislative support for the position that whereas a court (or tribunal) cannot adjust unreasonable provisions ex officio, a party should be considered to have invoked the unreasonableness of a clause if it contested the other party's claim and presented views on unreasonableness.

The award was challenged on the ground that arbitrators had based their ruling on general contract law although neither party had specifically invoked it. The Finnish Supreme Court had to decide if the tribunal had exceeded its authority or deprived a party of sufficient opportunity to present its case.

The Supreme Court decided not to set aside the award. In its reasoning it stated that the "burden of pleading" had been complied with, as the award was based on facts invoked by claimant and which respondent was able to comment on. Moreover, the Supreme Court applied the *iura novit curia* principle and clearly stated that "the Tribunal was not bound by the legal reasoning presented by the parties".[25]

Another case, *José Ignacio Urquijo Goitia v. Liedson da Silva Muñiz*, involved an agent that entered into an agreement with a Brazilian football player according to which the agent was accorded the exclusive right of representation in Europe. However, the player contracted with a Portuguese football club without the agent's involvement. The Court of Arbitration for Sport ruled based on a mandatory provision in the Swiss Federal Law on the Employment Exchange and the Hiring-out of Personnel, which had not been invoked by the parties. This provision provided that a person seeking employment, even if contractually bound to one broker, might use the services of other brokers.

The Swiss Federal Supreme Court ruled that: (i) the panel should have allowed the parties to comment on the legal provision that decided the outcome of the case; (ii) the

---

23. *Op. cit.*, fn. 5, p. 950.
24. Per RUNELAND, "Iura Novit Curia in Finnish and Swiss Arbitration", Sansfrontieres, bi-annual Newsletter of SJ Berwin's International Arbitration Group (Issue of 8 September 2009) pp. 5-7.
25. *Ibid.*

agent's right to be heard had been violated; and (iii) the award was annulled due to the violation of the right to be heard.[26]

Both the *Comesa* and *Silva Muñiz* cases relate to situations where the parties did not rely on a statute that was used by the tribunal or panel to decide the case. Per Runeland has amply analyzed this situation, highlighting the differences between both cases, indicating that "there is a material difference between the two cases"[27] which may be outlined as follows:

(a) In the Finnish case a basic principle of civil law was applied (which was in fact undoubtedly applicable to the dispute). In the Swiss case, a law was applied (which was not applicable), therefore the parties could not foresee that it would be applied.
(b) In the Finnish case the arbitrators knew the law, whereas in the Swiss case they did not and applied a provision in error without allowing the parties to comment.

As a practical solution, in a case where the parties have failed to raise such rules, the arbitral tribunal is encouraged to invite the parties to express their opinion on this issue, in order to guarantee due process.

This issue may further be exemplified by reference to two annulment procedures which reached the Paris Court of Appeal.

The first annulment procedure resolution was issued on 3 December 2009 and decided on the partial annulment of an arbitral award.[28] The background of the arbitration related to a contract for the fabrication of PET bottles about which the parties had a disagreement and initiated an arbitration proceeding before the ICC. The losing party to the award filed an annulment procedure, invoking breach of due process (*le principe de la contradiction*) stipulated in Art. 1502 of the French Code of Civil Procedure. Specifically, the party seeking the annulment claimed that the arbitral tribunal decided on the validity of the contract referring to a legal provision (a rule of Austrian law – *Wegfall der Geschäftsgrundlage* (frustration of contract)) not invoked by the parties and which was not subject to adversarial debate during the arbitration. The Paris Court of Appeal annulled the award, upon consideration that due process had been breached given that neither one of the parties had invoked the application of the aforementioned rule nor had been granted the opportunity to comment on such provision.

---

26. Commenting on this case Laurent Levy stated that:

> "So far the [Swiss Federal Tribunal] had always used "*jura novit curia*" to reject setting aside proceedings, namely to save awards which arbitrators had, arguably, based on legal reasons beyond the arguments of the parties.... Thus, it is not really a matter of substantive law but that the law is being applied without the parties' being able to make their submissions on that substantive law. As far as I am aware, the FT Decision of 9 February 2009 represents the first time the FT annulled an award in spite of "*jura novit curia*."

Op. cit., fn. 21.
27. *Op. cit.*, fn. 24, pp. 5-7.
28. Court of appeal of Paris, Pole 1 – Chamber 1, decision of 3 December, 2009, general docket no.: 08/13618, *Recours en Annulation, République Française*.

The second annulment resolution was issued on 25 March 2010 by the Paris Court of Appeal. The case related to the exploitation of nickel deposits in Cuba.[29] The party seeking the annulment of the award claimed that the arbitral tribunal did not comply with the mission conferred and violated the principles of due process and procedural public policy, as provided in Art. 1502 of the French Code of Civil Procedure. The Court of Appeal annulled the award on the ground that the arbitral tribunal issued the award substituting the indemnification claimed by one of the parties and omitted giving the parties an opportunity to comment on this point, neglecting due process.

These annulment decisions outline the importance of due process in the application of the law in order to secure enforceability of awards.

2. *Compliance with Mandatory Rules and Public Policy*

An award may also be set aside when it violates public policy, as may be the case when it contains provisions against mandatory rules, or fundamental principles of law:

(a) In addition to the rules of law chosen by the parties the arbitrator is also bound to apply "... a number of mandatory rules that are essential prerequisites of any dispute settlement system, private or public, which have a bearing on the duties of the arbitrator".[30]

(b) Moreover, arbitrators may also decide not to apply the governing law when this is contrary to public policy: "There is no doubt that arbitrators are entitled to disregard the provisions of the governing law chosen by the parties where they consider those provisions to be contrary to international public policy."[31]

Nonetheless, the fact remains that in practice it is rare for arbitrators to decide not to apply the rules of the governing law chosen by the parties.

According to Fouchard, Gaillard and Goldman, "The crux of the problem is the determination of the reasoning arbitrators should adopt when faced with an allegation that a contract is illegal in the light of rules other than those of the law governing the contract."[32]

In an English case, *Soleimany v. Soleimany*,[33] there is a useful illustration of public policy and illegalities of the law. The case related to an agreement concerning Persian carpets exported from Iran to England. The exporting of carpets was in contravention of the Iranian revenue laws. The award was ruled under Jewish law and the arbitral award decided that even if smuggling carpets was illegal this had no bearing on the contractual rights of the parties.

The Court of Appeal held that "Where public policy is involved, the interposition of an arbitration award does not isolate the successful party's claim from the illegality which

---

29. Court of appeal of Paris, Pole 1 – Chamber 1, decision of 25 March 2010, general docket no.: 08/23901, *Recours en Annulation, République Française*.
30. *Op. cit.*, fn. 4, p. 276.
31. *Op. cit.*, fn. 5, pp. 860-861.
32. *Ibid.*, p. 851.
33. *Soleimany v. Soleimany* [1998] 3 WLR 811, [1999] QB 785 (CA), [1999] 3 All ER 847, 859.

gave rise to it."³⁴ Therefore the court held that the agreement was illegal and it was contrary to public policy to enforce it in England.

Another case, *Westacre Investments, Inc.*,³⁵ involved the purchase of military equipment in Kuwait. The contract was governed by Swiss law. The arbitral tribunal dismissed allegations by respondents that the contract involved bribery and as such should be declared void.

The award was in favor of Westacre and respondents challenged it on public policy grounds. The Court of Appeal ruled that the award should be enforced because although it would be contrary to the public policy of Kuwait, its enforcement was not contrary to the public policy of Switzerland.

IV. PRACTICAL SOLUTION IN INTERNATIONAL ARBITRATION IN ESTABLISHING THE CONTENT OF THE CHOSEN LAW

Most arbitration laws empower the tribunal to determine proceedings with regard to ascertaining the facts and the law. Therefore, arbitrators are allowed considerable flexibility to decide how to establish the content of the law.

As a starting premise, arbitrators have broad discretion and flexibility to establish the content of the substantive law. The arbitral tribunal must therefore have access to the content of the applicable foreign law. In reaching this goal there appears to be a liberal approach taken in the forum.³⁶

Generally in practice, arbitral tribunals are able to resolve the dispute analyzing the evidence submitted by the parties, the facts in dispute and contractual terms. In such a case, arbitrators are not faced with the issue of establishing the content of the substantive applicable law, and may validly resolve the dispute by interpreting the contract terms and applying principles of law, as allowed, for example, under Art. 33(3), of the UNCITRAL Rules which provides that: "In all cases, the arbitral tribunal shall decide in accordance with the terms of the contract and shall take into account the usages of the trade applicable to the transaction."³⁷ Therefore, arbitral tribunals normally analyze the documents and other evidence submitted by the parties, as well as their subsequent conduct, in order to determine the parties' intention and understanding at the time of executing the contract.

When it is not possible to resolve the dispute solely according to contractual terms, arbitrators must apply a law which is often unknown or difficult to access. There is little doctrine on this point, regarding the methodology to be used, and no clear guidance is given by most arbitration rules.

In this typical scenario, the practice of arbitration on the American continent has evolved in that in cases where arbitrators are not familiar with the law, the parties will normally submit expert opinions on the applicable law. During the hearing arbitrators will examine legal experts and narrow the key issues of the dispute. Thereafter, if

---

34. *Op. cit.*, fn. 4, p. 724.
35. *Westacre Investments Inc. v. Jugoimport –SDPR Holding Co Ltd and Others* [1999] 3 All ER 864, 876.
36. See further: *op. cit.*, fn. 5, p. 689 and *op. cit.*, fn. 4, p. 282.
37. *Op. cit.*, fn. 10, pp. 20-21.

arbitrators require any submission on a specific point of law, they will request briefing from the parties.

In my experience, arbitrators must use all available methods which allow them to establish the contents of the law chosen by the parties to resolve the dispute. Among the methods which I have used in practice the following are worth mentioning:

(a) Seeking support from co-arbitrators, when they have specific knowledge on the applicable law.
(b) Studying thoroughly memorials and submissions by the parties in preparation for the oral phase of the proceeding, in order to have sufficient opportunity to spotlight and interrogate on key issues.
(c) Determine in a procedural order whether the proceedings will be conducted in an inquisitorial or adversarial style.[38]
(d) Where possible, combine the continental tradition and the common law approach, ensuring a flexible procedure. This methodology is effective, as it allows for combining independent study with expert reports and pleadings on the content of the foreign law submitted by the parties. This approach lightens the burden of the arbitral tribunal to establish the content of the law and is a practical solution which might lower costs in the arbitration.
(e) The examination of legal expert witnesses at the hearing is an important point (if not a crucial point) for the arbitrator to ascertain the law. In this phase the common law procedures, in which the parties plead and prove the applicable law, are most valuable.
(f) Arbitrators when addressing questions directly to expert witnesses may ascertain the contents of the applicable law or clarify any issue which comes from their independent research of the law. Therefore, arbitrators should use the hearing to interrogate witnesses regarding legal points. This is the perfect moment for arbitrators to question and confront legal experts with delicate and relevant points of law, both in the file or not mentioned therein.
(g) Also, in my experience calling the experts from both parties together for confrontation of legal points and to discuss and interpret their positions has rendered excellent results. This method has allowed me to narrow the discussion and be able to deliberate on specific and controversial issues of law. This is in line with a harmonizing approach, in which the tribunal will allow the parties to conduct their examinations, and after this the tribunal will use its broad discretion to interrogate both on the matters at issue as well as on other points of law that might be central to the dispute.
(h) Another valuable method of establishing the content of the law is posing additional questions to be answered by both parties, in closing briefs.

---

38. *Op. cit.*, fn. 4, pp. 725-726:

> "It is a continental European tradition that a court takes the initiative in directing the ascertainment of the facts and the law. For that purpose it may conduct its own examination of witnesses. Litigation in common law countries is, on the other hand, traditionally adversarial. In adversarial proceedings the principle is that the parties arrive at the truth by each leading evidence and then testing that evidence through cross-examination of the relevant witnesses."

(i) Furthermore, the arbitral tribunal should also conduct an independent study of the law where relevant.

(j) Arbitrators should make available for examination and critical analysis by the parties any specific legal points which have not been addressed by the parties and which will be part of the basis of the award.

In the application of a national law, the arbitral tribunal should: (i) be aware of the hierarchy of sources in such legal system; (ii) and as a general rule, apply the law in force.

Also, arbitrators should be allowed flexibility in the process of interpretation of the applicable law. In this exercise tribunals may consider international practice or international standards to help them interpret national rules. Morever, arbitrators may decide to apply international or transnational legal rules.

Even when parties select one law to apply, it might well be that the remedy they have requested is not contemplated in such law. In this scenario arbitrators are entitled to apply other laws different from the chosen law. Where the parties are silent as to the governing law, the arbitrators have complete freedom to determine and ascertain the law.[39]

In conclusion, in practice arbitrators have flexibility, and therefore they must use all available methods in order to arrive at the hearing with sufficient knowledge, which allows them to present relevant questions to the parties and focus on relevant and core issues. If and when the arbitral tribunal is able to spot these issues and question both the parties and experts during the hearing, this discussion will bring them a step closer to knowing the law and applying it.

V. THE ADVOCATE'S PERSPECTIVE

The role of counsel in presenting the case before the arbitral tribunal is relevant in that adequate briefing of the case allows arbitrators to spot key legal substantive issues and to guarantee that the expectations of the parties are met by the arbitral tribunal when resolving the dispute.

It is advisable that counsel take into consideration the following issues:

(a) The choice of arbitrators will impact the application of the law. A common question in this matter would be: should arbitrators know the applicable law? There is no correct answer to this question. It appears to be advisable that arbitrators know the applicable law. However, it is not indispensable. There may be other characteristics, such as experience in case management, which might be more relevant when choosing an arbitrator. Or the dispute may be more of a contractual nature or involve certain technicalities which do not revolve around the application of the governing law.

On the contrary, where the understanding and application of the law is key to the resolution of the dispute, there is no doubt that arbitrators who know the law should be preferred. Especially when the dispute involves complex legal points, it is advisable that

---

39. See further: *op. cit.*, fn. 5, pp. 881-882.

counsel ensure that there is a co-arbitrator who will guide the process of the applicable law or a chairman who is knowledgeable in the applicable law.

Moreover, the legal tradition of arbitrators will impact the resolution of the dispute. An arbitrator from a civil law tradition will generally consider that he or she should investigate the applicable law; whereas a common law counsel might expect the law to be proven by the parties. In this regard, counsel must have sufficient background regarding the dispute and its legal implications in order to take this into consideration when choosing an arbitrator. However, this is not the full story where the parties seek relief on a matter that is not covered by the law chosen or produced. In such a case the arbitrator's legal background might not cover any and every issue involved.

(b) Whenever there is doubt regarding the application by the arbitral tribunal of the substantive law, counsel should address this issue, especially at the procedural hearing.

(c) Counsel, even if not obliged, are expected to file sufficient legal evidence and make available legal materials (as well as good translations) given that arbitral practice has developed to expect that "the parties bring forth their legal arguments in their written submissions and 'prove' the content of the chosen law by various evidentiary means, such as documents (be it authorities, whether statutes, court decisions, arbitral awards or legal writings), or legal experts".[40]

(d) Counsel are responsible for defining a strategy, taking into consideration whether the arbitrators have knowledge of the applicable law and the legal cultures of the arbitrators and for defining whether and if, in the particular case, it is convenient to provide the arbitral tribunal with information on the applicable law. From the above analysis it will be determined whether or not to submit expert legal opinions or whether to trust the authority of arbitrators who have knowledge as to the applicable law.

(e) During the hearing counsel should examine expert legal witnesses efficiently, allowing arbitrators to spot and understand any issue relevant to their claim.

In conclusion, the hearing is the perfect moment for arbitrators to confront any legal issues and: (i) determine how to apply the law chosen by the parties; (ii) establish the contents of the law or address any error of law or clarify any issues relating to the remedy sought; (iii) give the parties sufficient opportunity to comment on provisions of the applicable law and (iv) thereby ensure the validity and enforcement of the award.

---

40. *Op. cit.*, fn. 21.

The Relative Merits of Oral Argument and Post-Hearing Briefs

*Alejandro A. Escobar**

TABLE OF CONTENTS	Page
I. Introduction	221
II. The Right to Oral Argument	221
III. The Limits of Oral Argument	222
IV. The Opportunity and Purpose of Post-hearing Briefs	225
V. Conclusions	228

I. INTRODUCTION

A full hearing on the merits has essentially two objectives: to hear live testimony from witnesses and experts, and to hear the oral submissions of the parties. This paper will focus on the making of oral arguments and compare this mode of advocacy to the submission of post-hearing briefs.

II. THE RIGHT TO ORAL ARGUMENT

Numerous arbitration rules acknowledge the right of the parties to make oral arguments to a tribunal. Art. 19(1) of the Rules of the LCIA (London Court of International Arbitration), for example, states: "Any party which expresses a desire to that effect has the right to be heard orally before the Arbitral Tribunal on the merits of the dispute, unless the parties have agreed in writing on documents-only arbitration."

Art. 15(2), first sentence, of the UNCITRAL Arbitration Rules also expressly provides for this right: "If either party so requests at any stage of the proceedings, the arbitral tribunal shall hold hearings for the presentation of evidence by witnesses, including expert witnesses, or for oral argument."[1]

Art. 32 of the Arbitration Rules of the International Centre for Settlement of Investment Disputes (ICSID) clearly entitles the parties to oral argument: "(1) The oral procedure shall consist of the hearing by the tribunal of the parties, their agents, counsel and advocates, and of witnesses and experts.... (3) The members of the Tribunal may, during the hearings, put questions to the parties, their agents, counsel and advocates, and ask them for explanations."

The same meaning is gleaned from Art. 16(1) of the American Arbitration Association (AAA) International Dispute Resolution Procedures, which grants broad powers to a tribunal to conduct the arbitration "provided that ... each party has the right to be heard and is given a fair opportunity to present its case".

---

* Partner, Baker Botts (UK) LLP.
1. See also Art. 24(1) of the UNCITRAL Model Law (2006).

Art. 15(2) of the Rules of the International Court of Arbitration of the International Chamber of Commerce (ICC) adopts a less categorical approach, calling instead on the tribunal to "ensure that each party has a reasonable opportunity to present its case".[2] Equivalent provisions are found in Arts. 19(2) and 34 of the Arbitration Rules of the Arbitration Institute of the Stockholm Chamber of Commerce. What is a reasonable opportunity in the circumstances of each case would in the first instance be left to the discretion of the arbitral tribunal. Even so, the scope of that discretion will likely be determined by the arbitration law at the seat, or legal place, of the arbitration. If the arbitration is seated in Sweden, for example, Art. 24, first paragraph, of the Swedish Arbitration Act will provide a more express recognition of the right to oral argument:

> "The arbitrators shall afford the parties, to the extent necessary, an opportunity to present their respective cases in writing or orally. Where a party so requests and provided that the parties have not otherwise agreed, an oral hearing shall be held prior to the determination of an issue referred to the arbitrators for resolution."

III. THE LIMITS OF ORAL ARGUMENT

The purpose of oral argument is closely linked to the purpose of oral evidence: to establish direct communication with the arbitral tribunal regarding the central issues of the matter, allowing the tribunal to interact fully with the parties' advocates.[3]

Three specific aims of oral argument would include:

(1) to set the context (including a party's case on the law) for the evidence to be heard (in opening statements);
(2) to summarize the central points of fact and their legal implications based on the evidence heard (in closing statements); and
(3) to answer specific questions put by the arbitral tribunal.[4]

The right to oral argument is not absolute, in the sense that it is not unrestrained.[5] The length of oral argument in a hearing on the merits can only ever extend to a reasonable proportion of the overall time available, as most of the time must be devoted

---

2. See, e.g., Y. DERAINS and E.A. SCHWARTZ, *A Guide to the ICC Rules of Arbitration*, 2nd edn. (2005) at p. 293; see also Art. 22(1) of the ICC Arbitration Rules.
3. See 1996 UNCITRAL Notes on Organizing Arbitral Proceedings, para. 75.
4. See "'Oral Argument': Report of the Session", in *International Arbitration 2006: Back to Basics?*, ICCA Congress Series no. 13 (2007) p. 829 at p. 830 (presentation by Mr. Robert BRINER), p. 832 (presentation by Ms. Teresa CHENG) and p. 835 (presentation by Mr. Yves FORTIER).
5. Although a truism in this specific context, the point is relevant to the overall conduct of international arbitration. "*All legal power is limited.... To claim legal power is to accept its limits.*" P. ALLOTT, *Eunomia* (1990) para. 11.20, at p. 173 (italics in original).

to the hearing of witness and expert evidence. This will of course remain under the control of the arbitral tribunal.[6]

Other issues that often arise in connection with the presentation of oral argument include:

(1) reliance on new authorities or, occasionally, new documents not previously available to a party, after the evidentiary record is closed;[7]
(2) the use of visual aids and whether they may be regarded as new documents not previously presented;[8] and
(3) the submission of skeleton arguments and whether they may be regarded as a distinct and unscheduled written pleading.[9]

1. *A Narrowing Window for Oral Argument*

In contrast to the introduction of new evidence, it is generally understood that a party is not prevented from introducing new legal theories for its claims or defences in the course of oral argument. The consequence of doing so, however, may include an adverse impact on the credibility of a party's case. Nonetheless, it is not difficult to imagine circumstances that could justify the introduction of new arguments during a hearing, such as the novelty or complexity of the facts, instruments or legal issues in dispute;[10] the late appointment of counsel to a matter; or (perhaps most frequently) the late introduction of arguments or documents by the opposing party during the written phase of proceedings.

This will likely be a critical juncture in the handling of the proceeding by a tribunal. A tribunal will not want the proceedings to be extended unnecessarily by the appearance of late arguments, especially if it senses that such arguments might be no more than last-ditch attempts to run a claim or a defence. In order to discourage or curtail the appearance of new legal theories during oral argument, a tribunal may limit the time for oral submission to a minimum (e.g., one hour per party at the beginning or at the end of the hearing).

The refusal of a tribunal to hear any oral argument, against the wishes of one or more of the parties, is unusual.[11] Because such a refusal potentially touches upon the

---

6. See 1996 UNCITRAL Notes on Organizing Arbitral Proceedings, paras. 78-80.
7. See "Techniques for Controlling Time and Costs in Arbitration", para. 76 (Cut-off date for evidence), 18 ICC International Court of Arbitration Bulletin (2007, no. 1), p. 23 at p. 41.
8. See "'Oral Argument': Report of the Session", fn. 4 above, at pp. 836-839 (presentation by Professor Albert Jan VAN DEN BERG).
9. See 1996 UNCITRAL Notes on Organizing Arbitral Proceedings, para. 84.
10. Counsel in one of the first arbitrations to be conducted under Chapter Eleven of the North American Free Trade Agreement (NAFTA), when articulating a new position on attribution of conduct to the State during the hearing, affirmed to have experienced a "legal epiphany" of the meaning of the NAFTA provisions.
11. It is not, however, unheard of, even in large cases. The author knows of a proceeding, in which the amount claimed runs to several hundreds of millions of dollars, where the tribunal has declined to hear any oral argument on the merits of the dispute.

fundamental right of a party to a full or fair opportunity to present its case, the circumstances that could justify a tribunal's decision to forego oral argument would probably be limited to cases where the tribunal is certain that oral argument (or at least oral argument by the party requesting such an opportunity) will have no material impact on the issues in dispute. For example, a tribunal might consider that the heads of liability and damage it has found to be viable are essentially uncontroversial within the overall context of the case, despite these questions being resisted as a matter of principle by the respondent party who seeks to make oral submission to the tribunal.

2. *The Opportunity to Respond in Oral Argument*

In the normal course, the parties will be allowed a complete opportunity for oral argument. Beyond the question of the timing of initial presentations, that opportunity typically entails two further dimensions in the conduct of the proceeding: (a) the opportunity to respond to the opposing party's submissions; and (b) the opportunity to answer questions posed by the tribunal to the parties.

The opportunity to respond to an opponent's oral submission, or to questions from the bench, is often associated with the core skill or art of oral advocacy. This is so because of the immediacy of the task. As regards responding to opposing counsel, the advocate must be able to identify the opponent's vulnerable points and construct an argument in a matter of minutes. Arbitration tribunals will seldom, if ever, be as exacting as certain national courts in expecting an uninterrupted flow of argument as between one side and the other. A tribunal will typically grant a reasonably brief pause between a respondent's principal argument and a claimant's rebuttal, and between the claimant's rebuttal and respondent's surrebuttal, to the extent not already marked by a scheduled pause in the order of proceedings.

A party's response to questions from the tribunal may be different, depending on the nature of the question. Certain questions may require an immediate answer, for example because they are meant to elucidate the meaning or implications of a specific point made by a party, which that party (or its advocate) would be expected to command. Certain questions may refer to the place in the record where a certain point is analyzed or a document is found, requiring a minor lapse before the answer is provided.

Other questions, however, may go the crux of the issues of the case, and these may be factually complex, legally novel or far-reaching, or concern the application of rules whose contours are particularly uncertain or ill-defined. As much as a party (or its advocate) may be prepared to provide an immediate response, the party may wish to be cautious and reserve the possibility of a written response.[12] Tribunals will often be aware of the sensitive character of this sort of question and some tribunals may readily offer the opportunity of a written response when putting the question to counsel.

As in other circumstances, procedural fairness will normally require the opposing party to be given the opportunity to respond to the first party's oral response to a question by the tribunal. Very rarely, a tribunal will not afford the opposing party that

---

12. See, e.g., A. REDFERN, M. HUNTER, N. BLACKABY and C. PARTASIDES, *Redfern and Hunter on International Arbitration* (2009) para. 6.247, at p. 429.

opportunity during the hearing (perhaps, for example, out of time pressure if the questions are asked at the end of the last day of the hearing).[13]

These and other circumstances may, and usually do, lead to a final and limited opportunity for the parties to state their respective positions on substantive questions posed by the arbitral tribunal, i.e., to do so in a post-hearing brief.

IV. THE OPPORTUNITY AND PURPOSE OF POST-HEARING BRIEFS

Unlike the right to submit oral argument to a tribunal, arbitration rules are normally silent on the opportunity of the parties to submit post-hearing briefs. This silence in itself denotes the secondary and contingent character of such presentations as a matter of affording due process to the parties, i.e., that post-hearing submissions normally are not a part of the full opportunity of a party to present its case.

This view is reflected clearly in the 1996 UNCITRAL Notes on Organizing Arbitral Proceedings, para. 40:

> "Practices differ as to whether, after the hearings have been held, written submissions are still acceptable. While some arbitral tribunals consider post-hearing submissions unacceptable, others might request or allow them on a particular issue. Some arbitral tribunals follow the procedure according to which the parties are not requested to present written evidence and legal arguments to the arbitral tribunal before the hearings; in such a case, the arbitral tribunal may regard it as appropriate that written submissions be made after the hearings."

Since 1996, the surge in the practice of international arbitration, both under institutional sets of rules (such as those of the ICC Court, the LCIA, the AAA and ICSID, to name just a few) and under rules governing ad hoc proceedings (notably the UNCITRAL Arbitration Rules), has brought with it the expectation that the parties will first put their entire case to the tribunal in writing, before the tribunal hears the parties orally on the merits of their dispute. The need for post-hearing submissions in light of this practice may not be obvious.[14]

As noted by leading commentators on the practice of the Iran-US Claims Tribunal, which established its rules of procedure on the basis of the UNCITRAL Arbitration Rules, that Tribunal revealed "a predisposition against post-hearing submissions" for the sake of the orderly conduct of proceedings.[15] Of course, the Iran-US Claims Tribunal had a unique mandate.

---

13. This was the case of an ICSID Convention proceeding in which the author acted as co-counsel for the respondent party.
14. See, e.g., "Techniques for Controlling Time and Costs in Arbitration", fn. 7 above, para. 47 (Avoiding repetition) p. 23 at p. 37.
15. D.D. CARON, L.M. CAPLAN, and M. PELLONPÄÄ, *The UNCITRAL Arbitration Rules: A Commentary* (OUP 2006) pp. 500-501.

1. The Prevalent Practice of Allowing Post-hearing Briefs

Today it is nevertheless possible to point to an opposite tendency, that is, towards the frequent use of post-hearing briefs in arbitration proceedings where substantial amounts or issues are in dispute. This seems to be true particularly in the field of investment treaty arbitration, as reflected in the arbitration proceedings pending before ICSID. Of the 125 ICSID arbitration proceedings pending as of 31 January 2010, 35 proceedings have held a hearing on the merits (which for these purposes means a hearing on liability or on liability and damages). Post-hearing briefs have been filed in twenty-eight of these thirty-five cases, that is, in eighty percent of the pending matters that have held a hearing on the merits. For the fifteen cases which have held hearings on issues other than liability and damages, post-hearing briefs were filed in nine of these cases, that is, in sixty percent of the total. While data for concluded ICSID cases and for arbitrations under other rules are not as readily available, the perception (as stated by one leading arbitrator) is that "closing written submissions" have become "universal practice".[16]

In this context, it might be said that post-hearing briefs have become a function of the multiplying demands on the time of those who serve as arbitrators and counsel.[17] Arbitrators who are approached more and more frequently to serve on tribunals can set aside fewer consecutive days on a calendar for a hearing on the merits. Counsel might thus not be able to present a party's entire oral evidence or argument in the time available.[18] Arbitrators who serve on multiple tribunals simultaneously might not find the necessary time to digest the document record or to structure and draft an award promptly after a hearing. They would thus seek to rely on the parties to condense their respective cases into a digestible form.

Thus, post-hearing briefs in today's arbitration landscape might be seen as a supplement to oral advocacy. As a supplement, it is normally used only as and when needed, and it would be exceptional for a tribunal to schedule post-hearing submissions in the procedural calendar.[19] Instead, they are normally ordered at the conclusion of a hearing. In the same way as oral argument, post-hearing submissions are subject to certain constraints. First and foremost, the evidentiary record would be closed and no new documents would be allowed.[20] Second, there is usually a page limit on the post-hearing brief, in order to ensure that it provides a summary and not a regurgitation or expansion of a party's main arguments.

---

16. See "'Oral Argument': Report of the Session", fn. 4 above, at p. 836 (intervention by Professor CAPPER).
17. See "Techniques for Controlling Time and Costs in Arbitration", fn. 7 above, para. 10 (Counsel with time), para.12 (Arbitrators with time) p. 23 at pp. 30-31.
18. A. REDFERN, M. HUNTER, N. BLACKABY and C. PARTASIDES, eds., *Redfern and Hunter on International Arbitration*, fn. 12 above, para. 6.243, at p. 428.
19. See "Techniques for Controlling Time and Costs in Arbitration", fn. 7 above, para. 84 (Closing submissions)", p. 23 at p. 42: "Consider whether post-hearing submissions can be avoided in order to save time and cost. If post-hearing submissions are required, consider providing for either oral or written closing submissions...."
20. See A. REDFERN, M. HUNTER, N. BLACKABY and C. PARTASIDES, eds., *Redfern and Hunter on International Arbitration*, fn. 12 above, para. 6.242, at p. 428.

Within these limits, a post-hearing brief may play an important role in assisting the tribunal in rendering its award. The roadmap such a brief could provide might consist roughly in issues of fact and issues of law.

As regards issues of fact, a post-hearing brief could:

– set out the undisputed facts of the matter;
– show how the evidence proves the key facts of the party's case;
– analyse the key aspects of the documentary record;
– point to central concordances and contradictions in the witness evidence, on the basis of the hearing transcript;
– point to, and distinguish between, sound and weak expert evidence, on the basis of the hearing transcript;
– update, and provide alternative, quantum calculations; and
– make cost submissions if so ordered by the tribunal.

As regards issues of law, a post-hearing brief could:

– provide a list of points at issue. A tribunal may keep a running list of points at issue consisting of an aggregate of points identified by each party. Some tribunals may invite the parties to submit, with their post-hearing briefs, an annotated list of issues making reference to the evidentiary record.
– set out the parties' agreement, the Tribunal's determination, or the submitting party's position on the applicable system of law, in general terms;
– identify the applicable rules of law in a more specific manner; and
– provide citation, web links or copies of pertinent authority.

2. *Focus v. Tactics*

As can be easily appreciated, these objectives could just as well, given sufficient time, be reached in the course of oral argument at the hearing. If this then confirms the view that post-hearing briefs are supplemental to oral argument and serve the same purposes, the question may arise as to how to make best use of one and the other. It would seem that there is no univocal answer. This is because, despite the plethora of rules and guidance concerning efficient use of time at the hearing, the decision-makers, the arbitrators, are individuals with their own preferences and their own perception of their mandated tasks. The basic rule of advocacy must prevail, namely, that the advocate must respond to the arbitrators' concerns.

The basic boundaries of the playing field are probably predictable in most instances of international arbitration today. One might expect a week-long hearing, with all or part of the first morning devoted to the parties' opening statements, and statements in rebuttal. Closing arguments might be provisionally scheduled for the last day or not at all. Assuming a transcript is made of the hearing, parties may be confident of the chance to make a closing submission on the basis of it. Unless there is a particular urgency, a final transcript will usually be completed only after the hearing, thus prompting post-hearing submissions.

Beyond this, however, much will depend on the persons sitting as arbitrators. If they are inclined to favour oral argument then the parties should prepare to make use of that opportunity at the hearing (or any extension or adjournment of the hearing), regardless of whatever else they may submit in their post-hearing briefs. If they wish to economize on time and prefer to hear the evidence instead of closing statements, then the parties should plan the hearing with that in mind.

What should probably always be kept in mind is that post-hearing submissions are ancillary. As such, they should be prepared with the same mindset as oral argument, and under the same rules of thumb. Most of all, these submissions should be focused. They are part of the same thought process as oral argument. They should therefore be conceived and outlined immediately following from oral argument.

To be sure, certain parties may use post-hearing tactics as much as they may use pre-hearing tactics. Parties may delay contributions to the costs of the hearing or proceedings. They may seek to introduce new documents or allegations. They may even retain new counsel for their post-hearing submissions and seek and obtain on this basis extensions of time (for example, because they wish to overcome an adverse impression given to the tribunal by their oral evidence). While all of these tactics may be opposed by the other party, the fundamental objective is to maintain the focus and direction of the post-hearing submission. That focus should already be clear by the end of the hearing.

V.   CONCLUSIONS

The relative importance of oral argument and post-hearing briefs is likely to be a function of the character and dynamics of the proceeding.

If the case needs to be handled swiftly (because the issues are straightforward, for example), or if the basic facts are undisputed, then the need for post-hearing briefs might not be great. The necessary evidence is marshalled at the hearing, legal submissions are made orally and any further submissions could be limited to a statement of costs. This pattern is not infrequently found, for example, in ICSID annulment proceedings.

If the evidence is complex and contested, or if the legal issues in dispute are novel or not well-defined, then the parties and the tribunal would likely be well served by post-hearing submissions that digest the central issues of fact and law. This will be true especially if time is scarce.

Post-hearing briefs, although in writing, are nonetheless not a different exercise from oral argument. They are a supplement to oral argument and are defined by counsel's experience before the tribunal. They require the same focus and should be part of the same endeavour to persuade to which advocates should devote their skill and their art.

Advocacy After the Issue of the Arbitral Award

Post-Award Advocacy: The Relationship Between Interim and Final Awards – Res Judicata Concerns

Eduardo Zuleta[*]

TABLE OF CONTENTS	Page
I. Introduction	231
II. The Concept of Res Judicata	234
III. Final, Partial and Interim Awards	242
IV. The Classification of Awards and Res Judicata: Advocacy for a Standard	252
V. Conclusions	273

I. INTRODUCTION

The parties in an existing or potential conflict resort to arbitration as a mechanism to obtain a final and binding resolution of their dispute. It is undisputed amongst scholars that one of the purposes of arbitration is to obtain a decision that is final and binding upon the parties.[1] To reach this objective, the decision of the arbitrators must have – at some point in time – a preclusive effect. As indicated by Gary Born, "… [e]ssential to achieving this objective is the preclusive effects of arbitral awards: if the parties are not bound by the arbitral awards made against them – either dismissing or upholding their claims or declaring their conduct wrongful or unlawful – then those awards do not achieve their intended purpose and are of limited practical value…".[2]

Arbitration and res judicata are, of course, closely linked. According to the International Law Association, res judicata issues may arise in the context of arbitration in at least four factual scenarios:

(i) within a single arbitral tribunal, as may be in the case of a tribunal facing the inconsistencies of a previous partial award;
(ii) between two arbitral tribunals (for example, where two arbitral proceedings have commenced pursuant to different arbitration agreements but in relation to a single legal relationship);

---

[*] Partner, Gómez-Pinzón Zuleta Abogados. The opinions contained in this paper are the opinions of the author exclusively and do not necessarily reflect the opinion of Gómez-Pinzón Zuleta Abogados. The author would like to thank Rafael Rincón and Sebastian Mantilla for their contribution in the preparation of this paper.
1. Nigel BLACKABY, Constantine PARTASIDES, Alan REDFERN and Martin HUNTER, *Redfern and Hunter on International Arbitration*, 5th edn. (Oxford University Press 2009) p. 30; Gary B. BORN, *International Commercial Arbitration*, Volume I (Wolters Kluwer 2009) pp. 64-65; E. GAILLARD and John SAVAGE, eds., *Fouchard Gaillard Goldman on International Commercial Arbitration* (Wolters Kluwer 1999) pp. 12 et seq (herein after *Fouchard Gaillard Goldman*).
2. Gary B. BORN, *International Commercial Arbitration*, fn. 1 above, Volume II, p. 2880.

(iii) in a court of law and an arbitral tribunal (for example where the award is being challenged); and

(iv) in a supra-national court and an arbitral tribunal.[3]

If the relevant issue is that an award must have preclusive effects, then the question arises as to what is an *arbitral award* and whether any decision putting an end to a controversy submitted to the arbitrators may be considered as such.

The 1958 New York Convention on the Recognition and Enforcement of Foreign Awards (the New York Convention) "... seeks to provide common legislative standards for the recognition of arbitration agreements and court recognition and enforcement of foreign and non-domestic arbitral awards...".[4] Other international conventions providing for the recognition and enforcement of decisions issued by arbitral tribunals, or governing particular issues of international commercial arbitration disputes, also refer to *awards*.[5] The same term (*award*) is used by the Convention on the Settlement of Investment Disputes between States and Nationals of Other States (the ICSID Convention)[6] and by other international treaties, such as the Energy Charter Treaty[7] and the North American Free Trade Agreement.[8]

The UNCITRAL Model Law on International Commercial Arbitration (the UNCITRAL Model Law) includes provisions on the making of the award,[9] available recourse[10] and recognition and enforcement.[11] Domestic laws, whether or not based on the UNCITRAL Model Law, generally use the same language.[12] International arbitration rules also refer to the content, structure and timing of the awards.[13] In turn, the Arbitration Rules of the International Chamber of Commerce (the ICC Rules) contain a special feature – the review of draft arbitral decisions by the International Court of Arbitration – which, according to these rules, is only applicable to awards.[14]

---

3. International Law Association (ILA), "Interim Report: Res Judicata and Arbitration" (Berlin Conference 2004) pp. 3-4.
4. New York Convention on the Recognition and Enforcement of Foreign Arbitral Awards, 1958.
5. See, for example: Inter-American Convention on International Commercial Arbitration, 1975; European Convention on International Commercial Arbitration, 1961.
6. See Convention on the Settlement of Investment Disputes between States and Nationals of Other States (1965) (the ICSID Convention), Arts. 48-55.
7. See Energy Charter Treaty, Art. 26.8.
8. See North American Free Trade Agreement, Arts. 1135-1136.
9. UNCITRAL Model Law (1985), Ch. VI.
10. UNCITRAL Model Law (1985), Ch. VII.
11. UNCITRAL Model Law (1985), Ch. VIII.
12. See: Peruvian Legislative Decree No. 1071 (1 September 2008), Arts. 52-68; Mexican Code of Commerce, Arts. 1445-1451 and 1457-1463; Chilean Law No. 19.971 (10 September 2004), Arts. 28-36; English Arbitration Act (1996), Sects. 46-58 and 66-71; French New Code of Civil Procedure, Arts. 1469-1507; US Federal Arbitration Act, Sects. 9-16, 204 and 304.
13. See: ICC Rules (1998), Arts. 24-29; UNCITRAL Arbitration Rules (1976), Arts. 31-37; LCIA (London Court of International Arbitration) Arbitration Rules (1998), Arts. 26-27; Hong Kong International Arbitration Centre (HKIAC) Rules, Arts. 29-35.
14. ICC Rules (1998), Art. 27.

In the course of arbitration, arbitrators have to decide on several different but related issues, such as:

(i) the dates for hearings or submission of documents;
(ii) the definition of the seat and language of the arbitration, as well as of the procedure to be followed, in the absence of an agreement of the parties (and the silence of the applicable rules);
(iii) the definition of their own jurisdiction;
(iv) interim measures;
(v) admission or rejection of evidence;
(vi) submissions made by the parties in the course of the proceedings; and, of course,
(vii) the points of law and fact submitted before the tribunal in the claim, the counterclaim and the defenses.

Neither the relevant international conventions nor international arbitration rules in general contain a definition of *award*. This is also the case in most national statutory law provisions. However, arbitration regulations refer to different types of awards[15] – final, interim, preliminary, partial or interlocutory – without providing a clear concept or definition of such terms and even using some of them as equivalent.

As stated by *Fouchard Gaillard Goldman*

> "... it is essential to identify precisely which of an arbitrator's decisions can be classified as awards and, in particular, to distinguish awards from procedural orders, from orders for provisional measures, and even from agreements between the parties. These distinctions have significant legal consequences, the main one being that only a genuine award can be the subject of an action to set it aside or to enforce it.... Similarly, only genuine awards are covered by international conventions on the recognition and enforcement of arbitral awards. The characterization of a decision as an award may also have an impact on the application of certain provisions of arbitration rules. For example, Article 27 of

---

15. Art. 32(1) of the UNCITRAL Rules provides that "... [i]n addition to making a final award, the arbitral tribunal shall be entitled to make interim, interlocutory, or partial awards...". Similarly, according to Art. 2(iii) of the ICC Rules "... '[A]ward' includes, inter alia, an interim, partial or final Award...." Sect. 44 of the Arbitration Rules of the China International Economic and Trade Arbitration Commission (CIETAC) treats interlocutory and partial awards as equivalent terms, which refer to awards deciding on one *issue of the case* in the course of arbitration. Sect. 21(2) of the Rules of the International Centre for Dispute Resolution (ICDR), whereby the interim measures of protection issued by the tribunal may take the form of an interim award. Turning to domestic statutory law, Sect. 37 of the Spanish Arbitration Law (Law 60/2003 of 2 December 2003) reads as follows "... unless otherwise agreed by the parties, the arbitrators shall decide the dispute in one single award or in as many partial awards as they consider necessary..."; on the other hand, pursuant to Sect. 1049 of the Netherlands Code of Civil Procedure "... the arbitral tribunal may render a final award, a partial award, or an interim award...".

the ICC Rules states that an 'award' must be submitted in draft form to the International Court of Arbitration for approval prior to being signed...."[16]

Currently there is no uniform definition of *final award*, *partial award*, or *interim award*. As discussed below, scholars draw distinguishing lines in different places, use different terms, and treat the same term differently. Likewise, international arbitration tribunals and particularly national courts define and treat them differently. What one jurisdiction considers an interim or interlocutory decision not subject to treatment as an award, another considers a partial or final award that must be treated as an award.

Differing standards matter. Indeed, they dictate the preclusive (res judicata) effect of the award. Additionally, the type of award or measure may impact the recourse against the decision and its recognition and enforcement. For example, and as will be explored below, the New York Convention does not necessarily provide for the enforcement of interim awards. In turn, the ICSID Convention states that interim measures have no res judicata effects and do not require enforcement.[17]

This paper first analyzes the concept of res judicata and, thereafter, refers to the differing definitions and understandings of final award, partial award, interim award and interim measure. Next, it attempts to create distinctions between the terms *final award*, *partial award* and *interim award* or *measure*. Finally the paper refers to the form in which courts in various jurisdictions have defined and differentiated the concept of award, even disregarding the classification, name or nature attributed to the decision by the arbitration tribunal.

There are inconsistencies in the treatment of final and interim awards, and inconsistencies may be advantageous to some advocates in certain circumstances – permitting two (or three) bites at the apple, for example. Where uncertainty exists, advocates may attempt to persuade a tribunal to construe a decision as an award so as to encourage or discourage enforcement and res judicata, depending upon whether they want the decision to be reviewed, challenged or enforced, or to bring the claim in another forum. Ultimately, however, this ambiguity could be seen as promoting an inefficient system. Indeed, as the ICC pointed out long ago, "... for businessmen to have confidence in arbitration as a method to resolve disputes, it is essential that they can trust that arbitral awards will be executed. It is here where one can question the effectiveness of the entire system of arbitration...."[18]

II.   THE CONCEPT OF RES JUDICATA

Generally, res judicata is understood as the institution whereby a claim that has already been decided by a competent authority may not be submitted again to it, nor to any other decision-maker. As expressed by the International Law Association, "... the term

---

16. *Fouchard Gaillard Goldman*, fn. 1 above, p. 736.
17. ICSID Convention (1965), Art. 54.
18. XXIV ICC News, Monthly Bulletin of the International Chamber of Commerce (World Trade) (April 1958, no. 3).

res judicata refers to the general doctrine that an earlier and final adjudication by a court or arbitration tribunal is conclusive in subsequent proceedings involving the same subject matter or relief, the same legal grounds and the same parties...".[19] Although this is an accurate statement, it may be seen as a description of one of the effects of res judicata rather than its *meaning*. The following section will refer to the nature of res judicata by addressing: (1) the origins and scope of res judicata as a rule in domestic systems and its recognition as such in litigation and arbitration; and (2) the acceptance and scope of res judicata as a principle of public international law.

1. *The Origins and Scope of Res Judicata as a Rule in Domestic Systems and its Recognition as Such in Litigation and Arbitration*

Res judicata is commonly associated with only one of its implications.[20] However, it has two effects: (a) a positive effect, whereby a final – or partial – judgment or award is binding upon the parties and must be implemented in good faith; and (b) a negative effect, preventing the parties from re-litigating issues decided in such a judgment or award.[21] Now, the doctrine under consideration applies whenever two requisites are met: (i) identity of the parties; and (ii) identity of the subject matter.[22] The latter is in turn generally divided into: (i) identity of the relief or object (*petitum*); and (ii) identity of cause (*causa petendi*).[23]

---

19. ILA, Berlin Conference Report (2004) p. 2.
20. William DODGE, "Res Judicata, 2006" in *Max Planck Encyclopedia of Public International Law*, para. 1.
21. *Ibid.*, para. 1. See also: ILA, Berlin Conference Report (2004) p. 2.
22. William DODGE, "Res Judicata", fn. 20 above, paras. 5-10. In this regard, the Permanent Court of International Justice stated: "... it must be remembered that the Court of Arbitration applied the doctrine of res judicata because not only the Parties but also the matter in dispute was the same...". Permanent Court of International Justice, *Polish Postal Service in Danzing* – Advisory Opinion, (6 May 1925) in *Collection of Advisory Opinions*, Series B – No. 11, p. 30. Similarly, the award rendered in the *Newchwang case* states: "... the doctrine of *res judicata* applies only where there is identity of the parties and of the question...". *Newchwang case (UK v. USA)* Arbitral Award (9 December 1921), United Nations, *Reports of International Arbitral Awards*, Volume VI, p. 65. In addition, the Statute of the International Court of Justice provides: "... the decision of the Court has no binding force except between the parties and in respect of that particular case...". International Court of Justice, Statute of the Court, Art. 59. National statutes have a similar approach. For example, the Colombian Code of Civil Procedure states: "... the judgment issued in a litigious proceeding has *res judicata* effects, as long as the new proceeding refers to the same object, is grounded on the same cause as the former and there is a juridical identity of the parties in both proceedings...". Código de Procedimiento Civil Colombiano, Art. 332.
23. William DODGE, "Res Judicata 2006", fn. 20 above, para. 5. See also: *Petrobart Ltd. v. Kyrgyzstan*, Award in SCC Case No. 126/2003-IIC 184 (29 March 2005), para. 295; M. ANZILIOTTI, Dissenting Opinion in the Interpretation of Judgments No. 7 and 8 – The *Chorzów Factory case* (16 December 1927); International Court of Justice, *Genocide Convention case (Bosnia and Herzegovina v. Serbia and Montenegro)*, Judgment (27 February 2007) para. 1.

Res judicata (literally meaning *a thing decided*)[24] has been traced to Roman law, under which a prior judicial decision had prejudicial effects (*prejudicium*) over a subsequent trial, as long as its contents were binding for the second judge (at least regarding the issues discussed and decided by the first decision-maker).[25] Today it is still recognized that the doctrine in question intends to avoid the duplication of proceedings whenever two state courts are seized with the same dispute between the same parties.[26] Since it seeks to rapidly restore a lasting juridical peace, it indicates that judicial decisions must remain unaltered and are binding for the parties if a later conflict arises,[27] as is usually provided in national statutes.[28]

In practice, the foregoing means that judgments can only be attacked or changed subject to the conditions and deadlines provided by each state's procedural civil law, which in turn pursues the maintenance of peace and of the rule of law.[29] This explains the reasons underlying res judicata and particularly its negative effect, which constitutes the *substantive finality* of this rule, whereby "... an action cannot be considered anew with respect to an identical object of dispute, which has already been adjudicated in the form of a final judgment...".[30]

What seemed to be clear became a matter of intense discussion when state courts were faced with res judicata objections based on decisions made by *foreign* courts.[31] The enforceability of a court judgment in another jurisdiction will generally depend upon the existence of a treaty between the relevant states establishing the duty to enforce; in common law countries, the principle of the most convenient forum would generally be applicable in this regard.[32]

Now, most jurisdictions recognize res judicata effects not only for judgments issued by courts of law, but also to arbitral awards. For example, the French New Code of Civil

---

24. Michelle SIMON, "Offensive Issue Preclusion in the Criminal Context: 'Two Steps Forward, One Step Back'", The University of Memphis Law Review (2004) p. 753.
25. Nattan NISIMBLAT, "*La cosa juzgada en la jurisprudencia constitucional colombiana y el principio del estoppel en el derecho anglosajón*", Revista Vniversitas (2009, no. 118) p. 252.
26. Christer SÖDERLUND, "*Lis Pendens, Res Judicata* and the Issue of Parallel Judicial Proceedings", 22 Journal of International Arbitration (2005, no. 4) p. 303.
27. Pierre LALIVE, "Absolute Finality of Arbitral Awards?", Revista Internacional de Arbitragem e Conciliação (2008) p. 9.
28. For example, the Swedish Code of Judicial Procedure provides: "... upon the expiration of the time for appeal, a judgment acquires legal force to the extent that it determines the matter at issue in respect of which the action was instituted.... A question thus determined cannot be adjudicated again...." Swedish Code of Judicial Procedure, Ch. 13, Art. 11. See also Sect. 322 (*Materielle Rechtskraft*) of the German *Zivilprozessordnung* (ZPO); Art. 480 of the French New Code of Civil Procedure; and Sect. 332 of the Colombian Code of Civil Procedure.
29. Pierre LALIVE, "Absolute Finality of Arbitral Awards?", fn. 27 above, p. 9.
30. Christer SÖDERLUND, "*Lis Pendens, Res Judicata* and the Issue of Parallel Judicial Proceedings", fn. 26 above, p. 302.
31. *Ibid.*, p. 303.
32. *Ibid.*, p. 303.

Procedure provides: "The arbitral award has force of res judicata with regard to the dispute it decides at the moment it is rendered."[33]

However, the consensual and private nature of arbitration may lead to the conclusion that state courts do not have a duty to examine ex officio any possible situation of res judicata related to an arbitral award.[34] In addition, certain legislations recognize res judicata effects only for final and partial awards. For example, the Netherlands Code of Civil Procedure states: "… only a final or partial award is capable of acquiring the force of *res judicata*…".[35]

There is a difference in the scope of res judicata between common law and civil law jurisdictions. Although both recognize the *substantive finality* or negative effect of the doctrine,[36] continental legal systems generally only grant res judicata effects to the dispositive part of the decision. The *ratio* is used just for interpretation purposes.[37] This feature is expressed in the French New Code of Civil Procedure, according to which: "… the judgment which decides in its operative part the whole or part of the main issue, or one which rules upon the procedural plea, a plea seeking a plea of non-admissibility or any other interlocutory application, will, from the time of its pronouncement, become res judicata with regard to the dispute which it determines…".[38] A recent decision of the First Civil Law Court of the Swiss Federal Tribunal reflected this view, holding that: "Res iudicata is limited to the holding of the judgment. It does not extend to its reasons. The reasons of a judgment have no binding effect as to another disputed issue, but they may have to be relied upon to clarify the scope of the holding of the judgment."[39]

On the other hand, "… the principle of the conclusiveness of judgments has been classified, through a very long period of English law, as a branch of the doctrine of estoppel"[40] and "the concepts of *collateral estoppel* (US law) and *issue estoppel* (English law) attach *res judicata* also to legal premises and issues".[41]

---

33. French New Code of Civil Procedure, Art. 1476. Similarly, the German ZPO provides in Art. 1055: "The arbitral award has the same effect between the parties as a final and binding court judgment." See also: Art. 1703 of the Belgian Judicial Code and Art. 1059 of the Netherlands Code of Civil Procedure.
34. Christer SÖDERLUND, "*Lis Pendens*, *Res Judicata* and the Issue of Parallel Judicial Proceedings", fn. 26 above, p. 304.
35. Netherlands Code of Civil Procedure, Art. 1059.
36. We identify the negative effect of res judicata with the *substantive finality* thereof, since the latter "… means that an action cannot be considered anew with respect to an identical object of dispute which has already been adjudicated in the form of a final judgment…". Christer SÖDERLUND, "*Lis Pendens*, *Res Judicata* and the Issue of Parallel Judicial Proceedings", fn. 26 above, p. 302.
37. *Ibid.*, p. 302.
38. French New Code of Civil Procedure, Art. 480.
39. Decision of 13 April 2009, *Club Atlético de Madrid SAD v. Sport Lisboa Benfica – Futebol SAD and Fédération Internationale de Football Association (FIFA)*
40. Henry Campbell BLACK, *A Treatise on the Law of Judgments Including the Doctrine of Res Judicata*. Quoted by Nattan NISIMBLAT, fn. 25 above, p. 249.
41. Christer SÖDERLUND, "*Lis Pendens*, *Res Judicata* and the Issue of Parallel Judicial Proceedings", fn. 26 above, p. 303.

Res judicata has also been recognized as a rule in arbitration. For example, the ICC Rules provide: "... every award shall be binding on the parties. By submitting to arbitration under these Rules, the parties undertake to carry out any award without delay and shall be deemed to have waived their right to any form of recourse insofar as such waiver can be validly made...."[42] The positive and negative effects of res judicata are included in the latter rule. Similar provisions appear in the Rules of the LCIA (London Court of International Arbitration)[43] and the Rules of the China International Economic Trade and Arbitration Commission (CIETAC).[44] However, other arbitration institutions only mention the positive effect of the doctrine.[45]

An additional relevant point is the acknowledgment by arbitrators of res judicata effects to prior judicial and arbitral decisions. With respect to a prior court judgment, arbitral tribunals do not base their decision on its enforceability at the place of arbitration, as state courts do. In fact, the threshold issue in arbitration is *competence*, i.e., whether the court was competent to decide on the claim submitted: if it was, no competence will be vested in the arbitrators.[46] If an arbitration agreement exists, it will be deemed to constitute a prima facie indication that the arbitrators, rather than the court which initially decided the case, are competent.[47] In any case, arbitral tribunals are autonomous in the determination of the issue.[48]

If a party fails to object to the jurisdiction of the court of law in a timely fashion,[49] it may be considered to have waived its right to arbitrate.[50] The question arises as to whether the appropriateness of the time in which the objection was raised must be determined relying on the law of the place of arbitration or on the procedural law applicable in the court's jurisdiction. Christer Söderlund submits that, since the court

---

42. ICC Rules (1998) Art. 28(6).
43. Indeed, they provide: "... all awards shall be final and binding on the parties. By agreeing to arbitration under these Rules, the parties undertake to carry out any award immediately and without any delay (subject only to Article 27); and the parties also waive irrevocably their right to any form of appeal, review or recourse to any state court or other judicial authority, insofar as such waiver may be validly made...". LCIA Arbitration Rules (1998) Art. 26(9).
44. The CIETAC Arbitration Rules (2005) read as follows: "... the arbitral award is final and binding upon both parties. Neither party may bring a suit before a law court or make a request to any other organization for revising the award..." (Art. 43(8)).
45. For example, the SCC Rules (2010) provide: "... an award shall be final and binding on the parties when rendered. By agreeing to arbitration under these Rules, the parties undertake to carry out any award without delay..." (Art. 40). A similar rule appears in Art. 33(2) of the Arbitration Rules of the Australian Centre for International Commercial Arbitration (ACICA).
46. Christer SÖDERLUND, "*Lis Pendens, Res Judicata* and the Issue of Parallel Judicial Proceedings", fn. 26 above, pp. 305-306.
47. *Ibid.*, pp. 306-307.
48. *Ibid.*, p. 306.
49. For example, Art. 8.1. of the UNCITRAL Model Law on International Commercial Arbitration (the Model Law) requires the party intending to object to the court's jurisdiction on grounds that a valid arbitration agreement exists, to do so not later than in the submission of its first statement on the substance of the dispute.
50. Christer SÖDERLUND, "*Lis Pendens, Res Judicata* and the Issue of Parallel Judicial Proceedings", fn. 26 above, p. 307.

proceedings were governed by the latter law, it should be applied in this regard.[51] Now, if the tribunal is faced with a court default judgment, the same scholar considers that arbitration ought to proceed: a party to an arbitration agreement cannot be required to appear before a court of law.[52] In addition, whenever a foreign state court holds that a matter is not arbitrable, bearing in mind that an arbitral tribunal located abroad will examine the arbitrability issue based on the law of the place of arbitration, it is possible for parallel proceedings to exist.[53]

Another scenario is one where arbitrators are faced with a prior arbitration award. The mere *existence* of an award between the same parties and on the same matter would bar the second arbitration: only the supervisory court, i.e., the court having jurisdiction in the place where arbitration takes place, may decide on the fate of the award.[54] Another interesting case appears when an award is in the process of being challenged: in such a situation, whether the challenge is successful or not may indicate if the dispute is subject to arbitration at all.[55] That is why "... if the challenge were based on any non-recurrent defect then the tribunal would have the choice of continuing the arbitration instead of holding it in the abeyance waiting for the court's decision...".[56]

Accordingly, it is clear that res judicata has arisen in municipal law with practical purposes and is plainly defined by national statutes and arbitration rules. Since a *rule* is essentially practical and clearly defined, while a *principle* expresses a more general truth and is broadly described,[57] it may be said that the doctrine under consideration is a *rule*. In this regard, the Supreme Court of California stated:

> "... The doctrine of res judicata precludes parties or their privies from relitigating a cause of action that has been finally determined by a court of competent jurisdiction. Any issue necessarily decided in such litigation is conclusively determined as to the parties or their privies if it is involved in a subsequent lawsuit on a different cause of action. The rule is based upon the sound public policy of limiting litigation by preventing a party who has had one fair trial on an issue from again drawing it into controversy...."[58]

---

51. *Ibid.*, pp. 307-308.
52. *Ibid.*, p. 308.
53. *Ibid.*, pp. 308-309.
54. *Ibid.*, p. 310.
55. *Ibid.*, pp. 310-111.
56. *Ibid.*, p. 311.
57. Joost PAUWELYN, *Conflict of Norms in Public International Law: How WTO Relates to Other Rules of International Law* (Cambridge University Press 2003) p. 132.
58. Supreme Court of California, *Bernhard v. Bank of America*, 19 Cal.2d 807, 122 P.2d 892 (1942), p. 2. Similarly, the American Bar Association has stated, referring to the Convention on the Limitation Period in the International Sale of Goods, that: "... a forum's legal rules, such as rules regarding res judicata and merger of the claim into the judgment, may prevent the assertion of the claim but the Convention leaves these questions to domestic law...". American Bar Association, Section of International Law and Practice Reports to the House of Delegates, Convention on the Limitation Period in the International Sale of Goods (1990) p. 592.

On the other hand, in the context of *private international law* "... the term international does not refer to the internationality of the source of law but to the internationality of the cases covered...".[59] Thus, it is clear that this field of law is the domestic law[60] governing legal relationships having a foreign element.[61] As has been shown, one of such rules is res judicata.

2. *The Acceptance and Scope of Res Judicata as a Principle of Public International Law*

It is hereby submitted that res judicata has been recognized in private international law as a rule and by public international law as a principle. Before going any further, it must be noted that these approaches are logical rather than contradictory. Indeed, in the *Antoine Fabiani case (France v. Venezuela)*, the arbitrator decided to apply the *general principles of the law of nations*, understanding them as "... the rules common to most legislation or taught by doctrines...".[62]

As the *rules* of private international law are part of domestic law, they may become *principles* of public international law, as long as they are common to most jurisdictions and applicable to the relationships governed by the latter. Res judicata has been applied for a long time in public international law. For example, in the *Corfu Channel case*, the

---

59. Thomas PFEIFFER, "Private International Law, 2008," in *Max Planck Encyclopedia of Public International Law*, para. 1. This scholar further states that:

    "... as to the civil law distinction between private law and public law, the prevailing viewpoint is that PIL is a part of private law: PIL rules do not constitute competences of national legal systems in the area of private law, which would be a legal effect typical for public law. In international cases, the rules of substantive private law would be incomplete without PIL rules. Together, they determine legal answers to private law questions so that PIL rules are understood best if considered as a part of private law...."

    Ibid., para. 1.
60. In fact: "... due to the limited role of public international law, PIL rules are a part of national laws.... Even if international conventions or other supra-national sources apply, the imperative behind these sources is eventually rooted in national law...." *Ibid.*, para. 6.
61. It must be emphasized that international private law does not refer solely to conflict of law rules since it

    "... includes, beside the law of conflict of laws, which constitutes its 'classical component', also what is known as direct rules, both of substantive law – either internationally unified or municipal only – and of procedural law, the latter specifically bearing in mind relations with an international element and constituting the international law of civil procedure. This trend is being generally manifested in the modern theory of private international law in contrast to older doctrine, especially German, which viewed private international law and the law of conflict of laws as synonyms...."

    Pavel KALENSKÝ, *Trends of Private International Law* (Academia 1971) p. 234.
62. *Antoine Fabiani case (France v. Venezuela)*, Arbitral Award, 31 July 1905, in X United Nations Reports of International Arbitral Awards, p. 117.

International Court of Justice (ICJ) considered that its own decision on jurisdiction had res judicata effect:

> "... [t]he Albanian Government disputed the jurisdiction of the court with regard to the assessment of damages. The Court may confine itself to stating that this jurisdiction was established by its Judgment of April 9th, 1949 ... That judgment is final and without appeal, and that therefore the matter is res judicata...."[63]

Today it seems undisputed that res judicata is a *principle* of public international law.[64] Indeed, the ICJ recently stated:

> "... [t]here is no dispute between the Parties as to the existence of the principle of *res judicata* ... the fundamental character of that principle appears from the terms of the Statute of the Court and the Charter of the United Nations.... That principle signifies that the decisions of the Court are not only binding on the parties, but are final, in the sense that they cannot be reopened by the parties as regards the issues that have been determined, save by procedures, of an exceptional nature, specially laid down for that purpose...."[65]

In public international law, it has also been accepted that the *ratio* of a decision most of the time is necessary to understand the operative part.[66] However, *dictum* is not binding upon the parties.[67] Finally, it is necessary to point out that, in investment arbitrations, res judicata has been consistently referred to as a *principle*. Indeed, in *Waste Management Inc. v. Mexico*, the arbitral tribunal held: "... there is no doubt that res judicata is a principle of international law, and even a general principle of law...".[68]

---

63. International Court of Justice, *Corfu Channel case (Albania v. UK)*, Judgment on Compensation, 15 December 1949, in International Court of Justice, Reports on Judgments, Advisory Opinions and Orders (1949) p. 248.
64. See: M. ANZILIOTTI, Dissenting Opinion in the Interpretation of Judgments No. 7 and 8, *The Chorzów Factory case*, 16 December 1927, para. 7; International Court of Justice, *Genocide Convention case (Bosnia and Herzegovina v. Serbia and Montenegro)*, Judgment, 27 February 2007, para. 114, et seq.
65. International Court of Justice, *Genocide Convention case (Bosnia and Herzegovina v. Serbia and Montenegro)* Judgment, 27 February 2007, para. 114, et seq. See also: M. ANZILIOTTI, Dissenting Opinion in the Interpretation of Judgments No. 7 and 8, The *Chorzów Factory case*, 16 December 1927.
66. *Ibid.*, para. 2.
67. In this regard, the Permanent Court of International Justice stated: "... the Court is unable to see any ground for extending the binding force attaching to the declaratory judgment on the point decided to reasons which were only intended to explain the declaration contained in the operative portion of this judgment and all the more so if these reasons relate to points of law on which the High Commissioner was not asked to give a decision...". Permanent Court of International Justice, *Polish Postal Service in Danzing* in *Collection of Advisory Opinions*, Series B – No. 11, p. 30.
68. *Waste Management, Inc. v. Mexico* (ICSID Case No. ARB(AF)/00/3-IIC 269), Decision on Mexico's Preliminary Objection Concerning the Previous Proceedings of 26 June 2002, para. 39. See also: *Petrobart Ltd. v. Kyrgyzstan*, Award on SCC Case No. 126/2003-IIC 184 (29 March 2005) para. 294

Bearing the foregoing in mind, res judicata may be regarded as *the rule of domestic and private international law and a principle of public international law, by which a partial or final judgment or award must be fulfilled in good faith by the parties and which bars any attempt by them to relitigate the issue thereby resolved.*

III.   FINAL, PARTIAL AND INTERIM AWARDS

1.   Final Awards

The term *final award* refers to a decision made by the arbitrators which is *final and binding* upon the parties,[69] so that it "… is conclusive as to the issues with which it deals, unless and until there is a successful challenge to the award…".[70] The latter understanding leads to the result that all awards are final regarding the particular issues the award deals with. This approach will not be the subject of discussion in this paper. In fact, our purpose here is to determine when a decision issued by an arbitral tribunal qualifies as a *final award*.

The issue may seem simple. One might think that *final award* is a self-evident concept: It is a *final* award. However, as debated below, the term *final award* has been the subject matter of intense discussions and multiple attempts at definition, the underlying question being: Final with respect to what? Final regarding the entire arbitration (it ends the arbitral proceedings)? Or final in relation to the issue decided (the award is binding and fully considered)?

That is why the attempts to define this expression have been unsuccessful so far. For example, the drafters of the UNCITRAL Model Law suggested the following definition:

> "… 'award' means a final award which disposes of all issues submitted to the arbitral tribunal and any other decision of the arbitral tribunal which finally determine[s] any question of substance or the question of its competence or any other question of procedure but, in the latter case, only if the arbitral tribunal terms its decision an award…".[71]

However, this approach was finally abandoned. The drafting group did not agree on whether decisions on jurisdiction or procedural issues would qualify as awards. However, traces of such definition may be found in Art. 32(1) of the UNCITRAL Model

---

et seq.; and *Industria Nacional de Alimentos SA and Indalsa Perú v. Peru* (ICSID Case No. ARB/03/4-IIC 300), Decision on Annulment of 13 August 2007, para. 86.

69. See for example the English Arbitration Act 1996 Sect. 58(1), according to which "… unless otherwise agreed by the parties, an award made by the tribunal pursuant to an arbitration agreement is final and binding both on the parties and on any persons claiming thorough or under them…".
70. David ST JOHN SUTTON, Judith GILL and Matthew GEARING, *Russell on Arbitration* (Thomson Sweet & Maxwell 2007) p. 274.
71. See Report of the Working Group on International Contract Practices on the Work of its Seventh Session (New York, 6-17 February 1984) UNCITRAL, 7th session, New York, UN Doc. A/CN.9/246 (6 Mar. 1984) para. 192.

Law, according to which the "... arbitral proceedings are terminated by the final award..."[72] and, of course, in legislation following this statute.[73]

In any case, it is evident that uncertainties surround the concept of *final award*, which in turn has given rise to several approaches.

A first approach is to submit that a final award is a decision resolving all aspects of a dispute, putting an end to the arbitrator's jurisdiction. Redfern and Hunter seem to follow this approach, proposing that the term "final award" must be reserved for

> "... an award that completes the mission of the arbitral tribunal. Subject to certain exceptions, the delivery of a final award renders the arbitral tribunal *functus officio*. It ceases to have any further jurisdiction over the dispute, and the special relationship that exists between the arbitral tribunal and the parties during the currency of the arbitration ends...."[74]

According to the foregoing, a final award would be equivalent to a *last award*, i.e., an award issued after all proceedings have taken place, all issues have been discussed and contested throughout and disposing on all the matters submitted to the arbitrators. The commentators on *Russell on Arbitration* consider that a final award would be one determining "... all outstanding issues in the arbitration, i.e., all those not previously dealt with in earlier awards...".[75] Thus, subject to exceptions usually contemplated in arbitral statutory law (such as the power of the tribunal to correct or clarify awards or to issue additional awards), once a final award has been issued, the tribunal is functus officio and its jurisdiction comes to an end. Rubino-Sammartano is of a similar view and defines a final award as one in which the arbitrators "... completely define the dispute which has been referred to them...".[76]

Conversely, other scholars consider that an award is final if it "... puts an end to at least one aspect of the dispute...".[77] According to them, "... in that sense, a final award is distinguished from an interim award (or procedural order), which do not terminate any aspect of the dispute, nor the last stage of that dispute.... Thus interpreted, a final award does not necessarily cover the entire dispute, nor the last stage of that dispute...."[78]

These authors draw a line between *final award* and measures that do not *terminate any aspect of the dispute*. Therefore, a final award would be the one putting an end to the

---

72. UNCITRAL Model Law (1985), Art. 32(1).
73. See, for example, Chilean Law No. 19.971 (10 September 2004), Art. 31(1); Brazilian Law No. 9.307 (23 September 1996), Art. 29; Mexican Commercial Code, Art. 1449.
74. Nigel BLACKABY, Constantine PARTASIDES, Alan REDFERN and Martin HUNTER, *Redfern and Hunter on International Arbitration*, fn. 1 above, p. 520.
75. David ST JOHN SUTTON, Judith GILL and Matthew GEARING, *Russell on Arbitration*, fn. 70 above, p. 273.
76. Mauro RUBINO-SAMMARTANO, *International Arbitration, Law and Practice* (Kluwer Law International 2001) p. 738.
77. *Fouchard Gaillard Goldman*, fn. 1 above, p. 741.
78. *Ibid.*

entire dispute or to a part thereof, without necessarily concluding the arbitration. To the extent that the decision is one which "... concludes the arbitration over a certain point of the dispute between the parties...",[79] other issues may remain still open and the tribunal may continue to perform its functions until the conclusion of the entire proceedings; however, the award will still be final.

This approach is followed, inter alia, by the Dutch Code of Civil Procedure, which provides in its Art. 1049 that "... the arbitral tribunal may render a final award, a partial final award, or an interim award...";[80] Art. 1699 of the Belgian Judicial Code, under which "... [t]he arbitral tribunal may make a final award or render interlocutory decisions in the form of one or more awards...";[81] and recent legislation such as the Spanish Arbitration Law (Law 60/2003),[82] and the Peruvian Arbitration Law of 2008.[83] These last two arbitration statutes authorize arbitrators to define, through awards that would be considered as final, not only the issues related to the merits of the dispute, but also matters such as the jurisdiction of the arbitral tribunal, and even the granting of interim measures.

A different classification suggests that the term *final*, when qualifying an award, has two meanings. On the one hand, "... it refers to the award, be it unique or the last one, which decides all the claims referred to the arbitrator, or at least those remaining to be decided, and thus puts an end to the proceedings...".[84] Under the latter classification, an award is such even if it does not end the mission of the arbitrators (functus officio). Therefore, an award will be final if, as a final judgment, it "... ends the arbitral proceedings for a procedural or substantive reason...".[85] On the other hand, with respect to awards on jurisdiction, they will be considered *final* depending on their content. If the arbitrators decline jurisdiction, the award is final; if they admit jurisdiction, it is an interim award.[86]

In sum, *final* is understood by a number of scholars as related to the end of all disputes submitted to the arbitral tribunal and the termination of the arbitrators' duty; others consider that *final* refers to the end of at least one aspect of the dispute.

Gary Born asserts that the expression *final award* is used in a number of different senses, so that care should be taken in the use of such terms; he proposes a terminological distinction under which

---

79. Domenico DI PIETRO and Martin PLATTE, *Enforcement of International Arbitration Awards, The New York Convention of 1958* (Cameron May 2001) p. 31.
80. Netherlands Code of Civil Procedure, Art. 1049.
81. Belgian Judicial Code, Art. 1699.
82. Art. 37(1) of the Spanish Arbitration Law provides that "... [u]nless otherwise agreed by the parties, the arbitrators shall decide the dispute in a single award or in as many partial awards as they deem necessary...".
83. Art. 54 of the Peruvian Arbitration Law is identical to Art. 31(1) of the Spanish Arbitration Law, quoted in the previous footnote.
84. Jean-Francois POUDRET and Sebastien BESSON, *Comparative Law of International Arbitration*, 2nd edn. (Sweet & Maxwell 2007) p. 646.
85. *Ibid.*, p. 647.
86. *Ibid.*, p. 644.

"... all arbitral awards can be regarded as 'final', in the sense that they finally resolve a particular claim or matter with preclusive effect. Even awards granting provisional relief can be considered to be 'final', notwithstanding the fact that they will be superseded by subsequent relief, because they finally dispose of a particular request for relief; much the same is true with regard to interim awards that decide a particular issue (e.g., choice of applicable law) without granting or denying a party's underlying claim. In this sense, every arbitral award rendered during the course of arbitration, before its final conclusion, is 'final' because of the preclusive effect that it enjoys...."[87]

The international arbitration conventions and national arbitration statutes requiring an award to be *final* in order to be subject to recognition and enforcement, lead to the conclusion that a *final award* refers only to one that has achieved a sufficient degree of finality in the arbitral seat (most obviously, by being granted confirmation or exequatur) or that is no longer subject to appeal or annulment in the arbitral seat.[88]

Finally, and also to avoid confusion,

"... the concept of a 'final award' must be distinguished from an 'award' that is 'final' (in the sense of no longer being subject to judicial review). As its name suggests, the term 'final award' refers to the last award in an arbitration, which disposes of all (or all remaining) claims and terminates the tribunal's mandate. This is a 'final' award in the sense used by Article 32(1) of the UNCITRAL Model Law. A 'final' award in this sense is also to be distinguished from 'partial awards', which 'finally' resolve part (but not all) of the parties' claims, and which may become sufficiently 'final' for recognition, in each case without terminating the arbitration...."[89]

In sum, under this last sense, both a final award and partial awards issued during the proceedings are final and, as such, will be subject to recognition and enforcement; however, "... only a 'final award' concludes the arbitration and renders the tribunal *functus officio*...".[90]

There is discussion as to whether *partial* awards are indeed *final*, since certain matters are still being considered by the arbitrators at the date when these awards are issued. For example, a German court recently held that a partial award finding liability but reserving the quantum of the damages for a subsequent award was not final and, thus, could not be subject to annulment proceedings.[91] Nonetheless, it may be generally stated that "... a

---

87. Gary B. BORN, *International Commercial Arbitration*, fn. 1 above, pp. 2428-2442.
88. *Ibid.* (footnotes omitted).
89. *Ibid.* (footnotes omitted).
90. *Ibid.* (footnotes omitted).
91. *Oberlandesgericht* Frankfurt, Schieds VZ 278 (10 May 2007).

partial award is final and is subject to the means of recourse every arbitration law makes applicable to final awards...".[92]

In this regard, the author has expressed his view that

> "... an award is final not only when it ends the entire proceedings, thus concluding the jurisdiction of the arbitrators, but also when it decides in a definitive manner one or more of the controversies submitted to the tribunal, or a portion of such controversy, putting an end to the litigious issue that is the subject matter of the decision...".[93]

However, as discussed later in this paper, while practitioners and scholars may try to define *award* and determine when it is *final*, tribunals may not. Many international arbitration rules permit tribunals to select the form and language of an order. Hence, tribunals may (and do) call procedural orders, interlocutory orders or other temporary requirements *awards*.[94] Arbitral tribunals want to ensure compliance. The best way to do so is to use the form of an award. Anything called *award* is more likely to be recognized and enforced by most domestic courts, given that the New York Convention seems generally to extend only to final and binding awards, not to cover interim measures.

National courts, in turn, resort to different criteria to define what an *award* is and when it is *final*. Some take the view that there may only be an award when the tribunal decides all issues pending before it and becomes functus officio. Others, as will be shown below, admit as *final award* any decision that puts an end to a controversy, but suggest that the controversy should be on the merits.

Award, then, lacks clarity. There is ambiguity both with respect to the expression *final award* and *award*, meaning that tribunals and domestic courts are left to draw the line where they see fit in the absence of guidance.

---

92. Julian LEW, Loukas MISTELIS and Stefan KRÖLL, *Comparative International Commercial Arbitration* (Kluwer Law International 2003) p. 634.
93. Original text in Spanish: "... *un laudo es final no solamente cuando pone fin a la totalidad del arbitraje, terminando también la jurisdicción de los árbitros, sino que igualmente final es el laudo que resuelve de manera definitiva una o más de las controversias que le han sido sometidas al tribunal, o una parte de dichas controversias, poniendo fin a la cuestión litigiosa materia de la decisión*" (free translation). Eduardo ZULETA, "*¿Qué es una sentencia o laudo arbitral? El laudo parcial, al laudo final y el laudo interino*" in Guido TAWIL and Eduardo ZULETA, eds., *El Arbitraje Comercial Internacional Estudio de La Convención de Nueva York con motivo de su 5 aniversario* (Abeledo Perrot 2008) p. 61.
94. This is easily explained: "... [t]he primary concern of ICC tribunals and the Court of Arbitration is to provide awards having international currency – awards which are recognized de facto in international business milieux as having the intrinsic value of persuasive and authoritative resolutions of disputes, and enforceable de jure in the greatest possible number of jurisdictions...". W.L. CRAIG, W.W. PARK and J.P. PAULSSON, *International Chamber of Commerce Arbitration*, 2nd edn. (New York, Oceana 1990) p. 327. (This explains why courts will tend to use the most binding form and language, even when issuing interim decisions.)

2. Interim and Partial Awards

The terminology with respect to interim and partial awards seems to be even more confusing.

There is lack of uniformity in the doctrine and practice of international arbitration as regards the criteria for delimitation of the different categories of awards. Moreover, terms such as "partial award" and "interim award" are used as synonymous without attributing to them a particular meaning. Interim measures and even rulings on purely procedural matters are named "awards". The ICC Commission on International Arbitration attempted to agree on a definition of the different terms, but "… [n]ot only did it find that in practice these terms are used often indiscriminately, but it was unable to reach a consensus with regard to the definition of an award, despite the fact that this is essential for determining which decisions have to be submitted to the ICC Court of Arbitration for scrutiny…".[95]

Lew, Mistelis and Kröll summarize the problem well and illustrate the inconsistencies explained above. They state:

> "… [a]ccording to the working group preparing the Model Law, an interim award or provisional award is an award which does not definitively determine an issue before the tribunal. This definition is in line with the general meaning of interim as opposed to final. However, the definition was not adopted in the final text of the Model Law. One of the reasons was that in practice the term 'interim award' is often used interchangeably with that of partial awards. Actually the majority of so-called interim awards are partial awards in the sense that they often contain final determinations of separate issues such as jurisdiction, damages or even questions of applicable law…."[96]

Others suggest that there should not be a distinction between final awards and partial awards. Any award that puts an end to at least one aspect of the dispute would be a final award and in such sense "… a final award is distinguished from an interim award (or from a procedural order) which do not terminate any aspect of the dispute, nor the last stage of that dispute. Thus interpreted, a final award does not necessarily cover the entire dispute, nor the last stage of that dispute…."[97] An award that puts and end to all or part of the dispute would be final with respect to that dispute; therefore, to avoid confusion "… partial awards should be contrasted with global awards, rather than with final awards…".[98]

---

95. Jean-Francois POUDRET and Sebastien BESSON, *Comparative Law of International Arbitration*, fn. 84 above, p. 635. For the discussion on the ICC Commission on terminology, see ICC, "Final Report on Interim and Partial Awards of a Working Party of the ICC's Commission on International Arbitration", 2 ICC International Court of Arbitration Bulletin (1990) pp. 26-30.
96. Julian LEW, Loukas MISTELIS and Stefan KRÖLL, *Comparative International Commercial Arbitration*, fn. 92 above, p. 634.
97. *Fouchard Gaillard Goldman*, fn. 1 above, p. 740.
98. *Ibid.*

Under this approach, if an award puts an end to all the disputes and terminates the duties of the arbitrators, it will be a global award; if it only decides in a final manner part of the dispute, it will be partial. Rubino-Sammartano seems to follow the same criteria; however, he uses the term *interim award* as equivalent to *partial award*. According to his view: "... there is an interim award only if there is a decision on a head of claim or on a preliminary issue which determines the entire proceeding. Decisions concerning the conduct of the proceedings should not be defined as interim awards...."[99]

Another proposed criterion for differentiating a partial and an interim award, is that the former is the one resolving all or part of the merits of the case, while the latter determines issues such as jurisdiction or the applicable law.[100] However, with respect to the tribunal's decisions on jurisdiction, as mentioned above, some scholars are of the view that a distinction should be drawn between the awards that admit jurisdiction, which would be *interim awards*, and those declining jurisdiction, which would be *final awards*.

However, the term *interim* is not only used in connection with awards, i.e., for decisions that resolve a dispute or controversy or a part thereof, but also for procedural decisions or measures taken by the tribunal.

Interim, as an adjective (modifying the noun *award* or *measure*) is defined as: "... for, during, belonging to, or connected with an intervening period of time; temporary; provisional...".[101] This definition includes two possibilities, which are used interchangeably but have different meanings. First, *interim* may be read as *belonging to or connected to* the intervening period of the dispute. In this sense, *interim* would be understood in temporal relationship to *final award*. The intervening period may be thought of as anything that occurs between the formation of the tribunal and the end of the proceedings. An interim *award* may be defined as any award disposing of an issue that precedes the final award (or any award putting an end to the dispute). In sum, it is a fully reasoned award that resolves an issue *connected with an intervening period*, as opposed to the end of the dispute. Second, *interim* means *temporary* or *provisional*. Under this reading, an interim award may be thought of as a temporary or provisional award. Therefore, such award is impermanent, merely a placeholder until the tribunal fully reviews the case and issues an award on the merits.

With very few exceptions, arbitration rules and national statutes do not contain a clear definition or standard for these awards. Art. 32(1) of the UNCITRAL Arbitration Rules simply authorizes the tribunal to issue interim, interlocutory or partial awards.[102] Similarly, Art. 2 of the ICC Rules provides that the term *award* includes, inter alia, interim, partial or final awards.[103] Art. 21(1) of the ICDR Rules authorizes the arbitral tribunal to take "... whatever interim measures it deems necessary, including injunctive

---

99. Mauro RUBINO-SAMMARTANO, *International Arbitration, Law and Practice*, fn. 76 above, p. 737.
100. Nigel BLACKABY, Constantine PARTASIDES, Alan REDFERN and Martin HUNTER, *Redfern and Hunter on International Arbitration*, fn. 1 above, p. 521.
101. Bryan GARNER, ed., *Black's Law Dictionary* (Thomson West, 2004).
102. UNCITRAL Arbitration Rules (1976), Art. 32(1).
103. ICC Rules(1998), Art. 2.

relief and measures for the protection or conservation of property...";[104] in addition, in Art. 21(2), the same Rules state that such interim measures "... may take the form of an award...",[105] so suggesting that arbitral tribunals may denominate *award* a decision that does not necessarily put an end to the dispute or a part thereof. Art. 57 of the CIETAC Rules refers to interlocutory and partial awards as those made on "... any issue of the case at any time in the course of arbitration before the final award is made...";[106] this understanding of *partial* and *interlocutory* as equivalent terms appears in relation to awards that resolve any matter, but not the entire case. Art. 26(7) of the LCIA Rules provides that the arbitrators may issue "... separate awards on different issues at different times. Such awards shall have the same status and effect as any other award made by the Arbitral Tribunal...";[107] in turn, Art. 25 authorizes the arbitral tribunal to issue interim and conservatory measures in one or more awards.[108] The Swiss Rules on International Arbitration follow a similar path by indicating, on the one hand, in Art. 32 that, "... in addition to the final award, the arbitral tribunal shall be entitled to make interim, interlocutory, or partial awards. If appropriate, the arbitral tribunal may also award costs in awards that are not final...."[109] Art. 26(2) of the same Rules, states that that interim measures "... may be established in the form of interim awards...".[110]

The arbitration rules, in general, grant ample discretion to arbitrators (sometimes subject to the request of the parties) to issue not only a final award that puts an end to the entire case, but also several awards issued during the proceedings. But they also seem to grant discretion to arbitrators to name as *awards* or to issue in the form of *awards* decisions that are provisional in nature, which the arbitrators may review and reverse or change during the proceedings, such as provisional measures related to costs or the preservation of evidence. However, the name *award* contained in the decision or the fact that the decision takes the form of an *award* is not sufficient, as discussed below, for it to be considered as such for purposes of: (i) challenge before the courts; (ii) recognition; and (iii) enforcement.

As mentioned elsewhere in this paper, the UNCITRAL Model Law contains neither a definition of "award", nor a reference to "awards" other than the "final award" mentioned in Art. 32(1). Other statutes, such as the French and German Codes of Civil Procedure refer to final awards, understood as those which terminate the proceedings.[111] The same can be said regarding Art. 29 of the Brazilian Arbitration Law.[112]

---

104. ICDR Rules, Art. 21(1).
105. *Ibid.*, Art. 21(2).
106. CIETAC Arbitration Rules (2005), Art. 57.
107. LCIA Arbitration Rules (1998), Art. 26(7).
108. *Ibid.*, Art. 25.
109. Swiss Chambers' Court of Arbitration and Mediation, Swiss Rules on International Arbitration, Art. 32.
110. *Ibid.*, Art. 26(2).
111. French New Code of Civil Procedure, Art. 1475(1); ZPO, Art. 1056(1).
112. Brazilian Law No. 9.307 (23 September 1996), Art. 29.

Other statutes entitle arbitrators to issue other types of awards, particularly during the course of the proceedings. However, "... they use different terminologies which render comparisons difficult...".[113] Art. 1699 of the Belgian Judicial Code provides that arbitrators "... may render a partial or a final decision by means of one or more awards...".[114] The English Arbitration Act (Art. 47) empowers the arbitrators, unless otherwise agreed by the parties, "... to make more than one award at different times on different aspects of the matters to be determined...";[115] the same Act, in Art. 39, authorizes the arbitrators, with the agreement of the parties, to make provisional awards "... subject to the tribunal's final adjudication...".[116] This means that, during the course of the proceedings, arbitrators may render awards on the matters provided for by Art. 39, which may be modified at a later stage by the tribunal itself. Art. 31(6) of the Indian Arbitration Act provides that the arbitral tribunal "... may, at any time during the arbitral proceedings, make an interim arbitral award on any matter with respect to which it may make a final award...".[117] The provision of Art. 188 of the Swiss Federal Code on Private International Law, according to which, except for an agreement of the parties to the contrary, the arbitral tribunal may issue partial awards,[118] has generated debate amongst Swiss scholars and practitioners: while some consider that the expression *partial* includes all interim and interlocutory awards, whether procedural or substantive, others support a restrictive definition of the term to include only awards deciding a part of the dispute.[119] The Spanish and Peruvian Arbitration Laws also empower arbitrators to issue partial or interim awards.[120]

Finally, the term *interim* is also used by several statutes and rules to refer to procedural measures issued by the arbitral tribunal (such as preservation of evidence). Specifically, they are "... intended to preserve a factual or legal situation so as to safeguard rights the recognition of which is sought from the court having jurisdiction as to the substance of the case...".[121] In these cases there is "... no pre-judgment of the case, and threat of irreparable or substantial harm which cannot be compensated for by damages...".[122] The expression *interim measures* is said to cover those measures related to the discovery, preservation and production of the evidence concerning the dispute; those intended to preserve the subject matter of the dispute and avoid prejudice to the rights of the parties during the pendency of the proceedings; and those destined to permit the effective

---

113. Jean-Francois POUDRET and Sebastien BESSON, fn. 19 above, p. 632.
114. Belgian Judicial Code, Art. 1699.
115. English Arbitration Act 1996, Art. 57.
116. *Ibid.*, Art. 39.
117. Indian Arbitration Act (1996), Art. 31(6).
118. Swiss Federal Code of Private International Law, Art. 188.
119. For the discussion see Jean-Francois POUDRET and Sebastien BESSON, fn. 19 above, p. 634.
120. Spanish Arbitration Law (Law 60/2003 of 2 December 2003), Art. 54; Peruvian Legislative Decree No. 1071 (1 September 2008), Art. 37(1).
121. Julian LEW, Loukas MISTELIS and Stefan KRÖLL, *Comparative International Commercial Arbitration*, fn. 92 above, p. 586
122. *Ibid.*, p. 604.

execution of the award. Together, these powers might be called investigatory, preservatory (of the status quo), and conservatory (of the award to be rendered).[123]

As has been discussed elsewhere, arbitral tribunals are often authorized to issue interim measures in the form of an award. The 2006 amendment to the UNCITRAL Model Law empowers the arbitrators to grant interim measures.[124] The interim measure is, according to the definition provided by Art. 17(2), a temporary measure issued at any time before the issuance of the award by which the dispute is finally decided, by means of which the arbitral tribunal orders a party to:

(i) maintain or restore the *status quo* pending determination of the dispute;
(ii) take an action that would prevent, or refrain from taking action that is likely to cause, current or imminent harm or prejudice to the arbitral process itself;
(iii) provide a means of preserving assets out of which a subsequent award may be satisfied; or
(iv) preserve evidence that may be relevant and material to the resolution of the dispute.[125]

Such interim measures may be issued in the form of an award or in any other form and are subject to recognition and enforcement under the provisions of Arts. 17H and 17I.[126] However, the arbitral tribunal may modify, suspend or terminate an interim measure or a preliminary order it has granted, upon application of any party or, in exceptional circumstances and upon prior notice to the parties, on its own initiative.[127] Finally, the 2006 amendment to the UNCITRAL Model Law indicates that the arbitrators may issue preliminary orders which shall be binding on the parties, but shall neither be subject to enforcement by a court nor constitute an award.[128] This chapter of the UNCITRAL Model Law on provisional measures has been adopted, inter alia, by the new Peruvian Arbitration Law.[129]

---

123. *Ibid.*, p. 595 et seq.
124. UNCITRAL Model Law (1985), Art. 17(1).
125. UNCITRAL Model Law (1985), Art. 17.
126. UNCITRAL Model Law (1985), Arts. 17, 17H and 17I.
127. UNCITRAL Model Law (1985), Art. 17D.
128. UNCITRAL Model Law (1985), Art. 17C.
129. Peruvian Legislative Decree No. 1071 (1 September 2008), Art. 47 et seq.

3. *Conclusions on the Classification of Awards*

A preliminary conclusion of the above discussion would be that neither the international arbitration rules, nor the national laws nor the international conventions, provide a definition or clear concept of *award*. However, from this set of norms and the different positions of scholars it would be possible to suggest some basic rules:

(i) It seems undisputed that a decision resolving all matters submitted to arbitration and putting an end to both the dispute and the duties of the arbitrators is a *final* award.
(ii) There seems to be a prevailing view that a ruling on some (but not all) the merits of the case qualifies as a *final* award too. Nevertheless, the terminology varies: some use the term partial (end even interim award) while others refer to *final awards*.
(iii) There is debate as to whether specific decisions on the jurisdiction of the arbitrators, the liability of a party or the applicable law, qualify as awards.
(iv) Even assuming that decisions on jurisdiction are final awards, debate exists as to whether such decisions are *final awards* in all circumstances, or only when they decline jurisdiction, so that awards admitting jurisdiction would be *interim*.
(v) Interim measures may take the form of an award, but they are not generally perceived as awards.
(vi) Decisions or orders of merely procedural or interlocutory nature (e.g., those fixing dates for hearings, summoning witnesses, admitting evidence and, in general, deciding on procedural pleadings), are generally not considered awards. However, a decision that is in appearance a procedural order but that puts an end to the proceedings, could be considered an award.

IV. THE CLASSIFICATION OF AWARDS AND RES JUDICATA: ADVOCACY FOR A STANDARD

One may master the theory, adopt or agree with one of the different approaches as to what is and what is not an award and whether or not a given decision has res judicata effects, or even develop a new doctrinal approach. But the real test, the confrontation of the theory with reality arises when the arbitrators have issued their decision and counsel faces the inevitable questions from the party. Can this decision be set aside? Can my opponent obtain a decision setting aside what the arbitrators decided? Can this decision be enforced when rendered? Elsewhere in the world? Is it final or could the issues that are the subject matter of the decision be revisited?

The immediate response would be that as a general rule awards are final, that only awards can be subject to an action to set aside, and only awards may be enforced under international conventions and particularly the New York Convention. Which leads to a new set of questions: Is this an award? Why, if the arbitration tribunal called the decision "award", is my counsel telling me that a court may decide otherwise? Who sets the standard?

International arbitrations are multi-layered proceedings. The forum rules, the tribunal composition, the laws of the arbitration (procedural and substantive), the laws of the state in which the arbitration is seated, and the laws of the enforcing state all impact an award. As between these overlapping rules, who determines what constitutes an interim award or final award? Secondarily, who determines what to do with each type of award? An advocate should understand how these conflicting rules interact. For example, where the tribunal determines the form of the award (e.g., they call it a partial award), how will the courts of the enforcing state interpret the award? To what extent are those courts bound by a partial award, versus an interim measure, versus a final award? Will those state courts look to the substance of the award, and decide based on that substance? Will that state's courts take the tribunal's language literally – e.g., if the tribunal calls the document an award will the state courts treat it as such? Does it even matter in that state because, for example, that state has a law that requires enforcing all measures, including interim measures? These are only some of a long list of issues that an advocate should consider once the decision is issued.

As mentioned above, the arbitrators enjoy a great degree of flexibility as to the form in which they issue their decisions. Arbitration rules often leave it to the tribunal to select the language and format of the decision. However, after the award is issued, the determination as to whether or not a decision issued by an arbitration tribunal qualifies as an award is no longer a matter for the arbitrators to determine. If the parties voluntarily comply with a decision that has been issued by the arbitration tribunal as an award or in the form of an award, the matter of whether or not such decision is an award becomes to some extent academic. The true problem, however, arises when the decision is submitted for scrutiny of the courts. Even though there are jurisdictions where awards may be subject to unusual means of review,[130] for purposes of this paper we will focus on the two basic cases of scrutiny of awards by the courts and thus the two main scenarios that the advocate should face after the award is issued:

(1) the possible action to set aside the award; and
(2) the action to obtain the recognition and enforcement of the award.

1. *The Action to Set Aside the Award*

It is almost undisputed that the courts having jurisdiction to set aside an award are the courts of the seat of the arbitration. This general rule is contained in the international

---

130. For example, in certain Latin American countries awards may be reviewed through constitutional actions (such as the *amparo* in Mexico or the *tutela* in Colombia) meant to protect fundamental rights. In other jurisdictions awards may be subject to appeal (particularly in domestic arbitration).

conventions on arbitration,[131] in the UNCITRAL Model Law[132] and under most arbitration statutes, even those not based on the UNCITRAL Model Law.[133]

The New York[134] and Panama[135] Conventions, however, provide for the possibility of annulment of an award by the court of the state under which law the award was made.

> "... The correct interpretation of Article V(1)(e)'s second alternative is that it refers exclusively to the procedural law of the arbitration which produced an award, and not to other possible laws (such as the substantive law governing the parties' underlying dispute or governing the parties' arbitration agreement). As with the definition of where an award is 'made' under Article V(1)(e)'s first alternative, this is a uniform international standard dictated by the New York Convention, which is not subject to divergent national law definitions...."[136]

---

131. Art. V(1)(e) of the New York Convention provides that

> "Recognition and enforcement of the award may be refused, at the request of the party against whom it is invoked, only if that party furnishes to the competent authority where the recognition and enforcement is sought, proof that:
> ...
> (e) The award has not yet become binding on the parties, or has been set aside or suspended by a competent authority of the country in which, or under the law of which, that award was made...."

According to Art. 5(1)(e) of the Panama Convention

> "The recognition and execution of the decision may be refused, at the request of the party against which it is made, only if such party is able to prove to the competent authority of the State in which recognition and execution are requested:
> ...
> (e) That the decision is not yet binding on the parties or has been annulled or suspended by a competent authority of the State in which, or according to the law of which, the decision has been made...."

In turn, under Art. IX(1) of the European Convention of 1961,

> "The setting aside in a Contracting State of an arbitral award covered by this Convention shall only constitute a ground for the refusal of recognition or enforcement in another Contracting State where such setting aside took place in a State in which, or under the law of which, the award has been made and for one of the following reasons...."

132. UNCITRAL Model Law (1985), Arts. 1(2), 6 and 34(2).
133. See for example Arts. 1037 and 1064(2) of the Netherlands Code of Civil Procedure; Art. 1717 of the Belgian Judicial Code; Art. 176, Swiss Private International Law Act; Sect. 46 of the 1999 Swedish Arbitration Act; Art. 8(4) of the Peruvian Arbitration Law; Art. 8(5) of the Spanish Arbitration Law of 2003.
134. New York Convention Art. V(1)(e).
135. Inter-American Convention on International Commercial Arbitration (1975) Art. 5(1)(e).
136. Gary B. BORN, *International Commercial Arbitration*, fn. 1 above.

In practice, however, the case where a court, other than the court of the seat, assumes jurisdiction to set aside the award because it was issued under its procedural law are rare and found more in the academic propositions of scholars than in case law.

Some arbitration statutes seem to require the award to be "final" in order for it to be subject to annulment.[137] For example, in *Postal Workers Union v. U.S. Postal Service*, the US District Court for the District of Columbia stated: "... [a]n award must be final and binding before a district court may vacate or enforce it...".[138] The reasons underlying this approach were explained by the US Court of Appeals for the Ninth Circuit in *Aerojet-General Corporation v. American Arbitration Association*, where it held that "... judicial review prior to the rendition of a final arbitration award should be indulged, if at all, only in the most extreme cases. The basic purpose of arbitration is the speedy disposition of disputes without the expense and delay of extended court proceedings.... To permit what is in effect an appeal of an interlocutory ruling of the arbitrator would frustrate this purpose...."[139] The vast majority of jurisdictions, however, do not seem to contain an express requirement of finality. The grounds available for setting aside an award in the seat of arbitration are defined normally by the national law of such place.

In short, as a general rule it is the court of the seat of the arbitration that defines – even before considering any of the available grounds – whether or not the decision presented to it qualifies as one subject to the annulment action usually available for arbitral awards. The court of the seat is the one that defines the standard to determine if a given decision issued by an arbitration tribunal may be considered an award or, in a more ample sense, may be considered as a decision for which an action to set aside is

---

137. See, for example: US Federal Arbitration Act, Sect. 10; US District Court for the District of Columbia, *Postal Workers Union v. U.S. Postal Serv.*, 422 F.Supp.2d 240 (2006); Swiss Federal Code of Private International Law, Art, 190.1; Stephen BERTI, Anton SCHNYDER, Heinrich HONSELL and Nedim Peter VOGT, *International Arbitration in Switzerland* (2000) Art. 190 and *Oberlandesgericht* Frankfurt, Schieds VZ 278 (10 May 2007).
138. US District Court for the District of Columbia, *Postal Workers Union v. U.S. Postal Serv.*, 422 F.Supp.2d 240 (2006).
139. US Court of Appeals for the Ninth Circuit, *Aerojet-General Corporation v. American Arbitration Association*, 478 F.2d 248, (30 April 1973). The same rule has been recognized regarding labor arbitration. Indeed, in *Millmen Local 550, et. al. v. Wells Exterior Trimp*, the US Court of Appeals for the Ninth Circuit held:

"... The question presented in this case is whether a labor arbitrator's decision determining liability, but reserving jurisdiction to determine the remedy in the future, is a final and binding award reviewable by the courts under section 301 of the Labor Management Relations Act.... We determine that such an award is not final and not reviewable. Accordingly, we vacate the district court's summary judgment confirming the decision of the labor arbitrator, and remand for the district court to dismiss the petition for confirmation.... The arbitrator's award must normally be final and binding before such review is undertaken.... To allow judicial intervention prior to the final award would contravene the fundamental federal labor policy of deference to contractual dispute resolution procedures, and would interfere with the purpose of arbitration: the speedy resolution of grievances without the time and expense of court proceedings...."

US Court of Appeals for the Ninth Circuit, *Millmen Local 550, et. al. v. Wells Exterior Trimp*, 828 F.2d 1373 (1987).

available. And the court generally determines such standard in accordance with its lex fori.

In theory one may attempt to construe a more international standard, a material rule, to define what an award is, and whether it has res judicata effects for purposes of the availability of the action to set aside. In practice, however, from the point of view of advocacy, the practitioner must consider that a court would likely apply its own standards – the law of the seat, the decisions of other local courts and the position of the scholars of the land – to define the issue.

2. Recognition and Enforcement of the Award

The determination of a standard as to whether a decision is an award, on the one hand, and whether it has res judicata effects, on the other, seems more complicated, from the point of view of advocacy, in the action for the recognition and enforcement of the award.

When an award is presented to a court for recognition and enforcement such court – as in the action to set aside – would have to first define if the decision presented to it qualifies as an award. In doing so the court would have to define which rule, law or set of standards would apply to qualify the decision as an award.

The international conventions and the generality of the laws that govern the matter refer to the recognition and enforcement of foreign awards, or to awards issued outside of the territory of the given State, or to awards subject to a law other than the law of recognition and enforcement, or to awards not considered national under the law of the state where recognition and enforcement are sought.[140] In addition, as discussed above, awards are subject to action to set aside before the courts of the seat of the arbitration and it would generally be the lex fori that would determine, for purposes of the annulment action, whether the given decision is an award.

The question becomes, then, how does the law of the seat interact with the law of the enforcing state, with the lex fori of the judge of recognition and enforcement. Should the court of the enforcing state simply apply its own set of rules to determine whether the decision submitted to it is an award? Under the rules that derive from the New York and Panama Conventions the response seems negative. Recognition and enforcement under those conventions require that the award be a foreign award. The same can be said with respect to the rules contained in the UNCITRAL Model Law and in national laws with respect to recognition and enforcement. They apply to awards that are foreign or not national: to awards issued in a seat or under a procedural law other than the law of recognition and enforcement.

Consequently, under the aforesaid international conventions where the law of the seat considers something an award, an enforcing judge should recognize it as such, even where the enforcing state law finds otherwise. The only exception would be the case in which considering it an award would violate international public order, because in such

---

140. See Arts. I(1) and V(1)(e) of the New York Convention; Art. 5(1) of the Panama Convention; Art. 36 of the UNCITRAL Model Law; Arts. 34 and 36 of the Brazilian Arbitration Law of 1996; Art. 46(1) of the Spanish Arbitration Law of 2003; Art. 75(2) of the Peruvian Arbitration Law.

event the pertinent court may refuse recognition and enforcement under Art. V(2)(b) of the New York Convention.

But, at least theoretically, the issue could be extended even further. An argument could be construed to the effect that since arbitration arises as a result of the agreement of the parties, and given that the grounds for annulment and for refusing recognition and enforcement are exceptional and limited in nature, both the court of annulment and the court of recognition and enforcement should look to the *lex loci arbitri* to determine whether the decision qualifies as an award.

However, for purposes of recognition and enforcement, the courts of the enforcing state make the ultimate determination of whether a decision constitutes an award; and, in doing so, such courts may also decide to look to their own law, to the lex fori of the court of enforcement and simply disregard the law of the seat.

If the court of recognition and enforcement considers that the classification of the decision by the arbitral tribunal as an award should be respected and may not be reviewed, then, of course, the view of the arbitral tribunal would govern. If, on the contrary, the court of recognition and enforcement considers that the classification of the decision as an award by the arbitral tribunal may be reviewed, then the court of recognition and enforcement would "reclassify" the decision (ether under the lex arbitri, the law of the seat or the lex fori of the state of enforcement). In this second scenario – review of the classification of the decision made by the arbitral tribunal – the court of enforcement normally looks to the content of the decision, and particularly to its res judicata effects to determine whether it may be considered an award.

Last but not least, the "state of the art" in arbitration in the given jurisdiction and the attitude of the courts towards arbitration play a fundamental role in the decision. It is not the same to advocate for a standard of what is an award or for a standard of finality in jurisdictions such as Belgium, England, France, Switzerland and the United States, as it is in Latin America, for example, where the laws on arbitration are relatively recent and the courts are generally not familiar with the principles and practices of arbitration.

Advocacy, thus, comes in at various levels. First the advocate should understand that the language a tribunal uses, the categorization of the decision by the tribunal and the lex arbitri may dictate the standard for recognition of an award in another forum. Tribunals, as seen above, do have a great deal of power and discretion. For example, an advocate may encourage the tribunal to use the term "partial award" for an interim measure. "Partial award" sends a message to the state that this is a binding decision and that the losing party is estopped from revisiting the issue. The other party, of course, might argue that the decision is an "interim measure", which is generally not binding on courts. Thus, an advocate who finds the classification of the decision under the lex arbitri favorable should attempt to emphasize the application of the lex arbitri throughout the arbitration, from classification of the decision by the tribunal to enforcement of the award.

Second, the advocate should consider the standard of the seat of the arbitration carefully. Either because he seeks to annul or enforce a decision and needs it to be considered an award by the court having jurisdiction,[141] or because opposition to the action to set aside or enforce is based on the decision that does not qualify as an award, a strategic decision may have to be made to disregard the lex arbitri and convince the court that it is exclusively the law of the seat that governs.

Third, where an advocate can choose from various states in which to enforce a decision, he should carefully consider the treatment of interim and final awards under the lex fori of the state of enforcement and attempt, if need be, to have the court of enforcement apply its local standards as opposed to the lex arbitri or the lex fori of the seat.

The approaches of state courts vary dramatically and successful advocacy within the complex interplay outlined above requires that an advocate analyze the situation on four levels: the arbitration agreement, the international conventions, domestic laws of the seat of arbitration and domestic laws of the enforcing state.

In addition, court decisions have generated additional debate as to the finality and enforceability of certain categories of awards which in turn raise concerns as to their preclusive effects. Such is the case of annulled awards and default awards, which will be referred to briefly later in this section.

In the United States, case law provides examples where awards annulled by the courts of the seat have been given preclusive effects. For example, in *Chromalloy Gas Turbine v. Arab Republic of Egypt*, the US District Court for the District of Columbia explains the reasoning underlying this approach:

> "... [i]n the present case, the award was made in Egypt, under the laws of Egypt, and has been nullified by the court designated by Egypt to review arbitral awards. Thus, [this] Court may, at its discretion, decline to enforce the award. While Article V [of the New York Convention] provides a discretionary standard, Article VII of the Convention requires that, '[t]he provisions of the present Convention shall not ... deprive any interested party of any right he may have to avail himself of an arbitral award in the manner and to the extent allowed by the law ... of the count[r]y where such award is sought to be relied upon'. In other words, under the Convention, CAS maintains all rights to the enforcement of this Arbitral Award that it would have in the absence of the Convention. Accordingly, the Court finds that, if the Convention did not exist, the [FAA] would provide CAS with a legitimate claim to enforcement of this arbitral award...."[142]

---

141. Exceptionally, such classification is not required because the applicable law permits the annulment of other arbitral decisions not considered awards. The action to set aside the arbitral award is discussed supra at pp. 253-256.
142. US District Court for the District of Columbia, *Chromalloy Gas Turbine v. Arab Republic of Egypt*, 939 F.Supp. 907 (1996).

A similar view was expressed by the US Court of Appeals for the Fifth Circuit in *Karaha Bodas Company [KBC] v. Perusahaan Pertambangan Minyak Dan Gas Bumi Negara, et.al, Pertamina.*[143]

However, a new trend not to execute such awards seems to have commenced with the *Baker Marine, Ltd. v. Chevron* decisions, where the US Court of Appeals for the Second Circuit denied the enforcement of two awards rendered in Nigeria, which had been annulled by the courts of that country. In that case, the US District Court for the Northern District of New York had concluded that "... it would not be proper to enforce a foreign arbitral award under the [New York] Convention when such an award has been set aside by the Nigerian courts...".[144] Baker Marine requested the Court of Appeals to reverse the latter decision; nevertheless, the Court confirmed the judgment and asserted: "... [i]t is sufficient answer that the parties contracted in Nigeria that their disputes would be arbitrated under the laws of Nigeria ... Baker Marine has shown no adequate reason for refusing to recognize the judgments of the Nigerian court...".[145] This line was also followed by the US District Court for the Southern District of New York in *Martin I. Spier v. Calzaturificio Tecnica SpA*[146] and by the US Court of Appeals for the District of Columbia Circuit in *Termorío S.A. ESP & LeaseCo Group LLC v. Electranta S.P. et. al.*[147]

French courts followed a similar path of enforcing annulled awards, granting them preclusive effects. For example, in *Ticaret v. Société Norsolor*, the French *Cour de Cassation* enforced an award rendered in Austria, which had been set aside by the Court of Appeals of Vienna. The French court held that, under Art. VII of the New York Convention, it was not entitled to deny the recognition of an award which would be valid and enforceable under its own national legislation.[148] In *Hilmarton v. OTV*, the *Cour de Cassation* enforced an award issued in Switzerland and declared null there, holding that: "... [t]he award rendered in Switzerland is an international award not incorporated to such State's system of law, so that its existence remains established despite its annulment, and its recognition in France is not contrary to international public policy...".[149] Another French example is found in the decision of the First Civil Section of the *Cour de Cassation* in *Polish Ocean Line v. Société Jolasry*.[150] This approach has been recently confirmed by the Paris Court of Appeals in *Direction Générale de l' Aviation Civile*

---

143. US Court of Appeals for the Fifth Circuit, *Karaha Bodas Company [KBC] v. Perusahaan Pertambangan Minyak Dan Gas Bumi Negara, et.al, Pertamina*, 335 F.3d 357 (18 June 2003).
144. This excerpt was quoted by the Court of Appeals in its judgment on the same case. See: US Court of Appeals for the Second Circuit, *Baker Marine Ltd. v. Chevron Ltd.*, 191 F.3d 194 (12 August 1999).
145. *Ibid.*
146. US District Court for the Southern District of New York, *Martin I. Spier v. Calzaturificio Tecnica SpA*, 71 F.2d 279 (1999).
147. US Court of Appeals for the District of Columbia Circuit, *Termorío S.A. ESP & LeaseCo Group LLC v. Electranta S.P. et. al.*, 487 F.3d 928 (25 May 2007).
148. *Cour de Cassation, Société Pabalk Ticaret, Ltd. Sirketi v. Société Norsolor* (9 October 1984).
149. *Cour de Cassation, Hilmarton v. Omnium de Traitement et de Valorisation [OTV]* (23 March 1994).
150. *Cour de Cassation, First-Civil Section, Société Polish Ocean Line v. Société Jolasry* (10 March 1983).

de l'Emirat de Dubai [DAC] v. Société International Bechtel, Co.,[151] as well as by the *Cour de Cassation* in *PT Putrabali Adyamulia v. Rena Holding.*[152] In sum, the fact that an award has been declared void does not automatically prevent courts from recognizing its res judicata effects.

Finally, the European Convention on International Commercial Arbitration (1961) provides: "... [t]he setting aside in a Contracting State of an arbitral award covered by this Convention shall only constitute a ground for the refusal of recognition or enforcement in another Contracting State where such setting aside took place in a State which, or under the law of which, the award has been made and for one of the following reasons...".[153] Therefore, if the award is annulled for a reason other that the ones listed in this Convention, such award may be enforced and considered preclusive despite the annulment decision of the court of the seat.

On the issue of default awards, it is well established that "... occasionally, international commercial arbitrations are held in which one party (usually the respondent) fails or refuses to take part...".[154] In such cases, the tribunal should not be expected to assist the reluctant party in delaying the resolution of the dispute and will generally render a *default award*. Taking into account that one of the parties did not participate in the arbitral proceedings, doubts may arise as to the preclusive effects of these awards. In *Glenn L. Rudell, et. al. v. Comprehensive Accounting Corporation*, the US Court of Appeals for the Seventh Circuit affirmed a decision confirming a default arbitral award, holding that:

> "... [t]he Rudells' case presents the issue of whether the doctrine of res judicata will, under certain circumstances, bar a party from subsequently raising claims based on facts which could have constituted a defense to a prior proceeding.... Both precedent and policy require that res judicata bar a counterclaim when its prosecution would nullify rights established by the prior action. Judicial economy is not the only basis for the doctrine of res judicata. Res judicata also preserves the integrity of judgments and protects those who rely on them ... by remaining silent during arbitration the Rudells are foreclosed from raising such a claim now...."[155]

The reasoning underlying this decision is that res judicata bars not only any attempt to relitigate issues which were decided pursuant to previous proceedings, but also refers to those matters which could have been raised therein.[156]

---

151. Paris Court of Appeals, *Direction Générale de l' Aviation Civile de l' Emirat de Dubai [DAC] v. Société International Bechtel, Co.*, RG2004/07636 (29 September 2005).
152. *Cour de Cassation, PT Putrabali Adyamulia v. Rena Holding* (29 June 2007).
153. European Convention on International Commercial Arbitration, 1961, Art. IX(1).
154. Nigel BLACKABY, Constantine PARTASIDES, Alan REDFERN and Martin HUNTER, *Redfern and Hunter on International Arbitration*, fn. 1 above, p. 524.
155. US Court of Appeals for the Seventh Circuit, *Glenn L. Rudell, et. al. v. Comprehensive Accounting Corporation*, 802 F.2d 926 (30 September 1986).
156. This idea was expressed in *Harper Plastics v. Amoco Chemicals* with the following words:

> "... [R]es judicata operates to bar litigation of matters that should have been raised in the prior

Nevertheless, it must be highlighted that the preclusive effects of default awards are not unlimited. In fact, in the same decision quoted above, the court avowed that "... [i]t is well-established that the doctrine of res judicata is applicable only in cases where the party against whom it is asserted had a full and fair opportunity to litigate the issue...".[157] That is why *ex parte* proceedings cause the arbitrators to assume a more active role, since they must assure that the absent party is given an opportunity to fully present its case, so that it will not succeed in a prospective attempt to challenge the award.[158]

3. *The Varying Standards in Recognition and Enforcement – Whose Nightmare?*

In enforcing awards different courts apply different standards, not only when the courts are located in different jurisdictions but also when they are within the same territorial jurisdictions. The name the arbitrators give to the decision is questioned; the finality and preclusive effects of the decision are put into question; the nature of the decision is defined under different standards and by applying different rules: the *lex arbitri*, the law of the site, the *lex fori*. Moreover, even though the category within which an award is classified plays a determining role in whether it has res judicata effects, the scope and use of the classificatory terminology remain unclear.

It is sometimes tempting to see those varying standards as a result of errors of the courts, inconsistencies in the interpretation of the rules of international arbitration or even misunderstandings of what scholarly writings see as crystal clear. But certainly this apparent chaos, those criticized contradictions are not, in most cases, spontaneously created by the courts. They are not the result of theories created by the courts in a vacuum without influence from the outside. Advocates act for their clients and in doing so, they have to convince the courts to enforce, or reject enforcement, of a given award. Not surprisingly, the first and most obvious strategy is to attempt to convince the court of enforcement that the decision of the arbitral tribunal is not an award or that, even if it is an award, it is not final, it does not have preclusive effects and therefore cannot be enforced under the applicable convention or law. Lawyers advocate for standards, and standards vary as jurisdictions vary – depending, inter alia, on culture, legal system, development and state of the art in arbitration.

In real life, the application of a given standard to define what is an award or what are its preclusive effects may result in chaos for the general practice of arbitration, or from an academic point of view, but at the same time prove extremely helpful from the point of view of the advocate and his client. The interaction of advocates and the courts has

---

proceeding. The prior judgment is conclusive not only in respect of every matter which was actually offered and received to sustain the demand or to make out a defense, but also as to every ground of recovery or defense which might have been presented...."

US Court of Appeals for the Seventh Circuit, *Harper Plastics v. Amoco Chemicals*, 657 F.2d 939 (1981).

157. US Court of Appeals for the Seventh Circuit, *Glenn L. Rudell, et. al. v. Comprehensive Accounting Corporation*, 802 F.2d 926 (30 September 1986).
158. Nigel BLACKABY, Constantine PARTASIDES, Alan REDFERN and Martin HUNTER, *Redfern and Hunter on International Arbitration*, fn. 1 above, p. 524.

resulted in the adoption by the latter of different standards – even different from those proposed by scholars and arbitration practitioners – to determine what is an award and when it has preclusive effects.

The following selected cases representing decisions taken in European countries, the United States and Latin America may illustrate the point of the varying, and sometimes contradictory, standards for definition of what is an award, whether or not it is final, what the treatment of interim awards should be and what are the preclusive effects of the different categories of awards.

a. *It is the content of the award and not its nomenclature that determines whether an award is final*

Two cases are mentioned as landmarks for this standard: one from the US Court of Appeals for the Seventh Circuit and the other from the Paris Court of Appeals.[159]

In the case of *Publicis Communications* (a French company) v. *True North Communications, Inc.* (a US corporation) a dispute arose between these corporations as to the termination of their joint venture. During arbitration the parties disputed whether the French company had to turn over tax records that the US corporation claimed were needed for it to file with the US Internal Revenue Service and the Securities and Exchange Commission. The arbitration tribunal ordered Publicis Communications to provide the tax information by a certain date. The French corporation failed to comply and True North Communications sought the US district court's confirmation of the arbitration decision, the first step toward federal court enforcement of an arbitration ruling. The ruling was confirmed. The French company appealed. The appellate court affirmed.

In its decision, the US Court of Appeals for the Seventh Circuit held:

> "... Publicis says the tribunal's decision was an interim order and, under the convention, only arbitral 'awards' are final and subject to confirmation. Publicis insists that until the order was final, True North was confined to seeking relief from the tribunal itself or the courts of England, the site of the arbitration. True North says the convention allows judicial confirmation of final rulings, whether they are termed 'awards' or 'orders', and insists that the tribunal's October 30 opinion was final. Although Publicis suggests that our ruling will cause the international arbitration earth to quake and mountains to crumble, resolving this case actually requires determining only whether or not this particular order by this particular arbitration tribunal regarding these particular tax records was final.... Publicis places great importance on the difference between an award and an order. True North requested an 'award' from the arbitration tribunal on the tax records issue, but the tribunal called its decision an 'order'.... The convention speaks only of recognizing and enforcing an arbitral 'award'; it does not refer to an arbitral order or any other comparable term...."[160]

---

159. The decision in *Merck et al v. Tecnoquimicas* discussed in the next section, adopts the same standard.
160. US Court of Appeals for the Seventh Circuit, *Publicis Communication, et. al. v. True North Communications, Inc.*, 206 F.3d 725 (14 March 2000).

In determining whether the wording used by the arbitration tribunal determines the nature of the decision the court considered that

> "... Publicis' position is that an arbitral ruling can be final in every respect, but unless the document bears the word 'award' it is not final and is unenforceable. This is extreme and untenable formalism. The New York Convention, the United Nations arbitration rules, and the commentators' consistent use of the label 'award' when discussing final arbitral decisions does not bestow transcendental significance on the term. Their treatment of 'award' as interchangeable with 'final' does not necessarily mean that synonyms such as decision, opinion, order or ruling could not also be final. The content of a decision – not its nomenclature – determines finality...."[161]

In *Braspetro Oil Services Co (Brasoil) v. The Management and Implementation Authority of the Great Man-Made River Project (Authority)*, the Paris Court of Appeals decided a case related to a contract whereby Brasoil agreed to drill certain wells in the Libyan Desert for the Authority. In 1990, the latter party terminated the contract. Therefore, Brasoil commenced ICC arbitration proceedings, which in turn led to the issuance of a partial award in 1995 declaring that the claimant was liable for the malfunctioning of the wells constructed. In 1997, during the damages phase of the arbitration, the Authority submitted a number of documents which, according to Brasoil, had been fraudulently withheld in the course of the liability phase. In light of the foregoing, Brasoil requested the arbitral tribunal to review its partial award on liability. However, in May 1998 the arbitrators issued an *order* denying such application.

Due to these circumstances, Brasoil sought the annulment of the *order* before the Paris Court of Appeals. The Court granted such request and asserted that

> "... [t]he qualification of [a decision as an] award does not depend on the terms used by the arbitrators or by the parties ... after a five-month deliberation, the arbitral tribunal rendered the 'order' of 14 May 1998, by which, after a lengthy examination of the parties' positions, it declared that there had been fraud as alleged. This reasoned decision – by which the arbitrators considered the contradictory theories of the parties and examined in detail whether they were founded, and solved, in a final manner, the dispute between the parties concerning the admissibility of Brasoil's request for a review, by denying it and thereby ending the dispute submitted to them – appears to be an exercise of its jurisdictional power by the arbitral tribunal.... Notwithstanding its qualification as an 'order', the decision of 14 May 1998 ... is thus indeed an award...."[162]

---

161. *Ibid.*
162. Paris Court of Appeals, *Braspetro Oil Services Co v. The Management and Implementation Authority of the Great Man-Made River Project* (1 July 1999).

b. *Only the award that resolves all matters and terminates the arbitration is final. An award on jurisdiction is not final and is not enforceable under the New York Convention or the local laws*

In *Merck & Co. Inc, et. al. v. Tecnoquímicas* the Supreme Court of Justice of Colombia set a particular standard to define whether or not a decision is an award, and concluded that only final awards are enforceable under the New York Convention and that only a decision where the arbitral tribunal resolves all pending matters qualifies as a final award. The Court denied res judicata effects to a decision on jurisdiction and an interim measure.

On 23 June 1986, Tecnoquímicas entered into five agreements with Merck & Co. Inc. and two of its affiliated companies (Merck) for the supply, licensing and distribution of certain products. The agreements contained an arbitration clause under which all disputes were to be submitted to arbitration under ICC Rules in Newark, New Jersey, United States, in English. The agreements further provided for the application of the laws of New Jersey.

Merck decided not to renew the agreements on their expiration, and the agreements expired on June 1996. Tecnoquímicas retained some amounts due Merck claiming the existence of a commercial agency agreement and the right of retention provided under Colombian law for commercial agents.[163]

On 3 February 1997, Merck commenced ICC arbitration seeking payment of the amounts retained. Tecnoquímicas challenged the jurisdiction of the ICC, claiming that its relationship with Merck was a commercial agency under Colombian law, that the provisions on commercial agency were a matter of public policy and that therefore only a Colombian arbitral tribunal had jurisdiction. On 7 March 1997, Tecnoquímicas filed a request for arbitration before the Center of Conciliation and Arbitration of the Chamber of Commerce of Bogotá against Merck. The Center appointed three arbitrators and on 19 March 1999, the arbitrators held that they had jurisdiction over the dispute, as the arbitration clauses providing for ICC arbitration in New Jersey were null and void pursuant to what the arbitral tribunal considered the public policy provisions of Colombian law on commercial agency.

In the meantime, in the ICC arbitration proceedings Merck had filed a request for the sole arbitrator to issue a decision on jurisdiction and to prevent Tecnoquímicas to continue the arbitration proceedings in Colombia. On 29 July 1998 the sole arbitrator, issued an Interim Award on Jurisdiction providing that:

(i) the arbitral clauses embedded within the agreements were valid;
(ii) he was empowered to examine and resolve the dispute submitted to arbitration;
(iii) he would proceed to examine the further aspects referred to in the Terms of Reference;

---

163. Arts. 1317 and following of the Commercial Code of Colombia grant special protection to commercial agents.

(iv) Tecnoquímicas shall abstain from pursuing any action in disregard of the the arbitration clauses, including the arbitration commenced before the Chamber of Commerce of Bogotá; and
(v) he would decide on the claim for damages filed by Merck in the final award.

On 18 December 1998, in an attempt to stop the arbitration proceedings taking place in Colombia, Merck filed a request for enforcement of the Interim Award on Jurisdiction with the Colombian Supreme Court. In its decision of 26 January 1999,[164] the Supreme Court considered that both the issue of the jurisdiction over the enforcement proceedings and the issue of the nature of the foreign decision to be enforced are primarily governed by the provisions of treaties – and in that particular case by the New York Convention – and, subsidiarily, by national law.

In its analysis of the New York Convention the Supreme Court considered that, since the Convention does not define the term "arbitral award", such term shall be given the meaning that better agrees with the spirit of the Convention and, in the absence thereof, the meaning ascribed to it under Colombian law. In its review of the spirit of the Convention, the Supreme Court stated that

> "... the Convention excludes from what it means by arbitral award 'domestic awards' which are so considered in the State where recognition and enforcement are sought. By so doing, it undoubtedly disregards, with respect to the meaning [which it gives to 'arbitral awards'], the legal definition which the award can be given in the country of enforcement. In other words, it is not the 'legal definition' which qualifies an award as such; rather, [such definition] is irrelevant in order to ascertain whether an act issued by the arbitrators is an 'arbitral award'. When the Convention provides that 'arbitral awards' must arise 'out of differences between persons, whether physical or legal' (Art. I(1), it undoubtedly adopts a material criterion: 'arbitral awards' are only those acts which are decisions, that is, which decide on or settle 'differences between persons, whether physical or legal' and that, as such, may be submitted for 'recognition and enforcement'...."[165]

Without further explanation as to why a decision on jurisdiction does not settle "differences between persons whether physical or legal" – differences related to jurisdiction – the Court proceeded to conclude that only decisions that settle the dispute on the merits qualify as an arbitral award. In the opinion of the Court

> "... a decision on jurisdiction, rendered by an arbitral tribunal in a State party to the New York Convention, is not an 'arbitral award' in the sense mentioned above when it merely decides on the jurisdiction over certain claims, establishing it or excluding it vis à vis the courts of that State or of another State. Even if it is formally defined an 'arbitral award', because it calls itself so or because it is so called by arbitration rules, still, according to Art. I(1) of the Convention, such a

---

164. Supreme Court of Justice of Colombia, *Merck & Co., et. al. v. Tecnoquímicas* (26 January 1999).
165. *Ibid.*

decision is not a foreign arbitral award enforceable in Colombia, since, independent of how it is called in the country of origin, it is simply a preliminary and preparatory interim decision, that is, it does not settle the dispute on the merits submitted to arbitration, which is the subject matter of a further decision...."[166]

The Supreme Court then undertook a detailed analysis of Colombian law to conclude that under the rules of procedure of the land, a decision on jurisdiction is merely a preliminary and preparatory decision "... which does not fully or partially settle the merits of the dispute ..."[167] and therefore may not be enforced in Colombia.[168]

A request for reconsideration was filed by Merck and on 1 March 1999 the Supreme Court upheld its original decision and included two additional considerations.

On the one hand, it held that the agreement of the parties and the applicable rules (ICC Rules, where an interim or partial award on jurisdiction was possible) cannot be interpreted in isolation but in conjunction with Art. V of the New York Convention, and specifically Sects. (*d*) and (*e*). According to the Court such sections – which Merck had claimed should be considered, amongst other sections of the Convention, as an indication that the definition of award should be made considering the lex arbitri and the law of the seat – do not list the decisions that can be recognized as awards nor were they meant to indicate which decisions may be submitted for recognition and enforcement.

On the other, the Supreme Court made a distinction between decisions that resolve *differences*, which means those disputes which arise from a conflict of interest that arises out of the claim and the response that are the subject matter of the case, from decisions which *settle* or *end* disputes.

> "... If we accepted this interpretation, we would read something in the Convention which is not there, that is, that an 'arbitral award' is not only a decision which settles 'differences between persons, whether physical or legal', but also a decision which settles the 'differences arising' out of 'the arbitration', such as jurisdiction and other issues. This may not be deduced from the system of the Convention...."[169]

The same conclusion was reached *obiter dicta* by the Colombian Council of State in *Empresa Colombiana de Vias Ferreas v. Drummond*.[170]

---

166. *Ibid.*
167. *Ibid.*
168. The court also dealt with the problem of the effects of its decision, that is, the continued existence of parallel arbitration proceedings. Its conclusion is surprising. If the parties disagree as to the validity of the arbitration clause, and each one commences arbitral proceedings – one in Colombia and the other in New Jersey – each party has the right to object to jurisdiction before the pertinent arbitration tribunal, but the decision of the Colombian arbitrators shall prevail.
169. Supreme Court of Justice of Colombia, *Merck & Co., et. al. v. Tecnoquímicas* (1 March 1999).
170. *Consejo de Estado, Sala de lo Contencioso, Administrativo, Sección Tercera, Empresa Colombiana de Vias Férreas v. Drummond Ltd.* (24 October 2003 and 22 April 2004).

c. *Only decisions on the merits can be recognized and enforced; but interim determinations in respect of claims that are binding on the parties can be subject to recognition just like final decisions on the merits*

On 8 August 2008, the Court of Appeal of Thuringia decided a dispute between a Japanese corporation and two German companies. The parties had entered into several agreements for the licensing and production of thin-film transistor glass, including a ten-year license agreement for the Japanese corporation's know-how. As the German parties established a plant in Germany, the Japanese corporation alleged that they were unlawfully using its know-how, since the license agreement had already expired. Thus, it commenced ICC arbitral proceedings in Zurich. On 30 January 2006, the tribunal issued an interim award containing binding decisions regarding the use of the know-how.

The German companies filed an appeal before the Swiss Federal Supreme Court, which was dismissed on 19 June 2006. In the meantime, the Japanese corporation sought the enforcement of the ICC award in Germany. The request was first submitted to the Koblenz Court of Appeal. However, it was later transferred to the Thuringia Court of Appeal, which was the court having territorial competence for deciding on the issue. The German parties requested the enforcement of the part of the award favorable to them, and opposed the execution of the unfavorable part for a number of reasons.

The Court held:

> "… It is true that the arbitral award at issue is only an interim award…. In principle, only decisions on the merits can be recognized and enforced (the same question arises for foreign interim orders by courts)…. In this case, the arbitral tribunal's determinations include interim determinations in respect of claims that are binding on the parties and therefore can be subject to recognition just like final decisions on the merits. They concern the [un]authorized use of know-how in respect of the new technologies and [the new technologies'] disclosure at the expiry of the agreements…."[171]

d. *An interim award may be enforced when it conclusively disposes of a separate independent claim, provided that the party seeking enforcement is able to identify an immediate need for relief*

In a decision dated 7 June 2009 the US District Court for the Eastern District of Michigan, Southern Division,[172] indicated that for an interim award to be considered final, and thus enforceable under the New York Convention, two requirements must be met. On the one hand, it must conclusively dispose of a separate independent claim; on the other, the party seeking enforcement must be able to identify an immediate need for relief.

The case concerned a dispute between Metalloyd, Ltd (a UK company) and Hall Steel Company (a US company) resulting from a sales contract pursuant to which the former

---

171. *Oberlandesgericht* Thüringen, 4 Sch 03/06, (8 August 2007).
172. US District Court for the Eastern District of Michigan, Southern Division, *Hall Steel, Co. v. Metalloyd, Ltd.* (7 June 2009).

sold steel coils to the latter. The contract included a clause for arbitration of disputes in London.

A dispute arose between the parties in connection with the contractual specifications of a delivery. The dispute was initially submitted by Hall Steel to the US District Court for the Eastern District of Michigan, Southern Division. Metalloyd applied for dismissal or a stay of the proceedings based on the arbitration clause; Hall Steel admitted that the dispute was subject to arbitration and finally the court referred the parties to arbitration.

Arbitration took place in London before a sole arbitrator. On 16 March 2006, the sole arbitrator issued an interim award holding that he had jurisdiction over the dispute and that Hall Steel was liable to Metalloyd for the costs of the US proceedings and possible related damages, as well as for Metalloyd's costs in arguing the issue of jurisdiction before the arbitrator. The costs and damages were to be assessed by the arbitrator if not agreed between the parties. Given that the parties did not agree on the amount payable under the interim award, on 29 November 2006, the sole arbitrator issued a second interim award directing Hall Steel to pay a certain amount in costs to Metalloyd.

On 1 March 2007, Metalloyd sought enforcement of the interim awards in the same Michigan district court. Hall Steel opposed enforcement on various grounds, the first one being that the two awards were not final and thus that the request for confirmation was premature. Hall Steel claimed that the arbitrator had named the awards *interim* and that they did not purport to resolve, or even address, the contractual dispute between the parties.

In its decision the District Court considered that whether enforcement is sought under the FAA or the New York Convention,

> "... the courts are agreed that the award in question must be 'final' in order to be eligible for judicial confirmation.... The New York Convention authorizes the courts to refuse confirmation of awards that are not yet ... binding on the parties.... Nonetheless, the courts have found that an arbitrator's award need not conclusively resolve all matters in dispute in order to qualify as 'final' and eligible for confirmation.... The Sixth Circuit has explained, for example, that 'an "interim" award that finally and definitively disposes of a separate independent claim may be confirmed notwithstanding the absence of an award that finally disposes of all the claims that were submitted to arbitration'.... Similarly, an arbitrator's characterization of an award as 'interim' does not necessarily disqualify it from judicial confirmation, because '[t]he content of a decision – not its nomenclature – determines finality'...."[173]

After citing the reasoning of *Hall Steel* to the effect that the award dealt simply with the matter of the costs incurred before the Michigan court, but neither disposed of all the claims that were submitted to arbitration nor finally and definitely disposed of a separate independent claim, the court indicated that in its view, the

---

173. *Ibid.*

"... requirement of a 'separate independent' claim is only a necessary, but not by itself sufficient, prerequisite to immediate confirmation of an interim award. Upon reviewing *Island Creek Coal Sales* and various other decisions in which the courts have found it appropriate to confirm interim awards, this Court discerns a common feature in addition to the 'separate [and] independent' nature of the issue addressed in the award – namely, that the party seeking confirmation was able to identify an immediate need for relief...."[174]

The Court concluded that:

"... [t]his justification for immediate confirmation is utterly lacking here. In the awards at issue, the London arbitrator assessed costs against Plaintiff for a threshold phase of the case, in which the parties litigated concerning the proper forum for resolving their contractual dispute. This was not the sort of prejudgment relief that a court might award to preserve the status quo during the ensuing proceedings, or to otherwise ensure that the arbitrator's final award on the merits is capable of meaningful enforcement ... the arbitrator's interim award of monetary relief in this case may readily be addressed along with his disposition of the parties' dispute on the merits, without any need for immediate judicial recourse in order to preserve the status quo while the arbitration proceedings are ongoing.... Indeed, there is a particularly compelling reason in this case for the Court to proceed with caution in considering whether to immediately enforce the arbitrator's interim awards. The interim award of costs here, totaling over $ 330,000, is almost half again as large as the roughly $ 700,000 amount in controversy in the parties' underlying breach-of-contract dispute. Yet, the arbitrator found that Defendant reasonably incurred this substantial amount of costs in litigating only the threshold issue of the arbitrator's jurisdiction to decide the parties' underlying dispute. Under these circumstances, there is a ring of truth to Plaintiff's contention that Defendant is using the arbitrator's award of costs as a 'whipsaw' to discourage or prevent Plaintiff from pursuing its breach-of-contract claim on the merits. Whether or not this is the case, the Court is unwilling to immediately confirm the arbitrator's sizable – and, in fact, rather staggering – award of costs, where Defendant does not face any sort of irreparable harm through delayed confirmation, but instead is protected by the accrual of interest as ordered by the arbitrator...."[175]

---

174. *Ibid.* In fact, in *Island Creek Coal Sales Company v. City of Gainesville*, the US Court of Appeals for the Sixth Circuit avowed: "... an 'interim' award that finally and definitively disposes of a separate independent claim may be confirmed notwithstanding the absence of an award that finally disposes of all the claims that were submitted to arbitration...". US Court of Appeals for the Sixth Circuit, *Island Creek Coal Sales Company v. City of Gainesville – Florida*, 729 F.2d 1046 (15 March 1984).

175. US District Court for the Eastern District of Michigan, Southern Division, *Hall Steel, Co. v. Metalloyd*, Ltd. (7 June 2009).

To the same effect, in *Publicis Communication, et. al. v. True North Communications*, the US Court of Appeals for the Seventh Circuit asserted that "... [r]equiring the unrelated issues to be arbitrated to finality before allowing True North to enforce a decision the tribunal called urgent would defeat the purpose of the tribunal's order. A ruling on a discrete, time-sensitive issue may be final and ripe for confirmation even though other claims remain to be addressed by arbitrators...."[176]

e. *The "interim arbitral award" on jurisdiction (or other procedural issues) is not a final decision on the merits and is binding only on the arbitral tribunal. It is not enforceable under the New York Convention or the local laws. The portion of the award related to costs is final and enforceable.*

In ICC arbitration in Switzerland, the arbitral tribunal issued a partial award on jurisdiction finding that it had jurisdiction over the dispute. The award ordered defendant to reimburse the costs of the claimant for the procedural phase dealing with the issue of jurisdiction. The claimant sought enforcement of that latter part of the award in Germany.

The Court of Appeal in Hamburg accepted the enforcement of the relevant part of the partial award. The defendant filed an appeal with the Federal Supreme Court. In its decision of 18 January 2007[177] the latter Court stressed that the question to be resolved was whether a foreign interim award on admissibility was subject to recognition and enforcement and found that the response to such question was traditionally answered in the negative. "... The interim award on jurisdiction [or other procedural issues] is not a [final] decision [on the merits] and is binding only on the arbitral tribunal...."[178]

However, the Supreme Court went further to consider that the decision directing the defendant to reimburse the claimant's costs was not an *interim arbitral award* but rather a partial decision meant to be final.

> "... [i]t is irrelevant to the qualification of this part of the 'Partial Award' as an interim decision or as an enforceable [partial] final decision of the arbitral tribunal whether the arbitral tribunal could finally decide on part of the costs [at this stage]. It is important that an arbitral award on such content, similar to a partial decision on costs, was issued.... The arbitral tribunal separated these considerable procedural costs and decided thereon in a final matter. A further decision on this point in the final arbitral award on the merits, which could be enforced in favor of the claimant, is not to be expected...."[179]

---

176. US Court of Appeals for the Seventh Circuit, *Publicis Communication, et. al. v. True North Communications, Inc.*, 206 F.3d 725 (14 March 2000) para. 12.
177. *Bundesgerichtshof*, III ZB 35/06, (18 January 2007).
178. *Ibid.*
179. *Ibid.*

f. Rulings from the arbitral tribunal ordering a party to provide accounting documents may be confirmed as awards to the extent that, according to the arbitration agreement or procedure, they finally dispose of a controversy between the parties

Mayer Zeiler and a group of his relatives (collectively referred to as Deitsch) decided to divide part of their jointly owned assets in Israel and the United States. They agreed to seek the assistance of a *Beth Din*.[180] The parties entered into an arbitration agreement calling for the appointment of three arbitrators.

The *Beth Din*, sitting in New York, issued a decision setting out a general plan for the division. The decision required the parties to pay, in certain proportions, the tax obligations of the US and Israeli companies. The parties commenced negotiations to implement the decision and the arbitral panel issued a total of eight rulings ordering that Deitsch provide Zeiler with an accounting in respect of jointly owned entities in the United States and Zeiler's life insurance policies, and reiterating the arrangement regarding the tax liability (collectively, the accounting rulings).

A dispute arose between the parties when Deitsch sought reimbursement of Zeiler's share of the taxes paid by Deitsch in the United States. Zeiler contended that Deitsch had failed to supply credible documentation in support of its request. Even though the arbitrator appointed by Zeiler had resigned, the two remaining arbitrators rendered an award stating that they retained authority over the arbitration and then issued a second award ordering Zeiler to pay Deitsch the amount of US$ 794,145.16.

Zeiler filed a petition in the New York Supreme Court to vacate the two awards and confirm the eight accounting orders. Deitsch removed the case to the federal district court, where it cross-moved for confirmation of the last award and argued that the eight accounting orders were merely interim orders.

The district court confirmed the eight accounting orders and the case went to the US Court of Appeals for the Second Circuit. After reviewing the issues related to the awards, the court focused on the nature of the eight procedural orders to determine whether they could be confirmed as awards.

The court concluded, admitting the reasoning of Zeiler, that all of the accounting orders were final orders requiring accounting and transfer of documents. "... The decisions require specific action and do not serve as a preparation or a basis for further decisions by the arbitrators. They have 'finally and conclusively disposed of a separate and independent claim' and therefore 'may be confirmed although [they do] not dispose of all the claims that were submitted to arbitration'...."[181]

The court granted special relevance to the particular nature of the arbitration:

"... If the parties agree that the panel is to make a final decision as to part of the dispute, the arbitrators have the authority and responsibility to do so. This was not a 'regular' arbitration, in which the arbitrators would hear all the evidence and

---

180. The *Beth Din* is a rabbinical tribunal that decides applying Jewish law. The tribunal is usually appointed by the *Zabla* method, according to which each party appoints an arbitrator and the two arbitrators appoint the presiding member of the panel.
181. US Court of Appeals for the Second Circuit, *Mayer Zeiler et. al. v. Deitsch*, Docket Nos. 06-1893-cv, 06-5617-cv (23 August 2007).

eventually reach a conclusive resolution of the entire case. Rather, the arbitrators were asked to preside over the continuing process of sorting out the details of a commercial relationship, entering operative decisions along the way. The various decisions entered since the 1999 Decision were practical orders to the parties to take various actions, including conducting accountings and providing documents. Each order was specific and final and did not need to be followed by a concluding award...."[182]

g.   *An interim order is enforceable where it is necessary for preventing a possible final award from becoming meaningless*

In *British Insurance Co. of Cayman v. Water Street Insurance Co.*, the US District Court for the Southern District of New York confirmed a prehearing security award and asserted:

"... courts in [the Second] Circuit have firmly established the principle that arbitrators operating pursuant to [provisions relieving the panel of judicial formalities and permitting them to abstain from following strict rules of law] have the authority to order interim relief in order to prevent their final award from becoming meaningless...".[183]

Similarly, in *Reinsurance Mgmt. Corp. v. Ohio Reinsurance Corp.*, the US Court of Appeals for the Ninth Circuit established that "... [t]emporary equitable orders calculated to preserve assets or performance needed to make a potential final award meaningful ... are final orders that can be reviewed for confirmation and enforcement...".[184]

To the same effect, in *Yasuda Fire & Marine Insurance v. Continental Casualty*, an arbitral tribunal had issued an interim order for security, whereby it obliged the claimant to open an interim letter of credit. When deciding on the confirmation of such order, the US Court of Appeals for the Seventh Circuit held:

"... [t]he arbitration panel in this case ordered Yasuda to post an interim letter of credit in order to protect a possible final award in favor of [Continental Casualty]. The panel concluded that if it did not order interim relief [Continental Casualty] would have to bear the risk that any final award it might win would be meaningless. Because this relief protects [Continental Casualty]'s interests, [Continental Casualty] has the right to confirm the order in district court, which it has done. Analogously, Yasuda should have the right to attack this relief if it believes that the panel exceeded its powers in granting the relief. The interim relief represents a 'temporary equitable order calculated to preserve assets ... needed to make a potential final award more meaningful'. Id. Accordingly, we find that the interim letter of credit constitutes an 'award' under section 10 [of the

---

182. Ibid.
183. US District Court for the Southern District of New York, *British Insurance Co. of Cayman v. Water Street Insurance Co.*, 93 F.Supp.2d 506 (2000).
184. US Court of Appeals for the Ninth Circuit, *Reinsurance Mgmt. Corp. v. Ohio Reinsurance Corp.*, 935 F.2d 1019 (1991).

FAA] and that the district court had jurisdiction to consider Yasuda's Petition to Vacate...."[185]

h.   An interim order is not truly final and binding on the parties, so that it is not enforceable
In *Resort Condominiums v. Bolwell*, the parties had concluded a licensing agreement for the use of know-how and trademarks related to time-sharing. The arbitrator issued an interim award ordering the respondent to refrain from using the know-how and trademark covered by the licensing agreement. When the claiming party sought enforcement of that award, the Supreme Court of Queensland stated:

> "... [i]t does not appear that the [1974 Australian International Commercial Arbitration] Act or [the New York] Convention contemplates any type of 'award' or 'order' of an arbitrator, other than an award which determines at least all or some of the matters referred to the arbitrator for decision.... Whilst it is true that a valid interlocutory order is in one sense 'binding' on the parties to the arbitration agreement at least until it is varied or discharged by the tribunal which made it.... An interlocutory order which may be rescinded, suspended, varied or reopened by the tribunal which pronounced it, is not 'final' and 'binding' on the parties...."[186]

V.   CONCLUSIONS

The lack of a definition of "award" in the laws and the international conventions, and the absence of a clear differentiation between final and interim awards, has left the definition and differentiation to the work of scholars and practitioners. A number of theories have been developed which, of course, are influenced by the cultural and legal background of the authors. Such theories move between extremes: from considering that any decision that puts an end to any dispute or difference may be an award, to restricting the concept only to the decision that solves all the issues submitted to the tribunal and puts an end to its jurisdiction.

This ample spectrum of definitions and classifications, in turn, creates obstacles to the creation of predictable rules on the res judicata effects of arbitral awards, and, of course, creates room for intense advocacy: advocacy before the arbitral tribunal so that a decision is termed award and its enforcement facilitated before the corresponding courts; advocacy before the court of the seat of the arbitration to convince it that a given decision is – or is not – an award and therefore that it has – or does not have – res judicata effects; and finally, advocacy before the court of recognition and enforcement so that the decision submitted to it is qualified – or not qualified – as an award.

But regardless of the theories of advocates and scholars, and irrespective of the names given to the decisions by the arbitrators, the courts seem the ones to have the final say

---

185. US Court of Appeals for the Seventh Circuit, *Yasuda Fire & Marine Insurance v. Continental Casualty*, 37 F.3d 345 (7 October 1994).
186. Supreme Court of Queensland, *Resort Condominiums v. Bolwell* (29 October 1993).

on the matter. It is the court of the seat or the court of recognition and enforcement, as the case may be, that will finally conclude whether a decision is an award, whether it has res judicata effects and which standards are to be applied. The question is, thus, whether we are providing the courts with certain basic clear standards to follow, or rather creating confusion with the terminology and the criteria for definition and classification of awards. The courts respond to what advocates submit and rely, inter alia, on scholarly writings and available publications to define whether or not a decision is an award and whether or not it has res judicata effects. Perhaps it is time to discuss some basic guidelines that, considering all that has been written on the issue, the different cultural backgrounds and legal systems, and the existing international conventions, may assist the courts in their decisions on this delicate and fundamental matter.

Correction and Clarification of Arbitral Awards

*Luiz Olavo Baptista**

TABLE OF CONTENTS	Page
I. Introduction	275
II. Requests for *Correction*	276
III. Requests for *Clarification*	284
IV. Conclusion	287

I. INTRODUCTION

In theory, the role of the arbitrator of the dispute terminates the moment the arbitral award is issued. However, this general principle must be taken with a grain of salt, because one could imagine situations in which the arbitral award contains omissions, mistakes or obscurities. That is why arbitration rules[1] and the legislation[2] of most jurisdictions allow the parties to request the arbitral tribunal to remove gaps, correct any material or clerical errors and clarify ambiguities in the award.

The arbitral tribunal's power to interpret its own awards is recognized by many civil law jurisdictions[3] and some common law states.[4] Requests for interpretation of arbitral

---

* Ph.D., H.C. Doctor; Founding partner, L.O. Baptista Advogados, São Paulo; Professor of International Law, University of São Paulo; member, WTO Appellate Body 2001-2009; chair, WTO Appellate Body, 2008.
  The author expresses his gratitude to Júlia Vita de Almeida, who helped him do the research for this paper. However, any mistakes or omissions are the author's own responsibility.
1. UNCITRAL Rules on International Commercial Arbitration (hereinafter the UNCITRAL Rules) (Arts. 35-37), ICC Rules (Art. 29), Stockholm Chamber of Commerce (SCC) Rules (Arts. 41 and 42), LCIA Rules (Art. 27), ICSID Convention Art. 50 and Rule 51 of the ICSID Arbitration Rules and Rules of the Mediation and Arbitration Chamber of São Paulo (Arts. 13.9 and 13.10), for instance.
2. UNCITRAL Model Law on International Commercial Arbitration (the UNCITRAL Model Law) (Art. 33), the 1996 English Arbitration Act (Sect. 57), the 1996 Brazilian Arbitration Act (Art. 30), the 1986 Netherlands Arbitration Act (Arts. 1060 and 1061 of the Code of Civil Procedure), the 1997 German Arbitration Statute (Art. 1058 of the *Zivilprozessordnung* – ZPO), the 1998 Belgian Arbitration Statute (new Art. 1702*bis* of the Judicial Code) and the 1999 Swedish Arbitration Act (Sect. 32), for instance. As FOUCHARD, GAILLARD and GOLDMAN point out, "other legal systems, including French international arbitration law, are silent, leaving these questions to the parties who are free to select an appropriate procedural law or arbitration rules". E. GAILLARD and J. SAVAGE, eds., *Fouchard Gaillard Goldman on International Commercial Arbitration* (Kluwer Law International 1999) p. 775.
3. Belgium, Brazil, Germany, Japan, Mexico, Netherlands, Spain and Sweden, for example.
4. Canada (Commercial Arbitration Act Art. 33), England (Sect. 57 of English Arbitration Act), Malaysia (Art. 35 of Arbitration Act 2005) and Scotland (the Scotland Arbitration Code Art. 23), for example.

awards have become popular among common law states due to the increasing acceptance of the UNCITRAL[5] Model Law and Rules.[6] Knutson reminds us that "the tribunal can go back and reconsider its award, but the exact scope of this power is unclear and rests uneasily with concepts common to most jurisdictions, civil- or common-law, such as *res judicata* and *functus officio*".[7] How the arbitral tribunal shall face this situation, independently of civil or common law provisions, and how it can prevent abuses by the parties, are issues to be further discussed in the present analysis.

A set of post-award motions is usually available to the parties in international commercial arbitration.[8] Among them, requests for *correction* and *clarification* of arbitral awards will be the focus of this review. *Correction* is employed here as meaning the rectification of omissions and of material or clerical errors. The word *clarification*, in its turn, is employed as a synonym for interpretation, seen as the pursuit of the real intent of the arbitral tribunal either in the motivation of the award, or in the *dictum* itself.

Therefore, it is convenient to examine, as regards the requests for *correction* (Part II below), first, the definition of gaps and how they can be filled and, second, the description of material and clerical errors and their correction. Finally, with respect to requests for *clarification* (Part III below), we will proceed to analyze obscurities and what is to be deemed an obscurity.

II. REQUESTS FOR *CORRECTION*

One of most common errors in arbitral awards is the omission of any claim that should have been decided – or in the very least addressed – as well as the absence of any word in the text (*1*); also, the existence of material and clerical mistakes is quite usual (*2*). These errors are subject to a request for *correction* and not *clarification* of the award, since the objective here is not to pursue the arbitrators' real intent, but to identify defects in the text resulting from a lapse of attention.

1. The Removal of Gaps

A gap is present whenever a claim or issue that should have been addressed in the proceedings, or simply a word or information, is omitted in the award.[9] The *correction* can be presented as an additional award in the first situation, or as an *addendum*, in the second one. Circumstances such as the composition of the arbitral tribunal, the rules

---

5. United Nations Commission on International Trade Law.
6. Since Arts. 35 to 37 of the 1976 UNCITRAL Arbitration Rules (the UNCITRAL Rules) provide for the interpretation, correction and the making-process of an additional award.
7. R.D.A. KNUTSON, "The Interpretation of Arbitral Awards – When Is a Final Award Not Final?", 11 Journal of International Arbitration (1994, no. 2) p. 99.
8. See A.N. VOLLMER and A.J. BEDFORD, "Post-Award Arbitral Proceedings", 15 Journal of International Arbitration (1998, no. 1) p. 37.
9. See A. REDFERN, M. HUNTER, N. BLACKABY and C. PARTASIDES, *Law and Practice of International Commercial Arbitration*, 4th edn. (Sweet and Maxwell 2004) pp. 1-36.

applicable to the *correction*, the procedural usages and customs and the extension and nature of the *lacuna* are taken into consideration by the arbitrators when making the choice between the additional award and the *addendum* remedies. What really matters is, actually, the substance.

Whenever a word or information is omitted in the text of the award, the usual solution is to make an *addendum*. This amendment follows the same procedure as the one provided for the correction of material and clerical errors. For this reason, it will be examined under Sect. II.2 below.

As regards the omission of a claim in the decision, the appropriate solution is the request for an additional award, as it usually is for this specific sort of flaw. The main purpose of the remedy "is to prevent a national court from setting aside an award for incompleteness or failure to dispose of a claim at issue".[10]

The peculiarity of such motion resides in the fact that a *correction* of omissions might avoid the need for further *clarification* of the arbitral award. Since the purpose of an additional award is to rectify an omission, once the gap is filled, the decision of the arbitrators will be better understood.

The motion for an additional award has a similar procedure in most arbitration rules and legislation. An important consideration to bear in mind is that it is usually not carried out on the initiative of the arbitral tribunal.[11]

After receipt of the arbitral award the parties usually have thirty days to request an additional award, on notice to the other party. However, terms are not timed so universally: pursuant to Art. 37(2) of the UNCITRAL Arbitration Rules of 1976 (the UNCITRAL Rules), "if the arbitral tribunal considers the request for an additional award to be justified and considers that the omission can be rectified without any further hearings or evidence, it shall complete its award within sixty days after the receipt of the request". The 1998 Rules of the LCIA (London Court of International Arbitration) also accords sixty days as the time limit for rendering an additional award. Under the American Arbitration Association Rules (AAA Rules) the delay is substantially shorter – the additional award must be issued within thirty days after the request.

The Brazilian Arbitration Act admits motions for an additional award in its Art. 32, II. The procedure is very similar to the one provided by the institutional rules described above, but the difference resides, once again, in the delays. The parties have only five days to file the request, while the arbitral tribunal shall respect the time limit of ten days

---

10. A.N. VOLLMER and A.J. BEDFORD, "Post-Award Arbitral Proceedings, fn. 8 above, p. 44.
11. An exception is, for instance, The English Arbitration Act Art. 57(3)(b):

"57. Correction of award or additional award:
(…)
(3) *The tribunal may on its own initiative* or on the application of a party
(…)
(b) *make an additional award* in respect of any claim (including a claim for interest or costs) which was presented to the tribunal but was not dealt with in the award. These powers shall not be exercised without first affording the other parties a reasonable opportunity to make representations to the tribunal." (Emphasis added.)

to issue the additional award. The English Arbitration Act of 1996 (English Arbitration Act) has similar provisions,[12] but the parties are bound to a twenty-eight-day time limit, while the arbitral tribunal is bound to a fifty-six-day time limit.

The table below[13] illustrates the comparative analysis of requests for additional awards in a few institutional rules and national arbitration legislation:

ADDITIONAL AWARDS

	Institutional Rules				Legislation			
	UNCITRAL	ICC	SCC	LCIA	UNCITRAL Model Law	Brazil	England	USA
Contemplate additional awards?	Yes	No	Yes	Yes	Yes	Yes	Yes	No
On the initiative of the arbitral tribunal?	No	—	No	No	No	No	Yes, within 28 days	—
Time limit granted to the parties for submission of request	30 days	—	30 days	30 days	30 days	5 days	28 days	—
Time limit granted to the arbitral tribunal for deciding	60 days	—	60 days	60 days	60 days	10 days	56 days*	—

* In this case the arbitral tribunal is granted 56 days *of the date of the original award.*

If the purpose of the additional award is to deal with claims that were omitted in the award's *dictum*, there are two conditions for its application. First, the request shall challenge an award that addresses *claims* and, second, the request shall not be used as an artifice to raise *new* claims.

The first condition means that an award dealing only with procedural issues, not touching the merits of the dispute, is not subject to a request for an additional award. It

---

12. See Art. 57(3)(b).
13. Other relevant institutional rules and legislation are not part of the present and subsequent tables because they were not analyzed in this paper.

seems irrelevant whether the award is final or partial,[14] since what really matters is the omission of any claim that supposedly had to be dealt with in the award's *dictum*.[15]

The second condition is related to the specific scope of the additional award: to decide a claim that was omitted in the award's *dictum* or, in other words, to remove a gap. The terms of reference shall be taken as parameters to determine whether the gap alleged by the parties concerns a claim previously defined or simply and erroneously an issue out of the scope of the arbitration. We agree with Trittmann and Duve in their statement that "in making use of its discretionary power, the arbitral tribunal has to examine whether the affected claim has actually been presented in the proceedings or whether the request affects a new claim".[16]

The request for an additional award being an unusual remedy and not foreseen by all institutional rules, such as the Arbitration Rules of the International Chamber of Commerce (ICC Rules) of 1998, there are not many examples[17] of it in case law. But one of them that is widely discussed by authorities is particularly worth a closer examination: *Lockheed Corp. v. Iran*.[18]

---

14. We agree with R.D.A. KNUTSON when he contends that "interim awards are final as to the matters they decide", in "The Interpretation of Arbitral Awards – When Is a Final Award Not Final?", fn. 7 above, p. 99.

15. In their mention of UNCITRAL Rules Art. 37, AAA Rules Art. 30 and Inter-American Arbitration Commission Rules Art. 37, N. VOLLMER and A.J. BEDFORD, fn. 8 above, affirm that

   "the use of the term 'claims' (rather than 'claim') and the reference to 'the award' could imply that the award referred to in these provisions is the final award. In other words, the term 'claims' could mean the totality of the claims (which only the final award will deal with) and the use of the term 'the award' could mean the final award (only one final award exists, but more than one interim or partial award may exist). This issue apparently has not been raised in practice. To the contrary, in one or perhaps two cases, tribunals have considered requests for additional awards when only a partial award had been issued."

   (e.g. *Harris Int'l Telecomms. Inc. v. Iran*, 18 Iran-US CTR 76-77 (1988); "Post-Award Arbitral Proceedings", fn. 8 above, p. 46.

16. In F.B. WEIGAND, ed., *Practitioner's Handbook on International Arbitration* (Verlag C.H. Beck, Munich/Copenhagen 2002) p. 366.

17. D.D. CARON and L.F. REED mention the following cases of the Iran-US Claims Tribunal as examples of requests for additional awards: *Hood Corp. v. Islamic Republic of Iran*; *Flexi-Van Leasing, Inc. v. Islamic Republic of Iran*; *International Schools Services, Inc. v. Islamic Republic of Iran*; *Exxon Research and Engineering Co. v. Islamic Republic of Iran*; *Sedco, Inc. v. NIOC*; *Harris International Telecommunications, Inc. v. Islamic Republic of Iran*; *Mohajer-Shojaee v. Islamic Republic of Iran*; *Saboonchian v. Islamic Republic of Iran*; *Collins Systems International, Inc. v. Navy of the Islamic Republic of Iran*; *Harold Birnbaum v. Islamic Republic of Iran*; *Unidyne Corporation v. Islamic Republic of Iran*. "Post Award Proceedings Under the UNCITRAL Arbitration Rules", 11 Arbitration International (1995, no. 4) pp. 442-443.

18. See *Ibid.*, p. 443; N. VOLLMER and A.J. BEDFORD, "Post-Award Arbitral Proceedings", fn. 8 above, p. 44; and R.D.A. KNUTSON, "The Interpretation of Arbitral Awards – When Is a Final Award Not Final?", fn. 7 above, p. 104.

The dispute arose when the North American Lockheed Corp. claimed recovery losses that resulted from its business activities with Iran and the Iranian Air Force.[19] The Iran-United States Claims Tribunal (Iran-US Claims Tribunal),[20] governed by the UNCITRAL Arbitration Rules, found against Iran's counterclaim. Iran, arguing that Lockheed should be ordered to return certain parts to Iran and asking for clarification as regards the status of certain other parts in Lockheed's possession, filed a post-award motion, but did not specify whether it was a request for *correction* or *clarification* of the arbitral award. The tribunal first noted that a request for *correction*[21] of errors was clearly not applicable to the case. Moreover, a request for *clarification*[22] could not be examined either: as Iran had only claimed damages during the course of the proceedings, a claim for physical delivery of the parts could not be the subject of the post-award requests. Finally, issuing an additional award[23] was also inappropriate, since Iran had not specified any claims from its original proceedings that the tribunal's award might have failed to address.

From the brief analysis of this case, it is possible to affirm that the request for an additional award has the limited scope of rectifying an omitted claim in the award's *dictum*. Any new issue raised by the parties in the post-award motion shall be considered an abuse and be rejected by the arbitral tribunal.

We proceed to examine the request for *correction* of material and clerical errors, the most usual among all post-award motions.

2. The Correction of Material and Clerical Errors

Material errors are computational, such as mistakes in the calculation of a certain amount. Clerical errors are purely typographical or of a similar technical nature, such as erroneous dates, inverted numbers and displaced words. Both must be self-evident.

In any case, errors are what theory calls *noises in communication*, and although they do not affect the intention of the arbitrators, they might lead to difficulties of comprehension to a less alert reader. For this reason, errors shall be corrected, "but the correction would not mean that the tribunal had changed its decision. Rather, it would only mean that the tribunal had incorrectly expressed its decision in the first place."[24]

Thus, it is clear that rectification of obvious mistakes is subject to a post-award motion for *correction*, and not *clarification*. Nothing will be interpreted again by the arbitral tribunal, which will only perform a formal technical review.

The motion for *correction* of any error in the award can arise on the initiative of the arbitral tribunal and also at the request of any of the parties.

---

19. J.D. FRY, "Islamic Law and the Iran-United States Claims Tribunal: The Primacy of the International Law over Municipal Law", 18 Arbitration International (2002, no. 1) p. 111.
20. This tribunal came into existence to govern the delicate relations between the Islamic Republic of Iran and the United States of America arising in November 1979. More information at <www.iusct.org/background-english.html>.
21. UNCITRAL Rules Art. 36.
22. UNCITRAL Rules Art. 35.
23. UNCITRAL Rules Art. 37.
24. A.N. VOLLMER and A.J. BEDFORD, "Post-Award Arbitral Proceedings", fn. 8 above, p. 39.

When the arbitral tribunal itself detects an error in the award, it can make an amendment. The ICC Rules allow the arbitral tribunal thirty days to submit an *addendum* for approval to the Court.[25] The time limit granted to *"sponte propria"* corrections by the arbitral tribunal is the same under UNCITRAL,[26] Arbitration Institute of the Stockholm Chamber of Commerce (SCC)[27] and LCIA[28] Rules.

The UNCITRAL Model Law[29] provides for the *correction* of errors on the arbitral tribunal's own initiative. The English Arbitration Act in its Art. 57(3)(A) also contemplates such possibility and there do not seem to be laws forbidding this practice in other countries.

The parties are also allowed to request the arbitral tribunal for *correction* of errors in the award. Under the ICC Rules,[30] the interested party shall make the application within thirty days of the receipt of the award. The arbitral tribunal will then grant the other party a short time limit, normally not exceeding thirty days, to submit any comments. Finally, the arbitral tribunal shall render its draft decision to the ICC Court in thirty days. As regards the procedure of *correction* under ICC Rules, M. Bühler and S. Jarvin interestingly note that

> "What is foreseen by the ICC Rules is exactly what does happen in practice: out of over 300 Awards approved each year by the Court, and despite ICC arbitrators using their best efforts in drafting Awards, only a handful pass such scrutiny without the Secretariat and/or the Court finding at least one typographical error....
>
> However, as practice has shown, the *system is not 100% 'safe'* and, on past experience, the need to have corrections made to an award has arisen even after the approval of the Award by the Court and most often after its notification to the parties."[31] (Emphasis in original.)

Other institutional rules also provide for *correction* of the award on the initiative of any of the parties. The UNCITRAL Rules' Art. 36.1, for instance, states that "within thirty days after the receipt of the award, either party, with notice to the other party, may request the arbitral tribunal to correct in the award any errors in computation, any clerical or typographical errors, or any errors of similar nature". Under SCC[32] and LCIA[33] Rules, not only the parties, but also the arbitral tribunal is bound to a thirty-day time limit to submit its decision thereon.

---

25. ICC Rules Art. 29(1).
26. UNCITRAL Rules Art. 36.
27. Art. 41(2) of the 2010 SCC Rules.
28. LCIA Rules Art. 27(2).
29. Art. 33(2) of 1985 UNCITRAL Model Law.
30. ICC Rules Art. 29(2).
31. In F.B. WEIGAND, ed., *Practitioner's Handbook on International Arbitration*, fn. 16 above, p. 276 (footnotes omitted).
32. SCC Rules Art. 41(1).
33. LCIA Rules Art. 27(1).

We find similar provisions, but with different time limits, in national legislation, such as the Brazilian Arbitration Act, Art. 30, and the English Arbitration Act, Art. 57.[34] In this sense, Born properly recalls that "even where legislative mechanisms do not exist, national courts have fashioned limited means of correcting mistaken awards. These various legislative and judicial actions are necessary in order to avoid the unacceptable possibility that a party find itself bound by an award ordering relief that the arbitrators did not intend and do not want to grant."[35]

As the 1958 New York Convention does not expressly require or forbid procedures for correction of arbitral awards, and considering that a mistaken award shall not be given effect, pursuant to basic conceptions of procedural fairness, it seems acceptable that, in the absence of applicable institutional rules or legislation, the parties be free to agree on a procedure for correction in the Terms of Reference of the dispute.[36] Likewise, in rare circumstances, national courts might be allowed to proceed to a formal review of the arbitral award, as provided by the US Federal Arbitration Act (FAA), Sect. 11.[37]

The following table summarizes the differences and similarities among institutional rules and legislation as regards the procedure for *correction* of arbitral awards.

---

34. "... the Swiss Law on Private International Law does not include a statutory provision on correction of awards. It is well settled, however, that this does not prevent an arbitral tribunal in an international arbitration seated in Switzerland from correcting its award. In the absence of contrary agreement, some Swiss commentators suggest that a thirty-day time limit is applicable to requests for corrections, although the better view adopts a more flexible analysis in the absence of legislative deadlines."

    G.B. BORN, *International Commercial Arbitration* (Kluwer Law International 2009) pp. 2521-2536.
35. *Ibid.*, p. 2521. The author, however, does not mention which other countries have such rules.
36. This possibility is also in accordance with the principle of party autonomy.
37. "Section 11. Same; modification or correction; grounds; order.
    In either of the following cases *the United States court in and for the district wherein the award was made may make an order modifying or correcting the award upon the application of any party to the arbitration* (a) Where there was an evident material miscalculation of figures or an evident material mistake in the description of any person, thing, or property referred to in the award. (b) Where the arbitrators have awarded upon a matter not submitted to them, unless it is a matter not affecting the merits of the decision upon the matter submitted. (c) Where the award is imperfect in matter of form not affecting the merits of the controversy. The order may modify and correct the award, so as to effect the intent thereof and promote justice between the parties." (Emphasis added)

Correction of the Award

	Institutional Rules				Legislation			
	UNCITRAL	ICC	SCC	LCIA	UNCITRAL Model Law	Brazil	England	USA
Contemplate correction of awards?	Yes	Yes	Yes	Yes	Yes	Yes	Yes	Yes*
On the initiative of the arbitral tribunal?	Yes, within 30 days	Yes, within 30 days	Yes, within 30 days	Yes, within 30 days	Yes, within 30 days	No	Yes, within 28 days	—
Time limit granted to the parties for submission of request	30 days	30 days	30 days	30 days	30 days	5 days	28 days	—
Time limit granted to the arbitral tribunal for deciding	—	30 days	30 days	30 days	30 days	10 days	28 days	—

* FAA provides for correction of arbitral awards carried out by the United States Court in and for the district wherein the award was made.

Although it seems to be clear that an award can be subject to amendment only when there is an obvious mistake, parties still attempt to use the request for *correction* as an opportunity to challenge the substance of the award.

For this reason, arbitral tribunals have quite often redefined the real purpose of an *addendum*, explaining to the parties that provisions for *correction* have a restricted meaning and should not be raised as an appeal of the arbitral award. The strict scope of Art. 36 of the UNCITRAL Rules, for instance, was re-affirmed in several decisions of the Iran-US Claims Tribunal:[38] *Harris Int'l Telecomms., Inc. v. Iran*;[39] *American Bell Int'l, Inc. v. Iran*;[40]

---

38. See more detailed commentaries at A.N. VOLLMER and A.J. BEDFORD, "Post-Award Arbitral Proceedings", fn. 8 above, pp. 38-40; and D.D. CARON and L.F. REED, "Post Award Proceedings Under the UNCITRAL Arbitration Rules", fn. 17 above, pp. 437-439.
39. *Harris Int'l Telecomms., Inc. v. Iran*, 18 Iran-US CTR 76-77 (1988).
40. *American Bell Int'l, Inc. v. Iran*, 14 Iran-US CTR 173, 174 (1987).

Unidyne Corp. v. Iran;[41] *Petrolane, Inc. v. Iran*;[42] *Picker International Corp. v. Iran*;[43] *Paul Donin de Rosiere v. Iran*;[44] *Sedco, Inc. v. NIOC*;[45] *Endo Laboratories, Inc. v. Iran*;[46] *Uiterwyk Corp v. Iran*[47] and *Avco Corp. v. Iran.*[48]

Moreover, the unusual provision of the FAA (which, as explained above, allows judicial courts to make the correction of arbitral awards), was also subject to interpretation on a case-law basis. On 29 August 2003, the Ninth Circuit of the US Court of Appeals found that Sects. 10 and 11 of the FAA allow a federal court to correct a technical error, to strike all or a portion of an award and to vacate an award only when it is completely irrational or exhibits manifest disregard of the law. In addition, the court held that

> "private parties have no authority to dictate the manner in which the federal courts conduct judicial proceedings. That power is reserved to Congress – and when Congress is silent on the issue, the courts govern themselves. Here, *because Congress has determined that federal courts are to review arbitration awards only for certain errors, the parties are powerless to select a different standard of review* – whether that standard entails review by seeking facts unsupported by substantial evidence and errors of law."[49] (Emphasis added.)

In conclusion, the narrow scope of requests for *correction* of omissions and material or clerical errors means that the arbitral tribunal shall not be invited to review the reasoning of its award's *dictum*. Requests for *clarification*, which will be discussed below, have that purpose.

III.   REQUESTS FOR *CLARIFICATION*

The text of the arbitral award often contains ambiguities, allowing more than one interpretation for a single statement. It can also be obscure, that is, unclear and difficult

---

41. Dec. No. DEC 122-368-3 (Iran-US Cl. Trib. 1994) (Westlaw, Int–Iran database).
42. 27 Iran-US CTR 264 (1991).
43. *Picker International Corp. v. Islamic Republic of Iran*, Dec. No. DEC 48-10173-3 (7 October 1986) reprinted in 12 Iran-US CTR 306, 307 (1986-II).
44. *Paul Donin de Rosiere v. Islamic Republic of Iran*, Dec. No. DEC 57-498-1 (10 February 1987) reprinted in 14 Iran-US CTR 100, 101 (1987-I).
45. *Sedco, Inc. v. NIOC*, Dec. No. DEC 64-129-3 (18 September 1987) reprinted in 16 Iran-US CTR 282, 284 (1987-III).
46. *Endo Laboratories, Inc. v. Islamic Republic of Iran*, Dec. No. DEC 74-366-3 (25 February 1988) reprinted in 18 Iran-US CTR 113, 114 (1988-I).
47. *Uiterwyk Corp v. Islamic Republic of Iran*, Dec. No. DEC 96-381-1 (22 November 1988) reprinted in 19 Iran-US CTR 171, 174-175 (1988-II).
48. *Avco Corp. v. Islamic Republic of Iran*, Decision and Correction to Partial Award, Award No. 377-261-3 (15 January 1989) reprinted in 19 Iran-US CTR 253, 255 (1988-II).
49. R.P. ALFORD, "29 August 2003 – Federal Court of Appeals for the Ninth Circuit", Digest by ITA Board of Reporters.

to understand. These flaws may be subject to a procedure of *clarification*, whereby the arbitral tribunal is invited to clarify or reveal the real meaning of what was written.

Thus, many institutional rules and national legislation contemplate post-award motions for *clarification* of arbitral awards. The arbitrators' power to interpret their own decisions may also be founded on the parties' agreement as well, since one of the guiding principles of arbitration is the parties' right to create the rules thereof.[50]

The object of a motion for *clarification* may explain why it is raised on the initiative of the parties: those who have trouble understanding the decision will be the ones interested in having a clearer award.

As explained above, the arbitrators' answer to requests for *correction* of awards can be a simple decision when they find it inappropriate to make an amendment, and an additional award, or an *addendum*, when they agree that an amendment is necessary. In respect to the requests for *clarification,* the arbitral tribunal may also make a decision denying interpreting the award. However, when an interpretation is necessary, it usually takes the form of an *addendum* and constitutes part of the award.

Pursuant to the UNCITRAL Rules[51] the parties are granted thirty days – counted from the receipt of the award – to request an interpretation. The arbitral tribunal must decide thereon in up to forty-five days after the receipt of the request. The procedure of *clarification* under the SCC and ICC Rules[52] follows the same deadlines provided for the above-described procedure for *correction*. It is interesting to note that the LCIA Rules are silent in respect to the clarification of awards, although they expressly provide for correction of material or clerical errors, as well as for an additional award in case of omissions.[53]

The Brazilian Arbitration Act also contemplates the *interpretation of obscurities, doubts or contradictions* in the award. But the time limits here are considerably shorter: five days for the parties to request it and ten days for the arbitral tribunal to decide on it. On the other hand, the English Arbitration Act prefers to refer to the *clarification or removal of ambiguities* and grants a twenty-eight-day time limit to both the parties and the arbitral tribunal.

The following table illustrates the previous considerations regarding requests for *clarification* of arbitral awards in institutional rules and national legislation.

---

50. R.D.A. KNUTSON, "The Interpretation of Arbitral Awards – When Is a Final Award Not Final?", fn. 7 above, p. 103.
51. UNCITRAL Rules Art. 35.
52. ICC Rules Art. 29.2.
53. "It is interesting to speculate as to whether an ambiguity or lacuna in the award could be thought of as an accidental mistake or omission. It seems doubtful that requests for interpretation could be thought to be included in the arbitrator's jurisdiction by this clause." R.D.A. KNUTSON, "The Interpretation of Arbitral Awards – When Is a Final Award Not Final?", fn. 7 above, p. 105.

CLARIFICATION OF THE AWARD

	Institutional Rules				Legislation			
	UNCITRAL	ICC	SCC	LCIA	UNCITRAL Model Law	Brazil	England	USA
Contemplate additional awards?	Yes	Yes	Yes	No	Yes*	Yes	Yes	No
On the initiative of the arbitral tribunal?	No	No	No	—	No	No	Yes, within 28 days	—
Time limit granted to the parties for submission of request	30 days	30 days	30 days	—	30 days	5 days	28 days	—
Time limit granted to the arbitral tribunal for deciding	45 days	30 days	30 days	—	30 days	10 days	28 days	—

* If so agreed by the parties.

Requests for *clarification*, as well as requests for *correction*, constitute an important instrument employed by the parties as an attempt to have the substance of the award reviewed. Again, although this practice is quite usual, it shall not be encouraged, since the interpretation has a very limited purpose, which was reinforced several times by case law.

The scope of the power to interpret was settled under the general principles of international law in two important cases: *U.K. – French Continental Shelf* and *Chorzów Factory*. In the first case, the Court of Arbitration held that interpretation is an auxiliary process that may not change what the Court has already settled with binding force. In the second case, the Permanent Court of International Justice laid down that the interpretation merely gives a precise definition of the meaning and scope of the decision, but does not add anything to it.[54]

Besides, Art. 35 of the UNCITRAL Rules was extensively discussed in the context of the Iran-US Claims Tribunal.[55] In *Pepsico, Inc. v. Iran*,[56] for instance, the tribunal affirmed that interpretation means clarification, and shall be employed when the language of the award is ambiguous. Other cases reinforced the idea that an interpretation is applicable

---

54. See *ibid.*, p. 106.
55. See D.D. CARON and L.F. REED, "Post Award Proceedings Under the UNCITRAL Arbitration Rules", fn. 17 above, pp. 433-434.
56. *Pepsico, Inc. v. Iran*, 13 Iran-US CTR 328, 329 (1986).

to remove an ambiguity in the text: *Ford Aerospace & Communications Corporation v. Air Force of Iran*;[57] *Paul Donin de Rosiere v. Iran*;[58] *Sedco, Inc. v. NIOC*;[59] *Phibro Corporation v. Iran*;[60] *Gabay v. Iran*[61] and *Eastman Kodak Co. v. Iran*.[62]

Caron and Reed suggest an interesting practical test to identify when the request for *clarification*, as provided for in Art. 35 of the UNCITRAL Rules, is applicable:

> "If specific language or punctuation in the award is unclear – meaning incomprehensible or susceptible to contradictory interpretations – ideally, to both client and attorney, then an Article 35 request for clarification is warranted. Under Article 35, counsel should be able in the written request to quote the ambiguous language in the award and define the ambiguity. True ambiguity is a high test, and one that definitely merits giving the panel a second chance to be understood. Particularly if the award is unclear as to the 'purport of the award and the resultant obligations and rights of the parties', clarification will increase the chances of voluntary compliance with the award. Ambiguity will not only stand in the way of satisfaction, but will also complicate any subsequent commercial relationship between the parties."[63]

IV. CONCLUSION

The requests for *correction* and *clarification* of arbitral awards stem from a characteristic of the human species itself – the impossibility of avoiding mistakes. Due to this trait, even procedural orders may contain slips or obscurities. However, those are in a secondary position, since procedural issues are ancillary to the merits of the case. Thus, they were not an object of our comments in the present article.

One could imagine the arbitrators' power to correct or interpret the arbitral award without the initiative of the parties. In theory, this power is comparable to any author's right to issue *errata* to correct errors his text may contain. Nevertheless, the silence of the parties renders the manifestation of the arbitrators unnecessary, and maybe this is why it is not usual that this practice be put into action.

---

57. *Ford Aerospace & Communications Corporation v. Air Force of Iran*, Dec. No. DEC 47-195-3 (2 October 1986) reprinted in 12 Iran-US CTR 304, 305 (1986-III).
58. *Paul Donin de Rosiere v. Islamic Republic of Iran*, Dec. No. DEC 57-498-1 (10 February 1987) reprinted in 14 Iran-US CTR 100, 101-102 (1987-I).
59. *Sedco, Inc. v. NIOC*, Dec. No. DEC 64-129-3 (18 September 1987) reprinted in 16 Iran-US CTR 283, 284 (1987-III).
60. *Phibro Corporation v. Islamic Republic of Iran*, Dec. No. DEC 97-474-3 (17 May 1991) reprinted in 26 Iran-US CTR 254-255 (1991-I).
61. *Gabay v. Islamic Republic of Iran*, Dec. No. DEC 99-771-2 (24 September 1991) reprinted in 27 Iran-US CTR 194, 195 (1991-II).
62. *Eastman Kodak Co. v. Islamic Republic of Iran*, Dec. No. DEC. 102-227-3 (30 December 1991) reprinted in 27 Iran-US CTR 269, 271 (1991-II).
63. D.D. CARON and L.F. REED, "Post Award Proceedings Under the UNCITRAL Arbitration Rules", fn. 17 above, p. 452.

Another issue linked to the *correction* and *clarification* of arbitral awards is the evaluation that must be carried out by lawyers before requesting it. If their request is granted, the rectification or interpretation – which implies costs – might lead to an eventual surprise. Moreover, sometimes the inability of lawyers who impolitely or aggressively address the tribunal could provoke a human reaction from the arbitrators, whose patience has already been tested by such lawyers' previously using inadequate language. As we know, rules of courtesy stand to human behavior as rules of hygiene stand to peoples' health.

In brief, the *correction* and *clarification* of arbitral awards is admissible only when it does not intend to modify the essence of the decision. Otherwise, it merely constitutes a manifestation of what was called "*jus sperniandi*"[64] in the past.

---

64. *Jus sperniandi* means a right to complain.

ICSID Annulment Procedure: A Balancing Exercise Between Correctness and Finality

*Gabriela Alvarez Avila**

TABLE OF CONTENTS	Page
I. Introduction	289
II. The Three Grounds Advocated in ICSID Annulment Proceedings	290
III. Conclusions	304

I. INTRODUCTION

One of the distinctive features of arbitration under the Convention on the Settlement of Investment Disputes Between States and Nationals of Other States (the ICSID Convention) is the annulment procedure, which is a self-contained process of review of an arbitral award[1] designed to ensure that the underlying arbitration was fundamentally fair.[2] The purpose of the annulment mechanism has been described as "the control of the fundamental integrity of the ICSID arbitral process in all its facets".[3] The annulment procedure is governed by Art. 52 of the ICSID Convention, which specifies five possible grounds for annulment of an award: (I) improper constitution of the tribunal; (ii) manifest excess of power; (iii) corruption on the part of a member of the tribunal; (iv) serious departure from a fundamental rule of procedure; and (v) failure to state reasons on which the award is based. Importantly, an ICSID award cannot be subject to an appeal

---

* Partner, Mexico City Office, Curtis, Mallet-Prevost, Colt & Mosle, LLP; member of the International Arbitration Group, Curtis, representing States in some ICSID arbitration proceedings. The views expressed in this paper are exclusively the author's views. The author wishes to thank Claudia Frutos-Peterson and Kate Brown for their valuable comments on this paper.
1. A. GIARDINA, "ICSID: A Self-Contained, Non-National Review System" in R.B. LILLICH and C.N. BROWER, eds., *International Arbitration in the 21st Century: Towards "Judicialization" and Uniformity?* (Hotei Publishing 1994) p. 199.
2. *Ad hoc* committees have frequently been preoccupied with the rationale behind the annulment procedure. In the *CDC* case, it was described as follows:

   "This mechanism protecting against errors that threaten the fundamental fairness of the arbitral process (but not against incorrect decisions) arises from the ICSID Convention's drafters' desire that Awards be final and binding, which is an expression of 'customary law based on the concepts of *pacta sunt servanda* and *res judicata*,' and is in keeping with the object and purpose of the Convention."

   CDC Group plc. v. Republic of Seychelles (ICSID Case No. ARB/02/14), Annulment Proceeding Decision of 29 June 2005, para. 36 (hereinafter *CDC*).
3. *Hussein Gnemon Soufraki v. The United Arab Emirates* (ICSID Case No. ARB/02/7), Decision of the *ad hoc* Committee on the Application for Annulment of Mr. Soufraki of 5 June 2007, para. 23 (hereinafter *Soufraki*).

or any other remedy, except as provided for in the ICSID Convention.[4] Of the remedies enumerated in the ICSID Convention, the annulment procedure is the one that has most frequently been invoked by parties.[5]

The growth in ICSID arbitration cases has brought an increase in the number of annulment procedures, leading some authors to suggest that there has been excessive use, and even abuse, of the procedure.[6] Whether or not the annulment procedure has been misused, the truth remains that states ratified the ICSID Convention, inter alia, because the procedure offered investors and states alike a mechanism for setting aside all or part of an arbitral award.

The purpose of this paper is to analyze how the annulment procedure has been used in practice, and in particular, to review certain decisions of *ad hoc* annulment committees interpreting and applying three grounds most frequently advanced by counsel in annulment applications: manifest excess of powers, departure from a fundamental rule of procedure and failure to state reasons.[7] As the analysis below shows, there are important aspects of these grounds for annulment that are far from settled. The uncertainty surrounding the application of these grounds by annulment committees has opened the door for criticism of the ICSID annulment procedure.

II. THE THREE GROUNDS ADVOCATED IN ICSID ANNULMENT PROCEEDINGS[8]

1. Manifest Excess of Powers

Art. 52(1)(b) of the ICSID Convention, entitles a party to annulment of an award if the tribunal "has manifestly exceeded its powers". As described by Dolzer and Schreuer, "[a]n excess of powers occurs where the tribunal deviates from the parties' agreement to arbitrate" and "[m]anifest means that the excess of powers [is] obvious".[9]

---

4. See Art. 53 of the ICSID Convention.
5. The other two remedies that can be invoked by a party are an interpretation under Art. 50 of the ICSID Convention and a revision under Art. 51 of the ICSID Convention.
6. Gaëtan VERHOOSEL, "Annulment and Enforcement Review of Treaty Awards: To ICSID or Not to ICSID" in *50 Years of the New York Convention*, ICCA Congress Series no. 14 (Kluwer Law International 2009) (hereinafter *ICCA Congress Series no. 14*) pp. 285-317.
7. "Only three of the grounds for annulment listed above have played a role in practice: excess of powers, serious departure from a fundamental rule of procedure, and failure to state reasons." R. DOLZER and C. SCHREUER, *Principles of International Investment Law* (Oxford University Press 2008) p. 281.
8. No reported decision by an *ad hoc* committee has addressed the other two grounds: improper constitution of the tribunal and corruption of a member of the tribunal.
9. R. DOLZER and C. SCHREUER, *Principles of International Investment Law*, supra fn. 7, p. 281.

Parties have argued, variously, that a manifest excess of powers exists when: (I) there is a lack or excess of jurisdiction;[10] (ii) a tribunal does not exercise its jurisdiction; or (iii) a tribunal fails "to apply the proper law".[11]

Commentators and tribunals alike have emphasized the requirement that the excess of powers must be "manifest", i.e. "easily understood or recognized by the mind",[12] or "highly probable" and not simply "possible".[13] The effect of the "manifest" requirement, however, has varied depending upon which of the three grounds constituting an excess of power (identified in the preceding paragraph) is alleged by the applicant.[14]

a. Lack or excess of jurisdiction as an excess of powers

Lack of jurisdiction has been characterized as the most obvious example of a manifest excess of powers.[15] This basis for annulment finds its rationale in Art. 25 of the ICSID Convention, which sets forth the scope of ICSID's jurisdiction. A tribunal that exercises jurisdiction when one of the requirements listed in Art. 25 of the ICSID Convention has not been met, either because (I) there was an absence of consent to arbitrate, (ii) the nationality requirements have not been met, or (iii) the ratione materiae condition is

---

10. *Ibid*.
11. *Principles of International Investment Law*, supra fn. 7, p. 282. The *MTD ad hoc* committee clearly stated that the excess of powers did not only constitute one regarding jurisdiction:

    "In the present case Chile does not deny that there was a protected investment or that there is a dispute concerning that investment. No question of the Tribunal's jurisdiction to decide that dispute is therefore raised. But the ground of manifest excess of powers is not limited to jurisdictional error; it is established that a complete failure to apply the law to which a Tribunal is directed by Article 42(1) of the ICSID Convention can constitute a manifest excess of powers, as also a decision given *ex aequo et bono* – that is to say, in the exercise of a general discretion not conferred by the applicable law – which is not authorized by the parties under Article 42(3) of the Convention. The Respondent claims that there was a manifest excess of powers in the present case on the ground that the Tribunal failed to apply international law or Chilean law as required, and that it effectively decided aspects of the dispute on an *ex aequo et bono* basis."

    MTD Equity Sdn. Bhd. and MTD Chile S.A. v. Republic of Chile (ICSID Case No. ARB/01/7), Decision on Annulment of 21 March 2007, para. 44 (hereinafter *MTD*).
12. C. SCHREUER, L. MALINTOPPI, A. REINISCH and A. SINCLAIR, *The ICSID Convention: A Commentary*, 2nd edn. (Cambridge University Press 2009) p. 938.
13. ICSID Case No. ARB/81/1, Decision on the Proposal to Disqualify an Arbitrator of 24 June 1982 (unreported). Referred to in *The ICSID Convention: A Commentary*, supra fn. 12, p. 1203.
14. C. SCHREUER, et al., *The ICSID Convention: A Commentary*, supra fn. 12, pp. 938-943. The *Soufraki ad hoc* committee rejected the idea that the term "manifest" should be disregarded when the question to be addressed relates to jurisdiction, stating that "Article 52(1)(b) of the Convention does not distinguish between findings on jurisdiction and findings on the merits", and quoted the *MTD ad hoc* Committee, which followed the same approach. *Soufraki*, supra fn. 3, para. 118.
15. Vladimir BALAS, "Review of Awards" in Peter MUCHLINSKI, Federico ORTINO and Christoph SCHREUER, *The Oxford Handbook of International Investment Law* (Oxford University Press 2008) p. 1138.

lacking, would be granting itself faculties which it evidently lacks, and therefore manifestly acting in excess of powers.[16]

In this regard, the *ad hoc* committee in *Klöckner* stated:

> "Clearly, an arbitral tribunal's lack of jurisdiction, whether said to be partial or total, necessarily comes within the scope of an 'excess of powers'.
>
> Consequently, an applicant for annulment may not only invoke lack of jurisdiction *ratione materiae* or *ratione personae* under Articles 25 and 26 of the Convention, but may also contend that the award exceeded the tribunal's jurisdiction as it existed under the appropriate interpretation for the ICSID arbitration clause."[17]

In the *Klöckner* case, although the *ad hoc* committee criticized the tribunal, it found that the tribunal's findings were "tenable and not arbitrary" and therefore rejected the applicant's request for annulment on this ground.[18]

In *Vivendi*, Argentina argued that the tribunal had exceeded its powers by upholding a jurisdiction that it did not have. The *ad hoc* committee rejected the State's arguments by affirming that the tribunal had indicated the basis for its finding on jurisdiction in the terms expressed in the award.[19] Nevertheless, the committee recognized as a general matter that proceeding with an arbitration despite a lack of jurisdiction would amount to an excess of powers and constitute grounds for annulment:

> "… Argentina also argued that the tribunal lacked jurisdiction in any event. If this is right, it was a manifest excess of power for the tribunal to proceed to consider the merits, and the whole Award must be annulled."[20]

In *Mitchell*, it was argued that the tribunal had committed a manifest excess of powers by assuming jurisdiction although the dispute had not arisen from an investment. The *ad hoc* committee held that an essential element of the concept of investment was a contribution to the host State's economic development. In this regard, it decided that there was no indication that the claimant's business, a legal counseling firm, had made such a contribution. In the *ad hoc* committee's own words:

> "The *ad hoc* Committee is thus inclined to believe that the Arbitral Tribunal forced the concept of investment in the case at hand in order to affirm its jurisdiction. This is perhaps attributable to the discomfort engendered in the Arbitral Tribunal

---

16. C. SCHREUER, "Three Generations of ICSID Annulment Proceedings" in Emmanuel GAILLARD and Yas BANIFATEMI, eds., *Annulment of ICSID Awards* (Juris Publishing, Inc. 2004) p. 17.
17. *Klöckner Industrie – Anlagen Gmbh and others v. Republic of Cameroon* (ICSID Case No. ARB/81/2), Decision on Annulment of 3 May 1985, para. 4. (hereinafter *Klöckner*)
18. *Ibid.*, para. 52.
19. *Compañía de Aguas del Aconquija S.A. and Vivendi Universal, S.A. v. Argentine Republic* (ICSID Case No. ARB/97/3), Decision on Annulment of 3 July 2002, paras. 73-80 (hereinafter *Vivendi*).
20. *Ibid.*, para. 72.

by the factual circumstances of the case, namely the violent dispossession of the Claimant's property and good will. The fact remains, however, that this combination of flaws in the Award is such that an excess of power on the part of the Arbitral Tribunal must be acknowledged."[21]

The *ad hoc* committee found that by "forcing the concept of investment" the tribunal committed an excess of powers. It based this conclusion on the "arbitrary reference, made two or even three times in the Award, to the returns collected by the claimant in the United States being treated as an element constituting the investment".[22] The reasoning of the *ad hoc* committee seems to shift between two elements: first, the existence of a contribution to the development of the host State as an element of the definition of investment, and, second, whether that element was satisfied by the tribunal's finding that returns collected by the claimant in the United States were considered an investment. This second step seems to have been the one that most influenced the *ad hoc* committee, which found that the tribunal's decision on this point was "arbitrary". It has been argued that the *Mitchell* tribunal's finding that there was an investment, and therefore jurisdiction, was "tenable and not arbitrary" according to the *Klöckner* test set out above. It also has been suggested that the *ad hoc* committee in this case may have crossed the line between annulment and appeal insofar as it reexamined the tribunal's finding of fact regarding the existence of an investment.[23]

b.   *Failure to exercise jurisdiction*

A failure by a tribunal to exercise its jurisdiction has also been found to constitute a manifest excess of powers. Indeed, the *ad hoc* committee in the *Vivendi* case stated the following:

"[t]he failure by a tribunal to exercise a jurisdiction given it by the ICSID Convention and a BIT, in circumstances where the outcome of the inquiry is affected as a result, amounts in the Committee's view to a manifest excess of powers ...".[24]

In *Vivendi* the tribunal had asserted jurisdiction under the France-Argentina bilateral investment treaty (BIT), but had not decided some treaty claims on the basis that this would entail an interpretation of the underlying contract, which included a jurisdictional

---

21. *Patrick Mitchell v. Democratic Republic of Congo* (ICSID Case No. ARB/99/7), Decision on the Application for Annulment of the Award of 1 November 2006, para. 46 (hereinafter *Mitchell*).
22. *Ibid.*
23. This decision has been criticized on the basis that the *ad hoc* committee's reasoning was similar to the reasoning of a Court of Appeals. See ICSID case law review in Chronique de Règlement Pacifique des Différends Internationaux (2004, no. 2); 3 Cases & Awards and Comment (December 2006, no. 5); "Provisional enforcement of ICSID Awards Pending ICSID Annulment Proceedings: An Analysis after the Recent Decisions Rendered by *ad hoc* Committees in the *CDC Group PLC v. The Republic of Seychelles* (ICSID Case No. ARB/02/14) and *Patrick Mitchell v. Congo* (ICSID Case No. ARB/99/7) Cases", 3 Cases & Awards and Comment (April 2006, no. 02).
24. *Vivendi*, supra fn. 19, para. 86.

clause in favor of the local courts. The *ad hoc* committee reached the following conclusion:

> "In the Committee's view, it is not open to an ICSID tribunal having jurisdiction under a BIT in respect of a claim based upon a substantive provision of that BIT, to dismiss the claim on the ground that it could or should have been dealt with by a national court ... the Committee concludes that the tribunal exceeded its powers in the sense of Article 52(1)(b), in that the tribunal, having jurisdiction over the Tucumán claims, failed to decide those claims."[25]

c. *Failure to apply the governing law*

Failure to apply the governing law to the case is widely recognized as a proper ground for annulling an ICSID award. The legal basis for this ground for annulment is found in Art. 42(1) of the ICSID Convention which establishes the tribunal's general obligation to apply the governing law to the dispute. Art. 42 provides as follows:

> "The tribunal shall decide a dispute in accordance with such rules of law as may be agreed by the parties. In the absence of such agreement, the tribunal shall apply the law of the Contracting State party to the dispute (including its rules on the conflict of laws) and such rules of international law as may be applicable."

In analyzing what is the proper standard for finding a failure to apply the proper law, *ad hoc* committees have discussed the difference between a failure to apply the governing law and an erroneous application of the law. As explained below, *ad hoc* committees have had divergent views on the issue of whether and in what circumstances the erroneous application of the law may justify annulment of an award.

If a tribunal does not apply any law, or applies a law different from the law to which Art. 42(1) of the ICSID Convention directs it, then it manifestly commits an excess of powers. In the words of the *ad hoc* committee in *CDC*,

> "Common examples of such 'excesses' are a tribunal deciding questions not submitted to it or refusing to decide questions properly before it. Failure to apply the law specified by the parties is also an excess of powers. Essentially, a tribunal's legitimate exercise of power is tied to the consent of the parties, and so it exceeds its powers where it acts in contravention of that consent (or without their consent, i.e., absent jurisdiction)."[26]

---

25. *Ibid.*, paras. 102, 115. The analysis made by the *ad hoc* committee regarding the difference between contract claims and treaty claims has been found to be fundamental for the analysis of this issue. See Bernardo CREMADES, "Litigating Annulment Proceedings – The *Vivendi* Matter: Contract and Treaty Claims" in E. GAILLARD and Y. BANIFATEMI, eds., *Annulment of ICSID Awards*, supra fn. 16.
26. *CDC*, supra fn. 2, para. 40.

The term "manifest" in the context of non-application of the governing law has been discussed by a number of *ad hoc* committees. For instance, the *ad hoc* committee in *MINE* stated that a failure to apply the law agreed upon by the parties, or a decision based on no law, is an excess of powers if the "derogation is manifest".[27]

Ad hoc committees have tried to define and give context to the term "manifest". The *ad hoc* committee in *CMS* found that a "complete failure to apply" the governing law can constitute a manifest excess of powers.[28]

The *ad hoc* committee in *MTD* stated:

> "An award will not escape annulment if the tribunal, while purporting to apply the relevant law actually applies another, quite different, law. But in such a case the error must be 'manifest', not arguable, and a misapprehension (still less mere disagreement) as to the content of a particular rule is not enough."[29]

This issue of when a failure to apply the governing law is "manifest" has proved to be fertile ground for applicants, who have sought annulment on the basis that the tribunals applied the governing law "incorrectly".

However, it has been found that a mistake in the application of the governing law does not warrant annulment of an award. For instance, the *ad hoc* committee in *MINE* observed:

> "Disregard of the applicable rules of law must be distinguished from erroneous application of those rules which, even if manifestly unwarranted, furnishes no ground for annulment."[30]

---

27. *Maritime International Nominees Establishment v. Republic of Guinea* (ICSID Case No. ARB/84/4), Decision on Annulment of 22 December 1989, para. 5.03 (hereinafter *MINE*).
28. *CMS Gas Transmission Company v. Argentine Republic* (ICSID Case No. ARB/01/8), Decision of the *ad hoc* Committee on the Application for Annulment of the Argentine Republic of 25 September 2007, para. 49 (hereinafter *CMS*).
29. *MTD*, supra fn. 11, para. 47.
30. *MINE*, supra fn. 27, para. 5.04. The *ad hoc* committee in *Amco v. Indonesia* explained very clearly that it viewed its task as limited to making sure the proper law was applied by the tribunal, and not whether the tribunal correctly applied that law:

    "The law applied by the Tribunal will be examined by the *ad hoc* Committee, not for the purpose of scrutinizing whether the Tribunal committed errors in the interpretation of the requirements of applicable law or in the ascertainment or evaluation of relevant facts to which such law has been applied. Such scrutiny is properly the task of a court of appeals, which the *ad hoc* Committee is not. The *ad hoc* Committee will limit itself to determining whether the Tribunal did in fact apply the law it was bound to apply to the dispute. Failure to apply such law, as distinguished from mere misconstruction of that law, would constitute a manifest excess of powers on the part of the Tribunal and a ground for nullity under Art. 52(1)(b) of the Convention. The *ad hoc* Committee has approached this task with caution, distinguishing failure to apply the applicable law as a ground for annulment and misinterpretation of the applicable law as a ground for appeal."

    AMCO Asia Corp. et al. v. Republic of Indonesia (ICSID Case No. ARB/81/1), Annulment Decision

Commentators have stated that "an error in the application of the proper law, even if it leads to an incorrect decision, is not a ground for annulment".[31]

The line between a "failure to apply the governing law" and an "error of law" was considered by both the *CMS* and *Soufraki ad hoc* committees.

In the *Soufraki* case, Mr. Soufraki requested the annulment of the award arguing, among other grounds, that the tribunal exceeded its powers by failing to apply the proper law to the question of Mr. Soufraki's nationality. The *ad hoc* committee confirmed that an error in the application of the law was not a ground for annulment, but recognized that there was a fine distinction between "non-application" of the applicable law and "mistaken" application of the law.[32] The *ad hoc* committee in this case analyzed whether the errors alleged by the claimant were "so egregious as to amount to a failure to apply the proper law",[33] and ultimately rejected the claimant's request for annulment.

In *CMS*, the *ad hoc* committee was called upon to decide whether, as contended by Argentina, the tribunal had committed an excess of powers while considering the interpretation of Art. XI of the Argentina-France BIT, which related to measures necessary for the maintenance of public order, and the defense of state of necessity argued by Argentina under customary international law. The *ad hoc* committee found that the tribunal had made two errors of law in its analysis, and that those errors could indeed have had an impact on the operative part of the award:

> "These two errors made by the tribunal could have had a decisive impact on the operative part of the Award. As admitted by CMS, the tribunal gave an erroneous interpretation to Article XI. In fact, it did not examine whether the conditions laid down by Article XI were fulfilled and whether, as a consequence, the measures taken by Argentina were capable of constituting, even *prima facie*, a breach of the BIT. If the Committee was acting as a court of appeal, it would have to reconsider the Award on this ground."[34]

Despite this, the *ad hoc* committee rejected Argentina's application for annulment, finding that the tribunal had applied the relevant law, although "cryptically and defectively".[35]

Finally in *Lucchetti*, the *ad hoc* committee had to consider whether there was a failure to apply the governing law because of alleged defects in the tribunal's reasoning. In this

---

of 16 May 1986, para. 9 (hereinafter *AMCO*).

31. R. DOLZER and C. SCHREUER, *Principles of International Investment Law*, supra fn. 7, p. 282. The *ad hoc* committee in *Soufraki* also indicated that "Errors in a tribunal's findings of facts, generated by, for instance, acceptance of evidence of no or insufficient probative value, do not provide a ground for annulment, save where such errors constitute or result in a 'serious departure from a fundamental rule of procedure' under Article 52(1)(d) of the ICSID Convention." *Soufraki*, supra fn. 3, para. 87.
32. *Soufraki*, supra fn. 3, para. 85.
33. *Ibid.*, para. 98.
34. *CMS*, supra fn. 28, para. 135.
35. *Ibid.*, para. 136.

case, the tribunal rejected jurisdiction on the basis that the dispute in question arose before the entrance into force of the BIT between Chile and Peru. In making this determination, the tribunal considered whether a dispute raised by Lucchetti before the Peruvian courts and decided by the Peruvian courts was in fact the same dispute brought by Lucchetti before the tribunal under the Chile-Peru BIT. The tribunal stated that "the subject matter of the earlier dispute" did not differ from the subject matter of the dispute brought by Lucchetti under the BIT and, on this basis, held that the dispute "crystallized by 1998".[36]

Lucchetti argued that the tribunal exceeded its powers by failing to apply the proper law (which, according to the claimant, consisted of the recognized principles of treaty interpretation), and by instead applying a "subject matter"[37] test which, in the claimant's view, was not a recognized legal principle. The *ad hoc* committee rejected the argument on the following rationale:

> "the Committee has no basis for concluding that the tribunal disregarded any significant element of the well-known and widely recognized international rules of treaty interpretation. In any event, the Committee, which has also carefully examined all other arguments put forward by Lucchetti, cannot find that the tribunal's reasoning in the Award, although summary and somewhat simplified in relation to the Vienna Convention, constituted an excess – and even less a manifest excess – of the tribunal's powers within the meaning of Article 52(1)(b) of the Convention."[38]

A synthesis of the reported annulment committee decisions to date suggests that an ICSID award will be annulled for failure to apply the governing law if a tribunal:

(a) mistakenly applies a different law than the one agreed by the parties or provided for by Art. 42 of the ICSID Convention;
(b) fails to apply the governing law;
(c) acts ex aequo et bono without the agreement of the parties;
(d) makes an "egregious" error of law.

However, no annulment is possible if a tribunal:

(a) applies the governing law in a "summary or somewhat simplified" way;
(b) makes a mere error of law.

---

36. *Industria Nacional de Alimentos, S.A. and Indalsa Perú, S.A. v. The Republic of Peru* (ICSID Case No. ARB/03/4), Award of 7 February 2005, para. 53.
37. *Lucchetti*, para. 31. Claimants also argue an excess of powers because the Tribunal failed to exercise the jurisdiction that it properly possessed. *Ibid.*
38. *Ibid.*, para. 116.

2. *Failure to State Reasons*

Pursuant to Art. 52(1)(e) of the ICSID Convention, a party may request annulment of the award if "the award has failed to state the reasons on which it is based".[39] This ground has been considered as "the most difficult ground for annulment to apply and to analyze",[40] since a total absence of reasons seems unlikely, given the tribunals' obligation to follow Art. 48(3) of the ICSID Convention.

For some commentators and *ad hoc* committees, insufficient reasons seem not to meet the threshold for annulment. However, if the stated reasons are such as to make it impossible to understand the manner in which a tribunal reached its conclusion, then the door may be open for annulment. Indeed, "[t]he purpose of a statement of reasons is to explain to the reader of the award, especially to the parties, how and why the tribunal reached its decision".[41]

This ground of annulment has caused great concern among commentators since, unlike the ground of excess of powers, it does not include any limiting terms such as "manifest", "serious" or "fundamental". In early *ad hoc* committees' decisions, this ground was interpreted as allowing inquiry into whether the reasons given by the tribunal were "reasonably sustainable and capable of providing a basis for the decision",[42] or whether there was a "reasonable connection between the basis invoked by the tribunal and the conclusions reached by it".[43]

In *MINE*, the *ad hoc* committee argued that the ICSID Convention requires only that the reader of the award be able "to follow the reasoning of the tribunal on points of fact and law". It maintained that investigation into "the adequacy of the reasoning is not an appropriate standard of review ... because it almost inevitably draws an *ad hoc* Committee into an examination of the substance of the tribunal's decision, in disregard of the exclusion of the remedy of appeal by Article 53 of the ICSID Convention".[44] The committee did note however that "the minimum requirement is in particular not satisfied by either contradictory or frivolous reasons".[45]

The *ad hoc* committee in *Wena Hotels* extended its understanding of stated reasons to reasons that could be elicited by the committee itself:

> "It is in the nature of this ground of annulment that in case the award suffers from a lack of reasons which can be challenged within the meaning and scope of Article 52(1)(e), the remedy need not be the annulment of the award. The purpose of this particular ground for annulment is not to have the award reversed on its merits. It is to allow the parties to understand the tribunal's decision. If the award does

---

39. This follows from Art. 48(3) of the ICSID Convention that establishes that "[t]he award ... shall state the reasons upon which it is based".
40. C. SCHREUER, "Three Generations of ICSID Annulment Proceedings", supra fn. 16, p. 33.
41. R. DOLZER and C. SCHREUER, *Principles of International Investment Law*, supra fn. 7, p. 284.
42. *Klöckner*, supra fn. 17, para. 120.
43. *Amco*, supra fn. 30, para. 29.
44. *MINE*, supra fn. 27, para. 5.08.
45. *Ibid.*, para. 5.09.

not meet the minimal requirement as to the reasons given by the tribunal, it does not necessarily need to be resubmitted to a new tribunal. If the *ad hoc* committee so concludes, on the basis of the knowledge it has received upon the dispute, the reasons supporting the tribunal's conclusions can be explained by the *ad hoc* Committee itself."[46]

More recently, the *Soufraki ad hoc* committee considered that "insufficient or inadequate reasons, which are insufficient to bring about the solution or inadequate to explain the result arrived at by the tribunal" could amount to a failure to state reasons.[47]

There is no doubt that the minimalist approach taken by some tribunals in their reasoning in awards has generated questions as to the legitimacy of some awards.[48] Parties can be expected to argue that, in the interest of the legitimacy of the investor-state arbitration system, if an *ad hoc* committee needs to explain the reasoning behind an award to the parties, and that explanation is not readily apparent on the face of an award, it would seem that the tribunal strayed rather close to a failure to state reasons and the award should then be annulled.

a. Inadequate, insufficient or contradictory reasons

The terms "inadequate", "insufficient" and "contradictory", used in connection with tribunal reasoning, are elusive concepts which represent a challenge for *ad hoc* committees.[49]

With respect to contradictory reasons, this issue was raised in the *Vivendi* annulment proceeding where the *ad hoc* committee commented:

> "It is frequently said that contradictory reasons cancel each other out, and indeed, if reasons are genuinely contradictory, so they might. However, tribunals must often struggle to balance conflicting considerations, and an *ad hoc* committee should be careful not to discern contradiction when what is actually expressed in a tribunal's reasons could more truly be said to be but a reflection of such conflicting considerations."[50]

As to "insufficient" reasons, the *Klöckner ad hoc* committee accepted that inadequate reasons, not "sufficiently relevant"[51] reasons or findings that are not "expressly justified", are grounds to annul an award for failure to state reasons.[52]

---

46. *Wena Hotels v. Arab Republic of Egypt* (ICSID Case No. ARB/98/4), Decision of 28 January 2002 on the Application by the Arab Republic of Egypt for Annulment of the Arbitral Award of 8 December 2000, para. 83 (hereinafter *Wena*).
47. *Soufraki*, supra fn. 3, para. 126.
48. See for instance T. LANDAU, "Reasons for Reasons: The Tribunal's Duty in Investor-State Arbitration" in *ICCA Congress Series no. 14*, supra fn. 6, pp. 187-205.
49. C. SCHREUER, "Three Generations of ICSID Annulment Proceedings", supra fn. 16, p. 35.
50. *Vivendi*, supra fn. 19, para. 65.
51. *Klöckner*, supra fn. 17, para. 128.
52. *Ibid.*, para. 171.

Other *ad hoc* committees have regarded their power in this regard as limited to analyzing whether the reasons set forth by the tribunal were sufficient, independently of their correctness. The approach of these committees was thus more formal, leaving substantive considerations to one side. The *ad hoc* committee in *Vivendi* stated:

> "In the Committee's view, annulment under Article (52)(1)(e) should only occur in a clear case. This entails two conditions: first, the failure to state reasons must leave the decision on a particular point essentially lacking in any expressed rationale; and second, that point must itself be necessary to the tribunal's decision."[53]

Finally, in the *CDC* case, the *ad hoc* committee stated that:

> "It thus appears that the more recent practice among *ad hoc* Committees is to apply Article 52(1)(e) in such a manner that the Committee does not intrude into the legal and factual decision-making of the tribunal. That is to say, Article 52(1)(e) requires that the tribunal have stated reasons, and that such reasons be coherent, i.e., neither 'contradictory' nor 'frivolous', but does not provide us with the opportunity to opine on whether the tribunal's analysis was correct or its reasoning persuasive. This conclusion is reinforced by reference to three other provisions of the Convention: Article 49(2), Article 50, and, as noted in the MINE decision, Article 53."[54]

Therefore, the test to find a failure to state reasons seems to have shifted from "relevant sufficient reasons" to reasons that follow a logical sequence in which the conclusions can be inferred from the premises. Illogical reasoning may be a ground for annulment, and may encompass, inter alia, (a) contradictory reasons,[55] and (b) *pseudo-reasons*. However, logical reasoning based on incorrect premises is easy to espouse, but difficult to apply in practice.

The *ad hoc* committee in *MINE* stated the foregoing in the following terms:

> "[T]he requirement to state reasons is satisfied as long as the award enables one to follow how the tribunal proceeded from point A to point B and eventually to its conclusion, even if it made an error of fact or of law. The minimum requirement is in particular not satisfied by either contradictory or frivolous reasons."[56]

---

53. *Vivendi*, supra fn. 19, para. 65.
54. *CDC*, supra fn. 2, para. 70.
55. "It is also accepted that contradictory reasons may amount to a failure to state reasons, since they will not enable the reader to understand the tribunal's motives. Genuinely contradictory reasons would cancel each other out." R. DOLZER and C. SCHREUER, *Principles of International Investment Law*, supra fn. 7, p. 285.
56. *MINE*, supra fn.27, para. 5.09.

[T]he requirement that an award has to be motivated implies that it must enable the reader to follow the reasoning of the tribunal on points of fact and law. It implies that, and only that. The adequacy of the reasoning is not an appropriate standard of review under paragraph 1(e)...."[57]

One interesting question which arises is whether the *Klöckner* test of "tenable and not arbitrary", or the test advocated by some commentators of "clearly inadequate set of reasons",[58] might be the most appropriate test to be applied by *ad hoc* committees in light of the problems related to defective or "minimalist" reasoning in some awards. This matter goes directly to the purpose of the annulment procedure itself and the legitimacy of the ICSID system as a whole. The question, then, is whether the principle that awards shall be final should prevail over ensuring that awards are supported by clear and adequate reasoning.

b.   Not dealing with a crucial issue

The basis for this ground for annulment is Art. 48(3) of the ICSID Convention, which provides that "the award shall deal with every question submitted to the tribunal".

Although the obligation to deal with every question submitted to the tribunal is not listed as a separate ground for annulment, *ad hoc* committees have found that it is implicit in the obligation to state reasons.[59] However, *ad hoc* committees have not required that tribunals deal with every single argument advanced by a party. Rather, they have stated that if an argument is of such importance that it could have affected the outcome of the award, then the tribunal should have addressed it.[60]

3.   Serious Departure from a Fundamental Rule of Procedure

Pursuant to Art. 52(1)(d) of the ICSID Convention, a party may request annulment of the award if "there has been a serious departure from a fundamental rule of procedure".

Not all departures from procedural rules will be considered sufficient to annul an award. As with the requirement that a tribunal's "excess of power" be "manifest", it is said that the departure must be "serious" and it must relate to a "fundamental" rule of procedure. According to Dolzer and Schreuer:

> "The seriousness of the departure requires that it is more than minimal and that it must have a material effect on a party.... A rule is fundamental only if it affects the fairness of the proceedings."[61]

---

57. *Ibid.*, para. 5.08.
58. P. LALIVE, "On the Reasoning of International Arbitral Awards", 1 Journal of International Dispute Settlement (2010) pp. 58-59.
59. R. DOLZER and C. SCHREUER, *Principles of International Investment Law*, supra fn. 7, p. 285. See also *MINE*, supra fn. 27, para. 5.13.
60. R. DOLZER and C. SCHREUER, *Principles of International Investment Law*, supra fn. 7, p. 285.
61. *Ibid.*, p. 283.

In the words of the *CDC ad hoc* committee:

> "A departure is serious where it is 'substantial and [is] such as to deprive the party of the benefit or protection which the rule was intended to provide.' In other words, 'the violation of such a rule must have caused the tribunal to reach a result substantially different from what it would have awarded had the rule been observed.' As for what rules of procedure are fundamental, the drafters of the Convention refrained from attempting to enumerate them, but the consensus seems to be that only rules of natural justice – rules concerned with the essential fairness of the proceeding – are fundamental." [62]

For its part, the *Wena ad hoc* committee considered that the main criterion was whether the observance of such rule would have made a difference in the final result. It stated that Art. 52(1)(d) of the ICSID Convention makes applicable to ICSID arbitrations the "minimal standards of procedure to be respected as a matter of international law",[63] and that, in order to be a serious departure, the violation "must have caused the tribunal to reach a result substantially different from what it would have awarded had such rule been observed".[64]

The *ad hoc* committee in *Repsol* followed the approach of the *Wena ad hoc* committee in this regard:

> "A departure from a rule of procedure is justification, therefore, for annulment of an ICSID award, only if the violation 'caused the tribunal to reach a result substantially different from what it would have awarded had such rule been observed'."[65]

The following matters have been raised as grounds for serious departures from a fundamental rule of procedure:

a.   Impartiality

The *Klöckner ad hoc* committee stated that a lack of impartiality will almost certainly constitute a departure from a fundamental procedural rule for annulment purposes:

> "Impartiality of an arbitrator is a fundamental and essential requirement. Any shortcoming in this regard, that is a sign of partiality, must be considered to constitute, within the meaning of Article 52(1)(d), a 'serious departure from a fundamental rule of procedure' in the broad sense of the term 'procedure', i.e.,

---

62. *CDC*, supra fn. 2, para. 49.
63. *Wena*, supra fn. 46, para. 57.
64. *Ibid.*, para. 58.
65. *Repsol YPF Ecuador, S.A. v. Empresa Estatal Petróleos del Ecuador (Petroecuador)* (ICSID Case No. ARB/01/10), Decision on the Application for Annulment, 8 January 2007, para. 81.

a serious departure from a fundamental rule of arbitration in general, and of ICSID arbitration in particular."[66]

The ground of "impartiality" was alleged in *Klöckner*[67] on the basis of the style, wording and general structure of the award, and in *Amco*[68] with respect to the tribunal's handling of the evidence, which was supposedly biased in favor of the claimant. In both cases, the allegations were rejected by the *ad hoc* committee.

b. Right to be heard

A failure by a tribunal to accord a party the right to be heard has been raised as a ground for annulment in several cases. This argument is premised on the rule that the tribunal is bound to decide a case on the basis of the parties' arguments and that, therefore, the parties shall be granted a meaningful opportunity to present their cases.

In *Klöckner*, the applicant argued that because the tribunal was bound to decide the case on the basis of the parties' arguments, the tribunal was not permitted to rely on legal arguments not addressed by the parties during the proceedings.[69] However, the *ad hoc* committee rejected this argument:

> "Within the dispute's 'legal framework', arbitrators must be free to rely on arguments which strike them as the best ones, even if those arguments were not developed by the parties (although they could have been). Even if it is generally desirable for arbitrators to avoid basing their decision on an argument that has not been discussed by the parties, it obviously does not follow that they therefore commit a 'serious departure from a fundamental rule of procedure'."[70]

In *Wena*, one of the parties argued that the fact that the tribunal had awarded compound interest without giving the parties a right to address the issue constituted a violation of the right to be heard. The *ad hoc* committee rejected this argument on the ground that claimant had requested the tribunal to award it interest. Therefore, according to the *ad hoc* committee, the parties must have been aware of the possibility that the tribunal could rule on compound interest:

> "In the light of this, the Committee cannot accept the complaint that the tribunal fixed interests by reference to a method not included in Wena's claim and on which the Applicant would have had no opportunity to express its views."[71]

---

66. *Klöckner*, supra fn. 17, para. 95.
67. *Klöckner*, supra fn. 17, paras. 93-113.
68. *AMCO*, supra fn. 30, para. 88.
69. *Ibid.*, para. 89.
70. *Ibid.*, para. 91.
71. *Wena*, supra fn. 46, para. 70.

In *Vivendi,* claimants argued that when the tribunal dismissed Tucuman's claims, it based its reasoning on a point not argued by the parties, and as a consequence came unannounced to the parties, without their having had the opportunity to present arguments on that decisive point. The *ad hoc* committee rejected this request, basing its reasoning on the fact that the alleged ground for annulment was "the manner in which the tribunal proceeded, not in the content of its decision".[72] The *ad hoc* committee then went on to state:

> "From the record, it is evident that the parties had a full and fair opportunity to be heard at every stage of the proceedings. They had ample opportunity to consider and present written and oral submissions on the issues, and the oral hearing itself was meticulously conducted to enable each party to present its point of view. The tribunal's analysis of issues was clearly based on the materials presented by the parties and was in no sense *ultra petita*. For these reasons, the Committee finds no departure at all from any fundamental rule of procedure, let alone a serious departure."[73]

The *Vivendi ad hoc* committee therefore focused on the form and not on the substance, as opposed to the approach of the *ad hoc* committees in *Klöckner* and *Wena*.

III. CONCLUSIONS

There are two aspects that need particular attention regarding the annulment procedure. The first relates to an excess of powers due to a "gross or egregious misinterpretation or misapplication of the law". Gross errors of law by a tribunal should indeed constitute an excess of powers and result in annulment of the award. The second aspect is the need for well-reasoned decisions. An *ad hoc* committee's task should not be to reconstruct a tribunal's reasoning when that reasoning is not apparent from an award itself. If an *ad hoc* committee has to spend several paragraphs trying to explain to the parties how a tribunal reached its conclusion, then the line has been crossed and such an award should be annulled. While the requirement to state reasons does not require "juridical perfection in the crafting"[74] of awards, parties expect tribunals to give thorough consideration to their arguments and to address disputed legal issues in a clear and coherent manner. This expectation is defeated if annulment is unavailable in the case of incoherent arbitral decisions or awards for which the legal basis is unascertainable or obviously flawed. Finality cannot prevail over legal certainty. Improving the application of these standards by *ad hoc* committees, in our view, would enhance the correctness principle, reinforcing the credibility and legitimacy of the system.

---

72. *Vivendi*, supra fn. 19, para. 83.
73. *Ibid.*, para. 85.
74. *Soufraki*, supra fn. 14, para. 127.

The existence of an annulment mechanism serves to reinforce the finality, integrity and stability of ICSID awards, but also the fairness and correctness of the outcome. This purpose is undermined, however, if the annulment mechanism ceases to be meaningful and *ad hoc* committees assess annulment applications on the basis of pure form rather than also considering substance.

Arbitration Advocacy and

Constitutional Law

Fundamental Rights and International Arbitration: Arbitral Awards and Constitutional Law

Laurence Boisson de Chazournes[*]

TABLE OF CONTENTS	Page
I. Introduction	309
II. The Hurdle of Constitutional Law as a "Fact"	310
III. The Hurdle of General International Law	314
IV. Constitutional Law as the "Primary Law" in Relation to Fundamental Rights: Possible Paths	318
V. Conclusion	323

I. INTRODUCTION

This paper aims at discussing and analyzing the scenarios in which constitutional law may or may not play a role in international arbitration. It will focus on international investment arbitration and is centered on the relationship between constitutional law, fundamental rights and arbitral awards. The aim is to explore when and how fundamental rights guaranteed by constitutional law provisions may be invoked by advocates in arbitral proceedings.

The intricacies of the relationship between constitutional law, fundamental rights and arbitral awards are appearing more and more in investment arbitration. One can think for instance of the *CMS Gas* case where Argentina asserted that the country's economic and social crisis affected fundamental rights and that giving effect to an investment treaty "would be in violation of such constitutionally recognized rights";[1] or also of the *Siemens* case in which Argentina argued that in light of the social and economic conditions prevailing at that time in Argentina, recognition of property rights would contravene fundamental rights incorporated in the Constitution.[2] Until now, the foray into the "constitutional order" by the arbitral tribunal in the *Sempra* case remained perhaps one of the most prominent examples of an arbitral award seeking to preserve a State's constitutional order. Dealing with the Argentine crisis, the tribunal considered that the "real issue is whether the constitutional order and the survival of the State were imperiled by the crisis" and found subsequently that "the constitutional order was not on the verge of collapse".[3]

---

[*] Professor, Faculty of Law, University of Geneva; Member, Permanent Court of Arbitration (PCA).
[1] *CMS Gas Transmission Co v. Argentina* (ICSID Case No. ARB/01/08), Award of 12 May 2005, para. 114.
[2] *Siemens v. Argentina* (ICSID Case No. ARB/02/08), Award of 6 February 2007, para. 75.
[3] *Sempra Energy International v. Argentina* (ICSID Case No. ARB/02/16), Award of 28 September 2007, para. 332.

Fundamental rights here do not only encompass the rights of investors (right to property, customary standards of investment protection, etc.) but also the rights of other stakeholders (such as local and indigenous communities). Fundamental rights here are also taken in a broader sense than human rights. Fundamental rights are a more generic category embracing human rights (right to life, right to a clean environment, freedom of expression, right to a fair trial, right to health, etc.) as well as other rights which may be labeled "public policy-related rights".

This latter category refers to rights that States have to guarantee as the primary custodians of the general interest within their jurisdiction but also as primary guardians of the public order on their territory. They are not subject to an exhaustive listing and may vary depending on the national constitutions in question. Furthermore they are not always rights in the classical legal perception of this term, and may include legal "values" on which a State must rely in formulating public policies and also in contracting with private actors such as investors.

As examples of "public-policy rights", one may mention the supremacy of the rule of law,[4] social justice, due process, distribution and redistribution of social goods and products,[5] accountability, transparency and prior consultation of local communities with respect to exploitation of natural resources.

The relationship between arbitral awards, fundamental rights and constitutional law will be seen through a public international law perspective. In other words, the general idea of this paper will be to identify how and to which extent international law "allows" constitutional law to play a role in international arbitration. Advocates may face hurdles invoking constitutional law (Sects. II and III below), but it is also noticeable that references to constitutional law in international arbitration may also occur through certain paths thus giving advocates room to refer to constitutional law (Sect. IV below).

II. THE HURDLE OF CONSTITUTIONAL LAW AS A "FACT"

In the *Polish Upper Silesia* case, the Permanent Court of International Justice (PCIJ) explained that

> "from the standpoint of International law and of the Court which is its organ, *municipal laws are merely facts* which express the will and constitute the activities of States, in the same manner as do legal decisions and administrative measures. The Court is certainly not called upon to interpret the Polish law as such, but there is nothing to prevent the Court's giving judgment on the question whether or not, in applying that law, Poland is acting in conformity with its obligations towards Germany under the Geneva Convention."[6]

---

4. See, e.g., South African Constitution (1996), Chapter I, Sect. I.
5. See, e.g., Bolivian Constitution (2009).
6. *Case concerning Certain German Interests in Polish Upper Silesia*, Merits, Judgment No. 7, 1926, PCIJ, Series A No. 7, p. 19 (italics added).

The concept of "municipal laws" as foreseen by the PCIJ embodies constitutional law. Constitutional law is a "fact" in the context of international arbitration. As it has been stressed, "International tribunals are properly reluctant to conclude that national law contradicts international law."[7] In those circumstances an advocate would only be allowed to ask an arbitral tribunal to determine whether a State in applying its constitutional law is acting in conformity with its international obligations.

An advocate may, a fortiori, refer to constitutional provisions in order to formulate claims of violations of international law with regard to fundamental rights. As stressed by the International Court of Justice (ICJ) in the *Lagrand* case, any international tribunal can hold that a domestic law (including constitutional law) has been the cause of the violation of international law.[8] The arbitrator in the *Georges Pinson* case emphasized that considering national constitutions as "facts" implies that "*tout tribunal international, de par sa nature, est obligé et autorisé à les examiner à la lumière du droit des gens*".[9]

In the *Bernardus Henricus Funnekotter* case, Zimbabwe attempted to invoke the argument that a state of necessity or emergency existed and that relieved it of its responsibility for complying with applicable provisions of the bilateral investment treaty (BIT) between The Netherlands and Zimbabwe. Among the reasons for justifying such a state of necessity, Zimbabwe referred to its "domestic law" (referring also implicitly to its constitutional law). The ICSID tribunal observed that, Zimbabwe domestic law may provide the tribunal "*useful information* on the situation which prevailed in Zimbabwe from 2002 to 2005".[10] However, the tribunal considered that

> "in any event, *it is on the basis of the applicable rules of International Law* that, in conformity with Article 9(3) of the BIT, the Tribunal must decide whether or not there was at the time a state of necessity which could have made lawful deprivation of property without compensation. In other words, *ultimately international law, not the domestic law of Zimbabwe*, must determine the effect any state of emergency would have on the dispute before the Tribunal."[11]

Besides these aspects, let's imagine a case in which an advocate attempts to prove that the mere fact that the constitutional standard of protection of a given fundamental right has been complied with by a State is tantamount *mutatis mutandis* to compliance with a said standard of protection as required by international law. To give a concrete example in the field of foreign investment protection, Art. 27 of the Mexican Constitution reads as follows:

---

7. *GAMI Investments, Inc. (Claimant) and The Government of the United Mexican States (Respondent)*, Final Award, 15 November 2004, para. 41.
8. *Lagrand (Germany v. United States of America)*, Judgment, I.C.J. Reports 2001, p. 513, para. 125.
9. *Georges Pinson (France) v. United Mexican States*, 24 April 1928, Reports of International Awards, vol. V, United Nations, p. 393, para. 32.
10. *Bernardus Henricus Funnekotter and Others v. Republic of Zimbabwe* (ICSID Case No. ARB/05/6), Award of 22 April 2009, para. 103 (italics added).
11. *Ibid.* (italics added).

311

"The laws of the Federation and the States, in their respective jurisdictions, will determine the cases in which public utility requires the occupation of private property. The procedures used by the administrative authority to acquire this property will be according to these laws. The price fixed for indemnification of the expropriated property will be based on its *fiscal value* as figured at the appraiser's or assessor's office."[12]

Mexico is a Party to the North American Free Trade Agreement (NAFTA). NAFTA Chapter 11 (Investment) includes a different wording than the Mexican Constitution with regard to the basis of compensation in case of expropriation. Indeed, NAFTA Art. 1110(2) reads as follows:

"Compensation shall be equivalent to the *fair market value* of the expropriated investment immediately before the expropriation took place ('date of expropriation'), and shall not reflect any change in value occurring because the intended expropriation had become known earlier. Valuation criteria shall include going concern value, asset value including declared tax value of tangible property, and other criteria, as appropriate, *to determine fair market value.*"

Could an advocate in a NAFTA dispute claim that Mexico would comply with its obligation under NAFTA Chapter 11 to provide compensation on the basis of the "fair market value" for the reason that it would have granted compensation on the basis of the "fiscal value" under the Mexican Constitution?

The answer appears to be negative. As stated by the ICJ in the *ELSI* case with respect to the legality of a requisition under the Treaty of Friendship, Commerce and Navigation between Italy and the United States of America (FCN (1948)), the

"question arises irrespective of the position in municipal law. *Compliance with municipal law and compliance with the provisions of a treaty are different questions*. What is a breach of treaty may be lawful in the municipal law and what is unlawful in the municipal law may be wholly innocent of violation of a treaty provision. Even had the Prefect held the requisition to be entirely justified in Italian law, this would not exclude the possibility that it was a violation of the FCN Treaty."[13]

A similar point of view involving an issue of fundamental rights arose in the *Avena* case before the ICJ. In casu, the question was whether the legality of clemency proceedings to review and reconsider convictions and sentences was to be assessed in light of the US Constitution or in light of international law (here, the Vienna Convention on Consular Relations). In other words, could a defendant be effectively barred from raising the issue

---

12. Quoted by Álvaro RAMÍREZ MARTÍNEZ, "The Mexican Constitution and Its Safeguards Against Foreign Investments", Cornell Law School Inter-University Graduate Student Conference (2009) p. 6.
13. *Case concerning Elettronica Sicula S.p.A (ELSI)*, Judgment, I.C.J. Reports 1989, p. 51, para. 73 (italics added).

of the violation of his rights under Art. 36 of the Vienna Convention on Consular Relations and be limited to seeking the vindication of his rights under the US Constitution?

The ICJ gave a clear-cut answer on the relationship between international law and constitutional law with respect to fundamental rights. According to the Court

> "in a situation of the violation of rights under Article 36, paragraph 1, of the Vienna Convention,[14] the defendant raises his claim in this respect not as a case of 'harm to a particular right essential to a fair trial' – *a concept relevant to the enjoyment of due process rights under the United States Constitution* – but as a case involving the infringement of his rights under Article 36, paragraph 1. *The rights guaranteed under the Vienna Convention are treaty rights which the United States has undertaken to comply with in relation to the individual concerned, irrespective of the due process rights under United States constitutional law.*"[15]

The Court pointed out that "what is crucial in the review and reconsideration process is the existence of a procedure which guarantees that *full weight is given to the violation of the rights set forth in the Vienna Convention*".[16]

Thus, no matter if the clemency proceedings are an integral part of the overall scheme for ensuring justice and fairness in the legal process within the US criminal justice system and Constitution. What matters is that "the clemency process as practiced within the criminal justice systems of different States in the United States can, in and of itself, qualify as an appropriate means for undertaking the effective review and reconsideration of the conviction and sentence"[17] fully taking into account the violation of the rights set forth in the Vienna Convention on Consular Relations.

What are the lessons that can be drawn from this in terms of arbitration advocacy? First of all, national constitutions are and remain "facts" from a public international law perspective. From that perspective, an advocate should rather invoke fundamental rights as incorporated in international legal instruments to formulate his or her strategy. A strategy consisting of relying on constitutional law to preclude the application of international obligations would be meaningless and susceptible of failing before an international arbitral tribunal. As the tribunal concluded in *LG&E v. Argentina*, "international law overrides domestic law when there is a contradiction since a State cannot justify non-compliance of its international obligations by asserting the provisions of its domestic law".[18]

---

14. Consular rights under Art. 36(1) of the Vienna Convention on Consular Relations are not prima facie fundamental rights. But when they pertain to fundamental rights such as the right to life, they present the characteristic of fundamental rights.
15. *Avena and Other Mexican Nationals (Mexico v. United States of America)*, Judgment, I.C.J. Reports 2004, p. 65, para. 139 (italics added).
16. *Ibid.* (italics added).
17. *Ibid.*
18. *LG&E Energy Corp. and Argentine Republic* (ICSID Case No. ARB/02/1), Decision on Liability of October 2006, para. 94.

It is not relevant prima facie that constitutional law guarantees fundamental rights if the threshold or standard of protection is lower or substantially different from the one required by international law. International law does not foresee any *renvoi* to the constitutional law in a State. Domestic law (including constitutional law) may play a role not in itself "but only as one factual element among others, or as evidence".[19] It is not possible to allude to a *continuum juris* between constitutional law and international law.

In other words, an advocate may refer to constitutional law to justify *performance* of international obligations. In those situations, constitutional law only qualifies as a "fact" and is not of such a nature as to exclude or override the application of international law (i.e., fundamental rights as being protected under international law) in international arbitration proceedings.

III.   THE HURDLE OF GENERAL INTERNATIONAL LAW

Another issue is when an advocate faces a hurdle when resorting to constitutional law to prevent the enforcement or execution of an international award or when invoking a constitutional provision which is in violation of international law.

Invoking constitutional law to challenge a right protected under international law or to defeat international arbitral awards may sound unorthodox. Coming to general international law, it suffices to mention Art. 27 of the Vienna Convention on the Law of Treaties (1969). This provision reads as follows: "A party may not invoke the provisions of its *internal law as justification for its failure to perform a treaty*" (italics added). Art. 27 is considered as reflecting customary international law and is thus binding on States whether or not they are parties to the Vienna Convention on the Law of Treaties.

What is its effect when an advocate is tempted to challenge international arbitral awards on the basis of constitutional law or to invoke a constitutional provision which is contrary to rights as protected under international law instruments? This question raises several issues.

An advocate when resorting to constitutional law to prevent the enforcement or the execution of an international award faces the hurdle of general international law. Let's take the example of the Convention on the Settlement of Investment Disputes between States and Nationals of Other States (the ICSID Convention). This instrument provides that an award shall be binding on the parties and shall not be subject to any appeal or to any other remedy except those provided for in the ICSID Convention. In other words the parties to an ICSID dispute are obliged to abide by and comply with the award and every Contracting State is required to recognize the award as binding and to enforce the pecuniary obligations imposed by the award as if it were a final decision of a domestic court.

Let's consider then that an advocate attempts to challenge an ICSID arbitral award before a domestic court on the basis of constitutional grounds, and that the challenge succeeds on those grounds. De facto, it appears that the domestic court (organ of the State under art. 4 of the ILC Articles on State Responsibility) has invoked "internal law"

---

19. *Frontier Dispute (Burkina Faso/Mali)*, Judgment, I.C.J. Reports 1983, para. 30.

to justify "failure to perform a treaty", i.e., the ICSID Convention. This constitutes a breach of international law,[20] as was said by the PCIJ in the *Polish Nationals in Danzig*[21] and in the *Free Zones*[22] cases several decades ago.

In particular, in the first case, the PCIJ stated that:

> "It should ... be observed that, while on the one hand, according to generally accepted principles, a State cannot rely as against another State, on the provisions of the latter's Constitution, but only on international law and international obligations duly accepted, on the other hand and conversely, *a State cannot adduce as against another State its own Constitution with a view to evading obligations incumbent upon it under international law or treaties in force.*"[23]

This finding is applicable by extension in the relations between States and foreign investors as governed by BITs and customary standards of investment protection.

Indeed, the PCIJ was dealing with fundamental rights conferred on individuals. The PCIJ noted that "the question of the treatment of Polish nationals or other persons of Polish origin or speech must be settled exclusively *on the bases of the rules of international law and the treaty provisions in force* between Poland and Danzig".[24] The Court moreover concluded that "the application of the Danzig Constitution may however result in the violation of an international obligation incumbent on Danzig towards Poland, whether under treaty stipulations or under general international law, as for instance in the case of *a denial of justice* in the generally accepted sense of that term in international law".[25] In casu, the PCIJ was referring implicitly to the right to a fair trial – a fundamental right under international legal instruments – that may have been denied by the application of the Danzig Constitution. Thus, the question of the relationship between constitutional law and fundamental rights is not new for international permanent jurisdictions.

Neither is it new in the context of international arbitration. In the *Georges Pinson* case (1928), the arbitrator had to deal with similar issues relating to the relationship between constitutional law and fundamental rights as defined under international law. The

---

20. By analogy, see *SGS Société Générale de Surveillance S.A. v. Islamic Republic of Pakistan* (ICSID Case No. ARB/01/13), Procedural Order No. 2 of 16 October 2002 in ICSID Review – Foreign Investment Law Journal (2003) p. 293 at p. 300. The tribunal said: "The right to seek access to international adjudication must be respected and cannot be constrained by an order of a national court. Nor can a State plead its internal law in defence of an act that is inconsistent with its international obligations. Otherwise, a Contracting State could impede access to ICSID arbitration by operation of its own law."
21. *Treatment of Polish Nationals and Other Persons of Polish Origin or Speech in the Danzig Territory*, PCIJ, Series A/B, Advisory Opinion of 4 February 1932.
22. *Case of the Free Zones of Upper Savoy and the District of Gex*, PCIJ, Series A/B, Judgment of 7 June 1932.
23. *Polish Nationals in Danzig, op. cit.*, fn. 21, p. 24 (italics added).
24. *Ibid.*, p. 25 (italics added).
25. *Ibid.* (italics added).

Mexican Constitution of 1857 provided that aliens who had Mexican children[26] were to be considered Mexican, unless they manifested the intention to conserve their foreign nationality. It also provided that Mexican citizenship would be lost by reason of serving officially the Government of another State. A law of 1886 provided that children born in Mexico of an alien father should be considered as Mexicans, unless within one year after reaching majority they should manifest their intention to retain the nationality of their parent before the political authority of the place of their residence.

The arbitrator held that the Constitution of 1857 was inapplicable to claimant's father, rejecting vehemently the Mexican Agent's position according to which "*si acaso legara a existir (una Constitución en el sentido de ordenar la confiscación de derechos de propiedad extranjeros), como ella sería la Ley Suprema del país tendría que acatarse por encima de los Tratados, pues éstos no pueden tener mayor fuerza que la misma Constitución*".[27] The arbitrator judged such an assertion as being against the "axioms of international law".[28]

He declared :

"*Je ne peux me dispenser d'examiner la question de savoir si la disposition constitutionnelle invoquée parl'agence mexicaine serait à l'abri de tout reproche de contradiction avec le droit des gens, si elle prétendait, en effet, imposer à l'étranger, par surprise et contre son gré, la nationalité mexicaine. Car s'il est vrai que, en règle générale, tout Etat est souverain pour déterminer quelles personnes il considérera comme ses ressortissants, il n'en est pas moins vrai [...] que cette souveraineté peut être limitée par des règles du droit des gens, règles qui peuvent s'enraciner non seulement dans des traités formels, mais encore dans une communis opinio juris sanctionnée par le droit coutumier.*"[29]

From the foregoing, it seems difficult to deduce that an advocate in international arbitration could challenge or defeat an international arbitral award on the basis of constitutional law grounds if those grounds are contrary to rules and principles of international law, including those protecting fundamental rights. The issue is not new or unknown in international practice and the solutions given in the cases referred above show some clear reluctance of international courts and tribunals (permanent and arbitral) to give such effect to constitutional law.

In the same vein, it seems illusory to consider that an advocate could invoke a provision of constitutional law to defeat the object and purpose of international legal instruments dealing with the protection of fundamental rights. For instance, it is not possible for an advocate to rely on a Constitution which provides for the acquisition of land without compensation. Zimbabwe tried to do so in February 2000. One remembers that that constitutional amendment (which was defeated in a referendum) was part of the "Land Acquisition Program" which authorized the Government of Zimbabwe to acquire

---

26. The facts of the case refer to "sons" instead of children. For the sake of clarity we will refer to "children" in the context of the present contribution.
27. *Georges Pinson (France) v. United Mexican States*, op. cit., fn. 9, p. 393, para. 32.
28. *Ibid.*
29. *Ibid.* (emphasis added). No English translation to our knowledge.

compulsorily any rural land when the acquisition was deemed reasonably necessary for agricultural settlement purposes, i.e., for public purposes.

One may indeed doubt the possibility for an advocate to invoke constitutional provisions such as the one contained in Sect. 16A(1)(c) of the April 2000 Zimbabwe Constitution. This provision was introduced to replace the amendment mentioned above and which was defeated in a referendum. Sect. 16A(1)(c) provided that "the former colonial power has an obligation to pay compensation for agricultural land compulsorily acquired for resettlement" and that, if the former colonial power fails to pay, then "the Government of Zimbabwe has no obligation to pay compensation for agricultural land compulsorily acquired for resettlement".[30] In the *Bernardus Henricus Funnekotter* case, it was for instance specified that the "Dutch Embassy in Harare repeatedly advised the Government of Zimbabwe of its obligations under the BIT concluded between The Netherlands and Zimbabwe"[31] and that "the Zimbabwean Ministry of Foreign Affairs sent to the Embassy a *Note Verbale*, dated 21 November 2000, stating that property protected by investment agreements would be exempt from acquisition".[32] This shows indication and acknowledgement (even from Zimbabwe in casu) that constitutional law cannot defeat treaty obligations, in particular when those obligations protect fundamental rights of investors such as the right to property and the right to compensation.

However this acknowledgement did not prevent Zimbabwe from contending before the arbitral tribunal, that the measures it took in depriving Dutch farmers of their properties were taken in conformity with its "Constitution"[33] and in pursuance of "public interest".[34] The tribunal did not address specifically that issue of "public interest" since it decided that violation of the obligation to pay just compensation as foreseen by the BIT between The Netherlands and Zimbabwe was sufficient to find violation of the BIT.[35]

This being said, one needs now to turn to another aspect of the question surrounding the relationship between constitutional law, fundamental rights and arbitral awards. We have dealt with some of the hurdles that an advocate may face when invoking constitutional law in international arbitration proceedings. Another dimension of the relationship between constitutional law, fundamental rights and arbitral awards arises when considering the situation in which some fundamental rights are only provided for in constitutional law but not in international treaties applicable in a specific dispute or customary law. Here there is a gap in international law which may be closed by constitutional law. The field of investment arbitration sheds some light on this issue.

---

30. Quoted in *Bernardus Henricus Funnekotter and Others v. Republic of Zimbabwe*, op. cit., fn. 10, para. 28.
31. *Ibid.*, para. 31.
32. *Ibid.*
33. *Ibid.*, para. 61.
34. *Ibid.*, para. 84.
35. *Ibid.*, para. 98.

IV.   CONSTITUTIONAL LAW AS THE "PRIMARY LAW" IN RELATION TO FUNDAMENTAL RIGHTS: POSSIBLE PATHS

A concrete path is for example Art. 42(1) of the ICSID Convention. This provision reads as follows: "The Tribunal shall decide a dispute in accordance with such rules of law as may be agreed by the parties. In the absence of such agreement, *the Tribunal shall apply the law of the Contracting State party to the dispute* (including its rules on the conflict of laws) and such rules of international law as may be applicable" (italics added).

From the elements developed in the first part of this paper, one may therefore disagree with the position of the *ad hoc* Committee in *Amco v. Indonesia* according to which: "Article 42(1) of the Convention authorizes an ICSID tribunal to apply rules of international law *only* to fill up lacunae in the applicable domestic law and to ensure precedence to international law norms where the rules of the applicable domestic law are in collision with such norms."[36]

This is a misleading affirmation. Both legal systems, i.e., international law and the host State law, have a role to play. As stated by the tribunal in the resubmitted case of *Amco v. Indonesia*:

> "Article 42(1) refers to the application of host-State law and international law. If there are no relevant host-State laws on a particular matter, a search must be made for the relevant international laws. And where, there are applicable host-State laws, they must be checked against international laws, which will prevail in case of conflict. Thus international law is fully applicable and to classify its role as 'only' 'supplemental and corrective' seems a distinction without a difference."[37]

If one may subscribe more easily to the position of the tribunal in the resubmitted case of *Amco v. Indonesia*, there is still a missing element in both quotations. It is related to the fact that the "host State law" (including constitutional law) may fill the gaps in international law in investment arbitration. An advocate is allowed to make claims based on constitutional law to sustain his or her argument of the "host State law" applicable to a dispute as long as that constitutional law is not contrary to international law and as long as that constitutional law is filling up the lacunae of international law (for instance with regard to fundamental rights to be taken into account in a particular dispute).

Let's take the example of a recent investment dispute, i.e., *Cementownia "Nowa Huta" S.A. v. Republic of Turkey*.[38] In casu, a new Electricity Market Law (Law 4628) was enacted by Turkey through which the entire transmission network would be operated by a State-owned company: the Turkish Electricity Transmission Joint Stock Company (TEIAS). After its enactment, Law 4628 became a matter of dispute in Turkish court proceedings. Various members of the Turkish Parliament challenged the law on the grounds that it violated the articles of the Turkish Constitution dealing with the safeguard

---

36. *Amco v. Indonesia* (ICSID Case No. Arb/81/1), Decision on Annulment of 16 May 1986, para. 20.
37. *Amco v. Indonesia*, Resubmitted case, Award of 5 June 1990, para. 40.
38. *Cementownia "Nowa Huta" S.A. v. Republic of Turkey* (ICSID Case No. ARB(AF)/06/2), Award of 17 September 2009.

of the rule of law, the freedom to conclude agreements and the protection of private property. Subsequently, provisional Art. 4 of Law 4628 was annulled by the Constitutional Court. The latter's decision reads as follows: "An agreement concluded by a company shall be deemed to have been nullified if the company has failed to complete transfer of a power generating and distribution plant owned by the government by June, 2001."[39]

A request for arbitration was filed by Cementownia, a Polish company, since both Poland and Turkey were signatories to the Energy Charter Treaty (ECT). According to Cementownia, by terminating Concession Agreements, Turkey had violated Art. 10(1) ECT, which provides that "investments of investors of other Contracting Parties shall enjoy the most constant protection and security and no Contracting Party shall in any way impair by unreasonable or discriminatory measures their management, maintenance, use, enjoyment or disposal"; as well as Art. 13 ECT, which provides that "investments may not be nationalized, expropriated or subjected to a measure or measures having effect equivalent to nationalization or expropriation except in certain specified conditions, one of which is that the nationalization or expropriation be accompanied by the payment of prompt, adequate and effective compensation".[40]

The arbitral tribunal did not reach a judgment on the merits since Cementownia did not fulfill the condition of being an investor of another Party under the ETC. Nevertheless, it is interesting to note that besides traditional standards relating to investment protection (most favored nation (MFN), expropriation, fair and equitable treatment, full protection and security), the ECT does not emphasize the protection of fundamental rights such as the protection of private property, the rule of law, the right to a fair trial, the freedom to conclude agreements, etc. Since one main aspect of the dispute between Cementownia and Turkey related to the legality of the latter's actions in light of the Turkish Constitution, it might be considered that an advocate could have been in the position to invoke the said Constitution to supplement and strengthen the provisions of the ECT with respect to the protection of foreign investment.

For example, more and more arbitral awards[41] hold that a denial of due process or procedural fairness may amount to a breach of the fair and equitable treatment (FET) standard. Due process is often guaranteed under national constitutions. The recourse to constitutional law by an advocate (or an arbitral tribunal) may permit substantiation of the content and scope of the FET standard and better identification the fundamental rights directly in linkage with the FET standard.

Nevertheless, the importance of relying on constitutional law appears more crucial in instances where an international treaty is not dealing with specific fundamental rights such as the rights of certain communities, e.g., rights of indigenous peoples. This is the

---

39. Quoted in *ibid.*, para. 10.
40. *Cementownia "Nowa Huta" S.A. v. Republic of Turkey*, *op. cit.*, fn. 38, para. 105.
41. See, for example, *Bayindir Insaat Turizm Ticaret Ve Sanayi A.S. v. Islamic Republic of Pakistan* (ICSID Case No. ARB/03/29), Award of 27 August 2009. See also, *The Loewen Group, Inc. and Raymond L. Loewen (Claimant) v. United States of America (Respondent)* (ICSID Case No. ARB(AF)/98/3), Award of 26 June 200.

case within the framework of NAFTA. The *Glamis Gold, Ltd.* case[42] is illustrative of that point. Glamis Gold, Ltd., a Canadian mining company, brought proceedings against the United States, claiming that the United States breached obligations owed to it under Chapter 11 of the NAFTA. In particular, Glamis claimed that the United States expropriated rights possessed by Glamis to mine gold in southeastern California and that the United States denied Glamis fair and equitable treatment in its attempts to utilize those rights.

In particular, the dispute raised a conflict between Quechan religious beliefs and the Glamis "Imperial Project". A First Amendment issue was raised by the Quechan, as explained in the Report of the US Director of the Bureau of Land Management quoted in the arbitral award:

> "'The Quechan believe that this is a conflict between their protected right to practice religion under the First Amendment to the Constitution and the 1872 Mining Law; that by allowing the mining to occur the government will have violated their rights under the First Amendment and destroyed their ability to practice their religion where it must be practiced. What are our responsibilities to ensure that we do not violate the First Amendment? What are our responsibilities to the mining claimant to ensure that his proprietary rights are protected?'"[43]

The US also asserted that it was confronted with "an issue of first impression and involving a conflict of alleged constitutional concerns".[44]

Here we are facing an interesting scenario. NAFTA Chapter 11 (Investment) does not refer to the "host State law" as part of the applicable law that an arbitral tribunal must apply to decide an investment dispute.[45] According to NAFTA Art. 1131, a tribunal "shall decide the issues in dispute in accordance with this Agreement and applicable rules of international law". Thus the "host State law" (including constitutional law) is not referred to expressly in the text of that provision.

This situation has not yet prevented NAFTA Chapter 11 tribunals from showing "deference" or "comity" to domestic law (and by extension to constitutional law), in particular with respect to fundamental rights issues. The arbitral tribunal in the *Glamis Gold, Ltd.* case considered for instance that there was no violation of the fair and equitable treatment under NAFTA Art. 1105 partially because the US government had to take into account indigenous communities' rights. In the words of the arbitral tribunal,

> "It is clear from the record that the bill addresses some, if not all, *of the harms caused to Native American sacred sites by open-pit mining*. The tribunal agrees with Respondent's assertion that governments *must compromise between the interests of*

---

42. *Glamis Gold, Ltd. (Claimant) and United States of America (Respondent)*, ICSID/UNCITRAL, Award of 8 June 2009.
43. *Ibid.*, para. 114.
44. *Ibid.*, para. 654.
45. Most BITs do not refer to the "host State law".

competing parties and, if they were bound to please every constituent and address every harm with each piece of legislation, they would be bound and useless."[46]

This highlights a certain tendency at recognizing the freedom of governments to make their own choices in ensuring the respect of fundamental rights within their jurisdiction. Any advocate dealing with international arbitration cannot ignore that state of facts. One may even presume that the application of constitutional law in the context of an arbitral award implies meta-juridical considerations and transcends advocacy's strategies or the powers of an arbitral tribunal. Indeed, as stated by the arbitral tribunal in *S.D. Myers*:

> "When interpreting and applying the 'minimum standard', a Chapter 11 tribunal does not have *an open-ended mandate to second-guess government decision-making*. Governments have to make many potentially controversial choices. In doing so, they may appear to have made mistakes, to have misjudged the facts, proceeded on the basis of a misguided economic or sociological theory, placed too much emphasis on some social values over others and adopted solutions that are ultimately ineffective or counterproductive. The ordinary remedy, if there were one, for errors in modern governments is through internal political and legal processes, including elections."[47]

Arbitral tribunals have been very keen to acknowledge obligations for States: obligation of due process, obligation to implement and/or national law as well as the obligation to control local authorities, etc. One can surely have in mind the award of the arbitral tribunal in the *GAMI* case. In that case, Mexico advanced that an ICSID tribunal does not have the mandate to control the application of national law (and thus, constitutional law) by national authorities. The tribunal through a straightforward answer declared that:

> "This contention misconceives the role of international law in the context of the protection of foreign investment. International law does not appraise the content of a regulatory programme extant before an investor decides to commit. *The inquiry is whether the State abided by or implemented that programme*. It is in this sense that a government's failure to implement or abide by its own law in a manner adversely affecting a foreign investor may but will not necessarily lead to a violation of Article 1105 (FET standard). Much depends on the context. The imposition of a new licence requirement may for example be viewed quite differently if it appears on a blank slate or if it is an arbitrary repudiation of a preexisting licensing regime *upon which a foreign investor has demonstrably relied*."[48]

---

46. *Glamis Gold, Ltd. (Claimant) and United States of America (Respondent)*, op. cit., fn. 42, para. 804 (italics added).
47. *S.D. Myers, Inc. (Claimant) and Government of Canada (Respondent)*, Partial Award, 13 November 2000, para. 261 (italics added).
48. *GAMI Investments, Inc. (Claimant) and The Government of the United Mexican States (Respondent)*, op. cit., fn. 7, para. 91 (italics added).

The last sentence in the quoted passage is of interest. It demonstrates that legal obligations do not operate in a vacuum. They are inherently linked to rights. In other words, the obligation of due process entails for example a right to due process; the obligation to implement and enforce national law implies a right to the rule of law, etc. This nexus of obligations and rights forms what may be called "legitimate expectations". It is exactly those legitimate expectations that may be taken into account by an advocate when relying on constitutional law in the context of international arbitration. Legitimate expectations allow piercing the veil of formalism. The question is no longer whether constitutional law (and the fundamental rights contained therein) is formally applicable in the context of international arbitration but whether private persons (e.g., investors) can (must?) expect States to comply with fundamental constitutional requirements.

It seems that the pathway of a reference to "legitimate expectations" may help better integrate constitutional law in the context of international arbitration. As stated by the tribunal in the *Tecmed* case, "in light of the good faith principle established by international law, [the FET] requires the Contracting Parties to provide to international investments treatment that does not affect the *basic expectations* that were taken into account by the foreign investor to make the investment".[49]

Constitutional law appears to be more and more relied upon in international arbitration through an "informal" path. The concept of "transnational public policy"[50] reflects such a development. At this level, constitutional law is not referred to expressly in arbitral awards. Arbitrators prefer to rely on a sort of "global constitutional law" (or global administrative law for others)[51] or "international public order of most States"[52] to

---

49. *Tecnicas Medioambientales Tecmed S.A. v. The United Mexican States*, (ICSID Case No. ARB (AF)/00/2), Award of 29 May 2003, para. 154 (italics added).
50. See Catherine KESSEDJIAN, "Transnational Public Policy" in *International Arbitration 2006: Back to Basics?*, ICCA Congress Series no. 13 (Kluwer Law International 2007) (hereinafter *ICCA Congress Series no. 13*) pp. 857-870.
51. See Benedict KINGSBURY and Stephan SCHILL, "Investor-State Arbitration as Governance: Fair and Equitable Treatment, Proportionality and the Emerging Global Administrative Law", in *ICCA Congress Series no. 13*, pp. 5-68 ; José E. ALVAREZ, "Common Language, Common Challenges: The Evolving International Investment Regime", in a speech at the International Law Weekend, New York, 23 November 2009, p. 2. explains that

   "Today, investor-State arbitral awards, ever more abundant, are building, atop the slender common language of the 'international minimum standard' or 'FET', an elaborate body of global principles of 'good governance' that the international community is increasingly coming to expect from States that purport to adhere to the rule of law. As my colleagues at NYU have suggested, the investment regime, along with other contemporary human rights regimes, is constructing a global administrative law. These tribunals are now elaborating a cluster of common normative principles ... (1) requiring States to respect the legal values of stability, predictability and consistency, (2) to protect legitimate expectations, (3) grant procedural and administrative due process and avoid denials of justice, (4) require transparency, and (5) insist on reasonableness and proportionality when deploying the power of the State."

   (On file with the author.)
52. Rudolf DOLZER and Christoph SCHREUER, *Principles of International Investment Law* (Oxford University Press 2008) p. 87.

give weight to certain norms or fundamental rights in the context of international arbitration. The concept of "transnational public policy" encompasses such a phenomenon.

Such a rationale was endorsed by the arbitral tribunal in *World Duty Free v. Kenya* in which the tribunal decided that:

> "In light of *domestic laws* and international conventions relating to corruption, and in light of the decisions taken on this matter by courts and arbitral tribunals, this Tribunal is convinced that bribery is contrary to the *international public policy* of most, if not all, States or, to use another formula, to *transnational public policy*. Thus, claims based on contracts of corruption or on contracts obtained by corruption cannot be upheld by this Arbitral Tribunal."[53]

Constitutional law can definitely play a major role in the field of international arbitration to ensure the respect of fundamental rights, to promote public interest and above all to root arbitral awards "in the real world where people live, work and die".[54] Indeed, as stated by the arbitral tribunal in the *Calenergy's Himpurna California Energy Ltd.* case:

> "The members of (an) Arbitral Tribunal do not live in an ivory tower. Nor do they view the arbitral process as one which operates in a vacuum, divorced from reality.... The arbitrators believe that cronyism and other forms of abuse of public trust do indeed exist in many countries, *causing great harm to untold millions of ordinary people in a myriad of insidious ways*. They would rigorously oppose any attempt to use the arbitral process to give effect to contracts contaminated by corruption."[55]

V.   CONCLUSION

What if constitutional law was always there? One cannot conclude a paper on constitutional law and its relevance for arbitration advocacy without taking into consideration that some BITs refer *expressis verbis* to the "laws and regulations" of the host State. We have already discussed above that the host State "law" may incorporate in our view constitutional law. When an international treaty embodies an expression such as "laws and regulations", the use of the plural form indicates in our sense that constitutional law is definitely to be scrutinized by advocates and arbitrators when dealing with fundamental rights in international arbitration. This is the only way of giving

---

53. *World Duty Free Company Limited (Claimant) v. Republic of Kenya* (ICSID Case No. ARB/00/7), Award of 4 October 2006, para. 157 (italics added).
54. "European Communities – Measures Concerning Meat and Meat Products (Hormones)", Report of the WTO Appellate Body, 16 January 1998, WT/DS26/AB/R, WT/DS48/AB/R, para. 184.
55. *Himpurna California Energy Ltd (Bermuda) v. PT. (Persero) Perusahaan Listruk Negara (Indonesia)*, Final Award, 4 May 1999, para. 219 (italics added).

effet utile to the expression "laws and regulations". In this context, one may disagree with restrictive interpretations tending at limiting that expression to "legislation specifically addressing investments by foreign investors" or to "general legal framework consisting of tax laws, labour laws, environmental laws, corporate laws, competition laws, and intellectual property laws".[56] Constitutions are "laws" of countries. The South African Constitution (1996), for example, states clearly that the "Constitution is the supreme law of the Republic".

So yes, constitutional law was and is always relevant in arbitration advocacy, and particularly when it comes to fundamental rights and public policy. Dealing with the relationship between constitutional law, fundamental rights and arbitral awards seems to be an "understandable fact of life".[57] Nevertheless, that relationship shows that more than ever international arbitrators are called to rule upon matters of transnational law and transnational public policies.

International law is not hermetic to such transnational concerns. In the field of international investment arbitration, international law more than in any other field needs that "global constitutional law" to substantiate the content of some fundamental standards. The content of standards like the "FET" standard or the "minimum standard of treatment" has evolved and will more and more evolve in the coming years in light of constitutional law developments in order to foster a better balance between public policy aspects and investment rights aspects.[58]

---

56. Anna JOUBIN-BRET, "Admission and Establishment in the Context of Investment Protection" in August REINISCH, ed., *Standards of Investment Protection* (Oxford University Press 2008) pp. 18-19.
57. Expression borrowed from Rosalyn HIGGINS, "International Courts and Tribunals. The Challenges Ahead: Conference Opening Speech", 7 The Law and Practice of International Courts and Tribunals (2009) p. 261.
58. See Michael REISMAN, "Keynote Address to the Conference", Foreign Investment: New Horizons in Asia, Seoul, South Korea, 13 April 2007, p. 5. Professor Reisman speaks about a "workable international system ... accommodating many conflicting interests". (On file with the author.)

On the Internationalization of Administrative Contracts, Arbitration and the Calvo Doctrine

Guido Santiago Tawil[*]

TABLE OF CONTENTS	Page
I. Introduction	325
II. The Traditional Local Nature of Administrative Law and Administrative Contracts	326
III. The Calvo Doctrine and the Calvo Clause	328
IV. Globalization, the Internationalization of Administrative Law and Administrative Contracts	333
V. Echoes of the Calvo Doctrine	342
VI. Internationalization: Moving Forwards or Backwards?	346

I. INTRODUCTION

The traditional gap existing between international and administrative law seems to be gradually diminishing. The progress of international trade and communications; the new political, commercial and legal structures resulting from the globalization process and the thousands of international agreements executed over the last fifty years have raised more than justified doubts about the survival – in the long run – of some of administrative law's typical features.

However, at the same time that international regulations increasingly erode what were traditionally thought inexpugnable municipal barriers and begin ruling on some State domestic actions,[1] views that were until recently considered outdated appear to be gaining new stamina.

The revival of the Calvo Doctrine, with certain variations, is one of the more remarkable ones. In the past few years, States, legal scholars and practitioners seem to have reshaped the century-old theory to advance their positions in litigation as well as in academic and legislative levels.

The reappearance of the Calvo Doctrine should, however, be read in context.

---

[*] Professor, University of Buenos Aires School of Law; Co-Chair, International Bar Association Arbitration Committee; Member, London Court of International Arbitration (LCIA); Attorney at Law, Partner, M.&M. Bomchil; Member of ICCA.

[1] Concerning some of the issues that the move towards internationalization has raised within States' boundaries see Sabino CASSESE, "Global Standards for National Administrative Procedure", The Emergence of Global Administrative Law, 68 Law and Contemporary Problems, Institute for International Law and Justice, New York University School of Law (Summer/Autumn 2005, nos. 3-4) p. 109 et seq.

As part of the globalization trend,[2] the execution of bilateral investment treaties (BITs), free trade agreements (FTAs), regional integration treaties and the incorporation of international arbitration clauses in administrative contracts have implied a significant shift in States' international policies and domestic legislation by providing private parties with the possibility of solving international disputes in a forum traditionally reserved to State-State disputes and subject to public international law.

While reactions were initially minimal, the increasing number of investor-State disputes submitted to international arbitration seemed to have raised stronger voices of concern towards a system that judges a State's actions outside the boundaries of its own courts.

Although such reactions should not necessarily be read as an attempt to retreat from the internationalization process, they should be observed with caution. As normally happens with major changes, certain reactions and resistance are not totally unexpected – particularly when they could involve changing the way State entities and organizations, governed in most cases by administrative practices developed during decades, shall conduct themselves.

II. THE TRADITIONAL LOCAL NATURE OF ADMINISTRATIVE LAW AND ADMINISTRATIVE CONTRACTS

A particular product of the French Revolution, *Droit Administratif* was considered for centuries the most local legal regime.

In fact, its local nature was typically considered one of its distinctive features.[3] For centuries, relations between States and private parties within its boundaries were exclusively governed by domestic public law. International obligations did not bind the State unless they were incorporated into national law through domestic legislation.[4] The concept of sovereignty prevented States from being restrained by a global or international administrative regime. Domestic bodies were purely local and exercised their powers subject to domestic public laws and regulations.[5]

Administrative contracts were no exception.[6] Initially developed in order to distinguish between those government contracts to be adjudicated by administrative

---

2. See Guido S. TAWIL, "*Sobre Don Miguel, la globalización y la pasión por el derecho administrativo*", 20 Revista de Derecho Administrativo (AbeledoPerrot, Buenos Aires 2008, no. 66) p. 1040 et seq.
3. The application of domestic public law to any relationship with the State was clearly seen, for example, in the ideas of the German scholar Otto MAYER (*Derecho administrativo alemán*, Vol. IV, translation from its French original of 1906, (Arayú,Buenos Aires 1954) pp. 356-358). See also, Guido S. TAWIL, "*El estudio del derecho comparado y su incidencia en el desarrollo del derecho público interno*", Revista de Derecho Administrativo (year 3, Depalma, Buenos Aires, January-April 1991, no. 6) p. 73 et seq.
4. See O. MAYER, *Derecho administrativo alemán*, vol. IV, *op. cit.*, fn. 3, pp. 356-359.
5. See G.S. TAWIL, *El estudio del derecho comparado y su incidencia en el desarrollo del derecho público interno*, *op. cit.*, fn. 3, p. 73 et seq.
6. See André DE LAUBADÈRE, *Traité théorique et pratique des contrats administratifs*, Vol. I (Librairie générale de droit et jurisprudence R. Pichon et R. Durand-Auzias, Paris 1956) p. 9.

courts (initially the *Conseil d'Etat*) and other types of government contracts considered as ordinary agreements subject to the competing jurisdiction of judicial courts,[7] the notion of *contrats administratifs* evolved into a special legal regime distinguishable from the one applicable to ordinary contracts.

Within the realm of the State's own public law, administrative contracts were regarded as being embodied within a *régime exorbitant*[8] which provides for the application of provisions that go beyond those applicable to private law contracts. As opposed to private contracts, the State party in an administrative contract holds certain prerogatives or powers over the private contractor – i.e., the powers to unilaterally change the contract terms within certain limits in line with the general-interest purpose pursued by it; to issue self-enforcing decisions or to terminate the contract pursuant to the public interest, among others.

French administrative law and its theory of administrative contracts were widely accepted in most civil law jurisdictions. Under such a system, public prerogatives place the State party in a different status than private counterparties, administrative contracts are governed by domestic law and disputes arising as a result of them are to be exclusively adjudicated by local courts.[9]

Notwithstanding some historical debates – as the one held at the end of the nineteenth century between Dicey and de Laferrière concerning the existence of a special domestic regime applicable to States similar to *droit administrative* in England and the United States –[10] States have been increasingly subject to special rules in their domestic relations even in common law countries.[11]

---

7. See Charles DEBBASCH, *Droit Administratif*, 6th edn. (Economica, Paris 2002) pp. 522-529.
8. See *ibid.*, p. 529; Jean RIVERO, *Droit Administratif*, 12th edn. (Dalloz, Paris 1987) pp. 144-145; André DE LAUBADÈRE, Jean-Claude VENEZIA, and Yves GAUDEMENT, *Traité de droit administratif*, Vol. 1, 12th edn. (L.G.D.J., Paris 1992) p. 11.
9. The dispute settlement restrictions, based on the idea of State sovereignty, could be seen in France as early as in 1806, when the French Code of Civil Procedure prohibited disputes concerning "the State, the public domain, local authorities and public entities" from being referred to arbitration. With limitations, this restriction still remains in relation to domestic disputes. Indeed, Art. 2060 of the Civil Code confirms the position that "disputes concerning public collectivities and public establishments" cannot be referred to arbitration. However, the *Conseil Constitutionnel* has established that inasmuch as such provision does not stand above other laws, those public entities could submit to arbitration if authorized by law (see Decision no. 2004-506 DC, 2 December 2004, *Cahiers du Conseil Constitutionnel* No. 18). In fact, since 1906 a number of laws have authorized public entities to resort to arbitration (i.e., Laws No. 82-1153, 86-972, 90-568 and 97-135; Decree No. 2001-210). For a discussion on the arbitrability of State contract disputes, see Emmanuel GAILLARD and John SAVAGE, eds., *Fouchard Gaillard Goldman on International Commercial Arbitration* (Kluwer, Netherlands 1999) pp. 313-329 and Guido S. TAWIL and Ignacio MINORINI LIMA, "*El Estado y el arbitraje: primera aproximación*", Régimen de la Administración Pública (year XXIX – 337, Buenos Aires) pp. 24-25.
10. See Albert Venn DICEY, *Introduction to the Study of the Law of the Constitution*, reproduction of the 8th edition published by Macmillan in 1915 (Liberty Classics, Indianapolis 1982) p. 215.
11. Even the use of the term "administrative law" has generated passionate debates in the common law world. In addition to Dicey, compare the expressions of Lord Hewart of Bury (cited by S.A. DE SMITH, *Judicial Review of Administrative Action*, 4th edn. (Stevens & Son Limited, London 1980) p. 6.) and the opposite view expressed by Felix Frankfurter ("Foreword", 47 Yale Law Journal (1938)

The fact that administrative contracts were traditionally subject to domestic laws and jurisdictions seems consistent with the circumstances in which such theory developed.

Agreements such as those related to the maintenance of the public lighting or the waste management of a small town in France were typically local and had no relationship whatsoever with transnational elements.

No international funding or financing was necessary to perform such contracts. International trade was highly under-developed and closed economies prevailed. In such circumstances, States usually contracted with their own nationals and entering into contracts with foreign nationals or corporations was clearly an exception.[12]

III.   THE CALVO DOCTRINE AND THE CALVO CLAUSE

1.   The Doctrine's Main Tenets, the Calvo Clause and Its Contacts with Administrative Law

At the same time that administrative law consolidated in France, the Calvo Doctrine[13] emerged in the second half of the nineteenth century within Latin American countries as a reaction against both the international minimum standard of treatment and the

---

p. 515 at p. 517). Frankfurter's view must be seen in the context of the New Deal, to which both he and James Landis were certainly not foreign. Concerning the existence of a system of administrative law in England see Lord Denning's opinion in *Breen v. Amalgated Engineering Union*, 2 Q.B. 175, 189 (1971) ("It may truly now be said that we have developed a system of administrative law..."). A more detailed discussion of this matter can be seen in Guido S. TAWIL, *Administración y Justicia*, I (Depalma, Buenos Aires 1993) pp. 11-30.

12. Among those exceptions should be noted in the first place those agreements related to public borrowing, in many cases with undisputed international effects. See G.S. TAWIL, "*Sobre Don Miguel, la globalización y la pasión por el derecho administrativo*", *op. cit.*, fn. 2, p. 1029 et seq.

13. There is some debate as to whether the set of principles which would ultimately become known as the Calvo Doctrine intellectually originated with the Argentine diplomat and scholar Carlos Calvo (1822-1906). It has been argued that the principal elements which form the Calvo Doctrine were first expressed by the Venezuelan scholar Andrés Bello as early as in 1832, when promoting immigration by eliminating all civil differences between nationals and aliens. Therefore, if foreign investors were provided with civil legal equality they could not ask for more than that equality. See Santiago MONTT, "Latin American Position on State Responsibility: Looking into the Past for Lessons on the Future", LEGS Seminar Paper, Princeton University, 9 February 2009, p. 2 et seq. Notwithstanding, there seems to be a rather general agreement that the intellectual basis for the Calvo Doctrine is found in Carlos Calvo's 1868 treatise *Derecho Internacional Teórico y Práctico de Europa y América* and the later 1896 French edition *Le Droit International Théorique et Practique*. See Gonzalo BIGGS, *La crisis de la deuda latinoamericana frente a los precedentes históricos* (Grupo Editor Latinoamericano, Buenos Aires 1987) p. 76. However, as nowhere in those works is there a clear and straightforward assertion of the doctrine, it should be assembled by taking together different passages which throw some light on Calvo's ideas. See Carlos CALVO, *Le Droit International Théorique et Practique precede d'un exposé historique des progress de la science du droit des gens*, Vol. III, 5th edn. (Arthur Rousseau, Paris 1986) pp. 138-142, inter alia.

remedy of diplomatic protection.[14] Those institutions were widely seen as a foreign interference contrary to the States' sovereignty[15] and their domestic legal regimes, in particular, their administrative law system which naturally called for the application of the States' own laws within the exclusive jurisdiction of their national courts.

The principle of equality between States and between foreigners and nationals is at the heart of the Calvo Doctrine.[16] The doctrine consists of one central idea and two corollary principles.[17]

The Calvo Doctrine's central tenet is that international law requires that foreigners who establish themselves in another country should have the same right of protection as nationals of that host country. Foreigners should receive the same treatment as nationals. While this aspect of the principle may be viewed positively, the negative aspect which complements this principle is that foreigners should receive only treatment equal to national treatment and no more.[18]

The two necessary corollaries to Calvo's idea were that disputes between a host State and a foreigner should be governed by the State's national law and should be subject to the State's ordinary courts. Taken together, the Calvo Doctrine's practical proposition was that foreigners should not have resort to the remedy of diplomatic protection.

By the mid-1970s, the Calvo Doctrine had gained wide acceptance in most Latin American States. This was reflected through several milestones, such as most States' reluctance to ratify international agreements that could be in any extent understood as

---

14. In the wake of America's independence movement, Latin American States sought to limit foreign intervention, particularly from European countries, by aspiring to establish new standards within public international law. In this path, the Calvo Doctrine was complemented and followed by the narrower proposition posed by the Argentine Minister of Foreign Affairs Luis María Drago in 1902. The Drago Doctrine constituted an attempt to exclude "gunboat diplomacy" as a means to forcefully collect public debts. See Amos S. HERSHEY, "The Calvo and Drago Doctrines", 1 The American Journal of International Law (Jan./Apr. 1907, no. 1) pp. 26-45.
15. As explained by Montt, at that time "diplomatic protection was a process associated with the 'exercise of military, political or economic pressure by stronger against weaker states'" (Santiago MONTT, *State Liability in Investment Treaty Arbitration. Global Constitutional and Administrative Law in the BIT Generation*, Studies in International Law series (2009) p. 32).
16. See *ibid.*, pp. 38-39.
17. While it is likely that Calvo's ideas evolved against the backdrop of specific events such as the 1838-1840 French blockade of Buenos Aires port and the intervention of the Anglo-French fleet arising out of the blockade of Montevideo (1843-1850), these were not the only examples of diplomatic protection in Latin America in this period. Perhaps the most extreme example is the "Jecker claim" in which France, in response to the Mexican government's default under a Fr 75m loan made by a Swiss-French bank, invaded Mexico and installed a new regime.
18. Perhaps, the clearest summary of the position represented by the Calvo Doctrine comes from Art. 1 of the Convention Relative to the Rights of Aliens adopted by the Second International Conference of the American States (1902): "First: Aliens shall enjoy all civil rights pertaining to citizens, and make use thereof in substance, form or procedure, and in the recourses which result therefrom, under exactly the same terms as the said citizens, except as may be otherwise provided by the Constitution of each country." See S. MONTT, "Latin American Position on State Responsibility: Looking into the Past for Lessons on the Future", *op. cit.*, fn. 13, p. 14.

limiting the domain of local jurisdiction.[19] Although not in direct conflict with the Calvo

---

19. The increasing acceptance of the Doctrine and use of Calvo Clauses during most of the twentieth century is evidenced by events such as:

(i) The 1926 decision of the US-Mexican Claims Commission in *North American Dredging Co. of Texas v. United Mexican States* (4 Rev. Int'l Arb. Awards (1926) p. 26). In this case, a US company brought a claim against Mexico before the US-Mexican Claims Commission, claiming damages arising out of the alleged breach of a dredging contract. Mexico challenged the jurisdiction of the Commission on the basis that the dredging contract contained a Calvo Clause which deprived the foreign investor of the right to submit any contractual claims to an international commission. The Commission accepted Mexico's argument and declined jurisdiction on the basis that the US corporation had waived its right to request diplomatic protection.
(ii) The 1933 Seventh International Conference of the American States, in which a unanimous resolution on the rights of aliens was passed, codifying principles related to the Calvo Doctrine. The Convention on Rights and Duties of States therein passed provided in its Art. 9 that "The jurisdiction of states within the limits of national territory applies to all the inhabitants. Nationals and foreigners are under the same protection of the law and the national authorities and the foreigners may not claim rights other or more extensive than those of nationals." The United States of America reserved its rights in the following terms:

"In the meantime in case of differences of interpretations and also until the [proposed doctrines] can be worked out and codified for the common use of every government, I desire to say that the United States Government in all of its international associations and relationships and conduct will follow scrupulously the doctrines and policies which it has pursued since March 4 which are embodied in the different addresses of President Roosevelt since that time and in the recent peace address of myself on the 15th day of December before this Conference and in the law of nations generally recognized and accepted."

On the reservation made by the United States, see Oscar M. GARIBALDI, "Carlos Calvo Redivivus: the Rediscovery of the Calvo Doctrine in the Era of Investment Treaties", 3 TDM (2006, no. 5) p. 26.
(iii) The 1970 Foreign Investment Code of the Andean Commission which set down the principle of national treatment and established a prohibition on any clause in an investment agreement which placed disputes or conflicts outside of national jurisdiction and competence. In December 1970, the Andean Commission, one of the main bodies of the Cartagena Agreement (Agreement on Andean Subregional Integration, opened for signature 26 May 1969, 8 ILM 910 (1969)) which created the Andean Common Market, issued its Decision 24, also known as the Foreign Investment Code (Decision 24 of 31 December 1970, 16 ILM 138 (1977)), in order to regulate the treatment of foreign capital investment in the region. On the Andean Common Market, see Christopher K. DALRYMPLE, "Politics and Foreign Direct Investment: The Multilateral Investment Guarantee Agency and the Calvo Clause", 29 Cornell Int'l L.J. (1996, no. 1) p. 161. Bolivia, Chile, Colombia, Ecuador and Peru signed the Cartagena Agreement in 1969 thereby creating the Andean Common Market (ANCOM). The Cartagena Agreement and the Andean Common Market were designed to develop "a coordinated procedure in ... development planning ... and a harmonization of ... economic and social policies, directed toward future adoption of a concerted planning system for the integrated development of the area" (Cartagena Agreement, Art. 26). ANCOM also intended to create "a common system for the treatment of foreign capital".
(iv) The 1974 UN Charter of Economic Rights and Duties of States (UN General Assembly Resolution 3281 (XXIX), 12 December 1974 (Charter of Economic Rights and Duties of States), 28 YBUN (1974)) which established in its Art. 2(2)(c) that any dispute which arose out of a State's

Doctrine, the 1958 New York Convention[20] was only ratified prior to 1971 by Ecuador and Mexico.[21] Similarly, the 1965 ICSID Convention,[22] was ratified for the first time by a Latin American State only in 1983.[23]

The practical implementation of the Calvo Doctrine was left to the so-called Calvo Clauses, inserted – with different variations – into national constitutions, legislation and typical administrative contracts such as concession and/or construction agreements between States and foreign investors.

The substantive content of Calvo Clauses was not uniform. However, standard Calvo Clauses shared certain common elements, namely (1) the courts of the host State were to have exclusive jurisdiction to determine the dispute, (2) the applicable law of the dispute was to be the local law and (3) rights to diplomatic protection and other international law rights were waived.[24]

It can be argued, therefore, that both the Calvo Doctrine and the Calvo Clauses in practice intended to enforce at the international level – that is, one step further – the administrative law regimes in force within the States' national boundaries. No matter the origin or nationality of the State's counterparty, disputes related to State contracts and regulations had to be settled according to the host State's laws and before such State's own courts. Although originated in different intellectual bases, both constructions appeared as consistent and produced similar practical results.

---

nationalization, expropriation or transfer of foreign property, should "be settled under the domestic law of the nationalizing State and by its tribunals…".

20. Convention on the Recognition and Enforcement of Foreign Arbitral Awards, done at New York, 10 June 1958 (the New York Convention). See <www.uncitral.org/uncitral/en/ uncitral_texts/ arbitration/NYConvention.html>.
21. Ecuador ratified the 1958 New York Convention in 1962 and Mexico in 1971, followed by Cuba (1974), Chile (1975), Colombia (1979), Uruguay (1983), Guatemala (1984), Panama (1984), Costa Rica (1987), Peru (1988), Argentina (1989), Venezuela (1995), Bolivia (1995), Paraguay (1997), El Salvador (1998), Honduras (2000), Brazil (2002) and Dominican Republic (2002). It should be noted, however, that the majority of Latin American States had ratified by the time of the later 1975 Panama Convention, which dealt with the recognition and enforcement of arbitral awards on an inter-American basis.
22. Convention on the Settlement of Investment Disputes between States and Nationals of Other States, done at Washington D.C., 18 March 1965. See <http://icsid.worldbank.org/ICSID/ ICSID/RulesMain.jsp>.
23. Paraguay was the first state to ratify the ICSID Convention in 1983. The majority of Latin American States ratified the Convention in the 1990s: El Salvador (1984), Ecuador (1986), Honduras (1989), Chile (1991), Costa Rica (1993), Peru (1993), Argentina (1994), Bolivia (1995), Nicaragua (1995), Venezuela (1995), Panama (1996), Colombia (1997), Uruguay (2000) and Guatemala (2003). Others, as Brazil, are not yet a party to the ICSID Convention.
24. See O.M. GARIBALDI, "Carlos Calvo Redivivus: the Rediscovery of the Calvo Doctrine in the Era of Investment Treaties", *op. cit.*, fn. 19, p. 2 et seq. The one that was the subject of dispute between the Republic of Venezuela and a foreign investor in the Orinoco Steamship Company arbitration constitutes a good example of a common Calvo Clause. It provided that "Disputes and controversies which may arise with regard to the interpretation or execution of this contract shall be resolved by the tribunals of the Republic in accordance with the laws of the nation, and shall not in any case be considered as a motive for international reclamations." (*The Orinoco Steamship Company in Venezuela Arbitration of 1903*, S. Doc. no. 316, 58th Cong., 2 Sess. 100 (1904)).

2. The Decline of the Calvo Doctrine

By the late 1980s and early 1990s, the position most Latin American States had pursued for nearly a century was largely abandoned. By 1995, a majority of the Latin American States had ratified both the New York and the ICSID Conventions. Most Latin American States had also accepted the Convention Establishing the Multilateral Investment Guarantee Agency (the MIGA Convention),[25] recognizing rights of subrogation.[26]

However, the decisive step in the abandonment of the Calvo Doctrine was the gradual acceptance and ratification of bilateral investment treaties and free trade agreements.[27] Thus, even those countries which traditionally have been perceived to be the most ardent supporters of the Calvo Doctrine have become part of the BIT and FTA generation.

Mexico's experience is telling. Having being historically averse to arbitration and an active Calvo Doctrine promoter,[28] in the last decades Mexico has made significant changes in its international policy on and approach towards arbitration. Based on the economic benefits associated with market-oriented policies and regional integration movements, Mexico accepted investment arbitration within NAFTA, entered into more than twenty BITs and further encouraged investor-State dispute settlement provisions in several free trade agreements, such as those executed with Japan, Uruguay, the Northern Triangle (El Salvador, Guatemala and Honduras) and Nicaragua.

---

25. The Convention Establishing the Multilateral Investment Guarantee Agency (MIGA) was opened for signature on 11 October 1985 and entered into force on 12 April 1988. The Multilateral Investment Guarantee Agency sponsored by the World Bank aims to enhance the flow of capital investment by issuing "guarantees against non-commercial risks in respect of investments in a member country which flow from other member countries" (MIGA Convention). For a detailed discussion of the relationship between the Calvo Doctrine and the MIGA, see C.K. DALRYMPLE, "Politics and Foreign Direct Investment: The Multilateral Investment Guarantee Agency and the Calvo Clause", *op. cit.*, fn. 19.
26. Further, the strict doctrinal position which had been taken by the governments of the Andean Common Market in 1970 was somewhat mitigated in 1987 and then further relaxed in 1991. In 1987 the Andean Commission repealed Decision 24, which prohibited the resolution of investment disputes outside of national courts, and issued Decision 220 (Commission of the Cartagena Agreement, Decision 220, 11 May 1987, 27 ILM 974 (1988)). Under the terms of Decision 220, the prohibition on the use of dispute resolution mechanisms other than the national courts was removed and the resolution of disputes in accordance with the local legislation of the member states was permitted. Further, although Decision 291 issued in 1991 contained the same provision in relation to the permitted forms of dispute resolution mechanism, Art. 2, which set out the applicable standard of treatment provided an exception for treatment other than national treatment if contained in the Member State's own legislation. It should be noted that Chile withdrew from the Andean Common Market in 1976.
27. This proliferation of treaties was reflected, even if to varying degrees, throughout most of Latin America. For example, by 2009, Chile had signed fifty-one BITs, Argentina fifty-eight and Cuba fifty-nine. For the list of BITs signed by Argentina, as at 1 June 2009, see <www.unctad.org/sections/dite_pcbb/docs/bits_argentina.pdf>. For the list of BITs signed by Chile and Cuba as at 1 June 2009 see <www.unctad.org/sections/dite_pcbb/docs/bits_chile[cuba].pdf>.
28. Mexico was the first Latin American country to embrace the Calvo Doctrine and began to apply it as early as 1873. See G. BIGGS, *La crisis de la deuda latinoamericana frente a los precedentes históricos*, *op. cit.*, fn. 13, p. 76.

On the multilateral front, the Mercosur investment protocols,[29] though not yet in force pending ratification by some States, have also taken an internationalist approach abandoning the Calvo principle of exclusive local remedies.

While under the Calvo Doctrine it had been proposed that disputes with foreign investors should be subject to national law and national jurisdiction, the execution of investment treaties has implied an acceptance of the principle that, under certain circumstances, foreign investors have a right to treatment in accordance with international standards and that such foreign investors have the right to enforce such rights before international tribunals and without reference to the national courts of the host country.[30]

IV. GLOBALIZATION, THE INTERNATIONALIZATION OF ADMINISTRATIVE LAW AND ADMINISTRATIVE CONTRACTS

Modern globalization can be traced back to the post-World War II era,[31] though it intensified in the late 1980s and beginning of the 1990s. Among others, two developments assumed particular relevance in the last decades.

First, the execution of multilateral agreements and the consolidation of regional unions started to erode traditional domestic legal barriers. The strong influence that they have exercised on domestic regulations has put into question the very same local nature of administrative law and administrative contracts.

---

29. Mercosur is the Common Market of the South comprising Argentina, Brazil, Paraguay and Uruguay (1991). The Colonia and the Buenos Aires Protocols (the former has not been ratified yet by any State party and the latter has been ratified by Argentina, Paraguay and Uruguay) seek to provide substantive guarantees to protected investors in a form very similar to those included within BITs and include investor-State dispute resolution clauses.
30. See Bernardo M. CREMADES, "Disputes Arising Out of Foreign Direct Investment in Latin America: A New Look at the Calvo Doctrine and Other Jurisdictional Issues", Dispute Resolution Journal (May-July 2004) p. 78 et seq.; Debra F. GUAJARDO, "Redefining the Expropriation of a Foreign Direct Investment in Mexico", South Texas Law Review (Fall 2001) p. 1309 et seq; Denise MANNING CABROL, "The Imminent Death of the Calvo Clause and the Rebirth of the Calvo Principle: Equality of Foreign and National Investors", Law and Policy in International Business (Summer 1995) p. 26.
31. Influenced by the causes and effects of the war, the international community realized the need to develop international institutions, address common issues from a global perspective – i.e., peace and security, economic development, poverty, mass migration, pollution and markets – and redefine, accordingly, state sovereignty. On the economic standpoint, the Bretton Woods Conference set out the basis of an international economic order, through the establishment of the World Bank, the International Monetary Fund (IMF) and the Organisation for Economic Cooperation and Development (OECD), and the adoption of the General Agreement on Tariffs and Trade. In addition, the expansion of multinational corporations and technology improvements played a key role in fueling globalization. Development and flourishing of mass media, international transport and telecommunications shortened distances and speeded up economic transactions, while transnational corporations fostered mobility of capital, goods, and services. See Jost DELBRUCK, "Globalization of Law, Politics, and Markets – Implications for Domestic Law – A European Perspective", 1 Ind. J. Global Legal Stud., p. 9, at pp. 10-19.

At the same time, as a result of the substantial increase of trade, commerce and foreign direct investment, countries competing for incoming capital started to abandon their protectionist positions[32] by embracing more liberal policies towards foreign investment, international law and the settlement of international disputes. In this process, the Calvo Doctrine lost support.

1. Internationalization of Administrative Law

As mentioned before, the globalization trend and its inherent internationalization process also reached administrative law and administrative contracts.

The State's discretion to develop its own system of administrative law has been gradually limited through the establishment of organizations whose policies should be followed either as best practices, mandatory international law, regulations at a supranational level or as conditions for obtaining access to international capital markets.[33]

International bodies such as the World Trade Organization (WTO), the International Monetary Fund (IMF), the World Bank, the Inter-American Development Bank (IDB), the Organization for Economic Cooperation and Development (OECD) or the Inter-

---

32. However, the ongoing world financial crisis has brought into question whether globalization will be derailed and more protectionist measures will again be adopted. While investment flows have slowed down and, certainly, some States will adopt – or have already adopted – policies aimed at impairing international trade, scholars debate whether the overall impact will actually mean the return of protectionist theories or if those policies will just be applied until world economic recovery reaches standard levels. To this respect, it has been said that

    "The apparent importance of finance in the trade collapse suggests, but doesn't prove, that concerns about increased protectionism are overblown. Protectionism today is more subtle than in the past, coming more frequently in the guise of non-tariff barriers rather than formal tariffs. One commonly resorted to protectionist measure is antidumping actions—and they give us a snapshot of protectionism in the past few years. In the second half of 2008, the World Trade Organization found a 17 percent increase in the number of new antidumping investigations, compared with the same period in 2007. However, these numbers are still well within the experience of the past decade and well short of the peaks seen in the 2001 recession. While some protectionist measures have been introduced, they haven't approached what the world experienced in the 1930s. That's due in no small part to the lessons of the Great Depression. But the scale of the current crisis and the likelihood of a sluggish recovery suggest the need for ongoing vigilance against protectionist measures."

    (Mark A. WYNNE and Erasmus K. KERSTING, "Trade, Globalization and the Financial Crisis", 4 Economic Letter – Insights from the Federal Reserve Bank of Dallas (November 2009, no. 8). In others' view, protectionism is likely to become widespread ("Attempts to solve the banking and fiscal problems at an international rather than a national level have up to now been fiascos: there is hyperactive diplomacy, but no real results. The big G-20 summit in Washington in November 2008 produced resounding denunciations of protectionism, but was followed immediately by a slew of protectionist measures. Such measures are likely to become more common." See Harold JAMES, "Globalization comes and goes. Right now, it's going", available at <http://whatmatters.mckinseydigital.com> (last accessed 30 January 2010))).
33. See S. CASSESE, "Global Standards for National Administrative Procedure", *op. cit.*, fn. 1, p. 109 et seq.

American Court of Human Rights have impinged on the realm of domestic regulations related to trade, monetary policy, development, environment and human rights, among others.[34]

The European Union's experience is a paramount example. Despite theoretical discussions on whether the European Union has given rise to a body of administrative law,[35] the influence of EU directives and decisions on national administrative systems displays an ongoing increase.[36]

First, European Community Law has taken over on matters traditionally proper of administrative law by establishing certain principles that should be followed by national administrations. Though many of those principles had already been incorporated in domestic legal systems, EU law has certainly fostered other efforts directed to obtain greater efficiency, transparency, open government or an increased use of mechanisms of cooperative decision-making processes.[37]

The European Union further adopted positions which have decisively shaped domestic law regimes in areas such as public utilities regulation (*service public*), public aid, environmental protection, State responsibility,[38] public procurement and antitrust law.[39] For instance, EU law has displaced the idea of *service public* as an activity primarily reserved to the State and reinforced the principles of free initiative and competition,[40] impacting strongly, particularly on regimes such as those of France[41] and Spain.[42]

This process of regional integration, establishment of transnational organizations and flourishing of international treaties related to public governance has influenced national administrative regimes and policies, given rise to what is today called Global

---

34. See Benedict KINGSBURY, Nico KRISCH and Richard B. STEWART, "The Emergence of Global Administrative Law", 68 Law and Contemporary Problems, Institute for International Law and Justice, New York University School of Law (Fall 2005, nos. 3-4) p. 15 et seq.
35. See Sabino CASSESE, "*Derecho administrativo comunitario y derechos administrativos nacionales*", Actualidad en Derecho Público (no. 7) p. 19 et seq.
36. See G.S. TAWIL, "*Sobre Don Miguel, la globalización y la pasión por el derecho administrativo*", op. cit., fn. 2, pp. 1044-1045.
37. See *ibid.*, p. 1045.
38. See Francette FINES, "*Droit comparé et droit administrative communautaire: L'exemple de la responbilité extracontractualle*" in Fabrice MELLERAY, ed., *L'argument de droit comparé en droit administratif français*, Collection Droit Administratif (Bruylant, Brussels 2007) p. 55 et seq.
39. See G.S. TAWIL, "*Sobre Don Miguel, la globalización y la pasión por el derecho administrativo*", op. cit., fn. 2, p. 1045.
40. See S. CASSESE, "*Derecho administrativo comunitario y derechos administrativos nacionales*", op. cit., fn. 35, p. 27.
41. See Jean Bernard AUBY, "*Introduction*" in F. MELLERAY, ed., *L'argument de droit comparé en droit administratif français*, Collection Droit Administratif, op. cit., fn. 38, p. 10; Marie-Claire PONTHOREAU, "*L'argument de droit comparé et les procesus d'hybridation des droits. Les réformes en droit administratif français*" in F. MELLERAY, ed., *L'argument de droit comparé en droit administratif français*, Collection Droit Administratif, op. cit., fn. 38, p. 24.
42. See Jaime RODRÍGUEZ ARANA MUÑOZ, "*Un nuevo derecho administrativo*", El Derecho (Buenos Aires, 21 May 2008) p. 3.

Administrative Law[43] and impacted on the heart of one of administrative law's main institutions: administrative contracts.

2. *Internationalization of Administrative Contracts*

In addition to the process described above, the need to develop large infrastructure projects that require access to international financial markets and the setting of open international public biddings have contributed to significant changes in the legal regimes and practices applicable to State contracts.

Compliance with international and supranational rules as well as directives and guidelines from international organizations have become mandatory requirements in order to access financing of international institutions and many of their principles, guidelines, model regulations and terms have been adopted in local procurement regimes and State organizations.

On the international law side, the government procurement market has increasingly become one of the main targets of trade negotiations.[44] In addition, the WTO

---

43. As explained by Stewart,

"The past several decades have witnessed an explosive development of a great variety of international economic and social regulatory regimes. These regimes have been created in response to the rise of a global market economy (itself constructed through private and public international law regimes), the consequences of economic, social, environmental, informational and other forms of interdependence, and the perceived inadequacies of purely national solutions in the problems generated by those consequences. These regulatory regimes encompass a wide variety of subject areas, including trade; finance and banking; environment, health, and safety; pharmaceuticals; transportation and communications; conditions of financial assistance; human rights; and unlawful or undesirable activities. These regimes respond to the failures of both markets and decentralized national systems of regulation to secure important economic and social values. They also often include bodies that are administrative in character and that make regulatory decisions and create regulatory law that is domestically implemented.... the traditional paradigms of international law and of administrative law at the domestic level cannot adequately account for or address these new global regulatory regimes, which are creating a new field of global administration and administrative law."

(Richard B. STEWART, "US Administrative Law: A Model for Global Administrative Law", 68 Law and Contemporary Problems, Institute for International Law and Justice, New York University School of Law (Fall 2005, no. 3-4) p. 63 et seq.)

44. As explained in this regard,

"NAFTA, in its Chapter 10, included commitments on this issue [government procurement contracts].... An agreement was also signed by Mexico, Venezuela and Colombia (the Group of Three), Mexico and Bolivia and Mexico and Costa Rica. A posteriori, several countries in the Hemisphere participated in trade negotiation processes that have included, albeit without necessarily having concluded, a chapter on government procurement: MERCOSUR, FTAA, MERCOSUR-European Union, Chile-European Union, and more recently in the case of CAFTA."

See Norberto IANNELLI, "Rules and Disciplines in Government Procurement Agreements", publication by the Inter-American Development Bank (August 2003) at p. 2, available at

Agreement on Government Procurement (GPA)[45] and integration bodies – such as the European Commission which has passed public procurement directives[46] or the *Consejo del Mercado Común* (Mercosur) which set forth a Protocol on Public Procurement[47] – have aimed at making regulations and practices more transparent and avoiding discrimination against non-nationals within domestic regimes.

Those efforts to level State rules up to certain minimum standards have been complemented by the execution of international conventions against corruption intended to promote greater transparency and accountability in public governance and, particularly, in public procurement proceedings.[48]

As mentioned above, domestic procurement rules and practices have also been strongly influenced by international conventions, rules and guidelines, in particular in the case of developing countries, where international funding becomes essential in order to pursue special projects or development policies. The World Bank,[49] the IDB[50] and

---

<http://idbdocs.iadb.org/wsdocs/getdocument.aspx?docnum=606991> (last accessed 30 January 2010). In addition, BITs and FTAs have set standards of treatment which limited, in practice, the exercise of the State's prerogatives within administrative contracts. To this respect, Dolzer states that:

"... jurisprudence of investment tribunals as a whole contains ingredients of a growing system of international administrative law for foreign investment. The rules are developed on the basis of very generally worded clauses in virtually all areas of administrative law, ranging from tax law to bankruptcy issues, from the law of governmental immunity to export rules and, in particular, the requirements of permit processes."

(Rudolf DOLZER, "The Impact of International Investment Treaties on Domestic Administrative Law", 37 International Law and Politics, p. 953 at p. 970).

45. Aruba, Canada, China, the European Community, Hong Kong, Iceland, Israel, Japan, Korea, Liechtenstein, Norway, Singapore, Switzerland and the United States are WTO members that have become party to the Government Procurement Agreement.
46. See the Public Sector Directive (European Commission Directive No. 2004/18) and the Utilities Directive (European Commission Directive No. 2004/17).
47. Decision of the *Consejo del Mercado Común* No. 23/06. The Protocol is not yet in force as it has only been ratified by Argentina which approved it through Law No. 26.443.
48. To number just a few of them: the United Nations Convention against Corruption, the United Nations Declaration against Corruption and Bribery in International Commercial Transactions, the UN International Code of Conduct for Public Officials, the OECD Convention on Combating Bribery of Foreign Public Officials in International Business Transactions, the Convention of the European Union on the fight against corruption involving officials of the European Communities or officials of Member States, the Council of Europe's Criminal Law Convention Against Corruption, the Inter-American Convention Against Corruption, and the African Union Convention on Preventing and Combating Corruption.
49. The World Bank's Guidelines Procurement under International Bank for Reconstruction and Development (IBRD) Loans and International Development Association (IDA) Credits establish that

"1.2. ... While in practice the specific procurement rules and procedures to be followed in the implementation of a project depend on the circumstances of the particular case, four considerations generally guide the Bank's requirements: (a) the need for economy and efficiency

other regional development institutions (i.e., the European Bank for Reconstruction and Development, the African Development Bank) have performed a relevant role in fostering common principles applicable to public procurement. They have conditioned financing to the State's abidance by standard policies and procedures grounded upon economy and efficiency benchmarks, disregarding political and other non-economic factors. Other institutions such as the IMF subject State financing to compliance with pre-defined minimum standards or the adoption of certain government policies, which limit State administrative organizations and decisions.[51]

In this way, the not-so-long-ago commonly accepted assertion that administrative contracts were a creature of domestic law and shared the local nature of administrative law seems to have been subject to increasing re-examination. Today, administrative contracts appear increasingly bound to a myriad of global regimes – by direct application of international and supranational rules or through incorporation in domestic legislation – dealing with transparency, public accountability, general guidelines on procurement and standards of treatment owed to State's counterparties which limit the exercise of the State's contractual prerogatives.[52]

---

in the implementation of the project, including the procurement of the goods and works involved; (b) the Bank's interest in giving all eligible bidders from developed and developing countries the same information and equal opportunity to compete in providing goods and works financed by the Bank; (c) the Bank's interest in encouraging the development of domestic contracting and manufacturing industries in the borrowing country; and (d) the importance of transparency in the procurement process.

1.3 Open competition is the basis for efficient public procurement. Borrowers shall select the most appropriate method for the specific procurement. In most cases, International Competitive Bidding (ICB), properly administered, and with the allowance for preferences for domestically manufactured goods and, where appropriate, for domestic contractors for works under prescribed conditions is the most appropriate method. In most cases, therefore, the Bank requires its Borrowers to obtain goods, works and services through ICB open to eligible suppliers and contractors. Section II of these Guidelines describes the procedures for ICB."

(available at <http://web.worldbank.org/WBSITE/EXTERNAL/PROJECTS/PROCUREMENT/0,,contentMDK:50002392~pagePK:84269~piPK:60001558~theSitePK:84266,00.html> (last accessed: 30 January 2010).

50. The IDB and the World Bank share information and audit tools on financial management and have harmonized standard procurement guidelines. See Policies for the Procurement of Goods and Works Financed by the Inter-American Development Bank, available at <www5.iadb.org/idbppi/aspx/ppProcurement.aspx?pLanguage=ENGLISH> (Last accessed 30 January 2010).

51. See Oscar R. AGUILAR VALDÉZ, "*Sobre las fuentes y principios del derecho global de las contrataciones públicas*", 75 Revista Derecho Administrativo (January-March 2011) pp. 1-32.

52. The so-called umbrella clauses found in many BITs – though their scope has not yet been uniformly settled – are a paramount example of the fusion of international and national legal systems. We have addressed some of the issues posed by umbrella clauses in a prior ICCA Report. See Guido S. TAWIL, "The Distinction Between Contract Claims and Treaty Claims: An Overview" in *International Arbitration 2006: Back to Basics?*, ICCA Congress Series no. 13 (Kluwer Law International 2006) p. 492.

3. *International Arbitration as Means of Administrative Contract's Internationalization*

The internationalization process is also leading to the decline of a feature closely related to the application of a pure domestic law regime to State contracts. The principle of the local court's exclusive jurisdiction to settle disputes related to administrative contracts has increasingly been questioned. Arbitration has emerged as an available means of adjudication, and has gradually been accepted by States, particularly with respect to their international contracts.[53]

As early as 1957, France – generally considered to be the cradle of administrative law – accepted that restrictions relating to the arbitrability of State contract disputes under French domestic law are not relevant in the international context.[54] Though subject to stringent requirements, Spain – whose administrative law system has been historically influenced by the French regime – has softened its rules and endorsed arbitration within government contracts.[55]

In Latin America, which traditionally has been reluctant towards arbitration, a number of countries have shown a remarkable development. Many Latin American States have established a pro-arbitration environment[56] and have particularly

---

53. See O.M. GARIBALDI, "Carlos Calvo Redivivus: the Rediscovery of the Calvo Doctrine in the Era of Investment Treaties", *op. cit.*, fn. 19, pp. 34-35.
54. In the *Myrtoon Steamship* case, the Paris Court of Appeals held that "the prohibition ... is confined to domestic contracts and does not apply to contracts which are international in nature" (*Myrtoon Steam Ship v. Agent judiciaire du Trésor*, JCP, Ed. G., Pt. II, No. 10,078 (1957) (Paris Court of Appeals, 10 April 1957)). This position was confirmed by the *Cour de Cassation's* 1966 decision in the *Galakis* case where the Court confirmed that the restrictions did not apply to international contracts entered into for the purposes of and in accordance with international trade. See *Galakis v. Agent judiciaire du Trésor*, JCP, Ed. G. , Pt. II, No. 14,798 (1966) (Cass. 1e civ, 2 May 1966). See also Eduardo SILVA ROMERO, "ICC Arbitration and State Contracts", 13 ICC International Court of Arbitration Bulletin (Spring 2002, no. 1) p. 48, para. 5.
55. The Law on Contracts for the Public Administrations has authorized arbitration provided that submission is established through a royal decree issued before the Ministry Council and once the State Council – the Spanish *Consejo de Estado* – has been heard. See Art. 60.2 of Royal Decree No. 2/2000 of 16 June 2003, and Art. 7.3 of the General Budget Law No. 47/2003 of 26 November 2003. See also G.S. TAWIL and I. MINORINI LIMA," *El Estado y el arbitraje: primera aproximación*", *op. cit.*, fn. 9, pp. 9-52 and 25 et seq.
56. Since 1989, Bolivia, Brazil, Chile, Colombia, Costa Rica, Dominican Republic, Ecuador, El Salvador, Guatemala, Honduras, Mexico, Nicaragua, Panama, Paraguay, Peru and Venezuela have passed specific laws on arbitration or modified their existing rules. As well, almost all Latin American countries have ratified the 1958 New York Convention. Member countries from Latin America include Argentina, Bolivia, Brazil, Chile, Colombia, Costa Rica, Cuba, Dominican Republic, Ecuador, El Salvador, Guatemala, Honduras, Mexico, Nicaragua, Panama, Paraguay, Peru, Uruguay and Venezuela. Four of these ratifications took place within the past decade (Bahamas, 2007; Brazil, 2002; Dominican Republic, 2002; Honduras, 2001; Jamaica, 2002; and Nicaragua, 2003), with the case of Brazil clearly standing out due to its impact on the development of commercial arbitration in the region. The growing relevance of international arbitration in Latin America may be further seen in the number of disputes involving parties from the region that have been submitted to arbitration before arbitral institutions such as the International Chamber of Commerce. Of the total number of parties from the Americas registered in 2007, fifty-six percent

acknowledged the State's and its public entities' capacity to enter into arbitration agreements.[57]

In the case of Mexico, in addition to having reviewed its international policy by entering into the NAFTA and executing numerous BITs and FTAs containing investor-State dispute settlement mechanisms – as referred to above – Mexico reformed its commercial code introducing provisions on arbitration in 1993[58] and has recently amended its public law regime to widen the availability of arbitration within administrative contracts.[59]

International arbitration is increasingly becoming an acceptable feature in administrative contracts, gradually setting aside the notion of local courts' exclusive

---

belonged to Caribbean and Latin American countries, with a strong presence of Brazilian and Mexican parties. See International Chamber of Commerce, 19 ICC International Court of Arbitration Bulletin (2008, no. 1) p. 5.

57. This is the case for Bolivia, Colombia, Costa Rica, Ecuador, El Salvador, Guatemala, Honduras, Nicaragua, Panama, Paraguay, Peru and Venezuela. See Alexis MOURRE, "Perspectives of International Arbitration in Latin America", 17 Am. Rev. Int'l Arb., p. 597 at p. 601. In Argentina, while arbitration clauses are not forbidden within administrative contracts, the Federal Supreme Court has generally required that submission to arbitration be authorized by law passed by Congress (Fallos 330:2215, LL 2007-D, 262. See also G.S. TAWIL and I. MINORINI LIMA, "El Estado y el arbitraje: primera aproximación", op. cit., fn. 9, pp. 9-52 and 27 et seq).

58. See A. MOURRE, "Perspectives of International Arbitration in Latin America", op. cit., fn. 57, p. 600.

59. As recently as 28 May 2009, Mexico amended the Law on the Public Sector's Acquisitions, Leases and Services (Arts. 80-86) and the Law on Public Works and Related Services in order to authorize arbitration to settle disputes related to long-term service contracts and public works agreements. While the new regime still excludes disputes regarding administrative rescission or early termination from the scope of arbitration, it nonetheless constitutes a step forward in promoting arbitration within the administrative law field. See Francisco GONZÁLEZ DE COSSÍO, "Desarrollos recientes sobre arbitraje en México", Nota para la Reunión del Grupo Latinoamericano de la CCI, Punta Cana, República Dominicana, 27 August 2009; Herfried WÖSS, "Arbitration, Alternative Dispute Resolution and Public Procurement in Mexico – The 2009 Reforms, Analysis and their Impact", 6 TDM (2009, no. 4). Even prior to this amendment, arbitration in Mexico was quite common in the petroleum and energy sector. State entities as Pemex – and its subsidiaries – and the Comisión Federal de Electricidad were, and still are, entitled under their own organization rules to submit to arbitration and they actually turned to this authorization in many instances. Art. 14 of former Pemex's Organic Law established that Pemex had full capacity to execute arbitration agreements or include arbitration clauses in any sort of agreements, whether domestic or international. The November 2008 Ley de Petróleos Mexicanos – which superseded the organic law – confirmed this capacity in its Art. 72 and the 2008 amendment to the Ley Reglamentaria del Artículo 27 Constitucional en el Ramo del Petróleo corroborated that Pemex's contracts for works and services may include arbitral agreements in accordance with Mexican laws and international treaties – though it limited Pemex's capacity to consent to foreign jurisdictions (i.e., foreign courts) with respect to disputes related to contracts for works and services in the national territory and in the areas where the Nation exercises sovereignty, jurisdiction or competence (Art. 6, para. 2). Further, pursuant to Art. 45 of the Ley del Servicio Público de Energía Eléctrica, the Comisión Federal de Electricidad is entitled to agree upon application of foreign law, submit to foreign jurisdictions and enter into arbitration agreements if convenient for its purposes.

jurisdiction on administrative law issues.[60] Legislation and case law, including that from several Latin American States[61] – where the Calvo Doctrine originated – have promoted arbitration as an alternative and effective means to settle government disputes.

---

60. In most cases, however, arbitral jurisdiction is limited to awarding damages. Claims pursuing annulment or reversal of administrative decisions are very rarely accepted or submitted before arbitral tribunals. A similar situation arises, in general, with ICSID or ad hoc arbitration panels hearing investment disputes.
61. In addition to Mexico, Peru and, to a lesser extent, Brazil constitute further landmark examples of a significant change with respect to the treatment of arbitration agreements within the context of the administrative law field. The Peruvian Political Constitution as amended in 1993 adopted a pro-arbitration stance. Art. 63 provides that the State and its entities can submit contractual-related disputes to arbitration in accordance with international treaties or Peruvian Law. The recent 2008 Peruvian Arbitration Law has consolidated this general endorsement, by authorizing the State and its entities to include international or national arbitration clauses in public contracts (international arbitration is available provided the contractual counterparty is not domiciled in Peru). See 2008 Peruvian Arbitration Law (Legislative Decree No. 1071) Art. 4. Confirming the State's commitment to honor international arbitration clauses as a binding and enforceable agreement, the Peruvian Arbitration Law – following the criterion on subjective arbitrability established by the Swiss Code on Private International Law (Art. 177(2)) – sets forth that the State party to an arbitration agreement cannot invoke its own prerogatives to withdraw from the obligations arising out of the arbitration agreement. 2008 Peruvian Arbitration Law (Legislative Decree No. 1071) Art. 2. Concerning Brazil, its policy change in the last fifteen years is remarkable, as nowadays arbitration agreements contained in public contracts can be found with increasing frequency. See Arnoldo WALD, "Arbitration and Brazilian State Entities at Peace – at last", 4 GAR (issue 6). The 1996 Arbitration Law was construed as allowing the State and its entities to submit to arbitration, provided the subject matter related to disposable rights – i.e., government entities acting as private agents engaged in economic activities. However, there was no clear provision on the matter other than the general statement that persons with capacity to contract may resort to arbitration (see the 1996 Brazilian Arbitration Law, Art. 1; Gilberto GIUSTI and Adriano DRUMMOND C. TRINDADE, "International Arbitration in Investment Disputes: The Washington Convention, ICSID and the Position of Brazil", 2 Revista de Arbitragem e Mediação (Oct./Dec. 2005, no. 7). The Brazilian Superior Court of Justice has endorsed arbitration as a legitimate means to settle disputes arising from agreements executed between a private company and a quasi-public corporation in the well-known case of *AES Uruguaiana Empreendimentos Ltda. v. Companhia Estadual de Energia do Rio Grande do Sul* (RESP 612.439 – RS, Rel. Min. João Otávio Noronha, j. 25.10.2005, DJ 14.09.2006). See also *TMC Terminal Multimodal de Coroa Grande v. Federal Government* and *Petróleo Brasileiro SA Petrobrás v. Tractebel Energía SA*. The recent laws on concessions – Law No. 11,196/05 – and public-private partnerships – Law No. 11,079/04 – introduced arbitration in typical administrative contracts. They authorize arbitration provided that arbitration proceedings are conducted in Brazil, in the Portuguese language and pursuant to the Brazilian Arbitration Law provisions. See Art. 23-A of Law 8,987/95, as amended by Law 11,196/05; and Art. 11(III) of Law No. 11,079/04.

V. ECHOES OF THE CALVO DOCTRINE

At the time the Calvo Doctrine was born, it did not reflect the prevailing status of general international law. Though it was endorsed by many Latin American States, it did not reach wide acceptance outside the region or by international tribunals.[62]

It is of little value to discuss whether, at that time, the Calvo Doctrine was merely a tool or an actual aspiration to become the law of the nations.

The Calvo Doctrine was born out of the need to respond to what was perceived as the injustice of diplomatic protection and Western gunboat diplomacy.[63] It was, in Drago's words, "*a principle of American diplomacy*" designed as a forceful response to what were perceived to be, in particular, unacceptable European interventions in Latin America. It was maintained throughout the greater part of the twentieth century because it suited the political and economic policies of the States which supported it.

However, with the advent of globalization and the liberalization of international trade, such policy was no longer tenable and the Calvo Doctrine was quickly set aside.

Globalization; the internationalization of administrative contracts; the acceptance of arbitration in the administrative law field; the execution of BITs, FTAs and regional integration treaties providing for investor-State dispute settlement mechanisms; and the birth of international entities and rules to administer investment disputes such as the ICSID Convention have presented a complete new international adjudication system.

Investment arbitration – in particular, under the ICSID Convention – has been devised as an alternative to diplomatic protection[64] and appeared as a compromise between capital-exporting and developing countries.[65] As acknowledged by the International Court of Justice (ICJ),[66] the system of bilateral and multilateral agreements

---

62. See O.M. GARIBALDI, "Carlos Calvo Redivivus: the Rediscovery of the Calvo Doctrine in the Era of Investment Treaties", *op. cit.*, fn. 19.
63. See A. MOURRE, "Perspectives of International Arbitration in Latin America", *op. cit.*, fn. 57, p. 598.
64. See ICSID Convention, Art. 27.
65. While ICSID provides direct access to an international settlement mechanism, it sets aside diplomatic protection, so strongly questioned under the Calvo Doctrine. See Christoph H. SCHREUER with Loretta MALINTOPPI, August REINISCH and Anthony SINCLAIR, *The ICSID Convention. A Commentary*, 2nd edn. (2009) at pp. 415-416; Stephen M. SCHWEBEL, "A BIT about ICSID", 23 ICSID Rev. – FILJ (2008, no. 1) p. 1, at p. 4; Ben JURATOWITCH, "The Relationship Between Diplomatic Protection and Investment Treaties", 23 ICSID Rev. – FILJ (2008, no. 1) p. 10, at pp. 14-16.
66. In the *Case Concerning Ahmadou Sadio Diallo (Republic Of Guinea v. Democratic Republic of The Congo)* (Judgment of 24 May 2007 on preliminary objections) the ICJ held (para. 88):

"The Court is bound to note that, in contemporary international law, the protection of the rights of companies and the rights of their shareholders, and the settlement of the associated disputes, are essentially governed by bilateral or multilateral agreements for the protection of foreign investments, such as the treaties for the promotion and protection of foreign investments, and the Washington Convention of 18 March 1965 on the Settlement of Investment Disputes between States and Nationals of Other States, which created an International Centre for Settlement of Investment Disputes (ICSID), and also by contracts between States and foreign investors. In that

has effectively diminished the role of diplomatic protection. In that context, the Calvo Doctrine was seen as deprived of any relevant meaning.[67]

Though in place since 1966, the new mechanism of investment arbitration started to be tested on a relevant scale in the last fifteen years. The increasing number of disputes being submitted to international arbitration – mostly subject to international law and outside the control of national laws, policies and courts – has generated a backlash, which some have called a rediscovery of the Calvo Doctrine.

Unlike the phenomenon that gave place to the Calvo Doctrine, these reactions have occurred both in capital-exporting and developing countries, which were faced with a number of international claims.[68] This is an entirely new development in international law.[69] International arbitration has affected both developed[70] and developing countries and triggered attempts to limit litigation risks on both sides.[71]

---

context, the role of diplomatic protection somewhat faded, as in practice recourse is only made to it in rare cases where treaty regimes do not exist or have proved inoperative."

67. As the tribunal in *AES Corporation v. the Argentine Republic* (ICSID Case No. ARB/02/17), Decision on Jurisdiction of 26 April 2005, explained (paras. 98-99):

"… this very clause [the Calvo clause] only made sense by reference to the general international law rule of diplomatic protection; the 'Calvo Clause' was in essence a clause by which private persons mistakenly pretended to renounce to a right which in law did not belong to them but to their national State: the right for this State to exercise in favor of its nationals its diplomatic protection. Since under the ICSID system of settlement of disputes, exercise of diplomatic protection is per definition put aside, it is irrelevant to compare it with a clause the rationale of which is inseparable from diplomatic protection."

68. Within those States' boundaries, State representatives have questioned the constitutionality of international arbitration and even challenged the standards of treatment granted to foreign investors as being discriminatory against nationals. Supremacy of national law over international law has also been sought by asserting the State's right to subject ICSID awards to an internal review process.
69. As referred by Professor Orrego Vicuña, BITs originally drafted in the belief that developing countries ought to be restrained prove to impact on developed countries as well. See Francisco ORREGO VICUÑA, "Carlos Calvo, Honorary NAFTA Citizen", Keynote remarks made at the Conference on Regulatory Expropriations in International Law, New York University School of Law, 26 April 2002.
70. The United States is a paramount example of a leading country which has seen itself being a party to a large number of international arbitration cases. As of December 2009, the United States has faced more than fifteen international arbitration proceedings under NAFTA Chapter 11.
71. As Guillermo Aguilar Alvarez and William Park have explained in a prior ICCA Congress, "Thirty years ago the line between host and investor states was fairly clear. Nations such as Libya and Mexico were the host states; the United States and Canada were the investors. Today, however, NAFTA Chapter 11 has led to a role reversal, with the United States and Canada learning the 'down side' of arbitration." (Guillermo AGUILAR ALVAREZ and William PARK, "The New Face of Investment Arbitration: Capital Exporters as Host States under NAFTA Chapter 11" in *International Commercial Arbitration: Important Contemporary Questions*, ICCA Congress Series no. 11 (Kluwer Law International 2002) p. 392 at p. 423.)

Particularly interesting is the approach followed by the United States. A historical opponent to the Calvo Doctrine, it has recently adopted policies that can be described as sympathetic to that doctrine.

The United States

(i) has agreed to soften the protection provided by the fair and equitable treatment standard within NAFTA following the decision rendered in *Pope & Talbot v. Canada*,[72]
(ii) has restricted the scope of that very same standard and limited the concept of indirect expropriation even below customary international law in the 2004 model BIT[73] and
(iii) has adopted as its international negotiating policy that foreign investors should not be placed in a better position than US investors in the United States.[74] The view adopted

---

72. On 21 July 2001, the NAFTA Free Trade Commission issued a binding interpretation on the fair and equitable treatment standard. According to it,

    "Article 1105(1) prescribes the customary international law minimum standard of treatment of aliens as the minimum standard of treatment to be afforded to investments of investors of another Party. The concepts of 'fair and equitable treatment' and 'full protection and security' do not require treatment in addition to or beyond that which is required by the customary international law minimum standard of treatment of aliens. A determination that there has been a breach of another provision of the NAFTA, or of a separate international agreement, does not establish that there has been a breach of Article 1105(1)."

73. US State Department, Press Statement (5 February 2004) at <http://bilaterals.org/article.php3?id_article=137>. In line with NAFTA's interpretation of Art. 1105(1), the 2004 model BIT subjects the fair and equitable standard to the minimum treatment provided under customary international law. With respect to expropriation, see Stephen M. SCHWEBEL, "The United States 2004 Model Bilateral Investment Treaty: An Exercise in the Regressive Development of International Law", 3 TDM (April 2006, issue 2). The United States has embarked upon a review of its 2004 Model BIT. In that context, a group of leading business associations has expressed its support for a new Model BIT providing for stronger protections:

    "… we urge your Administration to embrace a strengthened and reenergized BIT program and to ensure the highest standard for the Model BIT's core obligations with respect to, among other things, 'fair and equitable treatment,' 'full protection and security,' and the obligation to provide compensation for expropriation. It is also vital to ensure that all economic sectors are covered by the BIT's protections and that investors in all sectors have the ability to use neutral and objective arbitration to resolve disputes with host states."

    (available at <www.transnational-dispute-management.com/members/recentlypublished/welcome.asp?v0=330> (last accessed 30 January 2010)).

74. Sect. 2102(b)(3), Public Law 107-210, 6 Aug. 2002, 116 Stat. 1995 (the 2002 Trade Act)

    ("Foreign investment.–Recognizing that United States law on the whole provides a high level of protection for investment, consistent with or greater than the level required by international law, the principal negotiating objectives of the United States regarding foreign investment are to reduce or eliminate artificial or trade-distorting barriers to foreign investment, while ensuring that foreign investors in the United States are not accorded greater substantive rights with respect to investment protections than United States investors in the United States, and to secure for

by the United States on the issue of "national treatment" seems to hit hard at the very same foundation of the investment treaty system.

While still a minority in their region, some Latin American States have either adopted measures consistent with the Calvo Doctrine or resorted to related arguments mainly for litigation purposes.[75]

Bolivia withdrew from the ICSID Convention on 2 May 2007[76] and amended its

---

> investors important rights comparable to those that would be available under United States legal principles and practice, by—
>
> (A) reducing or eliminating exceptions to the principle of national treatment;
> (B) freeing the transfer of funds relating to investments;
> (C) reducing or eliminating performance requirements, forced technology transfers, and other unreasonable barriers to the establishment and operation of investments;
> (D) seeking to establish standards for expropriation and compensation for expropriation, consistent with United States legal principles and practice;
> (E) seeking to establish standards for fair and equitable treatment consistent with United States legal principles and practice, including the principle of due process;
> (F) providing meaningful procedures for resolving investment disputes;
> (G) seeking to improve mechanisms used to resolve disputes between an investor and a government through–
> (i) mechanisms to eliminate frivolous claims and to deter the filing of frivolous claims;
> (ii) procedures to ensure the efficient selection of arbitrators and the expeditious disposition of claims;
> (iii) procedures to enhance opportunities for public input into the formulation of government positions; and
> (iv) providing for an appellate body or similar mechanism to provide coherence to the interpretations of investment provisions in trade agreements; and
> (H) ensuring the fullest measure of transparency in the dispute settlement mechanism, to the extent consistent with the need to protect information that is classified or business confidential, by–
> (i) ensuring that all requests for dispute settlement are promptly made public;
> (ii) ensuring that–
> (I) all proceedings, submissions, findings, and decisions are promptly made public; and
> (II) all hearings are open to the public; and
> (iii) establishing a mechanism for acceptance of amicus curiae submissions from businesses, unions, and nongovernmental organizations.").

75. In the latter trend, Argentina resorted to what Professor Schreuer has called Calvo's grandchildren to contest investment protections (Christoph SCHREUER, "Calvo's Grandchildren: the Return of Local Remedies in Investment Arbitration", 4 The Law and Practice of International Courts and Tribunals (2005, no. 1)). Among other arguments, it summarily has argued that investment cases need to be settled according to Argentine law, that contractually agreed dispute settlement provisions should supersede arbitral jurisdiction established under BITs and that the BITs' standards of treatment should be construed pursuant to domestic law and cannot afford foreign investors better treatment than that provided to nationals.
76. See Damon VIS-DUNBAR, Luke Eric PETERSON and Fernando CABRERA DIAZ, "Bolivia Notifies World Bank of Withdrawal from ICSID, Pursues BIT Revisions", available at <www.bilaterals.org/article.php3?id_article=8221&lang=en> (last accessed 30 January 2010); Cristina VITERI TORRES, "Withdrawal of States' Consent to ICSID Arbitration. Perspectives

Constitution in February 2009, adopting principles similar to those existing under the Calvo Doctrine.[77] Ecuador followed a similar path. On 4 December 2007, it notified ICSID that it would not consent to submitting to ICSID any disputes arising out of economic activities related to natural resources such as oil, gas, minerals and others.[78] Later on, subsequent to the approval of a new constitution,[79] Ecuador notified its withdrawal from the ICSID Convention on 6 July 2009.

VI. INTERNATIONALIZATION: MOVING FORWARDS OR BACKWARDS?

The development of both international and administrative law shows that progress does not necessary means always moving forward. More frequently than less, steps in one direction are followed by movements to the opposite side.

The burst of international arbitration – particularly in the investment law field; the recent trend towards admitting arbitration agreements in administrative contracts; and the influence of international law upon domestic administrative law have posed a number

---

from the Bolivian and Ecuadorian Cases", 6 TDM (2009, no. 4).

77. Under the new constitution, (i) Bolivian investments shall take precedence over foreign ones; (ii) foreign investments shall be subject to domestic laws and jurisdiction and no one could appeal to diplomatic claims to be granted more favorable treatment; and (iii) States and foreign companies shall not be granted more favorable conditions than those established for nationals (Art. 320 of the new Bolivian Constitution reads:

"*I. La inversión boliviana se priorizará frente a la inversión extranjera.*

II. Toda inversión extranjera estará sometida a la jurisdicción, a las leyes y a las autoridades bolivianas, y nadie podrá invocar situación de excepción, ni apelar a reclamaciones diplomáticas para obtener un tratamiento más favorable.

III. Las relaciones económicas con estados o empresas extranjeras se realizarán en condiciones de independencia, respeto mutuo y equidad. No se podrá otorgar a Estados o empresas extranjeras condiciones más beneficiosas que las establecidas para los bolivianos.

IV. El Estado es independiente en todas las decisiones de política económica interna, y no aceptará imposiciones ni condicionamientos sobre esta política por parte de estados, bancos o instituciones financieras bolivianas o extranjeras, entidades multilaterales ni empresas transnacionales.").

78. It further added that any instrument containing any such previous stated will to submit such type of dispute and not perfected through the other party's consent prior to the date of this notice was immediately withdrawn. See Ecuador's 4 December 2007 notice to ICSID available at <http://icsid.worldbank.org/ICSID/FrontServlet?requestType=ICSIDPublicationsRH&actionVal=ViewAnnouncePDF&AnnouncementType=regular&AnnounceNo=9.pdf> (last accessed 30 January 2010).

79. Ecuador's 2008 Constitution established limitations to international arbitration involving the State as a party. It prohibited execution of treaties or other international instruments through which Ecuador consents to submit contractual or commercial disputes with private parties to international arbitration. (Ecuador's 2008 Constitution, Art. 422; an exception was made with respect to treaties or other international instruments providing for dispute settlement mechanisms between the State and citizens of Latin America). The new Constitution further set forth that State contracts executed with foreign persons or companies shall imply their waiver of any diplomatic claims. (Ecuador's 2008 Constitution, Art. 307.)

of novel issues to States, private companies and legal practitioners. Internationalization of State contracts and dispute settlement mechanisms have never before been seen on the scale of the last decade.

Attempts to restrict the availability of investment arbitration or establish limitations to treaty standards should not necessarily be seen as an attempt to reawaken Calvo and its underlying policies. While isolated exceptions may certainly exist, by adopting those measures, States do not seem to be seriously seeking to change general international law, to limit the effects of globalization or to revert to older economic and trade models.

In sum, we can reasonably conclude that:

(i) Although coincidental in time, the traditional restrictive view of administrative law and the Calvo Doctrine towards the use of international law and jurisdictions was the result of diverse causes;
(ii) Pragmatism – not ideology – steers the conduct and policies of most States. While the Calvo Doctrine emerged as an answer to the international minimum standard of treatment and diplomatic protection, recent restrictive measures can be explained in many cases as efforts to balance what some see as an unprecedented and still largely unknown system which goes against a long-standing maxim: the sovereign does not like to be judged or controlled;
(iii) Reawakening the Calvo Doctrine would not only be a major step backwards but could lead to the reinstatement of the very same non-effective means of diplomatic protection against which such doctrine was created;
(iv) While administrative law could be originally found as supporting the Calvo Doctrine, that is no longer the case;
(v) Although until a few decades ago administrative law did not conceive that international elements – i.e., international agreements, guidelines issued by international institutions, foreign and global practices – could influence local rules and institutions, such a view has been gradually changing. Today, administrative law is increasingly abandoning its traditional local nature in order to seek harmonization through international standards;
(vi) A return of the Calvo Doctrine would oppose this process. To support internationalization of administrative law and contracts – implying an opening to international law and jurisdictions – and seek, at the same time, the re-establishment of ideas based on the primacy of local courts and domestic laws do not appear consistent with such process; and
(vii) Unless the current crisis finally develops into protectionism schemes (which still remains to be seen), administrative law today seems more in support of international standards and jurisdictions than in any way backing Calvo's return.

Mandatory Rules: What's a Lawyer to Do?

Josefa Sicard-Mirabal*

TABLE OF CONTENTS	Page
I. Introduction and Focus	348
II. What Are Mandatory Rules?	349
III. How Theories of Arbitration View Mandatory Rules	351
IV. The Main Competing Interests in Assessing the Applicability of Mandatory Rules	352
V. Mandatory Rules at the Enforcement Stage	354
VI. Final Comments	360

I. INTRODUCTION AND FOCUS

As I delved into the study of mandatory rules, I realized that much has been written and debated about the complexities and problems of the nature, methodology and application of mandatory rules in international arbitration. A number of scholars and practitioners have addressed issues concerning their applicability and scope. The definitive answer to questions posed remains elusive, but nonetheless of paramount importance.

Most of what has been written about mandatory rules has been with a view to provide guidance to arbitrators. Using such writings and discussions as my platform I will endeavor to focus on the role of the advocate in international arbitration when faced with issues relating to mandatory rules.

This analysis will start by defining mandatory rules and exploring how competing theories of arbitration approach mandatory rules. It will highlight the main interests that clash in the mandatory rules debate in the context of enforcement. Thereafter, as the crux of mandatory rules is truly seen and tested at the enforcement stage, I will briefly discuss how a national court may approach and interpret its role with respect to mandatory rules in a recognition or enforcement proceeding under the United Nations Convention on the Recognition and Enforcement of Foreign Arbitral Awards, New York, 1 June 1958 (the New York Convention). And finally I will venture to provide practical suggestions for counsel when faced with mandatory rules issues.

This paper does not address how mandatory rules interact with treaties, because the existence of a treaty – as opposed to merely a contract – introduces a plethora of unique legal issues at the enforcement stage that largely depend on the jurisprudence of the host

---

* Director for Arbitration and ADR in North America, International Court of Arbitration of the International Chamber of Commerce (ICC). Victoria Shannon and Suzanne Ulicny, Deputy Directors for Arbitration and ADR in North America, for the International Court of Arbitration of the ICC provided invaluable insights and assistance in earlier drafts.

country with respect to the status of treaties within its hierarchy of national law.[1] Furthermore, often the method of enforcement is built into the treaty itself, and not based on the parties bringing a recognition or enforcement action in court. Generally, however, the contractual relationship between the parties arbitrating pursuant to a treaty provision – usually, an investor and a State, but not always – necessarily bears a strong relation to the laws of the host State, because the host State is usually the place of performance, so mandatory rules of the host State are very likely to apply. A unique twist on the treatment of mandatory rules arises if the treaty specifies that certain mandatory rules do not apply or if the host State changes relevant mandatory rules between the signing of the treaty and the commencement of the dispute. Interpreting the treaty and the applicability of the relevant mandatory rules requires an additional layer of analysis that, while interesting, is beyond what can be accomplished in this brief analysis.[2]

II.   WHAT ARE MANDATORY RULES?

The term "mandatory rules" in English is ambiguous. It is defined differently depending on the context. One may define mandatory rules as rules that purportedly cannot be waived or forfeited, while others may define them as rules that the parties cannot contract around or opt out of by agreement.[3] Mandatory rules can be found in the law of the seat of the arbitration (lex arbitri), the applicable law of the contract (lex contractus), the place of performance and the place of enforcement; and, in any given arbitration some or all of these may apply. Mandatory rules are generally divided into two categories: procedural and substantive mandatory rules. Procedural mandatory rules are those that govern the legal process, while substantive mandatory rules determine the rights and obligations of the parties. Counsel should be less concerned about whether the rule is procedural or substantive and more interested in understanding the public policy rationale of the rule of the enacting State and determining whether that aim comports

---

1. For an in-depth discussion of mandatory rules in investment treaty arbitration, see Andrea K. BJORKLUND, "Mandatory Rules of Law and Investment Arbitration, 18 Am. Rev. Int'l Arb. (2007, nos. 1-2) pp. 175-204; Donald DONOVAN, *The Relevance (or Lack Thereof) of the Notion of 'Mandatory Rules of Law' to Investment Treaty Arbitration*, 18 Am. Rev. Int'l Arb. (2007, nos. 1-2) pp. 205-215.
2. In addition, the reader should note that treaties and conventions such as the Rome Convention, the Hague Conventions on Agency, the International Monetary Fund Agreement of 1945 and others offer varied examples of the guidelines agreed upon among signatory nations for interpreting and applying foreign laws of other signatory nations and the public policy considerations raised by such interpretation and application. For a further discussion of these issues, see Hannah L. BUXBAUM, "Mandatory Rules in Civil Litigation: Status of the Doctrine Post-Globalization", 18 Am. Rev. Int'l Arb. (2007, nos. 1-2) pp. 27-28; Audley SHEPPARD, "Mandatory Rules in International Arbitration – An English Law Perspective", 18 Am. Rev. Int'l Arb. (2007, nos. 1-2) pp. 126-130.
3. For more on the definition of mandatory rules, see Andrew BARRACLOUGH and Jeff WAINCYMER, "Mandatory Rules of Law in International Commercial Arbitration", 6 Melb. J. Int'l L. (2005) pp. 205-207; Catherine KESSEDJIAN, "Mandatory Rules of Law in International Arbitration: What Are Mandatory Rules?", 18 Am. Rev. Int'l Arb. (2007, nos. 1-2) pp. 147-149.

with or clashes with the aims of the enforcing State.[4] Using the Dominican Republic as an example, rules relating to national security, parental rights, marriage and property ownership are substantive, while the obligation of the enforcing party to identify the assets that are the object of the enforcement is an example of a procedural mandatory rule.[5]

So, how "mandatory" are mandatory rules? The debate still continues as to what test or standard an arbitral tribunal should apply to determine whether a mandatory rule is truly mandatory.[6] The core of this debate remains whether the parties can choose to defy a mandatory rule, or whether the arbitral tribunal can choose to ignore a mandatory rule, and yet simultaneously expect that the award rendered will be enforceable in the relevant jurisdiction(s).

This, of course, begs the question, *what is the true test of enforceability?*[7] If both parties choose to voluntarily comply with the award as rendered,[8] then there is no petition to a court of law to test the enforceability of the award, nor is there any dissenting voice to contest the non-application or incorrect application of a mandatory rule. Furthermore,

---

4. Public policy is the infrastructure upon which States develop mandatory rules. Public policy or *ordre public* is the body of principles that underpin the operation of legal systems in each State. It addresses the social, moral and economic values that tie a society together; values that vary in different cultures and change over time. For a discussion on the notion of public policy, see Audley SHEPPARD, "Public Policy and the Enforcement of Arbitral Awards: Should There Be a Global Standard?", 1 Transnat'l Disp. Mgm't (Feb. 2004, no. 1) available at <www.transnational-disputemanagement.com/samples/freearticles/tv1-1article_67.htm>; Yves DERAINS, "Public Policy and the Law Applicable to the Dispute in International Arbitration" in *Comparative Arbitration Practice and Public Policy in Arbitration*, ICCA Congress Series no. 3 (1987) p. 227.

5. For a list of mandatory rules of procedure for recognition and enforcement of foreign arbitral awards, with reference to Arts. III and IV of the New York Convention on a country-by-country basis, please see *Guide to National Rules of Procedure for Recognition and Enforcement of New York Convention Awards: Report from the ICC Commission on Arbitration*, ICC Int'l Ct. Arb. Bull. Special Supplement (2008).

6. This paper addresses the author's formulation of a mandatory rules balancing test alluded to in Alexander K.A. GREENAWALT, "Does International Arbitration Need a Mandatory Rules Method?", 18 Am. Rev. Int'l Arb. (2007, nos. 1-2) pp. 110-119, 147-149 (describing the mandatory rules balancing test). However, there are several approaches and tests described in the vast literature on this subject. For example, for a discussion on the "special connection" and "parties' legitimate expectations" methods, see Andrew BARRACLOUGH and Jeff WAINCYMER, supra fn. 3, at pp. 227-235. For a comparison of the treatment of mandatory rules during the arbitration stage and the enforcement stage, see Catherine KESSEDJIAN, supra fn. 3, at pp. 151-153. For an example applying one version of "the mandatory rules method" to a case involving the United States' Racketeer Influenced and Corrupt Organizations Act (RICO), see Serge LAZAREFF, "Mandatory Extraterritorial Application of National Law", 11 Arb. Int'l (1995, no. 2) pp. 137-150.

7. For a discussion of enforceability in light of mandatory rules, see Andrew BARRACLOUGH and Jeff WAINCYMER, supra fn. 3, at pp. 215-216; Serge LAZAREFF, supra fn. 6, at pp. 137-143; Catherine KESSEDJIAN, supra fn. 3, at pp. 151-153.

8. In arbitrations under the Rules of Arbitration of the International Court of Arbitration of the International Chamber of Commerce (ICC), it is reported that in over eighty percent of ICC cases parties voluntarily comply with ICC awards.

a State cannot *sua sponte* enforce a mandatory rule; it must wait until one of the parties petitions the court for relief or brings an action to enforce the resulting award. It is highly doubtful that parties would advocate for the interests of the State enacting the mandatory rule, if the parties' dispute has been satisfactorily resolved.

Since the State must rely on the judgment of the arbitrators, and the contentiousness of the parties to raise the State's interests in its stead, or wait for an enforcement proceeding to be brought in its jurisdiction, *does compliance then substitute for enforceability by rendering the issue moot, even though perhaps the award may have been set aside had it been challenged for lack of compliance with a mandatory rule?* Leaving this question aside, it would appear that it is only when the parties do not voluntarily comply with the award that the enforcement stage and the methods of determining enforceability become the ultimate battleground of the mandatory rules debate.

Assessing the importance and compatibility of mandatory rules requires the arbitrator issuing the award, or the State court at the enforcement stage, to develop or adopt a rule or method for determining the position of mandatory rules in the hierarchy of law applicable to a particular arbitration. In addition to consulting the jurisprudence of the laws of the enacting and enforcing States, the decision-maker or counsel should consider the treatment of mandatory rules along the sliding scale of theories of arbitration.

III. HOW THEORIES OF ARBITRATION VIEW MANDATORY RULES

At the extreme ends of the spectrum lie the pure contractualist and the pure jurisdictionalist schools of thought, which respectively, espouse party autonomy and governmental interests as supreme. Reality, as is often the case in many arenas, is somewhere in between.

1. Pure Contractualists

Pure contractualists see arbitration as fully premised upon party autonomy with States having no right to impose their will upon the parties' contractually agreed-upon arbitral process.[9] A pure contractualist would declare that arbitrators are not bound to apply any mandatory rules, because the arbitrator's primary duty is to the will of the parties. The basic premise is that arbitration is a creature of agreement; mandatory rules not mentioned in the contract or not explicitly agreed to by the parties are thus unenforceable. An arbitrator is only obliged to enforce the parties' agreement and is not obliged to champion the State's interest in promulgating its mandatory rules.

2. Pure Jurisdictionalists

Pure jurisdictionalists, on the other hand, see arbitration as necessarily tied to the interests of the State. The State is always involved in the arbitration process whether it is through the governing law of the contract, the physical presence of the parties during

---

9. See Andrew BARRACLOUGH and Jeff WAINCYMER, supra fn. 3, at pp. 209-210.

the course of conduct, or by bringing an enforcement action in a State court. No arbitration is devoid of a connection to a State; every transaction or dispute is tied to a place within the boundaries of one or more States. Thus, a pure jurisdictionalist would affirm that arbitrators have a duty to enforce all applicable mandatory rules, because arbitration exists at the pleasure of the State. States have a sovereign interest in regulating conduct within their borders, whether that conduct be performing a contract (i.e., place of performance), holding arbitration (i.e., seat of arbitration) or enforcing an arbitral award (i.e., place of enforcement).

3.   *The Hybrid Theory*

The hybrid theory is a mixture of these two theories and has proven to be a much better approximation of what really happens, especially since international arbitration is a field of law in which common practice speaks just as much – or more – to what is acceptable as the academic theories themselves. The hybrid theory is not fully defined, as there is a vast universe of possibilities between the two aforementioned extremes.[10] What has emerged from all of this is a balancing test with common practical application called "the mandatory rules method".[11]

4.   *The Mandatory Rules Method*

The mandatory rules method states that the application and enforcement of mandatory rules depends on the balancing of: (1) party autonomy, (2) the relevance of the rule to the parties' transaction or contractual relationship, and (3) the State's interests, including its rationale for why its mandatory rule should apply to the parties' contractual dispute.[12] Let us further explore these competing interests and how they affect the treatment of mandatory rules.

IV.   THE MAIN COMPETING INTERESTS IN ASSESSING THE APPLICABILITY OF MANDATORY RULES

1.   *Party Autonomy*

The most highly touted advantage of arbitration is party autonomy, because parties have the flexibility and freedom to tailor the dispute resolution process to fit their specific case requirements. Parties have a plethora of choices in arbitration with respect to language, location, arbitrator selection, applicable arbitration rules and procedures and arbitral institutions. The logical question then is, *if arbitration is born out of party autonomy through*

---

10. *Ibid.* at pp. 210-211.
11. For a more in-depth treatment of the subject, see Andrew BARRACLOUGH and Jeff WAINCYMER, supra fn. 3, at pp. 206-209; Catherine KESSEDJIAN, supra fn. 3, at pp. 147-149.
12. See supra fn. 6.

the parties' contractual relationship, why should mandatory rules unspecified in the contract receive special treatment?

2. *Relevance of the Rule*

The answer, surprisingly, comes from contract law itself, which brings us to our second interest: the relevance of the rule to the parties' transaction or contractual relationship. Despite the impression of complete party autonomy, such autonomy can only exist under the legal framework of a State's laws. It is the State that defines capacity to contract in its laws and grants the parties the right to choose the law of the governing law of a contract. Yet, if the parties do not exercise the right to choose the law, that choice may be made for them by an arbitral tribunal or by a court when a dispute is commenced. Additionally, the place of performance of the contract may present laws and regulations that govern the specific conduct that is the subject of the contract, even if that place is not named in the contract. For example, if a Japanese car company purchases car parts manufactured in China for cars that will eventually be sold in the United States, then both the car parts and the parties must comply with the regulations of the National Highway Traffic Safety Administration in the United States. Finally, in order to enforce an award in a court of law, parties must comply with the procedural rules of the venue, wherever that may be.

Thus, States impliedly touch all aspects of both the transaction and the arbitration proceeding. The relevance of the rule to the parties' transaction or contractual relationship stems from the nexus between the parties' actions under a contract and the effects of such actions within the territory of a specific State. Therefore, the mandatory rules of the affected State have relevance to the subject matter of the contract, even if that State is not mentioned in the contract and, more particularly, when the affected State expressly regulates the conduct or industry in question.

3. *States' Interests*

As mentioned above, several States may have an interest in a particular arbitration, which brings us to our third competing interest: the State's interests, including its rationale for why a mandatory rule should apply to the parties' contractual dispute. In the context of mandatory rules, the States' interests generally fall within two categories: the interests of the enacting State and the interests of the enforcing State.

a.   Interests of the enacting State
The enacting State is the State that enacts the mandatory legislation in order to promote a particular public policy interest. The interests of the enacting State are given the most importance when the law of that State is chosen by the parties. The law applicable to the contract (lex contractus) holds the most influence over substantive aspects of the dispute, while the choice of the seat of arbitration (lex arbitri) holds the most influence over procedural aspects of the arbitration. Thus, the lex contractus is the primary source of substantive mandatory rules and the lex arbitri is the primary source of procedural mandatory rules.

When either the lex contractus or the lex arbitri is unspecified by the contract, or when there is disagreement among parties about which law to choose, the arbitral tribunal normally chooses.

b. Interests of the enforcing State

The second category of State interests that affect the importance of a mandatory rule are the interests of the enforcing State. Consideration of the enforcing State's interests is the most common scenario in what is known as the "the third State mandatory rule problem".[13] The "third State" is a State not specified in a contract but whose mandatory rules may be applicable to a given contract. The "third State" is usually the enforcing State or the State where the contract is to be performed (if that State is not specified by the lex contractus or lex arbitri). The place of enforcement is rarely specified in the contract, and it can be very difficult to predict which States will be the enforcing States during arbitral proceedings for several reasons, including, changes affecting a party's assets (the depletion, transfer or creation of new assets), or fundamental corporate changes affecting the corporation (insolvency, mergers, acquisitions or dissolutions).

Thus, for several reasons, the enforcing State may be a wildcard in international arbitration, particularly with respect to the application and effect of mandatory rules. If the mandatory rules applied during the arbitration proceeding complement (or at least do not conflict with) the mandatory rules of the enforcing State, then the award will likely be enforced, absent a grave procedural error. *However, what happens when the law of the enacting State conflicts with the law of the enforcing State?* This issue will be further expounded under the section discussing the enforcement stage in the following section.

V. MANDATORY RULES AT THE ENFORCEMENT STAGE

This section seeks to expand on the question raised above, *what happens when the law of the enacting State conflicts with the law of the enforcing State?* The goal of arbitration, in the end, is party compliance with the result, whether voluntary or compelled by court. As mentioned in the Introduction, when parties voluntarily comply with the award, issues with respect to the application or interpretation of mandatory rules become moot. Now I will turn to the second, increasingly more common scenario – the bringing of an enforcement action in a State court.

1. Treatment of Mandatory Rules Under the New York Convention

While an arbitral award may be enforced under one of several international conventions, or even under the domestic law of the enforcing State, I will only discuss enforcement under the New York Convention, because this is the most recognized international agreement for the enforcement of arbitral awards.

---

13. See George A. BERMANN, "Introduction: Mandatory Rules of Law in International Arbitration", 18 Am. Rev. Int'l Arb. (2007, nos. 1-2) pp. 7-15; Laurence SHORE, "Applying Mandatory Rules of Law in International Commercial Arbitration", 18 Am. Rev. Int'l Arb. (2007, nos. 1-2) p. 95.

Generally, the New York Convention mandates enforcement of an arbitral award by a national court in a signatory country, unless an exception applies. Defenses to enforcement under the New York Convention are construed narrowly, "to encourage recognition and enforcement of commercial arbitration agreement in international contracts".[14] Let us look at how mandatory rules intersect with those exceptions.

2. *The Uncontroversial Exceptions*

The exceptions enumerated under Art. V(1) of the New York Convention are general exceptions that are uncontroversial in their application and interpretation with respect to the application of mandatory laws. This list of exceptions addresses obvious procedural defects, jurisdictional defects and well-established universal principles of contract law and due process. There are five such "uncontroversial exceptions." Art. V(1)(*a*) addresses incapacity to contract or invalidity of the contract, which references general and universal principles of contract law. Art. V(1)(*b*) addresses lack of notice and the inability of a party to present its case, which references procedural due process. Art. V(1)(*c*) references ultra petita ruling, or a ruling beyond the scope of the authority given to the arbitrators in the arbitration clause. Art. V(1)(*d*) references the composition of the tribunal and the authority of the arbitral institution, which reference procedural and jurisdictional defects, respectively. Finally, Art. V(1)(*e*) addresses the situation when an award is not yet binding on the parties, or has been set aside or suspended, which references the procedural posture of the award (i.e., only final awards may be enforced under the New York Convention).

3. *The Authority of the Enforcing Court*

Art. V(2) of the New York Convention lists the two exceptions in favor of broad authority of the enforcing court. Under these two exceptions, the mandatory rule of the enforcing State trumps the mandatory rule of the enacting State.

Art. V(2)(*a*) states that the enforcing court may deny enforcement if the arbitrability of the subject matter of the dispute is barred or constrained by mandatory rules of the enforcing State.[15]

Art. V(2)(*b*) states that the enforcing court may deny enforcement if the award would be contrary to the public policy of the country where enforcement is sought. The New York Convention does not define "public policy", but defers to norms of the enforcing

---

14. See *Karaha Bodas Co., v. Perusahaan Petambangan Minyak Dan Gas Bumi Negara*, 364 F.3rd 274, 288 (5th), *cert.denied*, 543 U.S. 917 (2004).
15. See Donald DONOVAN, "The Public Policy Defense in Recognition of Enforcement of Foreign Arbitral Awards in US Courts" in *Global Reflections on International Law, Commerce and Dispute Resolution: Liber Amicorum in Honour of Robert Briner* (2005) p. 235.

State.[16] "Public policy" is translated as *orden público* in Spanish or *ordre public* in French, but the actual interpretation of those words is slightly different in each legal tradition.

For example, in the United States – a common law country – public policy arises at the legislative level through the interpretation of existing constitutional or federal law and at the judicial level, in the course of tracing prior case precedents that declare certain rights and obligations to be public policy norms. Shifts in public policy happen as new cases arise or as the sentiment of the populace, the electorate or the judiciary changes with the modernizing world. The United States is unique in this system of codified law co-existing with "judge-made" case law. Both types of law are relatively equal in stature, and public policy norms can arise through either or both. In this way, public policy in the United States is an ever-shifting target. What was acceptable public policy in the nineteenth century may not be acceptable or even relevant today. When looking to the New York Convention to enforce an arbitral award in the face of a public policy rule of the United States, usually the appropriate source is case law or legislative history, and this source is interpreted by examining how prior US courts have addressed the matter and built upon precedents. This analysis is further complicated by the unique dual legal framework of federalism in the United States, which allows both national public policy and individual states' public policies to be equally applicable to a given situation, with federal public policy reigning supreme in the event of a conflict.[17]

In the Dominican Republic – a civil law country – *orden público* is divided into domestic and international realms, in contrast to the American system of federalism. Under Dominican law, *orden público* must be expressed through the legal framework in an authoritative, codified text. Thus, while public policy in the United States can be instantly affected by the judge's pen in a precedential case in a given jurisdiction, *orden público* is far more concrete, established and identifiable in the Dominican Republic.[18]

As a third example, in France – also a civil law country – a rule of *ordre public* is defined as a rule that has the goal of protecting a fundamental interest of the society

---

16. Under existing US case law, a foreign arbitration award violates public policy within the meaning of Art. V(2)(b) of the New York Convention "only when the award violates some explicit public policy that is well-defined and ... is ascertained by reference to the laws and legal precedents and not from general consideration of supposed public interests". *Indus. Risk Insurers v. M.A.N. Gutehoffnungshütte GmbH*, 141 F.3d 1434, 1445 (11th Cir. 1998). "Public policy arguments [under the New York Convention] should be accepted with caution, so as not to discourage enforcement of United States arbitration awards by courts of other countries." *MGM Productions Group, Inc. v. Aeroflot Russian Airlines*, No. 03 Civ. 0500, 2003 WL 21108367, at *5 (S.D.N.Y. 14 May 2003), *aff'd*, 91 Fed. App. 716 (2d Cir.), *cert. denied*, 543 U.S. 956 (2004). It is important to note that under the New York Convention, the burden is on the party opposing enforcement of the award. See *Europcar Italia S.p.A. v. Maiellano Tours, Inc.*, 156 F.3d 310, 313 (2d Cir. 1998).
17. For further reading on the sources, evolution and interpretation of public policy in the United States, see James E. ANDERSON, *Public Policymaking: an Introduction*, 7th edn. (Wadsworth Publishing 2010); Thomas J. BIRKLAND, *An Introduction to the Policy Process: Theories, Concepts, and Models of Public Policy Making*, 2nd edn. (M.E. Sharpe 2005).
18. For further reading on the sources, evolution and interpretation of public policy in the Dominican Republic, see Jorge A. SUBERO ISA, *4 (I.E. Cuatro) Años De Jurisprudencia Analitica Dominicana, 1985-1988*, 1st edn. (Asociación Hipólito Herrera Billini, Santo Domingo 1993.); S. C. J., 16 April 1986, B. J. 905, p. 272 [Supreme Court of Justice of the Dominican Republic].

concerned.[19] Similarly to the Dominican Republic, in France, *ordre public* is divided into two categories: *ordre public interne* (domestic public policy) and *ordre public international* (international public policy).[20] Still, there are certainly areas of overlap. Under the heading *ordre public interne*, one finds concepts such as *dispositions imperatives* (mandatory rules in domestic law that cannot be derogated by contract) and *lois d'application immediate* (another name for *loi de police* applicable to domestic matters).[21] By contrast, under the heading *ordre public international*, one finds concepts such as *lois de police* (mandatory rules in private international law that cannot be derogated by contract) and *règles d'ordre public* (rules applicable after the conflict of laws analysis has deemed that foreign law applies).[22] In sum, the French concept of *ordre public* is a heading for a wide variety of mandatory laws that have differing levels of gravitas and differing methods of application.

Despite these differences in the sources and codification of public policy norms in various jurisdictions, the essence and application is the same. As mentioned above, under the New York Convention, an enforcing court will defer to the public policy norms of its own jurisdiction when applying the public policy exception of Art. V(2)(b). Thus, the enforcing court in each of the jurisdictions described above would be well versed in the sources, interpretation and application of its own State's public policy jurisprudence.

So, what's a lawyer to do?

Is there any "clear" guidance or consensus as to what mandatory rules may be applied? Fortunately, there is a dim light at the end of the tunnel. There are situations, albeit not without controversy, that have been generally accepted as warranting the application of mandatory rules: force majeure, transnational public policy, mandatory rules of the lex contractus and mandatory rules of the seat of the arbitration.

4. Force Majeure

Arbitrators may apply the principle of force majeure to mandatory rules which make performance of contractual obligations impossible. This application, however, is not applied based on force majeure as a mandatory rule, but rather as part of the lex contractus.[23]

---

19. See Catherine KESSEDJIAN, "Public Order in European Law", 1 Erasmus L. Rev. (2007, no. 1) p. 25, at p. 29.
20. See Marco PISTIS, "Italy: The Rome Convention: Different Approaches", MONDAQ, 4 June 2006, <www.mondaq.com/article.asp?articleid=40212>.
21. See Janeen CARRUTHERS and Elizabeth CRAWFORD, "Variations on a Theme of Rome II. Reflections on Proposed Choice of Law Rules for Non-Contractual Obligations: Part I", 9 Edinburgh L. Rev. (Jan. 2005) p. 65, at p. 92 ; Catherine Kessedjian, supra fn. 19, at p. 25.
22. See Janeen CARRUTHERS and Elizabeth CRAWFORD, supra fn. 21, at p. 92. For a discussion of the difference between a *loi de police* and a *règle d'ordre public*, see Catherine KESSEDJIAN, supra fn. 19, at pp. 26-27.
23. For further expansion, see Emmanuel GAILLARD and John SAVAGE eds., *Fouchard Gaillard Goldman on International Commercial Arbitration* (1999) pp. 847-858.

5. *Transnational Public Policy*

Transnational public policy, also called norms of *jus cogens*, encompasses the fundamental values, ethical and moral principles that are generally accepted by the international community.[24] *Jus cogens* (literally, "compelling law") refers to fundamental norms of transnational public policy that transcend and preempt other ordinary rules of international law. Norms of *jus cogens* limit the ability of States to create or change rules of international law and prevent States from committing violations of the fundamental rules of international public policy that would be seriously detrimental to the international legal system.[25]

The Vienna Convention on the Law of Treaties has recognized the norms of *jus cogens* in Art. 53, which states that:

> "A treaty is void, if, at the time of its conclusion, it conflicts with a peremptory norm of general international law. For the purpose of the present convention, a peremptory norm of general international law is a norm accepted and recognized by the international community of States as a whole, as a norm from which no derogation is permitted and which can be modified only by a subsequent norm of general international law having the same character."[26]

The Restatement on Foreign Relations of the United States ("Restatement") defines *jus cogens* to include the prohibition against genocide; slavery and the slave trade; murder or disappearance of individuals; torture or other cruel, inhuman or degrading treatment or punishment; prolonged arbitrary detention; systematic racial discrimination; and "the principles of the United Nations Charter prohibiting the use of force".[27] Because of the gravity of these and other recognized injustices, norms of *jus cogens* bind all States regardless of whether they have consented to the application of these norms, and it is considered virtually criminal for private parties or States to contract out of *jus cogens* rules or even to object to them.[28]

The concept of *jus cogens* is often mentioned in the same breath as the concepts of public policy, *orden público* or *ordre public*, discussed above. The distinction lies in the method of creation. Laws regarding public policy are either created by a single State unilaterally to protect fundamental societal values within its own borders or those

---

24. See Martin HUNTER and Gui CONDE E SILVA, "Transnational Public Policy and its Application in Investment Arbitrations", 4 J. World Inv. (June 2003, no. 3) p. 367.
25. See Kamrul HOSSAIN, "The Concept of *Jus Cogens* and the Obligation Under the U.N. Charter", 3 Santa Clara J. of Int'l L. (2005) p. 72 at p. 73.
26. *Ibid.*, at pp. 75-76; Evan CRIDDLE and Evan FOX-DECENT, "A Fiduciary Theory of Jus Cogens", 34 Yale J. of Int'l L. (2009) p. 331 at pp. 337-338.
27. See Evan CRIDDLE and Evan FOX-DECENT, supra fn. 26, at pp. 331-332.
28. For example, the International Law Commission (ILC) Commentary to Art. 19 of the Draft Articles on State Responsibility stated that the intent of Art. 19 was to ensure that violations of *jus cogens* "shall be recognized as an 'international crime', not only by some particular group of States, even if it constitutes a majority, but by all the essential components of the international community". See Kamrul HOSSAIN, supra fn. 25, at pp. 80-81.

affecting its society by business conducted outside its borders (e.g., place of performance), or they are created by multiple States at the regional or international level through treaties, conventions, or other international agreements.[29] In essence, rules of public policy are rules that have been *negotiated*, either by a lawmaking body within a State or between States by their leaders and delegates, and are often memorialized on paper. By contrast, norms of *jus cogens* arise within the international legal order. Such rules exist and apply to all States even without their agreement or consent.[30]

6.   *Mandatory Rules of the Lex Contractus*

It is important to distinguish whether the applicable law was chosen by the parties or selected by the arbitral tribunal. Under the former scenario, the arbitrator is bound to apply the law specified by the party, while under the latter, the response is not uniform. The majority of commentators agree that arbitrators should choose the substantive law that best accords with the parties' legitimate expectations. Then, the arbitral tribunal may apply the mandatory rules of the chosen country.[31]

7.   *Rules of the Seat*

As discussed above, the pure jurisdictionalists and the pure contractualists would hold opposing positions as to the application of mandatory rules of the seat of the arbitration. The pure contractualists would apply no mandatory rules and the pure jurisdictionalists would consent in applying all. Despite the apparent contraposition, both the pure contractualists and the pure jurisdictionalists agree in applying the procedural mandatory rules of the seat of the arbitration.

This position is aligned with Art. 35 of the Rules of Arbitration of the International Court of Arbitration (the ICC Court) of the International Chamber of Commerce (the ICC Rules) when it states that arbitrators should "make every effort to make sure that the Award is enforceable at law". In addition, under Art. 27 of the ICC Rules, after the closing of the proceedings, the arbitral tribunal draws up a draft award and submits it to the ICC Court for scrutiny. The ICC Court may lay down modifications as to form and, without affecting the arbitral tribunal's liberty of decision, may draw its attention to points of substance. In scrutinizing draft awards, the ICC Court considers, to the extent practicable, the requirements of mandatory rules at the place of arbitration.[32]

---

29. See Catherine KESSEDJIAN, supra fn. 19, at p. 26.
30. *Ibid.*
31. For further reading and expansion on this topic, see Yves DERAINS, supra fn. 4, at pp. 244-247.
32. See Art. 6, Internal Rules of the International Court of Arbitration app. II, ICC Rules of Arbitration (1998).

VI. FINAL COMMENTS

As we have surmised from this brief analysis of the application and implementation of mandatory rules, it is a complex and, for the most part, an unsettled subject. Thus, with the ever increasing number of arbitrations due to globalization, it behooves arbitration practitioners, users and arbitral institutions alike to develop a "global" standard for the application of mandatory rules.

There are a number of steps a counsel can take to prepare herself for the eventual application of mandatory rules:

First, *follow the money.* What good is a contract, if at the end you cannot enforce your rights and obligations? The expression "follow the money" comes from my early corporate transactional experience, when a former partner and friend would recommend that you always keep the money in view in a transaction by following the movement of the money from beginning to end. If you only focus on the amount you will obtain at the closing of the deal, you are not "following the money". Thus, following the money implies that you become whole if the transaction goes sour. The point to counsel here is that, during the due diligence stage, before a dispute should ever arise, counsel negotiating the deal should seek to find out where the other party's assets are located.

Second, **own the process**. Draft the arbitration clause and choose the seat of arbitration or the country of the applicable law of the contract where the assets lie. If your contract (which is the subject of the dispute) does not have a choice of law clause, the arbitrators will generally apply the choice of law principles of the jurisdiction in which they are sitting in order to determine which law to apply. Counsel should not take a chance on what law will be applied, because the results can be very different, and the legal debate and analysis on choice of law may turn out costly.

Third, **know the law**. As we have discussed, arbitration must occur in a physical place, i.e., within a State, and that State and its laws will necessarily affect the arbitration process. Even after you have chosen the law governing the dispute, counsel should become knowledgeable on the national law of the place where the arbitration will take place and the conflict of laws under that national law. The lex arbitri will be the law a party must resort to if it must compel or stay arbitration or if the arbitration organization's rules must be enforced in order to, for example, remove an arbitrator. In addition, if the award will be enforced in the jurisdiction where the arbitration occurred (and where the losing party has assets), the lex arbitri will have an effect on the extent to which the award may be challenged.

In addition, bearing in mind that public policy will play a major role under the New York Convention in the recognition and enforcement of the award, counsel should become familiar with the mandatory rules and public policy laws of countries where enforcement may be sought. Mandatory rules of the enforcing State will be honored over any choice of governing law made by the parties, so parties must determine where their award might be enforced and what mandatory law might apply in that jurisdiction in order to consider the extent to which that law should be presented and argued before the arbitral tribunal.

Finally, if counsel has to enforce an award in a jurisdiction with mandatory rules adverse to her position, "*agree with your adversary quickly*, while you are on the way with him, lest your adversary delivers you to the judge…".[33]

---

33. Matthew 5:25, New King James Bible version.

State Immunity, Public Policy and International Commercial Arbitration

*Teresa Cheng, SC**

TABLE OF CONTENTS	Page
I. Introduction	362
II. State Immunity	363
III. *Lex Lata* for a Practice to Acquire the Status of Customary International Law	364
IV. The Principle of Persistent Objector	367
V. Immunity From Suit and Immunity from Execution	370
VI. Enforcing Awards Against Foreign States Under the New York Convention	371
VII. Art. III of the New York Convention – Jurisdictional Question	373
VIII. Waiver	374
IX. Expressed Waiver	374
X. Public Policy	375
XI. Alleged Fraud	376
XII. Impossibility	376
XIII. Third-party Funding	377
XIV. Conclusion	379
XV. Postscript	380

I. INTRODUCTION

The relationship between State immunity and public policy in international commercial arbitrations in the context of enforcement of arbitral awards is reviewed below. As to public policy, one phenomenon that seems to have been prevailing is the funding of arbitrations or enforcement proceedings by third parties. Before proceeding to consider the arguments as to whether there are any grounds under the 1958 New York Convention to refuse enforcement in such situations, the threshold question of jurisdiction when a foreign State is impleaded will also be reviewed.

Whilst it is universally accepted that waiver of immunity from suit has been established when parties appear before an arbitral tribunal whether by reason of the arbitration agreement or conduct, the question of whether such arbitration agreement is tantamount to a waiver before a national court in enforcement proceedings under the New York Convention has to be considered as part of the determination of the jurisdictional question regarding State immunity. In relation to that, when and how a

---

* Senior Counsel; Vice President, ICC International Court of Arbitration; Vice Chair, Hong Kong International Arbitration Centre; Past President, Chartered Institute of Arbitrators; Adjunct Professor, Hong Kong University and Hong Kong Polytechnic University; Vice President of ICCA.

waiver is established differs and turns not only just on the wording of the arbitration agreement but importantly on the relevant legal principles applicable to each New York Convention State.

II. STATE IMMUNITY

It is unnecessary but nonetheless important to remind oneself of the origin of the rules of public international law that are applicable to the doctrine of State immunity: the rule *par in parem non habet imperium.*

Although States are by their nature not equal as regards power, territory and the like, they are, as members of the community of nations, in principle equal. This is a consequence of their sovereignty in the international sphere.[1]

A consequence of the legal equality of States is that no State can claim jurisdiction over another – according to the rule *par in parem non habet imperium.*[2]

In *Holland v. Lampen-Wolfe*,[3] Lord Millett said at 1583E:

> "… The immunity does not derive from the authority or dignity of sovereign states or the need to protect the integrity of their governmental functions. It derives from the sovereign nature of the exercise of the state's adjudicative powers and the basic principle of international law that all states are equal. The rule is '*par in parem non habet imperium*….'"

The essence of the general principle of State immunity can therefore be summarized in the form of two principles:

1. The leading principle of international law that there is a duty not to intervene in the internal affairs of other States or to apply measures of coercion to their property. This is a principle of subject-matter jurisdiction.
2. The forum State should not assume jurisdiction in respect of disputes involving States which have not submitted to the jurisdiction of the municipal courts of the forum. This is the basic principle of immunity.

When it is said that the common law (or public international law) recognizes the principle of absolute immunity this involves a conventional mode of expressing the law. In fact what is involved is the general principle of jurisdictional immunity. This principle has always admitted exceptions, based upon waiver of immunity or bilateral treaty provisions.

The basis of this general principle of jurisdictional immunity is the leading principle of public international law that there is a duty not to intervene in the internal affairs of other States, or to apply measures of coercion to their property. This is a principle of subject-matter jurisdiction.

---

1. *Oppenheim's International Law*, 9th edn., Vol. 1, Part 1 at Sect. 107.
2. *Ibid.*
3. [2000] 1 WLR 1573 (HL).

In the context of the constitutional framework of Hong Kong, the Basic Law is the supreme law governing its constitution, the preservation of the capitalist and social system and the limits of its autonomy. Hong Kong is a Special Administrative Region of the State of the People's Republic of China (PRC). It has an independent immigration, customs, police and tax system. It has autonomy on all matters save those relating to foreign affairs and national defence. There are matters for which the Central People's Government of the PRC is responsible as expressly set out in the Basic Law. The relevant principle of immunity applicable to Hong Kong is therefore that of the PRC. This is trite and in no way affected by the ability of Hong Kong to continue to adopt or apply the common law, for only such part of the common law that is not in contravention of the Basic Law can survive the resumption of sovereignty.[4] Foreign affairs of Hong Kong is a matter for the Central People's Government and for which Hong Kong has no autonomy.[5]

III. LEX LATA FOR A PRACTICE TO ACQUIRE THE STATUS OF CUSTOMARY INTERNATIONAL LAW

The conditions to be satisfied before a rule may properly be recognized as one of customary international law can be seen in the following authorities:

1. *R (European Roma Rights Centre) v. Prague Immigration Officer*,[6] where Lord Bingham stated that:

> "The relevant law was, I think, accurately and succinctly summarised by the American Law Institute in its Restatement of the Foreign Relations Law of the United States (Third) vol 1, 1986, para 102(2) and (3):
>
> '(2) Customary international law results from a general and consistent practice of states followed by them from a sense of legal obligation.
> (3) International agreements create law for the states parties thereto and may lead to the creation of customary international law when such agreements are intended for adherence by states generally and are in fact widely accepted.'
>
> This was valuably supplemented by a comment to this effect:
>
> 'c. *Opinio juris*. For a practice of states to become a rule of customary international law it must appear that the states follow the practice from a sense of legal obligation (*opinio juris sive necessitatis*); a practice that is generally followed but which states feel legally free to disregard does not contribute to customary law. A practice initially followed by states as a matter of courtesy or habit may become law when states generally come to believe that they are under a legal obligation

---

4. See Arts. 1, 8 and 12 of the Basic Law.
5. See Art. 13 of the Basic Law.
6. [2005] 2 AC 1, 35.

to comply with it. It is often difficult to determine when that transformation into law has taken place. Explicit evidence of a sense of legal obligation (e.g., by official statements) is not necessary; *opinio juris* may be inferred from acts or omissions.'"

2. The *North Sea Continental Shelf* case[7] which suggests that what is required is:

> "... the consent, express or tacit, of the generality of States.... It is therefore a question of enquiring whether such a practice is observed, not indeed unanimously, but ... by the generality of States with actual consciousness of submitting themselves to a legal obligation.
> The facts which constitute the custom in question are to be found in a series of acts, internal or international, showing an intention to adapt the law of nations to social and economic evolution and to the progress of knowledge...."

3. In *C v. Director of Immigration*,[8] Hartmann J (as he then was) having cited the speech of Lord Bingham in *R (European Roma Rights Centre) v. Prague Immigration Officer*, concluded that:

> "Accordingly, a settled and consistent practice among states, if it is to develop into a rule of customary international law, must be accompanied by conduct on the part of states – including those which are specially affected – acknowledging that the practice has acquired the force of law."

Stock J.A. in the Court of Appeal majority decision of *FG Hemisphere Associates LLC v. Democratic Republic of the Congo and Others*[9] further held:

> "A custom practised and accepted as law by the international community generally thereby crystallises into customary international law notwithstanding the fact that not every State observes the custom and accepts it as law. Whether a State chooses to observe the law as a matter of international obligation or whether it incorporates the law domestically is a different issue. The failure of an individual State to observe or to import that which has, by reason of the consensus of the international community generally, become customary international law does not denude the law of its proper categorisation as customary international law."

At this stage it is necessary to turn to the following question: What is the extent of State practice required in order for the doctrine of restrictive immunity to acquire the status of customary international law (i.e., as *lex lata*).

The standard of consistency and generality is recognized in the case law of the International Court of Justice (ICJ), but there are certain significant qualifications. The

---

7. [1969] ICJ Rep. 3.
8. [2008] 2 HKC 165.
9. [2010] 2 HKLRD 66.

most detailed statement of the position is to be found in *Nicaragua v. United States*,[10] in which the issue of sources was fully argued. In the words of the Court:

> "185. In the present dispute, the Court, while exercising its jurisdiction only in respect of the application of the customary rules of non-use of force and non-intervention, cannot disregard the fact that the Parties are bound by these rules as a matter of treaty law and of customary international law. Furthermore, in the present case, apart from the treaty commitments binding the Parties to the rules in question, there are various instances of their having expressed recognition of the validity thereof as customary international law in other ways. It is therefore in the light of this 'subjective element' – the expression used by the Court in its 1969 Judgment in the *North Sea Continental Shelf* cases (I.C.J. Reports 1969, p. 44) – that the Court has to appraise the relevant practice.
>
> 186. It is not to be expected that in the practice of States the application of the rules in question should have been perfect, in the sense that States should have refrained, with complete consistency, from the use of force or from intervention in each other's internal affairs. The Court does not consider that, for a rule to be established as customary, the corresponding practice must be in absolutely rigorous conformity with the rule. In order to deduce the existence of customary rules, the Court deems it sufficient that the conduct of States should, in general, be consistent with such rules, and that instances of State conduct inconsistent with a given rule should generally have been treated as breaches of that rule, not as indications of the recognition of a new rule. If a State acts in a way prima facie compatible with a recognised rule, but defends its conduct by appealing to exceptions or justifications contained within the rule itself, then whether or not the State's conduct is in fact justifiable on that basis, the significance of that attitude is to confirm rather than to weaken the rule."

(ICJ Reports, 1986, p. 98)

The standard is not especially rigorous, and thus complete consistency of practice is not required. However, a general level of consistency is called for. If the practice (and doctrine) relating to the doctrine of restrictive immunity does not exhibit an appropriate general consistency, it will not acquire the status of customary international law. *Quaere*: where is the exact delineation of the relevant act to be considered, and what are the bounds of the exception created by the general term "commercial exception". Different legislation in different jurisdictions seek to draw a different boundary to the commercial exception and is it therefore necessary to find the common boundary before concluding what is the restrictive immunity that should be followed by all States? In the seventh (2008) edition of *Brownlie's Principles*,[11] the current legal position is formulated as follows:

> "It is far from easy to state the current legal position in terms of customary or general international law. Recent writers emphasise that there is a *trend* in the practice of states towards the restrictive doctrine of immunity but avoid firm and

---

10. [1986] ICJ Rep. 14.
11. I. BROWNLIE, *Principles of Public International Law*, 7th edn. (Oxford UP 2008) at p. 330.

precise prescriptions as to the present state of the law. Moreover, the practice of states is far from consistent and, as the comments of governments relating to the draft articles produced by the International Law Commission indicate, there is persistent divergence between adherents of the principle of absolute immunity and that of restrictive immunity. This divergence of views and the unresponsive attitude of the Sixth Committee of the General Assembly is usually ignored in the academic sources."

The sources of the practice of States on the question of jurisdictional immunities of States and their property are from surveys conducted by international bodies such as the International Law Association through reviewing the national legislation, as well as textbooks which have conducted regional surveys of the position of States. These sources may be said to demonstrate the lack of consistency in the State practice.

The practice of States can of course be discerned from their national legislation. This removal of the jurisdictional barrier against a foreign State does not, however, affect other jurisdictional issues that may exist in the relevant local laws or procedures, such as personal or subject-matter jurisdiction.

Exceptions that are created by domestic legislation include the arbitration exception and the commercial exception. Yet, the scope of the exception or how the boundary of the exception is to be drawn differs from State to State and in some States is still developing. In other words, whether a particular transaction, activity or asset is within the boundary of the commercial exception is still a matter for the national court applying its national laws. Questions such as the identification of the "relevant act" or "asset", or whether the proper test is one as to the nature or purpose of that act in deciding whether it falls within the bounds of the commercial exception will have to be reviewed from jurisdiction to jurisdiction to ascertain the exact "settled and consistent practice" of States on restrictive immunity.

IV.   THE PRINCIPLE OF THE PERSISTENT OBJECTOR

The principle of the persistent objector was applied by the ICJ in a strong majority Judgment in the *Anglo-Norwegian Fisheries* case[12] in 1951. It is important to recall that both the Norwegian and UK Governments accepted the principle. Since the decision the principle has received general approval.

There are nonetheless some reservations about this principle of customary international law. It is perhaps relevant to consider the rationale of the principle of the persistent objector. Customary international law can be developed by general and consistent practice of States generally. It binds all States. If such customary international law is to have such overriding and overarching effect, it is important to also recognize the origins of public international law – equality of States. The balance between the two principles is struck through the creation of the rule of customary international law of persistent objector, enabling States to maintain the position when they have persistently objected to the creation of any rule of customary international law whilst creating a

---

12. [1951] ICJ Rep. 116.

public legal order for international persons. It is submitted that the doctrine of the persistent objector must therefore exist in the context of public international law to strike a sensible balance between the binding effect of customary international law and the equality of States.

In his Hague lectures in 1957 Sir Gerald Fitzmaurice, formerly the Chief Legal Adviser in the British Foreign Office, also made the following observations:

> "A question of great importance for the principle of the rule of law, is that of how far a State can, in the process of the formation of a new customary rule of international law, disassociate itself from that process, declare itself not to be bound, and maintain that attitude – and with what results on the applicability to it of the rule in question. This was in fact part of the Norwegian position in the *Fisheries* case before the International Court of Justice, Norway contending that certain alleged rules were not general rules of international law at all, but that if they were, they did not apply to Norway, because Norway had 'consistently and unequivocally manifested a refusal to accept them'.
> (....)
> The United Kingdom, while denying that Norway had in fact consistently and unequivocally manifested a refusal to accept the rule concerned, admitted the general principle of the Norwegian contention in the following sense: that is to say, it was conceded by the United Kingdom that if (a) it could be shown that at one time international law had given States wider rights or a greater freedom than they at present possessed under the actual rules now prevailing; and if also (b) the dissenting State could show that it had openly and consistently made known its dissent at the time when the new rule was in process of formation, or when it came into operation; and if further (c) that position had been consistently maintained since – then it might be that the State in question was not bound; but if on the other hand this dissent was not manifested at the time, then the State would have become bound, and a dissent subsequently manifested, however consistently maintained, would be unavailing to release it from the obligation. It is believed that the position jointly taken up by Norway and the United Kingdom on this point (for their disagreement regarding it related to the facts rather than to the principle) must be regarded as correct, provided it is strictly confined to the particular premises postulated – namely, open dissent, expressly manifested at the time of the formation of the rule, and consistently maintained subsequently."[13]

The literature indicates approval not least from writers whose credentials include experience as counsel, judges or arbitrators.

Thus in *Oppenheim's International Law*, 9th edition (1992) edited by Jennings and Watts, the principle is stated without qualification:

---

13. Hague Academy, *Recueil des cours*, Vol. 92 (1957, II) pp. 99-100.

> "For purposes of Article 38 of the Statute of the International Court of Justice, a practice must be general in order to constitute an international custom; and it would seem implicit that its acceptance as law must similarly be that of the international community generally – although in certain fields it is the practice and attitude of states directly concerned in that field which may be of most importance. Thus a practice does not have to be either observed or accepted as law, tacitly or expressly, by every state.
>
> It is for this reason that established rules of customary international law are binding on a new or existing state notwithstanding that it may dissent from some particular rule (although express dissent by a state in the formative stages of a potential rule of customary law may prevent it ever becoming established, at least as against the dissenting state)."

(at p. 29).

In the seventh edition of *Brownlie's Principles*, published in 2008, the legal picture is reported as follows:

> "The way in which, as a matter of practice, custom resolves itself into a question of special relations is illustrated further by the rule that a state may contract out of a custom in the process of formation. Evidence of objection must be clear and there is probably a presumption of acceptance which is to be rebutted. Whatever the theoretical underpinnings of the principle, it is well recognized by international tribunals, and in the practice of states. Given the majoritarian tendency of international relations the principle is likely to have increased prominence."[14]

Other authorities include the following:

- Waldock, Hague Academy, Recueil des cours, Vol. 106 (1962, II) pp. 49-50 (Member and then President, ICJ)
- Sorensen, Hague Academy, Recueil des cours, Vol. 101 (1960, III), pp. 43-44 (Member of the International Law Commission)
- Jiménez de Arechaga, Hague Academy, Recueil des cours, Vol. 159 (1978, I), p. 30 (Member and then President ICJ).

The Court of Appeal in Hong Kong also accepted and applied the doctrine of persistent objector to the position of the PRC and held that as a matter of law and fact, PRC is an absolutist.

---

14. See fn. 11 above, p. 11.

V. IMMUNITY FROM SUIT AND IMMUNITY FROM EXECUTION

The distinction between immunity from suit and immunity from execution is trite. Yet the question arises as to whether one can view the immunity to be invoked at the New York Convention enforcement proceedings stage as one from suit or one from execution.

It is sometimes said that so far as the arbitration as a whole is concerned, the stage of enforcing the award under the New York Convention must invoke considerations of immunity from execution. There may nonetheless be a different perspective to the issue.

Art. III of the New York Convention provides: "Each Contracting State shall recognize arbitral awards as binding and enforce them *in accordance with the rules or procedure of the territory where the award is relied upon*" (emphasis added). In most jurisdictions such as Hong Kong, there is a two-stage procedure. The first stage involves recognizing and converting an award into a municipal court judgment which is to be "as mechanistic" as possible subject to the grounds of refusal being made out as provided in the New York Convention. The second stage, that of execution, involves the domestic procedures of execution measures that may be taken to recover the proceeds of the judgment. In that context, the New York Convention enforcement proceedings against States can be viewed as follows: the first stage before a municipal court is one where immunity from suit is invoked, and the second, the execution stage, is where the immunity from execution may be invoked. The enforcement proceedings are probably not really a simple extension of the arbitration proceedings but a separate and distinct procedure before a different forum, not the arbitral tribunal but the enforcing court, and involving proceedings of a different nature from those of the arbitration itself. This is dealt with in the case of *Xiamen Xinjingdi Group Ltd v. Eton Properties Ltd & Another*[15] set out below in Sect. XII.

The concept that the enforcement proceedings invoke directly the immunity from execution nonetheless remains a viable argument. In Hong Kong, this was so decided by the Court of First Instance and the Court of Appeal and will be further considered by the Court of Final Appeal in *FG Hemisphere Associates LLC v. Democratic Republic of the Congo and Others*.[16]

The distinction between immunity from suit and immunity from execution is important in the context of considering waiver or the applicability or scope of the commercial exception (restrictive immunity) before the enforcing court. It is trite that waiver of one does not amount to waiver of another.

1. State immunity is granted for all phases of judicial process. It is a generally accepted doctrine and State practice by treating immunity from enforcement as a distinct regime from that of immunity from suit and therefore a separate waiver is required for immunity from execution than that given in relation to suit.[17]

---

15. [2008] 4 HKLRD 972, [2009] 4 HKLRD 353.
16. [2009] 1 HKLRD 410, [2010] 2 HKLRD 66.
17. Hazel FOX, QC, *The Law of State Immunity*, 2nd edn. (2008 Oxford UP) at p. 602 and *Oppenheim's International Law* (supra) at pp. 350-351.

2. Thus, *submission by a State to the local jurisdiction in the merits of a case does not mean that its property may be subjected to execution to enforce a subsequent judgment against it.*

3. In *Duff Development Company Ltd. v. Government of Kelantan & Anor*,[18] Viscount Finlay in considering whether a submission to arbitration amounted to a submission to enforcement of the award said at 817-819:

> "Apart from statute the award of an arbitrator on a reference by agreement could be enforced only by action. When this was the state of the law it could not have been contended that a reference by agreement to arbitration with a foreign Government even if made in England would involve any obligation on the part of the foreign Government to submit to the jurisdiction of the English Courts in an action to enforce the award. When such an action was brought it would be at the option of the foreign Government to appear or not, as it pleased. There would certainly be no obligation upon it to accept the jurisdiction and to submit to judgment and execution against any property belonging to it in England. There is nothing in an agreement for settlement by arbitration to import a waiver of the right of a sovereign Power to refuse the jurisdiction of the English Courts in an action upon the award.
>
> ... Section 12 [of the Arbitration Act][19] can be made operative only by leave of the Court. I fail to see how art. 21 [a clause in relation to submission to arbitration] can possibly be read as an agreement by the Government of Kelantan to consent to an Order for such leave being made. The leave of the Court being necessary before the award can be enforced as if it were a judgment, if a sovereign State claimed its immunity this would be a good reason for refusing the leave...."

VI. ENFORCING AWARDS AGAINST FOREIGN STATES UNDER THE NEW YORK CONVENTION

The interaction of one of the principles of public international law and that of the application of New York Convention is interesting. The agreement to arbitrate in a New York Convention State has been said to represent a waiver of State immunity before any of the New York Convention State courts when it comes to enforcement of that award. On first blush this sounds credible and logical and may be applicable and correct in the context of private international law. However, this proposition it seems is not applicable to States as it may infringe or contravene a principle in public international law, the *pacta tertiis* rule.

The *pacta tertiis* rule is a fundamental principle in international law which means that treaties do not create either obligations or rights for the third States without their consent. This is also set out in Art. 34 of the Vienna Convention on the Law of Treaties.

---

18. [1924] AC 797 (HL).
19. Sect. 12 of the Arbitration Act 1889 provided that an award on submission may by leave of the Court or a judge be enforced in the same manner as a judgment or Order to the same effect.

"A treaty does not create either obligations or rights for a third State without its consent."[20]

In *Foreign State Immunity and Arbitration*, Dhisadee Chamlongrasdr,[21] dealt with these arguments in the context of public international law at paras. 4.60 and 4.61:

> "However, it should be noted that where the foreign State defendant is not a party to the international agreement providing for an obligation to recognize and enforce an arbitration agreement or award, it is unlikely that the US courts will find that the foreign State defendant has waived its immunity even though the arbitration agreement or award is governed by the international agreement, or even though the State where the arbitration took place (in cases where the arbitration did not take place in the defendant's State) and the US are parties to the international agreement. This holding is consistent ... with Crawford's view that international agreements cannot be interpreted as waiving immunity of a State which is not a party to the international agreement 'since it would violate the *pacta tertiis* rule'.
>
> For example, in the case of the New York Convention, even if the award is governed and otherwise enforceable under the Convention, where the foreign State defendant is not a party to the Convention, it is unlikely that courts will find that a foreign State defendant has waived its immunity by agreeing to arbitrate under section 1605(a)(1). This is the case of *Creighton v. Qatar*, where ... [t]he Court of Appeals rejected the plaintiff's claim on the ground that Qatar was not a signatory to the New York Convention, and that only the agreement to arbitrate in France (a contracting State to the convention) without more, could not be regarded as an indication by Qatar that it intended to waive its immunity in the US."

The effect of the *pacta tertiis* rule on enforcement proceedings can be considered in the following terms and cannot be ignored. A State that is not a party to a convention could not be assumed to be subjected to or have accepted the rights and obligations created by that convention or treaty. Arguments that a submission to arbitration in a New York Convention State would preclude a State that is not a New York Convention State would contravene this principle of public international law, and has been described as a bootstrap argument.

Qatar is not a New York Convention State. The US Court of Appeal in *Creighton v. Qatar*[22] concluded that by reason of the USC Sect. 1605(a)(6), the arbitration exception from State immunity, it had subject-matter jurisdiction over the case. As to personal jurisdiction, which was required under the rules of procedures in the US court, the court rejected the argument that having waived personal jurisdiction in one jurisdiction by reason of the agreement to arbitrate in that State, one has implicitly waived the right to challenge personal jurisdiction in another. The court recognized the principle that there

---

20. There are established exceptions to this rule as that set out in Arts. 35 and 36 of the Vienna Convention, both of which require the assent of the third State.
21. (Cameron May 2007).
22. *Creighton Ltd v. Government of the State of Qatar*, 181 F 3d 118 (DC Cir 1999).

would be an implicit waiver of personal jurisdiction in a jurisdiction by reason of an agreement to arbitrate or litigate in that particular jurisdiction, but that waiver is only applicable within that jurisdiction. The court drew an analogy with a domestic arrangement between federal States:

> "It is implausible that the defendant in Connecticut who had agreed to arbitrate all disputes in New York, and thereby implicitly waived any objection to personal jurisdiction in a suit brought in New York to enforce the resulting arbitral award, also waived its objection to personal jurisdiction in such an action brought in California merely because the full faith and credit clause would make a valid New York judgment enforceable in the courts of California. Indeed, to accept such a bootstrap argument, under which the courts in every state would have personal jurisdiction over a defendant who had waived its objection in any one state.... It seems to us likewise implausible that Qatar, by agreeing to arbitrate in France, a signatory to a treaty containing a similar reciprocal 'recognition and enforcement' clause, should be deemed thereby to have waived its right to challenge personal jurisdiction in the United States. For these reasons we hold that Qatar did not waive its objection to personal jurisdiction in the United States by agreeing to arbitrate in France."

Similarly, the court continues that an agreement to arbitrate in France would probably mean that the State has implicitly submitted to jurisdiction of the French supervisory courts; it would be contrary to common sense and the *pacta tertiis* rule to say that by agreeing to arbitrate it has thereby waived immunity in 145 jurisdictions.

VII.   ART. III OF THE NEW YORK CONVENTION – JURISDICTIONAL QUESTION

The jurisdiction of the enforcing court in a New York Convention State over a foreign State would therefore be governed by its own procedures as well as its doctrine of State immunity. This is exactly why the English court or the US court would have jurisdiction over foreign States when the transaction or the activity is within the exceptions created in the relevant legislation. In States where the applicable doctrine is one of absolute immunity, a foreign State may still be impleaded only if they have waived their right or entitlement to plead State immunity when it comes to enforcement of arbitral awards.

In *AIC Ltd v. Federal Government of Nigeria and another*,[23] the court concluded that enforcement of a foreign judgment does not fall within the arbitration or commercial exception created in the State Immunity Act. The rationale is this. Given that it is the enforcement of the foreign judgment that they are concerned with, and not the underlying transaction or the dispute, and as the judgment does not fall within any of the statutory exceptions, the foreign State can plead and enjoys immunity before the English court. Bearing in mind that the origin of immunity that a State is entitled to rely on is one of absolute immunity subject to any such exceptions, the court effectively concluded

---

23. [2003] EWHC 1357.

that it has no jurisdiction over a foreign State when it comes to enforcing a foreign court judgment.

This rationale was approved by the Court of Appeal in the *Svenska Petroleum AB v. Government of the Republic of Lithuania (No 2)*.[24]

The procedures and the nature of the proceedings applicable in the enforcement of foreign judgment proceedings are identical to those of the enforcement of arbitral awards under the New York Convention. The court's jurisdiction is invoked when deciding whether or not to convert an arbitral award into a domestic court judgment for the purpose of further execution measures to be undertaken. In so doing, the court would not be concerned with the underlying transaction and would only be concerned with the award itself as well as its procedural errors, if any. It has no commercial element involved in the enforcement proceedings notwithstanding the commercial nature of the transaction itself.

These two English court decisions may pose difficulty in enforcement proceedings against foreign States in the common law jurisdictions.

VIII. WAIVER

In the context of considering the question of waiver in enforcement proceedings, it is first necessary to consider the nature of the enforcement proceeding itself. Where the adjudicative function of a national court is invoked where a foreign judgment is sought to be enforced, the court would seek to verify whether it has jurisdiction by considering what the relevant act is, and whether any exception has been created for such proceedings.

The requirements for a valid waiver depend on the national laws. Issues such as whether it has to be expressed or implied, whether a submission to jurisdiction has to be made before the relevant forum, whether there can be prospective waiver, the wordings and hence extent of waiver are often fraught with difficulties in the light of the numerous cases that have considered this matter.

Even if an award can be converted into a court judgment against a foreign State, notwithstanding the above hurdles, it may be just the immunity from suit that has been overcome. The State's entitlement to enjoy immunity from execution may remain. Even in the United Nations Convention on Jurisdictional Immunities of States and Their Properties of 2004, immunity from execution over State property remains a matter on which no consensus, even simply with a view to create harmony, can be reached.

IX. EXPRESSED WAIVER

The adoption of certain wording in a contract, whether incorporated into an arbitration clause or otherwise, may contain the requisite wordings for a waiver including that of waiver of immunity from suit and execution before a foreign national court. This is usually the best solution to the problems set out above.

---

24. [2007] QB 886 at paras. 134 to 137.

There is a diverse jurisprudence on whether the provisions in the International Chamber of Commerce Arbitration Rules or the UNCITRAL Arbitration Rules amount to a waiver of immunity in subsequent recognition of awards proceedings.

The US court in *Walker*[25] interpreted the ICC Rules as amounting to waiver, in a very short and not fully reasoned passage.

In the French case *Creighton v. Qatar*, the *Cour de Cassation* held that both immunity from suit and immunity from execution had been waived.

The *Orascom Telecom Holding*[26] case deals with an ICC award. By reason of Sect. 3 of the 1978 State Immunity Act, there is no issue as to immunity from suit. The only issue considered there was the immunity from execution dealt with under Sect. 13(3), which provides the waiver to be by written consent by the State. ICC Rules Art. 28(6) was relied upon. The English court considered the *Cour de Cassation* case of *Creighton v. Qatar* and did not draw much of a conclusion from it. It then looked at the US case of *Walker* and observed that the court's decision did not rest solely upon an interpretation of Art. 28(6) but on the written agreement where the Republic of Congo waived the right of immunity including that of execution. Further, in both jurisdictions, unlike in England, there is no statutory provision for exception to immunity from execution. In the absence of statutory provisions in that jurisdiction, the English court was

> "reluctant to conclude that, without more, interpretation by the French and/or US courts of the effect of article 28(6) (or the old 24(2)) in a situation where there is no statutory framework such as the 1978 Act, should be imported into this jurisdiction so as to expand the waiver of immunity beyond the commercial purposes exception in section 13(4): certainly without the full evidence of French and/or US law which, for the obvious reason that I had in fact resolved this application in favour of Orascom without regard to the second issue, would not be appropriate now, and in any event Mr. Landau would have sought more time for any definitive appreciation of French and/or US law."

What is clear, however, is that there is no established or consistent jurisprudence on how the ICC Rules would be interpreted in so far as the issue of waiver of immunity from suit and immunity from execution is concerned. It only reinstates the position that each national court will apply its laws to interpret the arbitration clause and consider whether it amounts to a waiver.

X.   PUBLIC POLICY

Turning then to the grounds of public policy. The Court of Final Appeal in Hong Kong has held in *Hebei Import & Export Corp. v. Polytek Engineering Co. Ltd.*[27] that the public policy applicable to Hong Kong is not international public policy but that policy which offends the most basic notions of justice and morality in Hong Kong. It recognizes that the public

---

25. *Walker International Holdings Limited v. Republic of Congo*, 395 F.3d 229, 233 (5th Cir. 2004).
26. *Orascom Telecom Holding SAE v. Republic of Chad & Anor* [2008] 2 Lloyd's Rep 396.
27. [1999] 1 HKLRD 665 (CFA).

policy of the supervising jurisdiction may be different from that of the enforcing jurisdiction.

XI. ALLEGED FRAUD

In the recent case of *Karaha Bodas*,[28] the Court of Appeal and the Court of Final Appeal in Hong Kong considered a late allegation of fraud that was committed during the transaction. Whether or not such late allegation could be included was considered and "the *Saudi Eagle*" test was to be applied. Furthermore, these words from the Court of Appeal illustrate the difficulties a party would face when raising arguments to refuse enforcement on the grounds of public policy.

XII. IMPOSSIBILITY

Impossibility of performance has been prayed in aid as a ground to resist enforcement. This has been rejected by the Hong Kong Court of Appeal, and rightly so bearing in mind that the first stage of any enforcement proceedings is merely that of converting an award into a court judgment. Whether any proceeds or assets could be seized is a matter for consideration at the execution stage. More importantly, damages in view of specific performance render any such arguments as to public policy futile.

In the Court of First Instance in *Xiamen Xinjingdi Group Ltd v. Eton Properties Ltd & Anor*,[29] the learned judge rejected the respondent's arguments seeking to go behind the award and reargue matters which were either argued before the arbitrators or (if not) ought to have been argued before them.

> "... The Court must be vigilant against such attempts to go behind an award, in the guise of dealing with questions of public policy.
> 52. I would go further. Take the argument of impossibility with which this case is concerned. Unless an award is plainly incapable of performance such that it would be obviously oppressive to order a party to comply with it, the Court cannot consistently with the 'mechanistic principle' hold that the award is contrary to public policy and refuse to convert the award into a judgement of the court.
> 53. This is because otherwise the Court would have to go behind the award. The Respondents would in effect be allowed to re-open that which the arbitrators had decided. The Court would be doing that which it ought not to do, namely, encroach upon the jurisdiction of an arbitral tribunal."

This argument of impossibility of performance was raised again in the Court of Appeal and was similarly rejected. Xiamen Xinjingdi emphasized the distinction of the execution

---

28. *Karaha Bodas Company LLC v. Persusahaan Pertambangan Minydak Dan Gas Bumi Negara*, [2007] 4 HKLRD 1002, (2009) 12 HKCFAR 84.
29. [2008] 4 HKLRD 972.

stage and the registration stage of an award, and at this stage of considering whether or not to register an award as a court judgment, the court held as follows:

> "28. In considering whether or not to refuse the enforcement of the award, the court does not look into the merits or at the underlying transaction. Its role is confined to determining whether or not grounds exist for refusing to enforce the award because it would be contrary to public policy. As the judge recognized, the court's role should be as 'mechanistic as possible'.
> 29. As regards public policy, the only ground the appellants rely on as justifying a refusal to enforce the award is impossibility of performance. It was said that it is now impossible to deliver the land and further, because of the restructuring, the shares could no longer be transferred. Since the conversion of an award into a judgment of the court does not involve going into the merits, it is difficult to see how impossibility of performance is relevant at the registration stage."

The court then dealt with how the Eton Group went ahead with restructuring notwithstanding that the arbitration had commenced.

> "32. The notion that the appellants would be at risk for contempt proceedings for failing to comply with an order that is impossible to carry out is equally misguided. It was suggested that enforcement of the award is tantamount to an order decreeing specific performance, thereby exposing the appellants to the risk of contempt proceedings with all its consequences, including imprisonment. But the order does not specify any time for performance and committal proceedings may only be commenced against a person who refuses or neglects to do an act within the time specified in the order. Further a person who genuinely is unable to carry out the order cannot be made liable for the contempt."

XIII. THIRD-PARTY FUNDING

A new argument that may soon arise in the international arbitral community regarding public policy and foreign States is that of enforcement of awards through funding by third parties. This brings into question the extent to which maintenance and champerty are illegal and therefore contravene the public policy of the enforcing State.

On 9 February 2007, the Court of Final Appeal delivered a judgment *Siegfried Adalbert Unruh v. Hans-Joerg Seeberger and Another*[30] looking at the origins and development of maintenance and champerty.

> "77. The origins of maintenance and champerty are ancient and obscure. English statutes from at least the 13th century were enacted to deal with champerty and maintenance, but there is a solid body of authority for concluding that they have their origins in the common law and were supplemented by statute....

---

30. (2007) 10 HKCFAR 31.

78. The view has generally been taken that maintenance and champerty form part of Hong Kong law.... The common law rules making maintenance and champerty criminal offences, torts and a ground of public policy for invalidating tainted contracts, were part of the Hong Kong law prior to 1997 and remain applicable by virtue of Article 8 of the Basic Law."

Having considered the development of excluded categories of situations where maintenance and champerty would not be in contravention of public policy, the Court of Final Appeal opined that:

"92. One category of excluded cases involves what may be called the 'common interest' category. Certain relationships have been judicially recognized as involving persons with a legitimate common interest in the outcome of litigation sufficient to justify one of them in supporting the litigation conducted by another without engaging the prohibition against maintenance and champerty.
(....)
94. Clearly, this 'common interest' category is not closed. Public policy is likely to regard groups and associations pursuing legitimate objectives as possessing a sufficient common interest in related litigation to warrant their exclusion from the scope of maintenance and champerty....
95. A second excluded category involves what might today be referred to as cases involving 'access to justice' considerations. In Hong Kong, Article [35] of the Basic Law recognizes access to the courts as a fundamental right. It has never been a defence to an action nor a ground for a stay to show that the plaintiff is being supported by a third person in an arrangement which constitutes maintenance or champerty. Neither does liability for maintenance or champerty depend on the action or the defence being bad in law. It follows that an attack on an arrangement said to constitute maintenance and champerty could well result in a claim which is perfectly good in law being stifled where the plaintiff, deprived of the support of such an arrangement, is unable to pursue it. This is a powerful argument for such cases to be excluded from the ambit of maintenance and champerty.
(....)
97. It is again obvious that this access to justice category is not static. The development of policies and measures to promote such access is likely to enlarge the category and to result in further shrinkage in the scope of maintenance and champerty. Different measures, whether statutory or judicial, may be taken in different jurisdictions....
98. Thirdly, there exists the miscellaneous category of practices accepted as lawful even though, as pointed out by Gummow, Hayne and Crennan JJ in the recent decision of the Australian High Court in *Campbells Cash and Carry Pty Ltd v. Fostif Pty Ltd*, such practices do not differ in substance from practices which have traditionally been roundly condemned...." (Footnotes omitted.)

These passages show the tendency of the courts in Hong Kong to be less conservative and restrictive when it comes to considerations relating to maintenance and champerty. Yet, given the developing nature of approaches to matters such as funded litigation, the general views of the society as represented in the discussions in the domestic arena as well as in international bodies such as the International Monetary Fund and the World Bank on these matters will have a bearing on whether third-party funding will be viewed as contrary to public policy.

In Hong Kong, whilst this Court of Final Appeal judgment was generally welcomed in the international commercial litigation field, domestically in 2008, twenty-one persons were arrested for champerty and maintenance. On 30 June 2009 a solicitor was convicted for sharing twenty-five percent of the proceeds of the damages paid and was sentenced to fifteen month imprisonment by the District Court in Hong Kong.

Hence, whilst the Court of Final Appeal in *Siegfried Adalbert Unruh v. Hans-Joerg Seeberger and Another* accepts that sufficient genuine commercial interest in the outcome of the arbitration proceedings would merit the maintenance and champerty argument to be excluded, at the same time, the Panel on Administration of Justice and Legal Services of the Legislative Council of Hong Kong was provided with a background brief regarding the illegal activities of recovery agents involved primarily in personal injury cases. Whilst prosecution has been stepped up, the paper revealed that the Administration did not rule out the possibility of introducing legislation against the activities of recovery agents in order to protect the public interest. It is repeated there that champerty and maintenance are common law offences in Hong Kong and offenders could be liable to prosecution, and the need for legislation pending the outcome of the prosecution actions will be reviewed.

Whilst on an entirely different scale, what has been described as third-party funding of litigation in the international commercial world, or as "vulture funds" in certain papers, may be likened to recovery agents in Hong Kong. Whether or not the acts of these third-party funding proceedings in the courts of Hong Kong would be held to be in contravention of public policy will have to be seen.

The common law offence of maintenance and champerty remains in Hong Kong although the grounds are gradually narrowed. In the *Nina Kung* case[31] the Court of Final Appeal in 2006 confirmed that any such maintenance or champerty actions may still be contrary to public policy. It remains to be seen whether the funding by a third party for enforcement of an arbitral award with which it has no relations against a foreign State will be contrary to public policy in Hong Kong.

XIV. CONCLUSION

The many hurdles that face a winning party when seeking to enforce an award against a foreign State have to be addressed internationally. The 2004 UN Convention is far from getting the necessary signatories and ratification thereby giving it any force of law. In any event, it is devoid of clear measures dealing with enforcement of arbitral awards.

The best approach, it seems, is to develop a standard and universally accepted waiver of arbitral immunity as well as subsequent immunity in enforcement proceedings. States, including those that are absolutists, would be prepared to waive their immunity on a case-by-case basis in the commercial transactions they enter into. This gives flexibility

---

31. *Nina Kung alias Nina T.H. Wang v. Wang Din Shin*, (2006) 9 HKCFAR 800.

and freedom of choice. It is in accord with private and public international laws. It is also supported by the fundamental principle of party autonomy in commercial contracts.

Who is then to take the lead?

XV. POSTSCRIPT

On 8 June 2011, the Hong Kong Court of Final Appeal rendered a judgment in the case of *Democratic Republic of the Congo and others v. FG Hemisphere Associates LLC*. The case is concerned with the nature and scope of state immunity which the courts of the Hong Kong Special Administrative Region (HKSAR) should recognize, as a matter of law, as applying to foreign States which are sued in the HKSAR.

The case concerns the enforcement of two arbitration awards obtained against the Democratic Republic of the Congo (DRC) in arbitrations held in Paris and Zurich. FG Hemisphere is a Delaware company who has acquired the right to enforce these two awards in place of the original claimant in the arbitrations.

The majority decision to be found in paras. 181 to 416 of the judgment concluded that both the common law on state immunity and the relevant provisions of the Basic Law, namely Arts. 13 and 19, compel the conclusion that the common law principle of state immunity, modified in accordance with the requirements of the Basic Law, to be applied in the courts of the HKSAR is that of "absolute" immunity. This is the principle of state immunity which has been consistently applied by the PRC in its relations with other sovereign States. The court also rejected FG's argument that HKSAR can have a separate state immunity policy as such argument fails to appreciate the fundamental importance of the status of HKSAR being an inalienable part of the PRC and the force of the "one State one immunity" argument. HKSAR cannot have a position of State immunity different from that of the PRC.

State immunity is concerned with relations between States and a State waives its immunity only when it voluntarily submits itself to the exercise of jurisdiction by the courts of the forum State. The common law position, based on the line of English authorities in *Duff Development Co Ltd v. Government of Kelantan* and *A Company Ltd. v. Republic of X*, requires such a voluntary submission to be unequivocal and made at the time when the courts of the forum State are being asked to exercise their jurisdiction against the foreign State in question. There is no basis for finding that the DRC has waived its state immunity before the HKSAR courts.

Keynote Address: Advocacy and Ethics in International Arbitration

Ethics in International Arbitration

*Doak Bishop**

TABLE OF CONTENTS	Page
I. Introduction	383
II. Insufficiency of Present Codes and Hypotheticals	383
III. Recent Developments	384
IV. The Compelling Need for a Code	387
V. Enforcing a Code of Ethics	388
VI. The Way Forward	389

I. INTRODUCTION

I am honored to have been invited to give the keynote address at this first ICCA Conference in South America. My topic is ethics in international arbitration advocacy. This is a topic fraught with many difficulties. I don't claim this presentation will solve all of the problems, but I will try to move the debate forward. So let me start with this:

> "International arbitration dwells in an ethical no-man's land. Often by design, arbitration is set in a jurisdiction where neither party's counsel is licensed. The extraterritorial effect of national ethical codes is usually murky.... There is no supra-national authority to oversee attorney conduct in this setting, and local bar associations rarely if ever extend their reach so far ... specialized ethical norms for attorneys in international arbitration are nowhere recorded. Where ethical regulations should be, there is only an abyss."

That is the way that Prof. Catherine Rogers began her 2002 article on Developing a Code of Conduct for International Arbitration.[1] And it is my thesis today that there is a current, compelling need for the development of a Code of Ethics in International Arbitration and for the adaptation of tribunals and institutions to the adoption of such a Code.

II. INSUFFICIENCY OF PRESENT CODES AND HYPOTHETICALS

Now it may be pointed out that there already exists a code of ethics for international lawyers. The International Bar Association (IBA) has published an International Code of

---

* Partner, King & Spalding, Houston office; Co-head, King & Spalding's International Arbitration Group.
1. Catherine ROGERS, "Fit and Function in Legal Ethics: Developing a Code of Conduct for International Arbitration", 23 Mich. J. Int'l Law (2001-2002) p. 341.

Ethics. But I would point out that this Code was last revised in 1988, and very importantly, is not specific to international arbitration. It simply does not address all of the issues that a Code for international arbitration needs to consider. Moreover, that Code begins with this first Rule:

> "A lawyer who undertakes professional work in a jurisdiction where he is not a full member of the local profession shall adhere to the standards of professional ethics in the jurisdiction in which he has been admitted. He shall also observe all ethical standards which apply to lawyers of the country where he is working."

This is the very definition of double deontology — the situation in which a lawyer may be subject to more than one code of ethics. This may be workable when the rules are not in conflict, but what happens when they are?

Let's take two hypothetical situations. First, with respect to document production, what are the applicable ethical rules for an Italian lawyer handling an international arbitration in New York for an Italian client when the opposing side requests the production of certain documents that are harmful to his client's case? And to turn it around, in the same situation what are the ethical duties of an American attorney handling an international arbitration in Italy? Does it matter if the client is Italian or American? It is my understanding that the ethical rules for American and Italian lawyers in this situation may be in direct conflict.

Second, what ethical principles apply to the preparation of fact and expert witnesses for giving testimony for a British barrister representing an American company in an international arbitration in Washington, D.C., or to German and American attorneys representing opposite sides in an international arbitration in London?

In an article written almost two decades ago on Standards of Conduct for Counsel in International Arbitration, Jan Paulsson raised the obvious question: "in cases where counsel come from two different countries where standards are quite inconsistent on a given point, does the client whose lawyer is subject to the lowest standard have an unfair advantage?"[2] In that article, Prof. Paulsson called for the development of a specific code of conduct for counsel in international arbitration, at least for fundamental or essential standards, but until now that call has gone unheeded. As one can readily see, the present IBA Code is not altogether satisfactory.

There is, however, another supra-national code that should be mentioned — the Code of Conduct for European Lawyers prepared by the Council of Bars and Law Societies of Europe (CCBE Code).[3] But this Code has only three substantive provisions relating to a lawyer's conduct in an international arbitration. First, a lawyer should have due regard for the fair conduct of proceedings; second, a lawyer should maintain due respect and courtesy toward the tribunal and defend the interests of the client honorably; and third, a lawyer should never knowingly give false or misleading information to the

---

2. Jan PAULSSON, "Standards of Conduct in International Arbitration", 3 Am. Review Int'l Arb (1992) pp. 214-222.
3. Available at <www.ccbe.eu/fileadmin/user_upload/NTCdocument/2006_code_enpdf1_1228293527.pdf>.

tribunal. Those provisions are fine as far as they go, but they do not resolve the many prickly problems that trouble many of us in practice, and thus, they simply do not go far enough. Now another provision of the CCBE Code attempts to fill this void by requiring a lawyer appearing before a tribunal to comply with the rules of conduct of that tribunal.

But for international arbitration, this begs the question: what are the applicable rules of conduct for lawyers appearing before an international arbitration tribunal? Johnny Veeder posed this very question in the 2001 Goff Lecture:

> "To the Q: What are the professional rules applicable to an Indian lawyer in a Hong Kong arbitration between a Bahraini claimant and a Japanese defendant represented by NY lawyers, the answer is no more obvious than it would be in London, Paris, Geneva and Stockholm. There is no clear answer."[4]

III. RECENT DEVELOPMENTS

I propose next to look at three recent ICSID cases in which questions of counsel conduct arose to see how the arbitrators handled those issues in practice. We must (of course) be sensitive to the context of those cases. These are all ICSID cases governed by an international treaty — the ICSID Convention — and involving the application of international law. Nevertheless, investment disputes are an important part of international arbitration, and I believe these cases may be generally instructive.

1. *Hrvatska v. Slovenia*

In *Hrvatska v. Slovenia*,[5] the tribunal was asked by the claimant that it "recommend to the Respondent that it refrain from using the services" of a British barrister who was a member of the same chambers as the President of the tribunal. The barrister had been added to the respondent's legal team after the case had begun and his involvement was only disclosed shortly before the final hearing.

The tribunal reasoned as follows: first, the ICSID Convention does not grant the tribunal any explicit power to exclude counsel, and there is a fundamental principle that parties may use the lawyers of their choice. But this principle is subject to an overriding principle of the immutability of properly constituted tribunals. In practice, what this means is that a party cannot amend its legal team after the constitution of the tribunal "in such a fashion as to imperil the Tribunal's status or legitimacy".

The tribunal found that it had inherent power to take measures necessary to preserve the integrity of the proceedings. And on the basis of the fundamental principle of the immutability of tribunals, the tribunal disqualified the barrister from the case although it was quick to point out, of course, that there is no "hard and fast rule" preventing barristers from the same chambers from acting as arbitrator and counsel in the same case.

---

4. V.V. VEEDER, "The 2001 Goff Lecture – The Lawyer's Duty to Arbitrate in Good Faith", 18 Arbitration International (2002, no. 4) p. 431.
5. *Hrvatska Elektroprivreda d.d. v. Republic of Slovenia* (ICSID Case No. ARB/05/24).

It is clear that the tribunal was strongly influenced by the very late disclosure of the barrister's role in the case.

Comment — From this case, one might draw the conclusion that tribunals have inherent power to disqualify counsel in order to protect the integrity of the proceedings, but let's dig a little deeper.

2. *Rompetrol v. Romania*

In *Rompetrol v. Romania*,[6] respondent asked the ICSID tribunal to disqualify counsel for the claimant who had been brought into the case after the case had begun – he had previously practiced at the same law firm as the arbitrator appointed by the claimant. In rejecting respondent's application, what stands out from the decision is that the tribunal was reluctant to endorse the view that tribunals have inherent power to remove counsel. In fact, without ever finding that it had such power, the tribunal said that if such power exists, and assuming such power, it can only be exercised rarely and in exceptional or compelling circumstances that would genuinely touch on the integrity of the arbitral process. Relevant to our purposes, the tribunal noted that "one would normally expect to see such a power specifically provided for in the legal texts governing the tribunal and its operation". But no such power is provided for in the ICSID Convention or Arbitration Rules. Absent such express rules, the tribunal found that "the only justification for the tribunal to award itself this power" is an overriding need to safeguard the essential integrity of the arbitral process. The tribunal distinguished counsel's role from that of the arbitrator and noted that counsel's role is to present his client's case "with diligence and with honesty, and in due compliance with the applicable rules of professional conduct and ethics". But having found that the ICSID Convention and Rules do not address this subject, the tribunal did not identify what rules of ethics are applicable or seek to address them. Instead, the tribunal then turned the question around to one dealing with the more familiar issue of arbitrator ethics to ask if the presence of claimant's counsel would cause the arbitrator to be biased and partial. The tribunal did not find that to be the case, and thus, decided that the integrity of the proceeding was not threatened and rejected the challenge.

Comment — Based on this decision, we might question whether there exists any inherent power of the tribunal to disqualify counsel, but conclude that if it does exist, it will likely be exercised only rarely and in exceptional circumstances.

3. *Unreported Annulment Proceeding*

The third case involves an unreported ICSID annulment proceeding in which claimant's counsel was challenged for having allegedly represented respondent in a related proceeding five years earlier. Claimant's counsel denied that he had represented Respondent or had ever received any confidential information.

---

6. *Rompetrol Group N.V. v. Romania* (ICSID Case No. ARB/06/3).

The Committee started its analysis very importantly by deciding that its duty to treat the parties fairly and equally necessarily includes the power to ensure that generally recognized principles of conflict of interest and the protection of confidential information is complied with by counsel. But it was quick to note that the Committee had no deontological responsibilities over the lawyers in their own capacities and had "no power to rule on an allegation of misconduct under any such professional rules as may apply". Its concern was limited to the fair conduct of the proceeding before it.

The Committee then reviewed the two national codes of ethics of the bar associations of which claimant's counsel was a member and also looked to the CCBE Code in order to find "common general principles which may guide the Committee," but it noted that as an international tribunal it was not bound by the national codes. It saw its task as finding "what general principles are plainly indispensable for the fair conduct of the proceedings". On the facts before it, the tribunal rejected the application to disqualify claimant's counsel.

Comment — This Committee had no trouble in finding not only the power but also a duty to resolve the conflict issue, which arose from its obligation to treat the parties fairly and equally, and to do so on the basis of general principles of ethics, but not on the basis of any specific national code.

In the Goff Lecture of 2001, Johnny Veeder noted that the fact that international arbitration practitioners do not usually share the same national legal culture "does not mean that international practitioners are pirates sailing under no national flag; it means only that on the high seas, navigators need more than a coastal chart".[7]

I fully agree. And extending this imagery to the three cases we just examined, I respectfully suggest that the arbitrators found themselves blown out to sea and ill-equipped with nothing more than a coastal chart. And therein lies the problem. The three tribunals – faced with similar issues – created three different solutions.

I do not criticize the tribunals at all; they did their job by using what they had before them, in our imagery: dead reckoning. But dead reckoning is the last resort of a careful navigator, and many a ship piloted by dead reckoning has floundered on the rocks. Simply put, the arbitrators needed a sextant and a star chart – a Code of Conduct for Counsel.

IV. THE COMPELLING NEED FOR A CODE

Let's pose the fundamental question directly: is there really a compelling need for a Code now? After all, the arbitrators in the three cases we just surveyed were able to muddle through and find a solution, however imperfectly. Why can't we just leave it to tribunals to intuit solutions using the coastal charts of national codes? Or we could increasingly invite national courts into arbitral proceedings to police counsel's conduct.

---

7. See fn. 4 above.

Another solution is for arbitrators to continue using the assessment of costs as a means of controlling the conduct of the lawyers.

But all of these potential solutions are flawed. Cost assessments are a blunt instrument for policing counsel. They are indirect, do not fully address the problems and ultimately target the parties, not counsel. Additional court proceedings interfere in the arbitral process with attendant delays and extra costs. And leaving it to tribunals to devise their own – perhaps idiosyncratic – solutions, is less than ideal, and certainly does not satisfy the need for a uniform and transparent solution. Professor Rogers has characterized the lack of transparency of such solutions by referring to them as "the clandestine techniques by which arbitrators undoubtedly regulate proceedings before them".[8]

Despite the many challenges, the international arbitration system has worked, and worked well, but while we have been busy arbitrating, the system itself has been growing and changing over the past many years. The stakes are getting larger – much larger. We now find arbitrations involving claims of billions of dollars – even tens of billions of dollars. And the involvement of States as parties in both investment and commercial cases has added a public interest factor to the equation, with increasing publication of investment awards and public scrutiny.

The lack of clarity as to which ethical rules apply, the existence of conflicting rules and obligations, the non-transparency and the increased size of many proceedings, combined with greater public scrutiny, creates a certain instability in the system that could result in a future crisis of confidence. It only takes one highly visible, public spectacle to shake confidence in the entire system. There are already critics of arbitration in various countries, and if a public spectacle does occur involving counsel, what easier target than to point to the fact that international arbitration does not even have a Code of Ethics for counsel.

The international arbitration system needs to be able to police itself. Public confidence is an essential element of the system, and as one commentator has noted, if that confidence is lost, it could take decades to rebuild.

I submit that a uniform, binding Code of Ethics is a necessary part of maintaining that public confidence. Such a Code can accomplish three major goals: first, it can clarify the applicable rules and reduce ambiguity; second, it can level the playing field so that conflicting obligations do not unduly benefit one party at the expense of the other; and third, it can provide greater transparency, thus building confidence in the system. Although there have been no catastrophes to this point, the international arbitration system is at least subject to reasonable criticism without its own transparent Code of Ethics, and we need to ensure the future integrity and legitimacy of the system

V. ENFORCING A CODE OF ETHICS

I want to pose one final question: how can the international arbitration system enforce a binding Code of Ethics? There are really two questions here: first, what is the legal basis for enforcement? and second, who will enforce the Code?

---

8. See fn. 1 above.

To the first question, the legitimacy of international arbitration derives from the consent of the parties to arbitrate their disputes. Johnny Veeder has gone a step further and suggested that there is a duty to arbitrate in good faith, which is derived from the general principle of law that parties must perform their contract in good faith. Based on the party's consent to arbitrate, and perhaps *sub silentio* relying upon a duty to arbitrate in good faith, at least two of the three ICSID tribunals concluded that they had the inherent power to enforce such rules as are necessary for a fair hearing – and that includes rules of conduct for counsel.

This might be a sufficient answer, at least for certain fundamental rules necessary to a fair hearing, but I would suggest there is a simpler answer — and that is for the major arbitral institutions to incorporate a uniform Code of Ethics into their Arbitral Rules, thus making the Code expressly binding as a matter of the parties' contractual consent.

Now for the second question: Who is to enforce a binding Code? There are only three possibilities: local courts and bar associations; tribunals; or arbitral institutions.

As we've seen, the application of national codes is unclear and at times even conflicting, and the involvement of courts is likely to lead to delays and extra expense. The *Hrvatska* tribunal found that for an international system, "it seems unacceptable for the solution to reside in the individual national bodies which regulate the work of professional service providers, because that might lead to inconsistent or arbitrary outcomes...".[9] By the process of elimination that leaves tribunals and institutions.

My answer is that as international arbitration changes – handling enormous cases and with increasing public scrutiny – our institutions must adapt to this changing environment. Part of that adaptation will be to take on the role of enforcement of a binding Code of Ethics. This will undoubtedly make some people nervous, but many of the rules – for example dealing with relationships with the tribunal and opposing counsel – will likely pose few real difficulties in practice. Other issues dealing with relations with the parties – such as those arising in the three cases we surveyed like conflicts of interest and the possession of confidential information – may be distasteful for institutions and tribunals, especially for arbitrators appointed by counsel. But it is precisely in this most difficult area that parties may have expectations of transparent, equally applicable, and binding rules, with an acute need for quick decisions. These are not problems to which our system can turn a blind eye.

VI. THE WAY FORWARD

Margrete Stevens and I have put forward with our paper a draft Code of Ethics for Lawyers Practicing Before International Arbitral Tribunals (see this Volume, pp. 408-420). Perhaps it can be simplified to fewer, essential rules, with other rules being considered secondary and perhaps unnecessary for an International Arbitration Code. This distinction between essential and secondary rules was made by Jan Paulsson in the

---

9. *Hrvatska Elektroprivreda d.d. v. Republic of Slovenia* (ICSID Case No. ARB/05/24), Tribunal's Ruling of 6 May 2008 Regarding the Participation of Counsel in Further Stages of the Proceedings, para. 23.

paper I referred to earlier.[10] To many people, portions of this Code may seem quite imperfect, but at least it can provide a starting point.

We suggest that an organization like ICCA, or perhaps the IBA, appoint a working group of lawyers from different legal systems and geographical areas, including representatives of the major arbitral institutions, to consider this proposal, perhaps along with others, with a view toward building a consensus around a Code of Ethics that will have widespread support and can be adopted.

We then suggest that the major arbitral institutions consider incorporating this Code into their Rules by reference. As we have seen, this would make the Code binding, creating uniformity and transparency. While there are difficult questions that might provoke a response that we should leave well enough alone – at least for now – I respectfully suggest that in the context of much larger cases and increasing public interest and scrutiny, failing to address and solve a real problem until it manifests itself in an embarrassing public spectacle creates much greater risks for the international arbitration system of which we are all a part. We all have an interest in the system, and we should all be vigilant to protect its integrity and legitimacy. And for that reason, I would suggest that we must take seriously and move forward – now and not later – the development and adoption of a uniform Code of Ethics for International Arbitration.

---

10. See fn. 2 above.

The Compelling Need for a Code of Ethics in International Arbitration: Transparency, Integrity and Legitimacy

Doak Bishop and *Margrete Stevens***

TABLE OF CONTENTS	Page
I. Introduction	391
II. Background	392
III. Divergences in National Rules and Double Deontology	394
IV. Recent Developments	398
V. The Legitimacy of Arbitral Proceedings	400
VI. Recent ICSID Decisions	401
VII. Conclusion	406

> "*[Persuasion is effected] by means of the moral character, when the speech shall have been spoken in such a way as to render the speaker worthy of confidence: for we place confidence in the good to a wider extent, and with less hesitation, on all subjects generally; but on points where no real accuracy exists, but there is room for doubt, we even entirely confide in them.*"[1]

I. INTRODUCTION

Several investor-State tribunals have recently been called on to rule on requests concerning counsel's conduct. The recent requests have sought to have one of the parties' legal representatives disqualified from appearing in the arbitral proceeding on grounds of conflict of interest. Two cases involved a relationship with one of the arbitrators, which was claimed to threaten the integrity of the tribunal.[2] A third case

---

* Partner, King & Spalding, Houston office; Co-head, King & Spalding's International Arbitration Group.
** Consultant, King & Spalding, Washington, D.C. office; Member, King & Spalding's International Arbitration Group.
   The authors are grateful to Alejandro Cremades, Foreign Attorney, and Tim Sullivan, Associate, both of King and Spalding, for their assistance in the drafting of the Commentary to the proposed International Code of Ethics for Lawyers Practicing Before International Arbitral Tribunals.
1. See ARISTOTLE, *Treatise on Rhetoric* (Prometheus Books 1995).
2. See *Hrvatska Elektroprivreda d.d. v. Republic of Slovenia* (ICSID Case No. ARB/05/24), Order Concerning the Participation of Counsel of 6 May 2008 (hereinafter *Hrvatska* Decision); and *The Rompetrol Group N.V. v. Romania* (ICSID Case No. ARB/06/3), Decision on the Participation of a Counsel of 14 Jan. 2010 (hereinafter *Rompetrol* Decision).

concerned an alleged access to confidential information of one of the counsel.[3] The rulings have raised interesting questions regarding the power and duty of tribunals to rule on such requests. Other problems addressed in the case law concern counsel's disclosure obligations, applicable standards of conduct, the role of national ethics rules or other principles in regulating counsel's conduct in arbitral proceedings, questions of procedural fairness and the integrity of the tribunal, consistency in the application of criteria governing ethics, and ultimately, the credibility of the arbitral system to deal with counsel's conduct and ethics issues.

While the recent rulings addressed challenges to the right of a party to appoint the counsel of its choice in a particular matter, other instances have arisen in which tribunals have been asked to regulate counsel's conduct. Such instances frequently occur in the form of a claim for costs on grounds of conduct that have resulted in unnecessary delays, and hence, additional costs. Such delays may be attributable to a myriad of causes, among them conduct incompatible with the practice of international arbitration.[4]

Bearing in mind that tribunals have considered that they have both the duty and the power to decide questions of counsel conduct, and cost-related consequences, one might ask what principles should be applied when allegations of misconduct arise in international arbitral proceedings.

This inquiry is not new. On the contrary, the rulings discussed in this paper resurrect a decades-old debate on whether there is a need for an ethics code for counsel appearing in international arbitration. What is new is that there is nowadays far greater transparency in arbitral proceedings leading to greater public scrutiny of both the conduct of lawyers and the discretion of tribunals.[5]

II. BACKGROUND

Philosophers since Socrates, Plato and Aristotle in the fifth and fourth centuries BC have debated what makes for moral virtue in human life.[6] Going back further, societies from the earliest recorded times have encouraged conduct consistent with social values, and the religions of the world have sought to codify rules of moral conduct – the Ten Commandments is but one example of an ethical code of conduct. Such codes have had utility for thousands of years.

Recent decades have seen a proliferation of ethical codes in various contexts. The private sector displays corporate values through individual companies' codes of conduct

---

3. Unpublished Decision of ICSID Annulment Committee (2008) (hereinafter Unpublished Annulment Committee Decision).
4. See *Víctor Pey Casado and President Allende Foundation v. Republic of Chile* (ICSID Case No. ARB/98/2), Award of 8 May 2008 (hereinafter *Pey Casado* Award).
5. See William SLATE II, *Luncheon Remarks at the AAA/AIPN Conference*, Houston, 20 Apr. 2010, noting that more transparency in private as well as in public arbitrations may be anticipated.
6. See Aristotle, *The Nichomachean Ethics* (Oxford University Press 2009). The Greek philosophers thereby established the philosophical field of deontology – the study of moral duty. On the importance of *moral character* in delivering persuasive speech, see Aristotle, *Treatise on Rhetoric* (Prometheus Books 1995) p. 12.

to guide their employees. Governments, which for years relied on detailed civil service regulations, now publish ethics codes as they give staff more responsibility for performance, and there can be few professional associations in developed countries that do not have a code of professional conduct for their members. Such codes go much further than a simple Hippocratic Oath to do no harm. They provide guidance on conflicts of interest, gifts, offer and receipt of bribes, abuse of office, false information, outside financial interests and post-service employment. As we all know, lawyers too have their codes, although up to now such codes have largely been elaborated under the ambit of national authorities.

The question should therefore be posed: Is a code of ethics needed for international arbitration? Or can we continue to rely on national ethical codes, unspoken values and the personal standards of counsel who represent the parties? Ethics codes are a means to an end, in the case of civil servants to implement good public policy in a transparent manner, and in the corporate world to improve company performance, avoid entanglements with government agencies and prevent liability lawsuits. In the case of international arbitration, the overriding goal would be to improve the fairness of the process and ensure the integrity of – and public respect for – the outcome.

While the system could continue with business as usual, without a code for international arbitration, we strongly believe the time has come for the adoption of an explicit code of conduct to guide counsel representing the parties. In addition to guiding counsel, such a code would ensure that arbitrators and administering institutions refer to a uniform and standardized set of rules in cases in which questions of counsel's conduct arise.[7]

The reasons are becoming increasingly clear. Although we may never get to the point of arbitration in a fishbowl, demands for a more transparent process are growing. Awards are increasingly published and scrutinized, and open hearings are beginning to take place in certain contexts. Global standards are changing, and national and international non-governmental organizations (NGOs) are taking a heightened interest in cross-border disputes, particularly when environmental, human rights or other public interest issues are at stake.[8] Even if external scrutiny were not a factor, in a growing

---

7. One commentator has pointed out – albeit in the context of considering arbitrator integrity – that "vigilance commends itself when lawyers take on various professional roles, making arguments as advocates in one case about propositions that remain open in other cases where they sit as arbitrators". See William PARK, "Arbitrator Integrity: The Transient and the Permanent", 46 San Diego Law Review (2009, no. 3) p. 630 at p. 631.

8. Governments, for their part, are adjusting to much more transparency in the way their business is conducted. More than eighty-five countries have now passed Freedom of Information laws. International NGOs now rate governments on various factors such as the transparency of their budget processes and the extent of corruption. Legislatures have passed laws mandating transparent and competitive public procurement. The Extractive Industries Transparency Initiative (EITI) provides for third-party verification of mineral revenues, and is being replicated in other sectors, such as pharmaceuticals. There are international programs for recovery of stolen assets, the control of money-laundering and financing of terrorism, all of which require higher standards of transparency and ethical behavior by financial intermediaries.

number of cases tribunals have been asked to adjudicate issues of counsel's conduct, but they have had to do so without the assistance of a clear and binding set of rules.

Case loads are increasing, as are the value and significance of awards. Arbitration is no longer the closed club of a limited number of international jurists, if it ever was.[9] New faces are emerging with different country backgrounds, perspectives on issues in dispute and legal traditions. While there might in the past have been a "club" consensus on matters like conflict of interest, ex parte communications, the sharing of information, or the treatment of witnesses, these areas are now more open to the interpretation of different organizations, institutions and tribunals. So far, international arbitration has largely escaped major ethical controversy, but this cannot be taken for granted in the future.[10]

The time has now come for a collective effort by those who practice international arbitration law to develop a consensual code of conduct to guide professional practice in this field, and to ensure it is adopted by all of the principal institutions that administer proceedings. What follows is an exploration of the case for a code of conduct, culminating in a suggested draft of the content of such a code.

III. DIVERGENCES IN NATIONAL RULES AND DOUBLE DEONTOLOGY[11]

For some decades commentators have pointed to the problem that arises in international arbitration when lawyers subject to different national ethics rules appear before an arbitral tribunal.[12] The problem is often approached on the basis that different national ethics rules may lead to what is referred to as an uneven playing field for the parties' legal representatives.[13] Examples are frequently cited to demonstrate how some rules

---

9. See Bernardo CREMADES, "Overcoming the Clash of Legal Cultures: The Role of Interactive Arbitration", 14 International Arbitration (1998, no. 2) p. 157 at p. 158, noting that "the considerable participation of jurists from very different origins and with very different approaches has caused arbitral procedure to evolve in an extraordinary manner".
10. One commentator has observed that "[a]nother major factor masking the full impact of conflicting ethical norms in arbitration is the clandestine techniques by which arbitrations undoubtedly regulate proceedings before them". See Catherine ROGERS, "Fit and Function in Legal Ethics: Developing a Code of Attorney Conduct for International Arbitration", 23 Michigan Journal of International Law (2002) p. 341 at p. 376.
11. National ethics rules, or rules of professional practice, are also referred to as national rules of deontology (moral obligation). Double deontology refers to situations in which a lawyer may be subject to more than one code of ethics.
12. See Michael REISMAN, *Nullity and Revision: The Review and Enforcement of International Judgments and Awards* (Yale University Press 1971) pp. 116-117.
13. See V.V. VEEDER, "The 2001 Goff Lecture – The Lawyer's Duty to Arbitrate in Good Faith", 18 Arbitration International (2002, no. 4) p. 431 at p. 441. In arbitration conducted under the ICSID Convention, the playing field may be even more uneven. See ICSID Arbitration Rule 18, "[e]ach party may be represented or assisted by ... counsel.... There is no requirement under the ICSID Arbitration Rules that a party select a lawyer to act on its behalf; and "no party can object to a lack of professional qualifications of the opponent's representative". See ICSID Regulations and Rules, 1 Jan. 1968, Arbitration Rule 18, Note B.

may work to the advantage of one side, while the same rule would lead to a disadvantage for the other side. This conundrum of different practices arising from different legal cultures implicates a number of rules respecting counsel's conduct. One of the most frequently cited examples concerns pre-testimonial preparation of a witness. In general, common law systems consider it legitimate to prepare a witness, while civil law systems on the whole do not permit communication with witnesses prior to trial.[14] In international arbitration it is now common practice for a potential witness to be questioned by counsel about the facts of the dispute, and for counsel to assist in the presentation of testimony. Some commentators have pointed to the necessity of this approach insofar as tribunals generally require the parties to submit written witness statements.[15]

Another question concerns the issue of who may appear as a fact witness since legal systems take different approaches in regard to whether a person affiliated with a party to the dispute may appear as a witness. The common law approach allows for this kind of testimony while civil law systems often do not.[16] In international arbitration it is generally accepted that any person can testify as a fact witness, and this approach is followed in the International Bar Association (IBA) Rules on the Taking of Evidence.

Considering another element of advocacy in international arbitration, one commentator has pointed out that legal systems vary in their consideration of what constitutes "truthful" conduct by lawyers.[17] US lawyers are recognized as having a wider margin of possible construction of the law, without consideration as to whether such construction will ultimately prevail. In contrast, civil law systems take a less permissive view in regard to creative arguments, tending towards a limitation on what sort of argument can be made. In international arbitration, there has developed a custom that allows for some creativity but that nevertheless must be reasonable and not fall within the realm of overzealous advocacy.[18]

Yet another example of divergence may be found in the approaches taken to ex parte communications by different legal systems. Some countries, for example Germany, permit such contacts while other countries, including the United States, maintain restrictions against such contact. The general rule that has developed in international arbitration prohibits ex parte contacts concerning the merits of the dispute, an approach also adopted by the Council of Bars and Law Societies of Europe in the 1988 Code of Conduct for European Lawyers, or CCBE Code, as an important element of assuring a

---

14. See Catherine ROGERS, "Fit and Function", *op. cit.*, fn. 10, at p. 359; and Reza MOHTASHAMI, "The Requirement of Equal Treatment with Respect to the Conduct of Hearings and Hearing Preparation in International Arbitration", 3 Dispute Resolution International (2009, no. 2) p. 124 at pp. 130-131.
15. Lucy REED and Jonathan SUTCLIFFE, "The 'Americanization' of International Arbitration?", 16 Mealey's International Arbitration Reporter (Apr. 2001, no. 4) p. 37 at p. 42.
16. *Ibid.*
17. Catherine ROGERS, "Fit and Function", *op. cit.*, fn. 10, at p. 361.
18. *Ibid.*

fair proceeding.[19] These are just a few examples of the kinds of divergences that may be found in rules originating in different legal systems.

A different problem arises when the same counsel is subject to more than one set of national ethics rules, resulting in the application of "double deontology".[20] Sometimes, for example, the same counsel may be subject to conflicting rules, and in other instances, being subjected to different sets of rules raises the prospect of having to comply with rules with which counsel has no particular familiarity. Perhaps reflecting these concerns, an ICSID tribunal has recently pointed out the risk of "inconsistent or indeed arbitrary outcomes" if decisions are made by national bodies.[21]

This view by a tribunal may be attributed to the fact that, alongside existing national ethics rules, international arbitration has developed its own customs and practices in regard to a range of procedural issues. As is well known, these procedures reflect a harmonization of Anglo-American or common law legal traditions, on the one hand, and European or civil law traditions, on the other hand. This trend has been described elsewhere and has led to the formation of a basic procedural structure which — with adjustments in individual proceedings — is used in many if not most international arbitrations.[22]

The development and recognition of a unique dispute settlement culture of international arbitration has led some to call for an ethics code for international arbitration counsel, a code that should be founded on the basis of the culturally delocalized nature of international arbitration. The elaboration of such a code, it is argued, is necessary because "international arbitration dwells in an ethical no-man's land".[23] According to this view, although arbitration physically takes place within the boundaries of one nation, the so-called "host State" may have no particular interest in regulating counsel conduct.[24] At the same time, it is suggested, most so-called "home-

---

19. See Code of Conduct for European Lawyers (CCBE Code), adopted on 28 Oct. 1988 and updated on 19 May 2006 (available at <www.ccbe.eu/index.php?id=32&L=0>). See Commentary on Art. 4.2 to the Code. See also ICSID Administrative and Financial Regulation 24, "[d]uring the pendency of any proceeding the Secretary-General shall be the official channel of written communications among the parties [... and the] Tribunal."
20. See IBA Code of Ethics, *infra* fn. 39, Rule 1:

    "A lawyer who undertakes professional work in a jurisdiction where he is not a full member of the local profession shall adhere to the standards of professional ethics in the jurisdiction in which he has been admitted. He shall also observe all ethical standards which apply to lawyers of the country where he is working."

    See also Catherine ROGERS, "Lawyers Without Borders", 30 University of Pennsylvania Journal of International Law (2008-2009) p. 1035 for a discussion of the application of Model Rules of Professional Conduct R. 8.5(b)(1) (2002).
21. See *Hrvatska* Decision, *op. cit.*, fn. 2, at para. 23.
22. See Lucy REED and Jonathan SUTCLIFFE, "The 'Americanization' of International Arbitration?", *op. cit.*, fn. 15, at p. 38.
23. See Catherine ROGERS, "Fit and Function", *op. cit.*, fn. 10, at pp. 341, 342.
24. Catherine ROGERS, "The Ethics of Advocacy" in D. BISHOP and E. KEHOE, eds., The *Art of Advocacy in International Arbitration*, text accompanying fn. 3 (Juris Publishing 2010).

State" ethical rules do not extend their reach to international arbitral proceedings.[25] In further support for international regulation of ethics standards, the argument is made that while certain universal norms inform all legal ethics, there is a wide discrepancy as to the specific obligations arising from such norms.[26] Core concepts such as truthfulness, fairness, independence, loyalty and confidentiality, it is said, mean different things to different people, and it would be helpful to all users of international arbitration to find common ground.[27]

Many of these observations are correct, and even compelling. The absence of international ethics regulation does indeed appear to leave the waters of international arbitration uncharted, or at least somewhat murky and confused. Having said that, the characterization of "an ethical no-man's land" appears to overlook the role that international arbitration tribunals play in regulating counsel conduct in specific cases. In addition, it can be asked whether regulation can achieve the desired homogeneity and bring about a playing field that is perceived by all participants as completely level. Judgment calls that must be made in the application of ethics rules do not exist in a void. Rather, they are manifestations of human values conditioned by education and tradition, both legal and non-legal, that cannot – with a stroke – be ordered into neat, consensual, global uniformity.

While some have advocated regulation in spite of these considerable normative obstacles, others have cautioned against such an approach.[28] This reluctance to embrace regulation as an answer to existing problems stems in part from the conviction that although national ethics rules differ, and their application to particular proceedings is far from clear, there is no real crisis compelling intervention. Under this view, the existing system is not broken and does not need to be fixed.[29] This conclusion is shared by another commentator who argues that national ethics rules do apply to counsel conduct in international arbitration, and a conflict-of-laws approach is the proper way to reconcile inconsistent national ethics rules.[30] According to this view, it is consistent with the structure of international arbitral proceedings to apply conflict-of-laws rules to determine which ethics rules should apply to the conduct of counsel in a particular proceeding. This commentator also argues that arbitral tribunals have the authority to rule on these questions, and that national authorities will defer to their decisions should disciplinary actions ensue.

---

25. Catherine ROGERS, "Fit and Function", *op. cit.*, fn. 10, at pp. 341, 342.
26. *Ibid.*
27. *Ibid.*, at pp. 358-373.
28. See V.V. VEEDER, "Is There Any Need for a Code of Ethics for International Commercial Arbitrators?", *Les Arbitres Internationaux, Colloque du 4 Février* (2005) p. 187 at pp. 190-192.
29. *Ibid.*
30. See Kirsten WEISENBERGER, "Peace is Not the Absence of Conflict: A Response to Professor Rogers's Article 'Fit and Function in Legal Ethics'", 25 *Wisconsin International Law Journal* (2007) p. 89 at p. 90.

Another approach is suggested by a commentator who has developed an "ethical checklist" that could be employed at the beginning of a case to ensure that the parties, their counsel and the tribunal are on the "same page" with respect to ethical standards.[31]

IV. RECENT DEVELOPMENTS

These diverging views suggest that the issue remains of interest and concern both to those who favor maintaining the status quo and to those who call for change, a situation reflected in a number of institutional initiatives. Since ICCA held its last congress in Dublin in 2008, the American Bar Association,[32] the International Bar Association,[33] the American Society of International Law[34] and the International Law Association have all taken steps to examine the question of standards of conduct for counsel in international arbitral proceedings.

A further development that also should be taken into consideration in the discussion of legal ethics in international arbitration is the 1988 CCBE Code, last amended in 2006 and now applicable, although in somewhat different forms, in forty-one European countries.[35] The CCBE Code was created to address issues arising in the context of cross-border practice and currently applies to more than 700,000 European lawyers.[36] It may be recalled that it was the increasing frequency of cross-border activities of lawyers within the European Economic Area that led to its elaboration because this increased activity made it necessary to define common rules of professional conduct. The express application of CCBE rules to arbitral proceedings is somewhat limited. It provides that a lawyer has a general duty of fair conduct towards an arbitral tribunal; that a lawyer has a duty of respect and courtesy towards an arbitral tribunal; and that a lawyer must not knowingly give false or misleading information to an arbitral tribunal.

Noting that the express provisions applicable to arbitral proceedings are limited in number, one commentator has pointed out that there are numerous provisions in the Code that nonetheless apply in the context of international arbitration, "either by explicit incorporation into national norms ... or as evidence of internationally accepted norms".[37]

---

31. See Cyrus BENSON, "Can Professional Ethics Wait? The Need for Transparency in International Arbitration", 3 Dispute Resolution International (2009, no. 1) p. 78 at p. 85.
32. See ABA Commission on Ethics 2020, *Preliminary Issues Outline* dated 19 Nov. 2009, posing the following questions: "Do the Model Rules adequately address ethical issues relating to international arbitration?"; "What, for example, should be the ethical rules that govern a U.S. lawyer engaged in an arbitral proceeding in another country where the governing law is not U.S. law?" and "Should it matter whether the lawyer's client is or is not a U.S. person or entity?"
33. See Janet WALKER, "Ethics in Arbitration for Counsel and Arbitrators," 14 IBA Arbitration Committee Newsletter (Mar. 2009) p. 10 at p. 11.
34. See American Society of International Law, *Proceedings of the Annual Meeting* (2008).
35. See Explanatory Memorandum to the CCBE Code, *op. cit.*, fn. 19.
36. See Introduction to Charter of Core Principles of the European Legal Profession and Code of Conduct for European Lawyers, Council of Bars and Law Societies of Europe, 31 Jan. 2008.
37. See Jan PAULSSON, "Standards of Conduct for Counsel in International Arbitration", 3 American Review of International Arbitration (1992) p. 214 at p. 221.

Such norms may, for example, include the Code's provisions on principles such as independence, trust, personal integrity and confidentiality. Other parts of the Code, for example in the sections on relations with clients and relations between lawyers, espouse principles that might find wider usage, both in international arbitral practice and beyond the borders of the European countries that have adopted the Code's principles.[38]

In addition to the CCBE Code, some of the norms that are of concern to international arbitration practitioners are dealt with in other instruments that are relevant to arbitral proceedings. These include the IBA International Code of Ethics[39] and the IBA Rules on the Taking of Evidence, a revised version of which came into force in May 2010.

The problems that international arbitration counsel are, or should be, concerned with today in regard to applicable standards of conduct, are multifaceted and complex. They involve questions of the best arbitral practice, guidelines such as those developed by the IBA, and binding rules emanating from the CCBE Code and national authorities.[40] Nearly twenty years ago, Jan Paulsson observed with prescience that "it would be desirable to have a specific code relating to international arbitration".[41]

Since then, international arbitration has grown exponentially, and in the last decade or so we have seen investor-State arbitration expand both in numbers and significance. Many of the procedural rules relied upon in these kinds of disputes have their origins in practices established in international commercial arbitration. Investment arbitration proceedings have undoubtedly benefited from the pragmatism and experience that arbitrators with a commercial arbitration background have introduced through their procedural rulings.[42]

Having said that, just as commercial arbitration has informed certain practices in investor-State proceedings, the opposite is true as well. The ongoing debate about transparency in international arbitration might never have evolved to where it is today had it not been for the frequent appearances of States as parties to arbitral proceedings. As is well known, investor-State proceedings have drawn attention to a number of disputes because of the public interest questions that these disputes have presented. But investor-State proceedings have also exposed the overall system of international arbitration to new levels of public scrutiny, a factor that must be taken into consideration as we reflect on the strengths and weaknesses of the system. An awareness of the implications of such scrutiny may be seen in that arbitral tribunals themselves attach

---

38. See Explanatory Memorandum, *op. cit.*, fn. 19, "it is also hoped that the Code will be acceptable to the legal profession of other non-member States in Europe and elsewhere so that it could also be applied by appropriate conventions between them and the Member States".
39. International Bar Association International Code of Ethics, first adopted 1956; revised 1988.
40. A recent development giving a further indication of the different sources of ethics rules governing arbitral proceedings may be found in the Closer Economic Partnership Agreement signed by Hong Kong, China and New Zealand on 29 March 2010. Annex 1 to Chapter 16 (Dispute Settlement) contains a provision that expressly prohibits ex parte communications between tribunal members and a party. See Annex 1 (to Chapter 16) on Model Rules of Procedure for Arbitral Tribunals.
41. See Jan PAULSSON, "Standards of Conduct for Counsel in International Arbitration", *op. cit.*, fn. 37, at p. 221.
42. See, e.g., Jan PAULSSON, "The Timely Arbitrator: Reflections on the Böckstiegel Method", 22 Arbitration International (2006, no. 9) p. 19 at pp. 19-26.

importance to the cohesive development of investment law, and are generally minded to take into consideration decisions issued by other tribunals on similar issues.[43]

Transparency, however, is only one factor in a broader concern for the overall legitimacy of the arbitral process as a sound, acceptable contemporary dispute settlement mechanism.

V.   THE LEGITIMACY OF ARBITRAL PROCEEDINGS

Legitimacy, in addition to transparency, often evokes notions of good governance and predictability. Particularly in arbitrations involving States, these are hallmarks of a system that users recognize as being capable of providing procedural fairness.[44] While the system may not be broken, it lends itself to criticism, at a minimum for being archaic. Applicable ethics rules are difficult to identify,[45] tensions are not readily resolved, and experienced practitioners – both among counsel and arbitrators – may have a considerable advantage over newcomers to the field. Moreover, the sanctions that inappropriate – or unethical – counsel conduct may invite from tribunals are far from clear. This could, as has been the case in the past, involve an award of costs.[46] More recently, however, tribunals have also been asked to disqualify counsel, raising the

---

43. See *Saipem S.p.A. v. People's Republic of Bangladesh* (ICSID Case No. ARB/05/7), Decision on Jurisdiction of 21 Mar. 2007, at para. 67, "[The Tribunal] ... believes that, subject to the specifics of a given treaty and of the circumstances of the actual case, it has a duty to seek to contribute to the harmonious development of investment law and thereby to meet the legitimate expectations of the community of States and investors towards certainty of the rule of law." See also *Glamis Gold, Ltd. v. United States of America*, NAFTA Case, Award dated 8 June 2009, at para. 5, "The ultimate integrity of the Chapter 11 system as a whole requires a modicum of awareness of each of these tribunals for each other and the system as a whole." See also Carrie MENKEL-MEADOW, "Are Cross-Cultural Ethics Standards Possible or Desirable in International Arbitration" in *Mélanges en l'honneur de Pierre Tercier* (2008) p. 883 at p. 886, noting that "[i]f the privately chosen decision makers ... do not adhere to a systematic understanding of proper relationships and behavior with each other and with the parties before them, then the system that has worked so well for decades will likely suffer a loss of confidence and perhaps use". It should be noted that feedback (in this instance, from previous tribunal decisions) and adaptation (from new decisions taking prior decisions into account) are characteristics of an adaptive, complex system, as elaborated by complexity theory.
44. One commentator has observed that while "no arbitration tribunal can guarantee perfection at all times in deciding substantive law or fact (because judges and arbitrators are not deities), arbitrators can reasonably be asked to always deliver procedural fairness". See V.V. VEEDER, "The 2001 Goff Lecture – The Lawyer's Duty to Arbitrate in Good Faith", *op. cit.*, fn. 13, at p. 435.
45. See John TOWNSEND, "Clash and Convergence on Ethical Issues in International Arbitration", 36 University of Miami Inter-American Law Review (2004-2005, no. 1) p. 1 at p. 2.
46. See, e.g., *Zhinvali Development Ltd. v. Republic of Georgia* (ICSID Case No. ARB/00/1), Award of 24 Jan. 2003, at para. 430; *Desert Line Projects LLC v. Republic of Yemen* (ICSID Case No. ARB/05/17), Award of 6 Feb. 2008, at para. 304; *Pey Casado* Award, *op. cit.*, fn. 4, at para. 729.

question of whether a tribunal has the power and duty to deny a party the legal representation of its choice, and if so, on what grounds.[47]

Much of the debate regarding counsel ethics has hitherto taken place in the abstract, focusing on rules, or the absence thereof, as well as on conflict-of-laws issues, with relatively little discussion of problems arising in practice. The publication of awards, decisions and procedural rulings in investor-State proceedings has introduced a new perspective on the problems that we are considering today. One consequence of this increased level of transparency in the proceedings is that greater scrutiny of not just substantive but also procedural issues may be expected in the future. This goes to the heart of the legitimacy of the international arbitral system.

VI. RECENT ICSID DECISIONS

Before discussing some recent rulings concerning applications to disqualify counsel in investor-State arbitrations, it may be useful to briefly recall that tribunals, in large part, rely on their power to award costs to control the procedure in an arbitral proceeding. Such decisions on costs may simply reflect a perceived need by the tribunal to make certain adjustments in the final financial outcome of a proceeding, which take into account instances in which one side or the other failed to contribute properly to an efficient proceeding. In some cases, such adverse cost rulings may reflect compensation for expenses attributable to unwarranted delays or lack of coordination. However, other cost rulings may reflect more serious flaws in the conduct of the parties. In a recent ICSID decision, the tribunal awarded costs on grounds of delays, and consequential additional costs incurred on account of one party's "case strategy".[48] The underlying reason for the delays appears to have been ex parte communications that took place between counsel and the party-appointed arbitrator.[49] This decision raises the question whether there was sufficient appreciation on the part of counsel of the extent to which such communications were incompatible with the customs and practices of international arbitration and the attendant risk of jeopardizing the tribunal's integrity. The decision also invites consideration of whether procedural irregularities, including counsel conduct that is incompatible with proper practices, ought to be dealt with by tribunals in a manner that creates a more transparent record of the wrongdoing.

Other recent rulings of ICSID tribunals concerning counsel conduct include the decisions rendered in the *Hrvatska v. Slovenia* and the *Rompetrol v. Romania* cases. In the *Hrvatska* case, the tribunal had been asked by the claimant "to recommend to the Respondent that it refrain from using the services" of a particular lawyer who would be assisting respondent's legal team at the hearing.[50] Claimant based its request on the ground that the lawyer in question and the presiding arbitrator were both members of

---

47. See *Hrvatska* Decision and *Rompetrol* Decision, *op. cit.*, fn. 2; See also Unpublished Annulment Committee Decision, *op. cit.*, fn. 3.
48. See *Pey Casado* Award, *op. cit.*, fn. 4, at para. 729.
49. *Ibid.*, at paras. 36 and 37.
50. *Hrvatska* Decision, *op. cit.*, fn. 2, at para. 10.

the same chambers in London, and that this relationship raised "great concern and cast a 'cloud over these proceedings'".[51] Claimant argued that the respondent had failed to make prompt disclosure as required by the IBA Guidelines because the relationship allegedly could give rise to justifiable doubts about conflicts of interest. Claimant added that "many throughout the world, [are] entirely unfamiliar with the English legal system" and that

> "... the community of participants in ICSID arbitrations is much broader than the English bar, and what may not, apparently, be cause for concern in London may well be viewed very differently by a reasonable third person from Africa, Argentina, or Zagreb, Croatia. The Claimant *is* concerned that the President, and a member of the Respondent's legal team, are from the same Chambers. Viewed from the Claimant's cultural perspective, such concerns are justified, and, indeed, they are unavoidable."[52]

The respondent took the position that it had no disclosure obligation under the IBA Guidelines, and moreover, that there was no professional or personal relationship with the presiding arbitrator, and that the lawyer in question had no facts or information known to the lawyer that could give a reasonable third person any justifiable doubts as to the presiding arbitrator's partiality or independence.

The tribunal started its analysis by noting that the ICSID Convention does not grant explicit power to tribunals to exclude counsel, and observed that it was a fundamental principle that parties could seek the representation they saw fit. The tribunal balanced this principle, however, with what it called the principle of the "immutability of properly constituted tribunals".[53] In practical terms, the tribunal said, this meant that a party could not amend its legal team in a way that would "imperil the Tribunal's status or legitimacy".[54] The concern with legitimacy and the need "to preserve the integrity of the proceedings and, ultimately, its Award"[55] appear to have guided the tribunal, which also observed that "the proceedings should not be tainted by any justifiable doubt as to the impartiality or independence of any tribunal member".[56] The tribunal went on to say that "[t]he justifiability of an apprehension of partiality depends on all relevant circumstances",[57] and in this case, that included the fact that the system of London Chambers was entirely "foreign" to the claimant.[58] Another factor that clearly played a role in the tribunal's decision was the very late disclosure of the barrister's role in the case, that is, shortly before the oral hearing.

---

51. *Ibid.*, at para. 7.
52. *Ibid.*, at para. 10.
53. *Ibid.*, at para. 25.
54. *Ibid.*, at para. 26.
55. *Ibid.*, at para. 30.
56. *Ibid.*
57. *Ibid.*, at para. 31.
58. *Ibid.*

The tribunal based its power to exclude counsel on what it referred to as "an inherent power to take measures to preserve the integrity of its proceedings".[59] The tribunal said that this inherent power was partly based on Art. 44 of the Convention, authorizing a tribunal to decide "any question of procedure" not expressly dealt with in the Convention, but that more broadly, there is an "inherent power of an international court to deal with any issues necessary for the conduct of matters fully within its jurisdiction", and that this power "exists independently of any statutory reference".[60] In other words, one might conclude from this case that tribunals have inherent power to disqualify counsel appearing before them in order to protect the integrity of proceedings.

A different approach was followed in the second case, *Rompetrol v. Romania*. In this proceeding the respondent had sought the disqualification of claimant's counsel on the ground that there had been a previous professional relationship with one of the arbitrators, and that this allegedly called into question "the integrity of the Tribunal and the arbitral process, as well as its total independence".[61] The challenged lawyer denied any disclosure obligation and denied "any reasonable basis for inferring an infringement of the Tribunal's independence".[62]

In line with the *Hrvatska* decision, the *Rompetrol* tribunal noted that the ICSID Convention contains no express power for a tribunal to exclude counsel.[63] However, the tribunal said that if such power existed, it could only be exercised in "extraordinary circumstances, these being circumstances which genuinely touch on the integrity of the arbitral process *as assessed by the Tribunal itself*".[64]

In assessing what would constitute a threat to "the essential integrity of the arbitral process", the tribunal considered the kind of advantage that might develop when "natural sympathy" was present on account of a prior association between counsel and the tribunal member.[65]

The *Rompetrol* tribunal, however, was reluctant to endorse the proposition of the *Hrvatska* tribunal that the "inherent authority" of an international tribunal to preserve the integrity of the proceedings extended to the exclusion of counsel.[66] It noted that "the only justification for such extension in the arbitral context would be a clear need to safeguard the essential integrity of the arbitral process, on the basis that such integrity would be compromised were the exclusion not ordered".[67]

The tribunal went on to observe that there does exist in "some limited circumstances a power to control a party's choice of counsel",[68] but that such power can only be exercised rarely, and in compelling circumstances. In the particular matter before it, the

---

59. *Ibid.*, at para. 33.
60. *Ibid.*
61. *Rompetrol* Decision, *op. cit.*, fn. 2, at para. 5.
62. *Ibid.*, at para. 6.
63. *Ibid.*, at para. 14.
64. *Ibid.*, at para. 15.
65. *Ibid.*, at para. 17.
66. *Ibid.*, at para. 22.
67. *Ibid.*
68. *Ibid.*, at para. 23.

tribunal found no basis for any suggestion that it should interfere with the choice of counsel.

In arriving at its conclusion, the tribunal paid heed to the role of national ethics rules. The tribunal observed that counsel's role is to present his client's case "with diligence and with honesty, *and in due compliance with the applicable rules of professional conduct and ethics*". The tribunal further said that it was "reluctant to lend encouragement to any practice over and above the accepted rules of professional conduct and ethics that might end up casting a blight over the investor's freedom to find the most appropriate person to represent it in promoting its claims within the ICSID system".

However, having found that the ICSID Convention and Rules do not address the subject, the tribunal did not identify what rules of ethics were applicable nor did it seek to address such rules. The *Rompetrol* decision therefore raises the question of whether there exists any inherent power of a tribunal to disqualify counsel, and cautions, that to the extent such power exists, it will likely be exercised only seldom and in exceptional circumstances. The hypothetical character of this decision is perhaps what explains the tentative reliance by the tribunal on "applicable rules of professional conduct and ethics", leaving this question unaddressed.

In the third, unpublished ICSID case, an *ad hoc* Annulment Committee was asked to disqualify counsel on the ground of conflict of interest. In that case, the respondent argued that claimant's counsel had at an earlier point in time represented respondent in a related proceeding. The respondent invoked concern for the legitimacy of the arbitral process, requesting the tribunal "to grant procedural due process to both parties during the proceedings, and to ensure that an eventual award [would not be] tainted by any procedural irregularities".[69]

Counsel for the claimant maintained that there was no conflict of interest and that he had not acquired confidential information through his earlier involvement with the respondent. In this case, the Committee determined that it had to decide the matter in accordance with the power given to it under Art. 44 of the ICSID Convention. The Committee further stated that it had the power and duty

> "to conduct the process before it in such a way that the parties are treated fairly and with equality ... and that [such] power and duty necessarily includes the power and obligation to make sure that generally recognized principles relating to conflict of interest and the protection of the confidentiality of information imparted by clients to their lawyers are complied with. Indeed [the Committee said], such principles are of fundamental importance to the fairness of the Committee's procedures, and such that the Committee has the power and duty to ensure that there is no serious departure from them."[70]

The Committee also confirmed that it did not have any "deontological responsibilities" or "jurisdiction over the parties' legal representation in their own capacities".[71] The

---

69. Unpublished Annulment Committee Decision, *op. cit.*, fn. 3, at para. 10.
70. *Ibid.*, at para. 37.
71. *Ibid.*, at para. 39.

Committee emphasized that it "had no power to rule on an allegation of misconduct under any such professional rules as [might] apply", and that its concern was "limited to the fair conduct of the proceedings before it".[72]

In this case, the Committee had before it two national codes of ethics, and at its own request had also been directed to the relevant provisions of the CCBE Code. The Committee observed that this material was valuable but only to "the extent it reveals common general principles which could guide the Committee".[73] It was observed, however, that "such codes could not bind the Committee, as an international tribunal".[74] The Committee said it had to consider "what general principles are plainly indispensable for the fair conduct of proceedings".[75]

In considering the facts of the case, the Committee rejected the request to disqualify counsel and highlighted that it could only do so if there was "clear evidence of prejudice".[76] In doing so, the Committee had no difficulty in finding not only the power but a duty to resolve the conflict issue. This duty arose from the obligation to treat the parties fairly and equally and had to be discharged on the basis of general principles of ethics, and not on the basis of any specific national code.

The above decisions are few in number but nevertheless illustrative. They show that the tribunals, faced with similar issues, arrived at three different solutions. One tribunal found an inherent power to disqualify counsel; one tribunal speculated that *if* an inherent power existed, it could only be exercised rarely and in exceptional circumstances; and one committee found that it had not only the power but also the duty to deal with a request for disqualification. In one decision the tribunal said that:

> "For an international system like that of ICSID, it seems unacceptable for the solution to reside in the individual national bodies which regulate the work of professional service providers, because that might lead to inconsistent or indeed arbitrary outcomes depending on the attitudes of such bodies, or the content (or lack of relevant content) of their rules. It would moreover be disruptive to interrupt international cases to ascertain the position taken by such bodies."[77]

The second tribunal called for counsel to present his client's case "in due compliance with the applicable rules of professional conduct and ethics". In the third case, where the parties had made extensive reference to different national rules on legal ethics, as well as the CCBE Code, the Committee said that:

> "This material is valuable to the extent that it reveals common general principles which may guide the Committee. But none of it directly binds the Committee, as an international tribunal. Accordingly, the Committee's consideration of the

---

72. *Ibid.*
73. *Ibid.*, at para. 41.
74. *Ibid.*
75. *Ibid.*
76. *Ibid.*, at para. 55.
77. *Hrvatska* Decision, *op. cit.*, fn. 2, at para. 23.

matter is not, and should not be, based upon a nice reading of any particular code of professional ethics, applicable in any particular national jurisdiction. Such codes may vary in their detailed application. Rather, the Committee must consider what general principles are plainly indispensable for the fair conduct of the proceedings."[78]

In considering whether there is a compelling need for an international ethics code, one might reflect on the counterarguments that can be advanced. For example, as shown, tribunals are not bound by precedent and have found ad hoc solutions to issues arising in individual cases. Another possibility in future cases would be to invite national courts into arbitral proceedings to oversee, or police, counsel's conduct. A further option would be for arbitrators to continue to use assessments of costs as a means of controlling the conduct of lawyers. These potential solutions, however, are flawed for a variety of reasons. First, cost assessments may be characterized as "blunt" instruments for policing counsel. Such assessments are deficient to the extent that they are indirect, they do not fully address the problems and ultimately target the parties, as opposed to counsel. Second, regulating counsel conduct through additional court proceedings would interfere in the arbitral process because such procedures would introduce inevitable delays and additional costs. The third option, to allow tribunals to fashion their own – perhaps idiosyncratic – solutions is far from ideal as it would abandon all aspirations towards uniform solutions.

The desirability for uniformity has increased as the involvement of States as parties in both investment and commercial cases has brought public interest into the picture. Such interest has, in turn, led to increased publication of investment awards and there is more recently both interest and willingness to publish also procedural decisions. These decisions, such as the ones discussed in this paper, are destined for a new level of intense scrutiny that parties and tribunals did not have to deal with in the past. As a consequence, the lack of clarity as to which ethical rules apply, the existence of conflicting rules and obligations, the non-transparency and increased monetary value of many proceedings, and complexity of claims, combined with greater public scrutiny, creates a dangerously unstable foundation that can be expected to challenge confidence in international arbitration as a sound dispute settlement system. Other areas of arbitral practice, for example with respect to challenges to arbitrators, show the importance of the arbitral system being able to police itself. In a similar vein, international arbitration must be able to articulate and enforce standards for counsel's conduct on the basis of clear rules of general application.

VII.   CONCLUSION

From the foregoing, it should be apparent that the risks of continuing on a business-as-usual basis are likely to grow, and that a uniform code of ethics is a necessary part of underpinning the international arbitral system and maintaining public confidence. In the

---

78. Unpublished Annulment Committee Decision, *op. cit.*, fn. 3, at para. 41.

short run, an ethics code would guide counsel on how they should conduct themselves and alert arbitrators with limited tribunal experience as to the customs and conventions. In the longer run, such a code would contribute to uniformity in arbitral jurisprudence, improve the efficiency of proceedings, the fairness of outcomes, and above all, it would enhance the credibility and legitimacy of the international arbitration process as a whole.

A draft set of ethics rules and draft commentary has been attached to this paper (see this volume, pp. 408-420).[79] The authors propose that the proper way forward is for a body like the IBA to establish a process by which the discussion, development and refinement of the draft code can be moved forward, with a view to developing a consensus on the substantive provisions. The first step would be for the IBA to appoint a working group of representatives from all the main stakeholders – counsel, arbitrators, international arbitration institutions, and perhaps others.

It is to be expected that the code would at least initially be non-binding, insofar as tensions with the rules of national Bar associations and Law Societies would have to be resolved as part of the process and before the code could attain binding status. In this connection it is instructive to note that the implementation of the CCBE Code has been a lengthy and uneven process. However, even if the code were non-binding initially, the elaboration of transparent provisions would nevertheless serve to highlight potential conflicts for individual lawyers as well as tensions between the rules that might apply between opposing counsel. The code would also clarify the rules and principles to which tribunals consider themselves bound and point to where such rules and principles might differ from applicable national ethics codes to which lawyers are generally bound. Questions of uncertainty could thus be addressed as a preliminary matter.

It is to be hoped that the ethics code would in due course be adopted by arbitral institutions and provide a common set of guidelines for all international arbitration disputes, both investment and commercial. We would thus be acknowledging the precept of John Stuart Mill, who observed in his *Principles of Political Economy* in 1848 that:

> "To human beings, who, as hitherto educated, can scarcely cultivate even a good quality without running it into a fault, it is indispensable to be perpetually comparing their own notions and customs with the experience and example of persons in different circumstances from themselves; and there is no nation which does not need to borrow from others, not merely particular arts or practices, but essential points of character in which its own type is inferior."[80]

---

79. The draft set of rules has principally been elaborated on the basis of the IBA Code of Ethics, *op. cit.*, fn. 39, and the CCBE Code, *op. cit.*, fn. 19.
80. Quoted by Kwame Anthony APPIAH in *The Ethics of Identity* (Princeton 2005) at p. 271.

International Code of Ethics for Lawyers Practicing Before International Arbitral Tribunals

I. Applicable Ethics Rules

Rule 1. This Code shall prevail over national ethics or other standards for the practice of law before international arbitral tribunals.
(Council of Bars and Law Societies of Europe (CCBE) Rule 1.4 and 1.5 Field of application *Ratione Personae/Ratione Materia*; See also International Bar Association (IBA) Int'l Code of Ethics Rule 1)

- *This Code provides a guide to international arbitration practitioners as to the ethical conduct expected in international arbitration, aiming to ensure greater fairness in arbitral proceedings. Furthermore, to the extent conflicts between different State legal systems arise in international arbitration, these rules aim to mitigate such conflicts by providing a consensus as to the appropriate ethical rules drawn from the differing practices of civil and common law states and the exigencies of international arbitration.*

II. General Principles

Independence

Rule 2. In the discharge of their professional duties, lawyers shall preserve their independence from their client.
(IBA Int'l Code of Ethics Rule 3; CCBE General Principle 2.1 – Independence)

- *The meaning of "independence" differs between civil law practice and American common law practice. This rule reflects an understanding of independence more closely related to that held in civil law jurisdictions than in the United States. In both practices, a lawyer's representation of a client should be motivated by concern for the client and the interests of justice, rather than personal motives. However in US practice, independence connotes a general separation of the legal profession from government, and contemplates that lawyers will have almost total loyalty to the client and the client's interests. By contrast, in civil law systems, lawyers are regarded as "quasi-government agents", and independence refers more to a lawyer's relationship to the client and other attorneys. This difference becomes evident by comparing the preambles of two prominent ethical codes: the Preamble to the American Bar Association (ABA) Model Rules of Professional Conduct, which emphasizes a lawyer's duty to his or her client, and the Preamble to the CCBE, which refers to a lawyer's obligations to society.*

> *An example of this different approach can be drawn from Rule 2.1.1 of the CCBE, upon which this rule is based. That Rule states that a lawyer should "be careful not to compromise his or her professional standards in order to please the client, the court or third parties". Although US practice is not directly in conflict with this rule, presumably US practice would not hold as strict a view on what constitutes a "compromise" of professional standards as a civil law court would, as is evident, for example, from the greater permissiveness of creative advocacy in US practice.*
>
> *The lawyer must in any case retain enough independence from his or her client that the lawyer will not be swayed to violate his or her ethical duties to the tribunal in order to ingratiate himself to the client or obtain other personal gain.*

Personal Integrity

Rule 3. Lawyers shall at all times maintain the dignity of their profession and act with honor and integrity.
(IBA Int'l Code of Ethics Rule 2; CCBE Rule 2.2)

- *As international arbitration has grown in popularity as an effective dispute-resolution mechanism, there has been an accompanying call for greater transparency and fairness. Trust in international arbitration and its practitioners requires that a lawyer abstain from behavior that discredits not only arbitral practice but the very institution. A lawyer's personal honor, honesty and integrity must be beyond doubt. For the lawyer, these traditional virtues are professional obligations.*

Confidentiality

Rule 4. All communications between attorney and client relating to the subject matter of the lawyer's representation are privileged and may not be disclosed without the client's express or implicit permission, except to the extent they relate to future conduct that may be criminal or fraudulent. In-house attorneys are included within the scope of this Rule.
(CCBE General Principle 2.3.1 and 2.3.2 – Confidentiality)

- *It is the essence of a lawyer's function that the lawyer should be told by his or her client things that the client would not tell to others, and that the lawyer should be the recipient of such information on the basis of confidence. Confidentiality is therefore a primary and fundamental right and duty of the lawyer. A lawyer should not reveal any information relating to his or her representation of the client, unless the client gives informed consent, disclosure is permitted to prevent future criminal or fraudulent conduct by the client, or when otherwise required by the law of the jurisdiction in which the lawyer is licensed.*

Legal systems take different views on the extensiveness of the duty of confidentiality. For example, in France, the notion of "professional secret" protects information communicated by the client to his or her attorney, but an attorney is not bound to keep confidential his or her communication to the client. The common law duty of confidentiality is much broader, and Islamic law imposes an even higher duty, requiring protection of all information relating to such representation, not just attorney-client communication.

Legal systems also differ in their treatment of confidentiality obligations in the face of client wrongdoing. Even within the United States, the practice among the states varies significantly. Most European legal systems do not address the issue, and the CCBE, though it acknowledges the problem, does not expressly recognize the tension between obligations to disclose wrongdoing and maintaining client confidences.

Rule 5. **Any oral or written communication between lawyers representing the same party or parties with similar interests in the case or similar cases shall be accorded a confidential character and be privileged as far as the arbitral tribunal is concerned.**
(IBA Int'l Code of Ethics Rule 5; CCBE Rule 5.3 Correspondence between Lawyers; see also CCBE Commentary)

- *In addition to the duty to maintain client confidences, some states impose other confidentiality obligations. For example, communications between lawyers, even including opposing counsel, are regarded as confidential. In France, when a lawyer receives a communication marked "confidential", the lawyer must keep it confidential, even from his or her own client. By contrast, in the United States or the United Kingdom, not disclosing confidential communications from opposing counsel to one's client could conflict with the lawyer's duty to keep his or her client informed. This rule requires that confidentiality be maintained only as to communications between counsel either representing the same parties or parties with similar interests.*

Rule 6. **Lawyers should never disclose, unless lawfully ordered to do so by a proper Court with jurisdiction or as required by Statute or in a lawsuit with the client, what has been communicated to them in their capacity as lawyers even after they have ceased to be the client's counsel. This duty extends to their partners, to junior lawyers assisting them and to their employees.**
(IBA Int'l Code of Ethics Rule 14; CCBE General Principle 2.3.2 – Confidentiality)

- *The duty of confidentiality is not limited in time, and is subject to the same conditions as discussed in the Commentary to Rule 4. States' treatment of post-representation confidentiality varies considerably. In the United States, a lawyer may not accept employment of a new client if the matter is "substantially related" to a matter involving the former client, and the old and* prospective clients are "materially adverse". The prospective client may waive the conflict, but the lawyer has little discretion to do so.

European practice affords the lawyer more discretion. For example, the CCBE only forbids a lawyer from accepting a new client if there would be a "risk" of breaching the former client's confidences, or if the lawyer's knowledge of the former client gives an unfair advantage to the new client. It is within the lawyer's discretion to assess the risk and prospect of unfair advantage.

As international arbitrations often involve large law firms, it is important that the duty of confidentiality extend not only to the lawyer's partners and junior lawyers assisting him or her, but also the legal support staff.

III. Relations with Clients

Acceptance and Withdrawal

Rule 7. A lawyer should never consent to handle a case unless: (a) the client gives direct instructions, or (b) instructions are given in any other permissible manner.
(IBA Int'l Code of Ethics Rule 9; CCBE Rule 3.1.1 Acceptance and Termination of Instructions)

- *This rule is designed to ensure that a relationship is maintained between lawyer and client, and that the lawyer in fact receives instructions from the client. The rule omits language from both the IBA and CCBE Rules that permits a lawyer to act in a case that has been forwarded by another lawyer or assigned by a competent body without express permission of the client.*

    Regarding cases forwarded by another lawyer, the omission of this language shows a distinction between European and US practice. In European practice, the lawyer has more of a prerogative in handling a client's case, and in some countries, this extends so far as to permit substitution of counsel without the knowledge or consent of the client. American practice requires that a lawyer show more deference to his or her client's decisions. In US practice, a lawyer could not substitute counsel without informing the client and obtaining permission, and therefore a lawyer could not consent to handle a case forwarded by another lawyer, unless the referring lawyer is acting on instructions from the client.

    A lawyer may consent to handle a case based upon instructions from the client given through a duly-authorized intermediary. It is the responsibility of the lawyer to satisfy him- or herself as to the authority of the intermediary and the wishes of the client.

Rule 8. It is improper for lawyers to accept a case unless they can handle it in a timely manner and with due competence.
(IBA Int'l Code of Ethics Rule 4; CCBE Rule 3.1.3 Acceptance and Termination of Instructions)

- *It is imperative, particularly when a lawyer represents a foreign client, that the lawyer understand that the client must depend on him or her much more than in the case of a lawyer from his own country. A foreign client may request the lawyer's representation in an international arbitration that may involve the law of the client's state, with which the lawyer may be unfamiliar. Alternatively, a foreign client may be unfamiliar with the law and practice of the lawyer's state, and request the lawyer's assistance in a proceeding in which that law is relevant. Under either scenario, the lawyer must be aware of either his/her or the client's lack of familiarity with the relevant law, and either refuse to accept the case or enlist the assistance of other lawyers in order to provide the client with competent and efficient representation.*

  The lawyer must also take into consideration the pressure of other work, and be candid with the client about his or her ability to handle the case in a timely manner and competently.

Rule 9. Lawyers shall render legal assistance to their clients with reasonable care and diligence. They shall at all times give clients a candid opinion on any matter.
(IBA Int'l Code of Ethics Rule 10(a); CCBE Rule 3.1.2 Acceptance and Termination of Instructions)

- *A lawyer must undertake personal responsibility for fulfilling the client's instructions, and keep the client informed as to the progress of the matter with which the lawyer has been entrusted.*

  This Rule does not necessarily require that the lawyer show the high degree of deference to the client's decisions as is common in American practice. However, although the lawyer may exercise more of a prerogative in his or her handling of the client's case, the lawyer must keep the client informed and be candid with the client on the status and/or outlook for the client's case. The lawyer must also be candid with the client in explaining the limits of his or her representation, and any ethical obligations that may limit what the client requests of the lawyer.

  A lawyer cannot avoid responsibility by delegation to others. However, this Rule does not prevent a lawyer from seeking to limit his or her legal liability to the extent that it is permitted by the relevant law governing the attorney-client relationship.

Rule 10. The loyal prosecution or defense of a client's case may never cause advocates to be other than perfectly candid, subject to any legal right or privilege to the contrary, which clients choose to exercise.
(IBA Int'l Code of Ethics Rule 10(d); CCBE General Principle 2.2 – Trust and Personal Integrity)

- *A relationship of trust can only exist if a lawyer's personal honor, honesty and integrity are beyond doubt. For a lawyer these are professional obligations.*

American and European practice differ in their views of client loyalty. In Europe, the lawyer tends to be seen as more akin to an officer of the court. According to the Declaration of Perugia, the lawyer's duties extend not only to the client, but also to:

"[T]he client's family and other people towards whom the client is under a legal or moral obligation; the courts and other authorities before whom the lawyer pleads his client's cause or acts on his behalf; the legal profession in general and each fellow member of it in particular; and the public, for whom the existence of a free and independent but regulated profession is an essential guarantee that the rights of man will be respected."

From the European perspective, the lawyer's duty of candor applies not only to the client, but also to the court and arguably to the other parties listed above.

American practice takes a somewhat different view of client loyalty, casting the lawyer as a strategist and lobbyist for the client, rather than a quasi-official of the court. Thus the lawyer's duty of candor extends more narrowly to the client. For example, the American lawyer may "urge any possible construction of the law favorable to his client, without regard to his professional opinion as to the likelihood that the construction will ultimately prevail".

This Rule requires a greater duty of candor than that required under the American rule. This is also reflected in Rule 22 below, limiting the creativity of a lawyer's advocacy to "reasonable" constructions of a law.

Rule 11. Lawyers shall at any time be free to refuse to handle a case.
(IBA Int'l Code of Ethics Rule 10(b))

- *A lawyer is under no obligation to accept a case. However, a lawyer should not decline representation simply because a client or cause is unpopular, or community reaction is adverse. A lawyer should decline to represent a client if the case is frivolous and intended to merely harass or maliciously injure another or is part of a fraudulent or criminal scheme. Likewise, a lawyer should decline employment if his or her intensity of personal feeling about the client or case may impair his or her effective representation.*

Rule 12. Lawyers should only withdraw from a case during its course for good cause, and if possible in such a manner that the client's interests are not adversely affected. Good cause includes lack of timely payment of invoices by the client, the client's failure to provide honest and timely information to the lawyer, or the client's failure to provide documents ordered to be produced by the arbitral tribunal.
(IBA Int'l Code of Ethics Rule 10(c); CCBE Rule 3.1.4 Acceptance and Termination of Instructions; CCBE Rule 3.5 Payment on Account)

- *As noted in Rule 11, a lawyer has the right to refuse to represent a client in the first place, but once the lawyer agrees to represent the client, he or she has an obligation not to withdraw without reasonably attempting to protect the client's interests. A lawyer should give the client due notice of his withdrawal, suggest employment of other counsel, deliver to the client all documents and property to which the client is entitled, cooperate with subsequently employed counsel, and otherwise endeavor to minimize the possibility of harm. The lawyer should also refund to the client any compensation not earned during the employment.*

Conflict of Interest

Rule 13. Lawyers should never represent conflicting interests in an arbitral proceeding without the prior informed consent of the client. Conflicting interest refers to the specific parties to the arbitral dispute. A lawyer may never use confidential information of a client or its affiliates against that client or its affiliates in subsequent arbitral proceedings. This Rule also applies to all lawyers in a firm.
(IBA Int'l Code of Ethics Rule 13; CCBE Rule 3.2.1 and 3.2.2 Conflict of Interest)

- *This issue has in fact come up before an arbitral tribunal. In an unpublished ICSID decision, the tribunal had to consider a request to disqualify claimant's counsel on the grounds that counsel had previously represented the respondent in a related proceeding. The tribunal's analysis focused largely on its power to rule on an allegation of misconduct; however, it concluded that it could only disqualify counsel if there was clear evidence of prejudice, and denied the request to disqualify counsel.*

  This case is more illustrative of the need for a clear rule than a guide for what the rule should be. Civil law and common law systems adopt different approaches to conflicts of interest. In civil law countries, conflicts of interest are often viewed as a matter of personal ethics, while in common law countries they are more often a matter of law. Reflective of this difference, the CCBE focuses on situations concerning the lawyer's independence from the client, and less on conflicts of interest.

  Furthermore, in civil law systems, the lawyer often has more discretion to determine whether a conflict in fact exists. By contrast, in common law systems, the lawyer has little discretion to determine if there is a conflict, but still may represent two or more clients in the same matter, if he or she discloses the potential conflict and the clients consent to the representation.

Rule 14. Lawyers should not acquire a financial interest in the subject matter of a case which they are conducting. Neither should they, directly or indirectly, acquire property that is the subject matter of an arbitration in which they are representing a party as

counsel. A contingent fee does not constitute a financial interest in the subject matter of the case.
(IBA Int'l Code of Ethics Rule 12; CCBE Rule 3.3.1 and 3.3.2 *Pactum de Quota Litis*)

- *A lawyer should not acquire any interest in a case that could put the lawyer's personal interests in conflict with the best interests of the client. As discussed in Rule 18 below, contingency fees are permitted in international arbitration, subject to the rules of the jurisdiction governing the attorney-client relationship.*

Fee Arrangements

Rule 15. **Lawyers' fees should, in the absence or non-applicability of official scales, be based on a consideration of the amount involved in the controversy and the interest of it to the client, the time and labor involved, the novelty and difficulty of the matter, and all other relevant personal and factual circumstances of the case.**
(IBA Int'l Code of Ethics Rule 17(c); CCBE Rule 3.4 Regulation of Fees)

- *A lawyer should put the interest of his or her client and the exigencies of justice before his or her right to compensation. The lawyer should fully disclose his or her fees to the client, such fees shall be fair and reasonable, and shall also be consistent with the law and professional rules to which the lawyer is subject.*

  The reasonableness of fees depends on a number of factors, including the time and labor required, the novelty and difficulty of the questions involved, the skill required, the likelihood that employment of the lawyer precludes other employment, the fee results obtained, the time limitation imposed by the client or circumstances, the nature and length of the professional relationship with the client, the experience, reputation and ability of the lawyer(s) performing the services, and whether the fee is fixed or contingent.

Rule 16. **Lawyers may require that an advance deposit be made to cover their fees and expenses, but the deposit should be in accordance with the estimated amount of their charges based on the probable expenses and labor required.**
(IBA Int'l Code of Ethics Rule 16; CCBE Rule 3.5 Payment on Account)

- *Requests for advance deposits should be made on the basis of good faith estimates of fees and expenses to be incurred.*

Rule 17. **The lawyer's right to ask for an advance deposit of fees or expenses, to demand payment of out-of-pocket expenses and commitments, or to be paid on a periodic and timely basis, failing payment of which the lawyer may withdraw from the case, should not be exercised at a moment at which the client may be unable**

to find other assistance in time to prevent irreparable damage being done.
(IBA Int'l Code of Ethics Rule 17(b); CCBE Rule 3.5 Payment on Account; CCBE Rule 3.1.4 Acceptance and Termination of Instructions)

- *If a lawyer requires an advance deposit which the client agrees to but fails to pay, or if the client fails to timely make agreed periodic payments, the lawyer has the right to withdraw. However, the lawyer should not exercise this right in a manner or at a time that will impede the client's ability to find other legal assistance. As noted in the Commentary to Rule 12, the withdrawing attorney must give the client due notice of his withdrawal, suggest employment of other counsel, deliver to the client all documents and property to which the client is entitled, cooperate with subsequently employed counsel, and otherwise endeavor to minimize the possibility of harm.*

Rule 18. Lawyers may charge their fees on a contingent basis to the extent permitted by the law that governs the attorney-client relationship. Such contingency fees should be reasonable under all of the circumstances of the case, including the risk and uncertainty of compensation or collection.
(IBA Int'l Code of Ethics Rule 18)

- *Civil and common law systems have traditionally differed in their rules regarding contingency fees. Most civil law countries prohibit such arrangements, believing contingency fees compromise the lawyer's independence and encourage speculative litigation. In the United States, however, such fees are permissible, subject to some ethical restrictions. The CCBE leans towards the civil law approach, but permits a form of contingency fees when bar-approved fee schedules may be used to supplement a lawyer's fee, if the lawyer turns out to be successful. Contingency fee arrangements have become increasingly accepted outside common law jurisdictions. The view taken here is that contingency fees may be necessary to prevent an injustice from being done by the inability of a client to fund a legitimate and meritorious claim.*

IV. Relations with the Tribunal

Rule 19. Lawyers shall always maintain due respect towards all members of the arbitral tribunal.
(IBA Int'l Code of Ethics Rule 6; CCBE Rule 4.3 Demeanour in Court)

- *In international arbitration, respect must be shown towards all members of the tribunal. Furthermore, the lawyer must keep in mind the necessary balance between the pursuit of his client's best interest, and the respect that must be shown to the arbitral tribunal. A lawyer must never deliberately mislead any or all of the arbitrators or act in any other manner conveying disrespect.*

INT'L CODE OF ETHICS FOR LAWYERS PRACTICING BEFORE INT'L ARBITRAL TRIBUNALS

Rule 20. Lawyers may not have any ex parte communications with any members of the arbitral tribunal about the merits of the case, except when the opposing party or its counsel have failed to attend a hearing either in person or by telephone. (CCBE Rule 4.2 Fair Conduct of Proceedings – See also CCBE Commentary)

- *In adversarial proceedings, a lawyer must not attempt to take unfair advantage of his or her opponent by discussing the merits of the arbitration with one or more of the arbitrators outside of the arbitral proceedings. If a lawyer needs to contact one of the arbitrators, he should first inform the counsel of the opposing party.*

  This Rule does not follow the approach of some jurisdictions in which ex parte communications with arbitrators are not banned. In China, it is not only permissible but probable that an arbitrator may act as a mediator in the same case in which he or she presides as the ultimate arbitrator.

  US litigation practice has traditionally required almost absolute restrictions against ex parte communication with judges or arbitrators on the merits of a case, in contrast to European informal practice, in which fraternization between the lawyers and arbitrators is more common.

Rule 21. Lawyers shall never knowingly make false factual representations to the arbitral tribunal.
(IBA Int'l Code of Ethics Rule 6(2); CCBE Rule 4.4 False or Misleading Information)

- *A lawyer must never knowingly mislead the tribunal. This requirement is necessary in order to ensure trust between the arbitrators, arbitration counsel and the parties. Such trust requires transparency and honesty.*

  In some states (such as Mexico and Saudi Arabia) a lawyer may make statements to the tribunal about the facts, even if this statement is not supported by any known evidence. This Rule suggests that a lawyer should avoid factual representations based on speculative evidence or a lack of evidence. Furthermore, a lawyer must not make a factual representation if he or she knows or believes it to be false.

V. Pleadings and Presentation of Evidence

Rule 22. Lawyers may argue any construction of a law, a contract or a treaty that they believe is reasonable.

- *This Rule attempts to balance differing American and European practices. American practice permits more zealous advocacy and greater creativity in arguing the interpretation of a law. A lawyer may even be "ethically impelled" to "urge any possible construction of the law favorable to his client, without regard to his professional opinion as to the likelihood that the construction will* ultimately prevail". Creativity is limited only by strategic considerations, credibility concerns and the stricture against wholly frivolous arguments.

By contrast, in European practice, creative arguments that are not, in the lawyer's opinion, likely to prevail, would be considered professionally irresponsible and possibly sanctionable.

This Rule is not as permissive of the American standard allowing "any possible construction", and limits a lawyer to arguments he or she believes are reasonable. Limiting frivolous and unreasonable arguments is necessary to ensure efficiency and integrity in arbitral proceedings.

Rule 23. In an arbitral proceeding, lawyers should not knowingly contend, argue for or examine a witness in order to establish the existence of facts that they know or believe not to be true.

- *A lawyer must never knowingly mislead the tribunal. The integrity and effectiveness of international arbitration require transparency and efficiency. Arguments and examinations seeking to establish facts known or believed to be false undermine these two essential elements of international arbitration, and thus must be avoided.*

Rule 24. The taking of evidence shall be conducted on the principle that each party shall act in good faith. Lawyers may not assist a party or a witness in giving false evidence to the arbitral tribunal, whether in oral testimony or in written witness statements.

- *This Rule raises an issue about attorney confidentiality obligations in the face of client perjury, or a client's threat to commit perjury. Most European codes do not include an obligation that an attorney disclose a client's intention to commit perjury. However, European attorneys are generally required to disclose unlawful conduct or potentially unlawful conduct by a client.*

    In the United States, there is relatively little agreement among the states regarding the scope of attorney confidentiality obligations in this situation. Under this Rule, the lawyer must make a good-faith effort to ascertain the truthfulness of his or her client's statements, as well as that of any witnesses. If the lawyer learns that any of these statements are false, the lawyer must seek the truth from the client or witness and seek to persuade them not to give false evidence. If the client or witness persists in giving false testimony, the lawyer should not assist them in doing so, should seek to withdraw from the case, or should reveal any known falsehood to the arbitral tribunal, unless the information is privileged.

Rule 25. Lawyers may communicate with a witness about facts and documents within the knowledge of that witness and about the witness's potential testimony, but lawyers may not directly or indirectly seek to influence witnesses to give testimony that is not accurate or true.

- *This topic is one of the instances of differing national practice most frequently cited in discussions of a need for an ethical code in international arbitration. In American practice, it is expected and perhaps even ethically required that a lawyer assist a witness in preparing testimony. In stark contrast, in Germany, attorneys are generally prohibited from engaging in any pre-testimonial communication with witnesses in judicial proceedings. Continental practitioners tend to perceive witness preparation as "coaching", which diminishes the reliability of a witness.*

  The relative informality of international arbitration as compared to litigation encourages conversation outside the hearing, which would make the German approach seem unnatural, and perhaps even impossible. On the other hand, arbitration values such as openness and efficiency should discourage behavior in witness preparation that might facilitate deceit and increase the time and expense of the arbitration.

  This conflict may not be as much of an issue in current practice, as more international arbitration practitioners have become accustomed to witness preparation. For example, German practitioners have professionally reoriented and developed a new norm of professional conduct that treats pre-trial communications between witness and counsel as ethically permissible in the international arbitration context.

Rule 26. **Lawyers may not conceal, or advise a client to conceal, documents that are ordered to be produced by the arbitral tribunal. Lawyers have a duty to the arbitral tribunal to be honest with it and the opposing party and counsel with respect to documents that are requested by the opposing party or ordered to be produced by the arbitral tribunal.**

- *Discovery and the exchange of information is, like witness preparation, another area of major difference between civil law and common law countries. Discovery is far less common in European practice and often viewed as a "fishing expedition" wasteful of both time and money.*

  This Rule takes no position on the scope of discovery or document exchanges. Nor does it address the grounds on which a party may refuse to produce a document requested by the arbitral tribunal or an opposing party. But it does require that a party make an honest refusal to produce a document that can be judged on its merits, and not conceal or attempt to conceal documents in an effort to mislead the tribunal and/or the opposing party as to their existence or relevance.

VI. Relations Between Lawyers

Rule 27. Lawyers shall treat their professional colleagues, including opposing counsel, with courtesy and respect.
(IBA Int'l Code of Ethics Rule 4; CCBE Rule 5.1.2 Corporate Spirit of the Profession)

- *International arbitration lawyers should recognize one another as professional colleagues and act fairly and courteously towards them. Because international arbitration lawyers hail from numerous and largely divergent legal systems and cultural backgrounds, all must keep in mind that no single State's legal system governs international arbitration, and differences in practice and misunderstandings may often reflect differences in legal culture rather than attempts to act unethically. Although the rules proposed here seek to mitigate these differences, the effort must be reinforced by respectful behavior among international arbitration practitioners.*

Rule 28. It is improper for lawyers to communicate about a particular case directly with the opposing party whom they know to be represented in that case by another lawyer without the latter's knowledge or consent.
(IBA Int'l Code of Ethics Rule 7; CCBE Rule 5.5 Communication with Opposing Parties)

- *This rule reflects a generally accepted principle, based on the need to prevent any attempt by a lawyer to take advantage of an opposing lawyer's client by communicating to that client without his or her lawyer's knowledge, and to promote the smooth conduct of business between lawyers. If a lawyer does mistakenly communicate with an opposing lawyer's client, the lawyer should inform that client's lawyer as soon as possible of the communication and its content.*

    State practice differs when the adverse party is a corporation. For example, a lawyer wanting to communicate with employees of an adverse corporate party that the lawyer knows is represented by counsel may do so in the United Kingdom, but it is absolutely prohibited in the United States. German lawyers would also have to refrain from such contact, whereas Mexican lawyers would likely feel free to do so, although Mexican law is silent on the issue.

List of Session Reporters

The General Editor would like to acknowledge the contribution of those who served as Session Reporters during the Congress. Although the size of this volume did not permit the publication of their Reports, thanks are due to:

Adryanna Chrystina Ferreira Toledo,	Câmara de Mediação e Arbitragem da CIESP
Ana Gerdau de Borja, Barretto Ferreira,	Kujawski, Brancher e Gonçalves Sociedade de Advogados
Andre Chateaubriand,	Escritório de Advocacia Sergio Bermudes
Arthur Gonzalez Cronemberger Parente,	Mundie e Advogados
Cristina Saiz Jabardo,	L.O. Baptista Advogados
Daniel Levy,	Ferro, Castro Neves, Daltro & Gomide Advogados
Eduardo Rabelo Kent Coes,	Tozzini Freire Advogados
Flavia Foz Mange,	Barretto Ferreira, Kujawski, Brancher e Gonçalves Sociedade de Advogados
Isabel Cantidiano,	Motta Fernandes Rocha Advogados
Luiz Claudio Aboim,	Freshfields Bruckhaus Deringer LLP
Mariana Cattel Gomes Alves,	L.O. Baptista Advogados
Petr Polášek,	White & Case LLP
Quinn Smith,	Câmara de Arbitragem e Mediação da Câmara de Comércio Brasil-Canadá
Silvia Bueno de Miranda,	L.O. Baptista Advogados

ICCA RIO CONGRESS LIST OF PARTICIPANTS

Angola

Fernandes de Souza Garcia, Patricia
Odebrecht – Construtora Norberto
Odebrecht AS

Argentina

Capparelli, Santiago
Baker & McKenzie
Avenida Leandro N. Alem 1110, piso 13
C1001AAT Buenos Aires

De Luca, Juan Pablo
Rattagan Macchiavello Arocena
& Peña Robirosa Abogados
Avenida de Mayo 701, piso 18
C1084AAC Buenos Aires

De San Martín, Inés
DSMS Abogados
Montevideo 666, piso 7
C1019ABN Buenos Aires

Minorini, Ignacio
Suipacha 268, piso 12
C1008AAF Buenos Aires

Rattagan, Michael R.
Rattagan, Macchiavello, Arocena
& Peña Robirosa Abogados
Avenida de Mayo 701, piso 18
C1084AAC Buenos Aires

Tawil, Guido Santiago
Member of ICCA
M&M Bomchil
Suipacha 268, piso 12
C1008AAF Buenos Aires

Australia

Bonnell, Max
Mallesons Stephen Jaques
Governor Phillip Tower, Level 61
1 Farrer Place
Sydney, NSW 2000

Jones, Doug
Clayton Utz
1 O'Connell Street
Sydney, NSW 2000

Megens, Peter
Mallesons Stephen Jaques
Bourke Place, Level 50
600 Bourke Street
Melbourne, Victoria 3000

Stephenson, Andrew
Clayton Utz
333 Collins Street
Melbourne, Victoria 3000

Waincymer, Jeff
Monash University
Wellington Road
Clayton
Melbourne, Victoria 3144

Austria

Baier, Anton
Baier Boehm Attorneys at Law
Kaerntner Ring 12
1010 Vienna

Haugeneder, Florian
Wolf Theiss
Schubertring 6
1010 Vienna

Herrmann, Gerold
Honorary President of ICCA
Reimersgasse 16 B2
1190 Vienna

Melis, Werner
Honorary Vice President of ICCA
International Arbitral Centre of the
Austrian Federal Economic Chamber
Wiedner Hauptstrasse 63
1045 Vienna

Pitkowitz, Nikolaus
Graf & Pitkowitz Rechtsanwälte GmbH

Stadiongasse 2
1010 Vienna

Belgium

Bassiri, Niuscha
Hanotiau & van den Berg
IT Tower, 9th Floor
Avenue Louise 480
1050 Brussels

Van den Berg, Albert Jan
Member of ICCA
Hanotiau & van den Berg
IT Tower, 9th Floor
Avenue Louise 480
1050 Brussels

Hanotiau, Bernard
Member of ICCA
Hanotiau & van den Berg
IT Tower, 9th Floor
Avenue Louise 480
1050 Brussels

Paulsson, Marike
Hanotiau & van den Berg
IT Tower, 9th Floor
Avenue Louise 480
1050 Brussels

Bermuda

Elkinson, Jeffrey
Conyers Dill and Pearman
2 Church Street
HM11 Hamilton

Bolivia

Moreno Gutierrez, Andres
Moreno Baldivieso Estudio de Abogados
Calle Capitan Ravelo No. 2366
La Paz

Zapata, Delfor
Moreno Baldivieso Estudio de Abogados
Calle Capitan Ravelo No. 2366
La Paz

Brazil

Abbud, André
Barbosa, Müssnich & Aragão
Al. Jaú, 1817, apto. 41
São Paulo 01420-002

Abby, Alexandre
Lobo & Ibeas Advogados
Av. Rio Branco, 125, 10º andar
Rio de Janeiro 20040-006

Abdalla, Letícia
Wald Associados Advogados
Av. Brigadeiro Faria Lima, 3729
7º andar
São Paulo 04538-133

Abreu, Paula
Embaixada Reino Unido
SES 801, Cj K, Lote 8
Brasilia 70673-426

Afonso de Assis, João
Xavier, Bernardes, Bragança,
Sociedade de Advogados
Av. Rio Branco, 1, 14º A andar
Rio de Janeiro 20090-003

Almeida, Ricardo
Lobo & Ibeas Advogados
Av. Rio Branco, 125, 10º andar
Rio de Janeiro 20040-006

Alvarenga, Maria Isabel
BCW Advogados
Rua Tabapuã, 1123, cj. 121/123
São Paulo 04533-014

Alvarenga, Vanessa
Universidade Mackenzie
Rua Manuel Guedes, 214, apto. 133
São Paulo 04536-070

Alves, Rafael
Comite Brasileiro de Arbitragem
Rua Joao Lourenco, 763, apto. 143
São Paulo 04508-031

Alves Ferreira Santos, Thiago
CCBC - Câmara de Comércio Brasil-Canadá
Rua do Rocio, 220, 12º andar, cj.121
São Paulo 04552-000

LIST OF PARTICIPANTS

Andrade, Flávia
TozziniFreire Advogados
Rua Borges Lagoa, 1328
São Paulo 04038-904

Aprigliano, Ricardo
USP
Rua Bela Cintra, 1149, 11° andar
São Paulo 01415-001

Arruda Silva, Carlos
Banco do Brasil S.A.
SBS QD 1, Bloco C, Lote 32, 21° andar
Brasilia 70073-901

Aun, Daniel
L.O. Baptista Advogados
Av. Paulista, 1294, 8° andar
São Paulo 01310-100

Balbino, Inez
CNC
Av. General Justo, 307
Rio de Janeiro 22420-041

Baltag, Crina
FGV – Fundação Getúlio Vargas
Rua Eurico Cruz, 11/202
Rio de Janeiro 22461-200

Bandeira, Paula
Gustavo Tepedino Advogados
Rua da Assembléia, 58
Rio de Janeiro 20011-000

Barbosa, Flávio
Mattos Filho, Veiga Filho, Marrey Jr.
e Quiroga Advogados
Al. Joaquim Eugênio de Lima, 447
São Paulo 01403-001

Barbosa, Joaquim Simões
Lobo & Ibeas Advogados
Av. Rio Branco, 125,10° andar
Rio de Janeiro 20040-006

Barbuto Neto, Antonio
TozziniFreire
Rua Borges Lagoa, 1328
São Paulo 04038-904

Barradas, Marcelo
Lefose Advogados
Rua General Furtado Nascimento, 66
São Paulo 05465-070

Barros, Augusto
Banco Itaú Unibanco S.A.
Praça Alfredo Egydio de Souza Aranha,100
Torre Conceição, 2° andar
São Paulo 04344-902

Barsanti, Jarbas
Escritorio Jharbas Barsanti Pericias
Judiciais e Arbitragens
Av. Presidente Wilson 164, 11° andar
Rio de Janeiro 20 030-020

Bartolomé, James P.
Escritório Jurídico Elísio de Souza
Av. Erasmo Braga, 227, gr. 301
Rio de Janeiro 20020-902

Basilio, João
Basilio Advogados
Av. Presidente Wilson, 210,12° andar
Rio de Janeiro 20030-021

Batista Martins, Pedro A.
Batista Martins Advogados
Av. Rio Branco, 103, 13° andar
Rio de Janeiro 22250-900

Bautista, Rogério
Odebrecht – Construtora Norberto
Odebrecht AS
Av. Pasteur, 110, 8° andar
Rio de Janeiro 22290-240

Beer, Veronica
Beer e Ayres Advocacia
Av. José Rocha Bonfim, 214
Campinas 13080-650

Bellocchi, Marcio
Nehring & Associados Advocacia
Av. Paulista, 1294, 12° andar
São Paulo 01310-915

Beneti, Ana
Pinheiro Neto Advogados
Rua Hungria, 1.100
São Paulo 01455-906

Berenguer, Caetano
Sergio Bermudes Advogados

425

Praça XV de Novembro 20, 8° andar
Rio de Janeiro 20010-010

Berezowski, Aluísio
Escritório de Advocacia Sergio Bermudes
Rua Frei Caneca, 1380, 5° andar
São Paulo 1309020

Bermudes, Sergio
Sergio Bermudes Advogados
Praça XV de Novembro, 7° andar
Rio de Janeiro 20010-010

Beyrodt Cardoso, Christiana
CCBC – Câmara de Comércio Brasil-Canadá
Rua Cel. Xavier de Toledo, 316, 5° andar
São Paulo 01048-000

Birchal, Leonardo
Lima Netto, Campos, Fialho, Canabrava Advogados
Av. Getúlio Vargas, 447, 6° e 7° andares
Belo Horizonte 30112-020

Bittar, Flávia
Grebler Advogados
Alvares Cabral, 1777, 14° andar
Belo Horizonte 30170-001

Bittencourt, Rafael
Universidade de São Paulo
Av. Paulista, 2584, apto. 37
Rio de Janeiro 01310-300

Blaso, Cristina
Banco Nacional de Desenvolvimento Econômico e Social – BNDES
Av. República do Chile, 100
São Paulo 20031917

Bosco Lee, João
Castro & Lee Sociedade de Advogados
Av. Nossa Senhora da Luz, 1755
Curitiba 82520-060

Braga, Carlos
Souza, Cescon, Barrieu & Flesch Advogados
Rua Funchal, 418, 11° andar
São Paulo 4551060

Braghetta, Adriana
L.O. Baptista Advogados

Av. Paulista, 1294, 8° andar
São Paulo 01310-100

Brechbühler, Gulherme
Basilio Advogados
Av. Presidente Wilson, 210, 12° andar
Rio de Janeiro 20030-021

Brumati, Carolina
Nehring & Associados Advocacia
Av. Paulista, 1294, 12° andar
São Paulo 01310-915

Bueno, Julio
Pinheiro Neto Advogados
Rua Hungria, 1100
São Paulo 01455-000

Calluf, Emir
Emir Calluf Advogados
Av. Jaime Reis, 152
Curitiba 80510-010

Campello, Caio
Lefosse Advogados
Rua General Furtado Nascimento, 66
São Paulo 05465-070

Cantidiano, Isabel
Motta Fernandes Rocha Advogados
Av. Almirante Barroso, 52, 5° andar
Rio de Janeiro 20031-000

Cantidiano, Maria Lúcia
Motta Fernandes Rocha Advogados
Av. Almirante Barroso, 52, 5° andar
Rio de Janeiro 20031-000

Carlos, Antonio
Brasil, Pereira Neto, Galdino e Macedo Advogados
Rua Olimpíadas, 100, 6° andar
São Paulo 04551-000

Carmelingo Alves, André
L.O. Baptista Advogados
Av. Paulista, 1294, 8°andar
São Paulo 01310-100

Carmona, Carlos Alberto
Marques Rosado Toledo Cesar e Carmona Advogados

Av. Brigadeiro Faria Lima, 1478
19º andar, cj. 1901
São Paulo 01452-001

Carmona Bianco, Rogerio
Lilla Huck Advogados
Av. Brigadeiro Faria Lima, 1744
6º andar
São Paulo 01451-001

Carpenter, Marcelo
Escritório de Advocacia Sergio Bermudes
Praça XV de Novembro, 20, 7º andar
Rio de Janeiro 20010-010

Carvalho, Lucila
Rua Felipe dos Santos, 365, apto. 700
Belo Horizonte 30180-160

Carvalho Morris, Jessica
Abengoa Bioenergia Brasil
Rua Funchal, 418, 36º andar, Vila Olimpia
São Paulo 04551-060,

Carvalho Passaro, Rafael
Machado, Meyer, Sendacz e Opice
Av. Brigadeiro Faria Lima, 3144, 11º andar
São Paulo 01451-000

Casado Filho, Napoleão
CCBC – Câmara de Comércio Brasil-Canadá
Rua Augusta, 1.939, 11º andar
São Paulo 01413-000

Catramby, Alexandre
Castro, Barros, Sobral, Gomes Advogados
Av. Rio Branco, 110, 14º andar
Rio de Janeiro 20040-001

Cattel Alves, Mariana
L.O. Baptista Advogados
Av. Paulista, 1294, 8º andar
São Paulo 01310-100

Cavalcante Moreira, Rodrigo
Laudelino da Costa Mendes Neto Advocacia
Rua da Candelária, 9, Centro
Rio de Janeiro 20220-390

Celso Pugliese, Antonio
Vella Pugliese Buosi Guidoni Advogados
Rua São Tomé, 86, 7º andar
São Paulo 04551-080

Cesario Alvim, Juliana
Rua da Assembléia, 58, 10º andar
Rio de Janeiro 20011-000

Chacel, Julian
Câmara FGV de Arbitragem
Praia de Botafogo, 190, 15º andar
Rio de Janeiro 22250-900

Chalfin, Eduardo
Chalfin, Goldberg & Vainboim Advogados
Rua da Assembleia, 98, 5º andar
Rio de Janeiro 20011000

Chateaubriand, André
Sergio Bermudes Advogados
Praça XV de Novembro, 20, 7º andar
Rio de Janeiro 20010-010

Chiabrando, Iva
Nehring & Associados Advocacia
Av. Paulista, 1294, 12º andar
São Paulo 01310-915

Chierighini, Marina
Castro Barros Subral Gomes Advogados
Rua do Rocio, 291, 11º andar
São Paulo 04552-020

Coelho Pitombo, Eleonora
Castro Barros Sobral Gomes Advogados
Rua do Rocio 291, 11º andar
São Paulo 04552-020

Cogo, Rodrigo
Ferro, Castro Neves, Daltro & Gomide Advogados
Rua Ramos Batista, 198, 8º andar
São Paulo 04552-020

Corrêa, Darwin
PCPC Advogados
Av. Nilo Peçanha, 11, 12º andar
Rio de Janeiro 20020-100

Corrêa, Fernanda
TozziniFreire Advogados
Praia de Botafogo, 228, 3º andar
Rio de Janeiro 22250-040

Corrêa, Leonardo
Machado, Meyer, Sendacz
e Opice Advogados

Av. Rio Branco, 1, 9° andar – Bloco B
Rio de Janeiro 20090-003

Correa Cardoso Coelho, Daniel
Justen, Pereira, Oliveira e Talamini –
Sociedade de Advogados
Av. Presidente Wilson, 231, 21° andar
Rio de Janeiro 20030-021

Costa, Caroline
CCBC – Câmara de Comércio Brasil-Canadá
Rua do Rocio, 220, 12° andar, cj.121
São Paulo 04552-000

Costa, Pedro
Barbosa, Müssnich & Aragão Advogados
Av. Almirante Barroso, 52, 29° andar
Rio de Janeiro 20031-000

Coutinho, Renato F.
L.O. Baptista Advogados
Av. Paulista, 1294, 8° andar
São Paulo 1310-100

Couto, Paulo Rogério
Machado, Meyer, Sendacz e
Opice Advogados
Av. Rio Branco, 1, 9° andar, Bloco B
Rio de Janeiro 20090-003

Cristofaro, Pedro Paulo
Motta Fernandes Rocha Advogados
Rua Baronesa de Poconé 75, apto. 202
Rio de Janeiro 22471-270

Cunha, Elina
Pinheiro Neto Advogados
Rua Humaitá, 275
Rio de Janeiro 22261-005

Da Graça Prado, Maria
Trench, Rossi e Watanabe Advogados
(Baker & McKenzie)
Av. Dr. Chucri Zaidan, 920, 13° andar
São Paulo 04583-904

Damasceno, Guilherme

Damiani, Gerson
International Relations Institute
University of Sao Paulo
Av. Nações Unidas, 4849, 242R
São Paulo 05477-000

Damião Gonçalves, Eduardo
BKBG Advogados Associados
Rua Dr. Eduardo de Souza Aranha, 387
15° andar
São Paulo 04543-121

De Alencar Machado, Pedro
Ferro & Castro Neves Advogados
Av. Rio Branco, 85, 13° andar
Rio de Janeiro 20040-004

De Andrade Lévy, Daniel
Ferro, Castro Neves, Daltro & Gomide
Advogados
Rua Ramos Batista, 198, 8° andar
São Paulo 4552-020

De Andrade Novaes, Luiz R.
Instituição
Av. Brigadeiro Faria Lima, 2601
10° andar
São Paulo 01452-000

De Campos Borges Filho, Daltro
UERJ
Rua S. Francisco Xavier, 524
Rio de Janeiro 20550-013

De Carolis, Roberta
Motta Fernandes Rocha Advogados
Av. Almirante Barroso, 52, 5° andar
Rio de Janeiro 20031-000

De Carvalho Jacintho, Gabriel
G. Jacintho Consultoria Contábil e Tributária
S/S Ltda.
Rua Luis Coelho, 223, 1° andar
São Paulo 01309-001

De Carvalho Pinto Pupo, Alvaro
Pinhão & Koiffman advogados
Av. Dr. Cardoso de Melo, 1340
12° andar
São Paulo 04548-004

De Castro Neves, Jose Roberto
Ferro & Castro Neves Advogados
Av. Rio Branco, 85, 13° andar
Rio de Janeiro 20040-004

De Gennari, Elisabeth
Di Pierro e De Gennari Advogados
Av. General Furtado do Nascimento, 740

cj. 75
São Paulo 05465-070

De Maria, Paulo
Mattos Filho, Veiga Filho, Marry Jr.
e Quiroga Advogados
Al. Joaquim Eugênio de Lima, 447
São Paulo 01403-001

De Miranda, Thales
Petrobras
Av. República do Chile 65, 16° andar
Rio de Janeiro 20521-160

De Moraes Miranda, Raphael
Sergio Bermudes Advogados
Praça XV de Novembro, 20, 8° andar
Rio de Janeiro 20010-080

De Oliveira, Henrique
Trigueiro Fontes Advogados
Av. Domingos Ferreira, 467, 8° andar Boa Viagem
Recife 51011-050

De Oliveira, Nelson
Nelson de Oliveira Advocacia
Rua Cubatão, 354, Marambaia
Vinhedo 13280-000

De Souza e Straube, Frederico Gustavo
CCBC – Câmara de Comércio Brasil-Canadá
Rua Coronel Xavier de Toledo, 316, 5° andar
São Paulo 01048-000

Della Valle, Martim
AmBev
Rua Teixeira da Silva, 240, 72° andar
São Paulo 04002-030

Deluiggi, Marco
Castro, Barros, Sobral, Gomes Advogados
Rua do Rocio, 291, 11° andar
São Paulo 04552-000

Di Franco, Angela
Levy & Salomao Advogados
Av. Brigadeiro Faria Lima, 2601, 12° andar
São Paulo 01452-924

Di Nizo, Rosana
Banco do Brasil S.A.

SBS - Qd 01 - Lt 32 - Ed. Sede III, 21° andar
Brasilia 70073-901

Domingues Moreno, Diego
FTI Consulting
Rua Tabapuã, 474, conjunto 52
São Paulo 04533-001

Donato, Milena
Gustavo Tepedino Advogados
Rua da Assembléia, 58, 10° andar
Rio de Janeiro 20011-000

Edson Fachin, Luiz
Fachin Advogados Associados
Candido de Abreu, 651
Curitiba 80530-907

Egashira, Fábio
Trigueiro Fontes Advogados
Av. Domingos Ferreira, 467, 8° andar
Recife 51011-050

Eizirik, Nelson
Carvalhosa e Eizirik Advogados
Rua Santa Luzia, 651, 34° andar
Rio de Janeiro 20021-903

Fachin, Melina
Fachin Advogados Associados
Av. Cândido de Abreu, 651
Curitiba 80530-907

Faleiro, Kelly
Odebrecht – Construtora Norberto Odebrecht AS
Av. Brigadeiro Faria Lima, 1912, Pinheiros
São Paulo 01451-000

Fávero, Ligia
Mattos Filho, Veiga Filho, Marrey Jr.
e Quiroga Advogados
Rua Joaquim Eugenio de Lima, 447
São Paulo 01403-001

Federici, Roberto
Demarest e Almeida Advogados
Praia do Flamengo, 78, 1° andar
Rio de Janeiro 22210-030

Felsberg, Thomas
Felsberg & Associados

Av. Paulista, 1294, 2°andar
São Paulo 01310-915

Fernandes, Gustavo
Sergio Bermudes Advogados
Praça XV de Novembro, 20, 7° e 8° andares
Rio de Janeiro 20010-010

Fernando, Luiz
Motta Fernandes Rocha Advogados
Av. Almirante Barroso, 52, 5° andar
Rio de Janeiro 20031-000

Fernando Fraga, Luiz
Barbosa, Müssnich & Aragão
Av. Almirante Barroso, 52, 29° andar
Rio de Janeiro 20031-000

Fernando Sant'Anna, Luiz
Demarest e Almeida Advogados
Av. Pedroso de Moraes, 1201, 3° andar
São Paulo 05419-001

Fernando Visconti, Luiz
Tozzini Freire Advogados
Av. Carlos Gomes, 222, 5° andar
Porto Alegre 90480-000

Ferraz, Rafaella
Araújo e Policastro Advogados
Av. Almirante Barroso, 139, sala 903
Rio de Janeiro 20031-005

Ferreira, Marcio
Sergio Bermudes Advogados
Praça XV de Novembro, 20, 7° andar
Rio de Janeiro 20010-010

Ferreira Lemes, Selma
Selma Lemes Advogados
Av. Brigadeiro Faria Lima, 1768, cj. 6D
Rio de Janeiro 01451-001

Ferreira Toledo, Adryanna Chrystina
CIESP – Adryanna Toledo
Rua Sao Paulo Antigo, 500, apto. 202
São Paulo 05684-011

Ferro, Marcelo
Ferro, Castro Neves, Daltro & Gomide Advogados
Av. Rio Branco, 85, 13° andar
Rio de Janeiro 20040-040

Fichtner, José Antonio
Andrade & Fichtner Advogados
Av. Almirante Barroso, 139
Rio de Janeiro 20031-005

Fichtner Pereira, Vivianne
Andrade & Fichtner Advogados
Av. Almirante Barroso, 139, 4° andar
Rio de Janeiro 20031-005

Figueiredo, Roberto
Sergio Bermudes Advogados
Praça XV de Novembro, 20, 7° Andar
Rio de Janeiro 20010-010

Fonseca, Luciana
Procuradoria–Geral do Distrito Federal
SQS 303-J-306
Brasilia 70336-100

Fonseca, Rodrigo
Wald Associados Advogados
Av. Almirante Barroso, 52, 8° andar
Rio de Janeiro 20031-000

Fontes, Marcos
Porto Advogados
Av. Nove de Julho, 5109, 3° andar
São Paulo 01407-200

Forbes, Carlos
Mundie e Advogados
Av. Presidente Juscelino Kubistchek, 50, 18° andar
São Paulo 04543-000

Fradera, Véra
Universidade Federal do Rio Grande do Sul
Av. Carlos Gomes, 403/405
Porto Alegre 90035-073

Fragata, Octavio
Barbosa, Müssnich & Aragão Advogados
Av. Almirante Barroso, 52, 32° andar
Rio de Janeiro 20031-000

Freitas, Pedro
Veirano Advogados
Av. Presidente Wilson, 231, 23° andar
Rio de Janeiro 20030-021

Gabardo, Rodrigo
Castro & Lee Sociedade de Advogados

Rua Prof. Pedro Viriato Parigot de Souza
2581, apto. 34
Curitiba 81200-100

Gabbay, Daniela
Direito GV
Rua Silvia, 23
São Paulo 01331-010

Gagliardi, Rafael
Demarest e Almeida Advogados
Av. Pedroso de Morais, 1.201, 3º andar
São Paulo 05419-001

Galea, Felipe
Barbosa, Müssnich & Aragão Advogados
Av. Presidente Juscelino Kubitschek, 1455
11º andar
São Paulo 04543-011

Galíndez, Valeria
BKBG Sociedade de Avogados
Rua Dr. Eduardo de Souza Aranha, 387
15º andar
São Paulo 04543-121

Gama Junior, Lauro
Binenbojm, Gama & Carvalho Britto Advocacia
Rua da Quitanda 50, 14º andar
Rio de Janeiro 20011-030

Gandelman, Marcelo
Barbosa, Müssnich & Aragão Advogados
Av. Almirante Barroso, 52, 29º andar
Rio de Janeiro 20031-000

Gerdau de Borja, Ana
BKBG Sociedade de Advogados
Rua Bandeira Paulista, 97, apto. 23
São Paulo 04532-010

Giusti, Gilberto
Pinheiro Neto Advogados
Rua Hungria, 1.100
São Paulo 01455-000

Goes, Monica

Goldberg, Karina
Ferro, Castro Neves, Daltro
e Gomide Advogados

Ramos Batista, 198, 8º andar
São Paulo 04552-020

Gomes, Raphael
Demarest e Almeida Advogados
Rua Barão de Itapagipe, 365, apto. 706, bl 1
Rio de Janeiro 20261-005

Gonçalves, Tatiana
Camarb Câmara de Arbitragem
Empresarial Brasil
Rua Paraíba, 1000, 16 º andar
Belo Horizonte 30130-141

Gondinho, André
Doria, Jacobina, Rosado e Gondinho
Advogados Associados
Rua da Assembléia, 98, 13º andar
Rio de Janeiro 20011-000

Gouvêa Vieira, Luciano
Ferro & Castro Neves Advogados
Av. Rio Branco, 85, 13º andar
Rio de Janeiro 20040-004

Grebler, Eduardo
Grebler Advogados
Av. Alvares Cabral, 1777, 14º andar
Belo Horizonte 30170-001

Gregorio Canelas, João Paulo
Oxiteno S.A. Indústria e Comércio
Av. Brigadeiro Luís Antônio, 1343, 7º andar
São Paulo 01317-910

Grion, Renato
Pinheiro Neto Advogados
Rua Hungria, 1100
São Paulo 01455-906

Gruenbaum, Daniel
Faculdade de Direito da Universidade do Estado do Rio de Janeiro
Rua São Francisco Xavier, 524, 7º andar
Bloco F, sala 7045
Rio de Janeiro 22421-030

Guerrero, Luis
Dinamarco e Rossi Advocacia
Rua Joaquim Floriano, 72, cj. 155
São Paulo 4630-010

Guimarães de Almeida Neto, Armando
Wald Associados Advogados
Av. Almirante Barros, 52, 8° Andar
Rio de Janeiro 20031-000

Guimarães Pereira, Cesar
Rua Visconde do Rio Branco, 237
Curitiba 80410-000

Guimarães Pessoa, Carlos Alexandre
Brandão Couto, Wigderowitz, Pessoa
e Alvarenga Advogados
Rua Dom Gerardo, 35, 4° andar
Rio de Janeiro 20090-905

Harger, Alissa
Unicuritiba
Rua Desembargador Motta, 2012, apto. 603
Curitiba 80420-190

Horta, Paulo Gustavo R.
Chalfin, Goldberg & Vainboim
Advogados Associados
Rua da Assembléia, 98, 5° andar
Rio de Janeiro 20011-000

Huck, Marcelo
Faculdade de Direito Universidade de São Paulo
Av. Brigadeiro Faria Lima, 1744, 6° andar
São Paulo 01451-910

Hueb Baroni, Maria Fernanda
Souza, Cescon, Barrieu e Flesch Advogados
Rua Funchal, 418, 11° andar
São Paulo 04551-060

Inglez de Souza, Marcelo
Demarest e Almeida Advogados
Av. Pedroso de Moraes, 1201
São Paulo 05419-001

Jardim de Paiva Barroso, Pedro
Petroleo Brasileiro S.A.
Av. Republica do Chile, 65
Rio de Janeiro 20031-912

Jucá, Adriano
Odebrecht – Construtora
Norberto Odebrecht AS
Av. Rebouças, 3.970, 28° andar
São Paulo 05402-600

Junqueira de Souza, Miriam Claudia

Kehdi Fagundes, Sergio
Av. Presidente Juscelino
Kubitschek, 1455, 11° andar
São Paulo 04543-011

Kent Coes, Eduardo
TozziniFreire Advogados
Rua Borges Lagoa, 1328
São Paulo 04038-904

Knoll Aymone, Priscila
Rua Pedroso Alvarenga, 505, apto.141
São Paulo 04532-011

Kobayashi, Patrícia
BKBG Sociedade de Advogados
Av. do Café, 77, apto. 33 II
São Paulo 4311-000

Kroetz, Tarcísio
Rua Lysímaco Ferreira da Costa, 80
Curitiba 80530-100

La Laina, Roberto
José Emilio Nunes Pinto Advogados
Av. Presidente Juscelino Kubitschek, 28
9° andar
São Paulo 5679-060

Lacreta, Isabela
Isabela Lacreta
Rua Mangabeiras 91, apto. 41
São Paulo 1233-010

Leão, Fernanda
Barreto Ferreira, Kujawski, Brancher e
Gonçalves Sociedade de Advogados
Av. Angelica, 2297, apto. 31
São Paulo 01227-200

Levy, Luciana
Lobo & de Rizzo Advogados
Rua Lauro Müller, 116, 42° andar
Rio de Janeiro 22290-906

Lima, Flávio
Mattos Filho, Veiga Filho, Marrey Jr.
e Quiroga Advogados
Al. Joaquim Eugênio de Lima, 447
São Paulo 01403-001

Linhares, Camila

Lopes, Marcelo Alexandre
Ferro, Castro Neves, Daltro & Gomide Advogados
Rua Ramos Batista, 198, 8° andar
São Paulo 4552-020

Lopes, Paulo Guilherme
Leite, Tosto e Barros Advogados
Rua Dr. Renato Paes de Barros, 1017
5° andar
São Paulo 04530-001

Loretti, Ricardo
Sergio Bermudes Advogados
Praça XV de Novembro, 20
Rio de Janeiro 20010-010

Lyra, Tomaz
Andrade & Fichtner Advogados
Av. Almirante Barroso 139, 4° andar
Rio de Janeiro 2003-105

Macedo, Leonardo
Advocacia Raul de Araujo Filho
Afonso Pena, 4121, 11° andar
Belo Horizonte 30130-008

Maciel, Pedro
Veirano Advogados
Av. Nações Unidas, 12995, 18° andar
São Paulo 04578-000

Makant, Barbara
Veirano Advogados
Av. Presidente Wilson, 231, 23° andar
Rio de Janeiro 20030-021

Malard, Luciana

Mambrini, Eduardo
Majella Jones Advogados
Av. Rio Branco, 181, SL 3604
Rio de Janeiro 20040-007

Mange, Flavia
BKBG Sociedade de Avogados
Al. Casa Branca, 1204, apto. 81
São Paulo 01408-000

Manieiro, Laura
Lefosse Advogados
Rua General Furtado Nascimento, 66
São Paulo 05465-070

Mannheimer, Sérgio
Andrade & Fichtner Advogados
Av. Almirante Barroso 139, 4° andar
Rio de Janeiro 20031-005

Mansur, Renata
Tribunal de Justiça do Estado do Rio de Janeiro

Marcondes, Fernando
F. Marcondes Advocacia
Rua Diogo de Quadros, 330, conjunto 73
São Paulo 04710-010

Marinho Nunes, Thiago
Sturzenegger e Cavalcante Advogados Associados
Rua Vergueiro, 2016, 6° andar
São Paulo 4102000

Martins Costa, Judith
Martins Costa Advogados
Rua Luciana de Abreu, 323, sala 204
Porto Alegre 90570-060

Martins de Almeida, Fabiana
Trindade Sociedade de Advogados
Av. Ataulfo de Paiva, 245, 8° Andar
Rio de Janeiro 22440032

Matias, Eduardo
L.O. Baptista Advogados
Av. Paulista, 1294, 8° andar
São Paulo 1310-100

Mattar, Eduardo A.
Pinheiro Guimarães Advogados
Av. Paulista 1842, 24° andar – TN
São Paulo 01310-923

Médici, Fernando
Mattos, Muriel e Kestener Advogados
Al. Santos, 1940, 1° andar
São Paulo 01418-200

Meira Moser, Luiz Gustavo
Universidade Federal do Rio Grande do Sul
Rua Dom Pedro II, 1445, 401
Porto Alegre 90550-143

Meirelles, José
Leite, Tosto e Barros Advogados
Rua Dr. Renato Paes de Barros, 1017
São Paulo 04530-001

Mello, Jaqueline
Mattos Filho, Veiga Filho, Marrey Jr.
e Quiroga Advogados
Al. Joaquim Eugênio de Lima, 447
São Paulo 01403-001

Migliore, Alfredo
Escritorio de Advocacia Sergio Bermudes
Rua Dionisio da Costa, 63, apto. 21
São Paulo 04117-110

Miranda, Isabel
Batista Martins Advogados
Av. Ataulfo de Paiva, 221, apto. 302
Rio de Janeiro 22440-032

Miranda, Marilia
USP
Rua dos Ingleses, 586, apto. 131
São Paulo 1329000

Miranda, Silvia
L.O. Baptista Advogados
Av. Paulista, 1294, 8° andar
São Paulo 01310-100

Monteiro, Andre Luís
Andrade & Fichtner Advogados
Av. Almirante Barroso, 139, 4° andar
Rio de Janeiro 20031-005

Monteiro, Antonio H.
Mattos, Muriel e Kestener Advogados
Al. Santos, 1940, 1° andar
São Paulo 01418-200

Monteiro de Barros, Vera Cecília
Selma Lemes Advogados
Rua Alves Guimarães, 518, apto. 194
São Paulo 05410-000

Montoro, Marcos
José Carlos de Magalhães
Advogados Associados
Av. Brigadeiro Faria Lima, 1306, 9° andar
São Paulo 01451-914

Moreira Franco, Alice
Ferro, Castro Neves, Daltro &
Gomide Advogados
Av. Rio Branco, 85, 13° andar
Rio de Janeiro 20040-004

Motta Pinto, Ana Luiza
José Emilio Nunes Pinto Advogados
Av. Presidente Juscelino Kubitschek, 28
9° andar
São Paulo 04543-000

Moura, Rodrigo
BG E&P Ltda
Rua Lauro Muller, 116, 17° andar
Rio de Janeiro 22290-160

Muglia, Vanessa
PUC–RIO
Rua Redentor 225/101, Ipanema
Rio de Janeiro 22421-030

Mundie, Kevin
Mundie e Advogados
Av. Presidente Juscelino Kubitschek, 50
18° andar
São Paulo 04543-000

Munhoz, Eduardo
Mattos Filho, Veiga Filho, Marrey Jr.
e Quiroga Advogados
Al. Joaquim Eugênio de Lima, 447
São Paulo 01403-001

Muniz, Joaquim
Trench, Rossi e Watanabe Advogados
(Baker & McKenzie)
Av. Dr. Chucri Zaidan, 920, 13° andar
Rio de Janeiro 20090-003

Muriel, Marcelo
Mattos, Muriel e Kestener Advogados
Al. Santos, 1940, 1° Andar
São Paulo 01418-200

Müssnich, Francisco
Barbosa, Müssnich & Aragão
Av. Presidente Juscelino Kubitschek, 1.455
10° andar
São Paulo 04543-01

Nacif, Mariana
Wald Associados Advogados
Av. Almirante Barroso, 52, 8° andar
Rio de Janeiro 20031-000

Nanni, Giovanni
TozziniFreire
Rua Borges Lagoa 1328
São Paulo 04038-904

Nasser, Rabih
Nasser Advogados
Av. Angélica, 2510, 3° andar
São Paulo 01228-200

Nehring Netto, Carlos
Advisory Member of ICCA
Nehring Advogados Associados
Av. Paulista, 1294, 12° andar
São Paulo 01310-100

Neves, Roberta
FGV
Rua José Debieux, 282, apto.143
São Paulo 02038-030

Nitschke, Guilherme
TozziniFreire Advogados
Av. Carlos Gomes, 222, 5° andar
Porto Alegre 90480-000

Nunes Ferreira, Ivan
Nunes Ferreira, Vianna Araújo, Cramer, Duarte Advogados
Presidente Wilson, 164, 6° andar
Rio de Janeiro 20030-020

Nunes Pinto, José Emilio
José Emilio Nunes Pinto Advogados
Av. Presidente Juscelino Kubitschek, 28
São Paulo 04543-000

Oertel, Roberta
Rangel Ribeiro Advogados Associados
Rua Haddock Lobo, 578, cj 92
São Paulo 01414-000

Olavo Baptista, Luiz
L.O. Baptista Advogados
Av. Paulista, 1294, 8° andar
São Paulo 01310-100

Oliveira, Augusto
UERJ
Rua Eduardo Guinle, 60, apto. 202
Rio de Janeiro 22260-090

Oliveira, Renata
Machado, Meyer, Sendacz e Opice Advogados
Av. Brigadeiro Faria Lima, 3.144, 13° andar
São Paulo 01451-000

Ozorio, Celina
Rua da Assembleia, 66, 17° andar
Rio de Janeiro 20011-000

Pacheco Neto, Renato
CAE–Eurocamaras
Al. Franca 1050, 11° andar
São Paulo 1422001

Parente, Arthur
Mundie e Advogados
Av. Presidente Juscelino Kubitschek, 50
18° andar
São Paulo 04543-000

Parente, Eduardo
Neumann, Salusse, Marangoni Advogados
Av. Paulista, 1842, Torre Norte
12° andar
São Paulo 01310-923

Pasqualin, Roberto
Pasqualin Advogados
Rua Gomes de Carvalho, 1327, 11° andar
São Paulo 04547-005

Passaro, Denise H.
Brandão Teixeira Ricardo e Foz Advogados
Rua Henrique Monteiro, 90, 7° andar
São Paulo 05423-020

Paulo de Almeida Salles, Marcos
CCBC – Câmara de Comércio Brasil-Canadá
Rua Coronel Xavier de Toledo, 316, 5° andar
São Paulo 01048-000

Pecoraro, Eduardo
Ferro, Castro Neves, Daltro & Gomide Advogados
Rua Ramos Batista, 198, 8° andar
São Paulo

Peixinho Gomes Corrêa, Fábio
Lilla, Huck, Otranto e Camargo Advogados
Av. Brigadeiro Faria Lima, 1744, 6° andar
São Paulo 01451-910

Perassi, Paulo
Rua Mourato Coelho, 50, apto. 104
São Paulo 05417-000

Peretti, Luis
Roner Guerra Fabris Adv. Assoc.
Al. Eduardo Guimarães, 27
Porto Alegre 91340-350

Perlingeiro, Marcus
TozziniFreire Advogados
Praia de Botafogo, 228, 3° andar
Rio de Janeiro 22250-040

Piau, Lara
Kuehne+Nagel
Praia do Flamengo, 78, 1° andar
Rio de Janeiro 22210-904

Pimentel Gomes, Joana
Mattos Filho, Veiga Filho, Marrey Jr.
e Quiroga Advogados
Al. Joaquim Eugênio de Lima, 447
São Paulo 1403001

Polto, Marcio
Trench, Rossi e Watanabe Advogados
(Baker & McKenzie)
Av. Dr. Chucri Zaidan, 920, 8° andar
São Paulo 04583-904

Portella, Gabriel
Gabriel Portella Advogados Associados
SHIS QL 26, conj. 04, casa 19 – Lago Sul
Brasilia 71665-145

Portugal, Wanessa
CIESP – Wanessa Portugal
Av. Paulista, 1313, 11° andar
São Paulo 01311-200

Prado, Maurício
L.O. Baptista Advogados
Av. Paulista, 1294, 8° andar
São Paulo 01310-100

Pucci, Adriana Noemi
Lucon Advogados
Al. Campinas, 977, 10° andar
São Paulo 01404-001

Reale Junior, Miguel
Martins Costa Advogados
Rua Luciana de Abreu, 323, sala 204
Porto Alegre 90570-060

Rebello Horta, Julio
Andrade & Fichtner Advogados
Av. Almirante Barroso, 139, 4° andar
Rio de Janeiro 20031-005

Refinetti, Domingos
Machado, Meyer Advogados
Av. Brigadeiro Faria Lima, 3144
São Paulo 1451000

Reiff, Paulo
Mattos Filho, Veiga Filho, Marrey Jr.
e Quiroga Advogados
Al. Joaquim Eugênio de Lima, 447
São Paulo 01403-001

Rennó, Leandro
PUC Minas
Rua do Ouro, 229/204 – Serra
Belo Horizonte 30220-000

Ribas, Marcel Alberge
Rua João Américo de Oliveira, 177
Curitiba 80730-390

Robalinho, Fabiano
Sergio Bermudes Advogados
Praça XV de Novembro, 20, 7° andar
Rio de Janeiro 20010-010

Rocha, Fabrício
PUC–SP
Rua Frei Caneca, 1380, 6° andar
São Paulo 13007-002

Rocha, José Paulo
Deloitte
Rua Alexandre Dumas, 1981
São Paulo 04717-906

Rodante, Marcello
Rodante e Scharlack Advogados
Rua Dr. Bacelar, 187, Vila Mariana
São Paulo 04026-000

Rodrigues P. Pachikoski, Silvia
CIESP – Silvia Rodrigues Pachikoski
Al. Santos, 2395, 4º Andar
Cerqueira Cesar
São Paulo 01419-002

Rosa, Beatriz V.X.S.
Tarobá Engenharia
Al. Itapecuru, 645, cj. 522
Barueri 6454-080

Rossani Garcez, José Maria
Escritório JM Garcez Advogados Associados
Rua Visconde de Inhaúma, 134/327
Rio de Janeiro 20091-000

Ruiz, Fernanda
Av. Padre Antonio José dos Santos, 495
apto. 33
São Paulo 04563-011

Saiz Jabardo, Cristina
L.O. Baptista Advogados
Av. Paulista, 1294, 8º andar
São Paulo 1310-100

Sampaio, Gisela
Barbosa, Müssnich & Aragão
Av. Almirante Barroso, 52, 32º andar
Rio de Janeiro 20031-000

Sampaio Carvalho, Antonio Luiz
CCBC – Câmara de Comércio Brasil-Canadá
Rua do Rocio, 220, 12º andar, cj.121
São Paulo 04552-000

Santana, Renata
Tojal, Teixeira Ferreira, Serrano & Renault Advogados Associados
Al. Itu 852, 14º andar
São Paulo 5683-020

Santos Kulesza, Gustavo
L.O. Baptista Advogados
Av. Paulista, 1294, 8º andar
São Paulo 01310-100

Saud, Salim
Tauil & Chequier Advogados
Rua do Carmo, 43, 8º e 9º andares
Rio de Janeiro 20011-020

Savi, Sérgio
Castro Barros Sobral Gomes Advogados
Av. Rio Branco, 110, 14º andar
Rio de Janeiro 20040-001

Seijo, Gabriel
Souza, Cescon, Barrieu & Flesch
Rua Funchal, 418, 11º andar
São Paulo 04551-060

Serec, Fernando
Tozzini Freire
Rua Borges Lagoa, 1328
São Paulo 04038-904

Silva, Eduardo
Uniritter
Rua Gal Caldwell 661, apto. 807
Porto Alegre 90050-130

Silva Seabra, Andre
Ferro & Castro Neves Advogados
Av. Rio Branco, 85, 13º andar
Rio de Janeiro 20040-004

Silveira, Vivian
Momsen, Leonardos & Cia.
Rua Teofilo Otoni, 63, 10º andar
Rio de Janeiro 20090-080

Sioufi, Alfred
Veirano Advogados
Av. Nações Unidas, 12995, 18º andar
São Paulo 04578-000

Skitnevsky, Karin H.
Karin Skitnevsky
Rua Mangabeiras, 91
São Paulo 01233-010

Smilgin, André
Pinto de Miranda, Smilgin, Teixeira Advogados
Av. Nilo Peçanha, 50, grupo 2011
Rio de Janeiro 20020-906

Soares, Rafael Vicente
L.O. Baptista Advogados
Av. Paulista, 1294, 8º andar
São Paulo 01310-100

Soares de Souza, Luciana
SSC Advogados
Rua Visconde de Pirajá, 595 / 807
Rio de Janeiro 22410-050

Souza Martins, Cintia Ramos
Machado, Meyer, Sendacz e Opice Advogados
Av. Brigadeiro Faria Lima, 3144, 11º andar
São Paulo 01451-000

Spadano, Lucas
Lima Netto, Campos, Fialho, Canabrava Advogados
Av. Getúlio Vargas, 447, 6º e 7º andares
Belo Horizonte 30112-020

Spyrides, Katherine S.
Trench, Rossi e Watanabe Advogados
(Baker & McKenzie)
Av. Rio Branco, 1, 19º andar – Setor B
Rio de Janeiro 20090-003

Stern, Karina
Andrade & Fichtner Advogados
Av. Almirante Barroso 139, 4º andar
Rio de Janeiro 20031-005

Stetner, Renato
Castro, Barros, Sobral, Gomes Advogados
Rua do Rócio, 291, 11º andar
São Paulo 04655-000

Straube, Frederico José
CCBC – Câmara de Comércio Brasil-Canadá
Rua Coronel Xavier de Toledo, 316, 5º andar
São Paulo 01048-000

Tannous, João Paulo
Souza, Cescon, Barrieu & Flesh – Advogados
Rua Funchal, 418
São Paulo 05083-030

Tannuri, Rodrigo
Sergio Bermudes Advogados
Praça XV de Novembro, 20, 7º andar
Rio de Janeiro 20010-010

Tassara, Patricia
Barbosa, Müssnich & Aragão Advogados
Av. Almirante Barroso, 52, 29º andar
Rio de Janeiro 20031-000

Tavares, Tiaia
Universidade de São Paulo
Largo São Francisco, 95
São Paulo 1005-010

Tavela Luís, Daniel
Nasser Advogados
Av. Angélica, 2510, 3º andar
São Paulo 01228-200

Tellechea, Rodrigo
Universidade de São Paulo
Rua Manoel da Nóbrega, 275, apto. 62
São Paulo 4001-081

Teixeira, Daniel
Sturzenegger e Cavalcante Advogados Associados
Rua Indiana, 310, 1º andar
São Paulo 04562-000

Telles, Eduardo
Neoenergia
Rua do Carmo, 43, 8º andar
Rio de Janeiro 20011-020

Tepedino, Gustavo
Gustavo Tepedino Advogados
Rua da Assembléia, 58, 10º andar
Rio de Janeiro 20011-000

Tepedino, Patrícia
Gustavo Tepedino Advogados
Rua da Assembléia 58, 10º andar
Rio de Janeiro 20011-000

Tepedino, Ricardo
Escritório de Advocacia Sergio Bermudes
Rua Frei Caneca, 1380, 5º andar
São Paulo 01307-002

Tess, Eduardo
Tess Advogados
Av. Brasil, 471
São Paulo 01431-000

Timm, Luciano
Carvalho, Machado, Timm & Deffenti
Av. Carlos Gomes, 1340, cj. 602
Porto Alegre 90480-001

Tipnis, Ketan
Sheraton Barra Hotel and Apartments

Av. Lúcio Costa, 3150
Rio de Janeiro 22630-010

Tolentino, Augusto
Hapner & Kroetz Advogados
Av. Cristóvão Colombo, 485, 13° andar
Belo Horizonte 30140-140

Tortorelli, Mauro
VRBG
Iguatemi, 192, 12° andar
São Paulo 01451-010

Trindade, Marcelo
Trindade Sociedade de Advogados
Av. Ataulfo de Paiva, 245, 8° andar
Rio de Janeiro 22440-032

Tripodi, Leandro
University of São Paulo
Rua Cayowaa 702, apto. 104
São Paulo 05018-001

Valdetaro, Guilherme
Sergio Bermudes Advogados
Praça XV de Novembro, 20, 8° andar
Rio de Janeiro 20010-010

Valença Filho, Clávio
Valença Advogados
Rua do Riachuelo, 105, 6° andar
Recife 50050-400

Valente, Helen
MacDowell Advogados
Travessa do Ouvidor, 50
Rio de Janeiro 20040-040

Valentiniano Benetti, Giovana
Universidade Federal do Rio Grande do Sul
Rua Salvador França, 1070, apto. 410
Porto Alegre 90690-000

Verçosa, Fabiane
ThyssenKrupp CSA Siderúrgica do Atlântico
Rua Voluntários da Pátria, 86, bloco B/ 808
Rio de Janeiro 22270-010

Verona, Carlo
Veirano Advogados
Av. das Nações Unidas, 12.995
18° andar
São Paulo 04578-000

Vicente de Assis, João
Pontificia Universidade Católica – RJ
Rua Henrique Cavaleiro, 123
Rio de Janeiro 22610-270

Videira, Fabiana
Campos Mello Advogados
Av. Almirante Barroso, 52, sala 1202
Rio de Janeiro 20031-000

Vieira, Paulo
Vieira, Rezende, Barbosa
e Guerreiro Advogados
Av. Presidente Wilson, 231, 18° andar
Rio de Janeiro 20030-021

Visconte, Debora
José Carlos de Magalhães Advogados Associados
Av. Brigadeiro Faria Lima, 1306, 9° andar
São Paulo 01451-914

Vita, Julia
L.O. Baptista Advogados
Av. Paulista, 1294, 8° andar
São Paulo 1310-100

Wald, Arnoldo
Wald Associados Advogados
Av. Brigadeiro Faria Lima, 3729, 7° andar
São Paulo 04538-133

Wald Filho, Arnoldo
Wald Associados Advogados
Av. Brigadeiro Faria Lima, 3729, 7° andar
São Paulo 04538-133

Weber, Ana Carolina
Carvalhosa e Eizirik Advogados
Rua Santa Luzia 651, 34° andar
Rio de Janeiro 20021-903

Wigderowitz Neto, Walter
Brandão Couto, Wigderowitz, Pessoa
e Alvarenga Advogados
Rua Dom Gerardo, 35, 4° andar
Rio de Janeiro 20090-905

Wink, Gabriela
TozziniFreire Advogados
Av. Carlos Gomes, 222, 5° andar
Porto Alegre 90480-000

Xavier, Celso
Demarest e Almeida Advogados
Av. Pedroso de Moraes, 1.201, 3° andar
São Paulo 05419-001

Zahr, Sergio
Nasser Sociedade de Advogados
Av. Angélica, 2510, 3° andar
São Paulo 01228-200

Zanatta, Andre
TozziniFreire Advogados
Rua Borges Lagoa, 1328
São Paulo 04038-904

Zanetti, Cristiano
L.O. Baptista Advogados
Av. Paulista, 1294, 8° andar
São Paulo 01310-100

Zanin Martins, Cristiano
Teixeira, Martins Advogados Associados
Rua Padre João Manuel, 755, 19° andar
São Paulo 01411-001

Canada

Bienvenu, Pierre
Norton Rose OR LLP
1 Place Ville Marie, Suite 2500
Montréal QC H3B 1R1

Cadieux, Rene
Fasken Martineau
The Stock Exchange Tower
PO Box 242, Suite 3700
800 Victoria Square
Montréal QC H4Z 1E9

Casey, J. Brian
Baker & McKenzie
181 Bay Street
Toronto ON M5J 2T3

Cicchetti, Tina Maria
Fasken Martineau
2900 – 550 Burrard Street
Vancouver BC V6C 0A3

Deane, Robert J.C.
Borden Ladner Gervais
1200 – 200 Burrard Street
Vancouver BC V7Z 1T2

Fortier, Yves
Member of ICCA
Norton Rose OR LLP
1 Place Ville Marie, Suite 2500
Montréal QC H3B 1R1

Haigh, David
Burnet, Duckworth & Palmer
1400, 350 – 7th Avenue SW
Calgary AB T2P 3N9

Hardin, Laura
FTI Consulting
79 Wellington Street West
Toronto ON M5K 1G8

Kotecha, Vimal
FTI Consulting
79 Wellington Street West
Toronto ON M5K 1G8

Lalonde, Marc
Advisory Member of ICCA
1155 René–Levesque Boulevard West
33rd Floor
Montréal QC H3B 3V2

Leon, Barry
Perley–Robertson, Hill & McDougall
1400 – 340 Albert Street
Ottawa ON K1R 0A5

Low, Robert
Deloitte & Touche
1400 – 181 Bay Street
Toronto ON L6J 1M1

McDougall, Andrew
Perley–Robertson, Hill & McDougall
340 Albert Street, Suite 1400
Ottawa ON K1R 0A5

McLaren, Richard H.
The University of Western Ontario
c/o 300 Dundas Street
London ON N6B 1T6

Prujiner, Alain
Université Laval
Bureau 7115

Pavillon Charles–De Koninck
Québec QC G1K 7P4

Smith, Murray
Smith Barristers
105 – 1008 Beach Avenue
Vancouver BC V6E 1T7

Theriault, Renee
Norton Rose OR LLP
45 O'Connor Street, Suite 1500
Ottawa ON K1P 1A4

Weiler, Todd
Investment Treaty Counsel
2014 Valleyrun Boulevard
Unit 19
London ON N6G 5N8

Chile

Biggs, Gonzalo
Law Firm Figueroa & Valenzuela
Moneda 970, Piso 5
Santiago

Figueroa, Juan Eduardo
Figueroa, Illanes, Huidobro y Salamanca
Apoquindo 3669
Santiago

Jana Wetzky, Andres
CNC
Av. Andrés Bello 2711, Piso 8
Las Condes Santiago

Jimenez, Dyalá
Bofill Mir & Alvarez Hinzpeter Jana
Av. Andrés Bello 2711, Piso 8
Las Condes Santiago

Mereminskaya, Elina
Cámara de Comercio de Santiago
Monjitas 392, Piso 11
Las Condes Santiago

Orrego Vicuña, Francisco
Member of ICCA
Instituto de Estudios Internacionales – IEI
Av. El Golf No. 40, Piso 6
Santiago 7550107

China PR

Ding Jianyoung
Beijing Arbitration Commission
16/F, China Merchants Tower
No. 118 Jianguo Road, Chaoyang District
100022 Beijing

Horrigan, Brenda
Salans
22F, Park Place Office Tower
1601 Nanjing West Road
200040 Shanghai

Leng Haidong
China International Economic and Trade Arbitration Commission
2 Huapichang Hutong, Xicheng District
100035 Beijing

Lu Xin
Beijing Arbitration Commission
16/F, China Merchants Tower
No. 118 Jianguo Road, Chaoyang District
100022 Beijing

Thorp, Peter
Allen & Overy, Beijing Office
1 Jianguomenwai Avenue
100004 Beijing

Xi Jin
China International Economic and Trade Arbitration Commission
2 Huapichang Hutong, Xicheng District
100035 Beijing

Zhao Jian
China International Economic and Trade Arbitration Commission
No. 2, Huapichang Hutong, Xicheng District
100035 Beijing

Colombia

Zuleta, Eduardo
Calle 67 No. 7-35
Oficiana 1204 Edificio Caracol
Bogotá

Czech Republic

Maisner, Martin
Rowan Legal
Na Pankráci 1683/127
14000 Prague

Olík, Milos
Rowan Legal
Na Pankraci 1683/127
14000 Prague

Denmark

Spiermann, Ole
Bruun & Hjejle
Bredgade 38
1260 Copenhagen

Ecuador

Andrade, Xavier
Andrade Veloz & Asociados
Av. República 396 y Diego de Almagro
Quito

Egypt

Hafez, Karim
5 Ibrahim Naguib Street
11451 Cairo

France

Aboim, Luiz Claudio
Freshfields Bruckhaus Deringer
2, rue Paul Cézanne
75008 Paris

El-Ahdab, Jalal
Orrick
31, avenue Pierre 1er de Serbie
75782 Paris Cedex 16

Banifatemi, Yas
Shearman & Sterling
114, avenue des Champs-Elysées
75008 Paris

Beechey, John
ICC International Court of Arbitration
38, cours Albert 1er
75008 Paris

Bühler, Michael
Jones Day
120, rue du Faubourg Saint-Honoré
75008 Paris

Cabrol, Emmanuelle
Herbert Smith
66, avenue Marceau
75008 Paris

Carducci, Guido
Carducci (Paris – Rome)
29, rue Montagne de l'Espérou
75015 Paris

Castello, James
King & Spalding
65-67, avenue des Champs-Elysées
75008 Paris

Clay, Thomas
University of Versailles
27, rue Bois-le-Vent
75016 Paris

Colaiuta, Virginie
Hughes Hubbard & Reed
47, avenue Georges Mandel
75116 Paris

De Boisséson, Matthieu
Darrois Villey Maillot Brochier
69, avenue Victor Hugo
75116 Paris

Degos, Louis
K&L Gates
78, avenue Raymond Poincaré
75116 Paris

Derains, Yves
Member of ICCA
25, rue Balzac
75009 Paris

Duprey, Pierre
Darrois Villey Maillot Brochier

LIST OF PARTICIPANTS

69, avenue Victor Hugo
75016 Paris

Feris, Jose Ricardo
ICC International Court of Arbitration
38, cours Albert 1er
75006 Paris

Fleuriet, Ken
King & Spalding
65-67, avenue des Champs-Elysées
75008 Paris

Gaillard, Emmanuel
Member of ICCA
Shearman & Sterling
114, avenue des Champs-Elysées
75008 Paris

Gelinas, Paul-A.
Cabinet Paul-A. Gelinas
69, avenue Victor Hugo
75116 Paris

Harb, Jean-Pierre
Baker & McKenzie
1, rue Paul Baudry
75008 Paris

Henry, Marc
Hughes Hubbard & Reed
8, rue de Presbourg
75116 Paris

Hertzfeld, J.
Salans
5, boulevard Malesherbes
75008 Paris

Kessedjian, Catherine
Université Panthéon-Assas
19, villa Seurat (boîte B)
75014 Paris

Kirby, Jennifer
Herbert Smith
66, avenue Marceau
75008 Paris

von Krause, Christophe
White & Case
19, Place Vendôme
75001 Paris

Legum, Barton
Salans
5, boulevard Malesherbes
75008 Paris

Leleu-Knobil, Nanou
International Arbitration Institute (IAI)
114, avenue des Champs-Elysées
75008 Paris

Mantilla-Serrano, Fernando
Shearman & Sterling
114, avenue des Champs-Elysées
75008 Paris

Marquardt, Alexander
Kramer Levin
47, avenue Hoche
75008 Paris

Mayer, Pierre
Dechert
32, rue de Monceau
75008 Paris

McNeill, Mark
Shearman & Sterling
114, avenue des Champs-Elysées
75008 Paris

Mendes Costa, Marina
Chenut Oliveira Santiago
63, avenue Franklin Roosevelt
75016 Paris

Michou, Isabelle
Herbert Smith
66, avenue Marceau
75008 Paris

Montans, Ana Paula
Derains & Gharavi
25, rue Balzac
75008 Paris

Mourre, Alexis
Castaldi Mourre & Partners
73, boulevard Haussmann
75008 Paris

Nairac, Charles
White & Case

19, Place Vendôme
75001 Paris

Ostrove, Michael M.
Debevoise & Plimpton
71, avenue George V
75008 Paris

Paulsson, Jan
President of ICCA
Freshfields Bruckhaus Deringer
2, rue Paul Cézanne
75008 Paris

Peterson, Patricia
Linklaters
25, rue de Marignan
75008 Paris

Picq, Caroline
USP
9 bis, route de Jouy
91570 Bièvres, France

Pinsolle, Philippe
Shearman & Sterling
114, avenue des Champs-Elysées
75008 Paris

Plump, Andrew R.
Darrois Villey
69, avenue Victor Hugo
75116 Paris

Procopiak, Maria Claudia
International Chamber of Commerce – ICC
38, cours Albert 1er
75008 Paris

Silva Romero, Eduardo
Dechert
32, rue de Monceau
75008 Paris

Stern, Brigitte
Université Paris 1
7, rue Pierre Nicole
75005 Paris

Stoyanov, Marie
Freshfields Bruckhaus Deringer
2, rue Paul Cézanne
75008 Paris

Tarré Bernini, Marcela
ICC International Court of Arbitration
38, cours Albert 1er
75008 Paris

Turner, Peter
Freshfields Bruckhaus Deringer
2, rue Paul Cézanne
75008 Paris

Vagenheim, Alexandre
Castaldi Mourre & Partners
73, boulevard Haussmann
75008 Paris

Vermal, Ana
Proskauer Rose
374, rue Saint-Honoré
75001 Paris

Vicien, Maria
UNESCO
7, Place de Fontenoy
75352 Paris

Wetmore, Todd
Shearman & Sterling
114, avenue des Champs-Elysées
75008 Paris

Ziade, Roland
Cleary Gottlieb Steen & Hamilton
12, rue de Tilsitt
75008 Paris

Germany

Böckstiegel, Karl-Heinz
Member of ICCA
Parkstrasse 38
51427 Bergisch-Gladbach

Bredow, Jens
German Institution for Arbitration (DIS)
Beethovenstrasse 5-13
50674 Cologne

Curschmann, Jan
Taylor Wessing
Am Sandtorkai 41
20457 Hamburg

LIST OF PARTICIPANTS

Kreindler, Richard
Shearman & Sterling
Gervinusstrasse 17
60322 Frankfurt

Sachs, Klaus Michael
CMS Hasche Sigle
Nymphenburger Strasse 12
80335 Munich

Schäfer, Erik G.W.
Cohausz & Florack
Patent- und Rechtsanwälte
Bleichstrasse 14
40211 Düsseldorf

Schilf, Sven
adesse anwälte
Stolzingstrasse 22
13465 Berlin

Trittmann, Rolf
Freshfields Bruckhaus Deringer
Bockenheimer Anlage 44
60322 Frankfurt

Umbeck, Elke
Heuking Kühn Lüer Wojtek
Bleichen Brücke 9
20354 Hamburg

Hong Kong SAR

Bao, Chiann
Hong Kong International Arbitration Centre
38/F, Two Exchange Square
8 Connaught Place

Barrington, Louise
Aculex Transnational Inc.
11A Greenwood Court
Discovery Bay

Cheng, Teresa
Vice President of ICCA
Des Voeux Chambers
38/F Gloucester Tower
The Landmark
Central

Kaplan, Neil
Member of ICCA
Mallesons Stephen Jaques
13/F Gloucester Tower – The Landmark
15 Queens Road
Central

Moser, Michael
Hong Kong International Arbitration Centre
Suite 3101-6, AIA Central
1 Connaught Road
Central

Van Eupen, Frances
Allen & Overy
9th Floor, Three Exchange Square
Central

Hungary

Kecskés, László
Arbitration Court attached to the Hungarian
Chamber of Commerce and Industry
Kossuth tér 6-8.
1055 Budapest

Szász, Iván
Honorary Vice President of ICCA
Eros Ugyvedi Iroda
Squire, Sanders & Dempsey
Roosevelt Irodaház – Roosevelt tér 7-8.
1051 Budapest

India

Dushyant, Dave
Member of ICCA
'Atlantis' Building
43, Prithviraj Road
110011 New Delhi

Ireland

Mansfield, Barry
145/151 Church Street
Dublin 7

445

O'Donoghue, James
Bluett & O'Donoghue Architects
No. 2 John Street
Kilkenny

Reichert, Klaus
Bar Council of Ireland/Brick Court Chambers
145-151 Church Street
Dublin 7

Italy

Azzali, Stefano
Chamber of Arbitration of Milan
Palazzo Turati, Via Meravigli, 9/B
20123 Milan

Benedettelli, Massimo
Freshfields Bruckhaus Deringer
Via dei Giardini 7
20121 Milan

Cicogna, Michelangelo
De Berti Jacchia Franchini Forlani
Via S. Paolo 7
20121 Milan

Crivellaro, Antonio
Bonelli Erede Pappalardo
Via Barozzi 1
20122 Milan

Fumagalli, Luigi
Studio Legale
Galleria San Babila 4/D
20122 Milan

Henke, Albert
Clifford Chance
Piazzetta M. Bossi 3
20122 Milan

Radicati Di Brozolo, Luca G.
Bonelli Erede Pappalardo
Via Barozzi 1
20122 Milan

Japan

Nakamura, Tatsuya
The Japan Commercial
Arbitration Association
3rd Floor, Hirose Building
3-17, Kanda Nishiki-cho, Chiyoda-ku
Tokyo 101-0054

Oghigian, Haig
Baker & McKenzie GJBJ
Tokyo Aoyama Aoki Koma Law Office
(Gaikokuho Joint Enterprise)
The Prudential Tower
13-10 Nagatacho 2-chome, Chiyoda-ku
Tokyo 100-0014

Sawai, Akira
Osaka Prefecture University
Gakuencho-1-1, Naka-ku
Sakai
Osaka 599-8531

Taniguchi, Yasuhei
Advisory Member of ICCA
Matsuo & Kosugi
Fukoku Seimei Building, 18th Floor
2-2-2 Uchisaiwai-cho, Chiyoda-Ku
Tokyo 100-0011

Yamashita, Rieko
Toyo University
Hakusan 5-28-20, Bunkyo-ku
Tokyo 112-8606

Kenya

Wako, Hon. S. Amos
Member of ICCA
State Law Office
PO Box 15053
Langata
Nairobi

Korea

Ahn, Keon Hyung
The Korean Commercial Arbitration Board
Room No. 4301
Korea World Trade Center
159 Samsung-dong, Kangnam-ku
Seoul 135-729

Doh, Jae Moon
The Korean Commercial Arbitration Board

LIST OF PARTICIPANTS

Room No. 4301
Korea World Trade Center
159 Samsung-dong, Kangnam-ku
Seoul 135-729

Kim, Kap-You (Kevin)
Secretary General of ICCA
Bae, Kim & Lee LLC
647-15 Yoksam-dong, Kangnam-gu
Seoul 135-723

Lee, Young Seok
Yulchon Attorneys at Law
Textile Center 12F
944-31 Daechi 2-dong, Gangnam-gu
Seoul 135-713

Lithuania

Nikitinas, Vilius
SC "Lithuanian Railways"
Mindaugo st. 12/14
03603 Vilnius

Tamaviciute, Vitalija
SC "Lithuanian Railways"
Mindaugo st. 12/14
03603 Vilnius

Malaysia

Abraham, Cecil
Member of ICCA
Zul Rafique & Partners
D3-3-8, Solaris Dutamas
No. 1 Jalan Dutamas 1
50480 Kuala Lumpur

Rajoo, Sundra
Kuala Lumpur Regional Centre
for Arbitration
No. 12, Jalan Conlay
50450 Kuala Lumpur

Mauritius

Hossen, Rashid
Employment Relations Tribunal
Level 18, Newton Tower
Sir William Newton Street
Port Louis

Mexico

Zamora, Rodrigo
Bufete Zamora Pierce
Porfirio Diaz 102-4
Mexico City 3720

Brown de Vejar, Kate
Curtis, Mallet-Prevost, Colt & Mosle LLP
Rubén Darío 281, Piso 9
Mexico City 11580

Basulto Barocio, Héctor
Baker & McKenzie Abogados, S.C.
Blvd. Puerta de Hierro 5090
Zapopan, Guadalajara 45110

Cortez, Alfonso
Baker & McKenzie Abogados, S.C.
Blvd. Antonio L. Rodríguez 1884 Pte
Torre I, Piso 10
Monterrey 64650

Navarro Velasco, Javier
Baker & McKenzie
Blvd. Antonio L. Rodríguez 1884 Pte
Torre I Piso 10
Monterrey 64650

Reyes-Retana, Juan Ygnacio
Baker & McKenzie Abogados, S.C.
Blvd. Agua Caliente 10611, Piso 1
Tijuana 22420

Von Wobeser, Claus
Von Wobeser y Sierra, S.C.
Guillermo Gonzalez Camarena 1100, Piso 7
Col. Santa Fe, Centro de Ciudad
Del. Álvaro Obregón
Mexico City 01210

Netherlands

Azpiroz, Maddi
Omni Bridgeway Holding B.V.
Tobias Asserlaan 5
2517 KC The Hague

Borelli, Silvia
ICCA Publications
Peace Palace
Carnegieplein 2
2517 KJ The Hague

Bosman, Lise
Permanent Court of Arbitration
Peace Palace
Carnegieplein 2
2517 KJ The Hague

Daly, Brooks
Permanent Court of Arbitration
Peace Palace
Carnegieplein 2
2517 KJ The Hague

De Ly, Filip
Erasmus University
c/o Johan Buziaulaan 33
3584 ZT Utrecht

Doe Rodríguez, Martin
Permanent Court of Arbitration
Peace Palace
Carnegieplein 2
2517 KJ The Hague

Grimmer, Sarah
Permanent Court of Arbitration
Peace Palace
Carnegieplein 2
2517 KJ The Hague

Le Cannu, Paul-Jean
Permanent Court of Arbitration
Peace Palace
Carnegieplein 2
2517 KJ The Hague

Leijten, Marnix
De Brauw Blackstone Westbroek
Claude Debussylaan 80
1082 MD Amsterdam

Levine, Judith
Permanent Court of Arbitration
Peace Palace
Carnegieplein 2
2517 KJ The Hague

Van der Bend, Bommel
De Brauw Blackstone Westbroek
Claude Debussylaan 80
1082 MD Amsterdam

Van Haersolte-van Hof, Jacomijn
HaersolteHof B.V.
Delistraat 27
2585 VX The Hague

Wielinga, Wieger
Omni Bridgeway Holding B.V.
Tobias Asserlaan 5
2517 KC The Hague

New Zealand

Williams, David
Member of ICCA
Bankside Chambers
Level 22, The Lumley Centre
88 Shortland Street
PO Box 405
1140 Auckland

Nigeria

Ojo, Bayo
Bayo Ojo & Co
4th Floor, ITF House
6 Adetokunbo Ademola Crescent
Wuse II
Abuja

Oyekunle, Tinuade
Honorary Vice President of ICCA
Sonotina Chambers
17 Olujobi Street
Gbagada, Phase I, (Near Anthony Bus Stop)
Lagos

Panama

González Arrocha, Katherine
ICC International Court of Arbitration
Calle 50 y 53
Edificio Banco Atlántico, Piso 5
Suite 11181, World Trade Center
Panama 0832-1236

Peru

Rubio, Roger
International Arbitration Centre – Amcham Peru
Av. Victor Andrés Belaunde 177
Lima 27

Poland

Gessel Kalinowska Vel Kalisz, Beata
Lewiatan Arbitration Court
Flory 9 lok. 3
00-586 Warsaw

Kalwas, Andrzej
Court of Arbitration at the
Polish Chamber of Commerce
4 Trebacka
00-074 Warsaw

Laszczuk, Maciej
Laszczuk & Partners
Plac Pilsudskiego 2
00-073 Warsaw

Morek, Rafal
Lewiatan Arbitration Court
Flory 9 lok. 3
00-586 Warsaw

Nowaczyk, Piotr
Court of Arbitration at the
Polish Chamber of Commerce
4 Trebacka
00-074 Warsaw

Okolski, Józef
Court of Arbitration at the
Polish Chamber of Commerce
4 Trebacka
00-074 Warsaw

Pieckowski, Sylwester
Lewiatan Arbitration Court
Flory 9 lok. 3
00-586 Warsaw

Pietkiewicz, Pawel
Lewiatan Arbitration Court
Flory 9 lok. 3
00-586 Warsaw

Szumanski, Andrzej
Lewiatan Arbitration Court
Flory 9 lok. 3
00-586 Warsaw

Wisniewski, Andrzej W.
Lewiatan Arbitration Court
Flory 9 lok. 3
00-586 Warsaw

Zbiegien, Tomasz
Lewiatan Arbitration Court
Flory 9 lok. 3
00-586 Warsaw

Portugal

Arantes Fontes, Tito
Uría Menéndez
Rua Duque de Palmela, 23
1250-097 Lisbon

Barrocas, Manuel P.
Barrocas Advogados
Amoreiras, Torre 2, 15° andar
1070-274 Lisbon

Caramelo, António S.
M.L.G.T.S. & Associados
Rua Castilho, 165
1070-050 Lisbon

Cavaleiro Brandão, Manuel
PLMJ
Rua S. João de Brito, 605-E, 1.2
4100-455 Porto

Duarte, Tiago
PLMJ
Av. da Liberdade, 224
1250-148 Lisbon

Gouveia, Rita
Cuatrecasas, Gonçalves Pereira
Praça Marquês de Pombal, 2
1250-160 Lisbon

Júdice, José Miguel
PLMJ
Av. da Liberdade, 224
1250-148 Lisbon

Larisma, Susana
Paulo de Almeida & Associados, RL
Av. da República, 14, 6° andar
1050-191 Lisbon

Lousa, Nuno Ferreira
Linklaters
Av. Fontes Pereira de Melo, 14, 15° andar
1050-121 Lisbon

Martins, Sofia
Uría Menéndez
Rua Duque de Palmela, 23
1250-097 Lisbon

Matos Martins, Ana Paula
PLMJ
Avenida 5 de Outubro, 17, 9° andar
1050-047 Lisbon

Metello de Nápoles, Pedro
PLMJ
Av. da Liberdade, 224
1250-148 Lisbon

Pinto Cardoso, Miguel
Linklaters
Av. Fontes Pereira de Melo, 14, 15° andar
1050-121 Lisbon

Pinto Leite, António
Morais Leitão, Galvão Teles,
Soares da Silva & Associados
Rua Castilho, 165
1070-050 Lisbon

Siza Vieira, Pedro
Linklaters
Av. Fontes Pereira de Melo 14, 15° andar
1050-121 Lisbon

Romania

Fruth, Despina
Fruth Oprisan & Associates
3, Corneliu Coposu
30601 Bucharest

Popa, Liliana
Fruth Oprisan & Associates
3, Corneliu Coposu
30601 Bucharest

Russian Federation

Lebedev, Sergei
Honorary Vice President of ICCA
Chamber of Commerce and Industry
of the Russian Federation
6, Ilyinka street
103684 Moscow

Singapore

Foxton, Rachel
Singapore International Arbitration Centre
32 Maxwell Road
Singapore 69115

Hwang, Michael
Member of ICCA
Michael Hwang S.C.
1 Finalayson Green #14-02
Singapore 18989

Lau, Christopher
32 Maxwell Road #02-04
Singapore 69115

Pryles, Michael
Member of ICCA
Singapore International Arbitration Centre
32 Maxwell Road
Singapore 069115

Tan, Chuan Thye
Baker & Mckenzie. Wong & Leow
8 Marina Boulevard
#05-01 Marina Bay Financial Centre
Tower 1
Singapore 018981

Spain

Alonso, José María
J&A Garrigues
Calle de Hermosilla, 3
28001 Madrid

Arias, David
Perez-Llorca
Alcalá, 61
28014 Madrid

LIST OF PARTICIPANTS

Cairns, David J.A.
B. Cremades y Asociados
Calle Goya, 18, planta 2
28001 Madrid

Calvo, Juan C.
CIMA
Calle de Hermosilla, 8
28001 Madrid

Claros, Pedro
Cuatrecasas, Gonçalves Pereira
Velázquez, 63
28001 Madrid

Conejero, Cristian
Cuatrecasas, Gonçalves Pereira
Velázquez, 63
28001 Madrid

Conthe, Manuel
Bird & Bird
Jorge Juan, 1
28001 Madrid

Cremades, Bernardo
Member of ICCA
B. Cremades y Asociados
Calle Goya 18, planta 2
28001 Madrid

Cremades Román, Alejandro
B. Cremades y Asociados
Calle Goya 18, planta 2
28001 Madrid

De Los Santos, Carlos
J & A Garrigues
Calle de Hermosilla, 2
28001 Madrid

Díez-Picazo, Ignácio Giménez
Herbert Smith
Paseo de la Castellana, 66
28046 Madrid

Fernandez Armesto, Juan
Armesto & Asociados
General Pardiñas, 102
28006 Madrid

Fernández-Ballesteros, Miguel Ángel
Fernández-Ballesteros Abogados

Serrano 22
28001 Madrid

Fröhlingsdorf, Josef
Fröhlingsdorf Abogados
Calle Nuria, 36 -1
28034 Madrid

Hamilton, Calvin
Hamilton Abogados
Espalter 15, 1° izquierda
28014 Madrid

López Ortiz, Alejandro
Hogan Lovells
Paseo de la Castellana, 51, planta 6a
28046 Madrid

Malaga, Francisco
Linklaters
Calle Zurbarán, 28
28010 Madrid

Mauleón, Santos
Abengoa, S.A.
Campus Palmas Altas
Parcela ZE-3 (Palmas Altas)
41012 Seville

Mendiola, Alvaro
Cuatrecasas, Gonçalves Pereira
Velázquez, 63
28001 Madrid

Pombo, Fernando
Gomez-Acebo & Pombo
Castellana, 216
28046 Madrid

Serra e Moura, Ana
Armesto & Asociados
General Pardiñas, 102
28006 Madrid

Sewell, Karen
Baker & McKenzie
Paseo de la Castellana, 92
28014 Madrid

Stampa, Gonzalo
Moscardo & Stampa
Calle Serrano, 6; 1°; 2ª
28001 Madrid

Venegas, Carmen
Club Español del Arbitraje
Paseo de la Castellana, 91
28046 Madrid

Virgós, Miguel
Uría Menéndez
Príncipe de Vergara, 187
28002 Madrid

Sweden

Almelöv, Jörgen
Setterwalls Advokatbyrå AB
Arsenalsgatan 6
111 47 Stockholm

Bagner, Hans
Frank Advokatbyrå AB
Birger Jarlsgatan 4
PO Box 55698
102 15 Stockholm

Bendrik, Mats
Nordenson Advokatbyrå AB
Grev Turegatan 13 A
114 46 Stockholm

Blomkvist, Christina
Advokatfirman Hammarskiöld & Co
PO Box 2278
103 17 Stockholm

Dahlberg, Hans
Setterwalls Advokatbyrå AB
Arsenalsgatan 6
111 47 Stockholm

Dandenell, Helena
Frank Advokatbyrå AB
Birger Jarlsgatan 4
Box 55698
102 15 Stockholm

Franke, Ulf
Honorary Secretary General of ICCA
Arbitration Institute of the Stockholm
Chamber of Commerce
Norr Malarstrand 68
103 21 Stockholm

Magnusson, Annette
Arbitration Institute of the Stockholm
Chamber of Commerce
PO Box 16050
103 21 Stockholm

Nilsson, Bo G. H.
Linddahl
PO Box 1065
101 39 Stockholm

Öhrström, Marie
Setterwalls Advokatbyrå AB
Arsenalsgatan 6
111 47 Stockholm

Shaughnessy, Patricia
Stockholm University
Department of Law
106 91 Stockholm

Söderlund, Christer
Advokatfirman Vinge
Smålandsgatan 20
Box 1703
111 87 Stockholm

Switzerland

Bärtsch, Philippe
Schellenberg Wittmer
15bis, rue des Alpes
1201 Geneva

Boisson de Chazournes, Laurence
40, boulevard du Pont d'Arve
1211 Geneva 4

De Castro, Ignacio
World Intellectual Property Organization
34, chemin des Colombettes
1211 Geneva

Habegger, Philipp
Walder Wyss Ltd.
PO Box 1236
Seefeldstrasse 123
8034 Zurich

Hirsch, Laurent
Hirsch Kobel
8, rue Eynard
1205 Geneva

Joory, Marc
Python & Peter
9, rue Massot
1206 Geneva

Kälin-Nauer, Claudia
Lavaterstrasse 98
8002 Zurich

Kaufmann-Kohler, Gabrielle
Member of ICCA
Lévy Kaufmann-Kohler
3-5, rue du Conseil Général
BP 552
1211 Geneva

Schneider, Michael E.
Lalive
35, rue de la Mairie
1207 Geneva

Schlaepfer, Anne Véronique
Schellenberg Wittmer
15bis, rue des Alpes
1201 Geneva

Tercier, Pierre
Member of ICCA
5, chemin Guillaume Ritter
1700 Fribourg

Thouvenin, André
Thouvenin Rechtsanwälte
Klausstrasse 33
8034 Zurich

Veit, Marc
Walder Wyss Ltd.
PO Box 1236
Seefeldstraase 123
8034 Zurich

Voser, Nathalie
Schellenberg Wittmer
Löwenstrasse 19
8021 Zurich

Wiebecke, Martin
Anwaltsbüro Wiebecke
Kohlrainstrasse 10
8700 Zurich

Thailand

Henderson, Alastair
Herbert Smith (Thailand) Ltd.
1403 Abdulrahim Place
990 Rama IV Road
10500 Bangkok

Ukraine

Perepelynska, Olena
Vasil Kisil & Partners
17/52A Bogdana Khmelnitskogo
1030 Kiev

United Arab Emirates

Mohtashami, Reza
Freshfields Bruckhaus Deringer
The Exchange Building, 5th Floor
Dubai International Financial Centre
Sheikh Zayed Road
PO Box 506 569
Dubai

Al Tamimi, Essam
Al Tamimi & Company
Sheikh Zayed Road
Dubai 9275

United Kingdom

Agaoglu, Cahit
School of International Arbitration
Queen Mary, University of London
67-69 Lincoln's Inn Fields
London WC2A 3JB

Alvey, Nicki
Chartered Institute of Arbitrators
12 Bloomsbury Square
London WC1A 2LP

Barratt, James
O'Melveny & Myers
5 Paternoster Square
London EC4M 7DX

Behan, Joe
Chartered Institute of Arbitrators
12 Bloomsbury Square
London WC1A 2LP

Brynmor Thomas, David
Herbert Smith
Exchange House, Primrose Street
London EC2A 2HS

De Oliveira, Leonardo V. P.
University of Essex
Wivenhoe Park
Colchester CO4 3SQ

Escobar, Alejandro
Baker Botts
41 Lothbury
London EC2R 7HF

Finizio, Steven P.
Wilmer Cutler Pickering Hale & Dorr
4 Carlton Gardens
London SW1Y 5AA

Forbes Smith, Michael
Chartered Institute of Arbitrators
12 Bloomsbury Square
London WC1A 2LP

Foster, David
O'Melveny & Myers
5 Paternoster Square
London EC4M 7DX

Gal, Daniel
Dechert
160 Queen Victoria Street
London EC4V 4QQ

Gardner, C. Hon.
Lamb Chambers
Temple
London EC4Y 7AS

Gill, Judith
Allen & Overy

One Bishops Square
London E1 6AD

Gómez-Acebo, Alfonso
Queen Mary, University of London
Lansdowne Terrace
London WC1N 1AS

Griffith, Nirada
CMS Cameron McKenna
160 Aldersgate Street
London EC1A 4DD

Hodges, Paula
Herbert Smith
Exchange House, Primrose Street
London EC2A 2HS

Holland, Ben
CMS Cameron McKenna
160 Aldersgate Street
London EC1A 4DD

Hunter, Ian
Essex Court Chambers
24 Lincoln's Inn Fields
London WC2A 3EG

Hunter, Martin
Member of ICCA
Essex Court Chambers
24 Lincoln's Inn Fields
London WC2A 3EG

Jagusch, Stephen
Allen & Overy
One Bishops Square
London E1 6AD

Key, Paul
Essex Court Chambers
24 Lincolns Inn Fields
London WC2A 3EG

Knox, Kate
DLA Piper UK
3 Noble Street
London EC2V 7EE

Landolt, Phillip
Charles Russell
5 Fleet Place London
London EC4M 7RD

LIST OF PARTICIPANTS

Kreindler, Richard
Shearman & Sterling
Gervinusstrasse 17
60322 Frankfurt

Sachs, Klaus Michael
CMS Hasche Sigle
Nymphenburger Strasse 12
80335 Munich

Schäfer, Erik G.W.
Cohausz & Florack
Patent- und Rechtsanwälte
Bleichstrasse 14
40211 Düsseldorf

Schilf, Sven
adesse anwälte
Stolzingstrasse 22
13465 Berlin

Trittmann, Rolf
Freshfields Bruckhaus Deringer
Bockenheimer Anlage 44
60322 Frankfurt

Umbeck, Elke
Heuking Kühn Lüer Wojtek
Bleichen Brücke 9
20354 Hamburg

Hong Kong SAR

Bao, Chiann
Hong Kong International Arbitration Centre
38/F, Two Exchange Square
8 Connaught Place

Barrington, Louise
Aculex Transnational Inc.
11A Greenwood Court
Discovery Bay

Cheng, Teresa
Vice President of ICCA
Des Voeux Chambers
38/F Gloucester Tower
The Landmark
Central

Kaplan, Neil
Member of ICCA
Mallesons Stephen Jaques
13/F Gloucester Tower – The Landmark
15 Queens Road
Central

Moser, Michael
Hong Kong International Arbitration Centre
Suite 3101-6, AIA Central
1 Connaught Road
Central

Van Eupen, Frances
Allen & Overy
9th Floor, Three Exchange Square
Central

Hungary

Kecskés, László
Arbitration Court attached to the Hungarian
Chamber of Commerce and Industry
Kossuth tér 6-8.
1055 Budapest

Szász, Iván
Honorary Vice President of ICCA
Eros Ugyvedi Iroda
Squire, Sanders & Dempsey
Roosevelt Irodaház – Roosevelt tér 7-8.
1051 Budapest

India

Dushyant, Dave
Member of ICCA
'Atlantis' Building
43, Prithviraj Road
110011 New Delhi

Ireland

Mansfield, Barry
145/151 Church Street
Dublin 7

Winstanley, Adrian
LCIA
70 Fleet Street
London EC4Y 1EU

United States

Abrahamson, Laura C.
Occidental Petroleum Corporation
10889 Wilshire Boulevard
Los Angeles, CA 90024

Aguilar-Alvarez, Guillermo
Vice President of ICCA
King & Spalding
1185 Avenue of the Americas
New York, NY 10036

Aguirre Luzi, Roberto
King & Spalding
1100 Louisiana Street, Suite 4000
Houston, TX 77002

Ali, Arif
Crowell & Moring
1001 Pennsylvania Ave., NW, 10th Floor
Washington, DC 20004

Altieri, Peter
Epstein Becker & Green PC
250 Park Avenue
New York, NY 10177

Arango, Maria-Elisa
Holland & Knight
2099 Pennsylvania Avenue, Suite 100
Washington, DC 20037

Astigarraga, Jose
Astigarraga Davis
701 Brickell Avenue, 16th floor
Miami, FL 33131

Barbosa Pechincha, Juliana
Hogan Lovells US
875 Third Avenue
New York, NY 10022

Bedard, Julie
Skadden, Arps, Slate, Meagher & Flom
Four Times Square
New York, NY 10036

Berghoff, Ethan
Baker & McKenzie
One Prudential Plaza
Chicago, IL 60601

Bishop, Doak
King & Spalding
1100 Louisiana Street
Suite 4000
Houston, TX 77002-5213

Blackaby, Nigel
Freshfields Bruckhaus Deringer
701 Pennsylvania Avenue, NW, Suite 600
Washington, DC 20004-2692

Boccuzzi, Carmine
Cleary Gottlieb Steen & Hamilton
One Liberty Plaza
New York, NY 10006

Burnett, Harry
Crowell & Moring
590 Madison Avenue, 20th Floor
New York, NY 10022

Cameron, Timothy
Cravath, Swaine & Moore
825 Eighth Avenue
New York, NY 10019

Cann, Frederic
Cann Lawyers, PC
1300 SW Fifth Avenue, Suite 2750
Portland, OR 97201-5617

Cardozo, Camilo
DLA Piper (US)
1251 Avenue of the Americas
New York, NY 10020

Carlson, Marinn
Sidley Austin
1501 K Street, NW
Washington, DC 20005

Davidson, George
Hughes Hubbard & Reed
1 Battery Park Plaza
New York, NY 10004

Davis Noll, Bethany
Debevoise & Plimpton

LIST OF PARTICIPANTS

919 Third Avenue
New York, NY 10022

De Miranda, Daniel C.
Mattos Filho, Veiga Filho, Marrey Jr.
e Quiroga Advogados
135 East 57th Street, 12th Floor
New York, NY 10022

Dombrowski, Lawrence
Dombrowski Forensic Engineers, P.A.
2310 NE 13 Street
Pompano Beach, FL 33062

Donovan, Donald
Honorary Vice President of ICCA
Debevoise & Plimpton
919 Third Avenue
New York, NY 10022

Duclos, Nicole
Allen & Overy
1221 Avenue of the Americas
New York, NY 10020

Enix-Ross, Deborah
Debevoise & Plimpton
919 Third Avenue
New York, NY 10022

Fernandez de la Cuesta, Isabel
King & Spalding
1100 Louisiana Street
Houston, TX 77002

Flower, Andrew
Deloitte Financial Advisory Services
One World Financial Center
New York, NY 10281

Franzetti, Erica
Crowell & Moring
1001 Pennsylvania Avenue, NW
Washington, DC 20004

Freitas, Andrea
Debevoise & Plimpton
919 Third Avenue
New York, NY 10022

Friedland, Paul
White & Case

1155 Avenue of the Americas
New York, NY 10036-2787

Frischtak, Ana L.
Debevoise & Plimpton
919 Third Avenue
New York, NY 10022

Frutos-Peterson, Claudia
Curtis, Mallet-Prevost, Colt & Mosle
1717 Pennsylvania Avenue, NW
Washington, DC 20006

Gardiner, John L.
Four Times Square
New York, NY 10036

Garfinkel, Barry
Skadden, Arps, Slate, Meagher & Flom
Four Times Square
New York, NY 10036

Goldberg, Michael
Baker Botts
910 Louisiana Street
Houston, TX 77002

Gomez-Pinzon, Enrique
Holland & Pinzon
2099 Pennsylvania Avenue, Suite 100
Washington, DC 20037

Gomm Santos, Mauricio
Smith International Legal Consultants, P.A.
175 SW 7th Street, Suite 2003
Miami, FL 33130

Gray, Scott
Navigant Consulting, Inc.
255 Alhambra Circle
Miami, FL 33134

Greenblatt, Jonathan
Shearman & Sterling
801 Pennsylvania Avenue, NW, Suite 900
Washington, DC 20004

Hamilton, Jonathan
White & Case
701 Thirteenth Street, NW
Washington, DC 20005

457

Hammond, Steven
Hughes Hubbard & Reed
One Battery Park Plaza
New York, NY 10004

Hanessian, Grant
Baker & McKenzie
1114 Avenue of the Americas
New York, NY 10036

Hayden, Don
Baker & McKenzie
1111 Brickell Avenue, Suite 1700
Miami, FL 33131

Hellmann, Betsy
Skadden, Arps, Slate, Meagher & Flom
Four Times Square
New York, NY 10036

Hodgson, Melida N.
Foley Hoag
1875 K Street, NW
Washington, DC 20006

Hosking, James
Chaffetz Lindsey
1350 Avenue of the Americas
New York, NY 10019

Hranitzky, Dennis
Dechert
1095 Avenue of the Americas
New York, NY 10036

Italiani, Fulvio
D'Empaire Reyna Abogados
PO Box 02-5210
Miami, FL 33102-5210

Kehoe, Edward G.
King & Spalding
1185 Avenue of the Americas
New York, NY 10036

Kerr, John
Simpson Thacher & Bartlett
425 Lexington Avenue
New York, NY 10017-3954

Kessler, Judd
Porter Wright
1919 Pennsylvania Avenue, NW
Washington, DC 20006

Kimmelman, Benno
Allen & Overy
1221 Avenue of the Americas
New York, NY 10020

Kinnear, Meg
3936 Georgetown Court NW
Washington, DC 20007

Knull, William H., III
Mayer Brown
700 Louisiana, Suite 3400
Houston, TX 77002

Kostadinova, Milanka
ICSID
1800 G Street, NW
Washington, DC 20423

Kuck, Lea Haber
Skadden, Arps, Slate, Meagher & Flom
Four Times Square
New York, NY 10036

Lamm, Carolyn
White & Case
701 Thirteenth Street, NW
Washington, DC 20005-3807

Leader, Jordan
Proskauer Rose
1585 Broadway
New York, NY 10023

Leathley, Christian
Curtis, Mallet-Prevost, Colt & Mosle
101 Park Avenue, 35th Floor
New York, NY 10178

Leite, Juliana
University of Miami
1311 Miller Drive
Coral Gables, FL 33146

Lindsey, David
Chaffetz Lindsey
1350 Avenue of the Americas
New York, NY 10019

LIST OF PARTICIPANTS

Martinez, Luis M.
ICDR/American Arbitration Association
1633 Broadway, 10th Floor
New York, NY 10019

Mattamouros, Jorge
King & Spalding
1100 Louisiana Street, Suite 4000
Houston, TX 77002

McCombs, Rick
Mayer Brown
71 S. Wacker Drive
Chicago, IL 60606

Menaker, Andrea
White & Case
701 Thirteenth Street, NW
Washington, DC 20005

Miles, Craig S.
King & Spalding
1100 Louisiana Street, Suite 4000
Houston, TX 77002

Moore, Allan
Covington & Burling
1201 Pennsylvania Avenue, NW
Washington, DC 20004

Nelson, Timothy
Skadden, Arps, Slate, Meagher & Flom
Four Times Square
New York, NY 10036

Paciaroni, Richard F.
K&L Gates
535 Smithfield Street
Pittsburgh, PA 15205

Parra, Antonio
Honorary Secretary General of ICCA
7500 Platter Terrace
Easton, ML 21601

Pearsall, Patrick W.
US State Department
2430 E Street, NW (SA-4), Suite 203
Washington, DC 20037-2851

Pierce, John V.H.
Wilmer Cutler Pickering Hale and Dorr
399 Park Avenue
New York, NY 10022

Polasek, Martina
ICSID
1818 H Street, SE
Washington, DC 20003

Polasek, Petr
White & Case
701 Thirteenth Street, NW
Washington, DC 20005

Prager, Dietmar W.
Debevoise & Plimpton
919 Third Avenue
New York, NY 10022

Rivkin, David W.
Debevoise & Plimpton
919 Third Avenue
New York, NY 10022

Rooney, John H., Jr.
Shutts & Bowen
201 S. Biscayne Boulevard 1500
Miami, FL 33131

Rostov, Gene
E. Rostov & Associates LLC
245 Catalonia Avenue
Coral Gables, FL 33134

Rovine, Arthur
Fordham Law School
1114 Avenue of the Americas
New York, NY 10036

Santens, Ank
White & Case
1155 Avenue of the Americas
New York, NY 10036

Schwebel, Stephen M.
Suite 410
1501 K Street, NW
Washington, DC 20005

Sherwin, Peter
Proskauer Rose
1585 Broadway
New York, NY 10036

Sicard-Mirabal, Josefa
USCIB
1212 Avenue of the Americas, 21st Floor
New York, NY 10036-1689

Slate, William K., II
Member of ICCA
American Arbitration Association
1776 Eye Street, NW, Suite 850
Washington, DC 20006

Slifkin, Daniel
Cravath, Swaine & Moore
825 Eighth Avenue
New York, NY 10019

Smith, Quinn
Smith International Legal Consultants, P.A.
175 SW 7th Street, Suite 2003
Miami, FL 33130

Smutny, Abby Cohen
White & Case
701 Thirteenth Street, NW
Washington, DC 20005-3807

Suarez Anzorena, Ignacio
Chadbourne & Parke
1200 New Hampshire Avenue, NW
Washington, DC 20036

Sussman, Edna
SussmanADR LLC
20 Oak Lane
Scarsdale, NY 10583

Tahbaz, Christopher K.
Debevoise & Plimpton
919 Third Avenue
New York, NY 10022

Tancula, James
Mayer Brown
71 S. Wacker Drive
Chicago, IL 60606

Taylor, Greig
Deloitte Financial Advisory Services
One World Financial Center, 17th Floor
New York, NY 10281

Thevenin, Nancy M.
Baker & McKenzie

1114 Avenue of the Americas
New York, NY 10036

Thomas, Peter C.
Simpson Thacher & Bartlett
1155 F Street, NW
Washington, DC 20004

Townsend, John
Hughes Hubbard & Reed
1775 I Street, NW
Washington, DC 20006

Valverde, Angel
Abogados Asesores & Asociados
3029 NE 188 Street, Apt. 519
Miami, FL 33180

Vickery, Howard L.
Boies, Schiller & Flexner
575 Lexington Avenue
New York, NY 10022

Weiss, David
King & Spalding
1100 Louisiana Street, Suite 4000
Houston, TX 77002

White, Brian
King & Spalding
1180 Peachtree Street
Atlanta, GA 30309

Wilbraham, Alexander John
Freshfields Bruckhaus Deringer
701 Pennsylvania Avenue, NW, Suite 600
Washington, DC 20004-2692

Yusem, Steve
527 Plymouth Road, Suite 416
Plymouth Meeting, PA 19462

Zaslowsky, David
Baker & McKenzie
1114 Avenue of the Americas
New York, NY 10036

Zelbo, Howard
Cleary Gottlieb Steen & Hamilton
One Liberty Plaza, 44th Floor
New York, NY 10312

Venezuela

De Jesus O., Alfredo
Venezuelan Arbitration Committee
Centro Lido
Avenida Francisco de Miranda
Caracas 1060

Droulers, Diana C.
Avenida La Cumbre
Qta Idefix, La Lagunita
El Hatillo 1083-A

Esis Villarroel, Ivette S.
Arbitration Centre of
Caracas Chamber of Commerce
Calle Andrés Eloy Blanco
Los Caobos
Caracas 1050

Frías, José H.
D'Empaire Reyna Abogados
Edificio Bancaracas, PH
Plaza La Castellana
Caracas 1060A

Gregorio Torrealba, José
Hoet Pelaez Castillo & Duque
Centro San Ignacio, Torre Kepler
Avenida Blandin, La Castellana
Caracas 1060

Martinez R., Edmundo
Baker & McKenzie
Torre Edicampo, PH
Avenida Francisco de Miranda
cruce con Avenida El Parque
PO Box 1286
Urbanización Campo Alegre
Caracas 1010-A

Saghy, Pedro
Macleod Dixon
Centro Comercial San Ignacio
Torreo Copérnico, Piso 8
Caracas 1060

Torrealba L., Henry
Baker & McKenzie
Torre Edicampo, PH
Avenida Francisco de Miranda
cruce con Avenida El Parque
PO Box 1286
Urbanización Campo Alegre
Caracas 1010-A

INTERNATIONAL COUNCIL FOR COMMERCIAL ARBITRATION (ICCA)

Correspondence address:
Mr. Kap-You (Kevin) Kim
Secretary General ICCA
Bae, Kim & Lee LLC
647-15 Yoksam-dong
Kangnam-gu
Seoul 135-723
Korea
Phone:+1-822 3404 0333
Fax:+1-822 3404 7306
E-mail: kevin.kim@bkl.kr

LIST OF OFFICERS AND MEMBERS

July 2011

OFFICERS

Honorary Presidents

THE HON. GIORGIO BERNINI (Bologna, Italy)
Former Minister of Foreign Trade and Member of Parliament; Former Member, Italian Antitrust Authority; Professor, University of Bologna, Chair of Arbitration and International Commercial Law; President, Association for the Teaching and Study of Arbitration and International Trade Law (AISA); Member, Executive Committee, Italian Arbitration Association; Senior Partner, Studio Bernini e Associati

DR. GEROLD HERRMANN (Vienna, Austria)
Former Secretary, United Nations Commission on International Trade Law (UNCITRAL); Honorary Professor, University of Vienna

MR. FALI S. NARIMAN (New Delhi, India)
President, Bar Association of India; Honorary Member, International Commission of Jurists; Past President, Law Association for Asia and the Pacific (LAWASIA); Member, Court of the LCIA; Past Vice Chairman, International Court of Arbitration of the International Chamber of Commerce (ICC); Past Co-Chair, Human Rights Institute of the International Bar Association (IBA); Senior Advocate, Supreme Court of India

PROF. PIETER SANDERS (Schiedam, The Netherlands)
Honorary President, Netherlands Arbitration Institute; Professor Emeritus, Faculty of Law, Erasmus University, Rotterdam

President

PROF. JAN PAULSSON (Paris, France)
General Editor, ICCA *International Handbook on Commercial Arbitration*; Michael Klein Distinguished Scholar Chair, University of Miami School of Law; Centennial Professor of Law, London School of Economics; Judge and Past President, World Bank Administrative Tribunal; President, Administrative Tribunal, European Bank for Reconstruction and Development; Past President, LCIA

Honorary Vice Presidents

MR. DONALD FRANCIS DONOVAN (New York, USA)
Adjunct Professor, New York University School of Law; former Vice President, American Society of International Law; former Chair, Institute for Transnational Arbitration; former Chair, U.S. National Committee, ICC International Court of Arbitration; Board of Directors, Human Rights First

JUDGE HOWARD M. HOLTZMANN (New York, USA)
Honorary Chairman of the Board, American Arbitration Association; Substitute Judge, Iran-United States Claims Tribunal, The Hague

PROF. SERGEI LEBEDEV (Moscow, Russian Federation)
President, Maritime Arbitration Commission; Member of the Presidium, International Commercial Arbitration Court of the Russian Federation Chamber of Commerce and Industry; Professor, Moscow Institute of International Relations (University); Former Commissioner, UN Compensation Commission; Member, UNCITRAL Working Group on Arbitration

DDR. WERNER MELIS (Vienna, Austria)
Honorary President, International Arbitral Centre of the Austrian Federal Economic Chamber, Vienna; Past Vice President, LCIA; Of Counsel, Baier Böhm

MS. TINUADE OYEKUNLE (Lagos, Nigeria)
Barrister and Solicitor of the Supreme Court of Nigeria, Arbitrator and Notary Public; Member, Association of Arbitrators of Nigeria; Fellow, Chartered Institute of Arbitrators, London; Member, Arbitration Committee of the Lagos Chamber of Commerce; Chartered Arbitrator; Member, Panel Membership Group (PMG), Chartered Institute of Arbitrators, London; former Chairman, Education & Training Committee of the Chartered Institute of Arbitrators, London; former Member, Board of Management of the Chartered Institute of Arbitrators, London; Regional Representative for Promotion of Arbitration in the West African Region; Past Chairman, Chartered Institute of Arbitrators, Nigeria Branch; former Member, London Court of International Arbitration; Correspondent of UNIDROIT

PROF. DR. IVÁN SZÁSZ (Budapest, Hungary)
Professor of Law, University of Economic Sciences, Budapest; Honorary Chairman, Legal Commission at the Hungarian Chamber of Commerce; Past Ambassador of Hungary to the European Communities; Past Member, ICC International Court of Arbitration; Of Counsel, Squire Sanders & Dempsey

Vice Presidents

MR. GUILLERMO AGUILAR-ALVAREZ (New York, USA)
Past General Counsel, ICC International Court of Arbitration; Principal Legal Counsel for the Government of Mexico for the Negotiation and Implementation of NAFTA; Visiting Scholar, Yale Law School; Partner, King & Spalding

MS. TERESA CHENG, BBS, SC, JP (Hong Kong)
Senior Counsel; Vice President of ICC International Court of Arbitration; Vice Chair, Hong Kong International Arbitration Centre; Past President, Chartered Institute of Arbitrators; Adjunct Professor, Hong Kong University and Hong Kong Polytechnic University

PROF. ALEXANDER S. KOMAROV (Moscow, Russian Federation)
Chairman, ICC Russia National Committee, Arbitration Commission; Professor, Russian Academy of Foreign Trade; President, International Commercial Arbitration Court at the Russian Federation Chamber of Commerce and Industry

Honorary Secretaries General

MR. ULF FRANKE (Stockholm, Sweden)
Past Secretary General, ICCA; Past Secretary General, Arbitration Institute of the Stockholm Chamber of Commerce; Past President, International Federation of Commercial Arbitration Institutions (IFCAI)

MR. ANTONIO R. PARRA (Washington, DC, USA)
Past Secretary General, ICCA; Past Deputy Secretary-General and Legal Adviser, International Centre for Settlement of Investment Disputes (ICSID); Fellow, Chartered Institute of Arbitrators; Consultant, World Bank

Secretary General

MR. KAP-YOU (KEVIN) KIM
Head of Arbitration Group, Bae, Kim & Lee LLC; Senior Advisor, Korea Commercial Arbitration Board (KCAB); Vice President, Korean Council for International Arbitration (KOCIA); Member, ICC International Court of Arbitration; Member, LCIA; Board Member, American Arbitration Association; Vice Chair, IBA Arbitration Committee; Member, Drafting Subcommittee for the revision of ICC Rules; Member, Subcommittee on revision of the IBA Rules on the Taking of Evidence; Panel of Arbitrators, ICSID

MEMBERS

MR. CECIL ABRAHAM (Seremban, Malaysia)
Fellow, Chartered Institute of Arbitrators; Fellow, Malaysian Institute of Arbitrators; Past Member, LCIA; Past President, Inter-Pacific Bar Association; Vice President, Asia Pacific Regional Arbitration Group (APRAG); Member, Malaysia National Committee, International Chamber of Commerce

PROF. DR. ALBERT JAN VAN DEN BERG (Brussels, Belgium)
General Editor, ICCA *Yearbook Commercial Arbitration*; Former President, Netherlands Arbitration Institute; Professor of Arbitration Law, Erasmus University, Rotterdam; Visiting Professor, University of Miami School of Law; Member, Amsterdam and Brussels Bars

INTERNATIONAL COUNCIL FOR COMMERCIAL ARBITRATION (ICCA)

PROF. DR. PIERO BERNARDINI (Rome, Italy)
Past Professor of Arbitration Law, LUISS University, Rome; Vice-President, Italian Arbitration Association; Past Vice-President, ICC International Court of Arbitration

PROF. DR. KARL-HEINZ BÖCKSTIEGEL (Bergisch-Gladbach, Germany)
Professor Emeritus of International Business Law, University of Cologne; Chairman, German Institution of Arbitration (DIS); Patron, Chartered Institute of Arbitrators; Past President, International Law Association (ILA); Past President, LCIA; Past President, Iran-United States Claims Tribunal, The Hague

PROF. DR. NAEL G. BUNNI (Dublin, Ireland)
Past President, Chartered Institute of Arbitrators; Member, Board of Trustees and Chairman, Executive Committee, Dubai International Arbitration Centre; Past Member, LCIA Board of Directors; Visiting Professor in Construction Law and Contract Administration, Trinity College, Dublin; Chartered Engineer and Chartered Registered Arbitrator

PROF. BERNARDO M. CREMADES (Madrid, Spain)
Professor, Faculty of Law, Madrid University; Member of the Madrid Bar

MR. DUSHYANT DAVE (New Delhi, India)
Senior Advocate at the Supreme Court of India; Member of the Board, American Arbitration Association; former member, LCIA; Vice Chair, Arbitration Committee, IBA; former member, National Legal Services Authority of India (NALSA)

M^E YVES DERAINS (Paris, France)
Past Secretary General, ICC International Court of Arbitration; Chairman, *Comité Français de l'Arbitrage*; Member of the Paris Bar

MR. L. YVES FORTIER, CC, QC (Montréal, Canada)
Chairman Emeritus and Senior Partner, Norton Rose OR Montreal; Former President and Honorary Vice President, LCIA; Chair, Hong Kong International Arbitration Court; former Ambassador and Permanent Representative of Canada to the United Nations; Judge ad hoc, International Court of Justice

PROF. DR. EMMANUEL GAILLARD (Paris, France)
Professor of Law, University of Paris XII; Chairman, International Arbitration Institute; Past Member, LCIA Court; Past Chairman, International Arbitration Committee, ILA

PROF. DR. BERNARD HANOTIAU (Brussels, Belgium)
Member, Brussels and Paris Bars; Professor of International Dispute Resolution, University of Louvain; Former Vice-President, LCIA; Vice-Chairman, Institute of Transnational Arbitration; Vice-Chairman, CEPANI (Belgium)

PROF. MARTIN HUNTER (London, United Kingdom)
Barrister; Professor of International Dispute Resolution, Nottingham Trent University; Visiting Professor, King's College London University; Chairman, Dubai International Arbitration Centre; Honorary Dean of Postgraduate Studies, T.M.C. Asser Instituut, The Hague

MR. MICHAEL HWANG, SC (Singapore)
Former Acting High Court Judge, Singapore; Advocate and Solicitor, Singapore; Member, Permanent Court of Arbitration; Chartered Arbitrator; Adjunct Professor, National University of Singapore; Former Vice Chair Committee D, International Bar Association; Former Vice Chair, ICC International Court of Arbitration; Member, International Council of Arbitration for Sport (ICAS); Member, LCIA; Deputy Chief Justice, Dubai International Financial Centre; President, Law Society of Singapore; Non-Resident Ambassador of Singapore to Switzerland

MR. NEIL KAPLAN, CBE, QC (Gloucestershire, United Kingdom)
Former Judge, High Court, Hong Kong; Chairman, Hong Kong International Arbitration Centre 1991-2004; Past President, The Chartered Institute of Arbitrators; Honorary Professor, City University of Hong Kong

PROF.DR. GABRIELLE KAUFMANN-KOHLER (Geneva, Switzerland)
Professor, Geneva University Law School; Director, Geneva Master in International Dispute Settlement; Partner, Lévy Kaufmann-Kohler; Honorary President, Swiss Arbitration Association (ASA)

DR. FATHI KEMICHA (Tunis, Tunisia)
Avocat à la Cour, Member of the Bars of Paris and Tunisia; Member, International Law Commission of the United Nations; Member, World Bank Group Sanctions Board; Member, Board of Trustees and Executive Committee, Dubai International Arbitration Centre; First appointed Secretary General, Constitutional Court of the Kingdom of Bahrain (January 2003 – December 2005); Former Vice President, LCIA

MR. ARTHUR MARRIOTT, QC (London, United Kingdom)
Board Member, Hong Kong International Arbitration Centre; Solicitor

PROF. FRANCISCO ORREGO VICUÑA (Santiago, Chile)
Professor of Law, University of Chile and first Director of the LL.M. on Investments, Trade and Arbitration offered jointly with the University of Heidelberg and the Max Planck Institute; Judge and former President, Administrative Tribunal of the World Bank; Member, Chairman's List of ICSID Arbitrators; former Vice President, LCIA; Member, Latin American Committee of Arbitrators of the ICC

PROF. WILLIAM W. PARK (Cohasset, USA)
Professor of Law, Boston University; General Editor, Arbitration International; President, LCIA; Past Chairman, ABA Committee on International Commercial Dispute Resolution

PROF. DR. MICHAEL PRYLES (Melbourne, Australia)
Chairman, Singapore International Arbitration Centre; Member, Board of Trustees, Dubai International Arbitration Centre; Former President, Australian Centre for International Commercial Arbitration; President, Asia Pacific Regional Arbitration Group; Former Commissioner, United Nations Compensation Commission; Member, LCIA Court

MR. WILLIAM K. SLATE II (Washington, DC, USA)
President and Chief Executive Officer, American Arbitration Association; Founder, Global Center for Dispute Resolution Research; Member, Arbitrator and Mediator, Panels of the International Court of Arbitration for Sport (Switzerland); Member, International Commercial Arbitration Court at the Ukraine Chamber of Commerce and Industry; Member, China International Economic and Trade Arbitration Commission (CIETAC)

PROF. DR. GUIDO SANTIAGO TAWIL (Buenos Aires, Argentina)
Professor, University of Buenos Aires School of Law; Co-Chair, IBA Arbitration Committee; Member, LCIA; Attorney at Law, Partner, M. & M. Bomchil

PROF. DR. DR. HC. PIERRE TERCIER (Fribourg, Switzerland)
Honorary Chairman, International Court of Arbitration of the International Chamber of Commerce; Professor Emeritus, Law Faculty, University of Fribourg; former Chairman, Swiss Antitrust Commission

MR. V.V. VEEDER, QC (London, United Kingdom)
Vice President, LCIA; Council Member, ICC Institute of World Business Law and of the Arbitration Institute of the Stockholm Chamber of Commerce; Visiting Professor on Investment Arbitration, King's College, University of London

THE HON. S. AMOS WAKO, F.C.I.ARB, SC (Nairobi, Kenya)
Attorney General, Republic of Kenya; Former Chairman, Arbitration Tribunal, Kenya Chamber of Commerce and Industry; Arbitrator, Vienna Convention on Law of Treaties, Centre for Settlement of Investment Disputes; former Vice President, LCIA-Africa Region; former Chairman, Law Society of Kenya; former Member, International Advisory Committee of WIPO Centre for Settlement of Disputes; former Commission Member, International Commission of Jurists, former Deputy Secretary General, IBA; former Secretary General, African Bar Association; former Senior Partner, Kaplan & Stratton; former President, Asian-African Legal Consultative Organisation; Member, International Law Commission (2007-2011)

DR. WANG SHENG CHANG (Beijing, People's Republic of China)
Former Vice Chairman and former Secretary General, CIETAC; former Vice Chairman, China Maritime Arbitration Commission (CMAC); Member, LCIA; Professor of Law, University of International Economics and Business, Beijing

MR. DAVID A.R. WILLIAMS, QC (Auckland, New Zealand)
Former Judge of the High Court of New Zealand; Former Chief Justice of the Cook Islands; Justice of the Cook Islands Court of Appeal; Judge, Court of Dubai International Financial Centre; Past President, Arbitrators and Mediators Institute of New Zealand; Former Member, ICC Court of International Arbitration; Former Member, LCIA; Board of Directors, American Arbitration Association; Honorary Professor of Law, University of Auckland, New Zealand

Advisory Members

MR. ROBERT COULSON (Riverside, USA)
Former President, American Arbitration Association

PROF. DR. RADOMIR DJUROVIČ (Belgrade, Serbia)
Former President, Arbitration Court of Yugoslavia; Professor of International Commercial Law, Belgrade University

DR. MAURO FERRANTE (Rome, Italy)
Secretary General, Italian Arbitration Association; Managing Director, ICC-Italy

PROF. AHMED S. EL-KOSHERI (Cairo, Egypt)
Former Professor of International Economic Law and Former President, International University for African Development (Université Senghor, Alexandria); Member, *l'Institut de Droit International*; Former Ad hoc Judge, International Court of Justice; Partner, Kosheri, Rashed & Riad Law Firm

PROF. DR. DR. HC. PIERRE LALIVE D'EPINAY (Geneva, Switzerland)
Senior Partner and Co-Founder, Lalive Attorneys, Geneva; Founder and Editor-in-Chief, Bulletin of the Swiss Arbitration Association (ASA); Professor Emeritus Geneva University; Member (elected) and Former President (1989-1991), Institut de Droit International; Honorary President of ASA and of the ICC Institute of World Business Law (Paris)

THE HON. MARC LALONDE (Montréal, Canada)
Former Ad Hoc Judge, International Court of Justice; Former Minister of Justice and Attorney General; Former Minister of Energy, Mines and Resources; Former Minister of Finance; Former President, LCIA North American Users Committee; Member, Institute of International Business Law and Practice

MR. MARK LITTMAN, QC (London, United Kingdom)
Barrister; Former Member, Royal Commission on Legal Services and Master Treasurer of Middle Temple

M^E CARLOS NEHRING NETTO (São Paulo, Brazil)
Founder, Nehring & Associados – Advocacia; Former Member, ICC International Court of Arbitration; Former Chairman, Arbitration Center of the American Chamber of Commerce in São Paulo

MR. ALAIN PLANTEY (Paris, France)
Former Member of the *Conseil d'État*; Member and Former President, *Institut de France*; Member and Former President, Academy of Moral and Political Sciences (*Institut de France*); Former Ambassador of France in Madagascar; Former Professor of Law, University of Paris I; *Président d'honneur*, ICC International Court of Arbitration

THE HON. ANDREW JOHN ROGERS, QC (Sydney, Australia)
Former Chief Judge, Commercial Division, Supreme Court of New South Wales; Adjunct Professor, University of Technology, Sydney; Deputy Chairman, International Legal Services Advisory Council (ILSAC); Foundation Chancellor of Southern Cross University; President of the Sydney University Foundation into Securities (now SIRCA Limited); Patron of the Australian Corporate Lawyers Association (NSW Division)

DR. JOSÉ LUIS SIQUEIROS (Mexico City, Mexico)
Past President, Mexican Academy of International Commercial Arbitration; Past President, Inter-American Bar Association; Past Chairman, Inter-American Juridical Committee (OAS); Professor, Universidad Iberoamericana, Mexico City; Member, NAFTA Advisory Committee on Private Commercial Disputes; Member, Advisory Board, Institute for Transnational Arbitration; Member, International Law Association

PROF. TANG HOUZHI (Beijing, People's Republic of China)
Honorary Vice Chairman, CIETAC; Vice Chairman, CCPIT/CCOIC Beijing Conciliation Centre; Professor, Law School of the People's University of China; Visiting Professor, Amoy University School of Law; Arbitration Adviser, UN International Trade Centre; Fellow and Chartered Arbitrator, Chartered Institute of Arbitrators; Former Court Member, LCIA; Honorary Professor, Hong Kong City University School of Law; Vice President, IFCAI; Adviser to the China International Law Society and the China Private International Law Society; Member, Executive Committee, China Maritime Law Association

PROF. YASUHEI TANIGUCHI (Tokyo, Japan)
Former Member, Appellate Body of the World Trade Organization Dispute Settlement Body; Professor of Law, Senshu University Law School, Attorney at Law; Professor Emeritus, Kyoto University; President, Japan Association of Arbitrators; Former President, Japanese Association of Civil Procedure; Former Vice-President, International Association of Procedural Law; Of Counsel, Matsuo & Kosugi